The Best Books for Academic Libraries

The Best Books for Academic Libraries
10 Volumes (ISBN 0-7222-0010-2)

Volume 1 — Science, Technology, and Agriculture
(ISBN 0-7222-0011-0)
Q	Science
S	Agriculture
T	Technology, Engineering

Volume 2 — Medicine
(ISBN 0-7222-0012-9)
BF	Psychology
R	Medicine
RM-RS	Therapeutics
RT	Nursing

Volume 3 — Language and Literature
(ISBN 0-7222-0013-7)
P	Language and Literature
PA	Classical Language and Literature
PB-PH	Modern European Languages and Slavic Languages and Literature
PJ-PL	Oriental Language and Literature
PN	Literature: General and Comparative
PQ	Romance Literatures
PR	English Literature
PS	American Literature
PT	German, Dutch and Scandinavian Literature
PZ	Juvenile Literature

Volume 4 — History of the Americas
(ISBN 0-7222-0014-5)
E	America
E151-E970	United States
F1-975	US Local History
F1001-3799	Canada, Latin America

Volume 5 — World History
(ISBN 0-7222-0015-3)
C	Auxiliary Sciences of History
D	History

Volume 6 — Social Sciences
(ISBN 0-7222-0016-1)
G-GF	Geography, Oceanography, Human Ecology
GN	Anthropology, Ethnology, Archaeology
GR-GT	Folklore, Customs, Costumes
GV	Recreation, Physical Training, Sports
H-HA	Social Sciences. General Statistics
HB-HJ	Economics, Population
HM-HV	Sociology, Social History, Social Pathology
HX	Socialism, Communism, Anarchism

Volume 7 — Political Science, Law, Education
(ISBN 0-7222-0017-X)
J	Political Science
L	Education
K	Law

Volume 8 — Religion and Philosophy
(ISBN 0-7222-0018-8)
B-BJ	Philosophy
BL-BX	Religion

Volume 9 — Music & Fine Arts
(ISBN 0-7222-0019-6)
ML, MT	Music
N-NX	Fine Arts

Volume 10 — General Works, Military & Naval, Library Science Author Index, Title Index, Subject Guide
(ISBN 0-7222-0020-X)
A	General Works
U	Military Science
V	Naval Science
Z	Bibliography, Library Science Author and Title Indexes Subject Guide

The Best Books for Academic Libraries

Medicine

Volume 2

First Edition

The Best Books, Inc.
P. O. Box 893520
Temecula, CA. 92589-3520

Copyright © 2002
The Best Books, Inc.

Printed in the United States of America

ISBN 0-7222-0010-2 (10 Volume Set)
ISBN 0-7222-0012-9 (Volume 2)

```
Library of Congress Cataloging-in-Publication Data


The best books for academic libraries.-- 1st ed.
      v. cm.
Includes indexes.
Contents: v. 1. Science, technology, and agriculture -- v. 2. Medicine
-- v. 3. Language and literature -- v. 4. History of the Americas -- v.
5. World history -- v. 6. Social sciences -- v. 7. Political science,
law, education -- v. 8. Religion and philosophy -- v. 9. Music & fine
arts -- v. 10. General works, military & naval, library science.
   ISBN 0-7222-0010-2 (set : alk. paper) -- ISBN 0-7222-0011-0 (v. 1 :
alk. paper) -- ISBN 0-7222-0012-9 (v. 2 : alk. paper) -- ISBN 0-7222-
0013-7 (v. 3 : alk. paper) -- ISBN 0-7222-0014-5 (v. 4 : alk.
paper) -- ISBN 0-7222-0015-3 (v. 5 : alk. paper) -- ISBN 0-7222-0016-1
(v. 6 : alk. paper) -- ISBN 0-7222-0017-X (v. 7 : alk. paper) -- ISBN
0-7222-0018-8 (v. 8 : alk. paper) -- ISBN 0-7222-0019-6 (v. 9 : alk.
paper) -- ISBN 0-7222-0020-X (v. 10 : alk. paper)
   1.  Academic libraries--United States--Book lists.  I. Best Books,
Inc.

Z1035 .B545 2002
011'.67--dc21  2002013790
```

For further information, contact:

The Best Books, Inc.
P.O. Box 893520
Temecula, CA 92589-3520
(Voice) 888-265-3531
(Fax) 888-265-3540

For product information/customer service, e-mail: <u>customerservice@thebbooks.net</u>

Visit our Web site: <u>www.bestbooksfor.com</u>

Table of Contents

Introduction

ABOUT THE PROJECT:

The Best Books for Academic Libraries was created to fill a need that has been growing in collection development for College and Academic Libraries since the late 1980s. Our editorial department organized *The Best Books* database (designed as a resource for University Libraries) by consulting the leading book review journals, bibliographies, and reference books with subject bibliographies.

PROCESSES FOR SUBJECT SELECTION AND COMPILATION:

To create *The Best Books for Academic Libraries*, the Editor conducted a comprehensive search of prominent Subject Librarians, experts in their area(s), to recommend the best books for undergraduate institutions. The editorial processes utilized by The Best Books editorial staff are as follows:

1. Subject Librarians and Subject Specialists were invited to participate in selecting the best books to recommend for Undergraduate libraries. Those who volunteered selected approximately one-third from over 170,000 books in our cumulative *The Best Books* database. These advisors made their recommendations from a complete list, organized by Library of Congress (LC) Classification Number. They identified approximately one-third of the books that they felt were essential to undergraduate work in their area(s) of expertise. They added their choices of titles that they felt were omitted from the surveys, and updated titles to the newest editions.

2. The Best Books' editorial staff tabulated the returned surveys and added the omissions into the database to arrive at a consensus of approximately the best 60,000 books to include in the cumulative surveys.

3. Senior Subject Advisors conducted a final review from the surveys and determined which books to add or delete from those lists. Senior Subject Advisors added any omitted titles they felt were essential to undergraduate work in their area(s) of expertise, and returned them to The Best Books editorial staff.

4. The final surveys were then tabulated and final omissions were added to create this First Edition of the 10 Volume set – *The Best Books for Academic Libraries*.

The Best Books database was organized based upon the LC MARC records, which were used as the bibliographic standard for this work. Each section was compiled based upon LC Classification, and their selected areas were given to the Subject Advisor(s) for their review.

The actual title selection was left to the Subject Advisors. Each advisor used the bibliographic resources available to them in their subject areas to make the best possible recommendations for undergraduate institutions. The Editor selected Advisors based upon their area(s) of expertise, working to see that each section was reviewed by two to three Subject Advisors to gain results that were well rounded. Advisors selected appropriate titles. Any titles that were deemed "omitted" from *The Best Books* database were added to the database, following the LC MARC record standard. When there was discrepancy in the LC sorting and/or the description of the "omitted" titles by the Advisors, The Best Books editorial staff defaulted to the information available on the LC MARC records.

The intention of The Best Books editorial staff was to include only books in this listing. However, in some cases other titles were included, based upon recommendations by Subject Advisors and Senior Subject Advisors. In some cases, Advisors did select annual reviews and multi-volume sets for inclusion in this work.

The editorial department has made every attempt to list the most recent publications for each title in this work. In the interest of maintaining a current core-collection list our Advisors were asked to note the most recent publications available, especially with regards to series and publishers that regularly produce new editions. Books were listed as the original edition (or latest reprint) when no information of a recent publication was available.

ERRORS, LACUNAE, AND OMISSIONS:

The Subject Advisors and Senior Subject Advisors were the sole source for recommending titles to include in the completed work, and no titles were intentionally added or omitted other than those that the Subject Advisors and Senior Subject Advisors recommended. There is no expressed or implied warranty or guarantee on this product.

The Best Books' editorial department requests that any suggestions or errors be sent, via e-mail or regular mail, to be corrected in future editions of this project.

BEST BOOKS EDITORIAL STAFF:

This work is the product of the group effort of a number of enthusiastic individuals: The Best Books editorial staff includes: Annette Wiles, Lee Anne Kawaguchi; Database Administrator, Richelle Tague; and Editor, Ashley Ludwig.

CONTRIBUTING ADVISORS:

This volume would not be possible without the dedicated work of our Subject Advisors and Senior Subject Advisors who donated their time, resources and knowledge towards creating this Best Books list. To them, we are truly grateful.

SUBJECT ADVISORS:

Michele Atlas — *Professor/Reference Librarian, Kornhauser Health Sciences Library, University of Louisville – Kentucky*

> Subject Advisor for the following sections: RA - Public Aspects of Medicine, RT - Nursing

Michelle Beattie — *Clinical Medical Librarian, University of Missouri Health Sciences Library*

> Subject Advisor for the following sections: RC - Internal Medicine, Practice of Medicine, RM - Therapeutics, Pharmacology

Dr. James Pat Craig — *Director, Health Sciences Library, Louisiana State University Health Sciences Center*

> Subject Advisor for the following sections: R – Medicine, RA - Public Aspects of Medicine, RX – Homeopathy, RZ – Other Systems of Medicine

Paula J. Craig — *Director, School of Nursing Library, Northwestern State University*

> Subject Advisor for the following sections: RT – Nursing, RX – Homeopathy, RZ - Other Systems of Medicine

Denise A. Garofalo — *Librarian, Astor Home for Children*

> Subject Advisor for the following sections: BF – Psychology, RA - Public Aspects of Medicine, RM - Therapeutics, Pharmacology, RX - Homeopathy

Jeff Gartman — *Reference Librarian, American Dental Association Library*

> Subject Advisor for the following section: RK - Dentistry

Julia Gelfand — *Applied Sciences & Engineering Librarian, University California, Irvine*

> Subject Advisor for the following sections: BF – Psychology, RA – Public Aspects of Medicine, RX - Homeopathy, and RZ – Other systems of medicine

David Juergens — *Acquisitions, Rowland Medical Library, University Of Mississippi Medical Center*

> Subject Advisor for the following sections: BF – Psychology, RT – Nursing

Bruce McClay — *Librarian, Librarian M.A., M.L.S., Walla Walla College School of Nursing*

> Subject Advisor for the following section: RT – Nursing

Kimberly Orr — *Library Manager, High Desert Hospital Library*

Subject Advisor for the following sections: R – Medicine, RC - Internal Medicine, Practice of Medicine, RT - Nursing

Brenda W. Quinn — *Education and Outreach Coordinator, Endometriosis Association Library*

Subject Advisor for the following section: RG - Gynecology & Obstetrics

Dr. Edwin Rather, M.D. — *Clinical Instructor, University of Arizona Medical School, Board Certified American Academy of Dermatology & American Society of Dermatopathology, Fellow, AAD, ASDP, ASDS, AMA, PDA, SWDS (Past President)*

Subject Advisor for the following section: RL - Dermatology

Ruth Schultz — *Reference Librarian, American Dental Association Library*

Subject Advisor for the following section: RK - Dentistry

Elizabeth M. Smigielski — *Acting Head of Technical Services, Kornhauser Health Sciences Library, University of Louisville*

Subject Advisor for the following sections: RC – Internal Medicine, Practice of Medicine, RX - Homeopathy

Joan Stoddart — *Deputy Director, Eccles Health Sciences Library, University of Utah*

Subject Advisor for the following section: RT - Nursing

Rajia Tobia — *Associate Director - Collection Development, University of Texas Health Sciences Center- San Antonio, University of Texas, San Antonio*

Subject Advisor for the following sections: RC - Internal Medicine, Practice of Medicine, RG - Gynecology and Obstetrics

SENIOR SUBJECT ADVISORS:

Michelle Beattie — *Clinical Medical Librarian, University of Missouri Health Sciences Library, University of Missouri.* Ms. Michelle Beattie earned her Masters of Library and Information Science from the University of Texas at Austin, and completed her Bachelor of Arts from the University of Kansas in Lawrence, Kansas. She is currently serving as a Clinical Medical Librarian at the Health Sciences Library, University of Missouri – Kansas City. Michelle has also served as a Clinical Medical Librarian at the Medical Dental Library and at the Truman Medical Center – Lakewood. Ms. Beattie's professional organizations include being a member of the Medical Library Association and member of the Hospital Libraries Section, the Medical Informatics Section, and the Corporate Information Services Section. She is also involved in the Mid-continental Chapter of the Medical Library Association and member of its Research Committee. Michelle is also a member of the Health Sciences Library Network of Kansas City, where she presently serves as the chair of the Educational/Professional Development Committee, and has served as Treasurer. She has belonged to the Kansas City Palm Users Group since 2001. Her Faculty Committee Assignments at the University of Missouri – Kansas City include serving on the University Libraries Staff Committee, the Librarians' Council Nominating and Elections Committee, the University Libraries Budget Advisory Task Force, and chairing the Librarians' Council University Libraries Budget Advisory Committee. She recently received the Grace and Harold Sewell Memorial Fund Stipend to attend the Annual Meeting of the American Association of Colleges of Pharmacy. Ms. Beattie has given numerous presentations regarding Palm OS Emulators and Personal Digital assistants, and their role in Health Sciences and Teaching.

Senior Subject Advisor for the following sections: BF – Psychology; R – Medicine (General); RA – Public Aspects of Medicine; RB – Pathology; RC – Internal Medicine; RD – Surgery; RE – Ophthalmology; RF – Otorhiolaryngology; RG – Gynecology & Obstetrics; RJ – Pediatrics; RK – Dentistry; RL – Dermatology; RM – Therapeutics. Pharmacology; RS – Pharmacy & Materia Medica; RT – Nursing; RV-Botanic, Thomsonian, and Eclectic Medicine; RX – Homeopathy; RZ – Other Systems of Medicine.

Denise A. Garofalo — *Library Director, Astor Home for Children, Rhinebeck, New York.* Ms. Denise A. Garoafalo received her Masters of Library Science from the State University of New York at Albany, where she also received her Bachelor of Arts Degree, cum laude. Denise is currently serving as the Library Director for the Astor Home for Children Library and the Astor Learning Center (ALC). Prior to her work with the ALC, she served as the Director for Telecommunications for the Mid-Hudson Library System, was Automation Consultant for the New Hampshire State Library, the Head of Technical Services for the Warwick Public Library, and began her employment as librarian for the Pawtucket Public Library. Denise is an adjunct professor for the State University of New York at Albany SISP, and is a member of the AAUW, ALA, ASIS, IEEE, NAFE, NELA, NYLA, and the Second Biennial Review Committee. Ms. Garofalo is a Grant Reviewer for Improving Literacy through School Libraries, National Leadership Grants, and the Regional Bibliographic Database Program. She is a reviewer for American Libraries, Library Journal, The Internet Encyclopedia, and other publications. Denise Garofalo also belongs to many professional associations, including the PC Weekly Advisory Board, the Professional Women's Advisory Board, and is a founding member of the Foundation for Hudson Valley Libraries.

Senior Subject Advisor for the following sections: BF – Psychology; R – Medicine (General); RA – Public Aspects of Medicine; RB – Pathology; RC – Internal Medicine; RF – Otorhiolaryngology; RJ – Pediatrics; RM – Therapeutics. Pharmacology; RS – Pharmacy & Materia Medica; RT – Nursing; RZ – Other Systems of Medicine.

David Juergens — *Head, Collection Development, Rowland Medical Library, University Of Mississippi Medical Center, University of Mississippi.* David Juergens received his Masters in Social Work from the Wayne State University in Detroit, Michigan, and his Bachelor of Arts degree from Elmhurst College. He has additional certification in Archival training, and Medical Terminology from the University of Mississippi Medical Center, and continues to further his education with library sciences and archival preservation and management training. He is currently serving as the Head of Collection Development for the University of Mississippi Medical Center, Rowland Medical Library in Jackson, Mississippi, where he also served as Acquisitions Librarian. David has experience as a Social Worker Supervisor, and a Psychiatric Social Worker. Mr. Juergens belongs to the Medical Library Association, the Southern Chapter/Medical Library Association, the Mississippi Library Association, and the Mississippi Biomedical Library Association. He belongs to many professional organizations, and has held offices and committee appointments in numerous local state, as well as regional appointments.

Senior Subject Advisor for the following sections: BF – Psychology; R – Medicine (General); RA – Public Aspects of Medicine; RB – Pathology; RC – Internal Medicine; RD – Surgery; RE – Ophthalmology; RF – Otorhiolaryngology; RG – Gynecology & Obstetrics; RJ – Pediatrics; RK – Dentistry; RL – Dermatology; RM – Therapeutics. Pharmacology; RS – Pharmacy & Materia Medica; RT – Nursing; RV-Botanic, Thomsonian, and Eclectic Medicine; RX – Homeopathy; RZ – Other Systems of Medicine.

Jean Liddell — *Reference Librarian, Ralph Brown Draughon Library, Auburn University, Alabama.* Jean Liddell received her Master of Arts in Library and Information Sciences from the University of Alabama, Tuscaloosa, in the College of Communication & Information Science. Her Undergraduate Studies were conducted at Memphis State University, graduating with a Bachelor of Arts in History from the University of Alabama at Birmingham. Jean began serving as Reference Librarian and Instructor at the Ralph Brown Draughon Library at Auburn University in November 2001. With a career history in the medical field, her liaison work includes Nursing, Nutrition, and Pharmacy. Jean's professional experience includes serving as a Reference Librarian and Instructor at the Delta State University in Cleveland, Mississippi, where she acted as Liaison for the Biology and Social Sciences Departments. Jean belongs to many professional associations, including the American Library Association, the Association of College and Research Libraries, the Alabama Library Association where she serves on the Reference and Adult Services Round Table, and the Southeast Library Association, where she works on the Professional Education and Continuing Education Committee. Jean's research interests include plagiarism, copyright, and public domain issues in academia and women's studies with a primary interest in spirituality.

Senior Subject Advisor for the following sections: BF – Psychology; R – Medicine (General); RA – Public Aspects of Medicine; RB – Pathology; RC – Internal Medicine; RD – Surgery; RE – Ophthalmology; RF – Otorhiolaryngology; RG – Gynecology & Obstetrics; RJ – Pediatrics; RK – Dentistry; RL – Dermatology; RM – Therapeutics. Pharmacology; RS – Pharmacy & Materia Medica; RT – Nursing; RV-Botanic, Thomsonian, and Eclectic Medicine; RX – Homeopathy; RZ – Other Systems of Medicine.

Bruce McClay — *Librarian, Librarian M.A., M.L.S., Walla Walla College School of Nursing.* Mr. McClay earned his Masters in Library and Information Science from the University of Missouri – Columbia in 1996. He also has his Masters degree in Religion (Church History) from Andrews University, Michigan, and earned his Bachelors Degree in History and Religion from Columbia Union College, in Maryland. Bruce McClay is currently working as an Assistant Librarian at the Walla Walla College School of Nursing Library in Walla Walla, Washington. Bruce previously worked as a Reference and Instructional Services Librarian at the University of Texas Pan American in Edinburg, Texas. McClay also has experience teaching at both the undergraduate and elementary school levels on a variety of subjects. He is currently a member of the School of Nursing Learning Resources Committee at the Walla Walla College School of Nursing Library. Bruce continues his education in his field of study, attending annual conferences and attending workshops, including the Annual Conference of the Association of Seventh-Day Adventist Librarians, of which he is a member. He has given numerous presentations and has published articles for professional publications, including the ASDAL and *Innovations in Special Education.* Mr. McClay's professional associations include the ASDAL, and the American Library Association.

Senior Subject Advisor for the following sections: RT – Nursing

Brenda W. Quinn — *Education and Outreach Coordinator, Endometriosis Association Library, Milwaukee, Wisconsin.* Quinn received her Masters Degree in Print Journalism, composing her thesis on media coverage of the 1918 flu epidemic, and was a fellow at the Institute of Humane Studies at Bryn Mawr College in Pennsylvania. Brenda received her Bachelor of Arts in Mass Communications from the University of Wisconsin at Milwaukee and she has won numerous awards for her publications, including the Council for Wisconsin Writers Leslie Cross Non-Fiction Book Award. . Brenda W. Quinn is currently serving as the education and outreach coordinator for the Endometriosis Association. She is currently at work on the biography of a Wisconsin Country Doctor.

Senior Subject Advisor for the following sections: RG – Gynecology & Obstetrics

Elizabeth M. Smigielski — *Acting Head of Technical Services, Kornhauser Health Sciences Library, University of Louisville, Louisville, Kentucky.* Elizabeth M. Smigielski is currently serving as the Acting Head of Technical Services and the Coordinator of Library Marketing at the Kornhauser Health Sciences Library at the University of Louisville. She received her Masters of Library Science at the University of Kentucky in Lexington, where she also earned her Masters in Foreign Language Education. Elizabeth attended both Wayne State University, and the Instituto de Lengua y Cultura Costarricense. Elizabeth has served as the Coordinator of Library Marketing, National Library of Medicine Associate Fellow for the Kornhauser Health Sciences Library, and as an Associate Fellow for the National Library of Medicine in Bethesda, Maryland. Ms. Smigielski has also worked in the area of molecular biology research, and her areas of research include epidemiology and infectious disease, the history of medicine, and alternative medicine. Elizabeth is affiliated with the Medical Library Association (MLA), the Medical Informatics Section, the Molecular Biology and Genomics Special Interest Group, and the Special Libraries Association (SLA), Kentucky Chapter, Leadership and Management Division. Her committee assignments include serving on the Gottlieb Prize Jury Committee for the MLA, and serving as the chair of the Diversity Leadership Development/Public Relations Committee, (SLA-Kentucky chapter). Her workshops and presentations have been given at the Midwest Chapter Medical Library Association, at the Medical Library Association Conference, and at the SLA-Kentucky Chapter Joint Spring Conference. She regularly attends conferences, and continues her education, serves the university library faculty on the Faculty Professional Travel Committee, and the Association for Research Libraries Planning Team. She also serves on the Archimedes Project Team, the Medical School First and Second Year Course Directors Committees, and the Health Sciences Center Web Committee.

Senior Subject Advisor for the following sections: BF – Psychology; R – Medicine (General); RA – Public Aspects of Medicine; RB – Pathology; RC – Internal Medicine; RD – Surgery; RG – Gynecology & Obstetrics; RJ – Pediatrics; RK – Dentistry; RM – Therapeutics. Pharmacology; RS – Pharmacy & Materia Medica; RT – Nursing; RV-Botanic, Thomsonian, and Eclectic Medicine; RX – Homeopathy; RZ – Other Systems of Medicine.

Joan M. Stoddart — *Deputy Director, Eccles Health Sciences Library, University of Utah, Salt Lake City, Utah.* Joan M. Stoddart earned her Master of Arts in Library Science from the Rosary College Graduate School in River Forest, IL. Her undergraduate studies were conducted at the University of Wisconsin, where she earned her Bachelor of Arts in History. Joan has continued her education regarding preservation of Library and Archival materials, courses related to Library administration and management, Research Methods, and History of Medicine Resources for Small Libraries. Ms. Stoddart currently is serving as Deputy Director of the Spencer S. Eccles Health Science Library at the University of Utah, where she has worked since 1979 and has received many academic promotions. Jean supervises the history of medicine collection, and has long been responsible for the Clinical Library and its services. Her professional experience has also included working as Reference Librarian at the University of Cincinnati, and as Library Manager for the Inhalation Toxicology Research Institute in Albuquerque, New Mexico. Joan has many professional associations and committee memberships. She is a member of the Medical Library Association (MLA) since 1973 – where she currently serves as the Continuing Education Liaison for History of the Health Sciences Section. Her memberships with the MLA have included serving on the National Program Committee for the 2002 Annual Meeting, the Credentialing Committee and the Chapter/Section Support Sub-Committee. For the MLA, she has also served as Liaison to CE Committee, Library Research Section, the Frank Bradway Rogers Information Advancement Award Jury, and has chaired the Membership Committee. She also belongs to the Mid-continental chapter, Medical Library Association (MLA), of which she has been a member since 1980. Joan is currently serving on the Nominating Committee, 2002-2004 and Chair, 2003. She has chaired and been active on many committees, including the Strategic Planning Committee, the Chair of the Honors and Awards Committee, and Co-Chair of the Annual Meeting Steering Committee. Stoddart has also been a member of the National Network of Libraries of Medicine, the Utah Library Association and the Utah State Library Division. She currently has duties and obligations with the University of Utah, the Utah Academic Library Council, and the Utah Health Science Library Consortium. She has acted as a consultant for the Consumer Health Information Center, the Association of Consulting Toxicologist as Search Analyst, and has consulted for Library Planning for the Cottonwood Hospital, the Western Rehabilitation Institute, and the Humana Davis North Hospital. Ms. Stoddart is also active in her community, having served on the Consumer Health Information Center Advisory Board, the East County Recreation Advisory Board, the Snowbird Ski Race Association Board of Directors, and as a Trustee for Families Involved in Adoption. Joan's publications have included writing papers and conducting presentations for such professional organizations as the Medical Library Association, InfoFairs, and columns for the *Health Sciences Report* for the Spencer S. Eccles Health Sciences Library as well as book reviews for *the Journal of the Medical Library*.

Ms. Stoddart has received awards and honors including: Continuing Education Award from the MLA, an Outstanding Achievement Award from the Mid-Continental Chapter, MLA, Distinguished Member for the Academy of Health Information Professionals, MLA, and Medical Librarian Certification from the MLA.

Senior Subject Advisor for the following sections: BF – Psychology; R – Medicine (General); RA – Public Aspects of Medicine; RB – Pathology; RC – Internal Medicine; RD – Surgery; RE – Ophthalmology; RF – Otorhiolaryngology; RG – Gynecology & Obstetrics; RJ – Pediatrics; RK – Dentistry; RL – Dermatology; RM – Therapeutics. Pharmacology; RS – Pharmacy & Materia Medica; RT – Nursing; RV-Botanic, Thomsonian, and Eclectic Medicine; RX – Homeopathy; RZ – Other Systems of Medicine.

BF11-891 Psychology

BF11 Societies

BF11.A68 1992
The American Psychological Association : a historical perspective / edited by Rand B. Evans, Virginia Staudt Sexton, Thomas C. Cadwallader. Washington, DC : American Psychological Association, c1992. xvi, 415 p.,
91-035825   150/.6/073   1557981361

BF20 Congresses

BF20.W28
Wann, T. W.,
Behaviorism and phenomenology; contrasting bases for modern psychology. Contributors: Sigmund Koch [and others. Chicago] Published for William Marsh Rice University [1964] xi, 190 p.
64-012257   150.19
Psychology -- Congresses.

BF21 Collected works (nonserial)

BF21.H8
Hunt, Joseph McVicker,
Personality and the behavior disorders, a handbook based on experimental and clinical research, edited by J. McV. Hunt. New York, The Ronald press company [1944] 2 v.
44-002163   616.89
Personality. Psychology, Pathological.

BF30 Directories

BF30.A56
Annual review of psychology. Stanford, Calif., Annual Reviews. v.
50-013143   150.58
Psychology -- Periodicals.

BF31 Dictionaries. Encyclopedias

BF31.C65 2001
Colman, Andrew M.
A dictionary of psychology / Andrew M. Colman. Oxford ; Oxford University Press, 2001. xiv, 844 p. :
01-133070   150/.3   0198662114
Psychology -- Dictionaries.

BF31.C67 1996
Concise encyclopedia of psychology / Raymond J. Corsini and Alan J. Auerbach, editors ; consulting editors, Anne Anastasi ... [et al.] ; associate editors, Mary Allen ... [et al.] ; managing editor, Becky Ozaki. New York : J. Wiley, c1996. xxi, 1035 p.
95-026497   150/.3   0471131598
Psychology -- Encyclopedias.

BF31.C72 1999
Corsini, Raymond J.
The dictionary of psychology / Raymond J. Corsini. Philadelphia, PA : Brunner/Mazel, c1999. xv, 1156 p. :
          150/.3   158391028X
Psychology--Dictionaries.

BF31.E5 1994
Encyclopedia of human behavior / editor-in-chief, V.S. Ramachandran. San Diego, CA : Academic Press, c1994. 4 v. :
93-034371   150/.3   0122269209
Psychology -- Encyclopedias.

BF31.E52 2000
Encyclopedia of psychology / Alan E. Kazdin, editor in chief. Washington, D.C. : American Psychological Association ; 2000. 8 v. ; 29 cm.
99-055239   150/.3   1557986509
Psychology -- Encyclopedias.

BF31.E52 2001
The Corsini encyclopedia of psychology and behavioral science / co-editors, W. Edward Craighead, Charles B. Nemeroff. New York : Wiley, c2001. 4 v. :
99-058006   150/.3   0471239496
Psychology -- Encyclopedias.

BF31.R625 1998
Roeckelein, Jon E.
Dictionary of theories, laws, and concepts in psychology / Jon E. Roeckelein. Westport, Conn. : Greenwood Press, 1998. xxvii, 548 p.
97-043941   150/.3   0313304602
Psychology -- Dictionaries.

BF31.Z87 1987
Zusne, Leonard,
Eponyms in psychology : a dictionary and biographical sourcebook / Leonard Zusne. New York : Greenwood Press, 1987. xxi, 339 p. ;
87-000255   150/.3/21   0313257507
Psychology -- Dictionaries. Biography -- Dictionaries. Eponyms -- Dictionaries.

BF38 Philosophy. Relation to other topics

BF38.A23
Adler, Mortimer Jerome,
What man has made of man; a study of the consequences of Platonism and positivism in psychology. With an introd. by Franz Alexander. New York, Ungar [1957, c1937] 246 p.
57-009409   150
Psychology. Psychology -- Philosophy. Psychology and philosophy.

BF38.A38
Allport, Gordon W.
Becoming; basic considerations for a psychology of personality. New Haven, Yale University Press, 1955. 106 p.
55-005975   137
Psychology.

BF38.B63 1999
Botterill, George.
The philosophy of psychology / George Botterill and Peter Carruthers. Cambridge, U.K. ; Cambridge University Press, 1999. xii, 297 p. :
98-033301   150/.1   0521551110
Psychology -- Philosophy.

BF38.D675 1988
Dretske, Fred I.
Explaining behavior : reasons in a world of causes / Fred Dretske. Cambridge, Mass. : MIT Press, c1988. xi, 165 p. ;
87-026158   150   0262040948
Psychology -- Philosophy. Human behavior. Causation.

BF38.F63 1987
Fodor, Jerry A.
Psychosemantics : the problem of meaning in the philosophy of mind / Jerry A. Fodor. Cambridge, Mass. : MIT Press, c1987. xiii, 171 p.
86-033173   128/.4   0262061066
Philosophy of mind. Representation (Philosophy) Causation.

BF38.G67
Gregory, R. L.
Mind in science : a history of explanations in psychology and physics / Richard L. Gregory. Cambridge [Cambridgeshire] : Cambridge University Press, 1981. xi, 641 p. :
81-007732   153/.01   0521243076
Psychology -- Philosophy. Science -- Philosophy. Physics -- Philosophy.

BF38.J87 1998
Justman, Stewart.
The psychological mystique / Stewart Justman. Evanston, Ill. : Northwestern University Press, 1998. 181 p. ;
98-029522   150/.1   0810116014
Psychology -- Philosophy. Ethnopsychology.

BF38.K23 1998
Kagan, Jerome.
Three seductive ideas / Jerome Kagan. Cambridge, Mass. : Harvard University Press, 1998. 232 p. ;
98-008169   150/.1   0674890337
Psychology -- Philosophy. Psychology.

BF38.K84 2001
Kukla, André,
Methods of theoretical psychology / André Kukla. Cambridge, Mass. : MIT Press, c2001. xii, 250 p. :
          150/.1   0262112612
Psychology--Philosophy. Psychology--Methodology.

BF38.W764 1982
Wittgenstein, Ludwig,
Last writings on the philosophy of psychology / Ludwig Wittgenstein ; edited by G.H. von Wright and Heikki Nyman ; translated by C.G. Luckhardt and Maximilian A.E. Aue. Chicago : University of Chicago Press, c1982-1992. 2 v. ;
82-042549   192   0226904458
Psychology -- Philosophy.

BF38.5 Philosophy. Relation to other topics — Methodology

BF38.5.R86 1982
Runyan, William McKinley.
Life histories and psychobiography : explorations in theory and method / William McKinley Runyan. New York : Oxford University Press, 1982. xiii, 288 p.
82-006458   155   019503189X
Psychology -- Methodology. Psychohistory. Personality.

BF38.5.R9
Rychlak, Joseph F.
A philosophy of science for personality theory [by] Joseph F. Rychlak. Boston, Houghton Mifflin [1968] xix, 508 p.
68-002021   155.2
Psychology -- Philosophy. Personality. Psychology -- Methodology.

BF39 Philosophy. Relation to other topics — Methodology — Mathematical and statistical methods. Psychometrics

BF39.C56 2001
Cohen, Barry H.,
Explaining psychological statistics / Barry H. Cohen. 2nd ed. New York : Wiley, c2001. xxxvii, 745 p. :
          150/.1/5195   0471345822
Psychometrics. Psychology--Mathematical models. Statistics--Study and teaching (Higher)

BF39.C67 1989
Cowles, Michael,
Statistics in psychology : an historical perspective / Michael Cowles. Hillsdale, N.J. : L. Erlbaum Associates, 1989. xvi, 218 p. :
89-011628   150/.72   080580031X
Psychology -- Statistical methods -- History. Social sciences -- Statistical methods -- History.

BF39.H26435 1993
A Handbook for data analysis in the behavioral sciences : methodological issues / edited by Gideon Keren, Charles Lewis. Hillsdale, N.J. : L. Erlbaum Associates, 1993. xii, 574 p. :
92-023007   150/.72   0805810366
Psychology -- Statistical methods. Social sciences -- Statistical methods. Psychology -- Research -- Methodology.

BF39.L79 1963
Luce, R. Duncan
Handbook of mathematical psychology, edited by R. Duncan Luce, Robert R. Bush [and] Eugene Galanter. New York, Wiley [1963-65] 3 v.
63-009428   150.151
Psychology -- Mathematical models. Psychometrics.

BF39.L83
Luce, R. Duncan
Readings in mathematical psychology. Edited by R. Duncan Luce, Robert R. Bush [and] Eugene Galanter. New York, Wiley [1963-65] 2 v.
63014066   150.151
Psychology -- Mathematical models. Psychometrics.

BF39.M545 1999
Michell, Joel.
Measurement in psychology :critical history of a methodological concept / Joel Michell. New York : Cambridge University Press, c1999. xvi, 246 p. ;
          150/.28/7   0521621208
Psychometrics--History. Psychology--Methodology--History.

BF39.4 Philosophy. Relation to other topics — Methodology — Biographical methods

BF39.4.E46 1994
Elms, Alan C.,
Uncovering lives : the uneasy alliance of biography and psychology / Alan C. Elms. New York : Oxford University Press, 1994. vi, 315 p. ;
94-016699   920/.001/9   0195082877
Psychology -- Biographical methods. Biography as a literary form. Psychologists -- Psychology -- Case studies.

BF39.5 Philosophy. Relation to other topics — Methodology — Electronic data processing. Computer models and simulation

BF39.5.B63 1988
Boden, Margaret A.
Computer models of mind : computational approaches in theoretical psychology / Margaret A. Boden. Cambridge [England] ; Cambridge University Press, 1988. xi, 289 p. :
87-025625   150/.724   052124868X
Psychology -- Computer simulation. Psychology -- Philosophy.

BF39.5.R49 1987
Reynolds, James H.,
Computing in psychology : an introduction to programming methods and concepts / James H. Reynolds. Englewood Cliffs, N.J. : Prentice-Hall, 1987. xii, 354 p. :
86-000593   150/.28/5526   0131658123
Psychology -- Data processing. Computer programming.

BF39.9 Philosophy. Relation to other topics — Critical psychology

BF39.9.C76 2000
Critical psychology : voices for change / edited by Tod Sloan. Houndmills [England] : Macmillan ; St. Martin's Press, 2000. xxvi, 256 p.
00-041508   150.19/8   0333794524
Critical psychology.

BF41 Philosophy. Relation to other topics — Relation to other topics — Relation to critical and speculative philosophy

BF41.P55 1996
The philosophy of psychology / edited by William O'Donohueand Richard F. Kitchener. London ; Sage Publications, 1996. xx, 395 p. ;
96-070152   150/.1   0761953043
Psychology and philosophy.

BF41.S57 1995
Slife, Brent D.
What's behind the research? : discovering hidden assumptions in the behavioral sciences / Brent D. Slife, Richard N. Williams. Thousand Oaks, Calif. : Sage Publications, 1995. xii, 251 p. ;
95-009376   300/.1   0803958625
Psychology and philosophy. Psychology -- Philosophy.

BF44 Philosophy. Relation to other topics — Relation to other topics — Relation to logic

BF44.K3
Kantor, J. R.
Psychology and logic. Bloomington, Ind., Principia Press, 1945-50. 2 v.
45001744   160
Logic. Behaviorism (Psychology) Psychology.

BF47 Philosophy. Relation to other topics — Relation to other topics — Relation to ethics and conduct

BF47.D45 1996
Deigh, John.
The sources of moral agency : essays in moral psychology and Freudian theory / John Deigh. Cambridge ; Cambridge University Press, 1996. xv, 254 p. ;
95-047292   155.2/32   0521556228
Freud, Sigmund, -- 1856-1939 -- Ethics. Psychology. Ethics. Moral development.

BF47.H6
Hollingworth, Harry Levi,
Psychology and ethics. New York, Ronald Press Co., 1949. ix, 247 p.
49007396   177.8
Psychology. Ethics.

BF56 Philosophy. Relation to other topics — Relation to other topics — Relation to economics, business, etc.

BF56.C65
Corsini, Raymond J.
Roleplaying in business and industry [by] Raymond J. Corsini, Malcolm E. Shaw [and] Robert R. Blake. [New York] Free Press of Glencoe [1961] 246 p.
61010897   150.13
Psychology, Industrial. Role playing.

BF57 Philosophy. Relation to other topics — Relation to other topics — Relation to sociology

BF57.D4 1930
Dewey, John,
Human nature and conduct; an introduction to social psychology, by John Dewey, with a new introduction by John Dewey. New York, The Modern library [c1930] ix, p., 1 l.,
30-019598   150
Social psychology -- Problems, exercises, etc.

BF57.H36 1998
Handbook of evolutionary psychology : ideas, issues, and applications / edited by Charles Crawford, Dennis L. Krebs. Mahwah, N.J. : Lawrence Erlbaum Associates, 1998. xii, 663 p. :
97-016301   155.7   0805816666
Psychology. Sociobiology. Genetic psychology.

BF64 Philosophy. Relation to other topics — Relation to other topics — Relation to natural sciences

BF64.A27 1998
Abra, Jock,
Should psychology be a science? : pros and cons / Jock Abra. Westport, Conn. : Praeger, 1998. xv, 249 p. :
97-021853   150/.1   0275954765
Science and psychology. Science and psychology -- History. Psychology -- Methodology.

BF76.4 Ethics in psychology and in psychological research

BF76.4.E814 1999
Ethical conflicts in psychology / Donald N. Bersoff. 2nd ed. Washington, DC : American Psychological Association, c1999. xxiv, 597 p. ;
       174/.915   155798591X
Psychology--Moral and ethical aspects. Psychologists--Professional ethics.

BF76.4.K55 1996
Kimmel, Allan J.
Ethical issues in behavioral research : a survey / Allan J. Kimmel. Cambridge, Mass., USA : Blackwell Publishers, 1996. xxi, 405 p. :
95-037163   174/.915   1557863946
Psychology -- Research -- Moral and ethical aspects. Human experimentation in psychology -- Moral and ethical aspects. Animal experimentation -- Moral and ethical aspects.

BF76.4.P75 1994
Prilleltensky, Isaac,
The morals and politics of psychology : psychological discourse and the status quo / Isaac Prilleltensky. Albany, NY : State University of New York Press, c1994. xiii, 283 p.
93-037494   150/.1   079142037X
Psychology -- Moral and ethical aspects. Psychology, Applied -- Moral and ethical aspects. Psychology -- Social aspects.

BF76.5 Research

BF76.5.D864 1999
Dunn, Dana.
The practical researcher : a student guide to conducting psychological research / Dana S. Dunn. Boston : McGraw-Hill College, c1999. xiv, 390 p. :
98-026089   150/.7/2   0070183236
Psychology -- Research -- Methodology. Psychology, Experimental.

BF76.5.E47 2001
The emotional nature of qualitative research / edited by Kathleen R. Gilbert. Boca Raton, Fla. : CRC Press, c2001. 201 p. ;
00-057984   150/.7/2   0849320755
Psychology -- Research -- Methodology. Qualitative research.

BF76.5.K68 1999
Using qualitative methods in psychology / Mary Kopala, Lisa A. Suzuki, editors. Thousand Oaks : Sage, c1999. xv, 237 p. ;
       150/.72   0761910379
Psychology--Research--Methodology.

BF76.7 Communication in psychology — General works

BF76.7.P83 2001
Publication manual of the American Psychological Association. 5th ed. Washington, DC : American Psychological Association, c2001. xxviii, 439 p. :
      808/.06615   1557988102
  Psychology--Authorship--Handbooks, manuals, etc. Social sciences--Authorship--Handbooks, manuals, etc. Psychological literature--Publishing--Handbooks, manuals, etc.

BF76.7.R67 2001
Rosnow, Ralph L.
Writing papers in psychology :a student guide / Ralph L. Rosnow, Mimi Rosnow. 5th ed. Belmont, CA : Wadsworth Thomson Learning, c2001. xii, 154 p. :
      808/.06615   0534529755
  Psychology--Authorship. Report writing.

BF80.5 Study and teaching — Equipment and supplies

BF80.5.K32
Katz, David,
Psychological atlas; with 400 illus. New York, Philosophical Library [1948] x, 142 p.
48005713   150.84
  Psychology -- Pictorial works. Psychology -- drawings

BF80.7 Study and teaching — By region or country, A-Z

BF80.7.U6.T43 1992
Teaching psychology in America : a history / edited by Antonio E. Puente, Janet R. Matthews, and Charles L. Brewer. Washington DC : American Psychological Association, c1992. xx, 578 p. :
92-032027   150/.71/173   1557981817
  Psychology -- Study and teaching (Higher) -- United States -- History. Psychology -- Training of -- United States -- History.

BF81 History — General works

BF81.P47 1997
A pictorial history of psychology / edited by Wolfgang G. Bringmann ... [et al.]. Chicago : Quintessence Pub., c1997. xix, 636 p. :
96-024728   150/.9/022   0867152923
  Psychology -- History -- Pictorial works.

BF81.R6
Roback, A. A.
History of psychology and psychiatry.   New York, Philosophical Library [1961] 422 p.
61-010613   150.9
  Psychology -- History. Psychiatry -- History.

BF81.W35 1968
Watson, Robert Irving,
The great psychologists from Aristotle to Freud [by] Robert I. Watson. Philadelphia, Lippincott [1968] xiv, 613 p.
68-015731   150/.922
  Psychology -- History.

BF95-105 History — By period — Modern

BF95.F5 1964
Flugel, J. C.
A hundred years of psychology,1833-1933, additional part: 1933-1963, by Donald J. West. by J.C. Flugel. With an New York, Basic Books [1964] 394 p.
      150.9
  Psychology--History.

BF95.S73 1982
Stevens, Gwendolyn.
The women of psychology / by Gwendolyn Stevens and Sheldon Gardner. Cambridge, Mass. : Schenkman Pub. Co., 1982. 2 v. :
81-014394   150/.88042   0870734431
  Psychology -- History. Women psychologists. Psychology -- United States -- History.

BF98.B23
Basic writings in the history of psychology / [compiled by] Robert I. Watson, Sr. New York : Oxford University Press, 1979. xviii, 420 p.
78-007274   150/.8   0195024435
  Psychology -- History -- Addresses, essays, lectures. Psychology -- Early works to 1850 -- Addresses, essays, lectures.

BF103.T73 2001
The transformation of psychology : influences of 19th century philosophy, technology, and natural science / edited by Christopher D. Green, Marlene Shore, and Thomas Teo. Washington, DC : American Psychological Association, c2001. xvii, 245 p.
00-068985   150/.9/034   1557987769
  Psychology -- History -- 19th century -- Congresses.

BF103.W6
Wolman, Benjamin B.
Historical roots of contemporary psychology, edited by Benjamin B. Wolman. New York, Harper & Row [1968] viii, 376 p.
68-010810   150
  Psychology -- History -- Addresses, essays, lectures.

BF105.E87 2002
Evolving perspectives on the history of psychology / edited by Wade E. Pickren and Donald A. Dewsbury. 1st ed. Washington, DC : American Psychological Association, c2002. ix, 608 p. :
      150/.9   155798882X
  Psychology--History--20th century. Psychology--History--19th century.

BF105.G66 1999
Goodwin, C. James.
   A history of modern psychology / C. James Goodwin. New York : J. Wiley, c1999. xix, 491 p. :
               150/.9/04   0471128058
   Psychology--History--20th century. Psychology--History--19th century.

BF105.K44 1996
Keehn, J. D.
   Master builders of modern psychology : from Freud to Skinner / J.D. Keehn. Washington Square, N.Y. : New York University Press, 1996. xi, 202 p. :
   95-051968   150/.9   0814746853
   Psychology -- History -- 20th century. Psychology -- History -- 19th century. Behaviorism (Psychology) -- History.

BF105.K45 2001
Keen, Ernest,
   A history of ideas in American psychology / Ernest Keen. Westport, Conn. : Praeger, 2001. xiv, 267 p. ;
               150/.973   0275972054
   Psychology--United States--History--20th century.

BF105.P79 1987
   Psychology in twentieth-century thought and society / edited by Mitchell G. Ash, William R. Woodward. Cambridge ; Cambridge University Press, 1987. ix, 320 p. ;
               150/.9   0521325234
   Psychology--History--20th century. Psychology--history.

BF105.W6 1964
Woodworth, Robert Sessions,
   Contemporary schools of psychology, by Robert S. Woodworth in collaboration with Mary R. Sheehan. 3d ed. New York, Ronald Press Co. [1964] viii, 457 p.
   Psychology.

BF108 By region or country, A-Z

BF108.A3.H65 2000
Holdstock, T. Len.
   Re-examining psychology :critical perspectives and African insights / T. Len Holdstock. London ; Routledge, 2000. xi, 255 p. ;
               155.8   0415187923
   Psychology--Africa, Sub-Saharan.

BF108.A92.G37 1992
Gardner, Sheldon.
   Red Vienna and the golden age of psychology, 1918-1938 / Sheldon Gardner and Gwendolyn Stevens ; foreword by Rudolf Ekstein. New York : Praeger, 1992. xiv, 285 p. ;
   91-036401   150/.9436/1309042
   0275940136
   Psychology -- Austria -- Vienna -- History -- 20th century. Vienna (Austria) -- Intellectual life.

BF108.S65.J67 1989
Joravsky, David.
   Russian psychology : a critical history / David Joravsky. Oxford, UK ; Blackwell, 1989. xxii, 583 p.,
   88-016833   150/.947   0631163379
   Psychology -- Soviet Union -- History. Communism and psychology -- Soviet Union -- History.

BF108.S65.K68 1984
Kozulin, Alex.
   Psychology in Utopia : toward a social history of Soviet psychology / Alex Kozulin. Cambridge, Mass. : MIT Press, c1984. xi, 179 p. :
   83-022264   150/.947   0262110873
   Psychology -- Soviet Union -- History. Psychology -- Soviet Union -- Philosophy. Psychology -- Social aspects -- Soviet Union.

BF108.U5.H66 1989
Hoopes, James,
   Consciousness in New England : from Puritanism and ideas to psychoanalysis and semiotic / James Hoopes. Baltimore : Johns Hopkins University Press, c1989. viii, 294 p.
   89-002663   155.2/0974   080183824X
   Psychology -- United States -- History. Psychology -- New England -- History. Consciousness -- History. New England -- Intellectual life.

BF108.U5.I58 1997
   Inventing the psychological : toward a cultural history of emotional life in America / edited by Joel Pfister and Nancy Schnog. New Haven, [Conn.] : Yale University Press, c1997. xiv, 329 p. :
   96-023275   150/.973   0300068093
   Psychology -- United States -- History. Social psychology -- United States -- History. Psychoanalysis and culture.

BF108.U5P67 1994
Popplestone, John A.
   An illustrated history of American psychology / John A. Popplestone, Marion White McPherson. Madison, Wis. : Brown & Benchmark Publishers, c1994. xii, 222 p. :
               150/.973   0697211274
   Psychology--United States--History. Psychologists--United States--History.

BF109.A1 Biography — Collective

BF109.A1.B56 1997
   Biographical dictionary of psychology / edited by Noel Sheehy, Antony J. Chapman, Wendy A. Conroy. London ; Routledge Reference, 1997. xvii, 675 p.
   96-034333   150/.92/2   0415099978
   Psychologists -- Biography -- Dictionaries. Psychology -- History.

BF109.A1.P67 1991
   Portraits of pioneers in psychology / edited by Gregory A.Kimble, Michael Wertheimer, Charlotte White. Washington, DC : American Psychological Association ; 1991-c1998 v. 1-3 :
   91-007226   150/.92/2   0805806202
   Psychologists -- Biography. Psychology -- History.

BF109.A1S56 2002
Simonton, Dean Keith.
    Great psychologists and their times :scientific insights into psychology's history / Dean Keith Simonton. 1st ed. Washington, DC : American Psychological Association, 2002. p. cm.
                    150/.92/2   155798896X
    Psychologists--Psychology.

BF109.A1.W65 1990
    Women in psychology : a bio-bibliographic sourcebook / edited by Agnes N. O'Connell and Nancy Felipe Russo. New York : Greenwood Press, 1990. x, 441 p. ;
89-025787   150/.92/2   0313260915
    Women psychologists -- Biography. Psychologists -- Biography. Psychology -- Bio-bibliography.

BF109.A1.Z85 1984
Zusne, Leonard,
    Biographical dictionary of psychology / Leonard Zusne. Westport, Conn. : Greenwood Press, 1984. xxi, 563 p. ;
83-018326   150/.92/2   0313240272
    Psychologists -- Biography -- Dictionaries. Psychology -- History.

BF109.A4-V95 Biography — Individual, A-Z

BF109.A4B62 1957a
Bottome, Phyllis,
    Alfred Adler, a portrait from life, by Phyllis Bottome. New York, Vanguard, 1957. 300 p.
58009249
    Adler, Alfred, -- 1870-1937.   Psychology -- biography.

BF109.D48.S29 1991
Sayers, Janet.
    Mothers of psychoanalysis : Helene Deutsch, Karen Horney, Anna Freud, Melanie Klein / Janet Sayers. New York : W.W. Norton, 1991. xiii, 319 p.
91-018644   150.19/5/0922   0393030415
    Deutsch, Helene, -- 1884- Horney, Karen, -- 1885-1952. Freud, Anna, -- 1895- Psychoanalysis. Women -- Psychology.

BF109.E7.S73 1983
Stevens, Richard.
    Erik Erikson, an introduction / Richard Stevens. New York : St. Martin's Press, 1983. 148 p. ;
83-003256   150.19/5/0924   0312258127
    Erikson, Erik H. -- (Erik Homburger), -- 1902-   Psychoanalysis. Psychoanalysis -- Social aspects. Psychoanalysis -- Biography.

BF109.E7W45 2000
Welchman, Kit.
    Erik Erikson : his life, work, and significance / Kit Welchman. Philadelphia : Open University Press, 2000. p. cm.
                    150.19/5/092   0335201571
    Erikson, Erik H. (Erik Homburger), 1902-   Psychoanalysts--United States--Biography. Psychanalysis--History.

BF109.F74.A25 1995
Freud, Sigmund,
    Psychological writings and letters / Sigmund Freud ; edited by Sander L. Gilman. New York : Continuum, 1995. xli, 281 p. ;
93-047191   150.19/52   0826407226
    Freud, Sigmund, -- 1856-1939 -- Correspondence.   Psychoanalysis. Psychoanalysts -- Austria -- Correspondence.

BF109.F74.A4 1993b
Freud, Sigmund,
    The correspondence of Sigmund Freud and Sandor Ferenczi / edited by Eva Brabant, Ernst Falzeder, and Patrizia Giampieri-Deutsch, under the supervision of Andre Haynal ; transcribed by Ingeborg Meyer-Palmedo ; translated by Peter T. Hoffer ; introduction by Andre Haynal. Cambridge, Mass. : Belknap Press of Harvard University Press, 1993-1996 v. 1-2 ;
93-017479   150.19/52/0922   0674174186
    Freud, Sigmund, -- 1856-1939 -- Correspondence. Ferenczi, Sandor, -- 1873-1933 -- Correspondence.   Psychoanalysts -- Correspondence. Psychoanalysis.

BF109.F74.A82513 1996
Althusser, Louis.
    Writings on psychoanalysis : Freud and Lacan / Louis Althusser ; edited by Olivier Corpet and Francois Matheron ; translated and with a preface by Jeffrey Mehlman. New York : Columbia University Press, c1996. ix, 194 p. :
96-025626   150.19/5   0231101686
    Freud, Sigmund, -- 1856-1939. Lacan, Jacques, -- 1901- Psychoanalysis.

BF109.F74.G39 1988
Gay, Peter,
    Freud : a life for our time / Peter Gay. New York : Norton, c1988. xx, 810 p., [
87-020454   150.19/52   0393025179
    Freud, Sigmund, -- 1856-1939.   Psychoanalysts -- Austria -- Biography. Psychoanalysis -- History.

BF109.F74.G55 1993
Gilman, Sander L.
    The case of Sigmund Freud : medicine and identity at the fin de siecle / Sander L. Gilman. Baltimore : Johns Hopkins University Press, c1993. xiii, 298 p.
92-039662   305.8/924   0801845351
    Freud, Sigmund, -- 1856-1939 -- Religion. Freud, Sigmund, -- 1856-1939. Antisemitism -- Austria -- Vienna -- History. Medicine -- Austria -- Vienna -- History. Judaism and psychoanalysis.

BF109.F74.G7813 1996
Grubrich-Simitis, Ilse.
    Back to Freud's texts : making silent documents speak / Ilse Grubrich-Simitis ; translated by Philip Slotkin. New Haven : Yale University Press, c1996. xv, 322 p. :
96-008117   150.19/52/092   0300066317
    Freud, Sigmund, -- 1856-1939 -- Manuscripts.   Criticism, Textual.

BF109.F74.H845 1994
Hughes, Judith M.
From Freud's consulting room : the unconscious in a scientific age / Judtih M. Hughes. Cambridge, Mass. : Harvard University Press, 1994. x, 235 p. :
93-047172   150.19/52/092   0674324528
Freud, Sigmund, -- 1856-1939.   Subconsciousness -- History.
Psychoanalysis -- History. Clinical psychology -- History.

BF109.F74.R55 1998
Rizzuto, Ana-Maria.
Why did Freud reject God? : a psychodynamic interpretation / Ana-Maria Rizzuto. New Haven : Yale University Press, c1998. xxi, 297 p. :
97-049877   200/.92   0300075251
Freud, Sigmund, -- 1856-1939 -- Religion.

BF109.F74.R632 1995
Roazen, Paul,
How Freud worked : first-hand accounts of patients / Paul Roazen. Northvale, N.J. : J. Aronson, c1995. xxvi, 301 p.
95-011733   150.19/52/092   1568215568
Freud, Sigmund, -- 1856-1939.   Psychoanalysis -- Case studies.

BF109.F76.B87 1991
Burston, Daniel,
The legacy of Erich Fromm / Danmiel Burston. Cambridge, Mass. : Harvard University Press, 1991. p. cm.
90-005348   150.19/57/092   0674521684
Fromm, Erich, -- 1900-   Psychoanalysis.

BF109.F76.K59 1989
Knapp, Gerhard Peter.
The art of living : Erich Fromm's life and works / Gerhard P. Knapp. New York : P. Lang, c1989. vi, 270 p. ;
88-038026   150.19/57/0924   0820410349
Fromm, Erich, -- 1900-   Psychoanalysts -- United States --
Biography.

BF109.J8.D7
Dry, Avis M
The psychology of Jung; a critical interpretation. London, Methuen; [1961] 329 p.
62003771   131.3464
Jung, C. G. -- (Carl Gustav), -- 1875-1961.

BF109.J8 H39 2001
Hayman, Ronald,
A life of Jung / Ronald Hayman. New York : W.W. Norton, 2001. xxi, 522 p. :
00-054802   150.19/54/092   0393019675
Jung, C. G. -- (Carl Gustav), -- 1875-1961.   Psychoanalysts --
Switzerland -- Biography. Jungian psychology -- History.
Psychoanalysis -- History.

BF109.L28.R6613 1997
Roudinesco, Elisabeth,
Jacques Lacan / Elisabeth Roudinesco ; translated by Barbara Bray. New York : Columbia University Press, c1997. xix, 574 p. :
96-030125   150.19/5/092   0231101465
Lacan, Jacques, -- 1901-   Psychoanalysts -- France -- Biography.
Psychoanalysis -- France -- History.

BF109.M33.H63 1988
Hoffman, Edward,
The right to be human : a biography of Abraham Maslow / Edward Hoffman. Los Angeles : J.P. Tarcher ; c1988. xviii, 382 p.
87-033518   150/.92/4   0874774616
Maslow, Abraham H. -- (Abraham Harold)   Psychologists -- United
States -- Biography.

BF109.M49.A4 1990
Meyer, Adolf,
Defining American psychology : the correspondence between Adolf Meyer and Edward Bradford Titchener / edited by Ruth Leys and Rand B. Evans. Baltimore, Md. : Johns Hopkins University Press, c1990. xiv, 292 p. :
89-033535   150/.973   0801838657
Meyer, Adolf, -- 1866-1950 -- Correspondence. Titchener, Edward
Bradford, -- 1867-1927 -- Correspondence. Psychologists -- United
States -- Correspondence. Psychology -- Philosophy. Psychology --
Methodology.

BF109.P5.M47 1996
Messerly, John G.
Piaget's conception of evolution : beyond Darwin and Lamarck / John G. Messerly ; foreword by Richard J. Blackwell. Lanham, Md. : Rowman & Littlefield Publishers, c1996. xiv, 166 p. ;
96-013049   155.4/13/092   0847682420
Piaget, Jean, -- 1896- -- Views on evolution.   Evolution.

BF109.R38.A3 1988
Reich, Wilhelm,
Passion of youth : an autobiography, 1897-1922 / Wilhelm Reich ; edited by Mary Boyd Higgins and Chester M. Raphael ; with translations by Philip Schmitz and Jerri Tompkins. New York : Farrar, Straus, Giroux, 1988. 177 p., [6] p
88-011286   150.19/5/0924   0374229953
Reich, Wilhelm, -- 1897-1957 -- Childhood and youth.
Psychoanalysts -- United States -- Biography. Sex (Psychology)

BF109.R63.E9 1975
Evans, Richard I.
Carl Rogers : the man and his ideas / Richard I. Evans. New York : Dutton, 1975. lxxxviii, 195
74-023270   150/.19/5   052507645X
Rogers, Carl R. -- (Carl Ransom), -- 1902-   Psychologists -- United
States -- Biography. Client-centered psychotherapy.

BF109.S55.A33 1976
Skinner, B. F.
Particulars of my life / B. F. Skinner. New York : Knopf, 1976. 319 p., [4] l
75-034927   150/.19/4340924   0394400712
Skinner, B. F. -- (Burrhus Frederic), -- 1904-   Psychologists -- United States -- Biography.

BF109.S55.B33 1996
B.F. Skinner and behaviorism in American culture / edited by Laurence D. Smith and William R. Woodward. Bethlehem : Lehigh University Press ; c1996. 348 p. :
95-042466   150.19/434/092   0934223408
Skinner, B. F. -- (Burrhus Frederic), -- 1904-   Behaviorism (Psychology) -- United States -- History.

BF109.S55.B46 1993
Bjork, Daniel W.
B.F. Skinner : a life / Daniel W. Bjork. New York : Basic Books, c1993. xiv, 298 p.,
92-054522   150.19/434/092   0465006116
Skinner, B. F. -- (Burrhus Frederic), -- 1904-   Psychologists -- United States -- Biography. Behaviorism (Psychology) -- United States -- History.

BF109.S55.M63 1995
Modern perspectives on B.F. Skinner and contemporary behaviorism / edited by James T. Todd & Edward K. Morris ; foreword by Ernest R. Hilgard. Westport, Conn. : Greenwood Press, 1995. xxviii, 283 p
94-042729   150.19/434/092   0313296014
Skinner, B. F. -- (Burrhus Frederic), -- 1904-   Behaviorism (Psychology)

BF109.T39.M56 1988
Minton, Henry L.
Lewis M. Terman : pioneer in psychological testing / Henry L. Minton. New York : New York University Press, 1988. xiv, 342 p. :
88-012274   153.9/3/0924   0814754422
Terman, Lewis Madison, -- 1877-1956.   Psychologists -- United States -- Biography. Stanford-Binet Test -- History. Intelligence levels -- United States -- History -- 20th century.

BF109.V95.R38 1991
Ratner, Carl.
Vygotsky's sociohistorical psychology and its contemporary applications / Carl Ratner. New York : Plenum Press, c1991. xi, 368 p. :
90-025506   150/.92   0306436566
Vygotskii, L. S. -- (Lev Semenovich), -- 1896-1934.   Psychology. Social psychology.

BF121 1851- — General works, treatises, and advanced textbooks

BF121.E95 1994
Eysenck, Michael W.
Perspectives on psychology / Michael W. Eysenck. Hove, East Sussex, UK ; L. Erlbaum Associates, c1994. 182 p. :
93-195433   150   0863772544
Psychology.

BF121.H78 2002
Huffman, Karen.
Psychology in action / Karen Huffman. 6th ed. New York : John Wiley & Sons, c2002. 1 v. (various pagings) :
150   0471394955
Psychology.

BF121.I56443 2000
International handbook of psychology / edited by Kurt Pawlik and Mark R. Rosenzweig. London ; Sage Publications, 2000. xxxii, 629 p. :
150   0761953299
Psychology.

BF121.I5645 1992
International psychology : views from around the world / edited by Virginia Staudt Sexton and John D. Hogan. Lincoln : University of Nebraska Press, c1992. x, 524 p. ;
91-032299   150/.9   0803241844
Psychology. Psychology -- History.

BF121.J2 1981
James, William,
The principles of psychology / William James ; [Frederick H. Burkhardt, general editor ; Fredson Bowers, textual editor ; Ignas K. Skrupskelis, associate editor]. Cambridge, Mass. : Harvard University Press, 1981. 3 v. (lxviii,
81-004194   150   0674705599
Psychology. Psychology.

BF121.M598 1998
Morris, Charles G.
Psychology :an introduction / Charles G. Morris with Albert A. Maisto. 10th ed. Upper Saddle River, N.J. : Prentice Hall, c1998. xxiv, 724 p. :
150   0136765378
Psychology.

BF121.R8
Russell, Bertrand,
Analysis of mind, by Bertrand Russell, F.R.S. London, G. Allen & Unwin ltd.; [1921] 310 p.
21016449
Psychology. Consciousness. Knowledge, Theory of.

1851- — Handbooks, manuals, etc.

BF131.S226 1965
Sargent, S. Stansfeld
Basic teachings of the great psychologists [by] S. Stansfeld Sargent. In collaboration with Kenneth R. Stafford. Rev. ed. Garden City, N.Y., Dolphin Books [1965] xv, 382 p.
150
Psychology.

BF149 1851- — Addresses, essays, lectures

BF149.B4
Bertalanffy, Ludwig von,
   Robots, men, and minds; psychology in the modern world. New York, G. Braziller [1967] x, 150 p.
67-027524   150
   Psychology -- Addresses, essays, lectures. Science -- Addresses, essays, lectures.

BF149.C36 1985
   A Century of psychology as science / edited by Sigmund Koch, David E. Leary. New York : McGraw-Hill, c1985. xi, 990 p. :
83-009836   150/.9   0070352496
   Psychology. Psychology -- History.

BF149.K37
Kaplan, Bernard,
   Perspectives in psychological theory; essays in honor of Heinz Werner. Edited by Bernard Kaplan and Seymour Wapner. New York, International Universities Press [1960] 384 p.
60008303   150.82
   Psychology.

BF161 1851- — Mind and body — 1851-

BF161.L28
Langer, Susanne Katherina Knauth,
   Mind; an essay on human feeling [by] Susanne K. Langer. Baltimore, Johns Hopkins Press [1967]-c1982. 3 v.
66-026686   128/.2   0801803608
   Mind and body. Emotions. Psychology -- Philosophy.

BF161.M45 1991
McGinn, Colin,
   The problem of consciousness : essays towards a resolution / Colin McGinn. Oxford, UK ; B. Blackwell, 1991. viii, 216 p.
90-036247   128/.2   0631176985
   Mind and body. Consciousness. Philosophy of mind.

BF161.M5 1999
Milner, Peter M.
   The autonomous brain : a neural theory of attention and learning / Peter M. Milner. Mahwah, N.J. : L. Erlbaum Associates, 1999. x, 155 p. :
99-019772   153.1   0805832114
   Mind and body. Brain -- Psychophysiology. Attention.

BF161.S352 1984
Searle, John R.
   Minds, brains, and science / John Searle. Cambridge, Mass. : Harvard University Press, 1984. 107 p. ;
84-025260   128/.2   0674576314
   Mind and body. Brain. Thought and thinking.

BF161.T94 1989
Tye, Michael.
   The metaphysics of mind / Michael Tye. Cambridge [England] ; Cambridge University Press, 1989. viii, 215 p.
88-015301   128/.2   0521354706
   Mind and body. Philosophy of mind.

BF173 Psychoanalysis — General works

BF173.A3 1979
Abraham, Karl,
   Selected papers of Karl Abraham, M.D. / with an introductory memoir by Ernest Jones ; translated by Douglas Bryan and Alix Strachey. New York : Brunner/Mazel, [1979] c1927. 527 p. :
79-011443   150/.19/52   0876302061
   Psychoanalysis.

BF173.A47
Adler, Alfred,
   The individual psychology of Alfred Adler; a systematic presentation in selections from his writings. Edited and annotated by Heinz L. Ansbacher and Rowena R. Ansbacher. New York, Basic Books [1956] xxiii, 503 p.
55-006679   131.3463
   Adlerian psychology.

BF173.A5 1932
Adler, Alfred,
   The practice and theory of individual psychology; translated by P. Radin. New York, Humanities Press; 1951. viii, 352 p.
52-007959
   Psychoanalysis. Psychology, Pathological.

BF173.A52 1929
Adler, Alfred,
   The science of living. New York, [c1929]
29020528   150.19/53
   Personality. Psychoanalysis.

BF173.A55.W3
Way, Lewis Malcolm.
   Adler's place in psychology. Introd. by Alexandra Adler. London, Allen & Unwin [1950] 334 p.
63025908   131.3463
   Adler, Alfred, -- 1870-1937. Psychology, Pathological.

BF173.A575
   Searchlights on delinquency; new psychoanalytic studies dedicated to Professor August Aichhorn on the occasion of his seventieth birthday, July 27, 1948. Managing editor: K. R. Eissler: chairman of the editorial board: Paul Federn. New York, International Universities Press [1949] xiii, 456 p.
49-007622   132.6
   Aichhorn, August, -- 1878-1949. Crime. Psychoanalysis.

BF173.E646 1985
Erdelyi, Matthew Hugh.
Psychoanalysis : Freud's cognitive psychology / Matthew Hugh Erdelyi. New York : W.H. Freeman, c1985. xv, 303 p. :
84-006056   150.19/52   0716716178
Freud, Sigmund, -- 1856-1939.   Psychoanalysis. Psychotherapy.

BF173.E9
Eysenck, H. J.
Handbook of abnormal psychology, an experimental approach. New York, Basic Books [1961] 816 p.
61-007077   132
Psychology, Pathological. Psychology, Experimental.

BF173.F58 1947
Flugel, J. C.
Men and their motives; psycho-analytical studies, by J. C. Flugel. With two essays by Ingeborg Flugel. New York, N.Y., International Universities Press, Inc. [1947] 289 p.
47002740   131.3462
Psychoanalysis. Psychoanalysis

BF173.F6173 1946
Freud, Anna,
The ego and the mechanisms of defence [by] Anna Freud, translated from the German by Cecil Baines. New York, N.Y., International Universities Press, inc. [1946] 2 p. l., vii-
47000430   131.34124
Psychoanalysis Defense Mechanisms Denial (Psychology)

BF173.F625
Freud, Sigmund,
The basic writings of Sigmund Freud; translated and edited, with an introduction, by Dr. A. A. Brill. New York, The Modern library [c1938] vi, 1001 p.
38-027462   150.19/52
Psychoanalysis.

BF173.F6253
Freud, Sigmund,
The standard edition of the complete psychological works of Sigmund Freud. Translated from the German under the general editorship of James Strachey, in collaboration with Anna Freud, assisted by Alix Strachey and Alan Tyson. London, Hogarth Press [19 v.
          131.3462
Psychoanalysis.

BF173.F6255
Freud, Sigmund.
Delusion and dream, and other essays. Beacon Pr., 1956.
56007108   131.3462
Psychoanalysis. Dreams.

BF173.F626
Freud, Sigmund,
Dictionary of psychoanalysis, edited by Nandor Fodor and Frank Gaynor. With a pref. by Theodor Reik. New York, Philosophical Library [1950] xii, 208 p.
50009853   131.34
Psychoanalysis. Psychoanalysis -- dictionaries

BF173.F6265 1986
Freud, Sigmund,
The essentials of psycho-analysis / Sigmund Freud ; selected with an introduction and commentaries by Anna Freud ; translated from the German by James Strachey. London : Hogarth Press and the Institute of Psycho-Analys 1986. xc, 597 p. :
86-180524   150.19/52   0701207205
Psychoanalysis.

BF173.F627 1957a
Freud, Sigmund,
A general selection from the works of Sigmund Freud. Edited by John Rickman. With an appendix by Charles Brenner. New York, Liveright Pub. Corp., 1957. xii, 294 p.
57010753   131.3462
Psychoanalysis.

BF173.F62913 1970
Freud, Sigmund,
An outline of psycho-analysis. Translated and newly edited by James Strachey. New York, W. W. Norton [1970, c1969] xi, 75 p.
72-108329   150.19/52   039301083X
Psychoanalysis.

BF173.F62943
Freud, Sigmund,
The origins of psycho-analysis; letters to Wilhelm Fliess, drafts and notes, 1887-1902. Edited by Marie Bonaparte, Anna Freud [and] Ernst Kris; authorized translation by Eric Mosbacher and James Strachey. Introd. by Ernst Kris. New York, Basic Books [1954] xi, 486 p.
54-008148   131.3462
Psychoanalysis.

BF173.F64 1936a
Freud, Sigmund,
The problem of anxiety. Trans. from the German by Henry Alden Bunker. New York, The Psychoanalytic quarterly press and W.W. Nort c1936. 127 p.
37027065   131.3462
Anxiety. Psychoanalysis. Fear.

BF173.F645 1961
Freud, Sigmund,
The ego and the id. Newly translated from the German and edited by James Strachey. New York, Norton [1961, c1960] 88 p.
61005935   131.341
Psychoanalysis.

BF173.F65 1970
Freud, Sigmund,
Beyond the pleasure principle. Translated and newly edited by James Strachey. Introd. by Gregory Zilboorg. New York, Liveright [1970, c1961] xx, 68 p.
70-114388   150.19/52
Pleasure principle (Psychology) Psychoanalysis.

BF173.F662 1975
Freud, Sigmund,
 Group psychology and the analysis of the ego / Sigmund Freud ; translated and edited by James Strachey. New York : Norton, [1975] c1959. viii, 85 p. ;
74-023610   150/.19/52   0393011178.
 Psychoanalysis. Social psychology. Psychoanalysis.

BF173.F673
Freud, Sigmund,
 Collected papers. Authorized translation under the supervision of Joan Riviere. New York, Basic Books [1959] 5 v.
59-008642   150/.19/5208
 Psychoanalysis.

BF173.F678
Freud, Sigmund,
 The origin and development of psychoanalysis / Introd. by Eliseo Vivas. [Chicago] : Regnery, [c1970] xxxv, 69 p. ;
55004350
 Psychoanalysis.

BF173.F682 1930
Freud, Sigmund,
 Civilization and its discontents [by] Sigmund Freud ... authorized translation by Jean Riviere. New York, J. Cape & H. Smith [1930] 144 p.
30023433   131
 Psychoanalysis. Social psychology. Civilization.

BF173.F7 1966
Freud, Sigmund,
 The complete introductory lectures on psychoanalysis. Translated and edited by James Strachey. New York, W. W. Norton [1966] 690 p.
66-016766   150.1952
 Psychoanalysis.

BF173.F76
Freud, Sigmund,
 New introductory lectures on psycho-analysis / by Sigmund Freud ; translated by W.J.H. Sprott. New York : W.W. Norton, c1933. 257 p. ;
33027464   131.3462
 Psychoanalysis Psychoanalysis.

BF173.F825
Freud, Sigmund,
 The psychopathology of everyday life. Translated from the German by Alan Tyson. Edited with an introd. and additional notes by James Strachey. New York, Norton [1966, c1965] xiii, 310 p.
65-021619   157
 Psychoanalysis. Memory. Parapraxis.

BF173.F85.A3 1952
Freud, Sigmund,
 An autobiographical study; authorized translation by James Strachey. New York, Norton [1952] 141 p.
52012426
 Psychoanalysis.

BF173.F85.A4 1985
Freud, Sigmund,
 The complete letters of Sigmund Freud to Wilhelm Fliess, 1887-1904 / translated and edited by Jeffrey Moussaieff Masson. Cambridge, Mass. : Belknap Press of Harvard University Press, 1985. xv, 505 p., [
84-024516   150.19/52   0674154207
 Freud, Sigmund, -- 1856-1939 -- Correspondence. Fliess, Wilhelm, -- 1858-1928 -- Correspondence. Psychoanalysts -- Correspondence. Psychoanalysis.

BF173.F85.A7
Arlow, Jacob A.
 The legacy of Sigmund Freud. New York, International Universities Press, 1956. 96 p.
56009746
 Freud, Sigmund, -- 1856-1939.

BF173.F85.D6 1988
Donn, Linda.
 Freud and Jung : years of friendship, years of loss / Linda Donn. New York : Scribner, c1988. xvi, 238 p.,
88-019739   150.19/52   0684189623
 Freud, Sigmund, -- 1856-1939 -- Friends and associates. Jung, C. G. -- (Carl Gustav), -- 1875-1961 -- Friends and associates. Psychoanalysts -- Austria -- Biography. Psychoanalysts -- Switzerland -- Biography. Psychoanalysis -- History.

BF173.F85.F55
Fisher, Seymour.
 The scientific credibility of Freud's theories and therapy / Seymour Fisher & Roger P. Greenberg. New York : Basic Books, c1977. x, 502 p. ;
76-030453   150/.19/52   0465073859
 Freud, Sigmund, -- 1856-1939. Psychoanalysis.

BF173.F85.J6
Jones, Ernest,
 The life and work of Sigmund Freud. New York, Basic Books [1953-57] 3 v.
53-008700   926.1
 Freud, Sigmund, -- 1856-1939.

BF173.F85.L4 1971
Levitt, Morton,
 Freud and Dewey on the nature of man. Westport, Conn., Greenwood Press [1971, c1960] 180 p.
76-138157   150/.1/952   0837156149
 Freud, Sigmund, -- 1856-1939. Dewey, John, -- 1859-1952. Human beings.

BF173.F85.N37
Nelson, Benjamin,
 Freud and the 20th century. New York, Meridian Books, 1957. 314 p.
57-006682   131.3462
 Freud, Sigmund, -- 1856-1939.

BF173.F85W46
Wittels, Fritz,
 Freud and his time; New York, H. Liveright, inc., 1931. 4 p.
 Freud, Sigmund, 1856-1939. [from old catalog]   Psychoanalysis. [from old catalog]

BF173.F866413 1992
Fromm, Erich,
   The revision of psychoanalysis / Erich Fromm ; edited by Rainer Funk. Boulder, Colo. : Westview Press, 1992. xiv, 149 p. ;
92-018300   150.19/57   0813314518
   Psychoanalysis. Subconsciousness -- Social aspects. Social psychology.

BF173.G496 1994
Gill, Merton Max,
   Psychoanalysis in transition : a personal view / Merton M. Gill. Hillsdale, NJ : Analytic Press, 1994. xvii, 179 p.
94-017701   150.19/5   0881631124
   Psychoanalysis.

BF173.G76 1984
Grunbaum, Adolf.
   The foundations of psychoanalysis : a philosophical critique / Adolf Grunbaum. Berkeley : University of California Press, 1984. xiv, 310 p. ;
83009264   150.19/52   0520050169
Freud, Sigmund, -- 1856-1939. -- cn Freud, Sigmund, -- 1856-1939. -- cn Psychoanalysis -- Philosophy. Psychoanalytic theory.

BF173.H737 1989
Holt, Robert R.
   Freud reappraised : a fresh look at psychoanalytic theory / Robert R. Holt. New York : Guilford Press, c1989. xiii, 433 p.
88-035623   150.19/52   0898623871
Freud, Sigmund, -- 1856-1939.   Psychoanalysis. Psychoanalytic Theory.

BF173.H7625
Horney, Karen,
   Self-analysis [by] Karen Horney, M. D. New York, W. W. Norton & company, inc. [1942] 309 p.
42-006940   131.342
   Psychoanalysis. Self-analysis (Psychoanalysis)

BF173.J6623 1983
Jung, C. G.
   The essential Jung / selected and introduced by Anthony Storr. Princeton, N.J. : Princeton University Press, c1983. 447 p. :
82-061441   150.19/54   0691024553
   Psychoanalysis.

BF173.J67
Jung, C. G.
   Basic writings. Edited with an introd. by Violet Staub de Laszlo. New York, Modern Library [1959] xxiii, 552 p.
59-005910   131.3464
   Psychoanalysis.

BF173.J74 1950
Jung, C. G.
   Modern man in search of a soul. [Translated by W. S. Dell and Cary F. Baynes] New York, Harcourt, Brace [n. d.] ix, 244 p.
50004826
   Psychoanalysis. Therapeutics, Suggestive.

BF173.J8 1963
Jung, C. G.
   Psychology of the unconscious : a study of the transformations and symbolisms of the libido, a contribution to the history of the evolution of thought ; authorized traslation, with introd., by Beatrice M. Hinkle. N.Y., Dodd, Mead, 1957 [c1916] 566 p.
59001537
   Subconsciousness. Sex. Psychology, Pathological.

BF173.J85.C15 1990
   C.G. Jung and the humanities : toward a hermeneutics of culture / edited by Karin Barnaby and Pellegrino D'Acierno. Princeton, NJ : Princeton University Press, c1990. xxx, 372 p. :
88-034257   001.3   0691086168
Jung, C. G. -- (Carl Gustav), -- 1875-1961 -- Influence -- Congresses. Psychoanalysis and culture -- Congresses. Hermeneutics -- Congresses.

BF173.J85.J32 1968
Jacobi, Jolande (Szekacs)
   The psychology of C. G. Jung: an introduction with illustrations, by Jolande Jacobi; [translated by Ralph Manheim from the German]. London, Routledge & K. Paul, 1968. xvi, 199 p.
79-407669   150.19/54/0924   0710015976
Jung, C. G. -- (Carl Gustav), -- 1875-1961.

BF173.J85.P7 1969
Progoff, Ira.
   Jung's psychology and its social meaning; an introductory statement of C. G. Jung's psychological theories and a first interpretation of their significance for the social sciences. New York, Julian Press [1969, c1953] xxiv, 335 p.
71-092327   150/.19/54
Jung, C. G. -- (Carl Gustav), -- 1875-1961.   Psychoanalysis. Social sciences and psychology.

BF173.K47
Klein, George Stuart,
   Psychoanalytic theory : an exploration of essentials / George S. Klein. New York : International Universities Press, [1976] x, 330 p. ;
75-018508   150/.19/5   0823650596
   Psychoanalysis.

BF173.K83 1989
Kurzweil, Edith.
   The Freudians : a comparative perspective / Edith Kurzweil. New Haven : Yale University Press, c1989. xii, 371 p. ;
89-008897   150.19/52   0300040091
Freud, Sigmund, -- 1856-1939.   Psychoanalysis -- History.

BF173.M3593 2000
Meissner, W. W.
   Freud & psychoanalysis / W.W. Meissner. Notre Dame, Ind. : University of Notre Dame Press, c2000. xv, 279 p. :
00-025639   150.19/52   0268028540
Freud, Sigmund, -- 1856-1939.   Psychoanalysis.

BF173.M36 1945
Menninger, Karl A.
The human mind [by] Karl A. Menninger. New York, A. A. Knopf, 1945. xvii, 517, xi
45-003595   132
Psychoanalysis. Psychology, Pathological. Mental health.

BF173.M82
Mullahy, Patrick,
Oedipus, myth and complex : a review of psychoanalytic theory / by Patrick Mullahy ; introd., Erich Fromm. New York : Hermitage Press, 1948. xix, 538 p. ;
49000530   131.34123
Oedipus (Greek mythology) Oedipus complex. Psychoanalysis

BF173.P75
Progoff, Ira.
The death and rebirth of psychology; an integrative evaluation of Freud, Adler, Jung, and Rank and the impact of their culminating insights on modern man. New York, Julian Press [1956] 275 p.
56012609   131.346   0070508909
Psychoanalysis -- History.

BF173.R35 1952
Rank, Otto,
The trauma of birth. New York, R. Brunner 1952. xv, 224 p.
52009510   131.3462
Psychoanalysis.

BF173.R425
Reik, Theodor,
The secret self; psychoanalytic experiences in life and literature. New York, Farrar, Straus and Young [c1952] 329 p.
52013917   131.34
Psychoanalysis Psychoanalysis.

BF173.R515 1990
Ritvo, Lucille B.,
Darwin's influence on Freud : a tale of two sciences / Lucille B. Ritvo. New Haven : Yale University Press, c1990. xii, 267 p. :
89-016672   150.19/52   0300041314
Freud, Sigmund, -- 1856-1939. Darwin, Charles, -- 1809-1882 -- Influence.

BF173.R5513 2001
Roazen, Paul,
The historiography of psychoanalysis / Paul Roazen. New Brunswick, N.J. : Transaction Publishers, c2001. xiii, 480 p.
00-064757   150.19/52/09   0765800195
Freud, Sigmund, -- 1856-1939. Psychoanalysis -- History -- 20th century.

BF173.R63.S3
Schafer, Roy.
Psychoanalytic interpretation in Rorschach testing: theory and application. New York, Grune & Stratton, 1954. xiv, 446 p.
54009030   137.8   0808904043
Psychoanalysis. Rorschach Test.

BF173.S326
Sarbin, Theodore R.
Studies in behavior pathology; the experimental approach to the psychology of the abnormal. New York, Holt, Rinehart and Winston [c1961] 341 p.
61014604   132
Psychology, Pathological.

BF173.S387 1999
Schwartz, Joseph,
Cassandra's daughter : a history of psychoanalysis / Joseph Schwartz. New York : Viking, 1999. 339 p. ;
99-019938   150.19/5/09   0670886238
Psychoanalysis -- History.

BF173.S674 1998
Stein, Murray,
Jung's map of the soul : an introduction / Murray Stein. Chicago : Open Court, c1998. 244 p. :
97-051485   150.19/54   0812693760
Jung, C. G. -- (Carl Gustav), -- 1875-1961. Jungian psychology. Psychoanalysis.

BF173.U55 2000
Horney, Karen,
The unknown Karen Horney : essays on gender, culture, and psychoanalysis / edited with introductions by Bernard J. Paris. New Haven : Yale University Press, c2000. xiv, 362 p. ;
99-039715   150.19/5   0300080425
Horney, Karen, -- 1885-1952. Psychoanalysis.

BF173.W549 1991
Wisdom, J. O.
Freud, women, and society / J.O. Wisdom. New Brunswick [N.J.], U.S.A. : Transaction Publishers, c1992. xi, 149 p. ;
91-013593   155.3   0887384447
Freud, Sigmund, -- 1856-1939. Psychoanalysis. Women -- Psychology. Sex (Psychology)

BF175 Psychoanalysis — General special

BF175.A25
Abraham, Karl,
On character and libido development; six essays, edited with an introd. by Bertram D. Lewin. Translated by Douglas Bryan and Alix Strachey. New York, W. W. Norton [1966] 206 p.
66014075   155.31
Psychoanalysis. Sex (Psychology)

BF175.E29 1984
Edelson, Marshall.
Hypothesis and evidence in psychoanalysis / Marshall Edelson. Chicago : University of Chicago Press, c1984. xiv, 179 p. ;
83-009281   616.89/17   0226184323
Psychoanalysis. Psychoanalysis -- Research. Psychoanalytic theory.

BF175.F77513 1990
Freud, Sigmund,
   Freud on women : a reader / edited and with an introduction by Elisabeth Young-Bruehl. New York : W.W. Norton, c1990. xii, 399 p. ;
89-035686   155.3/33   0393028224
Freud, Sigmund, -- 1856-1939 -- Views on women.   Women and psychoanalysis. Women -- Psychology. Sex (Psychology)

BF175.M485 1998
Miller, Martin A.
   Freud and the Bolsheviks : psychoanalysis in Imperial Russia and the Soviet Union / Martin A. Miller. New Haven : Yale University Press, c1998. xvii, 237 p.
98-003630   150.19/5/09470904
0300068107
Freud, Sigmund, -- 1856-1939.   Psychoanalysis -- Russia -- History -- 20th century. Psychoanalysis -- Soviet Union -- History -- 20th century.

BF175.R4
Reik, Theodor,
   Myth and guilt; the crime and punishment of mankind. New York, G. Braziller, 1957. 432 p.
57013807   131.34
   Fall of man. Psychoanalysis. Guilt.

BF175.T68 1992
Torrey, E. Fuller
   Freudian fraud : the malignant effect of Freud's theory on American thought and culture / E. Fuller Torrey. New York, NY : HarperCollins, c1992. xvi, 362 p. ;
91-058343   150.19/52/0973   0060168129
Freud, Sigmund, -- 1856-1939 -- Influence.   Psychoanalysis -- Social aspects -- United States -- History. Nature and nurture -- History. Science and psychology -- History. United States -- Intellectual life -- 20th century.

BF175.4 Psychoanalysis — Relation to other topics, A-Z

BF175.4.P45.L42 2000
Lear, Jonathan.
   Happiness, death, and the remainder of life / Jonathan Lear. Cambridge, Mass. : Harvard University Press, 2000. 189 p. ;
00-039705   150.19/5   0674003292
Freud, Sigmund, -- 1856-1939. Aristotle.   Psychoanalysis and philosophy. Ethics.

BF175.4.F45.F46 1989
   Feminism and psychoanalysis / edited by Richard Feldstein and Judith Roof. Ithaca, N.Y. : Cornell University Press, 1989. ix, 359 p. :
88-043235   150.19/5/088042   080149558X
   Psychoanalysis and feminism -- Congresses. Women and psychoanalysis -- Congresses. Psychoanalysis and literature -- Congresses.

BF175.4.F45.F462 1992
   Feminism and psychoanalysis : a critical dictionary / edited by Elizabeth Wright ; advisory editors, Diane Chisholm, Juliet Flower MacCannell, Margaret Whitford. Oxford, UK ; Blackwell, 1992. xix, 485 p. ;
92-006812   150.19/5/082   0631173129
   Psychoanalysis and feminism -- Dictionaries.

BF175.4.F45.N48 1994
Neumann, Erich.
   The fear of the feminine and other essays on feminine psychology / Erich Neumann ; translated from the German by Boris Matthews ... [et al.]. Princeton, N.J. : Princeton University Press, c1994. xiv, 296 p. ;
93-032444   155.3/33   0691034745
   Femininity. Psychoanalysis.

BF175.4.F45.S65 1996
Smith, J. C.
   The castration of Oedipus : feminism, psychoanalysis, and the will to power / J.C. Smith and Carla Ferstman ; with an introduction by Ann Scales. New York : New York University Press, c1996. xii, 316 p. :
95-041726   150.19/5   0814780180
   Psychoanalysis and feminism. Feminist theory. Postmodernism.

BF175.4.P45.B6813 1995
Bouveresse, Jacques.
   Wittgenstein reads Freud : the myth of the unconscious / Jacques Bouveresse ; translated by Carol Cosman ; with a foreword by Vincent Descombes. Princeton, N.J. : Princeton University Press, 1995. xx, 143 p. ;
94-040607   150.19/52   0691034257
Wittgenstein, Ludwig, -- 1889-1951 -- Views on psychoanalysis. Freud, Sigmund, -- 1856-1939 -- Influence. Freud, Sigmund, -- 1856-1939. Psychoanalysis and philosophy.

BF175.4.P45.C38 1993
Cavell, Marcia,
   The psychoanalytic mind : from Freud to philosophy / Marcia Cavell. Cambridge, Mass. : Harvard University Press, 1993. x, 276 p. ;
93-007325   150.19/52   0674720954
Freud, Sigmund, -- 1856-1939.   Subjectivity. Philosophy of mind. Psychoanalysis and philosophy.

BF175.4.P45.N34 1990
Nagy, Marilyn.
   Philosophical issues in the psychology of C.G. Jung / Marilyn Nagy. Albany, NY : State University of New York Press, c1991. ix, 321 p. ;
89-078451   150.19/54   079140451X
Jung, C. G. -- (Carl Gustav), -- 1875-1961.   Psychoanalysis and philosophy.

BF175.4.R44.D53 1999
DiCenso, James,
   The other Freud : religion, culture, and psychoanalysis / James J. DiCenso. London ; Routledge, 1999. vi, 174 p. ;
98-023772   150.19/52/092   0415196582
Freud, Sigmund, -- 1856-1939 -- Religion.   Psychoanalysis and religion.

BF175.4.R44.J65 1991
Jones, James William,
   Contemporary psychoanalysis and religion : transference and transcendence / James W. Jones. New Haven : Yale University Press, c1991. x, 144 p. ;
90-041776   200/.1/9   0300049161
   Psychoanalysis and religion. Transference (Psychology) Transcendence (Philosophy)

BF175.4.R44.P37 1999
Parsons, William Barclay,
   The enigma of the oceanic feeling : revisioning the psychoanalytic theory of mysticism / William B. Parsons. New York : Oxford University Press, 1999. ix, 252 p. ;
97-018199   291.4/22/019   0195115082
   Freud, Sigmund, -- 1856-1939. Psychoanalysis and religion.

BF175.4.R44.S65 1990
Smith, Curtis D.,
   Jung's quest for wholeness : a religious and historical perspective / Curtis D. Smith. Albany : State University of New York Press, c1990. ix, 169 p. ;
89-011313   150.19/54   0791402371
   Jung, C. G. -- (Carl Gustav), -- 1875-1961. Psychology, Religious -- History. Psychoanalysis and religion -- History.

BF175.4.R44.S94 1994
Symington, Neville.
   Emotion and spirit : questioning the claims of psychoanalysis and religion / Neville Symington. New York : St. Martin's Press, 1994. viii, 197 p.
94-014210   150.19/5   0312122209
   Psychoanalysis and religion. Psychology, Religious.

BF175.5 Psychoanalysis — Special topics, A-Z

BF175.5.A33G74 1998
Grey, Loren.
   Alfred Adler, the forgotten prophet :a vision for the 21st century / Loren Grey. Westport, Conn. : Praeger, 1998. x, 158 p. ;
               150.19/53   0275960722
   Adler, Alfred, 1870-1937. Adlerian psychology. Psychoanalysis-- History.

BF175.5.A72.S54 1988
Shelburne, Walter A.,
   Mythos and logos in the thought of Carl Jung : the theory of the collective unconscious in scientific perspective / Walter A. Shelburne. Albany : State University of New York Press, c1988. xi, 180 p. ;
87-010210   150.19/54   0887066933
   Jung, C. G. -- (Carl Gustav), -- 1875-1961. Archetype (Psychology)

BF175.5.C37
Taylor, Gary,
   Castration : an abbreviated history of western manhood / Gary Taylor. New York : Routledge , 2000. 307 p. ;
00-029105   155.3/32   0415927854
   Castration anxiety. Masculinity. Men -- Psychology.

BF175.5.C65.A97 1990
Aziz, Robert,
   C.G. Jung's psychology of religion and synchronicity / Robert Aziz. Albany : State University of New York Press, c1990. 269 p. ;
89-030039   150.19/54   0791401669
   Jung, C. G. -- (Carl Gustav), -- 1875-1961.   Coincidence. Psychology, Religious.

BF175.5.F48.S55 1993
Slipp, Samuel.
   The Freudian mystique : Freud, women, and feminism / Samuel Slipp. New York : New York University Press, c1993. viii, 240 p.
92-035872   150.19/52/082   0814779689
   Freud, Sigmund, -- 1856-1939 -- Contributions in psychology of femininity. Freud, Sigmund, -- 1856-1939 -- Relations with women. Femininity -- History. Psychoanalysis and feminism. Women -- Psychology -- History.

BF175.5.L68.K47 1995
Kernberg, Otto F.,
   Love relations : normality and pathology / Otto F. Kernberg. New Haven : Yale University Press, c1995. xiii, 203 p.
94-038369   155.3/4   0300060319
   Love. Object relations (Psychoanalysis). Psychoanalysis.

BF175.5.M37.R87 1992
Rutherford, Jonathan.
   Mens silences : predicaments in masculinity / Jonathan Rutherford. London ; Routledge, c1992. x, 227 p. ;
92-002801   155.3/32   0415075432
   Masculinity. Men -- Psychology. Men -- Identity.

BF175.5.M37.S74 1993
Steinberg, Warren,
   Masculinity : identity, conflict, and transformation / Warren Steinberg. Boston : Shambhala ; 1993. viii, 228 p.
93-002978   155.3/32   0877736200
   Jung, C. G. -- (Carl Gustav), -- 1875-1961 -- Contributions in psychology of masculinity.   Men -- Psychology. Sex role. Masculinity.

BF175.5.M95.W35 1995
Walker, Steven F.
   Jung and the Jungians on myth : an introduction / Steven F. Walker. New York : Garland Pub., 1995. xiii, 198 p.
94-015753   291.1/3/019   0824034430
   Jung, C. G. -- (Carl Gustav), -- 1875-1961.   Myth -- Psychological aspects.

BF175.5.O24.E87 1986
   Essential papers on object relations / Peter Buckley, editor. New York : New York University Press, 1986. xxv, 477 p. ;
85-013882   150.19/5   0814710794
   Object relations (Psychoanalysis) Psychoanalysis -- History.

BF175.5.O24.K44 1990
Klein, Randall S.,
Object relations and the family process / Randall S. Klein. New York : Praeger, 1990. xiii, 189 p.
89-016226   158/.24   0275932680
Object relations (Psychoanalysis) Family -- Psychological aspects.

BF175.5.P75.T35 1996
Tal, Kali.
Worlds of hurt : reading the literatures of trauma / Kali Tal. Cambridge [England] ; Cambridge University Press, 1996. x, 296 p. ;
96-112813   0521445043
Psychic trauma. Victims -- Psychology. Violence -- Psychological aspects.

BF175.5.P75.T73 1995
Trauma : explorations in memory / edited with introductions by Cathy Caruth. Baltimore : Johns Hopkins University Press, 1995. ix, 277 p. ;
94-046167   155.9/35   0801850096
Psychic trauma. Post-traumatic stress disorder. Recovered memory.

BF176 Psychological tests and testing

BF176.C76 1990
Cronbach, Lee J.
Essentials of psychological testing / Lee J. Cronbach. 5th ed. New York : Harper & Row, c1990. xxvi, 726 p. :
150/.28/7   0060414189
Psychological tests.

BF176.G85 1987
Gulliksen, Harold.
Theory of mental tests / Harold Gulliksen. Hillsdale, N.J. : L. Erlbaum Associates, 1987. xix, 486 p. ;
86-029350   150/.28/7   0805800247
Psychological tests -- Evaluation. Psychological Tests.

BF176.M45 1994
Meier, Scott T.,
The chronic crisis in psychological measurement and assessment : a historical survey / Scott T. Meier. San Diego : Academic Press, c1994. xvi, 290 p. :
94-014626   150/.28/7   0124884407
Psychological tests. Behavioral assessment. Psychological tests -- History.

BF176.T418
Test critiques. Kansas City, Mo. : Test Corporation of America, c1984- v. ;
150/.28/7
Psychological tests--Evaluation--Collected works. Educational tests and measurements--Evaluation. Occupational aptitude tests--Evaluation--Collected works.

BF176.T43 2003
Tests : a comprehensive reference for assessment in psychology, education, and business / [edited by] Taddy Maddox. 5th ed. Austin, Tex. : Pro-Ed, 2003. p. cm.
150/.28/7   0890798974
Psychological tests. Educational tests and measurements. Occupational aptitude tests.

BF176.5 Psychological tests and testing — Behavioral assessment

BF176.5.D53 1988
Dictionary of behavioral assessment techniques / edited by Michel Hersen, Alan S. Bellack. New York : Pergamon Press, 1988. Lxxi, 519 p.
86-025352   150/.28/7   0080319750
Behavioral assessment -- Dictionaries. Mental Disorders -- diagnosis -- handbooks. Personality Assessment.

BF181-182 Experimental psychology — General works

BF181.D27 1990
Danziger, Kurt.
Constructing the subject : historical origins of psychological research / Kurt Danziger. Cambridge ; Cambridge University Press, 1990. ix, 254 p. :
89-022160   150/.72   0521363586
Psychology, Experimental -- History.

BF181.F5
The First century of experimental psychology / edited by Eliot Hearst. Hillsdale, N.J. : L. Erlbaum Associates ; 1979. xxiii, 693 p.
79-016970   150/.7/24   0470268158
Psychology, Experimental -- History. Psychology, Experimental -- History.

BF181.H336 2002
Steven's handbook of experimental psychology / Hal Pashler, editor-in-chief. 3rd ed. New York : John Wiley & Sons, c2002. 4 v. :
150   0471378887
Psychology, Experimental.

BF181.L48 1994
Levine, Gustav.
Experimental methods in psychology / Gustav Levine, Stanley Parkinson. Hillsdale, N.J. : L. Erlbaum, 1994. xv, 474 p. :
93-035652   150/.724   0805814388
Psychology, Experimental -- Methodology. Psychology -- Research.

BF182.F7423
Fraisse, Paul.
   Experimental psychology; its scope and method, edited by Paul Fraisse and Jean Piaget. New York, Basic Books [1968-1969 v. 1, 4-5, 7
67-029581   152
   Psychology, Experimental.

BF199 Behaviorism. Neobehaviorism. Behavioral psychology

BF199.D52 1988
Dilman, Ilham.
   Mind, brain, and behaviour : discussions of B.F. Skinner and J.R. Searle / Ilham Dilman. London ; Routledge, 1988. xiv, 142 p. ;
89-103381   150.19/434   0415000068
Skinner, B. F. -- (Burrhus Frederic), -- 1904- Searle, John R. Behaviorism (Psychology) Mind and body.

BF199.M3
Maslow, Abraham H.
   Motivation and personality. New York, Harper [1954] xiv, 411 p.
54-010712   158.734
   Motivation (Psychology) Self-actualization (Psychology)

BF199.M485 1998
Mills, John A.
   Control : a history of behavioral psychology / John A. Mills. New York : New York University Press, c1998. xii, 246 p. ;
98-019699   150.19/43/09   0814756115
   Behaviorism (Psychology) -- History.

BF199.O39 2001
O'Donohue, William T.
   The psychology of B.F. Skinner / William O'Donohue, Kyle E. Ferguson. Thousand Oaks, Calif. : Sage, c2001. x, 286 p. :
00-011616   150.19/434/092   0761917586
Skinner, B. F. -- (Burrhus Frederic), -- 1904-   Behaviorism (Psychology)

BF199.S45 1988
   The Selection of behavior : the operant behaviorism of B.F. Skinner : comments and consequences / edited by A. Charles Catania and Stevan Harnad. Cambridge ; Cambridge University Press, 1988. xxii, 563 p.
87-033750   150.19/434   0521343887
Skinner, B. F. -- (Burrhus Frederic), -- 1904- Skinner, B. F. -- (Burrhus Frederic), -- 1904- Behaviorism (Psychology) Behaviorism.

BF199.S74 1996
Staats, Arthur W.
   Behavior and personality : psychological behaviorism / Arthur W. Staats. New York : Springer, c1996. xvii, 442 p.
96-017801   150.19/43   0826193110
   Behaviorism (Psychology) Personality.

BF199.W3 1958
Watson, John Broadus,
   Behaviorism. Chicago] University of Chicago Press [1958, c1930] 308 p.
58014680   150.1943
   Behaviorism (Psychology) Behaviorism

BF199.Z88 1985
Zuriff, G. E.
   Behaviorism : a conceptual reconstruction / G.E. Zuriff. New York : Columbia University Press, 1985. xiii, 369 p.
84-012657   150.19/43   0231059124
   Behaviorism (Psychology) Behaviorism (Psychology) -- Philosophy. Behaviorism (Psychology) -- History.

BF201 Cognitive psychology

BF201.B37 1992
Barsalou, Lawrence W.
   Cognitive psychology : an overview for cognitive scientists / Lawrence W. Barsalou. Hillsdale, N.J. : L. Erlbaum Associates, 1992. xi, 410 p. :
91-037192   153   0805806911
   Cognitive psychology.

BF201.P37 2000
Parkin, Alan J.
   Essential cognitive psychology / Alan J. Parkin. Hove, East Sussex : Psychology Press ; xiv, 354 p. :
              153   0863776736
   Cognitive psychology.

BF201.4 Feminist psychology

BF201.4.G47 2001
Gergen, Mary M.
   Feminist reconstructions in psychology : narrative, gender, and performance / Mary Gergen. Thousand Oaks, Calif. : Sage, c2001. vii, 229 p. :
00-010058   150/.82   0761911502
   Feminist psychology.

BF201.4.P73 2000
   Practicing feminist ethics in psychology / edited by Mary M. Brabeck. Washington, DC : American Psychological Association, c2000. xi, 285 p. ;
99-041175   174/.915/082   1557986231
   Feminist psychology. Feminism. Women -- Psychology.

BF203 Gestalt psychology. Gestalt perception

BF203.E48
Ellis, Willis Davis.
   A source book of gestalt psychology, prepared by Willis D. Ellis, with an introduction by Professor K. Koffka. London, K. Paul, Trench, Trubner & Co., ltd. [1938] 2 p. l., vii-
38030784   150.1924
   Gestalt psychology.

BF203.H43
Henle, Mary,
Documents of Gestalt psychology. Berkeley, University of California Press, 1961. 352 p.
61-014554   150.1924
Gestalt psychology.

BF203.K313
Katz, David,
Gestalt psychology; its nature and significance. Tr. by Robert Tyson. New York, Ronald [c1950] x, 175 p.
50006467   150.1924
Gestalt psychology.

BF204 Humanistic psychology

BF204.D4 1991
DeCarvalho, Roy Jose.
The founders of humanistic psychology / Roy Jose DeCarvalho.; foreword by Stanley Krippner. New York : Praeger, 1991. x, 221 p. ;
91-000444   150.19/8   027594008X
Humanistic psychology. Psychologists -- United States -- Biography.

BF204.F756 1994
Fromm, Erich,
On being human / Erich Fromm ; foreword by Rainer Funk. New York : Continuum, 1994. 180 p. ;
93-009243   150.19/57   0826405762
Humanistic psychology. Humanism -- 20th century. Social psychology.

BF204.H36 2001
The handbook of humanistic psychology : leading edges in theory, research, and practice / [edited] by Kirk J. Schneider, James F.T. Bugental, J. Fraser Pierson. Thousand Oaks, Calif. : Sage Publications, c2001. p. cm.
01-000095   150.19/8   0761921214
Humanistic psychology.

BF204.M34
Mahrer, Alvin R.
Experiencing : a humanistic theory of psychology and psychiatry / by Alvin R. Mahrer. New York : Brunner/Mazel, c1978. 884 p. :
77-027269   150/.19/2   087630160X
Humanistic psychology. Developmental psychology. Experiential psychotherapy.

BF204.5 Phenomenological psychology. Existential psychology

BF204.5.P65 1997
Pollio, Howard R.
The phenomenology of everyday life / Howard R. Pollio, Tracy B. Henley, Craig J. Thompson with James Barrell ... [et al.]. Cambridge, U.K. ; Cambridge University Press, 1997. x, 400 p. :
96-040020   150.19/2   0521462053
Phenomenological psychology.

BF204.5.S68
Spiegelberg, Herbert.
Phenomenology in psychology and psychiatry; a historical introduction. Evanston [Ill.] Northwestern University Press, 1972. xlv, 411 p.
     150/.19/2   0810103575
Phenomenological psychology. Psychiatry.

BF204.7 Transpersonal psychology

BF204.7.T72 2000
Transpersonal knowing : exploring the horizon of consciousness / edited by Tobin Hart, Peter L. Nelson, and Kaisa Puhakka. cAlbany, N.Y. : State University of New York Press, 2000. x, 341 p. ;
99-049022   150.19/8   0791446158
Transpersonal psychology.

BF204.7.W37 1995
Washburn, Michael,
The ego and the dynamic ground : a transpersonal theory of human development / Michael Washburn. Albany : State University of New York Press, c1995. xiv, 272 p. :
94-001379   150.19/8   0791422550
Transpersonal psychology. Ego (Psychology)

BF207 Psychotropic drugs and other substances

BF207.C28 1983
Carlton, Peter Lynn,
A primer of behavioral pharmacology : concepts and principles in the behavioral analysis of drug action / Peter L. Carlton. New York : W.H. Freeman, c1983. 301 p. :
83-009083   615/.78   0716714515
Psychopharmacology -- Research. Behavioral assessment. Behavior -- Drug effects.

BF209 Psychotropic drugs and other substances — Special drugs and other substances, A-Z

BF209.C3.A23
Abel, Ernest L.,
  Marihuana, the first twelve thousand years / Ernest L. Abel.
New York : Plenum Press, c1980. xi, 289 p. ;
80-015606   615/.7827   0306404966
  Marijuana -- History. Marijuana. Cannabis.

BF209.L9.B5
Blum, Richard H.
  Utopiates; the use & users of LSD 25 [by] Richard Blum &
associates. Foreword by Nevitt Sanford. [New York, Atherton
Press, 1964] xvi, 303 p.
64-023746   153.8
  LSD (Drug)

BF233 Sensation. Aesthesiology — General works — 1801-

BF233.C59 1994
Coren, Stanley.
  Sensation and perception / Stanley Coren, Lawrence M.
Ward, James T. Enns. 4th ed. Fort Worth, TX : Harcourt
Brace College Publishers, c1994. xi, 747 p. :
            153.7   0155001035
  Senses and sensation. Perception.

BF233.H35
Hayek, Friedrich A. von
  The sensory order; an inquiry into the foundations of
theoretical psychology, with an introd. by Heinrich Kluver.
Chicago, University of Chicago Press [1952] xxii, 209 p.
52014469   152
  Senses and sensation. Psychology. Mind and body.

BF241-242 Sensation. Aesthesiology — Special senses — Vision. Visual perception

BF241.B29 1997
Barry, Ann Marie.
  Visual intelligence : perception, image, and manipulation in
visual communication / Ann Marie Seward Barry. Albany :
State University of New York Press, c1997. viii, 425 p.
96-042465   302.2   0791434354
  Visual perception. Visual communication. Image processing.

BF241.D4
Dember, William N.
  Visual perception: the nineteenth century [by] William N.
Dember. New York, Wiley [1964] xii, 222 p.
64025895   152.1
  Visual perception.

BF241.E28 1999
Edelman, Shimon.
  Representation and recognition in vision / Shimon Edelman.
Cambridge, Mass. : MIT Press, c1999. xxiii, 335 p. :
            152.14   0262050579
  Visual perception. Mental representation. Visualization.

BF241.E45 1996
Elkins, James,
  The object stares back : on the nature of seeing / James
Elkins. New York : Simon & Schuster, c1996. 271 p. :
95-044872   152.14   0684800950
  Visual perception. Vision. Visual communication.

BF241.M26 1998
Mack, Arien.
  Inattentional blindness / Arien Mack and Irvin Rock.
Cambridge, Mass. : MIT Press, c1998. xiv, 273 p. :
97-028254   153.7/33   0262133393
  Visual perception. Attention. Visual discrimination.

BF241.P435 1987
  The Perception of illusory contours / Susan Petry and Glenn
E. Meyer, editors. New York : Springer-Verlag, c1987. xvi,
320 p. :
87-004572   153.7/4   0387965181
  Visual perception. Optical illusions.

BF241.P437 1998
  Perceptual constancy : why things look as they do / edited
by Vincent Walsh, Janusz Kulikowski. Cambridge, UK ;
Cambridge University Press, 1998. viii, 551 p.
97-006655   152.14   0521460611
  Visual perception.

BF241.U865 1998
Uttal, William R.
  Toward a new behaviorism : the case against perceptual
reductionism / William R. Uttal. Mahwah, N.J. : L. Erlbaum,
1998. xix, 249 p. :
97-019624   152.1   0805827382
  Visual perception. Behaviorism (Psychology)

BF241.W32 1991
Wade, Nicholas.
  Visual perception : an introduction / Nicholas J. Wade &
Michael Swanston. London ; Routledge, 1991. p. cm.
90-047530   152.14   041501042X
  *Visual perception. Visual discrimination. Motion perception
(Vision)*

BF241.W33 1990
Wade, Nicholas.
  Visual allusions : pictures of perception / Nicholas Wade.
Hare : Erlbaum, 1990. ix, 288 p.
90024332   152.14   0863771300
  Visual perception. Visual perception. Perception.

BF242.J64 1991
Johnson, Mark H.
 Biology and cognitive development : the case of face recognition / by Mark H. Johnson and John Morton. Oxford, UK ; B. Blackwell, 1991. x, 180 p. :
91014953   153.7/5   0631174540
 Cognition -- Physiological aspects. Developmental psychobiology. Face perception -- Physiological aspects.

BF242.S63 1988
 Social and applied aspects of perceiving faces / edited by Thomas R. Alley. Hillsdale, N.J. : Lawrence Erlbaum Associates, 1988. cvii, 285 p.
87-024611   302/.12   0805801634
 Face perception. Face perception -- Social aspects.

**BF251 Sensation. Aesthesiology — Special senses —
Hearing. Auditory perception**

BF251.C66 1989
 The Comparative psychology of audition : perceiving complex sounds / edited by Robert J. Dooling, Stewart H. Hulse. Hillsdale, N.J. : L. Erlbaum Associates, 1989. xii, 482 p. :
88-033576   156/.215   0805800204
 Auditory perception. Psychology, Comparative.

BF251.H35 1997
Hartmann, William M.
 Signals, sound, and sensation / William M. Hartmann. Woodbury, N.Y. : American Institute of Physics, c1997. xvii, 647 p.
96-043808   152.1/5   1563962837
 Auditory perception. Psychoacoustics. Signal theory (Telecommunication)

**BF271 Sensation. Aesthesiology — Special senses —
Smell**

BF271.M5
Millen, James Knox.
 Your nose knows; a study of the sense of smell. Los Angeles, Cunningham Press [1960] 166 p.
60002492   152.3
 Smell.

**BF275 Sensation. Aesthesiology — Special senses —
Touch and other cutaneous senses**

BF275.K3713 1989
Katz, David,
 The world of touch / David Katz ; edited and translated by Lester E. Krueger. Hillsdale, N.J. : L. Erlbaum Associates, c1989. xii, 260 p. :
89-011868   152.1/82   080580529X
 Touch.

BF275.P35 1996
 Pain and touch / edited by Lawrence Kruger. San Diego : Academic Press, c1996. xvii, 394 p.
96-022523   152.1/82   0124269109
 Touch -- Psychological aspects. Pain -- Psychological aspects.

BF275.P79 1992
 The Psychology of touch / edited by Morton A. Heller, William Schiff. Hillsdale, N.J. : L. Erlbaum, 1991. xi, 354 p. :
91-014484   152.1/82   0805807500
 Touch -- Psychological aspects.

**BF292 Sensation. Aesthesiology — Special senses —
Sense perceptions (General)**

BF292.A4
Alpern, Mathew.
 Sensory processes [by] Mathew Alpern, Merle Lawrence [and] David Wolsk. Belmont, Calif., Brooks/Cole Pub. Co. [1967] vii, 151 p.
67-012818   152.1
 Senses and sensation.

**BF293 Sensation. Aesthesiology — Special senses —
Form perception**

BF293.R63 1973
Rock, Irvin.
 Orientation and form. New York, Academic Press, 1973. ix, 165 p.
72-013618   152.1/423   0125912501
 Form perception. Orientation (Psychology) Form perception.

**BF295 Sensation. Aesthesiology — Special senses —
Movement. Motor ability. Motor learning**

BF295.C72
Cratty, Bryant J.
 Social dimensions of physical activity [by] Bryant J. Cratty. Englewood Cliffs, N.J., Prentice-Hall [1967] xi, 139 p.
67-020227   152.3
 Movement, Psychology of.

BF295.O9
Oxendine, Joseph B.
 Psychology of motor learning [by] Joseph B. Oxendine. New York, Appleton-Century-Crofts [1968] xi, 366 p.
68-012786   152.3/34
 Motor learning.

BF295.P43 1990
 Perception & control of self-motion / edited by Rik Warren, Alexander H. Wertheim. Hillsdale, N.J. : L. Erlbaum, 1990. xxi, 647 p. :
90-037125   153.7/54   0805805176
 Perceptual-motor processes.

BF311 Consciousness. Cognition — General works

BF311.A5
Allport, Floyd Henry,
Theories of perception and the concept of structure; a review and critical analysis with an introduction to a dynamic-structural theory of behavior. New York, Wiley [1955] 709 p.
55-006130   152.7
Perception.

BF311.A797 2000
Auyang, Sunny Y.
Mind in everyday life and cognitive science / Sunny Y. Auyang. Cambridge, Mass. : MIT Press, c2000. viii, 529 p.
00-064591   153   0262011816
Cognitive science. Intellect. Thought and thinking.

BF311.B227 1997
Baars, Bernard J.
In the theater of consciousness : the workspace of the mind / Bernard J. Baars. New York : Oxford University Press, 1997. xi, 193 p. :
96-010379   153   0195102657
Consciousness. Intellect. Human information processing.

BF311.C5395 1999
Clancey, William J.
Conceptual coordination :how the mind orders experience in time / William J. Clancey. Mahwah, N.J. : L. Erlbaum Associates, 1999. xix, 395 p. ;
      153   0805831436
Cognitive science. Cognition. Knowledge, Theory of.

BF311.C55115 1994
Cognitive approaches to human perception / edited by Soledad Ballesteros. Hillsdale, N.J. : L. Erlbaum Associates, 1994. xiii, 301 p.
93-006805   153.7   0805810439
Perception. Form perception. Visual perception.

BF311.C578 1998
A companion to cognitive science / edited by William Bechtel and George Graham ; advisory editors, David A. Balota ... [et al.]. Malden, Mass. : Blackwell, 1998. p. cm.
97-038757   153   1557865426
Cognitive science.

BF311.D39 2001
The dawn of cognitive science :early European contributors / edited by Liliana Albertazzi. Boston : Kluwer Academic Publishers, 2001. p. cm.
      153   0792367995
Cognitive science--Europe--History.

BF311.D568 2000
Dodwell, P. C.
Brave new mind :a thoughtful inquiry into the nature and meaning of mental life / Peter Dodwell. New York : Oxford University Press, 2000. ix, 250 p. :
      153   0195089057
Cognitive science. Creative thinking. Consciousness.

BF311.D57 2001
Donald, Merlin,
A mind so rare : the evolution of human consciousness / Merlin Donald. New York : Norton, c2001. xiv, 371 p. :
00-053721   153   0393049507
Consciousness.

BF311.D84 1993
Dunlop, Charles E. M.,
Glossary of cognitive science / Charles E.M. Dunlop, James H. Fetzer. New York, N.Y. : Paragon House, 1993. xii, 146 p. ;
92-027750   153.4/03   155778566X
Cognitive science -- Dictionaries.

BF311.D84513 2000
Dupuy, Jean Pierre,
The mechanization of the mind :on the origins of cognitive science / Jean-Pierre Dupuy ; translated by M.B. DeBevoise. Princeton : Princeton University Press, c2000. xiv, 210 p. ;
      153   0691025746
Cognitive science--History.

BF311.F423 2001
Fetzer, James H.,
Computers and cognition : why minds are not machines / by James H. Fetzer. Dordrecht [Netherlands] ; Kluwer Academic Publishers, c2001. xix, 323 p. ;
00-064705   153   0792366158
Cognitive science.

BF311.F66 2001
The foundations of cognitive science / edited by João Branquinho. Oxford : Clarendon Press ; xlvii, 235 p. :
      153   0198238894
Cognitive science.

BF311.F89 1997
The future of the cognitive revolution / edited by David Martel Johnson and Christina E. Erneling. New York : Oxford University Press, 1997. x, 401 p. :
96-023813   153   0195103335
Cognition. Cognitive science. Philosophy and cognitive science.

BF311.G714 1997
Greenspan, Stanley I.
The growth of the mind : and the endangered origins of intelligence / Stanley I. Greenspan with Beryl Lieff Benderly. Reading, Mass. : Addison-Wesley Pub., c1997. xi, 364 p. ;
96-031512   153   0201483025
Emotions and cognition. Emotional maturity. Intellect.

BF311.H334
Handbook of learning and cognitive processes / edited by
W. K. Estes. Hillsdale, N.J. : L. Erlbaum Associates ; 1975-
1978. 6 v. :
75-020113   153   0470245859
Cognition. Learning, Psychology of. Cognition.

BF311.H339 2001
Harnish, Robert M.
Minds, brains, computers :an historical introduction to the
foundations of cognitive science / Robert M. Harnish. Malden,
MA : Blackwell Publishers, 2001. p. cm.
                  153/.09   0631212604
Cognitive science--History.

BF311.I564 1996
Interactive minds : life-span perspectives on the social
foundation of cognition / edited by Paul B. Baltes, Ursula M.
Staudinger. Cambridge ; Cambridge University Press, 1996.
xii, 457 p. :
95-019302   302/.12   0521481066
Cognition and culture. Social perception.

BF311.K45 2001
Keijzer, Fred A.,
Representation and behavior / Fred Keijzer. Cambridge,
Mass. : MIT Press, c2001. viii, 276 p. ;
                  150.19/43   0262112590
Cognitive science. Human behavior. Mental representation.

BF311.K57 1990
Kitcher, Patricia.
Kant's transcendental psychology / Patricia Kitcher. New
York : Oxford University Press, 1990. xiii, 296 p.
89-078463   128/.092   0195059670
*Kant, Immanuel, -- 1724-1804 -- Contributions in psychology. Kant,
Immanuel, -- 1724-1804 -- Kritik der reinen Vernunft.   Cognition.*

BF311.L59 1989
Lloyd, Dan Edward,
Simple minds / Dan Lloyd. Cambridge, Mass. : MIT Press,
c1989. xiv, 266 p. :
88-026808   153   0262121409
Cognition. Human information processing. Neuropsychology.

BF311.M553 1995
Mind as motion : explorations in the dynamics of cognition /
edited by Robert F. Port and Timothy van Gelder. Cambridge,
Mass. : MIT Press, c1995. x, 590 p. :
94-023127   153   0262161508
*Cognition. Cognition -- Research -- Methodology. Cognitive
science.*

BF311.M556 1999
The MIT encyclopedia of the cognitive sciences / edited by
Robert A. Wilson and Frank C. Keil. Cambridge, Mass. : MIT
Press, c1999. cxxxii, 964 p
99-011115   153/.03   026273124X
Cognitive science -- Encyclopedias.

BF311.N488
Neumann, Erich.
The origins and history of consciousness / Erich Neumann ;
with a foreword by C. G. Jung ; translated from the German by
R. F. C. Hull. Princeton, N.J. : Princeton University Press,
1970, c1954. xxiv, 493 p.,
53012527
Mythology Personality Development Consciousness.

BF311.N68 1993
Norwich, Kenneth H.
Information, sensation, and perception / Kenneth H.
Norwich. San Diego, CA : Academic Press, c1993. xix, 326 p.
:
93-016692   152.1   0125218907
*Perception -- Mathematical models. Senses and sensation --
Mathematical models.*

BF311.P31363 1999
Parker, Sue Taylor.
Origins of intelligence : the evolution of cognitive
development in monkeys, apes, and humans / Sue Taylor
Parker and Michael L. McKinney. Baltimore, Md. : Johns
Hopkins University Press, c1999. xv, 404 p. :
98-037428   156/.3   0801860121
Cognition. Cognition in animals. Animal intelligence.

BF311.P31367 1995
Parkinson, Brian,
Ideas and realities of emotion / Brian Parkinson. London ;
Routledge, 1995. xii, 333 p. :
95-001096   152.4   0415028582
Emotions. Interpersonal communication.

BF311.R62 1995
Rogers, William,
"Recovered memory" and other assaults upon the mysteries
of consciousness : hypnosis, psychotherapy, fraud, and the
mass media / by William Rogers. Jefferson, N.C. : McFarland,
c1995. viii, 144 p.
95-015794   150   0786401095
*Consciousness. Altered states of consciousness. Recollection
(Psychology)*

BF311.S385 2000
Schulkin, Jay.
Roots of social sensibility and neural function / Jay
Schulkin. Cambridge, Mass. : MIT Press, c2000. xviii, 206 p.
00-026950   153   0262194473
*Cognition -- Social aspects. Cognition and culture. Human
information processing -- Social aspects.*

BF311.S5686 1997
Situated cognition : social, semiotic, and psychological
perspectives / edited by David Kirshner, James A. Whitson.
Mahwah, N.J. : L. Erlbaum, 1997. ix, 323 p. :
96-034120   153   080582037X
Cognition. Cognitive learning theory. Cognition and culture.

BF311.S6778 1997
Sternberg, Robert J.
   Thinking styles / Robert J. Sternberg. Cambridge, U.K. ;
Cambridge University Press, 1997. xi, 180 p. ;
97-001586   153.4/2   0521553164
   Cognitive styles. Thought and thinking. Human information
processing.

BF311.T28
Tart, Charles T.,
   Altered states of consciousness; a book of readings. Charles
T. Tart, editor. New York, Wiley [1969] 575 p.
69-016040   154
   Altered states of consciousness.

BF311.T354 1999
Taylor, John Gerald,
   The race for consciousness / John G. Taylor. Cambridge,
Mass. : MIT Press, c1999. viii, 380 p.
98-037294   153   0262201151
   Consciousness.

BF311.V624 1993
Von Eckardt, Barbara.
   What is cognitive science? / Barbara Von Eckardt.
Cambridge, Mass. : MIT Press, c1993. x, 466 p. :
92-010167   153   0262220466
   Cognitive science.

BF311.W2695 2002
Ward, Lawrence M.
   Dynamical cognitive science / Lawrence M. Ward.
Cambridge, Mass. : MIT Press, c2002. xv, 355 p. :
                   153   0262232170
   Cognitive science. Change (Psychology) Time--Psychological
aspects.

BF315 Consciousness. Cognition — The unconscious mind, etc. Subconsciousness

BF315.I46 1996
   Implicit cognition / edited by Geoffrey Underwood. Oxford
; Oxford University Press, 1996. x, 305 p. :
95-018291   153   0198523114
   Subconsciousness. Cognition. Implicit learning.

BF316.6 Consciousness. Cognition — Mental representation

BF316.6.C64 2000
   Cognitive dynamics :conceptual and representational change
in humans and machines / edited by Eric Dietrich, Arthur B.
Markman. Mahwah, NJ : L. Erlbaum Associates, 2000. xiii,
380 p. :
                   153   0805834087
   Mental representation. Thought and thinking. Cognitive science.

BF316.6.T48 1996
Thagard, Paul.
   Mind : introduction to cognitive science / Paul Thagard.
Cambridge, Mass. : MIT Press, c1996. x, 213 p. :
96-017499   153   0262201062
   Mental representation. Intellect. Thought and thinking.

BF317 Consciousness. Cognition — Reactions. Reaction time, etc.

BF317.L3 1968
Laming, D. R. J.
   Information theory of choice-reaction times, by D. R. J.
Laming. London, Academic P., 1968. ix, 172 p.
68-019259   152.8/3
   Reaction time. Choice (Psychology) Information theory in
psychology.

BF318 Consciousness. Cognition — Learning

BF318.B68 1989
Bower, T. G. R.,
   The rational infant : learning in infancy / T.G.R. Bower.
New York, N.Y. : W.H. Freeman, c1989. ix, 176 p. :
88-031082   155.4/22   0716720051
   Learning, Psychology of. Reasoning in infants.

BF318.B79 1999
Bruer, John T.,
   The myth of the first three years : a new understanding of
early brain development and lifelong learning / John T. Bruer.
New York : Free Press, c1999. x, 244 p. :
99-034934   155.4/13   0684851849
   Learning, Psychology of. Educational psychology. Pediatric
neuropsychology.

BF319-319.5 Consciousness. Cognition — Learning — Conditioned response

BF319.B5 1961
Birney, Robert Charles,
   Reinforcement, an enduring problem in psychology;
selected readings. Edited by Robert C. Birney and Richard C.
Teevan. Princeton, N.J., Van Nostrand [1961] 230 p.
61-009251   154.4
   Reinforcement (Psychology)

BF319.5.I45.H68 1997
   How implicit is implicit learning? / edited by Dianne C.
Berry. Oxford ; Oxford University Press, 1997. viii, 245 p.
97-037706   153.1/5   0198523521
   Implicit learning.

BF319.5.O6.H37 1998
   Handbook of research methods in human operant behavior /
edited by Kennon A. Lattal and Michael Perone. New York :
Plenum Press, c1998. xi, 669 p. :
98-028963   153.1/526   0306456680
   Operant behavior. Operant conditioning. Behavior.

BF323 Consciousness. Cognition — Apperception. Attention — Special topics, A-Z

BF323.E8.I68 1993
Interpersonal expectations : theory, research, and applications / edited by Peter David Blanck. Cambridge [England] ; Cambridge University Press ; 1993. xviii, 500 p.
92-036925   158/.2   052141783X
Expectation (Psychology) Interpersonal relations.

BF323.L5.N53 1995
Nichols, Michael P.
The lost art of listening / Michael P. Nichols. New York : Guilford Press, c1995. viii, 251 p.
94-038111   153.6/8   0898622670
Listening. Interpersonal relations. Interpersonal communication.

BF323.S63K86 1999
Kunda, Ziva.
Social cognition :making sense of people / Ziva Kunda. Cambridge, Mass. : MIT Press, c1999. xi, 602 p. :
       302/.12   0262611430
Social perception.

BF323.S63.S44 1991
The Self-society dynamic : cognition, emotion, and action / edited by Judith A. Howard, Peter L. Callero. Cambridge [England] ; Cambridge University Press, 1991. xi, 337 p.:
90-041672   302.5   0521384338
Social perception -- Congresses. Social interaction -- Congresses. Social psychology -- Congresses.

BF323.S63.S74 1989
Stereotyping and prejudice : changing conceptions / Daniel Bar-Tal ... [et al.] editors. New York : Springer-Verlag, c1989. x, 273 p. :
88-038198   305   0387968830
Stereotype (Psychology) Prejudices.

BF323.S63.Z47 1997
Zerubavel, Eviatar.
Social mindscapes : an invitation to cognitive sociology / Eviatar Zerubavel. Cambridge, Mass. : Harvard University Press, 1997. viii, 164 p.
97-022037   302/.1   067481391X
Social perception. Knowledge, Sociology of.

BF327 Consciousness. Cognition — Attitude. Conscious attitudes

BF327.E19 1993
Eagly, Alice Hendrickson.
The psychology of attitudes / Alice H. Eagly, Shelly Chaiken. Fort Worth, TX : Harcourt Brace Jovanovich College Publishers, c1993. xxii, 794 p.
92-052667   153.8   0155000977
Attitude (Psychology) Attitude change.

BF335 Consciousness. Cognition — Habit. Adjustment — General works

BF335.H4
Helson, Harry,
Adaptation-level theory; an experimental and systematic approach to behavior. New York, Harper & Row [1964] xvii, 732 p.
64012786   150
Adjustment (Psychology) Adaptability (Psychology) Behavior.

BF335.L35
Lazarus, Richard S.
Patterns of adjustment and human effectiveness [by] Richard S. Lazarus. New York, McGraw-Hill [1968, c1969] xxiii, 680 p.
68-030976   155.2/4
Adjustment (Psychology)

BF341 Consciousness. Cognition — Nature and nurture — General works

BF341.C55 1999
Cohen, David B.,
Stranger in the nest : do parents really shape their child's personality, intelligence, or character? / David B. Cohen. New York : J. Wiley & Sons, 1999. p. cm.
98-031371   155.2/34   0471319228
Nature and nurture. Nativism (Psychology)

BF341.C57 1994
Collier, Gary.
Social origins of mental ability / Gary Collier. New York : Wiley, c1994. xii, 300 p. :
93-003625   155.9/2   0471304077
Nature and nurture. Intellect -- Social aspects.

BF341.N374 1994
Nature and nurture during middle childhood / [edited by] John C. DeFries, Robert Plomin, David W. Fulker. Oxford, UK ; Blackwell, 1994. xix, 368 p. :
93-022617   155.42/48234   1557863938
Individual differences in children -- Longitudinal studies. Adopted children -- Colorado -- Psychology -- Longitudinal studies. Nature and nurture -- Longitudinal studies.

BF341.R68 1994
Rowe, David C.
The limits of family influence : genes, experience, and behavior / David C. Rowe. New York : Guilford Press, c1994. viii, 232 p.
93-021876   155.7   0898621321
Nature and nurture. Behavior genetics. Socialization.

BF353 Consciousness. Cognition — Environmental psychology

BF353.B3
Barker, Roger G.
Ecological psychology; concepts and methods for studying the environment of human behavior [by] Roger G. Barker. Stanford, Calif., Stanford University Press, 1968. vi, 242 p.
68-021287   155.9
Environmental psychology. Psychology.

BF353.G355 1993
Gallagher, Winifred.
The power of place : how our surroundings shape our thoughts, emotions, and actions / Winifred Gallagher. New York : Poseidon Press, c1993. 240 p. ;
92-038022   155.9/1   067172410X
Environmental psychology. Human beings -- Effect of environment on.

BF353.H85
Human behavior and environment : advances in theory and research / edited by Irwin Altman and Joachim F. Wohlwill. New York : Plenum Press, c1976-c1990 v. 1-4, 6-11
76-382942   155.9   0306333015
Environmental psychology.

BF353.P44
Perspectives on environment and behavior :theory, research, and applications / edited by Daniel Stokols. New York : Plenum Press, c1977. xiv, 360 p. :
          155.9   0306309548
Environmental psychology. Psychology--Research.

BF353.R44 1996
Reed, Edward
Encountering the world : toward an ecological psychology / Edward S. Reed. New York : Oxford University Press, 1996. vii, 214 p. :
95-031908   155.9   0195073010
Environmental psychology.

BF353.5 Consciousness. Cognition — Environmental psychology — Special topics, A-Z

BF353.5.N37.E26 1995
Ecopsychology : restoring the earth, healing the mind / edited by Theodore Roszak, Mary E. Gomes, and Allen D. Kanner ; forewords by Lester R. Brown and James Hillman. San Francisco : Sierra Club Books, c1995. xxiii, 338 p.
94-031179   155.9   0871564998
Environmental psychology. Nature -- Psychological aspects. Environmentalism -- Psychological aspects.

BF365 Consciousness. Cognition — Association and reproduction of ideas — General works

BF365.D47 1993
The development and meaning of psychological distance / edited by Rodney R. Cocking, K. Ann Renninger. Hillsdale, N.J. : L. Erlbaum, 1993. xviii, 266 p.
92-049448   153   0805807470
Mental representation. Learning, Psychology of. Cognition.

BF367-378 Consciousness. Cognition — Association and reproduction of ideas — Special

BF367.R65 1989
Rollins, Mark,
Mental imagery : on the limits of cognitive science / Mark Rollins. New Haven : Yale University Press, c1989. xvii, 170 p.
88-036541   153.3/2   0300044917
Imagery (Psychology) Cognition. Cognitive science.

BF371.B59 1988
Bolles, Edmund Blair,
Remembering and forgetting : an inquiry into the nature of memory / Edmund Blair Bolles. New York : Walker and Co., 1988. xvii, 315 p.
87-014791   153.1/2   0802710042
Memory.

BF371.D6813 2000
Draaisma, D.
Metaphors of memory : a history of ideas about the mind / Douwe Draaisma. Cambridge ; Cambridge University Press, 2000. p. cm.
99-088502   153.1/2   0521650240
Memory -- History.

BF371.H757 1982
Human memory and amnesia / edited by Laird S. Cermak. Hillsdale, N.J. : L. Erlbaum Associates, 1982. x, 388 p. :
80-039586   616.85/232   0898590957
Memory. Memory disorders. Amnesia.

BF371.N55 1994
Noll, Richard,
The encyclopedia of memory and memory disorders / Richard Noll and Carol Turkington. New York, NY : Facts on File, c1994. 265 p. ;
94-001590   153.1/2/03   0816026106
Memory -- Encyclopedias. Memory disorders -- Encyclopedias.

BF371.P277 1993
Parkin, Alan J.
Memory : phenomena, experiment, and theory / Alan J. Parkin. Oxford, UK ; Blackwell, 1993. viii, 231 p.
92-035260   153.1/2   0631157115
Memory. Memory -- Age factors.

BF371.S29 1996
Schacter, Daniel L.
  Searching for memory : the brain, the mind, and the past / Daniel L. Schacter. New York, NY : BasicBooks, c1996. xiii, 398 p.
96-019521   153.1/2   0465025021
  Memory. Recollection (Psychology) Memory disorders.

BF371.W385 1987
Warnock, Mary.
  Memory / Mary Warnock. London ; Faber, 1987. ix, 150 p. ;
87017020   128/.3   0571147836
  Memory.

BF376.S33 2001
Schacter, Daniel L.
  The seven sins of memory : how the mind forgets and remembers / Daniel L. Schacter. Boston : Houghton Mifflin, 2001. x, 272 p. :
00-053885   153.1/2   0618040196
  Memory disorders. Memory. Recollection (Psychology)

BF378.A75.R57
Rokeach, Milton.
  The open and closed mind; investigations into the nature of belief systems and personality systems. In collaboration with Richard Bonier [and others] New York, Basic Books [1960] xv, 447 p.
60-005888   157.5
  Attitude (Psychology) Dogmatism.

BF378.I55.I46 1996
  Implicit memory and metacognition / edited by Lynne M. Reder. Mahwah, N.J. : Lawrence Erlbaum, c1996. xii, 362 p. :
96-029383   153.1/2   0805818596
  Implicit memory -- Congresses. Explicit memory -- Congresses. Metacognition -- Congresses.

BF378.S65
Gross, David,
  Lost time : on remembering and forgetting in late modern culture / David Gross. Amherst : University of Massachusetts, c2000. xii, 199 p. ;
00-036383   128/.3   1558492542
  Memory -- Social aspects. Memory.

BF378.S65.C65 1997
  Collective memory of political events : social psychological perspectives / edited by James W. Pennebaker, Dario Paez, Bernard Rime. Mahwah, N.J. : Lawrence Erlbaum Associates, 1997. xi, 303 p. :
96-029389   153.1/3   0805821821
  Memory -- Social aspects. Autobiographical memory. Social psychology.

BF408 Consciousness. Cognition — Creative processes. Imagination. Invention — General works

BF408.C5
University of Chicago.
  The works of the mind, by Mortimer J. Adler [and others] Ed. for the Committee on Social Thought by Robert B. Heywood; with a pref. by John U. Nef. Chicago, University of Chicago Press [1947] xi, 245 p.
47011992   155
  Creation (Literary, artistic, etc.)

BF408.E53 1999
  Encyclopedia of creativity / editors-in-chief, Mark A. Runco, Steven R. Pritzker. San Diego, Calif. : Academic Press, c1999. 2 v. (xvii, 8
99-061534   153.3/5/03   0122270754
  Creative ability -- Encyclopedias. Creation (Literary, artistic, etc.) -- Encyclopedias.

BF408.G33 1993
Gardner, Howard.
  Creating minds : an anatomy of creativity seen through the lives of Freud, Einstein, Picasso, Stravinsky, Eliot, Graham, and Gandhi / Howard Gardner. New York : BasicBooks, c1993. xvi, 464 p. :
92-056172   153.3/5/0922   0465014550
  Creative ability -- Case studies. Gifted persons -- Biography.

BF408.H285 1999
  Handbook of creativity / edited by Robert J. Sternberg. Cambridge, U.K. ; Cambridge University Press, 1999. ix, 490 p. :
98-035205   153.3/5   0521572851
  Creative ability. Creative thinking.

BF408.O74 1997
Oremland, Jerome D.
  The origins and psychodynamics of creativity : a psychoanalytic perspective / Jerome D. Oremland. Madison, Conn. : International Universities Press, c1997. xvi, 200 p. :
96-043194   153.3/5   0823639053
  Creative ability. Dream interpretation. Psychoanalysis and art.

BF408.P87 1992
Piirto, Jane,
  Understanding those who create / Jane Piirto. Dayton, Ohio : Ohio Psychology Press, 1992. iii, 360 p. ;
91-041971   153.3/5   0910707197
  Creative ability. Creative ability -- Testing. Creative ability -- Case studies.

BF408.R682 1990
Rothenberg, Albert,
  Creativity and madness : new findings and old stereotypes / Albert Rothenberg. Baltimore, Md. : Johns Hopkins University Press, c1990. vii, 199 p. :
90-030770   153.3/5   0801840112
  Creative ability. Mental illness.

BF408.S76 1995
Sternberg, Robert J.
   Defying the crowd : cultivating creativity in a culture of
conformity / Robert J. Sternberg, Todd I. Lubart. New York,
N.Y. : Free Press, c1995. ix, 326 p. ;
94-041129   153.3/5   0029314755
   Creative ability. Originality.

BF408.W384 2000
Weiner, Robert,
   Creativity & beyond : cultures, values, and change / Robert
Paul Weiner. Albany, NY : State University of New York
Press, c2000. xii, 353 p. :
99-052763   153.3/5   0791444775
   Creative thinking. Creative ability.

BF412 Consciousness. Cognition — Creative processes. Imagination. Invention — Genius. Gifted

BF412.E97 1995
Eysenck, H. J.
   Genius : the natural history of creativity / H.J. Eysenck.
Cambridge ; Cambridge University Press, 1995. 344 p. :
94-032136   153.9/8   0521480140
   Genius. Creative ability.

BF412.G27 1997
Gardner, Howard.
   Extraordinary minds : portraits of exceptional individuals
and an examination of our extraordinariness / Howard
Gardner. New York : BasicBooks, c1997. xii, 178 p. :
96-045069   153.9/8   0465045154
   *Mozart, Wolfgang Amadeus, -- 1756-1791. Freud, Sigmund, -- 1856-
1939. Woolf, Virginia, -- 1882-1941. Gifted persons. Gifted persons -
- Case studies.*

BF412.G435 1998
   Genius and the mind : studies of creativity and temperament
/ edited by Andrew Steptoe. Oxford ; Oxford University Press,
1998. vi, 274 p. :
97-051708   153.3/5   0198523734
   Genius. Creative ability. Nature and nurture.

BF412.S56 1994
Simonton, Dean Keith.
   Greatness : who makes history and why / Dean Keith
Simonton. New York : Guilford, c1994. x, 502 p. :
93-048127   153.9/8   0898623707
   Genius -- History. Genius -- Philosophy. History -- Philosophy.

BF416 Consciousness. Cognition — Creative processes. Imagination. Invention — Studies of men and women of genius. By name, A-Z

BF416.A1.T38 1995
Taylor, Benjamin,
   Into the open : reflections on genius and modernity /
Benjamin Taylor. New York : New York University Press,
c1995. xii, 145 p. ;
94-041349   155.9/8   0814782132
   *Pater, Walter, -- 1839-1894. Valery, Paul, -- 1871-1945. Freud,
Sigmund, -- 1856-1939. Genius -- Case studies. Gifted persons --
Case studies.*

BF423 Consciousness. Cognition — Creative processes. Imagination. Invention — Genius and mental illness

BF423.H474 1998
Hershman, D. Jablow.
   Manic depression and creativity / D. Jablow Hershman and
Julian Lieb. Amherst, N.Y. : Prometheus Books, c1998. v, 230
p. :
98-027043   153.3/5   1573922412
   *Genius and mental illness. Manic-depressive illness. Genius and
mental illness -- Case studies.*

BF423.L83 1995
Ludwig, Arnold M.
   The price of greatness : resolving the creativity and madness
controversy / Arnold M. Ludwig. New York : Guilford Press,
c1995. x, 310 p. :
94-044905   153.3/5   0898628393
   Genius and mental illness. Creative ability.

BF426 Consciousness. Cognition — Creative processes. Imagination. Invention — Genius and mental retardation

BF426.H78 1989
Howe, Michael J. A.,
   Fragments of genius : the strange feats of idiots savants /
Michael J.A. Howe. London ; Routledge, 1989. x, 178 p. :
89-010380   153.9   041500781X
   Savants (Savant syndrome) Savant syndrome.

BF431 Consciousness. Cognition — Intelligence. Mental ability. Intelligence testing. Ability testing — General works

BF431.A44 1990
Adler, Mortimer Jerome,
   Intellect : mind over matter / Mortimer J. Adler. New York :
Macmillan ; c1990. xvi, 205 p. ;
89-015924   128/.2   002500350X
   Intellect. Philosophy of mind. Mind and body.

BF431.B97 1998
Eysenck, H. J.
Intelligence : a new look / Hans J. Eysenck. New Brunswick, NJ : Transaction Publishers, c1998. 227 p. :
98-014308   153.9   156000360X
Intellect. Intelligence tests. Nature and nurture.

BF431.C66 1997
Contemporary intellectual assessment : theories, tests, and issues / edited by Dawn P. Flanagan, Judy L. Genshaft, Patti L. Harrison. New York : Guilford Press, c1997. xvi, 598 p. :
96-022622   153.9/3   1572301473
Intelligence tests. Intelligence tests -- History.

BF431.E59 1994
Encyclopedia of human intelligence / Robert J. Sternberg, editor in chief. New York : Macmillan ; c1994. 2 v. (1235 p)
93-046975   153.9/03   0028974077
Intellect -- Encyclopedias. Intelligence levels -- Encyclopedias.

BF431.F47
Flavell, John H.
The developmental psychology of Jean Piaget. With a foreword by Jean Piaget. Princeton, N.J., Van Nostrand [1963] 472 p.
63-002423   136.72
Piaget, Jean, -- 1896-   Intellect.

BF431.H398 1994
Herrnstein, Richard J.
The bell curve : intelligence and class structure in American life / Richard J. Herrnstein, Charles Murray. New York : Free Press, c1994. xxvi, 845 p.
94-029694   305.9/082   0029146739
Intellect. Nature and nurture. Intelligence levels -- United States.

BF431.I513 1996
Inequality by design : cracking the bell curve myth / Claude S. Fischer ... [et al.]. Princeton, NJ : Princton University Press, 1996. xii, 318 p. :
96-002171   305.9/082   0691028990
Herrnstein, Richard J. -- Bell curve.   Nature and nurture.
Intelligence levels -- United States. Intelligence levels -- Social aspects -- United States.

BF431.K3646
Kamin, Leon J.
The science and politics of I.Q., by Leon J. Kamin. Potomac, Md., L. Erlbaum Associates; distributed by Halsted Pr 1974. vii, 183 p.
74-013883   153.9/3   0470455748
Intellect -- Social aspects. Intelligence tests. Nature and nurture.

BF431.M4123 1996
Measured lies : The bell curve examined / edited by Joe L. Kincheloe, Shirley R. Steinberg, and Aaron D. Gresson III. New York : St. Martin's Press, 1996. x, 454 p. ;
95-047522   305.9/082   0312129297
Herrnstein, Richard J. -- Bell curve.   Nature and nurture.
Intelligence levels -- United States. Intelligence levels -- Social aspects -- United States.

BF431.P365 1995
Perkins, David N.
Outsmarting IQ : the emerging science of learnable intelligence / by David Perkins. New York : Free Press, c1995. x, 390 p. :
94-045954   153.9   0029252121
Intellect. Intelligence levels -- Social aspects. Nature and nurture.

BF431.P48272
Piaget, Jean,
The psychology of intelligence. [Translated from the French by Malcolm Piercy and D. E. Berlyne] London, Routledge & Paul [1950] viii, 182 p.
51-000991   151
Intellect.

BF431.S19
Sagan, Carl,
Broca's brain :reflections on the romance of science / Carl Sagan. 1st ed. New York : Random House, c1979. xv, 347 p. ;
128/.2   0394501691
Broca, Paul, 1824-1880.   Intellect. Brain. Space sciences.

BF431.S285 1986
Schiff, Michel.
Education and class : the irrelevance of IQ genetic studies / Michel Schiff, Richard Lewontin, with contributions from A. Dumaret ... [et al.]. Oxford [Oxfordshire] : Clarendon Press ; 1986. xxiii, 243 p.
86-002563   153.9/2   0198575998
Intellect -- Genetic aspects. Intelligence levels -- Social aspects. Nature and nurture.

BF431.S7382 1990
Sternberg, Robert J.
Metaphors of mind : conceptions of the nature of intelligence / Robert J. Sternberg. Cambridge ; Cambridge University Press, 1990. xvi, 344 p. ;
89-039370   153.9   0521355796
Intellect. Psychology -- Philosophy. Metaphor.

BF431.W35 1958
Wechsler, David,
The measurement and appraisal of adult intelligence. Baltimore, Williams & Wilkins, 1958. ix, 297 p.
58-008896   151.2
Wechsler Adult Intelligence Scale. Intellect.

BF431.W35 1972
Wechsler, David,
Wechsler's Measurement and appraisal of adult intelligence [by] Joseph D. Matarazzo. Baltimore, Williams & Wilkins [1972] x, 572 p.
72-077316   153.9/3   0683055954
Wechsler Adult Intelligence Scale.

BF431.W37 1952
Wechsler, David,
The range of human capacities. Baltimore, Williams & Wilkins, 1952. 190 p.
52003462   151
Variation (Biology) Ability. Psychophysiology.

BF431.5 Consciousness. Cognition — Intelligence. Mental ability. Intelligence testing. Ability testing — By region or country, A-Z

BF431.5.U6.I87 1994
Itzkoff, Seymour W.
The decline of intelligence in America : a strategy for national renewal / Seymour W. Itzkoff. Westport, Conn. : Praeger, 1994. viii, 242 p.
93-005416   153.9/0973   0275944670
Intelligence levels -- United States -- History -- 20th century. Intellect -- Genetic aspects -- History -- 20th century.   United States -- Intellectual life -- 20th century.

BF432 Consciousness. Cognition — Intelligence. Mental ability. Intelligence testing. Ability testing — By specific group of people, A-Z

BF432.A1.J46
Jensen, Arthur Robert.
Bias in mental testing / Arthur R. Jensen. New York : Free Press, c1980. xiii, 786 p.
79-007583   153.9/3   0029164303
Intelligence tests. Educational tests and measurements. Minorities -- Psychological testing.

BF432.A1.L6
Loehlin, John C.
Race differences in intelligence / John C. Loehlin, Gardner Lindzey, J. N. Spuhler. San Francisco : W. H. Freeman, [1975] xii, 380 p. :
75-001081   155.8/2   0716707543.
Intelligence levels -- United States. Race. Ethnic groups.

BF432.3 Consciousness. Cognition — Intelligence. Mental ability. Intelligence testing. Ability testing — Multiple intelligences

BF432.3.G378 1999
Gardner, Howard.
Intelligence reframed : multiple intelligences for the 21st century / Howard Gardner. New York, NY : Basic Books, c1999. x, 292 p. ;
99-042468   153.9   0465026109
Multiple intelligences.

BF433 Consciousness. Cognition — Intelligence. Mental ability. Intelligence testing. Ability testing — Special topics, A-Z

BF433.A6.B4
Bellak, Leopold,
The thematic apperception test and the children's apperception test in clinical use [by] Leopold Bellak, with the assistance of Marjorie Bristol. New York, Grune & Stratton, 1954. x, 282 p.
54009652
Apperception -- Testing.

BF433.A6.M82
Murstein, Bernard I.
Theory and research in projective techniques, emphasizing the TAT. New York, Wiley [1963] xiii, 385 p.
63020636   137.843
Thematic Apperception Test. Projection (Psychology) Thematic Apperception Test.

BF433.G45.J46 1998
Jensen, Arthur Robert.
The g factor : the science of mental ability / Arthur R. Jensen. Westport, Conn. : Praeger, 1998. xiv, 648 p. :
97-022815   153.9   0275961036
General factor (Psychology) Intellect. Nature and nurture.

BF441 Consciousness. Cognition — Thoughts and thinking

BF441.B29 1988
Baron, Jonathan,
Thinking and deciding / Jonathan Baron. New York : Cambridge University Press, 1988. xi, 516 p. :
87-035238   153.4/2   0521342538
Thought and thinking. Decision making.

BF441.J3
Janis, Irving Lester,
Decision making : a psychological analysis of conflict, choice, and commitment / Irving L. Janis, Leon Mann. New York : Free Press, c1977. xx, 488 p. :
76-019643   153.8/3   0029161606
Decision making. Conflict (Psychology) Stress (Psychology)

BF441.T465 1994
Thinking and problem solving / edited by Robert J. Sternberg. San Diego : Academic Press, c1994. xix, 461 p. :
94-004844   153.4/2   0121619524
Thought and thinking. Problem solving.

BF441.W46 1995
What might have been : the social psychology of counterfactual thinking / edited by Neal J. Roese and James M. Olson. Mahwah, N.J. : Lawrence Erlbaum Associates, 1995. xi, 408 p. :
95-008025   153.4   0805816135
Thought and thinking.

BF442 Consciousness. Cognition — Thoughts and thinking — Reasoning

BF442.R56 1994
Rips, Lance J.
The psychology of proof : deductive reasoning in human thinking / Lance J. Rips. Cambridge, Mass. : MIT Press, c1994. xiii, 449 p.
93-005811   160   0262181533
Reasoning (Psychology) Logic.

BF444 Consciousness. Cognition — Thoughts and thinking — Information processing

BF444.B37 1995
Baron-Cohen, Simon.
Mindblindness : an essay on autism and theory of mind / Simon Baron-Cohen. Cambridge, Mass. : MIT Press, c1995. xxii, 171 p.
94-036470   616.89/82   0262023849
Human information processing. Philosophy of mind. Genetic psychology.

BF444.C68 1995
Cowan, Nelson.
Attention and memory : an integrated framework / Nelson Cowan. New York : Oxford University Press ; 1995. xv, 321 p. :
94-012555   153.1   0195067606
Human information processing. Memory. Attention.

BF444.J33 1987
Jackendoff, Ray S.
Consciousness and the computational mind / Ray Jackendoff. Cambridge, Mass. : MIT Press, c1987. xvi, 356 p. :
87-002661   153   0262100371
Human information processing. Cognition. Consciousness.

BF444.J333 1992
Jackendoff, Ray S.
Languages of the mind : essays on mental representation / Ray Jackendoff. Cambridge, Mass. : MIT Press, c1992. ix, 200 p. :
91-045159   153.2   0262100479
Human information processing. Mental representation. Psycholinguistics.

BF448 Consciousness. Cognition — Thoughts and thinking — Decision making

BF448.R33 1989
Rachlin, Howard,
Judgment, decision, and choice : a cognitive/behavioral synthesis / Howard Rachlin. New York : W.H. Freeman, c1989. xiv, 288 p. :
88-016329   153.8/3   0716719908
Decision making. Choice (Psychology) Psychology, Comparative.

BF449 Consciousness. Cognition — Thoughts and thinking — Problem solving

BF449.E94 1989
Everyday problem solving : theory and applications / edited by Jan D. Sinnott. New York : Praeger, 1989. xvii, 314 p.
88-015537   153.4/3   0275926915
Problem solving.

BF449.W34 2002
Wagman, Morton.
Problem-solving processes in humans and computers :theory and research in psychology and artificial intelligence / Morton Wagman. Westport, Conn. : Praeger, 2002. xvii, 230 p. :
153.4/3   0275970876
Problem solving. Problem solving--Data processing. Artificial intelligence.

BF455 Consciousness. Cognition — Psycholinguistics. Psychology of meaning — General works

BF455.B75 1986
Bruner, Jerome S.
A study of thinking / Jerome S. Bruner, Jacqueline J. Goodnow, George A. Austin ; with a new preface by Jerome S. Bruner and Jacqueline J. Goodnow ; appendix on language by Roger W. Brown. New Brunswick, N.J., U.S.A. : Transaction Books, c1986. xx, 330 p. :
86-001913   153.4/2   0887386563
Thought and thinking.

BF455.S53
Skinner, B. F.
Verbal behavior.   New York, Appleton-Century-Crofts [1957] 478 p.
57-011446   158.83
Verbal behavior.

BF455.S58 1995
Speech, language, and communication / edited by Joanne L. Miller, Peter D. Eimas. San Diego : Academic Press, c1995. xviii, 415 p.
94-039355   401/.9   0124977707
Psycholinguistics. Speech perception. Language acquisition.

BF456 Consciousness. Cognition — Psycholinguistics. Psychology of meaning — Psychology of reading, spelling, etc., A-Z

BF456.R2.E65
Ephron, Beulah (Kanter)
Emotional difficulties in reading; a psychological approach to study problems. New York, Julian Press [1953] 289 p.
53008738   158.84
Reading, Psychology of.

BF456.R2.G63
Goodman, Kenneth S.
Language and literacy : the selected writings of Kenneth S. Goodman ; edited and introduced by Frederick V. Gollasch. Boston ; Routledge & Kegan Paul, 1982. 2 v. ;
81-011848   153.6   0710008759
Reading, Psychology of. Psycholinguistics.

BF456.R2.R33 1989
Rayner, Keith.
   The psychology of reading / Keith Rayner, Alexander Pollatsek. Englewood Cliffs, N.J. : Prentice Hall, 1989. xi, 529 p. :
88-022419   418   0137330073
   Reading, Psychology of. Reading.

BF458 Consciousness. Cognition — Psycholinguistics. Psychology of meaning — Symbolism

BF458.S74 1999
Stevens, Anthony.
   Ariadne's clue : a guide to the symbols of humankind / Anthony Stevens. Princeton, N.J. : Princeton University Press, 1999. xii, 464 p. :
98-039389   302.2/223   0691004595
   Symbolism (Psychology) Imagery (Psychology) Dream interpretation.

BF463 Consciousness. Cognition — Psycholinguistics. Psychology of meaning — Special topics, A-Z

BF463.M4.H37 1998
Hardy, Christine.
   Networks of meaning : a bridge between mind and matter / Christine Hardy. Westport, Conn. : Praeger, c1998. vii, 217 p. :
98-014932   128/.2   0275960358
   Meaning (Psychology) Cognition.

BF467 Consciousness. Cognition — Time, space, causality, etc.

BF467.C35 1994
Campbell, John,
   Past, space, and self / John Campbell. Cambridge, Mass. : MIT Press, c1994. x, 270 p. ;
93-014038   153.7   0262032155
   Space and time. Mental representation. Schemas (Psychology)

BF468 Consciousness. Cognition — Time, space, causality, etc. — Time

BF468.C6
Cottle, Thomas J.
   The present of things future; explorations of time in human experience [by] Thomas J. Cottle and Stephen L. Klineberg. New York, Free Press [1974] xiii, 290 p.
73-005292   153.7/53   0029068207
   Time -- Psychological aspects. Behavior. Time.

BF468.F75 1990
Friedman, William J.
   About time : inventing the fourth dimension / William Friedman. Cambridge, Mass. : MIT Press, c1990. x, 147 p. :
90-030771   153.7/53   0262061333
   Time perception. Space and time.

BF468.T544 1996
   Time and mind / edited by Hede Helfrich. Seattle : Hogrefe & Huber Publishers, c1996. ix, 209 p. :
96-008729   153.7/53   0889371733
   Time perception -- Congresses. Memory -- Congresses. Time perception -- Cross-cultural studies -- Congresses.

BF469 Consciousness. Cognition — Time, space, causality, etc. — Space

BF469.E42 1987
Eliot, John,
   Models of psychological space : psychometric, developmental, and experimental approaches / John Eliot ; with contributions by Heinrich Stumpf. New York : Springer-Verlag, c1987. viii, 203 p.
87-009770   153.7/52   0387965491
   Space perception. Psychometrics. Psychology, Experimental.

BF469.H34 1990
Hatfield, Gary C.
   The natural and the normative : theories of spatial perception from Kant to Helmholtz / Gary Hatfield. Cambridge, Mass. : MIT Press, c1990. xii, 366 p. ;
90-032191   153.7/52/09033   0262080869
   Space perception -- History.

BF469.H45 1999
Hershenson, Maurice.
   Visual space perception : a primer / Maurice Hershenson. Cambridge, Mass. : MIT Press, c1999. xvi, 238 p. :
98-004970   152.14/2   0262581671
   Space perception. Visual perception.

BF469.S685 1993
   Spatial representation : problems in philosophy and psychology / edited by Naomi Eilan, Rosaleen McCarthy, and Bill Brewer. Oxford [England] ; Blackwell, 1993. xi, 409 p. :
92-043144   153.7/52   0631183558
   Space perception. Mental representation.

BF481 Consciousness. Cognition — Work

BF481.I5 1991
   In the mind's eye : enhancing human performance / Daniel Druckman and Robert A. Bjork, editors. Washington, D.C. : National Academy Press, 1991. x, 291 p. ;
91-023941   158   0309043980
   Performance -- Psychological aspects.

BF481.W67 1988
   Work experience and psychological development through the life span / edited by Jeylan T. Mortimer and Kathryn M. Borman. Boulder, Colo. : Westview Press, 1988. viii, 306 p.
87-028190   158.7   0813374677
   Work -- Psychological aspects. Developmental psychology.

BF491 Consciousness. Cognition — Normal illusions

BF491.N5613 2001
Ninio, Jacques.
The science of illusions / Jacques Ninio ; translated by Franklin Philip. Ithaca : Cornell University Press, c2001. 211 p. :
00-011899   153.7/4   0801437709
Hallucinations and illusions.

BF495 Consciousness. Cognition — Synesthesia — General works

BF495.D36 1998
Dann, Kevin T.,
Bright colors falsely seen : synaesthesia and the search for transcendental knowledge / Kevin T. Dann. New Haven : Yale University Press, c1998. xi, 225 p. ;
98-015990   152.1   0300066198
Synesthesia.

BF503 Motivation — General works

BF503.B73 1982
Brenner, Charles,
The mind in conflict / by Charles Brenner. New York : International Universities Press, c1982. 266 p. ;
82-021391   150.19/5   0823633659
Conflict (Psychology) Psychoanalysis. Psychology, Pathological.

BF503.L63 1990
Locke, Edwin A.
A theory of goal setting & task performance / Edwin A. Locke, Gary P. Latham with contributions by Ken J. Smith, Robert E. Wood. Englewood Cliffs, N.J. : Prentice Hall, c1990. xviii, 413 p.
89-016372   153.8   0139131388
Goal (Psychology) Performance.

BF511 Affection. Feeling. Emotion

BF511.G3 1970
Gardiner, H. Norman
Feeling and emotion; a history of theories, by H. M. [sic] Gardiner, Ruth Clark Metcalf [and] John G. Beebe-Center. Westport, Conn., Greenwood Press [1970] xiii, 445 p.
74-098223   152.4   0837136830
Emotions.

BF511.H34 2001
Handbook of affect and social cognition / edited by Joseph P. Forgas. Mahwah, N.J. : L. Erlbaum Associates, c2001. xviii, 457 p.
00-034779   152.4   0805832173
Affect (Psychology) Cognition -- Social aspects.

BF511.J65 1999
Johnston, Victor S.
Why we feel : the science of human emotions / Victor S. Johnston. Reading, Mass. : Perseus Books, c1999. ix, 210 p. :
98-089426   152.4   073820109X
Emotions.

BF515 Affection. Feeling. Emotion — Pleasure and pain

BF515.B83 1962
Buytendijk, F. J. J.
Pain, its modes and functions. Translated by Eda O'Shiel. [Chicago] University of Chicago Press [1962] 189 p.
62009737   152.5
Pain.

BF515.G74 2000
Greenfield, Susan.
Private life of the brain : emotions, consciousness, and the secret of the self / Susan Greenfield. New York : John Wiley & Sons, c2000. xi, 258 p. ;
99-046191   152.4/2   0471183431
Pleasure. Emotions.

BF521 Affection. Feeling. Emotion — The feelings. Sensibility. Mood

BF521.M67 1989
Morris, William N.
Mood : the frame of mind / William N. Morris, in association with Paula P. Schnurr. New York : Springer-Verlag, c1989. xii, 261 p. ;
89-021739   152.4   0387969780
Mood (Psychology) Affective disorders. Affect.

BF531 Affection. Feeling. Emotion — Emotion — General works

BF531.B43 2000
Ben-Zeev, Aharon.
The subtlety of emotions / Aaron Ben-Zeev. Cambridge, Mass. : MIT Press, c2000. xv, 611 p. :
99-023903   152.4   0262024632
Emotions. Affect (Psychology) Mood (Psychology)

BF531.E55 1999
Encyclopedia of human emotions / edited by David Levinson, James J. Ponzetti, Jr., Peter F. Jorgensen. New York : Macmillan Reference USA, c1999. 2 v. :
99-031198   152.4/03   0028647661
Emotions -- Encyclopedias. Affect (Psychology) -- Encyclopedias. Mood (Psychology) -- Encyclopedias.

BF531.E79 2001
Evans, Dylan,
Emotion : the science of sentiment / Dylan Evans. Oxford ; Oxford University Press, 2001. xvi, 204 p. :
01-269239   152.4   019285433X
Emotions. Emotions (Philosophy)

BF531.H316 1996
Handbook of emotion, adult development, and aging / edited by Carol Magai, Susan H. McFadden. San Diego : Academic Press, c1996. xxi, 470 p. :
96-022522   152.4   0124649955
Emotions. Emotions and cognition. Adulthood.

BF531.K38 1999
Katz, Jack,
How emotions work / Jack Katz. Chicago : University of Chicago Press, 1999. xii, 407 p. :
99-032675   152.4   0226425991
Emotions -- Social aspects.

BF531.S314
Sartre, Jean Paul,
The emotions : outline of a theory / by Jean-Paul Sartre ; translated from the French by Bernard Frechtman. New York : Philosophical Library, c1948. 97 p. ;
48009080   157
Emotions. Emotions.

BF531.S35 1997
Scheff, Thomas J.
Emotions, the social bond, and human reality : part/whole analysis / Thomas J. Scheff. Cambridge [England] ; Cambridge University Press ; 1997. ix, 249 p. :
96-051847   302   0521584914
Emotions -- Social aspects. Interpersonal relations. Psychology -- Research -- Methodology.

BF531.T52 2001
Theories of mood and cognition : a users handbook / edited by Leonard L. Martin, Gerald L. Clore. Mahwah, N.J. : L. Erlbaum Associates, 2001. viii, 221 p.
00-042191   152.4   0805827838
Emotions and cognition.

BF531.T87 2000
Turner, Jonathan H.
On the origins of human emotions : a sociological inquiry into the evolution of human affect / Jonathan H. Turner. Stanford, Calif. : Stanford University Press, c2000. xiii, 189 p.
99-086427   304.5   0804737193
Emotions. Emotions -- Social aspects.

BF561 Affection. Feeling. Emotion — Emotion — Popular works. The "passions," etc. — 1851-

BF561.E95
Explaining emotions / edited by Amelie Oksenberg Rorty. Berkeley : University of California Press, 1980. vi, 543 p. ;
78-062859   152.4   0520037758
Emotions.

BF561.L38 1994
Lazarus, Richard S.
Passion and reason : making sense of our emotions / Richard S. Lazarus, Bernice N. Lazarus. New York : Oxofrd University Press, 1994. x, 321 p. ;
94-009320   152.4   0195087577
Emotions. Affect (Psychology) Adjustment (Psychology)

BF575 Affection. Feeling. Emotion — Emotion — Special forms of emotion, etc., A-Z

BF575.A3.A513 1989
Aggression and war : their biological and social bases / edited by Jo Groebel, Robert A. Hinde. Cambridge [England] ; Cambridge University Press, 1989. xvi, 237 p. ;
88-020426   302.5/4   0521353564
Aggressiveness. Aggressiveness -- Physiological aspects. Aggressiveness -- Social aspects.

BF575.A3.A52 1983
Aggression in global perspective / edited by Arnold P. Goldstein, Marshall H. Segall. New York : Pergamon Press, c1983. viii, 496 p.
82-010131   302.5/4   0080263461
Aggressiveness -- Cross-cultural studies.

BF575.A3.R46 1997
Renfrew, John W.
Aggression and its causes : a biopsychosocial approach / John W. Renfrew. New York : Oxford University Press, 1997. xi, 274 p. :
95-031920   302.5/4   019508229X
Aggressiveness.

BF575.A3.S76
Stepansky, Paul E.
A history of aggression in Freud / Paul E. Stepansky. New York : International Universities Press, c1977. ix, 201 p. ;
76-053907   152.5/2   0823623262
Freud, Sigmund, -- 1856-1939.   Psychoanalysis. Aggressiveness. Aggression.

BF575.A5R45 1999
Reiser, Christa,
Reflections on anger :women and men in a changing society / Christa Reiser. Westport, Conn. : Praeger, 1999. x, 156 p. ;
                   152.4/7   0275957772
Anger. Anger--Case studies. Man-woman relationships.

BF575.A6.L387 1995
Leary, Mark R.
Social anxiety / Mark R. Leary, Robin M. Kowalski. New York : Guilford Press, c1995. xii, 244 p. ;
95-032612   152.4/6   1572300078
Anxiety. Self-presentation. Interpersonal relations.

BF575.A86.A8 1998
Attachment theory and close relationships / Jeffry A. Simpson, W. Steven Rholes, editors. New York : Guilford Press, c1998. x, 438 p. :
97-037552   158.2   1572301023
Attachment behavior. Interpersonal relations. Intimacy (Psychology)

BF575.A86.F44 1996
Feeney, Judith.
Adult attachment / Judith Feeney, Patricia Noller. Thousand Oaks : Sage Publications, c1996. xiii, 176 p.
96-004527   155.6   0803972237
Attachment behavior. Attachment behavior in children. Interpersonal relations.

BF575.A86.H36 1999
Handbook of attachment : theory, research, and clinical applications / edited by Jude Cassidy, Phillip R. Shaver. New York : Guilford Press, c1999. xvii, 925 p.
98-053527   155.9/2   1572300876
Attachment behavior. Attachment behavior in children.

BF575.D35B67 1999
Boss, Pauline.
Ambiguous loss :learning to live with unresolved grief / Pauline Boss. Cambridge, Mass. : Harvard University Press, 1999. 155 p. ;
          155.9/3   0674017382
Loss (Psychology) Grief. Family--Psychological aspects.

BF575.E53.M55 1996
Miller, Rowland S.
Embarrassment : poise and peril in everyday life / Rowland S. Miller New York : Guilford Press, c1996. viii, 232 p.
96-021200   152.4   1572301279
Embarrassment.

BF575.F2.G73 1987
Gray, Jeffrey Alan.
The psychology of fear and stress / Jeffrey Alan Gray. Cambridge ; Cambridge University Press, 1987. x, 422 p. :
86-033387   156/.2432   0521249589
Fear. Stress (Psychology) Environmental psychology.

BF575.G7.A79 1996
Attig, Thomas,
How we grieve : relearning the world / Thomas Attig. New York : Oxford University Press, 1996. xviii, 201 p.
95-031907   155.9/37   0195074556
Bereavement -- Psychological aspects. Bereavement -- Psychological aspects -- Case studies. Grief.

BF575.G7.B68 1969b
Bowlby, John.
Attachment and loss. New York, Basic Books [1969-1980] 3 v.
70-078464   155.4/18
Maternal deprivation. Grief in children. Bereavement in children.

BF575.G7.H355 2001
Handbook of bereavement research : consequences, coping, and care / edited by Margaret S. Stroebe ... [et al.]. Washington, DC : American Psychological Association, c2001. xv, 814 p. ;
00-067633   155.9/37/072   155798736X
Grief. Bereavement -- Psychological aspects. Death -- Psychological aspects.

BF575.G7.J625 1987
Johnson, Sherry E.
After a child dies : counseling bereaved families / Sherry E. Johnson. New York : Springer Pub. Co., c1987. xiv, 216 p. :
87-016637   155.9/37   0826156908
Children -- Death -- Psychological aspects. Bereavement -- Psychological aspects. Parents -- Counseling of.

BF575.G7.S77 1987
Stroebe, Wolfgang.
Bereavement and health : the psychological and physical consequences of partner loss / Wolfgang Stroebe and Margaret S. Stroebe. Cambridge [Cambridgeshire] ; Cambridge University Press, 1987. xii, 288 p. ;
87-011627   155.9/37   0521244706
Bereavement -- Physiological aspects. Loss (Psychology) Grief -- Physiological aspects.

BF575.H27.C848 1997
Csikszentmihalyi, Mihaly.
Finding flow : the psychology of engagement with everyday life / Mihaly Csikszentmihalyi. New York : BasicBooks, c1997. ix, 181 p. :
97-002008   158   0465045138
Happiness. Conduct of life.

BF575.H27.P37 1995
Parducci, Allen.
Happiness, pleasure, and judgment : the contextual theory and its applications / Allen Parducci. Mahwah, N.J. : L. Erlbaum Associates, 1995. ix, 225 p. ;
95-014486   150   080581891X
Happiness. Pleasure. Judgment.

BF575.I5H66 2001
Honeycutt, James M.
Cognition, communication, and romantic relationships / James M. Honeycutt, James G. Cantrill. Mahwah, N.J. : L. Erlbaum Associates, c2001. xxiii, 198 p. :
          158.2   0805835776
Intimacy (Psychology) Interpersonal relations. Love.

BF575.I5.J36 1998
Jamieson, Lynn,
Intimacy : personal relationships in modern societies / Lynn Jamieson. Cambridge ; Polity Press, 1998. ix, 209 p. ;
97-038761   158.2   0745615732
Intimacy (Psychology)

BF575.I5.P73 1995
Prager, Karen Jean,
The psychology of intimacy / Karen J. Prager. New York : Guilford Press, c1995. x, 367 p. :
95-037284   158/.2   157230006X
Intimacy (Psychology)

BF575.J4.P79 1991
The Psychology of jealousy and envy / edited by Peter Salovey. New York : Guilford Press, c1991. xviii, 293 p.
90-023329   152.4   0898625556
Jealousy. Envy.

BF575.J4.W48 1989
White, Gregory L.
Jealousy : theory, research, and clinical strategies / Gregory L. White, Paul E. Mullen ; foreword by Philip Shaver. New York, NY : Guilford Press, c1989. xii, 340 p. :
89-007534   152.4   0898623855
Jealousy. Love. Psychotherapy.

BF575.L3.G78 1997
Gruner, Charles R.
The game of humor : a comprehensive theory of why we laugh / Charles R. Gruner. New Brunswick, N.J. : Transaction Publishers, c1997. 197 p. ;
97-002825   128/.3   1560003138
Laughter. Wit and humor -- Psychological aspects.

BF575.L3.H36 1983
Handbook of humor research / edited by Paul E. McGhee and Jeffrey H. Goldstein. New York : Springer-Verlag, c1983. 2 v. :
83-006675   152.4   0387908528
Wit and humor -- Psychological aspects. Wit and humor -- Social aspects. Wit and humor -- Research.

BF575.L7.A68
The Anatomy of loneliness / edited by Joseph Hartog, J. Ralph Audy, and Yehudi A. Cohen. New York : International Universities Press, c1980. xiv, 617 p. ;
79-053591   158/.2   0823601463
Loneliness -- Addresses, essays, lectures.

BF575.L8.P36 1988
Passionate attachments : thinking about love / edited by Willard Gaylin and Ethel Person. New York : Free Press ; c1988. xvi, 136 p. ;
87-020185   306.7   0029114306
Love. Interpersonal relations. Psychoanalysis.

BF575.L8.P78 1988
The Psychology of love / edited by Robert J. Sternberg and Michael L. Barnes. New Haven : Yale University Press, c1988. xii, 383 p. :
87-010656   302   0300039506
Love -- Psychological aspects.

BF575.R33.L36 1993
Landman, Janet.
Regret : the persistence of the possible / Janet Landman. New York : Oxford University Press, 1993. xxviii, 366 p
93-015209   152.4   0195071786
Regret.

BF575.S45.W87
Wurmser, Leon.
The mask of shame / Leon Wurmser. Baltimore : Johns Hopkins University Press, c1981. xiii, 345 p.
81-000964   152.4   080182527X
Shame. Psychoanalysis. Psychotherapy.

BF575.S75.H35 1982
Handbook of stress : theoretical and clinical aspects / edited by Leo Goldberger and Shlomo Breznitz. New York : Free Press ; c1982. xxi, 804 p. :
82-008448   155.9   0029120306
Stress (Psychology) Stress (Physiology) Stress, Psychological.

BF575.S75.H623 1998
Hobfoll, Stevan E.,
Stress, culture, and community : the psychology and philosophy of stress / Stevan E. Hobfoll. New York : Plenum Press, c1998. xvi, 296 p. :
98-039939   155.9/042   0306459426
Stress (Psychology) Stress (Psychology) -- Social aspects.

BF575.S75.L315 1999
Lazarus, Richard S.
Stress and emotion : a new synthesis / Richard S. Lazarus. New York : Springer Pub. Co., c1999. xiv, 342 p. :
98-045782   155.9/042   0826112501
Stress (Psychology) Emotions.

BF575.S9.S32 1970
Scheler, Max,
The nature of sympathy. Translated from the German by Peter Heath. With a general introd. to Max Scheler's work by W. Stark. [Hamden, Conn.] Archon Books, 1970. liv, 274 p.
71-016090   152.4   0208010203
Sympathy.

BF591-592 Affection. Feeling. Emotion — Emotion — Expression of the emotions

BF591.G45 2000
Gender and emotion : social psychological perspectives / edited by Agneta H. Fischer. Cambridge [England] ; Cambridge University Press ; 2000. xi, 331 p. ;
99-029140   155.3/3   0521630150
Expression -- Sex differences. Emotions -- Sex differences.

BF592.F33.P78 1997
The psychology of facial expression / edited by James A. Russell, Jose Miguel Fernandez-Dols. Cambridge ; Cambridge University Press, 1997. xiii, 400 p.
96-036250   153.6/9   0521496675
Facial expression. Body language.

BF632 Will. Volition. Choice. Control — Self-control. Willpower. Self-help techniques

BF632.E55 2001
Ellis, Albert.
Feeling better, getting better, staying better : profound self-help therapy for your emotions / Albert Ellis. Atascadero, Calif. : Impact Publishers, c2001. 259 p. ;
      152.4   1886230358
Self-help techniques.

BF632.K36 1993
Kaminer, Wendy.
I'm dysfunctional, you're dysfunctional : the recovery movement and other self-help fashions / Wendy Kaminer. New York : Vintage Books, 1993. xxvi, 180 p.
92-050677   158   0679745858
Self-help techniques -- United States. Psychological literature -- United States. Psychology -- United States.

BF632.R3 2000
Rachlin, Howard,
The science of self-control / Howard Rachlin. Cambridge, Mass. : Harvard University Press, 2000. 220 p. :
99-045204   153.8   0674000935
Self-control. Habit.

BF632.S73 1989
Starker, Steven,
Oracle at the supermarket : the American preoccupation with self-help books / Steven Starker. New Brunswick, N.J. : Transaction Publ., c1989. xi, 204 ;
88-001324   646.7   0887382339
Self-help techniques -- United States. Psychological literature -- United States. Psychology -- United States.

BF632.5 Will. Volition. Choice. Control — Manipulation or control by others

BF632.5.L36 1983
Langer, Ellen J.,
The psychology of control / Ellen J. Langer ; foreword by Irving L. Janis ; collaborators, Robert P. Abelson ... [et al.]. Beverly Hills : Sage Publications, c1983. 311 p. :
83-011224   153.8/3   080391962X
Control (Psychology) Behavior. Choice behavior.

BF633 Will. Volition. Choice. Control — Manipulation or control by others — Brainwashing

BF633.M4
Meerloo, Joost Abraham Maurits,
The rape of the mind; the psychology of thought control, menticide, and brainwashing. Cleveland, World Pub. Co. [1956] 320 p.
56-009252   131.33
Brainwashing.

BF633.W45 1990
Weinstein, Harvey.
Psychiatry and the CIA : victims of mind control / Harvey M. Weinstein. Washington, DC : American Psychiatric Press, c1990. xviii, 312 p.
90-000707   616.89/00973   0880483636
Cameron, Ewen, -- 1901-1967. Cameron, Ewen, -- 1901-1967. Psychiatric ethics -- Quebec (Province) -- Montreal. Brainwashing -- Quebec (Province) -- Montreal. Human experimentation in psychology -- Quebec (Province) -- Montreal.

BF634 Will. Volition. Choice. Control — Manipulation or control by others — Confession

BF634.R6
Rogge, O. John
Why men confess / O. John Rogge. New York : Nelson, c1959. 298 p. ;
59008613   159.4
Confession -- Psychology.

BF636 Applied psychology — General works

BF636.S77
Sullivan, Harry Stack,
The interpersonal theory of psychiatry; edited by Helen Swick Perry and Mary Ladd Gawel, with an introd. by Mabel Blake Cohen. New York, Norton [1953] xviii, 393 p.
53-009402   616.89*
Interpersonal relations. Psychiatry.

BF637 Applied psychology — Special topics (not otherwise provided for), A-Z

BF637.B4.H45 1986
Helping people change : a textbook of methods / edited by Frederick H. Kanfer, Arnold P. Goldstein. New York : Pergamon Press, c1986. x, 490 p. ;
85-006267   158   0080316018
Behavior modification. Personality. Behavior Therapy.

BF637.B4.H46 1998
Helping socially withdrawn and isolated children and adolescents / Maurice Chazan ... [et al.]. London ; Cassell, 1998. viii, 216 p.
98-220794   362.74/86   0304339695
Problem children -- Great Britain. Behavior modification -- Great Britain. Behavioral disorders in children -- Great Britain.

BF637.B4.M32
Mahoney, Michael J.
Cognition and behavior modification [by] Michael J. Mahoney. Cambridge, Mass., Ballinger Pub. Co., [1974] xv, 351 p.
74-013019   153.8/5   0884105008
Behavior modification. Cognition. Behavior therapy -- Cognition.

BF637.C4.M29 1991
Mahoney, Michael J.
  Human change processes : the scientific foundations of psychotherapy / Michael J. Mahoney. New York : BasicBooks, c1991. xiii, 590 p.
  90-080675   155   0465031188
  Change (Psychology) Developmental psychology. Psychotherapy.

BF637.C4M55 2001
Miller, William R.
  Quantum change :when epiphanies and sudden insights transform ordinary lives / William R. Miller, Janet C'de Baca ; afterword by Ernest Kurtz. New York : Guilford Press, c2001. xii, 212 p. ;
              155   1572305053
  Change (Psychology) Epiphanies. Insight.

BF637.C45.B57
Birdwhistell, Ray L.,
  Kinesics and context; essays on body motion communication [by] Ray L. Birdwhistell. Philadelphia, University of Pennsylvania Press [1970] xiv, 338 p.
  77-122379   153   0812276051
  Body language.

BF637.C45.B86 1995
Burgoon, Judee K.
  Interpersonal adaptation : dyadic interaction patterns / Judee K. Burgoon, Lesa A. Stern, Leesa Dillman. Cambridge ; Cambridge University Press, 1995. xvi, 334 p. :
  94-043249   153.6   0521451205
  Interpersonal communication. Adaptability (Psychology) Interpersonal relations.

BF637.C45.H283 1998
  Handbook of communication and emotion : research, theory, applications, and contexts / edited by Peter A. Andersen, Laura K. Guerrero. San Diego : Academic Press, c1998. xxxii, 590 p.
  97-023315   153.6   0120577704
  Interpersonal communication. Expression. Emotions.

BF637.C45.H29 1982
  Handbook of methods in nonverbal behavior research / edited by Klaus R. Scherer and Paul Ekman. Cambridge [Cambridgeshire] ; Cambridge University Press ; 1982. xiii, 593 p.
  81-009940   152.3/84   0521236142
  Body language -- Research. Psychology -- Research -- Methodology.

BF637.C45.S63 1998
  Social and cognitive approaches to interpersonal communication / edited by Susan R. Fussell, Roger J. Kreuz. Mahwah, N.J. : Lawrence Erlbaum Associates, 1998. ix, 298 p. :
  97-021638   302.2   0805822690
  Interpersonal communication. Cognition. Psycholinguistics.

BF637.C5.M36 1990
McCrae, Robert R.
  Personality in adulthood / Robert R. McCrae, Paul T. Costa, Jr. New York : Guilford Press, c1990. ix, 198 p. ;
  89-078494   155.6   0898624290
  Personality. Maturation (Psychology) Adulthood -- Psychological aspects.

BF637.C6D35 1999
D'Ardenne, Patricia.
  Transcultural counselling in action / Patricia d'Ardenne and Aruna Mahtani. 2nd ed. London ; SAGE Publications, 1999. xv, 142 p. ;
              158/.3   0761963154
  Counseling. Psychotherapy.

BF637.C6.H313 1987
  Handbook of counseling & psychotherapy with men / [edited by] Murray Scher ... [et al.]. Newbury Park, Calif. : Sage Publications, c1987. 400 p. :
  87-016578   158/.3   0803929919
  Counseling. Psychotherapy. Men -- Counseling of.

BF637.C6.H316 1996
  Handbook of counselling psychology / edited by Ray Woolfe and Windy Dryden. London ; Sage Publications, 1996. x, 662 p. :
  96-067251   158/.3   0803989911
  Counseling.

BF637.C6.H3174 1995
  Handbook of multicultural counseling / editors Joseph G. Ponterotto ... [et al.] ; foreword by Thomas A. Parham. Thousand Oaks, Calif. : Sage Publications, c1995. xvi, 679 p. :
  95-012874   158/.3   0803955065
  Cross-cultural counseling. Multiculturalism -- United States. Minorities -- Counseling of -- United States.

BF637.C6.K493 1999
  Key words in multicultural interventions : a dictionary / edited by Jeffrey Scott Mio ... [et al.]. Westport, Conn. : Greenwood Press, 1999. x, 306 p. ;
  99-014839   303.48/2/03   0313295476
  Cross-cultural counseling -- Dictionaries. Psychotherapy -- Dictionaries.

BF637.C6.P275 1997
Parrott, Les.
  Counseling and psychotherapy / Les Parrott III. New York : McGraw-Hill Companies, c1997. xiii, 431 p.
  96-027915   158/.3   007048581X
  Counseling. Psychotherapy.

BF637.C6.S755 1990
Stein, Ronald H.
  Ethical issues in counseling / Ronald H. Stein. Buffalo, N.Y. : Prometheus Books, 1990. 174 p. ;
  89-049689   174/.915   0879755571
  Counseling -- Moral and ethical aspects. Counselors -- Professional ethics.

BF637.C6.S85
Sue, Derald Wing.
Counseling the culturally different : theory and practice / Derald W. Sue, with chapter contributions by Edwin H. Richardson, Rene A. Ruiz, Elsie J. Smith. New York : Wiley, c1981. xvi, 303 p. ;
80-024516   158/.3   0471042188
Cross-cultural counseling.

BF637.D42.F67 1996
Ford, Charles V.,
Lies!, lies!!, lies!!! : the psychology of deceit / Charles V. Ford. Washington, DC : American Psychiatric Press, c1996. xiii, 333 p.
95-025312   153.8/3   0880487399
Deception. Self-deception. Truthfulness and falsehood.

BF637.H4.B39 1991
Batson, C. Daniel
The altruism question : toward a social psychological answer / C. Daniel Batson. Hillsdale, N.J. : L. Erlbaum, Associates, 1991. ix, 257 p. ;
91-006758   155.2/32   0805802452
Altruism. Altruism. Empathy.

BF637.I48.I57 1990
Intimates in conflict : a communication perspective / edited by Dudley D. Cahn. Hillsdale, N.J. : L. Erlbaum Associates, 1990. xv, 264 p. ;
89-071494   302.3/4   0805807357
Interpersonal conflict. Interpersonal communication. Communication.

BF637.I48M39 2000
Mayer, Bernard S.,
The dynamics of conflict resolution :a practitioner's guide / Bernard S. Mayer. 1st ed. San Francisco : Jossey-Bass Publishers, c2000. xvi, 263 p. :
                   303.6/9   078795019X
Interpersonal conflict. Conflict (Psychology) Conflict management.

BF637.L4
Popper, Micha,
Hypnotic leadership : leaders, followers, and the loss of self / Micha Popper. Westport, Conn. : Praeger, 2001. xx, 118 p. ;
00-064942   303.3/4   0275971384
Leadership. Control (Psychology) Dominance (Psychology)

BF637.L53.I5413 1991
Inglehart, Marita Rosch,
Reactions to critical life events : a social psychological analysis / Marita R. Inglehart. New York, NY : Praeger, 1991. xvi, 221 p. :
90-027790   302   0275938751
Life change events -- Psychological aspects. Cognitive consistency. Attribution (Social psychology)

BF637.N66.F47 1991
Feyereisen, Pierre.
Gestures and speech : psychological investigations / Pierre Feyereisen, Jacques-Dominique de Lannoy. Cambridge [England] ; Cambridge University Press ; 1991. vii, 210 p. ;
90-028283   153.6/9   0521377625
Gesture. Speech.

BF637.N66.N66 1997
Nonverbal communication : where nature meets culture / edited by Ullica Segerstrale, Peter Molnar. Mahwah, N.J. : Lawrence Erlbaum Associates, 1997. viii, 309 p.
96-002148   153.6/9   0805821791
Body language. Nonverbal communication. Psychology, Comparative.

BF637.P4.P39 1993
Perloff, Richard M.
The dynamics of persuasion / Richard M. Perloff. Hillsdale, N.J. : L. Erlbaum, 1993. xii, 411 p. :
92-035942   153.8/52   0805804900
Persuasion (Psychology) Mass media -- Psychological aspects. Attitude change.

BF637.S64.S65 1988
Storr, Anthony.
Solitude : a return to the self / Anthony Storr. New York : Free Press, 1988. xv, 216 p. ;
88-007187   155.9/2   0029316200
Solitude. Creation (Literary, artistic, etc.) Adjustment (Psychology)

BF671 Comparative psychology. Animal and human psychology — 1871-

BF671.A4
Altman, Joseph,
Organic foundations of animal behavior. New York, Holt, Rinehart and Winston [1966] xiv, 530 p.
65-018350   156.2
Animal behavior. Psychophysiology.

BF671.C615 1998
Comparative psychology : a handbook / Gary Greenberg, Maury M. Haraway, editors. New York : Garland Pub., 1998. xvi, 914 p. :
98-011939   156   0815312814
Psychology, Comparative.

BF671.H37
Harlow, Harry Frederick,
The human model : primate perspectives / Harry F. Harlow and Clara Mears. Washington : V. H. Winston ; 1979. viii, 312 p.
78-027597   156   0470266422
Psychology, Comparative. Primates -- Behavior. Ethology -- Collected works.

BF671.U53 1991
Understanding behavior : what primate studies tell us about human behavior / edited by James D. Loy and Calvin B. Peters. New York : Oxford University Press, 1991. ix, 264 p. :
90-039539   156   0195060202
Psychology, Comparative. Behavior evolution. Primates -- Behavior.

BF683 Comparative psychology. Animal and human psychology — Motivation

BF683.A8
Atkinson, John William,
An introduction to motivation, by John W. Atkinson. Princeton, N.J., Van Nostrand [1964] xiii, 335 p.
64023961   159.4
Motivation (Psychology)

BF683.M37 1970
Maslow, Abraham H.
Motivation and personality [by] Abraham H. Maslow. New York, Harper & Row [1970] xxx, 369 p.
76-113490   152.5
Motivation (Psychology) Self-actualization (Psychology)

BF683.T7 1967
Troland, Leonard T.
The fundamentals of human motivation. New York, Hafner Pub. Co., 1967. xiv, 521 p.
67-026458   152.5
Motivation (Psychology)

BF685 Comparative psychology. Animal and human psychology — Instinct

BF685.A24 1989
Abel, Donald C.,
Freud on instinct and morality / Donald C. Abel. Albany, N.Y. : State University of New York Press, c1989. xix, 123 p. ;
88-028247   150.19/52   0791400247
Freud, Sigmund, -- 1856-1939.   Instinct. Instinct -- Moral and ethical aspects.

BF685.B5
Birney, Robert Charles,
Instinct, an enduring problem in psychology; selected readings edited by Robert C. Birney and Richard C. Teevan. Princeton, N.J., Van Nostrand [1961] 181 p.
61-009250   158.424
Instinct.

BF692 Psychology of sex. Sexual behavior — General works

BF692.B38 1990
Beere, Carole A.,
Sex and gender issues : a handbook of tests and measures / Carole A. Beere. New York : Greenwood Press, 1990. xiv, 605 p. ;
90-032466   155.3/028/7   0313274622
Sex (Psychology) -- Testing -- Handbooks, manuals, etc.

BF692.F53 1989
Fisher, Seymour.
Sexual images of the self : the psychology of erotic sensations and illusions / Seymour Fisher. Hillsdale, N.J. : L. Erlbaum Associates, 1989. xi, 345 p. ;
88-022303   155.3   0805804390
Sex (Psychology) Body image. Psychosexual development.

BF692.M274
Maccoby, Eleanor E.,
The psychology of sex differences / Eleanor Emmons Maccoby and Carol Nagy Jacklin. Stanford, Calif. : Stanford University Press, 1974. xiii, 634 p.
73-094488   155.3/3   0804708592
Sex differences (Psychology) Sex differences (Psychology) -- Bibliography.

BF692.M34
May, Rollo.
Love and will. New York, Norton [1969] 352 p.
66-012799   152.4/32   0393010805
Sex (Psychology) Love -- Psychological aspects. Will.

BF692.M4
Menninger, Karl A.
Love against hate [by] Karl Menninger, M.D., with the collaboration of Jeanetta Lyle Menninger. New York, Harcourt, Brace and company [1942] ix p., 1 l.,
42-050183   131.341
Sex (Psychology) Psychoanalysis. Instinct.

BF692.15 Psychology of sex. Sexual behavior — Sexual animosity

BF692.15.S36 1989
Schoenewolf, Gerald.
Sexual animosity between men and women / Gerald Schoenewolf. Northvale, N.J. : Aronson, c1989. xii, 249 p. ;
88-019353   155.3   0876689330
Sexual animosity. Masculinity. Femininity.

BF692.2 Psychology of sex. Sexual behavior — Sex role. Sex differences — General works

BF692.2.C4713 1990
Christen, Yves.
Sex differences : modern biology and the unisex fallacy / Yves Christen ; translated by Nicholas Davidson. New Brunswick, N.J., U.S.A. : Transaction Publishers, c1991. 141 p. ;
90-011196   155.3/3   0887388698
Sex differences (Psychology) Sex differences. Feminism.

BF692.2.M33 1998
Maccoby, Eleanor E.,
The two sexes : growing up apart, coming together / Eleanor E. Maccoby. Cambridge, Mass. : Belknap Press of Harvard University Press, 1998. viii, 376 p.
97-030594   155.3/3   0674914813
Sex differences (Psychology) Gender identity. Man-woman relationships.

BF692.2.P764 1993
The psychology of gender / edited by Anne E. Beall, Robert J. Sternberg ; foreword by Ellen Berscheid. New York : Guilford Press, c1993. xxiv, 278 p.
93-011508   155.3/3   0898622867
Sex differences (Psychology) Gender identity. Sex (Psychology)

BF692.2.P77 1987
The Psychology of sex roles / edited by David J. Hargreaves and Ann M. Colley. Cambridge [Cambridgeshire] ; Hemisphere Pub. Corp., c1987. xiii, 323 p.
87-017708   155.3/3   0891167765
Sex role -- Psychological aspects. Identification (Psychology) Identification (Psychology)

BF692.5 Psychology of sex. Sexual behavior — Sex role. Sex differences — Psychology of men. Masculinity

BF692.5.D67 1993
Doty, William G.,
Myths of masculinity / William G. Doty. New York : Crossroad, 1993. ix, 243 p. :
93-025481   155.3/32   0824512332
Masculinity. Mythology -- Psychological aspects.

BF692.5.H83 1992
Hudson, Liam.
The way men think : intellect, intimacy, and the erotic imagination / Liam Hudson & Bernadine Jacot. New Haven : Yale University Press, 1991. xii, 219 p. :
91-021918   155.3/32   0300049978
Men -- Psychology. Intellect. Sex (Psychology)

BF692.5.S36 1993
Schoenberg, B. Mark,
Growing up male : the psychology of masculinity / B. Mark Schoenberg. Westport, Conn. : Bergin & Garvey, 1993. viii, 148 p.
93-018137   155.3/32   0897893441
Masculinity. Men -- Psychology.

BF697 Differential psychology. Individuality. Self — General works

BF697.A3
Adler, Gerhard,
The living symbol; a case study in the process of individuation. [New York] Pantheon Books [c1961] xii, 463 p.
61009310   131.3464
Obsessive-Compulsive Disorder. Psychoanalytic Interpretation. Individuation (Philosophy) -- Cases, clinical reports, statistics.

BF697.A55 1999
Aiken, Lewis R.,
Human differences / Lewis R. Aiken. Mahwah, N.J. : Lawrence Erlbaum Associates, 1999. xv, 337 p. :
99-011092   155.2/2   080583091X
Individual differences.

BF697.E7
Erikson, Erik H.
Identity, youth, and crisis [by] Erik H. Erikson. New York, W. W. Norton [1968] 336 p.
67-017681   155.2
Identity (Psychology)

BF697.G39 1991
Gergen, Kenneth J.
The saturated self : dilemmas of identity in contemporary life / Kenneth J. Gergen. [New York] : Basic Books, c1991. xiv, 295 p. :
90-055597   155.2   0465071864
Self. Identity (Psychology) Self -- Social aspects.

BF697.M32 1998
Margolis, Diane Rothbard.
The fabric of self : a theory of ethics and emotions / Diane Rothbard Margolis. New Haven, CT : Yale University Press, c1998. xi, 207 p. ;
97-034298   155.2   0300069901
Self. Self -- Social aspects. Emotions.

BF697.P765 2000
Psychological perspectives on self and identity / edited by Abraham Tesser, Richard B. Felson, and Jerry M. Suls. Washington, DC : American Psychological Association, c2000. x, 252 p. :
00-021139   155.2   1557986789
Self. Self -- Social aspects.

BF697.S672 1997
Socor, Barbara J.
   Conceiving the self : presence and absence in psychoanalytic theory / by Barbara J. Socor. Madison, Conn. : International Universities Press, c1997. xiv, 310 p. ;
96-029441   155.2   0823610306
   Self. Psychoanalysis. Self psychology.

BF697.W47
Whyte, William Hollingsworth.
   The organization man. New York, Simon and Schuster, 1956. 429 p.
56-009926   301.15
   Individuality. Loyalty.

BF697.W92 1974
Wylie, Ruth C.
   The self-concept, by Ruth C. Wylie. Lincoln, University of Nebraska Press [1974-79] 2 v.
72-097165   155.2   0803208308
   Self-perception. Self-perception -- Bibliography. Psychology -- Research.

BF697.5 Differential psychology. Individuality. Self — Special aspects, A-Z

BF697.5.B63.G76 1999
Grogan, Sarah,
   Body image : understanding body dissatisfaction in men, women, and children / Sarah Grogan. London ; Routledge, 1999. xii, 225 p. :
98-004036   155.9/1   0415147840
   Body image -- Social aspects -- United States. Body image -- Social aspects -- Great Britain.

BF697.5.B63.H47 1996
Hesse-Biber, Sharlene Janice.
   Am I thin enough yet? : the cult of thinness and the commercialization of identity / Sharlene Hesse-Biber. New York : Oxford University Press, 1996. ix, 191 p. :
95-011812   306.4   0195082419
   Body image. Leanness -- Psychological aspects. Eating disorders -- Social aspects.

BF697.5.B63L83 2001
Luciano, Lynne,
   Looking good :male body image in modern America / Lynne Luciano.1st ed. New York : Hill and Wang, 2001. x, 259 p. :
                306.4   0809066378
   Body image in men.

BF697.5.B63.P48 1997
   The physical self : from motivation to well-being / Kenneth R. Fox, editor. Champaign, IL : Human Kinetics, c1997. xiii, 329 p.
97-000128   155.2   0873226895
   Body image. Physical education and training -- Psychological aspects. Sports -- Psychological aspects.

BF697.5.S43.H365 1993
Hanson, F. Allan,
   Testing testing : social consequences of the examined life / F. Allan Hanson. Berkeley : University of California Press, c1993. ix, 378 p. :
92-032639   150/.28/7   0520080602
   Self-perception -- Social aspects -- United States. Examinations -- United States -- Psychological aspects. Examinations -- Social aspects -- United States.

BF697.5.S43.S434 1998
   Self-awareness : its nature and development / edited by Michel Ferrari, Robert J. Sternberg. New York : Guilford Press, c1998. xiv, 430 p. :
97-052300   126   1572303174
   Self-perception.

BF697.5.S46.M78 1995
Mruk, Christopher J.
   Self-esteem : research, theory, and practice / Chris Mruk. New York : Springer Pub. Co., c1995. vii, 230 p. :
94-035992   155.2/32   0826187501
   Self-esteem.

BF697.5.S46.S63 1989
   The Social importance of self-esteem / edited by Andrew M. Mecca, Neil J. Smelser, and John Vasconcellos. Berkeley : University of California Press, c1989. xxi, 346 p. :
89-004821   361.1   0520067088
   Social problems -- Psychological aspects. Deviant behavior. Self-esteem -- Social aspects -- United States. United States -- Social conditions -- 1945-

BF697.5.S46.S83 1996
Swann, William B.
   Self-traps : the elusive quest for higher self-esteem / William B. Swann, Jr. New York : W. H. Freeman, c1996. xiii, 236 p ;
96-005265   155.2   0716728982
   Self-esteem. Self-defeating behavior.

BF697.5.S65.L53 1993
Lifton, Robert Jay,
   The protean self : human resilience in an age of fragmentation / Robert Jay Lifton. -- New York, NY : BasicBooks, c1993. x, 262 p.
93027068   155.2   0465064205
   Resilience (Personality trait) Self -- Social aspects -- History -- 20th century. Civilization, Modern -- 20th century -- Psychological aspects.

BF698 Personality — General works

BF698.C323 vol. 1
Cattell, Raymond B.
   The structure of personality in its environment / Raymond B. Cattell. New York : Springer Pub. Co., c1979. xxiv, 421 p.
79-000593   155.2 s   0826121209
   Personality. Personality. Personality development.

BF698.E97 1970
Eysenck, H. J.
The structure of human personality [by] H. J. Eysenck. London, Methuen [1970] viii, 476 p.
70-494620   155.2/64   0416180302
Personality.

BF698.F585 1996
The five-factor model of personality : theoretical perspectives / edited by Jerry S. Wiggins. New York : Guilford Press, c1996. xiii, 216 p.
96-004859   155.2   157230068X
Personality. Individuality. Personality.

BF698.G56 1970
Goble, Frank G.
The third force; the psychology of Abraham Maslow [by] Frank G. Goble. Foreword by Abraham Maslow. New York, Grossman, 1970. xii, 201 p.
71-114940   150/.924   0670700657
Maslow, Abraham H. -- (Abraham Harold)   Personality. Social psychology.

BF698.K58 1953
Kluckhohn, Clyde,
Personality in nature, society, and culture.   New York, Knopf, 1953. xxv, 701, xv
52-012410   137.082
Personality.

BF698.M338 1968
Maslow, Abraham H.
Toward a psychology of being [by] Abraham H. Maslow. Princeton, N.J., Van Nostrand [1968] xvi, 240 p.
68-030757   155.2/5
Personality. Motivation (Psychology) Humanistic psychology.

BF698.M63
Montagu, Ashley,
Touching: the human significance of the skin.   New York, Columbia University Press, 1971. viii, 338 p.
75-151290   152.1/82   0231034881
Touch. Skin. Body language.

BF698.P256
Parsons, Talcott,
Social structure and personality.   [New York] Free Press of Glencoe [1964] 376 p.
64-011218   137.33
Socialization. Personality and culture. Social structure.

BF698.R8544 1996
Robinson, David L.,
Brain, mind, and behavior : a new perspective on human nature / David L. Robinson ; foreword by H.J. Eysenck. Westport, Conn. : Praeger, 1996. xviii, 171 p.
95-043765   155.2   0275954684
Personality. Temperament. Intellect.

BF698.S85
Symonds, Percival Mallon,
Adolescent fantasy; an investigation of the picture-story method of personality study.   New York, Columbia Univ. Press, 1949. xii, 397 p.
49009055   137.8
Adolescence. Personality tests.

BF698.W29
Wallace, Anthony F. C.,
Culture and personality.   New York, Random House [1961] ix, 213 p.
61-008788   137.33
Personality and culture. Ethnopsychology.

BF698.Z825 1991
Zuckerman, Marvin.
Psychobiology of personality / Marvin Zuckerman. Cambridge ; Cambridge University Press, 1991. xv, 482 p. :
90-045367   155.2   0521350956
Personality. Psychobiology.

BF698.3 Personality — Personality types. Typology — General works

BF698.3.L94 1987
Lyons, Joseph,
Ecology of the body : styles of behavior in human life / Joseph Lyons. Durham : Duke University Press, 1987. xvi, 338 p. :
87-009080   155.2/64   0822307103
Typology (Psychology) Personality. Somatotypes.

BF698.35 Personality — Personality types. Typology — Special personality traits or aspects, A-Z

BF698.35.O57.S45 1995
Seligman, Martin E. P.
The optimistic child / Martin E.P. Seligman ; with Karen Reivich, Lisa Jaycox, and Jane Gillham. Boston, Mass. : Houghton Mifflin, 1995. 336 p. :
95-012619   155.4/124   0395693802
Optimism. Depression in children -- Prevention.

BF698.35.O57.V38 2000
Vaughan, Susan C.
Half empty, half full : understanding the psychological roots of optimism / Susan C. Vaughan. New York : Harcourt, c2000. xiv, 240 p. ;
99-058575   152.4   0151004013
Optimism.

BF698.4 Personality — Personality assessment. Research

BF698.4.K56 1983b
Kline, Paul.
   Personality : measurement and theory / Paul Kline. New York : St. Martin's Press, 1983. 174 p. ;
83-013798   155.2/8   0312602308
   Personality assessment. Personality tests. Personality.

BF698.5-698.8 Personality — Personality assessment. Research — Personality testing

BF698.5.B87
Buros, Oscar Krisen,
   Personality tests and reviews;including an index to The mental measurements yearbooks. Edited by Oscar Krisen Buros. Highland Park, N.J., Gryphon Press [1970-75] 2 v.
          155.28   0910674108
   Personality tests. Personality tests--Bibliography.

BF698.5.C45
Chun, Ki-Taek.
   Measures for psychological assessment : a guide to 3,000 original sources and their applications / Ki-Taek Chun, Sidney Cobb, John R. P. French, Jr. ; with a foreword by E. Lowell Kelly. Ann Arbor, Mich. : Survey Research Center, Institute for Social Res 1975. xxiv, 664 p.
74-620127   016.1552/8   0879441682
   Psychological tests -- Directories.

BF698.8.M5.B86 1999
Butcher, James Neal,
   A beginner's guide to the MMPI-2 / James N. Butcher. Washington, DC : American Psychological Association, c1999. xiii, 225 p.
98-041100   155.2/83   1557985642
   Minnesota Multiphasic Personality Inventory.

BF698.8.M5.C65 1992
Colligan, Robert C.
   The MMPI : a contemporary normative study of adolescents / Robert C. Colligan, Kenneth P. Offord. Norwood, NJ : Ablex Pub., c1992. xxvi, 619 p.
92-024378   155.2/83   0893918725
   Minnesota Multiphasic Personality Inventory. Minnesota Multiphasic Personality Inventory for Adolescents.

BF698.8.R5.K56
Klopfer, Bruno.
   Developments in the Rorschach technique [by] Bruno Klopfer [and others] Yonkers-on-Hudson, N.Y., World Book Co. [1954-70] 3 v.
54-008471   137.8   0155176285
   Rorschach Test.

BF698.8.T5.B4 1971
Bellak, Leopold,
   The Thematic Apperception Test and the Children's Apperception Test in clinical use [by] Leopold Bellak, with the assistance of Ann Noll and Lynn Lustbader. New York, Grune & Stratton, 1971. xvi, 328 p.
76-139363   155.28/44   0808906755
   Thematic Apperception Test. Children's Apperception Test.

BF698.9 Personality — Special topics, A-Z

BF698.9.B5.E9
Eysenck, H. J.
   The biological basis of personality, by H. J. Eysenck. Springfield, Ill., Thomas [1967] xvii, 399 p.
67-018338   155.2
   Personality.

BF698.9.C8P54 1999
   Personality and person perception across cultures / edited by Yueh-Ting Lee, Clark McCauley, Juris Draguns. Mahwah, N.J. : L. Erlbaum Associates, 1999. ix, 314 p. :
          155.8   0805828133
   Personality and culture. Ethnopsychology.

BF698.9.C8.S57
Skinner, B. F.
   Beyond freedom and dignity [by] B. F. Skinner. New York, Knopf, 1971. 225 p.
75-098652   150.19/434   0394425553
   Personality and culture. Conditioned response. Control (Psychology)

BF698.9.I6.I57 1995
   International handbook of personality and intelligence / edited by Donald H. Saklofske and Moshe Zeidner. New York : Plenum Press, c1995. xxiv, 776 p.
95-001086   153.9   0306447495
   Personality and intelligence.

BF698.9.I6.P47 1994
   Personality and intelligence / edited by Robert J. Sternberg, Patricia Ruzgis. Cambridge ; Cambridge University Press, 1994. xii, 337 p. ;
93-021757   153.9/3   0521417902
   Personality and intelligence. Personality and intelligence -- Testing.

BF701-706 Genetic psychology — General works — 1881-

BF701.B56 2000
   Biology, brains, and behavior : the evolution of human development / edited by Sue Taylor Parker, Jonas Langer, and Michael L. McKinney. Santa Fe, N.M. : School of American Research Press, 2000. xiii, 386 p.
00-030123   155.7   0933452640
   Genetic psychology. Developmental psychology.

BF701.B57 2002
Bjorklund, David F.,
The origins of human nature :evolutionary developmental psychology / David F. Bjorklund & Anthony D. Pellegrini. Washington, DC : American Psychological Association, c2002. xi, 444 p. :
        155.7   1557988781
Genetic psychology. Developmental psychology.

BF701.C676 1993
Csikszentmihalyi, Mihaly.
The evolving self : a psychology for the third millennium / Mihaly Csikszentmihalyi. New York, NY : HarperCollins Publishers, c1993. xviii, 358 p.
92-056220   155.7   0060166770
Genetic psychology. Behavior evolution. Social evolution.

BF701.J3 1926a
Jascalevich, Alejandro A
Three conceptions of mind, their bearing on the denaturalization of the mind in history, by Alexander A. Jascalevich, PH. D. New York, Columbia university press, 1926. ix, 107 p., 1
27000678
Augustine, -- Saint, Bishop of Hippo. Descartes, Rene, -- 1596-1650. Aristotle. Intellect.

BF701.M6 1969
Morris, Desmond.
The human zoo. New York, McGraw-Hill [1969] 256 p.
78-091684   156
Psychology, Comparative. Human behavior.

BF702.P52.W6
Wolff, Peter H.
The developmental psychologies of Jean Piaget and psychoanalysis. New York, International Universities Press, 1960. 181 p.
60050064   136.5
Piaget, Jean, -- 1896-   Genetic psychology. Psychoanalysis.

BF706.V9413 1993
Vygotskii, L. S.
Studies on the history of behavior : ape, primitive, and child / L.S. Vygotsky, A.R. Luria ; edited and translated by Victor I. Golod and Jane E. Knox ; with introduction by Jane E. Knox. Hillsdale, N.J. : Lawrence Erlbaum Associates, 1993. xvi, 246 p. :
92-023404   156   0805810145
Genetic psychology. Behavior evolution. Psychology, Comparative.

BF710 Genetic psychology — Maturation. Maturity

BF710.A53 1995
Anderson, Clifford.
The stages of life : a groundbreaking discovery : the steps to psychological maturity / Clifford Anderson. New York : Atlantic Monthly Press, c1995. xiv, 222 p. :
94-043724   155.2/5   0871134810
Maturation (Psychology) Emotional maturity. Developmental psychology.

BF710.S22 1999
Saarni, Carolyn.
The development of emotional competence / Carolyn Saarni. New York : Guilford Press, c1999. xviii, 381 p. ;
        155.2/5   1572304340
Emotional maturity. Maturation (Psychology) Interpersonal relations.

BF713 Developmental psychology — General works

BF713.D33 1999
Dacey, John S.
Human development across the lifespan / John S. Dacey, John F. Travers. 4th ed. Boston : McGraw-Hill, c1999. xxvii, 580 p. :
        155   0697364291
Developmental psychology.

BF713.E47 1984
Emotions, cognition, and behavior / edited by Carroll E. Izard, Jerome Kagan, and Robert B. Zajonc. Cambridge [Cambridgeshire] ; Cambridge University Press, 1984. x, 620 p. :
83-007765   153.4   0521256011
Developmental psychology. Emotions. Cognition.

BF713.E73 1997
Erikson, Erik H.
The life cycle completed / Erik H. Erikson. New York : W.W. Norton, c1997. 134 p. ;
96-034622   155   039303934X
Developmental psychology. Psychoanalysis. Personality.

BF713.T97 1990
Tyson, Phyllis,
Psychoanalytic theories of development : an integration / Phyllis Tyson, Robert L. Tyson ; foreword by Robert S. Wallerstein. New Haven, CT : Yale University Press, c1990. xvi, 398 p. ;
90-032688   155   0300045786
Developmental psychology. Psychoanalysis.

BF713.5 Developmental psychology — Addresses, essays, lectures

BF713.5.C66 1997
Comparisons in human development : understanding time and context / edited by Jonathan Tudge, Michael J. Shanahan, Jaan Valsiner. Cambridge [Cambridgeshire] : Cambridge University Press, 1997. x, 368 p. :
96-012287   155   052148202X
Developmental psychology. Developmental psychology -- Cross-cultural studies. Developmental psychology -- Longitudinal studies.

BF713.5.L524 1996
The lifespan development of individuals : behavioral, neurobiological, and psychosocial perspectives : a synthesis / edited by David Magnusson, in collaboration with Torgny Greitz ... [et al.]. Cambridge [England] ; Cambridge University Press, 1996. xx, 526 p. :
95-013924   155   0521470234
Developmental psychology -- Congresses. Developmental biology -- Congresses. Developmental neurophysiology -- Congresses.

BF714 Developmental psychology — Context effects. Person-context relations

BF714.D48 1995
Development of person-context relations / edited by Thomas A. Kindermann, Jaan Valsiner. Hillsdale, N.J. : L. Erlbaum Associates, 1995. ix, 256 p. :
95-006935   155.9   0805815686
Context effects (Psychology) Developmental psychology.

BF714.L48 1997
Lewis, Michael,
Altering fate : why the past does not predict the future / Michael Lewis. New York : Guilford Press, c1997. xii, 238 p. ;
96-052568   155   0898628563
Context effects (Psychology) Developmental psychology -- Philosophy. Determinism (Philosophy)

BF717 Developmental psychology — Psychology of play

BF717.S514 1990
Singer, Dorothy G.
The house of make-believe : children's play and the developing imagination / Dorothy G. Singer and Jerome L. Singer. Cambridge, Mass. : Harvard University Press, 1990. ix, 339 p. :
90-035503   155.4/18   0674408748
Play -- Psychological aspects. Imagination in children. Developmental psychology.

BF717.S93 1997
Sutton-Smith, Brian.
The ambiguity of play / Brian Sutton-Smith. Cambridge, Mass. : Harvard University Press, 1997. x, 276 p. ;
97-021713   155   0674017331
Play -- Psychological aspects.

BF719 Developmental psychology — Infant psychology. Newborn infant psychology

BF719.F74 1997
Freedman, David A.
On infancy and toddlerhood : an elementary textbook / David A. Freedman. Madison, Conn. : International Universities Press, c1997. xiii, 247 p.
96-037168   155.42/2   0823637859
Infant psychology. Toddlers -- Psychology. Psychoanalysis.

BF719.M4413 1994
Mehler, Jacques.
What infants know : the new cognitive science of early development / Jacques Mehler and Emmanuel Dupoux ; translated by Patsy Southgate. Cambridge, MA : Blackwell, 1994. ix, 212 p. :
93-010147   155.42/23   1557863695
Infants (Newborn) -- Psychology. Genetic psychology. Cognition in children.

BF719.R63 2001
Rochat, Philippe,
The infant's world / Philippe Rochat. Cambridge, Mass. : Harvard University Press, 2001. ix, 262 p. :
00-054268   155.42/2   0674003225
Infant psychology. Infants -- Development.

BF719.S75 1985
Stern, Daniel N.
The interpersonal world of the infant : a view from psychoanalysis and developmental psychology / Daniel N. Stern. New York : Basic Books, c1985. x, 304 p. ;
85-047553   155.4/22   0465034039
Infant psychology. Psychoanalysis. Developmental psychology.

BF720 Developmental psychology — Infant psychology. Newborn infant psychology — Special topics, A-Z

BF720.P37.B72 1990
Brazelton, T. Berry,
The earliest relationship : parents, infants, and the drama of early attachment / T. Berry Brazelton, Bertrand G. Cramer. Reading, Mass. : Addison-Wesley, c1990. xix, 252 p. ;
89-039839   306.874   0201106396
Parent and infant. Parents -- Psychology. Infant psychology.

BF720.P47.K45 1998
Kellman, Philip J.
The cradle of knowledge : development of perception in infancy / Philip J. Kellman and Martha E. Arterberry. Cambridge, Mass. : MIT Press, c1998. xiv, 369 p. :
97-034269   155.42/2   0262112329
Perception in infants.

BF720.S67.J87 1997
Jusczyk, Peter W.
The discovery of spoken language / Peter W. Jusczyk. Cambridge, Mass. : MIT Press, c1997. xii, 314 p. :
96-029015   401/.93   0262100584
Speech perception in infants. Speech perception in newborn infants. Language acquisition.

BF721 Developmental psychology — Child psychology — General works

BF721.C213
Carmichael, Leonard,
Carmichael's manual of child psychology. Paul H. Mussen, editor. New York, Wiley [1970]- v. 1-
69-016127   155.4   0471626953
Child psychology.

BF721.F692
Freud, Anna,
The writings of Anna Freud. New York : International Universities Press, 1967-c1981 v. 1-5, 7-8
67-009514   618.92/89   0823668703
Child psychology. Child analysis. Psychoanalysis.

BF721.F692 vol. 2
Freud, Anna,
The ego and the mechanisms of defense. New York, International Universities Press [1967, c1966] ix, 191 p.
66-030463   154.2/2
Ego (Psychology) Defense mechanisms (Psychology)

BF721.G4652 1996
Gemelli, Ralph J.
Normal child and adolescent development / Ralph Gemelli. Washington, DC : American Psychiatric Press, c1996. xiv, 582 p. :
95-037815   155.4   0880482583
Child psychology. Adolescent psychology. Child development.

BF721.G5
Gesell, Arnold,
The mental growth of the pre-school child; a psychological outline of normal development from birth to the sixth year, including a system of developmental diagnosis. Illustrated with 200 action photos. New York, Macmillan, 1930 [c1925] x, 447 p.
25004215   155.41/3
Learning, Psychology of. Child study. Psychophysiology.

BF721.G64
Goodenough, Florence Laura,
Exceptional children / Florence L. Goodenough with the assistance of Lois M. Rynkiewicz. New York : Appleton-Century-Crofts [1956] 428 p. :
56005895   136.76
Child study.

BF721.H243
Handbook of cross-cultural human development / edited by Ruth H. Munroe, Robert L. Munroe, Beatrice B. Whiting. New York : Garland STPM Press, c1981. xiv, 888 p. :
79-012028   155.8   0824070453
Child psychology. Child psychology -- Cross-cultural studies.

BF721.I473
Inhelder, Barbel.
The growth of logical thinking from childhood to adolescence; an essay on the construction of formal operational structures [by] Barbel Inhelder and Jean Piaget. Translated by Anne Parsons and Stanley Milgram. [New York] Basic Books [1958] 356 p.
58-006439   136.7354
Child psychology. Logic. Cognition in children.

BF721.J6
Josselyn, Irene Milliken,
Psychosocial development of children.   Family Service Association of America, 1948. 134 p.
49000531   136.7
Child psychology. Socialization. Child development.

BF721.K158 1984
Kagan, Jerome.
The nature of the child / Jerome Kagan. New York : Basic Books, c1984. xvii, 309 p.
83-045263   155.4   0465048501
Child psychology.

BF721.M196 1969
Maier, Henry W.
Three theories of child development: the contributions of Erik H. Erikson, Jean Piaget, and Robert R. Sears, and their applications [by] Henry W. Maier. New York, Harper & Row [1969] ix, 342 p.
69-014983   155.41/0922
Erikson, Erik H. -- (Erik Homburger), -- 1902- Piaget, Jean, -- 1896- Sears, Robert R. -- (Robert Richardson) Child psychology.

BF721.P43
Piaget, Jean,
The child's conception of physical causality, by Jean Piaget. London, K. Paul, Trench, Trubner & co. ltd.; 1930. viii, 309 p.
30-017187   136.72
Causation. Physics. Child psychology.

BF721.P452 1951
Piaget, Jean,
Play, dreams, and imitation in childhood. Translated by C. Gattegno and F. M. Hodgson. London, W. Heinemann [1951] 296 p.
52003385   136.7
Imitation. Play. Symbolism.

BF721.P473
Piaget, Jean,
The origins of intelligence in children; translated by Margaret Cook. New York, International Universities Press [c1952] 419 p.
52-014807   136.72
Child psychology. Intellect.

BF721.P4813
Piaget, Jean,
The psychology of the child [by] Jean Piaget and Barbel Inhelder. Translated from the French by Helen Weaver. New York, Basic Books [1969] xiv, 173 p.
73-078449   155.4
Child psychology.

BF721.P5
Piaget, Jean,
The child's conception of the world, by Jean Piaget. London, K. Paul, Trench, Trubner & co., ltd.; 1929. ix, 397 p.
29-005717
Child psychology. Imagery (Psychology) in children -- Congresses. Drawing ability in children -- Congresses.

BF721.S485 1994
Shatz, Marilyn.
A toddler's life : becoming a person / Marilyn Shatz. New York : Oxford University Press, 1994. xiv, 221 p. :
93-029053   155.42/3   0195084179
Child psychology -- Longitudinal studies. Cognition in children -- Longitudinal studies. Toddlers -- Language -- Longitudinal studies.

BF721.S577 1961
Spock, Benjamin,
Dr. Spock talks with mothers; growth and guidance. Boston, Houghton Mifflin, 1961. 306 p.
61013338   136.7
Juvenile delinquency. Child Psychology. Child study.

BF721.S82 1968
Stone, L. Joseph
Childhood and adolescence; a psychology of the growing person [by] L. Joseph Stone [and] Joseph Church. New York, Random House [1968] xvi, 616 p.
67-022333   155
Child psychology. Adolescent psychology.

BF721.V25
Valentine, Charles Wilfred,
The normal child and some of his abnormalities; a general introduction to the psychology of childhood. [Harmondsworth, Penguin Books [1956] 290 p.
57000460   136.7
Child study.

BF721.Y3 1940
Yale university.
The first five years of life; a guide to the study of the preschool child, from the Yale clinic of child development. New York, Harper & brothers [c1940] xiii, 58 p.,
40-008731   136.7352
Child psychology. Psychophysiology. Learning, Psychology of.

BF722 Developmental psychology — Child psychology — Philosophy. Methodology. Relation to other subjects

BF722.J643
Johnson, Orval G.,
Tests and measurements in child development : handbook II / Orval G. Johnson. San Francisco : Jossey-Bass Publishers, 1976. 2 v. (xii, 13
76-011890   155.4/1   0875892787
Psychological tests for children.

BF722.V34 1997
Valsiner, Jaan.
Culture and the development of children's action : a theory of human development / Jaan Valsiner. New York : John Wiley & Sons, c1997. xx, 364 p. :
96-046293   155.4   0471135909
Child psychology -- Philosophy. Children -- Nutrition -- Psychological aspects. Children -- Nutrition -- Social aspects.

BF723 Developmental psychology — Child psychology — Special topics, A-Z

BF723.A25.H69 1999
Howe, Michael J. A.,
The psychology of high abilities / Michael J.A. Howe. New York : New York University Press, c1999. x, 198 p. ;
99-024049   153.9/8   0814736122
Ability in children. Gifted children. Nature and nurture.

BF723.A35.G76 1976
Growing up to be violent : a longitudinal study of the development of aggression / Monroe M. Lefkowitz ... [et al.]. New York : Pergamon Press, c1977. ix, 236 p. :
75-044349   155.4/18   0080195156
Aggressiveness in children. Aggressiveness. Longitudinal method.

BF723.A75.W38 1987
Watkins, Kathleen Pullan.
Parent-child attachment : a guide to research / Kathleen Pullan Watkins. New York : Garland Pub., 1987. xi, 190 p. ;
87-023614   306.8/74   0824084659
Attachment behavior in children. Parent and child. Object Attachment.

BF723.C5.B74 1974b
Bryant, Peter,
Perception and understanding in young children; an experimental approach [by] Peter Bryant. New York, Basic Books [1974] viii, 195 p.
73-092722   155.4/13   0465054889
Cognition in children.

BF723.C5.G56 1988
Ginsburg, Herbert.
 Piaget's theory of intellectual development / Herbert P. Ginsburg, Sylvia Opper. Englewood Cliffs, N.J. : Prentice-Hall, c1988. viii, 264 p.
87-017353   155.4/13/0924   0136751660
Piaget, Jean, -- 1896-   Intellect. Education -- Philosophy.
Cognition in children.

BF723.C5.P494
Piaget, Jean,
 The essential Piaget / edited by Howard E. Gruber and J. Jacques Voneche. New York : Basic Books, c1977. xlii, 881 p.
76-009337   155.4/13/08   0465020585
Cognition in children. Knowledge, Theory of. Biology.

BF723.C5.P5
Piaget, Jean,
 Genetic epistemology. Translated by Eleanor Duckworth. New York, Columbia University Press, 1970. 84 p.
74-100665   155.41/3   0231033869
Cognition in children. Genetic epistemology.

BF723.C5.S53 1996
Siegler, Robert S.
 Emerging minds : the process of change in children's thinking / Robert S. Siegler. New York : Oxford University Press, 1996. viii, 278 p.
95-042099   155.4/13   0195077873
Cognition in children. Cognitive styles in children. Human information processing in children.

BF723.C5.W66 1988
Wood, David J.
 How children think and learn / David Wood. Oxford, UK ; B. Blackwell, 1988. 238 p. :
87-035531   155.4/13   0631161384
Cognition in children. Learning, Psychology of.

BF723.C57.G37 1989
Garbarino, James.
 What children can tell us : eliciting, interpreting, and evaluating information from children / James Garbarino, Frances M. Stott, and Faculty of the Erikson Institute. San Francisco : Jossey-Bass, 1989. xxviii, 373 p
89-008192   155.4/136   1555421636
Interpersonal communication in children. Children and adults.

BF723.D3.S58 2000
Silverman, Phyllis R.
 Never too young to know : death in children's lives / Phyllis Rolfe Silverman. New York : Oxford University Press, 2000. xv, 271 p. ;
98-050158   155.9/37   0195109546
Children and death.

BF723.D54.P79 1983
 The Psychology of discipline / edited by Darwin Dorr, Melvin Zax, Jack W. Bonner, III. New York, N.Y. : International Universities Press, c1983. xv, 263 p. :
81-020775   649/.64   0823655814
Discipline of children -- Psychological aspects.

BF723.D7.P513 1967
Piaget, Jean,
 The child's conception of space, by Jean Piaget and Barbel Inhelder. Translated from the French by F. J. Langdon & J. L. Lunzer. New York, W. W. Norton [1967] xii, 490 p.
67-005864   155.4
 Space perception in children. Drawing ability in children. Imagery (Psychology) in children.

BF723.E9H35 1999
 Handbook of psychosocial characteristics of exceptional children / edited by Vicki L. Schwean and Donald H. Saklofske. New York : Kluwer Academic/Plenum Publishers, c1999. xxiii, 622 p. :
               155.45   0306460637
 Exceptional children--Psychology. Exceptional children--Mental health.

BF723.F28.D38 1952
Davidson, Audrey,
 Phantasy in childhood, by Audrey Davidson and Judith Fay. London, Routledge & Paul [1952] 188 p.
52-004507   155.4/13
 Fantasy. Child psychology.

BF723.F68.C66 1996
 The company they keep : friendship in childhood and adolescence / edited by William M. Bukowski, Andrew F. Newcomb, Willard W. Hartup. Cambridge [England] ; Cambridge University Press, 1996. x, 426 p. ;
95-016855   302.3/4   0521451981
 Friendship in children -- Congresses. Friendship in adolescence -- Congresses. Interpersonal relations in children -- Congresses.

BF723.G5.M36 1999
 The many faces of giftedness : lifting the masks / [edited by] Alexinia Young Baldwin, Wilma Vialle. Belmont, CA : Wadsworth Pub. Co., c1999. xxiii, 296 p.
98-010691   371.95   0766800067
 Gifted children -- Psychology -- United States. Gifted children -- Psychology -- Australia. Gifted children -- Psychology -- Case studies.

BF723.G5.S48 1992
Shurkin, Joel N.,
 Terman's kids : the groundbreaking study of how the gifted grow up / Joel N. Shurkin. Boston : Little, Brown, c1992. x, 317 p. ;
91-037572   155.45/5/0973   0316788902
Terman, Lewis Madison, -- 1877-1956.   Gifted persons -- United States -- Longitudinal studies. Gifted children -- United States -- Longitudinal studies.

BF723.G75.W67 1996
Worden, J. William
 Children and grief : when a parent dies / J. William Worden. New York : Guilford Press, c1996. x, 225 p. ;
96-029010   155.9/37/083   1572301481
 Bereavement in children. Parents -- Death -- Psychological aspects. Grief in children.

BF723.I5.C63 1990
Cohen, David,
  The development of imagination : the private worlds of childhood / David Cohen and Stephen A. MacKeith. London ; Routledge, 1991. vii, 119 p. :
90-008329   155.4/133
  Imagination in children.

BF723.I6.B67
Brody, Sylvia,
  Patterns of mothering; maternal influence during infancy. Introd. by Rene A. Spitz. New York, International Universities Press [1956] 446 p.
56-008839   155.4/22
  Infants. Mothers.

BF723.I6.G42
Gesell, Arnold,
  Infant development; the embryology of early human behavior. New York, Harper [1952] xi, 108 p.
51011915   136.7352
  Infants. Child study.

BF723.I6.P76 1963
Provence, Sally,
  Infants in institutions: a comparison of their development with family-reared infants during the first year of life [by] Sally Provence [and] Rose C. Lipton. Pref. by Milton J. E. Senn. New York, International Universities Press [1963, c1962] 191 p.
62021560   136.7352
  Infants. Growth. Children -- Institutional care.

BF723.M54.A66 1993
  Approaches to moral development : new research and emerging themes / edited by Andrew Garrod. New York : Teachers College Press, c1993. xi, 244 p. :
92-044918   155.2/5   0807732478
  Moral development.

BF723.M54.C63 1997
Coles, Robert.
  The moral intelligence of children / Robert Coles. New York : Random House, c1997. xv, 218 p. ;
96-020992   155.4/1825   067944811X
  Moral development. Moral education. Children -- Conduct of life.

BF723.P25.B53
Biller, Henry B.
  Father, child, and sex role; paternal determinants of personality development [by] Henry B. Biller. Lexington, Mass., Heath Lexington Books [1971] xi, 193 p.
74-145580   155.9/2/4
  Father and child. Sex role.

BF723.P25.H65 1997
Holden, George W.
  Parents and the dynamics of child rearing / George W. Holden. Boulder, Colo. : Westview Press, 1997. xvii, 235 p.
96-043122   155.6/46   0813330300
  Parent and child. Parenting.

BF723.P36.S84 1987
Sugarman, Susan.
  Piaget's construction of the child's reality / Susan Sugarman. Cambridge ; Cambridge University Press, 1987. vi, 258 p. ;
87-010959   155.4   0521341647
  Piaget, Jean, -- 1896-   Perception in children. Reality in children. Child Psychology.

BF723.P4.F87 1992
Furman, Erna.
  Toddlers and their mothers : a study in early personality development / Erna Furman. Madison, Conn. : International Universities Press, c1992 viii, 414 p.
91-035415   155.42/382   0823665550
  Child analysis. Personality development. Mother and child.

BF723.P75.A24 1989
Aboud, Frances E.
  Children and prejudice / Frances Aboud. Oxford, OX, UK ; B. Blackwell, 1989. x, 149 p. :
87-031472   305.2/3   0631149392
  Prejudices in children. Ethnicity in children. Race awareness in children.

BF723.P75.E94 1996
  Everyday acts against racism : raising children in a multiracial world / edited by Maureen T. Reddy. Seattle, Wash. : Seal Press ; c1996. xiii, 270 p.
96-031501   305.8/0083   1878067850
  Prejudices in children -- United States. Race awareness in children -- United States. Child rearing -- United States.

BF723.R46.C48 1989
  The Child in our times : studies in the development of resiliency / edited by Timothy F. Dugan and Robert Coles. New York : Brunner/Mazel, c1989. xv, 224 p. ;
89-000515   155.4/182   0876305281
  Resilience (Personality trait) in children. Resilience (Personality trait) in adolescence.

BF723.S43.B36 1982
Bank, Stephen P.,
  The sibling bond / Stephen P. Bank, Michael D. Kahn. New York : Basic Books, c1982. xiii, 363 p.
81-068401   155.9/24   0465078184
  Brothers and sisters. Developmental psychology. Sibling relations.

BF723.S43.D85 1990
Dunn, Judy,
  Separate lives : why siblings are so different / Judy Dunn and Robert Plomin. [New York] : Basic Books, c1990. xiii, 210 p.
90-080254   155.44/3   0465076882
  Brothers and sisters. Individual differences. Nature and nurture.

BF723.S6.D86 1988
Dunn, Judy,
The beginnings of social understanding / Judy Dunn. Cambridge, Mass. : Harvard University Press, 1988. vi, 212 p. :
88-000766   155.4/23   0674064534
Social perception in children. Social interaction in children. Family.

BF723.S75.E44 1981
Elkind, David,
The hurried child : growing up too fast too soon / David Elkind. Reading, Mass. : Addison-Wesley Pub. Co., c1981. xiii, 210 p.
81-014842   305.2/3   0201039664
Stress in children. Child mental health. Child rearing.

BF723.T53.K34 1994
Kagan, Jerome.
Galen's prophecy : temperament in human nature / by Jerome Kagan with the collaboration of Nancy Snidman, Doreen Arcus, J. Steven Reznick. New York, NY : Basic Books, c1994. xxiv, 376 p.
93-042664   155.2/6   0465084052
Temperament in children. Inhibition in children. Temperament in children -- Physiological aspects.

BF723.T9.I53 2001
Infancy to early childhood : genetic and environmental influences on developmental change / edited by Robert N. Emde, John K. Hewitt ; section editors, Jerome Kagan ... [et al.]. Oxford ; Oxford University Press, 2001. xiv, 393 p. :
00-022514   155.44/4   019513012X
Twins -- Psychology. Twins -- Longitudinal studies. Nature and nurture -- Longitudinal studies.

BF723.T9P56 2002
Piontelli, Alessandra,
Twins :from fetus to child / Alessandra Piontelli. New York : Routledge, 2002. p. cm.
               155.44/4   0415262275
Twins--Psychology.

BF723.T9S44 2000
Segal, Nancy L.,
Entwined lives :twins and what they tell us about human behavior / Nancy L. Segal. New York : Plume, 2000. p. cm.
               155.44/4   0452280575
Twins--Psychology. Nature and nurture.

BF723.T9.W75 1997
Wright, Lawrence,
Twins : and what they tell us about who we are / Lawrence Wright. New York : J. Wiley, 1997. vi, 202 p. ;
97-038827   155.44/4   0471252204
Twins -- Psychology. Nature and nurture.

BF724 Developmental psychology — Adolescence. Youth

BF724.H33 1980
Handbook of adolescent psychology / edited by Joseph Adelson. New York : Wiley, c1980. xiv, 624 p. :
79-021927   155.5   0471037931
Adolescent psychology. Adolescent psychology.

BF724.3 Developmental psychology — Adolescence. Youth — Special topics, A-Z

BF724.3.I3.K76 1989
Kroger, Jane,
Identity in adolescence : the balance between self and other / Jane Kroger. London ; Routledge, 1989. xiv, 217 p. :
88-032551   155.5   0415010888
Identity (Psychology) in adolescence.

BF724.3.S86.A36 1991
Adolescent stress : causes and consequences / Mary Ellen Colten, Susan Gore, editors. New York : Aldine de Gruyter, c1991. xii, 330 p. :
90-047963   155.5/18   0202304205
Stress in adolescence -- Congresses. Interpersonal relations in adolescence -- Congresses. Teenagers -- Mental health -- Congresses.

BF724.5 Developmental psychology — Adulthood — General works

BF724.5.E53 1993
Encyclopedia of adult development / edited by Robert Kastenbaum. Phoenix, Ariz. : Oryx Press, 1993. xviii, 574 p.
92-046666   155.6   0897746694
Adulthood -- Psychological aspects -- Encyclopedias. Developmental psychology -- Encyclopedias.

BF724.5.K55
Kimmel, Douglas C.
Adulthood and aging; an interdisciplinary, developmental view [by] Douglas C. Kimmel. New York, Wiley [1974] ix, 484 p.
73-013557   155.6   0471477001
Adulthood -- Psychological aspects. Aging -- Psychological aspects. Adulthood.

BF724.55 Developmental psychology — Adulthood — Special topics, A-Z

BF724.55.A35.B44 1990
Belsky, Janet,
The psychology of aging : theory, research, and interventions / Janet K. Belsky. Pacific Grove, Calif. : Brooks/Cole Pub. Co., c1990. xiv, 386 p. :
89-009990   155.67   0534121144
Aging -- Psychological aspects. Aged -- Psychology. Aged -- Mental health services.

BF724.55.A35.L68 1990
Lowenthal, Marjorie Fiske.
   Change and continuity in adult life / Marjorie Fiske, David A. Chiriboga. San Francisco : Jossey-Bass Publishers, 1990. xx, 342 p. ;
90-004966   155.6   1555422497
   Aging -- Psychological aspects -- Longitudinal studies. Adulthood -- Psychological aspects -- Longitudinal studies. Adult -- psychology.

BF724.55.A35.P794 2000
   Psychology and the aging revolution : how we adapt to longer life / edited by Sara Honn Qualls and Norman Abeles. Washington, D.C. : American Psychological Association, c2000. ix, 313 p. :
00-036265   155.67   1557987076
   Aging -- Psychological aspects. Aging. Aged -- Psychology.

BF724.85 Developmental psychology — Adulthood — Old age

BF724.85.C64.H36 1992
   The handbook of aging and cognition / edited by Fergus I.M. Craik, Timothy A.Salthouse. Hillsdale, N.J. : L. Erlbaum Associates, c1992. ix, 586 p. :
91-040681   155.67   0805807136
   Cognition in old age. Cognition -- Age factors.

BF724.85.L64
Gibson, H. B.
   Loneliness in later life / Hamilton B. Gibson ; foreword by Peter Laslett. Houndsmills [England] : Macmillan ; 2000. xvi, 150 p. ;
00-042238   155.67/18   0333920171
   Loneliness in old age.

BF724.85.M45.L36 1988
   Language, memory, and aging / edited by Leah L. Light and Deborah M. Burke. New York : Cambridge University Press, 1988. xi, 281 p. :
88-001068   155.67/1   0521329426
   Memory in old age. Aged -- Language. Psycholinguistics.

BF740 Class psychology — Race and ethnic psychology

BF740.S8 1961
Stonequist, Everett V.
   The marginal man; a study in personality and culture conflict. New York, Russell & Russell, 1961 [c1937] 228 p.
61013767   136.45
   Race relations. Culture conflict. Miscegenation.

BF755 Psychology of nations — By nation

BF755.A5.R5
Riesman, David,
   The lonely crowd; a study of the changing American character, by David Riesman in collaboration with Reuel Denney and Nathan Glazer. New Haven, Yale University Press, 1950. xvii, 386 p.
50-009967   136.4973
   National characteristics, American. Ethnopsychology -- United States.

BF755.A5.R525
Lipset, Seymour Martin.
   Culture and social character; the work of David Riesman reviewed. Edited by Seymour Martin Lipset and Leo Lowenthal. [New York, Free Press of Glencoe, 1961] xiv, 466 p.
61009169   301.082
Riesman, David, -- 1909- -- The lonely crowd.   Sociology.

BF773 Psychology of belief, faith, etc.

BF773.S75 1983
Stich, Stephen P.
   From folk psychology to cognitive science : the case against belief / Stephen P. Stich. Cambridge, Mass. : MIT Press, c1983. xii, 266 p. ;
82-025883   153/.01   0262192152
   Belief and doubt. Psychology -- Philosophy. Cognition.

BF778 Psychology of values, meaning

BF778.K56 1977
Klinger, Eric,
   Meaning & void : inner experience and the incentives in people's lives / Eric Klinger. Minneapolis : University of Minnesota Press, c1977. xiv, 412 p. ;
77-081425   155.2   0816608113
   Meaning (Psychology) Incentive (Psychology) Alienation (Social psychology)

BF789 Psychology of other special subjects, A-Z

BF789.C7.B49 1961
Birren, Faber,
   Color psychology and color therapy; a factual study of the influence of color on human life. New Hyde Park, N.Y., University Books [1961] 302 p.
61-014266   150
   Color -- Psychological aspects.

BF789.D4.G5
Glaser, Barney G.
　　Awareness of dying, by Barney G. Glaser and Anselm L. Strauss. Chicago, Aldine Pub. Co. [1965] xi, 305 p.
65012454　　　　　301.1522　　　　　0202300013
　　Death -- Psychological aspects. Physician and patient. Sick -- Psychology.

BF789.D4.K8
Kubler-Ross, Elisabeth.
　　On death and dying. [New York] Macmillan [1969] viii, 260 p.
69-011789　　　　　155.9/3
　　Death -- Psychological aspects.

BF789.E94.B38 1997
Baumeister, Roy F.
　　Evil : inside human cruelty and violence / Roy F. Baumeister. New York : W.H. Freeman, c1997. ix, 431 p. ;
96-041940　　　　　155.2/32　　　　　0716729024
　　Good and evil -- Psychological aspects.

BF818 Character

BF818.R5
Riesman, David,
　　Faces in the crowd; individual studies in character and politics, by David Riesman in collaboration with Nathan Glazer. New Haven, Yale University Press, 1952. xii, 751 p.
52-005357　　　　　136.4973
　　Personality and culture. National characteristics, American.

BF833 Character — Popular works — 1851-

BF833.A4
Adler, Alfred,
　　Understanding human nature, by Alfred Adler. Translated by Walter Beran Wolfe. New York, Greenberg [c1927] xiii, 286 p.
27-027582
　　Psychology. Characters and characteristics.

BF891 Graphology. Study of handwriting — General works — 1851-

BF891.O59
Olyanova, Nadya.
　　The psychology of handwriting. New York Sterling Pub. Co. [1960] 224 p.
59013005　　　　　137.75　　　　087980128X
　　Graphology.

BF1025-1389 Parapsychology

BF1025 Psychic research. Psychology of the unconscious — Dictionaries. Encyclopedias

BF1025.B47 1991
Berger, Arthur S.,
　　The encyclopedia of parapsychology and psychical research / Arthur S. Berger and Joyce Berger. New York : Paragon House, 1991. xi, 554 p. ;
89-028857　　　　　133/.03　　　　　1557780439
　　Parapsychology -- Encyclopedias.

BF1026-1027 Psychic research. Psychology of the unconscious — Biography

BF1026.B46 1988
Berger, Arthur S.,
　　Lives and letters in American parapsychology : a biographical history, 1850-1987 / by Arthur S. Berger. Jefferson, N.C. : McFarland, c1988. x, 381 p. :
88-042537　　　　　133.8/092/2　　　　0899503454
　　Psychics -- United States -- Biography. Parapsychology -- Research -- United States -- History.

BF1027.R5.A3
Rinn, Joseph Francis,
　　Sixty years of psychical research ; Houdini and I among the spiritualists. New York, Truth Seeker Co. [1950] xviii, 618 p.
50014838
　　Houdini, Harry, -- 1874-1926.   Psychical research.

BF1028 Psychic research. Psychology of the unconscious — History

BF1028.M38
Mauskopf, Seymour H.
　　The elusive science : origins of experimental psychical research / Seymour H. Mauskopf and Michael R. McVaugh ; afterword by J. B. and L. E. Rhine. Baltimore : Johns Hopkins University Press, c1980. xvi, 368 p. :
80-007991　　　　　133.8/01/5　　　　0801823315
　　Parapsychology -- History.

BF1029 Psychic research. Psychology of the unconscious — Report of commissions, investigations, etc.

BF1029.B37 1984
　　The Basic experiments in parapsychology / compiled and edited by K. Ramakrishna Rao. Jefferson, N.C. : McFarland, c1984. viii, 264 p.
83-042883　　　　　133.8/072　　　　0899500846
　　Parapsychology. Parapsychology.

BF1031 Psychic research. Psychology of the unconscious — General works

BF1031.I79 1999
Irwin, H. J.
An introduction to parapsychology / by H.J. Irwin. Jefferson, N.C. : McFarland, c1999. ix, 396 p. :
98-051001   133.8   0786406712
Parapsychology.

BF1031.M537 1987
Men and women of parapsychology : personal reflections / edited by Rosemarie Pilkington ; foreword by Stanley Krippner. Jefferson, N.C. : McFarland, c1987. viii, 173 p.
87-042517   133.8   0899502601
Parapsychology.

BF1031.S84 1997
Stokes, Douglas M.,
The nature of mind : parapsychology and the role of consciousness in the physical world / Douglas M. Stokes. Jefferson, N.C. : McFarland, c1997. ix, 259 p. ;
97-002510   133.8   0786403446
Parapsychology. Consciousness.

BF1031.V37 2000
Varieties of anomalous experience : examining the scientific evidence / edited by Etzel Cardena, Steven J. Lynn, Stanley C. Krippner. Washington, DC : American Psychological Association, c2000. xi, 476 p. :
99-045473   133   1557986258
Parapsychology.

BF1040-1042 Psychic research. Psychology of the unconscious — General special

BF1040.M326 1984
McClenon, James.
Deviant science : the case of parapsychology / James McClenon. Philadelphia : University of Pennsylvania Press, c1984. xiii, 282 p.
83-014680   133.8   0812211782
Parapsychology.

BF1042.H96 1989
Hyman, Ray.
The elusive quarry : a scientific appraisal of psychical research / Ray Hyman. Buffalo, N.Y. : Prometheus Books, c1989. 447 p. ;
89-003918   133   0879755040
Parapsychology. Parapsychology -- Book reviews.

BF1045 Psychic research. Psychology of the unconscious — Special topics, A-Z

BF1045.C7.P79 1994
Psychic sleuths : ESP and sensational cases / edited by Joe Nickell. Buffalo, N.Y. : Prometheus Books, 1994. 251 p. :
93-043069   133.8   0879758805
Parapsychology in criminal investigation -- Evaluation. Parapsychology -- Investigation. Psychics -- Rating of.

BF1045.N4.E57 1997
Elsaesser Valarino, Evelyn.
On the other side of life : exploring the phenomenon of the near-death experience / Evelyn Elsaesser Valarino ; translated by Michelle Herzig Escobar. New York : Insight Books, c1997. xiii, 353 p.
96-049353   133.9/01/3   0306455617
Near-death experiences.

BF1045.N4.K45 1996
Kellehear, Allan,
Experiences near death : beyond medicine and religion / Allan Kellehear. New York : Oxford University Press, 1996. xii, 230 p. ;
95-003947   133.9/01/3   0195091949
Near-death experiences. Near-death experiences -- Social aspects.

BF1045.S33.A42 1990
Alcock, James E.
Science and supernature : a critical appraisal of parapsychology / James E. Alcock. Buffalo, N.Y. : Prometheus Books, c1990. 186 p. ;
89-070033   133.8   0879755482
Parapsychology and science.

BF1071 Sleep. Somnambulism — 1801-

BF1071.F73
Foulkes, David,
The psychology of sleep [by] David Foulkes. New York, Scribner [1966] xii, 265 p.
66-015978   154.6
Sleep.

BF1078 Dreaming — General works — 1801-

BF1078.E63 1993
Encyclopedia of sleep and dreaming / Mary A. Carskadon, editor in chief. New York : Macmillan Pub. Co. ; c1993. xxx, 703 p. :
92-038048   154.6/03   0028970853
Dreams -- Encyclopedias. Sleep -- Encyclopedias. Sleep disorders -- Encyclopedias.

BF1078.F693
Freud, Sigmund,
    Dreams in folklore, by Sigmund Freud and D. E. Oppenheim. Translated from the German [by A. M. O. Richards; edited with an introd., by James Strachey] and [with] the original German text. New York, International Universities Press, 1958. 111 p.
57014990   131.3462
    Dreams. Psychoanalysis Folklore

BF1078.F72 1950
Freud, Sigmund,
    The interpretation of dreams; translated by A. A. Brill. New York, Modern Library [1950] 477 p.
50-006784   154.6/34
    Dream interpretation. Psychoanalysis.

BF1078.F773
Freud, Sigmund,
    On dreams; Translated by James Strachey. New York, Norton [1952] 120 p.
52006730   135.383
    Dreams.

BF1078.F84
Fromm, Erich,
    The forgotten language; an introduction to the understanding of dreams, fairy tales, and myths. New York, Rinehart [1951] 263 p.
51-013653   135
    Dream interpretation. Fairy tales -- Psychological aspects. Mythology -- Psychological aspects.

BF1078.U44
Ullman, Montague.
    Working with dreams / Montague Ullman and Nan Zimmerman. New York : Delacorte Press/Eleanor Friede, c1979. xii, 335 p. :
79-012866   154.6/3   0440092825
    Dreams.

BF1091 Dreaming — Popular works. Dream books, etc. — 1801-

BF1091.B94 1999
Bulkeley, Kelly,
    Visions of the night : dreams, religion, and psychology / Kelly Bulkeley. Albany, NY : State University of New York Press, c1999. ix, 217 p. cm
98-053601   154.6/3   0791442837
    Dreams. Dreams -- Religious aspects. Dream interpretation.

BF1091.G84 1993
Guiley, Rosemary.
    The encyclopedia of dreams : symbols and interpretations / Rosemary Ellen Guiley. New York : Crossroad, 1993. xiii, 206 p.
92-043098   154.6/3/03   0824512405
    Dreams. Symbolism (Psychology)

BF1091.L53 1995
Lewis, James R.
    The dream encyclopedia / James R. Lewis. New York : Gale Research, c1995. xxi, 416 p. :
95-010759   154.6/3/03   0787601551
    Dreams -- Dictionaries. Dream interpretation -- Dictionaries.

BF1099 Dreaming — Special topics, A-Z

BF1099.N53.H37 1984
Hartmann, Ernest,
    The nightmare : the psychology and biology of terrifying dreams / Ernest Hartmann. New York : Basic Books, c1984. viii, 294 p.
83-046070   154.6/32   046505109X
    Nightmares. Nightmares -- Physiological aspects. Dreams.

BF1101 Visions — 1801-

BF1101.H8
Huxley, Aldous,
    Heaven and hell. New York, Harper [1956] 103 p.
55010694   135.3
    Visions.

BF1125 Hypnotism. Animal magnetism. Odylic force. Biomagnetism. Mesmerism. Subliminal projection — History

BF1125.G38 1992
Gauld, Alan.
    A history of hypnotism / Alan Gauld. Cambridge ; Cambridge University Press, 1992. xvii, 738 p.
92-005106   154.7/09   0521306752
    Hypnotism -- History. Mesmerism -- History. Animal magnetism -- History.

BF1141 Hypnotism. Animal magnetism. Odylic force. Biomagnetism. Mesmerism. Subliminal projection — General works — 1871-

BF1141.W38
Weitzenhoffer, Andre M.
    Hypnotism; an objective study in suggestibility. New York, Wiley [1953] xvi, 380 p.
53011388   134
    Mental suggestion. Hypnotism.

BF1156 Hypnotism. Animal magnetism. Odylic force. Biomagnetism. Mesmerism. Subliminal projection — Special topics, A-Z

BF1156.S83.H53
Hilgard, Josephine (Rohrs)
   Personality and hypnosis; a study of imaginative involvement [by] Josephine R. Hilgard. Chicago, University of Chicago Press [1970] x, 304 p.
77-095656   154.7   0226334414
   Hypnotism.

BF1171 Telepathy. Mind reading. Thought transference — General works — 1871-

BF1171.S6
Soal, S. G.
   Modern experiments in telepathy, by S.G. Soal and F. Bateman. With an introductory note by G.E. Hutchinson. New Haven, Yale University Press, 1954. xv, 425 p.
54010093
   Telepathy.

BF1389 Spiritualism. Communication — Physical phenomena of spiritualism. Telekinesis. Psychokinesis — Special topics

BF1389.A7.B53 1982
Blackmore, Susan J.,
   Beyond the body : an investigation of out-of-the-body experiences / Susan J. Blackmore. London : Heinemann, 1982. xv, 271 p., [
82-222062   133.9   0434074705
   Astral projection.

BF1389.A7.G66 1990
Goodman, Felicitas D.
   Where the spirits ride the wind : trance journeys and other ecstatic experiences / Felicitas D. Goodman ; with drawings by Gerhard Binder. Bloomington : Indiana University Press, c1990. xii, 242 p. :
89-045567   133.9   0253327644
   Astral projection -- Case studies. Shamanism -- Case studies. Posture in worship -- Case studies.

BF1407-2050 Occult sciences

BF1407 Dictionaries. Encyclopedias

BF1407.D78 1992
Drury, Nevill,
   Dictionary of mysticism and the esoteric traditions / Nevill Drury. Santa Barbara, Calif. : ABC-CLIO, c1992. 328 p. :
92-023484   133/.03   0874366992
   Occultism -- Encyclopedias. Mysticism -- Encyclopedias.

BF1407.G85 1991
Guiley, Rosemary.
   Harper's encyclopedia of mystical & paranormal experience / Rosemary Ellen Guiley ; foreword by Marion Zimmer Bradley. [San Francisco] : HarperSanFrancisco, c1991. xiii, 666 p.
90-021718   133/.03   0062503650
   Occultism -- Encyclopedias. Parapsychology -- Encyclopedias. Supernatural -- Encyclopedias.

BF1411 General works — 1801-

BF1411.E82 1991
Evangelista, Anita.
   Dictionary of hypnotism / Anita Evangelista. New York : Greenwood Press, 1991. xiv, 273 p.,
90-036941   154.7/03   0313259674
   Hypnotism -- Dictionaries.

BF1483 Ghosts. Apparitions. Hauntings — House spirits. Hobgoblins

BF1483.S5 1959
Sitwell, Sacheverell,
   Poltergeists; an introduction and examination followed by chosen instances. With decorations by Irene Hawkins and silhouettes by Cruikshank. New York, University Books [1959] 418p.
59008686
   Ghosts.

BF1556 Demonology — Incubi. Succubi. Vampires

BF1556.V36 1991
   Vampires, werewolves, and demons : twentieth century reports in the psychiatric literature / [edited by] Richard Noll. New York : Brunner/Mazel, c1992. xxv, 244 p. ;
91-026933   616.89   0876306326
   Vampires -- Case studies. Werewolves -- Case studies. Demonomania -- Case studies.

BF1566 Witchcraft — General works — 1801-

BF1566.A56 2000
Aoumiel.
   Origins of modern witchcraft : the evolution of a world religion / Ann Moura. St. Paul, Minn. : Llewellyn Publications c2000. xx, 282 p. :
00-057483   133.4/3   1567186483
   Witchcraft -- History. Paganism -- History.

BF1566.F27 1993
Faber, M. D.
   Modern witchcraft and psychoanalysis / M.D. Faber. Rutherford : Fairleigh Dickinson University Press ; c1993. 191 p. ;
91-058949   133.4/3/019   0838634885
   Witchcraft. Psychoanalysis. Witchcraft -- History.

BF1566.G85 1999
Guiley, Rosemary.
The encyclopedia of witches and witchcraft / Rosemary Ellen Guiley. New York : Facts On File, c1999. xi, 417 p. :
98-054386   133.4/3/03   0816038481
Witchcraft -- Encylopedias. Witches -- Encyclopedias.

BF1566.W739 2001
Witchcraft in Europe, 400-1700 : a documentary history / edited by Alan Charles Kors and Edward Peters ; revised by Edward Peters. Philadelphia : University of Pennsylvania Press, 2001. p. cm.
00-064934   133.4/3/094   0812217519
Witchcraft -- Europe -- History -- Sources.

BF1576 Witchcraft — By region or country — United States

BF1576.S43 1995
Sebald, Hans.
Witch-children : from Salem witch-hunts to modern courtrooms / Hans Sebald. Amherst, N.Y. : Prometheus Books, 1995. 258 p. :
94-044760   133.4/3/083   0879759658
Witchcraft -- Massachusetts -- Salem -- History. Trials (Witchcraft) -- Massachusetts -- Salem -- History. Witchcraft -- Europe -- History.

BF1581 Witchcraft — By region or country — Other regions or countries

BF1581.H88 1999
Hutton, Ronald.
The triumph of the moon : a history of modern pagan witchcraft / Ronald Hutton. Oxford ; Oxford University Press, 1999. xv, 486 p. ;
99-031586   133.4/3/0941   0198207441
Witchcraft -- Great Britain -- History -- 19th century. Witchcraft -- Great Britain -- History -- 20th century. Neopaganism -- Great Britain -- History. Great Britain -- Religion -- 19th century. Great Britain -- Religion -- 20th century.

BF1623 Magic (White and Black). Shamanism. Hermetics. Cabala. Necromancy — Special topics, A-Z

BF1623.M43W65 2001
Moondance, Wolf.
Wolf medicine :Native American shamanic journey into the mind / by Wolf Moondance ; [illustrated by Jim Sharpe & Sky Starhawk]. New York : Sterling Pub., c2001. 192 p. :
          299/.7   0806936436
Medicine wheels--Miscellanea. Spiritual life--Miscellanea.

BF1623.P9.E55 1992
Schimmel, Annemarie.
The mystery of numbers / Annemarie Schimmel. New York : Oxford University Press, 1993. x, 314 p. :
90-022456   133.3/35   0195063031
Symbolism of numbers.

BF1655 Astrology — Dictionaries. Encyclopedias

BF1655.L485 1994
Lewis, James R.
The astrology encyclopedia / James R. Lewis. Detroit : Gale Research, c1994. xxvii, 603 p.
94-003067   133.5/03   0810389002
Astrology -- Encyclopedias. Natal astrology -- Encyclopedias.

BF1701 Astrology — General works — 1881-1970

BF1701.M2 1970
McCaffery, Ellen.
Astrology, its history and influence in the Western world. New York, S. Weiser, 1970. xvii, 408 p.
76-142497   133.5/09   0877280371
Astrology -- History.

BF1768 Oracles. Sibyls. Divinations — General works. History — Ancient

BF1768.P67 1994
Potter, D. S.
Prophets and emperors : human and divine authority from Augustus to Theodosius / David Potter. Cambridge, Mass. : Harvard University Press, 1994. viii, 281 p.
94-025982   133.3/248/0937   0674715659
Divination -- Rome. Oracles, Roman. Sibyls. Rome -- Religion.

BF1775 Oracles. Sibyls. Divinations — Popular superstitions

BF1775.D53 1989
A Dictionary of superstitions / edited by Iona Opie and Moira Tatem. Oxford [England] ; Oxford University Press, 1989. xiii, 494 p.
89-032327   001.9/6/03   0192115979
Superstition -- Great Britain -- Dictionaries. Folklore -- Great Britain -- Dictionaries. Superstition -- Ireland -- Dictionaries.

BF1786 Seers. Prophets. Prophecies — Dictionaries

BF1786.A84 2001
Ashe, Geoffrey.
Encyclopedia of prophecy / Geoffrey Ashe. Santa Barbara, Calif : ABC-CLIO, 2001. p. cm.
01-001067   133.3/03   1576070794
Prophecies (Occultism) -- Encyclopedias.

BF1815 Seers. Prophets. Prophecies — Biographies and prophecies of individual seers, A-Z

BF1815.N8.R35 1990
Randi, James.
   The mask of Nostradamus / James Randi. New York : Scribner, c1990. xiii, 256 p.
89-070189   133.3/092   0684190567
Nostradamus, -- 1503-1566.   Prophets -- France -- Biography.

BF1999 Miscellaneous — General works

BF1999.O94 1994
   The Oxford book of the supernatural / chosen and edited by D.J. Enright. Oxford ; Oxford University Press, 1994. 555 p. ;
93-032896   133   0192142011
   Supernatural.

BF2050 Human-alien encounters. Contact between humans and extraterrestrials — General works

BF2050.B35 2000
Baker, Alan,
   The encyclopedia of alien encounters / Alan Baker. New York : Facts on File, c2000. 283 p. :
99-086105   001.942/03   0816042268
   Human-alien encounters -- Encyclopedias.

BF2050.M36 1998
Matheson, Terry.
   Alien abductions : creating a modern phenomenon / Terry Matheson. Amherst, N.Y. : Prometheus Books, 1998. 317 p. ;
98-030816   398/.4   1573922447
   Alien abduction.

R Medicine (General)

R15 Societies. Serials — America — English

R15.A55.C36 1984
Campion, Frank D.,
The AMA and U.S. health policy since 1940 / Frank D. Campion. Chicago : Chicago Review Press, c1984. ix, 603 p. :
84-007817   610/.6/073   0914091573
Medical policy -- United States -- History -- 20th century. Medical care -- United States -- History -- 20th century. Health Policy -- History -- United States.

R15.A55.G3 1961
Garceau, Oliver,
The political life of the American Medical Association. Hamden, Conn., Archon Books, 1961 [c1941] 186 p.
61004986   610.6273
American Medical Association -- history Societies, Medical -- history -- United States

R15.B9
Burrow, James Gordon,
AMA: voice of American medicine.   [Baltimore] Johns Hopkins Press, 1963. xii, 430 p.
63015347   610.6273
Societies, Medical -- hist. American Medical Association

R15.R26 1967
Rayack, Elton,
Professional power and American medicine; the economics of the American Medical Association. Cleveland, World Pub. Co. [1967] xvii, 298 p.
67013628   610/.62/73
Education, Medical -- United States Insurance, Health Medicine

R111 Collected works (nonserial) — Several authors

R111.M423
Mainstreams of medicine; essays on the social and intellectual context of medical practice. Edited by Lester S. King. Introd. by David A. Kronick. Austin, Published for the University of Texas Medical Sc [1971] x, 186 p.
78-149564   610   0292701128
Medicine -- Addresses, essays, lectures.

R111.S25
Sanders, Marion K.
The crisis in American medicine. New York, Harper [1961] x, 149 p.
61007928   610.82
Medicine -- United States. Physician-Patient Relations Medical economics -- United States.

R118 Communication in medicine — General works

R118.C615 1990
Communication and health : systems perspective / edited by Eileen Berlin Ray, Lewis Donohew. Hillsdale, N.J. : L. Erlbaum Associates, 1990. x, 219 p. :
89-030978   610/.141   0805801545
Communication in medicine.

R118.K73 1984
Kreps, Gary L.
Health communication : theory and practice / Gary L. Kreps, Barbara C. Thornton. New York : Longman, c1984. xi, 287 p. :
83-000958   610/.141   0582284112
Communication in medicine -- Case studies. Delivery of health care.

R118.4 Communication in medicine — Information centers — By region or country, A-Z

R118.4.U6.C37 1987
Carper, Jean.
Health care U.S.A. / Jean Carper. New York, NY : Prentice Hall, c1987. xiv, 653 p. ;
86-025556   362.1/02573   0136096867
Medical care -- United States -- Information services -- Directories. Diseases -- United States -- Information services -- Directories. Medical centers -- United States -- Directories.

R118.4.U6.M38 1985
Medical and health information directory : a guide to associations, agencies, companies, institutions, research centers, hospitals, clinics, treatment centers, educational programs, publications, au Detroit, Mich. : Gale Research Co., c1985- v.
85148281   362.1/025/73   0810302683
Health Services -- United States -- directories. Information Services -- United States -- directories. Medicine -- United States -- directories.

R118.6 Communication in medicine — Medical literature

R118.6.G43 2002
Gehlbach, Stephen H.
Interpreting the medical literature / Stephen H. Gehlbach. 4th ed. New York : McGraw-Hill, Medical Pub. Division, c2002. xi, 296 p. :
          610/.72   0071387625
Medical literature. Medicine--Research. Epidemiology--Terminology.

R118.6.K49 1990
Keyguide to information sources in paramedical sciences / edited by John F. Hewlett. London ; Mansell, 1990. xii, 270 p. ;
90-005863   610   0720120578
Medical literature. Medicine -- Bibliography. Health Occupations -- bibliography.

R119 Communication in medicine — Medical writing. Abstracting and indexing

R119.F55 1972
Fishbein, Morris,
   Medical writing; the technic and the art. Springfield, Ill., Thomas [1972] xi, 203 p.
73-165883   808/.066/61021   0398022798
   Medical writing.

R119.S38 1991
Schwager, Edith.
   Medical English usage and abusage / by Edith Schwager. Phoenix, Ariz. : Oryx Press, 1991. xiv, 216 p. ;
90-007644   808/.06661   0897745906
   Medical writing. English language -- Medical English.

R119.S773 1994
Strickland-Hodge, Barry.
   How to use Index medicus, Psychological abstracts, Excerpta medica / Barry Strickland-Hodge. Aldershot, Hampshire ; Gower, c1994. xiii, 114 p.
94-013011   016.61   0566075555
   Medicine -- Bibliography -- Methodology. Medicine -- Abstracting and indexing. Abstracting and Indexing.

R119.9-119.95 Communication in medicine — Medical telecommunication. Television in medicine — General works

R119.9.C48 2000
Chellen, Sydney S.,
   Essential guide to the Internet for health professionals / Sydney S. Chellen. London ; Routledge, 2000. xiv, 215 p. :
99-054706   025.06/61   041522747X
   Medicine -- Computer network resources. Internet. Medical informatics.

R119.9.H39 2000
   Health care resources on the internet : a guide for librarians and health care consumers / M. Sandra Wood, editor. New York : Haworth Information Press, c2000. xxi, 205 p. ;
99-037569   025.06/61   0789006324
   Medicine -- Computer network resources. Internet. Medical care -- Computer network resources.

R119.95.M344 2001
Maheu, Marlene M.
   E-Health, telehealth, and telemedicine :a guide to start-up and success / Marlene M. Maheu, Pamela Whitten, Ace Allen ; foreword by Evan Melrose.1st ed. San Francisco : Jossey-Bass, c2001. xix, 380 p. :
              362.1/028   0787944203
   Telecommunication in medicine. Medical informatics. Medicine--Communication systems.

R121 Dictionaries

R121.D73
   Dorland's illustrated medical dictionary. London: W.B. Saunders Co., .: 2000 xxiii, 2087p.
00-006383   610/.3/21   0721682618
   Medicine -- Dictionaries. Dictionaries, Medical Reference Books, Medical

R121.H232 1987
Hamilton, Betty.
   The medical word finder : a reverse medical dictionary / Betty Hamilton and Barbara Guidos. New York : Neal-Schuman, c1987. vii, 177 p. ;
86-028462   610/.3/21   155570011X
   Medicine -- Dictionaries. Synonyms. Nomenclature.

R121.J86 1996
Juo, Pei-Show.
   Concise dictionary of biomedicine and molecular biology / Pei-Snow Juo. Boca Raton, Fla. : CRC Press, c1996. 983 p. :
95-038363   610/.3   0849324602
   Medical sciences -- Dictionaries.

R121.M564 2002
   Merriam-Webster's medical desk dictionary. Springfield, Mass. : Merriam-Webster, 2002. p. cm.
              610/.3   1401811884
   Medicine--Dictionaries.

R121.M89 2002
   Mosby's medical, nursing, & allied health dictionary / Douglas M Anderson ... [etal.]. 6th ed. St. Louis : Mosby, c2002. 2134 p. :
              610/.3   0723432252
   Medicine--Dictionaries. Nursing--Dictionaries.

R121.R626 1997
Rogers, Glenn T.
   English-Spanish, Spanish-English medical dictionary =Diccionario médico, inglés-español, español-inglés / Glenn T. Rogers.2nd ed. New York : McGraw-Hill, Health Professions Division, c1997. xxx, 230 p. ;
              610/.3   0070536805
   Medicine--Dictionaries. English language--Dictionaries--Spanish. Medicine--Dictionaries--Spanish.

R121.S398 1999
Sebastian, Anton.
   A dictionary of the history of medicine / Anton Sebastian. New York : Parthenon Pub. Group, c1999. vi, 781 p. :
98-032249   610/.9   1850700214
   Medicine -- History -- Dictionaries. History of Medicine -- dictionaries.

R121.S8 2000
Stedman, Thomas Lathrop,
   Stedman's medical dictionary. 27th ed. Philadelphia : Lippincott Williams & Wilkins, c2000. xxxvi, [127], 2098 p. :
              610/.3   0683400088
   Medicine--Dictionaries. Medicine--Dictionary--English.

R121.T18 2001
Taber's cyclopedic medical dictionary. Ed. 19, illustrated in full color / editor, Donald Venes ; coeditor, Philadelphia : F.A.Davis Co., c2001. xxxiii, 2770 p. :
      610/.3   0803606567
Medicine--Dictionaries. Medicine--Dictionary--English.

R121.W358 1999
Webster's new explorer medical dictionary : created in cooperation with the editors of Merriam-Webster. Springfield, Mass. : Federal Street Press, 1999. 27a, 767 p. ;
99-062652   610/.3   1892859076
Medicine -- Dictionaries. Medicine, Popular -- Dictionaries.

R123 Nomenclature. Terminology. Abbreviations

R123.H29 1997
Haubrich, William S.
Medical meanings : a glossary of word origins / William S. Haubrich. Philadelphia, Pa. : American College of Physicians, c1997. xi, 253 p. ;
96-029494   610/.1/4   0943126568
Medicine -- Terminology. English language -- Etymology -- Dictionaries. Dictionaries, Medical.

R123.L46 2001
Leonard, Peggy C.
Building a medical vocabulary :with Spanish translations / Peggy C. Leonard. 5th ed. Philadelphia, Pa. : W.B. Saunders, c2001. xvii, 590 p. :
      610/.1/4   072168954X
Medicine--Terminology. Human anatomy--Terminology. English language--Glossaries, vocabularies, etc.

R123.M394 2001
Medical terminology made incredibly easy. Springhouse, Pa. : Springhouse Corp., c2001. vi, 354 p. :
00-041974   610/.1/4   1582550417
Medicine -- Terminology. Medical sciences -- Terminology. Terminology.

R123.S69 1999
Stedman's abbreviations, acronyms & symbols. Baltimore : c1999. p. cm.
98-031525   610/.148   0683404598
Medicine -- Abbreviations. Medicine -- Acronyms -- Dictionaries. Medicine -- abbreviations.

R126 General works — Through 1800 — Ancient Greek

R126.A1.B7613 1972
Brock, Arthur John,
Greek medicine, being extracts illustrative of medical writers from Hippocrates to Galen, translated and annotated by Arthur J. Brock. London, Dent;New York, Dutton. [New York, AMS Press, 1972] xii, 256 p.
76-179302   610/.938   0404078060
Medicine, Greek and Roman.

R130 General works — 1801- — Theories. Principles

R130.M346 1996
Marcuse, Peter M.,
Disease : in search of remedy / Peter M. Marcuse. Urbana : University of Illinois Press, c1996. x, 156 p. ;
95-019707   610/.1   0252022157
Medicine -- Philosophy. Medicine -- History.

R130.5 General works — 1801- — Juvenile works

R130.5.D57 1997
Diseases / Bryan Bunch, editor. Danbury, CT : Grolier Educational, 1997. 8 v. :
96-027606   616/.003   0717276171
Diseases -- Encyclopedias, Juvenile. Diseases -- Encyclopedias.

R130.5.P369 1998
Parker, Steve.
Medical advances / Steve Parker. Austin, Tex. : Raintree Steck-Vaughn, c1998. 48 p. :
97-017985   610   081724896X
Medicine -- Juvenile literature. Medicine -- Forecasting -- Juvenile literature. Medicine -- History.

R130.5.W67 2000
World of health / Brigham Narins, editor. Detroit : Gale Group, c2000. viii, 1424 p.
99-031918   610   0787636495
Medicine -- Juvenile literature. Health -- Juvenile literature. Health -- Encyclopedias.

R131.A173 History — Societies. Serials

R131.A173
Ackerknecht, Erwin Heinz,
History and geography of the most important diseases, by Erwin H. Ackerknecht. Pref. by George Rosen. New York, Hafner Pub. Co. 1965. xii, 210 p.
65-020093   610.9
Diseases -- History. Medical geography.

R131.A34-W47 History — General works

R131.A34 1982
Ackerknecht, Erwin Heinz,
A short history of medicine / Erwin H. Ackerknecht. Baltimore : Johns Hopkins University Press, 1982. xx, 277 p. :
81-048194   610/.9   0801827264
Medicine -- History. History of medicine.

R131.B5
Bettmann, Otto.
A pictorial history of medicine; a brief, nontechnical survey of the healing arts from Aesculapius to Ehrlich, retelling with the aid of select illustrations the lives and deeds of great physicians With a foreword by Philip S. Hench. Springfield, Ill., Thomas [1956] xiii, 318 p.
54-010781   610.9
Medicine -- History. Medicine -- History -- Pictorial works.

R131.C233 1993
The Cambridge world history of human disease / editor, Kenneth F. Kiple ; executive editor, Rachael Rockwell Graham ; associate editors, David Frey ... [et al.] ; assistant editors, Alicia Browne ... [et al.]. Cambridge ; Cambridge University Press, 1993. xxiv, 1176 p.
92-004173   610/.9   0521332869
Medicine -- History. Medical geography. Epidemiology.

R131.C613 1960
Clendening, Logan,
Source book of medical history.   New York, Dover Publications [1960, c1942] 685 p.
60-002873   610.9
Medicine -- History.

R131.D79 1991
Duke, Martin.
The development of medical techniques and treatments : from leeches to heart surgery / Martin Duke. Madison, Conn. : International Universities Press, c1991. xvii, 252 p.
90-004666   610/.9   0823612325
Medicine -- History. Alternative Medicine. Cardiology -- trends.

R131.G3 1929
Garrison, Fielding H.
An introduction to the history of medicine, with medical chronology, suggestions for study and bibliographic data, by Fielding H. Garrison. Philadelphia, W. B. Saunders, 1929. 996 p.
29003665   0721640303
Medicine -- History. Bibliography of medicine. Physicians -- Biography.

R131.L95
Lyons, Albert S.,
Medicine : an illustrated history / by Albert S. Lyons and R. Joseph Petrucelli II, with special sections by Juan Bosch ... [et al.], and contributions by Alan H. Barnert ... [et al.]. New York : H. N. Abrams, [1978] 616 p. :
77-012912   610/.9   0810910543
Medicine -- History. Medicine -- History -- Pictorial works. History of medicine.

R131.M179 1992
Magner, Lois N.,
A history of medicine / Lois N. Magner. New York : M. Dekker, c1992. xvi, 393 p. :
92-004425   610/.9   0824786734
Medicine -- History. History of Medicine.

R131.M26
Major, Ralph Hermon,
A history of medicine. Springfield, Ill., Thomas [1954] 2 v.
54-006571   610.9
Medicine -- History.

R131.P59 1998
Porter, Roy,
The greatest benefit to mankind : a medical history of humanity / Roy Porter. New York : W. W. Norton, 1998. xvi, 831 p. :
98-010219   610/.9   0393046346
Medicine -- History. Social medicine -- History.

R131.S55 1962
Singer, Charles Joseph,
A short history of medicine, by Charles Singer and E. Ashworth Underwood. New York, Oxford University Press, 1962. 854 p.
62-021080   610.9
Medicine -- History.

R131.W47 1995
The Western medical tradition : 800 B.C.-1800 A.D. / by members of the Academic Unit, the Wellcome Institute for the History of Medicine, London: Lawrence Conrad ... [et al.]. Cambridge, Eng. ; Cambridge University Press, c1995. xiv, 556 p. :
94-034823   610/.94   0521381355
Medicine -- History.

R133 History — General special

R133.A85 1995
Atkinson, Paul,
Medical talk and medical work : the liturgy of the clinic / Paul Atkinson. London : Sage, 1995. x, 164 p. ;
95-068384   610   080397731X
Medicine. Social medicine.

R133.G656 1994
Golub, Edward S.,
The limits of medicine : how science shapes our hope for the cure / Edward S. Golub. New York : Times Books, c1994. xii, 258 p. :
94-010016   610   0812921410
Medicine -- History. Social medicine. Medicine -- Philosophy.

R133.H36 2000
Harding, Anne S.
Milestones in health and medicine / by Anne S. Harding. Phoenix : Oryx Press, 2000. xii, 267 p. :
00-032660   610/.9   1573561401
Medicine -- History.

R133.H455 2001
Hellman, Hal,
Great feuds in medicine :ten of the liveliest disputes ever / Hal Hellman. New York : Wiley, c2001. xiii, 237 p. ;
                    610/.9   20   041
Medicine--History--Miscellanea. Vandetta--Case studies. History of Medicine, Modern.

R133.M26 1997

Making medical history : the life and times of Henry E. Sigerist / edited by Elizabeth Fee and Theodore M. Brown. Baltimore : Johns Hopkins University Press, 1997. xiii, 387 p.
96-008862   610/.9   0801853559
Sigerist, Henry E. -- (Henry Ernest), -- 1891-1957. Sigerist, Henry E. -- (Henry Ernest), -- 1891-1957. Medicine -- History. Medical historians -- Biography. Physicians -- biography.

R133.M717 1997
Morton, Leslie T.

A chronology of medicine and related sciences / Leslie T. Morton and Robert J. Moore. Aldershot, England : Scolar Press ; c1997. 784 p. ;
96-042257   610/.9   1859282156
Medicine -- History -- Chronology. Medical sciences -- History -- Chronology. Medicine -- Bibliography.

R133.N77 2000
Nuland, Sherwin B.

The mysteries within : a surgeon reflects on medical myths / Sherwin B. Nuland. New York : Simon & Schuster, 2000. p. cm.
99-088659   610   0684854864
Body, Human -- Folklore. Body, Human -- Mythology. Human anatomy -- Mythology.

R133.W459 1992
Wilkinson, Lise.

Animals and disease : an introduction to the history of comparative medicine / Lise Wilkinson. Cambridge ; Cambridge University Press, 1992. x, 272 p. :
92-198312   363.089/09   0521375738
Medicine, Comparative -- History. Veterinary medicine -- History.

R134 History — Biography — Collective

R134.B455 1990
Bendiner, Jessica.

Biographical dictionary of medicine / Jessica Bendiner and Elmer Bendiner. New York : Facts on File, c1990. 284 p. ;
89-023604   610/.92/2   0816018642
Physicians -- Biography -- Dictionaries. Physicians -- biography.

R134.B55 1999
Bliss, Michael.

William Osler : a life in medicine / Michael Bliss. Oxford ; Oxford University Press, 1999. xiv, 581 p. :
99-032066   610/.92   0195123468
Osler, William, -- Sir, -- 1849-1919.   Physicians -- Canada -- Biography.

R134.D594 1996

The doctor-activist : physicians fighting for social change / edited by Ellen L. Bassuk, with the assistance of Rebecca W. Carman. New York : Plenum Press, c1996. xxii, 254 p.
96-003873   610/.92/2   0306452677
Physicians -- Biography. Health reformers -- Biography. Social action -- Case studies.

R134.F69 1990
Fox, Daniel M.

Nobel laureates in medicine or physiology : a bigraphical dictionary/ edited by Daniel M. Fox, Marcia Meldrum and Ira Rezak. New York : Garland Pub., 1990. xviii, 595 p.
90013907   610/.92/2   0824078926
Medicine -- History -- Dictionaries. Physiologists -- Biography -- Dictionaries. Physicians -- Biography -- Dictionaries.

R134.N633 1991

The Nobel Prize winners. edited by Frank N. Magill. Pasadena, Calif. : Salem Press, c1991. 3 v. :
91-012143   610/.92/2   0893565717
Medical scientists -- Biography. Nobel Prizes.

R134.N85 1988
Nuland, Sherwin B.

Doctors : the biography of medicine / Sherwin B. Nuland. New York : Knopf, 1988. xxi, 519 p. :
88-009337   610.92/2   0394551303
Physicians -- Biography. Medicine -- History.

R134.8-138.5 History — By period — Ancient

R134.8.A93 1998
Aufderheide, Arthur C.

The Cambridge encyclopedia of human paleopathology / by Arthur C. Aufderheide & Conrado Rodrigues-Martin ; including a dental chapter by Odin Langsjoen. Cambridge, UK ; Cambridge University Press, c1998. xviii, 478 p.
97-016223   616.07   0521552036
Paleopathology -- Encyclopedias. Paleopathology -- encyclopedias.

R134.8.H86 1991

Human paleopathology : current syntheses and future options / edited by Donald J. Ortner and Arthur C. Aufderheide. Washington : Smithsonian Institution Press, c1991. viii, 311 p.
90-010348   616.07   1560980397
Paleopathology -- Congresses. Paleopathology -- congresses.

R134.8.R62 1995
Roberts, Charlotte A.

The archaeology of disease / Charlotte Roberts and Keith Manchester. Ithaca, N.Y. : Cornell University Press, 1995. x, 243 p. :
95-015961   616/.009/01   0801484480
Paleopathology. Paleopathology.

R134.8.W427 1995
Webb, Stephen.

Palaeopathology of aboriginal Australians : health and disease across a hunter-gatherer continent / Stephen Webb. Cambridge [England] ; Cambridge University Press, 1995. xii, 324 p. :
94-015247   616.07/0994   0521460441
Paleopathology -- Australia. Australian aborigines -- Health and hygiene.

R135.S83513 1998
Western medical thought from antiquity to the Middle Ages / edited by Mirko D. Grmek ; coordinated by Bernardino Fantini ; translated by Antony Shugaar. Cambridge, Ma. : Harvard University Press, 1998. 478 p. ;
98-008462   610/.9   067440355X
Medicine, Ancient. Medicine, Medieval.

R138.5.J33 1988
Jackson, Ralph.
Doctors and diseases in the Roman Empire / Ralph Jackson. Norman : University of Oklahoma Press, c1988. 207 p. :
88-040206   610.937   080612167X
Medicine, Greek and Roman. History of Medicine, Ancient.

R141 History — By period — Medieval

R141.K4
Kealey, Edward J.
Medieval medicus : a social history of Anglo-Norman medicine / by Edward J. Kealey. Baltimore : Johns Hopkins University Press, c1981. x, 211 p. :
80-021870   362.1/0942   0801825334
Medicine, Medieval -- England. Physicians -- England -- Biography. Hospitals, Medieval -- England. England -- Social conditions -- 1066-1485.

R141.P7 1994
Practical medicine from Salerno to the black death / edited by Luis Garcia-Ballester ... [et al.]. Cambridge ; Cambridge University Press, 1994. xiii, 402 p.
92-049013   616/.0094/0902   0521431018
Medicine, Medieval -- History -- Congresses. History of Medicine, Medieval -- congresses.

R141.S546 1990
Siraisi, Nancy G.
Medieval & early Renaissance medicine : an introduction to knowledge and practice / Nancy G. Siraisi. Chicago : University of Chicago Press, c1990. xiv, 250 p. :
89-020368   610/.902   0226761290
Medicine, Medieval. Renaissance.

R145-149 History — By period — Modern

R145.A46 1989
Altschule, Mark D.
Essays on the rise and decline of bedside medicine / by Mark D. Altschule ; with a foreword by Stewart G. Wolf, Jr. Bangor, PA : Totts Gap Medical Research Laboratories ; 1989. x, 458 p. :
88-201683
Medicine -- History.

R145.F75 1998
Friedman, Meyer,
Medicine's 10 greatest discoveries / Meyer Friedman, and Gerald W. Friedland. New Haven, Conn : Yale University Press, c1998. xiii, 263 p.
98-019921   610/.9   0300075987
Medicine -- History. Medical scientists.

R145.S45 1947
Shryock, Richard Harrison,
The development of modern medicine; an interpretation of the social and scientific factors involved ... New York, Knopf, 1947. xv, 457, xv p
47-000049   610.9
Medicine -- History.

R148.K5
King, Lester Snow,
The medical world of the eighteenth century. [Chicago] University of Chicago Press [1958] 346 p.
58007332   610.903
History of Medicine, 18th Century Medicine -- History.

R148.S45
Shryock, Richard Harrison,
Medicine and society in America, 1660-1860. [New York] New York University Press, 1960. 182 p.
60-006417   610.973
Medicine -- United States -- History.

R149.G53 1997
Glasser, Ronald J.
The light in the skull : an odyssey of medical discovery / Ronald Glasser. Boston : Faber & Faber, 1997. 209 p. ;
96-051607   610/.9   057119916X
Medicine -- History.

R150 History — By region or country — America

R150.W5
American men of medicine. Farmingdale, N.Y. [etc.] Institute for Research in Biography. v.
45004406

R151-210 History — By region or country — United States

R151.B58
Bordley, James,
Two centuries of American medicine, 1776-1976 / James Bordley III, A. McGehee Harvey. Philadelphia : Saunders, 1976. xv, 844 p. :
75-019841   610/.973   0721618731
Medicine -- United States -- History. History of medicine, Modern -- United States.

R151.C375 1991
Cassedy, James H.
Medicine in America : a short history / James H. Cassedy. Baltimore : Johns Hopkins University Press, c1991. xi, 187 p. ;
91-007058   610/.973   0801842077
Medicine -- United States -- History. History of Medicine -- United States.

R151.K47
Kett, Joseph F.
The formation of the American medical profession; the role of institutions, 1780-1860, by Joseph F. Kett. New Haven, Yale University Press, 1968. xi, 217 p.
68-013914   610/.973
Medicine -- United States -- History -- 18th century. Medicine -- United States -- History -- 19th century.

R151.K56 1991
King, Lester S.
Transformations in American medicine : from Benjamin Rush to William Osler / Lester S. King. Baltimore : Johns Hopkins University Press, c1991. 268 p.
90-004662   610/.973/09034   0801840570
Rush, Benjamin, -- 1745-1813. Osler, William, -- Sir, -- 1849-1919. Rush, Benjamin, -- 1745-1813. Medicine -- History -- 18th century. Medicine -- United States -- History -- 20th century. History of Medicine, 18th Cent. -- United States.

R151.P12 1963
Packard, Francis R.
History of medicine in the United States. New York, Hafner Pub. Co., 1963. 2 v. (xxv, 13
63-018176   610.973
Medicine -- United States -- History.

R151.S52
Sigerist, Henry E.
American medicine, by Dr. Henry E. Sigerist ... translated by Hildegard Nagel. New York, W.W. Norton & company, inc. [c1934] xix, 316 p.
34-040281   610.973
Medicine -- United States. Physicians -- United States.

R152.H354
Haller, John S.
American medicine in transition 1840-1910 / by John S. Haller, Jr. Urbana : University of Illinois Press, c1981. xii, 457 p.,
80-014546   610/.9/034   0252008065
Medicine -- United States -- History -- 19th century. Medicine -- History -- 19th century. History of Medicine, 19th century.

R152.L56 1992
Link, Eugene P.,
The social ideas of American physicians (1776-1976) : studies of the humanitarian tradition in medicine / Eugene Perry Link. Selinsgrove [Pa.] : Susquehanna University Press ; c1992. 317 p. :
91-050603   610/.973   0945636342
Medicine -- United States -- History. Physicians -- United States -- Attitudes -- History. Humanitarianism.

R152.S58 1998
Smith-Cunnien, Susan L.
A profession of one's own : organized medicine's opposition to chiropractic / Susan L. Smith-Cunnien. Lanham : University Press of America, c1998. xii, 208 p. :
97-038181   610/.973/0904   0761809430
Chiropractic -- United States -- History -- 20th century. Professions -- United States -- Sociological aspects. Interprofessional relations -- United States.

R153.D53 1984
Dictionary of American medical biography / Martin Kaufman, Stuart Galishoff, Todd L. Savitt, editors ; Joseph Carvalho III, editorial associate. Westport, Conn. : Greenwood Press, 1984. 2 v. (xvi, 10
82-021110   610/.92/2   031321378X
Medicine -- United States -- Biography -- Dictionaries. Public health personnel -- United States -- Biography -- Dictionaries. Healers -- United States -- Biography -- Dictionaries.

R153.D63 1997
Doctors, nurses, and medical practitioners : a bio-bibliographical sourcebook / edited by Lois N. Magner. Westport, Conn. : Greenwood Press, 1997. xiii, 371 p.
97-002232   610/.92/2   0313294526
Medicine -- Bio-bibliography -- Dictionaries.

R153.D86 1996
Duncan, David Ewing.
Residents : the perils and promise of educating young doctors / David Ewing Duncan. New York, NY : Scribner, c1996. 302 p. ;
96-005907   610/.71/55   068419709X
Residents (Medicine) -- United States -- Biography. Residents (Medicine) -- Training of -- United States. Physician and patient -- United States

R153.K24 1993
Kaufman, Sharon R.
The healer's tale : transforming medicine and culture / Sharon R. Kaufman. Madison, Wis. : University of Wisconsin Press, c1993. x, 354 p. :
92-034798   610/.973/0922   0299135500
Physicians -- United States -- Biography.

R153.T32
Thacher, James,
American medical biography / by James Thacher ; with a new introduction and a bibliography by Whitfield J. Bell. New York : Da Capo Press ; 1967. 2 v. :
67-025447
Physicians -- United States -- Biography -- Dictionaries. Medicine -- United States -- Biography -- Dictionaries.

R154.A545.A3
Alvarez, Walter C.
Incurable physician, an autobiography. Englewood Cliffs, N.J., Prentice-Hall [1963] xiii, 274 p.
63-020033   926.1
Alvarez, Walter Clement, -- 1884- Physicians -- United States -- Biography.

R154.B3317.W37 1994
Ward, Patricia Spain.
Simon Baruch : rebel in the ranks of medicine, 1840-1921 / Patricia Spain Ward. Tuscaloosa : University of Alabama Press, c1994. xiv, 399 p. ;
93-031300   610./92   0817305890
Baruch, Simon, -- 1840-1921. Physicians -- United States -- Biography. Medicine -- Southern States -- History -- 19th century. Balneology -- United States -- History.

R154.B779.A3 1993
Brand, Paul W.
   Pain : the gift nobody wants / Paul Brand and Philip Yancey.
New York : HarperCollins Publishers ; c1993. x, 352 p. ;
92-056225   610/.92   0060170204
*Brand, Paul W.   Surgeons -- United States -- Biography. Surgeons -
- Great Britain -- Biography. Surgeons -- India -- Biography.*

R154.C83.A3
Crumbine, Samuel Jay,
   Frontier doctor; the autobiography of a pioneer on the
frontier of public health. Philadelphia, Dorrance [c1948] ix,
284 p.
48004882   926.1
   *Physicians -- Correspondence, reminiscences, etc. History of
Medicine -- biography Public Health -- history -- United States*

R154.C96.F8
Fulton, John F.
   Harvey Cushing, a biography, by John F. Fulton.
Springfield, Ill., C.C. Thomas, 1946. xii, 754 p.,
46-000151   926.1
Cushing, Harvey, -- 1869-1939.

R154.F65.A3
Fishbein, Morris,
   Morris Fishbein, M.D.; an autobiography. Garden City,
N.Y., Doubleday, 1969. xii, 505 p.
69-015180   610/.924
*Fishbein, Morris, -- 1889- Fishbein, Morris, -- 1889- Physicians --
United States -- Biography.*

R154.G827.K63 1997
Koch, Jean.
   Robert Guthrie--the PKU story : crusade against mental
retardation / by Jean Holt Koch. Pasadena, Calif. : Hope Pub.
House, 1997. p. cm.
97-002457   610/.92   0932727913
*Guthrie, Robert, -- 1916- Guthrie, Robert, -- 1916- Medical
scientists -- United States -- Biography. Phenylketonuria -- Diagnosis.
Mental retardation -- Prevention.*

R154.H238.A34 1985
Hamilton, Alice,
   Exploring the dangerous trades : the autobiography of Alice
Hamilton, M.D. / with a foreword by Barbara Sicherman ; with
illustrations by Norah Hamilton. Boston, Mass. : Northeastern
University Press, 1985. xx, 433 p., [
85-018876   616.9/803/0924   0930350812
*Hamilton, Alice, -- 1869-1970.   Physicians -- United States --
Biography. Women physicians -- United States -- Biography.
Toxicologists -- United States -- Biography.*

R154.H238.S53 1984
Sicherman, Barbara.
   Alice Hamilton, a life in letters / Barbara Sicherman.
Cambridge, Mass. : Harvard University Press, 1984. xiv, 460
p. :
83-026521   616.9/803/0924   0674015533
*Hamilton, Alice, -- 1869-1970.   Physicians -- United States --
Biography. Toxicologists -- United States -- Biography.*

R154.H39.A3 1970
Hertzler, Arthur E.
   The horse and buggy doctor. Lincoln, University of
Nebraska Press [1970, c1938] xiv, 322 p. :
78-105646   610/.924   0803257171
   Physicians -- United States -- Biography.

R154.H62.A33
Hoffman, Charles Anthony,
   God, man, and medicine / by Charles A. "Carl" Hoffman ;
edited by Elizabeth A. Nichols. Parsons, W. Va. : McClain
Printing Co., 1978. vii, 205 p. :
77-083436   616.6/0092/4   0870122851
*Hoffman, Charles Anthony, -- 1904-1982.   Urologists -- West
Virginia -- Biography.*

R154.J315.J2 1972
Jackson, James,
   A memoir of James Jackson, Jr., M.D., with extracts from
his letters to his father, and medical cases, collected by him.
New York, Arno Press, 1972. 444 p.
72-180579   610/.92/4   0405039565
*Jackson, James, -- 1810-1834. Jackson, James, -- 1810-1834 --
Correspondence. Physicians -- United States -- Biography.*

R154.J33.A33
Jackson, Ulys,
   The autobiography of Ulys Jackson, M.D., Harrison,
Arkansas, 1905-19--- / compiled by Mrs. Ulys Jackson (Mary
Ruth). Harrison, Ark. : Jackson, 1977, c1978. iii, 178 p. :
79-108086   610/.92/4
*Jackson, Ulys, -- 1905-   Physicians (General practice) -- Arkansas -
- Harrison -- Biography.   Harrison (Ark.) -- Biography.*

R154.M33.A3
Mayo, Charles W.
   Mayo; the story of my family and my career [by] Charles W.
Mayo. Garden City, N.Y., Doubleday, 1968. viii, 351 p.
68-022502   610/.924
Mayo, Charles W. -- (Charles William), -- 1898-1968.

R154.M33.C3 1954
Clapesattle, Helen.
   The Doctors Mayo. Minneapolis, University of Minnesota
Press [1954, c1941] 426 p.
54-011771   926.1
*Mayo, William Worrall, -- 1819-1911. Mayo, Charles Horace, --
1865-1939. Mayo, William James, -- 1861-1939.*

R154.M648.A3 1994
Mitchell, George T.
   Dr. George : an account of the life of a country doctor /
George T. Mitchell. Carbondale : Southern Illinois University
Press, c1994. xv, 359 p., [
93-016589   610/.92   0809319152
*Mitchell, George T.   Physicians (General Practice) -- Illinois --
Biography. Medicine, Rural -- Illinois. Physicians -- personal
narratives.*

R154.M734.A3
Moorman, Lewis Jefferson,
   Pioneer doctor.   Norman, University of Oklahoma Press
[1951] xvii, 252 p.
51-010218   926.1
Moorman, Lewis Jefferson, -- 1875-   Physicians -- United States --
Biography. Pioneers -- West (U.S.) -- Biography.

R154.R767.A3 1994
Rowland, Mary Canaga,
   As long as life : the memoirs of a frontier woman doctor,
Mary Canaga Rowland, 1873-1966 / edited, with a foreword
by F.A. Loomis. Seattle, Wash. : Storm Peak Press, c1994. xiii,
178 p.
94-066409   610/.92   0964135701
Rowland, Mary Canaga, -- 1873-1966.   Women physicians -- Great
Plains -- Biography.

R154.R92.A3
Rusk, Howard Archibald,
   A world to care for; the autobiography of Howard A. Rusk,
M.D. New York, Random House [1972] xii, 307 p.
72-005263   610/.92/4   0394481984
Rusk, Howard A., -- 1901- Rusk, Howard A., -- 1901- Physicians --
United States -- Biography.

R154.W32.F5
Fleming, Donald,
   William H. Welch and the rise of modern medicine. Boston,
Little, Brown [1954] 216 p.
54006867   926.1
Welch, William Henry, -- 1850-1934.   Physicians -- biography --
United States History of Medicine, 19th Century -- United States
History of Medicine, 20th Century -- United States

R154.W32.F6
Flexner, Simon,
   William Henry Welch and the heroic age of American
medicine, by Simon Flexner and James Thomas Flexner. New
York, The Viking press, 1941. x, 539 p.
41-020339   926.1
Welch, William Henry, -- 1850-1934.

R154.Y24.S77 1998
Straus, Eugene.
   Rosalyn Yalow, Nobel laureate : her life and work in
medicine : a biographical memoir / by Eugene Straus. New
York : Plenum Trade, c1998. xv, 277 p. :
98-002749   610/.92   0306457962
Yalow, Rosalyn S. -- (Rosalyn Sussman), -- 1921-   Women medical
scientists -- United States -- Biography. Nobel Prizes.

R154.Z39.A3 1993
Zazove, Philip,
   When the phone rings, my bed shakes : memoirs of a deaf
doctor / Philip Zazove. Washington, D.C. : Gallaudet
University Press, c1993. xiv, 295 p. ;
93-006384   610/.92   1563680246
Zazove, Philip, -- 1951-   Deaf physicians -- United States --
Biography.

R154.5.S68.S35 1989
   Science and medicine in the Old South / edited by Ronald L.
Numbers and Todd L. Savitt. Baton Rouge : Louisiana State
University Press, c1989. xii, 370 p. :
88-032648   610/.975   0807114642
   Medicine -- Southern States -- History -- 19th century --
Congresses. Science -- Southern States -- History -- 19th century --
Congresses. History of Medicine, 19th Cent. -- United States --
congresses.

R154.5.W47.D57 1998
   Disease and medical care in the mountain West : essays on
region, history, and practice / edited by Martha L. Hildreth &
Bruce T. Moran. Reno : University of Nevada Press, c1998.
xix, 154 p. :
97-026959   610/.979   0874173043
   Medicine -- West (U.S.) -- History.

R172.S24.I57 2000
   Institutional change and healthcare organizations : from
professional dominance to managed care / W. Richard Scott ...
[et al.]. Chicago : University of Chicago Press, 2000. xxv, 427
p. :
99-048850   362.1/09764/6   0226743098
   Health services administration -- California -- San Francisco Bay
Area -- History -- 20th century. Medical care -- California -- San
Francisco Bay Area -- History -- 20th century. Medicine -- California
-- San Francisco Bay Area -- History -- 20th century.

R210.C4.B6 1991
Bonner, Thomas Neville.
   Medicine in Chicago, 1850-1950 : a chapter in the social
and scientific development of a city / Thomas Neville Bonner ;
with a foreword by Robert C. Hamilton. Urbana : University of
Illinois Press, c1991. xvi, 335 p.,
90-011121   610/.9773/11   0252017609
   Medicine -- Illinois -- Chicago -- History. History of Medicine --
Chicago.

R463-652 History — By region or country — Other regions or countries

R463.N8.M37 1993
Marble, Allan Everett.
   Surgeons, smallpox, and the poor : a history of medicine and
social conditions in Nova Scotia, 1749-1799 / Allan Everett
Marble. Montreal ; McGill-Queen's University Press, c1993.
xvi, 356 p. :
94-233680   362.1/09716/09033
0773509887
   Medicine -- Nova Scotia -- History -- 18th century. Small pox --
Nova Scotia -- History -- 18th century. Poor -- Medical care -- Nova
Scotia -- History -- 18th century. Nova Scotia -- Social conditions --
History -- 18th century. Nova Scotia -- Social conditions -- To 1867.
Nouvelle-Ecosse -- Conditions sociales -- Jusqu'a 1867.

R464.L36.D84 1993
Duffin, Jacalyn.
   Langstaff : a nineteenth-century medical life / Jacalyn
Duffin. Toronto : University of Toronto Press, c1993. xv, 383
p., [
94-147960   610/.92   0802029086
*Langstaff, James Miles, -- 1825-1889.   Medicine -- Ontario --
Richmond Hill -- History -- 19th century. Physicians -- Ontario --
Richmond Hill -- Biography.*

R484.B95 1994
Bynum, W. F.
   Science and the practice of medicine in the nineteenth
century / W.F. Bynum. Cambridge [England] ; Cambridge
University Press, 1994. xvi, 283 p. :
93-029827   610/.9/034   0521251095
   *Medicine -- Europe -- History -- 19th century. Medicine -- North
America -- History -- 19th century.*

R487.G47 1998
Getz, Faye Marie,
   Medicine in the English Middle Ages / Faye Getz.
Princeton, NJ : Princeton University Press, 1998. xiv, 174 p. :
98-003534   160/.942/0902   0691085226
   *Medicine, Medieval -- England -- History. Medicine -- England --
History.*

R488.L8.L38 1996
Lawrence, Susan C.
   Charitable knowledge : hospital pupils and practitioners in
eighteenth-century London / Susan C. Lawrence. Cambridge ;
Cambridge University Press, 1996. xiv, 390 p. :
95-017710   610/.942/09033   0521363551
   *Medicine -- England -- London -- History -- 18th century.
Teaching hospitals -- England -- London -- History -- 18th century.
Medical education -- England -- London -- History -- 18th century.*

R489.B693.K37 1993
Kaplan, Barbara Beigun,
   Divulging of useful truths in physick : the medical agenda of
Robert Boyle / Barbara Beigun Kaplan. Baltimore : Johns
Hopkins University Press, c1993. xii, 216 p. ;
92-048468   610/.92   0801846013
*Boyle, Robert, -- 1627-1691. Boyle, Robert, -- 1627-1691.   Medicine
-- Great Britain -- History -- 17th century. History of Medicine, 17th
Cent. -- England. Philosophy, Medical -- England.*

R489.C9.T5
Thornton, Robert D.
   James Currie, the entire stranger, & Robert Burns.
Edinburgh, Oliver & Boyd, 1963. xvi, 459 p.
66-000039
*Currie, James, -- 1756-1805. Burns, Robert, -- 1759-1796.
Scotland -- History -- 18th century -- Biography.*

R489.G79.C66 1994
Cook, Harold John.
   Trials of an ordinary doctor : Joannes Groenevelt in
seventeenth-century London / Harold J. Cook. Baltimore :
Johns Hopkins University Press, c1994. xviii, 301 p.
93-039733   610/.92   0801847788
*Groeneveld, Joannes, -- 1647-1710?   Physicians -- Netherlands --
Biography. Physicians -- England -- Biography. Dutch -- England.*

R489.J5
Bazin, H.
   The eradication of smallpox : Edward Jenner and the first
and only eradication of a human infectious disease / Herve
Bazin ; translated by Andrew and Glenise Morgan. San Diego,
Calif. : Academic Press, c2000. xx, 246 p. :
99-065521   0120834758
*Jenner, Edward, -- 1749-1823.   Physicians -- England -- Biography.
Smallpox vaccine -- History. Smallpox -- Prevention -- History.*

R489.O7.C8 1940
Cushing, Harvey,
   The life of Sir William Osler, by Harvey Cushing ...
London, Oxford university press, 1940. xviii, 1417 p
40-027751   926.1
*Osler, William, -- Sir, -- 1849-1919.   Physicians -- Canada --
Biography.*

R489.S78
Greene, Gayle,
   The woman who knew too much : Alice Stewart and the
secrets of radiation / Gayle Greene ; foreword by Helen
Caldicott. Ann Arbor, MI : University of Michigan Press,
c1999. x, 321 p. :
99-051898   610/.92   0472111078
*Stewart, Alice M., -- 1906- Stewart, Alice M., -- 1906- -- Political
activity. Women physicians -- England -- Biography. Radiation
injuries -- Prevention -- Political aspects. Radiation -- Health aspects.*

R504.R36 1988
Ramsey, Matthew,
   Professional and popular medicine in France, 1770-1830 :
the social world of medical practice / Matthew Ramsey.
Cambridge ; Cambridge University Press, 1988. xvii, 406 p.
87-015882   610/.944   0521305179
   *Medicine -- France -- History -- 18th century. Medicine -- France
-- History -- 19th century. Medicine, Magic, mystic, and spagiric --
France -- History -- 18th century.*

R505.E44 1990
Ellis, Jack D.
   The physician-legislators of France : medicine and politics
in the early Third Republic, 1870-1914 / Jack D. Ellis.
Cambridge ; Cambridge University Press, 1990. xii, 305 p. :
89-025357   610/.944   0521382084
   *Physicians -- France -- History -- 19th century. Physicians --
France -- History -- 20th century. Legislators -- France -- History --
19th century. France -- History -- Third Republic, 1870-1940.*

R505.W55 1993
Wilson, Lindsay B.
   Women and medicine in the French Enlightenment : the
debate over "maladies des femmes" / Lindsay Wilson.
Baltimore : Johns Hopkins University Press, c1993. vii, 246 p.
;
92-015475   306.4/61/094409033
080184438X
   *Medicine -- France -- History -- 18th century. Women -- Health
and hygiene -- France -- History -- 18th century. Medical
jurisprudence -- France -- History -- 18th century.*

R506.P3.W45 1993
Weiner, Dora B.
   The citizen-patient in revolutionary and imperial Paris / Dora B. Weiner. Baltimore : Johns Hopkins University Press, c1993. xvi, 444 p. :
92-049007   362.1/0944/3609033
0801844835
   Medicine -- France -- Paris -- History -- 18th century. Medicine -- France -- Paris -- History -- 19th century. Delivery of Health Care -- history -- Paris.

R507.L193.W46 1992
Wellman, Kathleen Anne,
   La Mettrie : medicine, philosophy, and enlightenment / Kathleen Wellman. Durham : Duke University Press, 1992. xiv, 342 p. ;
91-023992   610/.92   0822312042
La Mettrie, Julien Offray de, -- 1709-1751.   Physicians -- France -- Biography. Philosophers -- France -- Biography.

R507.L25.D84 1998
Duffin, Jacalyn.
   To see with a better eye : a life of R.T.H. Laennec / Jacalyn Duffin. Princeton, N.J. : Princeton University Press, c1998. xvii, 453 p.
97-019779   610/.92   0691037086
Laennec, R. T. H. -- (Rene Theophile Hyacinthe), -- 1781-1826. Physicians -- France -- Biography.

R511.B33.T8 1993
Tuchman, Arleen,
   Science, medicine, and the state in Germany : the case of Baden, 1815-1871 / Arleen Marcia Tuchman. New York : Oxford University Press, 1993. viii, 200 p.
92-023470   610/.7/04346409034
0195080475
   Research -- Germany -- Baden -- History -- 19th century. Medicine -- Research -- Germany -- Baden -- History -- 19th century.

R557.A7.M38 1993
McVaugh, M. R.
   Medicine before the plague : practitioners and their patients in the crown of Aragon, 1285-1345 / Michael R. McVaugh. Cambridge [England] ; Cambridge University Press, 1993. xvi, 280 p. :
92-049626   610/.946/5509023
0521412358
   Medical care -- Spain -- Aragon -- History. Social medicine -- Spain -- Aragon -- History. Medicine, Medieval -- Spain -- Aragon.

R566.T57.E43 1992
Emch-Deriaz, Antoinette Suzanne.
   Tissot : physician of the Enlightenment / Antoinette Emch-Deriaz. New York : P. Lang, c1992. ix, 339 p. ;
91-046129   610/.92   0820418196
Tissot, S. A. D. -- (Samuel Auguste David), -- 1728-1797. Physicians -- Switzerland -- Biography.

R601.F64 1993
Fogelman, Betsy.
   The oriental medicine resource guide : an information sourcebook / edited by Betsy Fogelman. Santa Fe, NM, U.S.A. : InWord Press, c1993. xviii, 151 p.
93-085029   610/.951/0973   1566903114
   Medicine, Chinese -- Directories. Acupuncture -- Directories.

R601.H5 1983
Hillier, S. M.
   Health care and traditional medicine in China, 1800-1982 / S.M. Hillier and J.A. Jewell. London ; Routledge & Kegan Paul, 1983. xix, 453 p.,
83-003188   362.1/0951   0710094256
   Medicine -- China -- History. Medicine, Chinese -- History. Medical care -- China -- History.

R601.S58 1995
Sivin, Nathan.
   Medicine, philosophy and religion in ancient China : researches and reflections / Nathan Sivin. Aldershot, Hampshire, Great Britain ; Variorum, 1995. 1 v. (various
95-019571   610/.951   0860784932
   Medicine, Chinese -- History. Science -- China -- History. Taoism.

R602.M56 1994
Minden, Karen.
   Bamboo stone : the evolution of a Chinese medical elite / Karen Minden. Toronto ; University of Toronto Press, c1994. xiv, 201 p.,
94-205783   610/.951   0802005500
   Missionaries, Medical -- China. Missionaries, Medical -- Canada. Medical education -- China -- History -- 20th century.

R603.T5.T45 1992
   Tibetan medical paintings : illustrations to the blue beryl treatise of Sangye Gyamtso (1653-1705) / edited by Yuri Parfionovitch, Gyurme Dorje, Fernand Meyer ; foreword by the Fourteenth Dalai Lama ; introduction by Fernand Meyer. New York : H.N. Abrams, Inc., 1992. 2 v. (ix, 336
92-009016   610/.951/5022   0810938618
   Medicine, Tibetan -- Illustrations.

R604.H37.P67 1997
Porter, Edgar A.
   The people's doctor : George Hatem and China's revolution / Edgar A. Porter. Honolulu : University of Hawai'i Press, c1997. xii, 342 p.,
96-034018   951.05/092   0824818407
Hatem, George, -- 1910- Physicians -- China -- Biography. China -- History -- 20th century.

R606.A75 1993
Arnold, David,
   Colonizing the body : state medicine and epidemic disease in nineteenth-century India / David Arnold. Berkeley : University of California Press, c1993. xii, 354 p. :
92-025623   362.1/0954/09034
0520081242
   Medicine -- India -- History -- 19th century. Medicine -- Political aspects -- India. Social medicine -- India -- History.

R651.V38 1991b
Vaughan, Megan.
   Curing their ills : colonial power and African illness / Megan Vaughan. Stanford, Calif. : Stanford University Press, 1991. xii, 224 p. :
91-065562   610/.96/0934   0804719705
   Medicine -- Africa -- History -- 19th century. Medicine -- Africa -- History -- 20th century. Colonies -- Africa.

R652.P38 1996
Patton, Adell,
   Physicians, colonial racism, and diaspora in West Africa / Adell Patton. Gainesville : University Press of Florida, c1996. xx, 343 p. :
95-045070   610/.966   0813014328
   Physicians -- Africa, West -- History. Medicine -- Africa, West -- History. Physicians -- Africa, West -- Political activity. Africa, West -- Race relations.

R690 Medicine as a profession. Physicians — General works

R690.B58 1990
Birenbaum, Arnold.
   In the shadow of medicine : remaking the division of labor in health care / Arnold Birenbaum. Dix Hills, N.Y. : General Hall, c1990. 174 p. ;
90-080203   610/.6   0930390288
   Medicine. Social medicine.

R690.E97 2002
   Exploring health care careers / writers, Carole Bolster ... [et al.]. 2nd ed. Chicago : Ferguson Pub. Co., c2002. 2 v. (xvii, 949 p.) ;
          610.69   0894343114
   Medicine--Vocational guidance--Juvenile literature. Medicine--Vocational guidance. Vocational guidance.

R690.F713 1989
Franck, Irene M.
   Healers / by Irene M. Franck and David M. Brownstone. New York : Facts on File, c1989. viii, 232 p. :
          610.69   0816014469
   Medical personnel--History--Juvenile literature. Healers--History--Juvenile literature. Medical personnel--History.

R692 Medicine as a profession. Physicians — Women in medicine. Women physicians

R692.B66 1992
Bonner, Thomas Neville.
   To the ends of the earth : women's search for education in medicine / Thomas Neville Bonner. Cambridge, Mass. : Harvard University Press, 1992. xiv, 232 p. :
91-020826   610/.71/1   0674893034
   Women in medicine -- History. Women medical students -- History. Education, Medical -- history.

R692.B745 1994
Briles, Judith.
   The Briles report on women in healthcare : changing conflict to collaboration in a toxic workplace / Judith Briles. San Francisco : Jossey-Bass, c1994. xvi, 261 p. :
94-012540   158/.26/082   1555426719
   Women in medicine. Work environment. Work -- Psychological aspects.

R692.D34 1992
Dakin, Theodora P.
   A history of women's contribution to world health / Theodora P. Dakin. Lewiston, N.Y. : Edwin Mellen Press, c1991. iv, 116 p. ;
91-046383   610/.82   0773496246
   Women in medicine -- History. History of Medicine. Women -- history.

R692.L65
Lopate, Carol.
   Women in medicine. Baltimore, Published for the Josiah Macy, Jr., Foundation b [1968] xvii, 204 p.
68-019526   610/.23
   Women physicians.

R692.M64 2000
Morantz-Sanchez, Regina Markell.
   Sympathy and science : women physicians in American medicine / Regina Morantz-Sanchez ; with a new preface by the author. Chapel Hill : University of North Carolina, 2000. p. cm.
00-027309   610/.82/0973   0807848905
   Women physicians -- United States -- History. Physicians -- United States -- History. Medicine -- United States -- History.

R692.M645 1999
More, Ellen Singer,
   Restoring the balance : women physicians and the profession of medicine, 1850-1995 / Ellen S. More. Cambridge, Mass. : Harvard University Press, 1999. xi, 340 p. :
99-038185   610.69/52/0820973
067476661X
   Women physicians -- United States -- History -- 19th century. Women physicians -- United States -- History -- 20th century. Women in medicine -- United States -- History -- 19th century.

R692.S586 1997
Silverthorne, Elizabeth,
   Women pioneers in Texas medicine / Elizabeth Silverthorne & Geneva Fulgham. College Station : Texas A&M University Press, c1997. xxvi, 238 p.
97-018885   610/.9764   089096789X
   Women in medicine -- Texas -- History.

R692.W45 2001
Wells, Susan.
Out of the dead house : nineteenth-century women physicians and the writing of medicine / Susan Wells. Madison : University of Wisconsin Press, c2001. xii, 312 p. :
00-010614   610/.82/097309034
0299171701
Preston, Ann, -- 1813-1872. Jacobi, Mary Putnam, -- 1842-1906. Longshore, Hannah, -- 1819-1901. Women physicians -- United States. Women in medicine -- United States -- History -- 19th century.

R692.W656 1996
Women in medical education : an anthology of experience / Delese Wear, editor. New York : State University of New York Press, 1996. xiii, 183 p.
95-049902   610.82   0791430871
Women in medicine. Medical teaching personnel.

R692.W676 1997
Women healers and physicians : climbing a long hill / Lillian R. Furst, editor. Lexington, Ky. : University Press of Kentucky, c1997. vii, 274 p. ;
96-032389   610.69/52/082   081312011X
Women in medicine -- History.

R694 Medicine as a profession. Physicians — Minorities in medicine — Jews in medicine. Jewish physicians

R694.E376 2001
Efron, John M.
Medicine and the German Jews : a history / John M. Efron. New Haven : Yale University Press, c2001. viii, 343 p.
00-011315   610/.89/924043   0300083777
Jewish physicians -- Germany -- History. Jews -- Medicine -- Germany -- History. Medicine -- Germany -- History.

R694.S52 1994
Shatzmiller, Joseph.
Jews, medicine, and medieval society / Joseph Shatzmiller. Berkeley : University of California Press, c1994. xi, 241 p. ;
93-002810   610.69/52/08992404
0520080599
Jewish physicians. Medicine, Medieval.

R695 Medicine as a profession. Physicians — Blacks in medicine. Black physicians

R695.C86 1971
Curtis, James L.,
Blacks, medical schools, and society [by] James L. Curtis. Ann Arbor, University of Michigan Press [1971] xv, 169 p.
76-148249   610/.71/173   0472269003
Afro-Americans in medicine. Medical education -- United States.

R695.W38 1999
Watson, Wilbur H.
Against the odds : Blacks in the profession of medicine in the United States / Wilbur H. Watson. New Brunswick (U.S.A.) : Transaction Publishers, c1999. xi, 198 p. :
98-034953   610.69/52/08996073
1560003766
Afro-American physicians -- History. Race discrimination -- United States -- History.

R697 Medicine as a profession. Physicians — Other personnel, A-Z

R697.A4
Badasch, Shirley A.,
Introduction to health occupations : today's health care worker / Shirley A. Badasch, Doreen S. Chesebro. Upper Saddle River, N.J. : Prentice Hall Health, c2000. xxxix, 724 p.
99-038341   610.69   0130131474
Allied health personnel -- Vocational guidance.

R697.P45B66 1995
Bonewit-West, Kathy.
Clinical procedures for medical assistants / Kathy Bonewit-West. 4th ed. Philadelphia : Saunders, c1995. xvii, 667 p., 18 p. of plates :
         610.73/7   0721654134
Physicians' assistants. Clinical medicine. Physicians' Assistants.

R697.P45P488 2001
Physician assistant's guide to research and medical literature / edited by J. Dennis Blessing. Philadelphia, PA : F.A. Davis Co., c2001. viii, 110 p. :
         610.69/53   0803607687
Physicians' assistants. Physicians' assistants--Research. Medical literature.

R705 Anecdotes, humor, etc.

R705.M465 2000
Medicine in quotations : views of health and disease through the ages / edited by Edward J. Huth, T. Jock Murray. Philadelphia, PA : American College of Physicians, c2000. xvi, 524 p. ;
99-057212   610   0943126835
Medicine -- Quotations, maxims, etc. Health -- Quotations, maxims, etc.

R707 Personal life of physicians — General works

R707.S75
Strauss, Maurice Benjamin,
Familiar medical quotations, edited by Maurice B. Strauss. Boston, Little, Brown [1968] xix, 968 p.
68-021620   610/.2
Medicine -- Quotations, maxims, etc.

R712 Directories — By region or country — North America

R712.A1D47 1993
 Directory of deceased American physicians, 1804-1929 :a genealogical guide to over 149,000 medical practitioners providing brief biological sketches drawn from the American Medical Association's Deceased physician masterfile / Arthur W. Hafner, editor ; Fred W. Hunter, project manager ; E. Michael Tarpey, data entry specialist. Chicago : American Medical Association, c1993. 2 v. :
　　　　　610/.92/273　　　　0899705340
 Physicians--United States--Directories. Physicians--United States--Biography. History of Medicine, Modern--United States--directories.

R712.A1A8
 AAMC directory of American medical education. Washington, Association of American Medical Colleges, -1994. v.
　　　　　610/.7/1173
 Medical colleges--United States--Directories. Schools, Medical--Canada--Directories. Schools, Medical--United States--Directories.

R722.32 Missionary medicine. Medical missionaries — Biography — Individual, A-Z

R722.32.A45.A3 1994
Allison, Mary Bruins,
 Doctor Mary in Arabia : memoirs / by Mary Bruins Allison ; edited by Sandra Shaw ; introduction by Lucie Wood Saunders and John Clarke Saunders. Austin : University of Texas Press, 1994. xxvii, 329 p.
 93-031393　　　　610.69/5/092　　　　0292704542
 Allison, Mary Bruins, -- 1903- Missionaries, Medical -- United States -- Biography. Missionaries, Medical -- Arabian Peninsula -- Biography. Missionaries, Medical -- India -- Biography.

R722.32.D66.F57 1997
Fisher, James T.,
 Dr. America : the lives of Thomas A. Dooley, 1927-1961 / James T. Fisher. Amherst : University of Massachusetts Press, c1997. x, 304 p. :
 96-048652　　　　610/.92　　　　1558490671
 Dooley, Thomas A. -- (Thomas Anthony), -- 1927-1961. Missionaries, Medical -- Asia, Southeastern -- Biography. Missions, Medical -- Asia, Southeastern -- Biography. United States -- Civilization -- 1945- Asia, Southeastern -- History -- 1945-

R722.32.S35.A4 1996
Schweitzer, Albert,
 Brothers in spirit : the correspondence of Albert Schweitzer and William Larimer Mellon, Jr. / translated by Jeannette Q. Byers ; foreword by Gwen Grant Mellon and Rhena Schweitzer Miller. Syracuse, N.Y. : Syracuse University Press, 1996. xviii, 188 p.
 96-007388　　　　610/.92　　　　0815603444
 Schweitzer, Albert, -- 1875-1965 -- Correspondence. Mellon, William Larimer, -- 1910- -- Correspondence. Missionaries, Medical -- Gabon -- Lambarene (Moyen-Ogooue) -- Correspondence. Missionaries, Medical -- Haiti -- Correspondence.

R723 Medical philosophy. Medical logic — General works

R723.C42828 1991
Cassell, Eric J.,
 The nature of suffering : and the goals of medicine / by Eric J. Cassell. New York : Oxford University Press, 1991. p. cm.
 90-007657　　　　610/.1　　　　0195052226
 Medicine -- Philosophy. Suffering. Physician and patient.

R723.L35 1997
Lantos, John D.
 Do we still need doctors? / John D. Lantos. New York : Routledge, 1997. x, 214 p. ;
 97-011424　　　　610/.1　　　　0415918529
 Medicine -- Philosophy. Physician and patient. Medical innovations.

R723.M617 1983
Moore, Michael C.,
 The complete handbook of holistic health / Michael C. Moore, Lynda J. Moore. Englewood Cliffs, N.J. : Prentice-Hall, 1983. xiii, 253 p.
 82-013284　　　　615.5　　　　0131610260
 Holistic medicine. Health. Consumer education.

R723.N387 1994
Nesse, Randolph M.
 Why we get sick : the new science of Darwinian medicine/ Randolph M. Nesse and George C. Williams. New York : Times Books, c1994. xi, 291 p. :
 94-027651　　　　610/.1　　　　0812922247
 Medicine -- Philosophy. Human evolution. Human biology.

R723.P38
Pellegrino, Edmund D.,
 Humanism and the physician / Edmund D. Pellegrino. Knoxville : University of Tennessee Press, c1979. xiii, 248 p.
 78-023174　　　　610/.1　　　　0870492187
 Medicine -- Philosophy. Medicine and the humanities. Humanism.

R723.P3813
Pellegrino, Edmund D.,
 A philosophical basis of medical practice : toward a philosophy and ethic of the healing professions / Edmund D. Pellegrino, David C. Thomasma. New York : Oxford University Press, 1981. xvii, 341 p.
 80-036735　　　　610/.1　　　　0195027906
 Medicine -- Philosophy. Ethics, Medical. Philosophy, Medical.

R723.W355 1995
Weatherall, D. J.
 Science and the quiet art : the role of medical research in health care / David Weatherall. New York : W.W. Norton, c1995. 378 p. :
 94-016483　　　　610/.1　　　　0393037444
 Medicine -- Philosophy. Medical sciences. Social medicine.

R723.W39 1998
Weisse, Allen B.

The staff and the serpent : pertinent and impertinent observations on the world of medicine / Allen B. Weisse. Carbondale : Southern Illinois University Press, c1998. ix, 147 p. ;
97-005480   610   0809321491
Medicine -- Philosophy. Medicine -- Anecdotes. Medicine -- essays.

R723.5 Medical philosophy. Medical logic — Decision making

R723.5.B47 1997
Berg, Marc.

Rationalizing medical work : decision-support techniques and medical practices / Marc Berg. Cambridge, Mass. : MIT Press, c1997. x, 238 p. :
96-029283   610   0262024179
Medicine -- Decision making. Patient Care Planning. Decision Support Techniques.

R723.5.D44 1987
Degner, Lesley F.,

Life-death decisions in health care / Lesley F. Degner, Janet I. Beaton. Washington : Hemisphere Pub. Corp., c1987. xiv, 159 p. ;
86-031818   610   0891163999
Medicine -- Decision making. Life and death, Power over -- Decision making. Decision Making.

R723.5.G48 1998

Getting doctors to listen : ethics and outcomes data in context / edited by Philip J. Boyle. Washington, D.C. : Georgetown University Press, c1998. viii, 234 p.
97-009533   174/.2   0878406549
Medicine -- Decision making -- Moral and ethical aspects. Outcome assessment (Medical care) -- Moral and ethical aspects. Medical protocols -- Moral and ethical aspects.

R723.5.R67 1991
Rothman, David J.

Strangers at the bedside : a history of how law and bioethics transformed medical decision making / David J. Rothman. [New York, NY] : BasicBooks, c1991. xi, 303 p. ;
90-055598   610/.72   0465082092
Medicine -- United States -- Decision making -- History. Medicine -- Research -- United States -- Decision making -- History. Medical ethics -- United States -- History.

R724 Medical ethics. Medical etiquette — General works

R724.A32 1992

African-American perspectives on biomedical ethics / edited by Harley E. Flack and Edmund D. Pellegrino ; with editorial assistance by Dennis McManus. Washington, D.C. : Georgetown University Press, c1992. xx, 203 p. ;
92-017638   174/.2/08996073   0878405321
Medical ethics. Afro-American philosophy.

R724.B4585 2000

Bioethics : ancient themes in contemporary issues / edited by Mark G. Kuczewski and Ronald Polansky. Cambridge, Mass. : MIT Press, c2000. xiii, 304 p.
00-020815   174/.2   026211254X
Medical ethics. Philosophy, Ancient. Medicine, Greek and Roman.

R724.B49 2001

Biomedical ethics / [edited by] Thomas A. Mappes, David DeGrazia. 5th ed. Boston : McGraw-Hill, c2001. xii, 707 p. ;
          174/.2   0072303654
Medical ethics. Bioethics. Ethics, Medical--Collected Works.

R724.B497 1996

Birth to death : science and bioethics / edited by David C. Thomasma and Thomasine Kushner. Cambridge [England] ; Cambridge University Press, 1996. xvi, 382 p. ;
95-048006   174/.9574   0521462975
Medical ethics. Bioethics.

R724.B73 1991
Brennan, Troyen A.

Just doctoring : medical ethics in the liberal state / Troyen Brennan. Berkeley : University of California Press, c1991. xiv, 287 p. ;
91-010146   174/.2   0520073339
Medical ethics.

R724.B753 1993
Brock, Dan W.

Life and death : philosophical essays in biomedical ethics / Dan W. Brock. -- Cambridge ; Cambridge University Press, 1993. xi, 435 p. ;
92002092   174/.24   0521428335
Medical ethics.

R724.B77 1992
Brody, Howard.

The healer's power / Howard Brody. New Haven : Yale University Press, c1992. xiii, 311 p.
91-024291   174/.2   0300051743
Medical ethics. Ethics, Medical. Physician-Patient Relations.

R724.C337 1997
Caplan, Arthur L.

Am I my brother's keeper? : the ethical frontiers of biomedicine / Arthur L. Caplan. Bloomington : Indiana University Press, c1997. xiii, 241 p.
97-019268   174/.2   025333358X
Medical ethics.

R724.C338 1998
Caplan, Arthur L.

Due consideration : controversy in the age of medical miracles / Arthur Caplan. New York : Wiley, c1998. xi, 282 p. ;
97-029022   174/.2   047118344X
Medical ethics.

R724.C34 1992
Caplan, Arthur L.
If I were a rich man could I buy a pancreas? : and other essays on the ethics of health care / by Arthur L. Caplan. Bloomington : Indiana University Press, c1992. xvii, 348 p.
91-032112   174/.2   0253313074
Medical ethics. Bioethics.

R724.C45 1984
Chapman, Carleton B.
Physicians, law, and ethics / Carleton B. Chapman. New York : New York University Press, 1984. xviii, 192 p.
84-002130   174/.2   0814713920
Medical ethics -- History. Medical laws and legislation -- History. Ethics, Medical.

R724.C455 1993
Charlesworth, M. J.
Bioethics in a liberal society / Max Charlesworth. New York, NY, USA : Cambridge University Press, 1993. 172 p. ;
93-018160   174/.2   0521445035
Medical ethics. Bioethics. Ethics, Medical.

R724.C477 1997
Childress, James F.
Practical reasoning in bioethics / James F. Childress. Bloomington : Indiana University Press, c1997. xiv, 385 p. ;
96-025001   174/.2   0253332184
Medical ethics. Bioethics. Ethics, Medical.

R724.D3826 2000
A primer for health care ethics :essays for a pluralistic society / [edited by] Kevin O'Rourke. 2nd ed. Washington, DC : Georgetown University Press, 2000. xiii, 323 p. ;
          174/.2   0878408029
Medical ethics. Medical ethics--Case studies.

R724.D48 1995
Devettere, Raymond J.
Practical decision making in health care ethics : cases and concepts / Raymond J. Devettere. Washington, D.C. : Georgetown University Press, c1995. xix, 487 p. ;
95-006353   174/.2   0878405895
Medical ethics. Decision Making. Ethics, Medical.

R724.E5 1991
Emanuel, Ezekiel J.,
The ends of human life : medical ethics in a liberal polity / Ezekiel J. Emanuel. Cambridge, Mass. : Harvard University Press, 1991. x, 307 p. ;
91-007090   174/.2   0674253256
Medical ethics. Liberalism. Ethics, Medical.

R724.F59 1997
Flynn, Eileen P.
Issues in medical ethics / Eileen P. Flynn. Kansas City, MO : Sheed & Ward, c1997. vii, 384 p. ;
96-039109   174/.2   1556129173
Medical ethics.

R724.H49 1992
Heyd, David.
Genethics : moral issues in the creation of people / David Heyd. Berkeley : University of California Press, c1992. xiii, 276 p.
91-030300   174/.2   0520077148
Medical ethics. Human reproductive technology -- Moral and ethical aspects. Creation.

R724.H59 1997
Holm, Soren.
Ethical problems in clinical practice : the ethical reasoning of health care professionals / Soren Holm. Manchester ; Manchester University Press ; 1997. p. cm.
97-013570   174/.2   0719050499
Medical ethics. Clinical medicine -- Decision making. Ethics, Medical.

R724.H784 1997
Human lives : critical essays on consequentialist bioethics / edited by David S. Oderberg and Jacqueline A. Laing. New York, N.Y. : St. Martin's Press, 1997. viii, 244 p.
96-009136   174/.2   0312160992
Medical ethics. Bioethics. Consequentialism (Ethics)

R724.K54 1990
Kilner, John Frederic.
Who lives? who dies? : ethical criteria in patient selection / John F. Kilner. New Haven : Yale University Press, c1990. 359 p. ;
89-016542   174/.2   0300046804
Medical ethics. Decision Making. Ethics, Medical.

R724.K82 1997
Kuczewski, Mark G.
Fragmentation and consensus : communitarian and casuist bioethics / Mark G. Kuczewski. Washington, D.C. : Georgetown University Press, c1997. xi, 177 p. ;
97-006087   174/.2   0878406484
Medical ethics. Bioethics. Communitarianism.

R724.L496 1995
Life choices : a Hastings Center introduction to bioethics / edited by Joseph H. Howell and William F. Sale ; foreword by Daniel Callahan. Washington, DC : Georgetown University Press, c1995. xiii, 537 p.
94-035031   174/.2   0878405771
Medical ethics.

R724.L63 1986
Loewy, Erich H.
Ethical dilemmas in modern medicine : a physician's viewpoint / Erich H. Loewy. Lewiston, N.Y., USA : Edwin Mellen Press, c1986. 343 p. ;
86-023460   174/.2   0889461333
Medical ethics.

R724.M16135 1993
Macklin, Ruth,
   Enemies of patients / Ruth Macklin. New York : Oxford University Press, 1993. viii, 250 p.
92-016894   174/.2   0195072006
   Medical ethics. Physician and patient.

R724.M2654 1994
   A Matter of principles? : ferment in U.S. bioethics / edited by Edwin R. DuBose, Ronald P. Hamel, Laurence J. O'Connell. Valley Forge, Pa. : Trinity Press International, 1994. xviii, 381 p.
94-000033   174/.2/0973   1563380811
   Medical ethics -- United States. Bioethics -- United States.

R724.M285 1991
May, William F.
   The patient's ordeal / William F. May. Bloomington : Indiana University Press, c1991. xii, 218 p. ;
90-045841   174/.2   0253337178
   Medical ethics. Patients -- Psychology. Decision making -- Moral and ethical aspects.

R724.M2922 1997
McKenny, Gerald P.
   To relieve the human condition : bioethics, technology, and the body / Gerald P. McKenny. Albany, N.Y. : State University of New York Press, c1997. x, 279 p. ;
96-045998   174/.2   0791434737
   Medical ethics. Bioethics.

R724.M677 1995
Moreno, Jonathan D.
   Deciding together : bioethics and moral consensus / Jonathan D. Moreno. New York : Oxford University Press, 1995. xv, 165 p. :
94-026756   174/.2   019509218X
   Bioethics. Medical ethics committees.

R724.N43 1995
Nelson, Hilde Lindemann.
   The patient in the family : an ethics of medicine and families / Hilde Lindemann Nelson and James Lindemann Nelson. New York : Routledge, 1995. xii, 251 p. ;
94-033652   174/.2   0415911281
   Medical ethics. Family. Family medicine.

R724.P34 1993
Pellegrino, Edmund D.,
   The virtues in medical practice / by Edmund D. Pellegrino and David C. Thomasma. New York : Oxford University Press, 1993. xiv, 205 p. ;
92-049073   174/.2   0195082893
   Medical ethics. Bioethics. Ethics, Medical.

R724.P436 1996
Petrinovich, Lewis F.
   Living and dying well / Lewis Petrinovich. New York : Plenum Press, c1996. xi, 362 p. ;
96-006465   174/.2   0306451719
   Medical ethics.

R724.P665 1993
Post, Stephen Gerrard,
   Inquiries in bioethics / Stephen G. Post. Washington, D.C. : Georgetown University Press, c1993. xii, 179 p. ;
93-017564   174/.2   0878405380
   Medical ethics.

R724.Q35 1990
   Quality of life : the new medical dilemma / edited by James J. Walter, Thomas A. Shannon. New York : Paulist Press, c1990. vi, 357 p. :
90-041235   174/.24   0809131919
   Medical ethics. Quality of life.

R724.S48 1992
Sherwin, Susan,
   No longer patient : feminist ethics and health care / Susan Sherwin. Philadelphia : Temple University Press, 1992. xi, 236 p. ;
91-014499   174/.2   0877228892
   Medical ethics. Feminism -- Moral and ethical aspects. Women -- Health and hygiene.

R724.S57 2000
Smith, Wesley J.
   Culture of death : the assault on medical ethics in America / Wesley J. Smith. San Francisco, Calif. : Encounter Books, c2000. xv, 285 p. ;
00-052068   174/.2/0973   1893554066
   Medical ethics -- United States. Bioethics -- United States.

R724.S598 1995
   Society's choices : social and ethical decision making in biomedicine / Ruth Ellen Bulger, Elizabeth Meyer Bobby, and Harvey V. Fineberg, editors ; Committee on the Social and Ethical Impacts of Developments in Biomedicine, Division of Health Sciences Policy, Institute of Medicine. Washington, D.C. : National Academy Press, 1995. xv, 541 p. ;
94-039354   174/.2   0309051320
   Medical ethics. Bioethics.

R724.S599 1998
   Source book in bioethics / edited by Albert R. Jonsen, Robert M. Veatch, LeRoy Walters. Washington, D.C. : Georgetown University Press, c1998. ix, 510 p. ;
97-041521   174/.2/09   0878406832
   Medical ethics -- History -- Sources.

R724.S84 2000
Stevens, M. L. Tina.
   Bioethics in America : origins and cultural politics / M.L. Tina Stevens. Baltimore : Johns Hopkins University Press, c2000. xvi, 204 p. ;
00-008389   174/.2/0973   0801864259
   Medical ethics -- United States -- History. Bioethics -- United States -- History.

R724.T38 1999
Tauber, Alfred I.
Confessions of a medicine man : an essay in popular philosophy / Alfred I. Tauber. Cambridge, Mass. : MIT Press, c1999. xviii, 159 p.
98-027288   174/.2   0262201143
Medical ethics. Medicine -- Philosophy. Physician and patient -- Moral and ethical aspects.

R724.U55 1982
United States.
Making health care decisions : a report on the ethical and legal implications of informed consent in the patient-practitioner relationship. Washington, D.C. : President's Commission for the Study of Ethical 1982- v. 1-3   :
82-600637   362.1/042
Medical ethics -- United States. Informed consent (Medical law) -- United States. Physician and patient -- United States.

R725 Medical ethics. Medical etiquette — Codes of ethics

R725.A56 1999
The American medical ethics revolution : how the AMA's code of ethics has transformed physicians' relationships to patients, professionals, and society / edited by Robert B. Baker ... [et al.]. Baltimore : Johns Hopkins University Press, 1999. xxxix, 396 p.
99-029636   174/.2/0973   0801861705
Medical ethics -- United States. Medical ethics -- Social aspects -- United States.

R725.5 Medical ethics. Medical etiquette — Special aspects

R725.5.B76 1988
Brody, Baruch A.
Life and death decision making / Baruch A. Brody. New York : Oxford University Press, 1988. xii, 250 p. ;
87-023965   174/.24   019505007X
Medical ethics -- Decision making. Life and death, Power over -- Decision making. Medical ethics -- Decision making -- Case studies.

R725.5.C76 2000
Cross-cultural perspectives in medical ethics / edited by Robert M. Veatch. Boston : Jones and Bartlett, c2000. xx, 380 p. ;
99-089318   174/.2   0763713325
Medical ethics -- Cross-cultural studies. Medical ethics.

R725.5.F75 2000
Freedman, Benjamin.
The roles and responsibilities of the ethics consultant : a retrospective analysis of cases / Benjamin Freedman ; edited by Francoise Baylis. Hagerstown, Maryland : University Publishing, 2000. xii, 159 p. ;
00-1270163   1555720587
Medical ethics. Ethics, Medical

R725.5.G67 1991
Gorovitz, Samuel.
Drawing the line : life, death, and ethical choices in an American Hospital / Samuel Gorovitz. New York : Oxford University Press, 1991. xiv, 195 p. ;
90-007089   174/.2   0195044282
Hospital care -- Moral and ethical aspects. Medical ethics.

R725.5.H37 2000
Hardwig, John.
Is there a duty to die? : and other essays in bio-ethics / John Hardwig, with Nat Hentoff ... [et al.]. New York : Routledge, 2000. ix, 212 p. ;
99-013222   174/.24   0415922410
Death -- Moral and ethical aspects. Medical ethics.

R725.5.H44 1999
Hedges, Richard
Bioethics, health care, and the law : a dictionary / Richard Hedges. Santa Barbara, Calif. : ABC-CLIO, c1999. xii, 234 p. ;
99-050382   174/.2/03   0874367611
Medical ethics -- Dictionaries. Bioethics -- Dictionaries. Medical care -- Dictionaries.

R725.5.M465 2000
The medical profession and human rights : handbook for a changing agenda : report of a Working Party / British Medical Association. New York : Zed Books, 2000. p.
00043429   174/.2 21
Physicians -- Professional ethics. Human rights advocacy.

R725.5.P45 1988
Pellegrino, Edmund D.,
For the patient's good : the restoration of beneficence in health care / Edmund D. Pellegrino, David C. Thomasma. New York : Oxford University Press, 1988. xii, 240 p. ;
87-015214   174/.2   0195043197
Medical ethics. Benevolence. Physician and patient.

R725.5.R33 2000
Radest, Howard B.,
From clinic to classroom : medical ethics and moral education / Howard B. Radest. Westport, Conn. : Praeger, 2000. xiii, 199 p.
99-037525   174/.2   027596194X
Medical ethics. Moral education.

R725.5.R83 1998
Rubin, Susan B.,
When doctors say No : the battleground of medical futility / Susan B. Rubin. Bloomington, Ind. : Indiana University Press, 1998. x, 191 p. ;
98-006798   174/.2   0253334632
Medical ethics. Therapeutics -- Decision making -- Moral and ethical aspects. Care of the sick -- Decision making -- Moral and ethical aspects.

R725.5.S58 2001

Slow cures and bad philosophers : essays on Wittgenstein, medicine, and bioethics / edited by Carl Elliott. Durham, NC : Duke University Press, 2001. p. cm.

00-063661   174/.2/01   0822326574

Wittgenstein, Ludwig, -- 1889-1951.   Medical ethics -- Philosophy. Bioethics -- Philosophy.

R725.5.W37 1997
Warren, Mary Anne.

Moral status : obligations to persons and other living things / Mary Anne Warren. Oxford : Clarendon Press ; 1997. 265 p. ;

97-007803   179.7   0198236689

Euthanasia -- Moral and ethical aspects. Abortion -- Moral and ethical aspects. Animal rights.

R725.5.W55 2000
Wildes, Kevin Wm.

Moral acquaintances : methodology in bioethics / Kevin Wm. Wildes. Notre Dame, Ind. : University of Notre Dame Press, c2000. x, 214 p. ;

00-036489   174/.2   0268034508

Medical ethics -- Methodology. Bioethics -- Methodology.

R725.56 Medical ethics. Medical etiquette — Religious aspects — Christian ethics

R725.56.E54 2000
Engelhardt, H. Tristram

The foundations of Christian bioethics / H. Tristram Engelhardt, Jr. Lisse (Netherlands) ; Swets & Zeitlinger, c2000. xxiv, 414 p.

00-033848   174/.2   902651557X

Medical ethics. Christian ethics. Medicine -- Religious aspects -- Christianity.

R725.56.K44 1991
Kelly, David F.

Critical care ethics : treatment decisions in American hospitals / David F. Kelly. Kansas City, MO : Sheed & Ward, c1991. ix, 214 p. :

90-062086   174/.2   155612371X

Medical ethics. Medicine -- Religious aspects -- Catholic church. Catholic hospitals.

R725.56.P45513 1997
Pellegrino, Edmund D.,

Helping and healing : religious commitment in health care / Edmund D. Pellegrino, David C. Thomasma. Washington, DC : Georgetown University Press, c1997. viii, 168 p.

96-046598   174/.2   0878406433

Medical ethics. Christian ethics.

R725.57 Medical ethics. Medical etiquette — Religious aspects — Jewish ethics

R725.57.J45 1999

Jewish and Catholic bioethics : an ecumenical dialogue / edited by Edmund D. Pellegrino and Alan I. Faden. Washington, D.C. : Georgetown University Press, c1999. xviii, 154 p.

99-012407   296.3/642   0878407456

Bioethics -- Religious aspects -- Judaism. Medicine -- Religious aspects -- Judaism. Suffering -- Religiouis aspects -- Judaism.

R726 Medical ethics. Medical etiquette — Prolongation or termination of life-sustaining care. Euthanasia. Assisted suicide

R726.B25 1990
Bailey, Don V.,

The challenge of euthanasia : an annotated bibliography on euthanasia and related subjects / Don V. Bailey. Lanham, Md. : University Press of America, c1990. xvi, 395 p. ;

89-070604   179/.7   0819177113

Euthanasia -- Abstracts. Death -- Abstracts. Euthanasia -- Bibliography.

R726.B288 1994
Barry, Robert Laurence.

Breaking the thread of life : on rational suicide / Robert L. Barry. New Brunswick : Transaction Publishers, c1994. xxii, 353 p.

93-036053   241/.697   1560001429

Suicide -- Moral and ethical aspects. Suicide -- Religious aspects -- Catholic Church. Right to die.

R726.B325 1996
Basta, L.

A graceful exit : life and death on your own terms / Lofty L. Basta with Carole Post. New York : Insight Books, c1996. xviii, 350 p.

96-001283   174/.24   0306452707

Right to die. Terminal care -- Moral and ethical aspects.

R726.B33 1994
Battin, M. Pabst.

The least worst death : essays in bioethics on the end of life / Margaret Pabst Battin. New York : Oxford University Press, c1994. 305 p. :

93-008276   179/.7   0195085922

Terminal care -- Moral and ethical aspects. Right to die. Assisted suicide -- Moral and ethical aspects.

R726.C46 1991

Choosing death : active euthanasia, religion, and the public debate / edited by Ron P. Hamel. Philadelphia : Trinity Press International, c1991. ix, 163 p. ;

91-024448   179/.7   1563380315

Euthanasia -- Moral and ethical aspects. Euthanasia -- Religious aspects. Euthanasia -- Social aspects.

R726.E794 1989
Euthanasia : the moral issues / edited by Robert M. Baird and Stuart E. Rosenbaum. Buffalo, N.Y. : Prometheus Books, 1989. 182 p. ;
89-024042   179/.7   0879755555
Euthanasia. Ethics, Medical. Euthanasia.

R726.F45 1998
Filene, Peter G.
In the arms of others : a cultural history of the right-to-die in America / Peter G. Filene. Chicago : I.R. Dee, 1998. xvii, 282 p.
97-042583   174/.24   1566631882
Death. Euthanasia -- History -- United States.

R726.F69 1999
Fox, Elaine.
Come lovely and soothing death : the right to die movement in the United States / Elaine Fox, Jeffrey J. Kamakahi, Stella M. Capek. New York : Twayne Publishers, c1999. xviii, 216 p.
99-029556   179.7   0805716459
Euthanasia -- Social aspects -- United States. Right to die -- Social aspects -- United States. Right to Die -- United States.

R726.L6 1993
Logue, Barbara.
Last rights : death control and the elderly in America / Barbara J. Logue. New York : Lexington Books ; c1993. xi, 372 p. ;
92-039452   179/.7   0669273708
Life and death, Power over -- Moral and ethical aspects. Frail elderly -- Moral and ethical aspects -- United States -- Death. Frail elderly -- Care -- Moral and ethical aspects -- United States.

R726.M315 1998
Manning, Michael,
Euthanasia and physician-assisted suicide : killing or caring? / by Michael Manning. New York : Paulist Press, c1998. ix, 120 p. ;
98-017655   179.7   0809138042
Euthanasia -- Religious aspects -- Catholic Church. Assisted suicide -- Religious aspects -- Catholic Church. Euthanasia -- Religious aspects.

R726.M355 1999
McKhann, Charles F.
A time to die : the place for physician assistance / Charles F. McKhann. New Haven : Yale University Press, c1999. xi, 268 p. ;
98-022193   179.7   0300076312
Assisted suicide.

R726.R53 1996
Roberts, Carolyn S.,
Euthanasia : a reference handbook / Carolyn S. Roberts, Martha Gorman. Santa Barbara, Calif. : ABC-CLIO, c1996. xix, 348 p. :
96-028833   179/.7   0874368316
Euthanasia.

R726.S336 1999
Scherer, Jennifer M.,
Euthanasia and the right to die : a comparative view / Jennifer M. Scherer and Rita J. Simon. Lanham : Rowman & Littlefield Publishers, c1999. viii, 151 p.
98-041535   179.7   0847691667
Euthanasia -- Cross-cultural studies. Right to die -- Cross-cultural studies.

R726.U39 1999
Ulrich, Lawrence P.
The Patient Self-Determination Act : meeting the challenges in patient care / Lawrence P. Ulrich. Washington, D.C. : Georgetown University Press, c1999. xii, 351 p. ;
99-019307   174/.24   0878407472
Right to die -- United States. Patients -- Legal status, laws, etc. -- United States. Treatment Refusal -- legislation & jurisprudence -- United States.

R726.V4
Veatch, Robert M.
Death, dying, and the biological revolution : our last quest for responsibility / Robert M. Veatch. New Haven : Yale University Press, 1976. ix, 323 p. ;
75-043337   174/.24   0300019491
Terminal care -- Religious aspects. Terminal care -- Moral and ethical aspects. Medical policy -- United States.

R726.W655 1998
Woodman, Sue.
Last rights : the struggle over the right to die / Sue Woodman. New York : Plenum Trade, c1998. 293 p. ;
98-028439   174/.24   0306459957
Right to die. Assisted suicide.

R726.5 Medicine as a disease in relation to psychology — General works

R726.5.C354 1997
Cambridge handbook of psychology, health, and medicine / edited by Andrew Baum ... [et al.]. Cambridge, UK ; Cambridge University Press, 1997. xvii, 660 p.
96-044596   616/.001/9   0521430739
Medicine and psychology. Psychology, Medical -- handbooks. Behavioral Medicine -- handbooks.

R726.5.P63 1999
Pollack, Robert,
The missing moment : how the unconscious shapes modern science / Robert Pollack. Boston : Houghton Mifflin, 1999. x, 240 p. ;
99-026241   610/.1   0395709857
Medicine and psychology. Medicine -- Philosophy.

R726.5.S25 1999
Sallis, James F.
Physical activity & behavioral medicine / James F. Sallis, Neville Owen. Thousand Oaks, Calif. : Sage Publications, c1999. xxvii, 210 p.
98-025362   613/.7   0803959966
Medicine and psychology. Physical fitness -- Physiological aspects. Physical fitness -- Psychological aspects.

R726.5.S66 1998
Spiro, Howard M.
   The power of hope : a doctor's perspective / Howard Spiro. New Haven, CT : Yale University Press, c1998. xi, 288 p. ;
98-018731   610/.1/9   0300074107
   Medicine and psychology. Hope -- Psychological aspects. Placebo (Medicine)

R726.5.S825 1996
   Suffering / [edited by] Betty Rolling Ferrell. Sudbury, Mass. : Jones and Bartlett Publishers, c1996. x, 238 p. :
95-000544   155.9   086720723X
   Sick -- Psychology. Suffering. Pain.

R726.7 Medicine as a disease in relation to psychology — Clinical health psychology

R726.7.H356 1996
   Handbook of diversity issues in health psychology / edited by Pamela M. Kato and Traci Mann. New York : Plenum Press, c1996. xxviii, 439 p
96-032564   610/.8/693   0306453258
   Clinical health psychology. Clinical health psychology -- United States -- Cross-cultural studies. Minorities -- United States -- Health and hygiene.

R726.7.H3645 2001
   Handbook of health psychology / [edited by] Andrew Baum, Tracey A. Revenson, Jerome E. Singer. Mahwah, N.J. : Lawrence Erlbaum Associates, c2001. xx, 961 p. :
00-063628   616/.001/9   0805814957
   Clinical health psychology -- Handbooks, manuals, etc. Medicine and psychology -- Handbooks, manuals, etc. Behavioral Medicine.

R726.7.M55 1999
Miley, William M.,
   The psychology of well being / William M. Miley. Westport, Conn. : Praeger, 1999. xiv, 258 p. :
98-044533   610   027596275X
   Clinical health psychology. Mental health. Health behavior.

R726.8 Medicine as a disease in relation to psychology — Terminal care. Dying

R726.8.B467 1995
Berger, Arthur S.,
   When life ends : legal overviews, medicolegal forms, and hospital policies / Arthur S. Berger ; foreword by Louis Lemberg. Westport, Conn. : Praeger, 1995. xiv, 188 p. ;
94-043173   362.1/75   0275946207
   Terminal care. Terminal care -- Law and legislation -- United States. Terminally ill -- Hospital care.

R726.8.C76 2000
   Crossing over : narratives of palliative care / David Barnard ... [et al.]. Oxford ; Oxford University Press, c2000. xii, 451 p. ;
99-029317   362.1/75   0195123433
   Palliative treatment -- Case studies.

R726.8.D3785 2000
   Death and dying sourcebook : basic consumer health information for the layperson about end-of-life care and related ethical and legal issues ... / edited by Annemarie S. Muth. Detroit, Mich. : Omnigraphics, c2000. xiii, 641 p.
99-044810   362.1/75   0780802306
   Death. Terminal care.

R726.8.F33 1996
   Facing death : where culture, religion, and medicine meet / edited by Howard M. Spiro, Mary G. McCrea Curnen, and Lee Palmer Wandel. New Haven : Yale University Press, c1996. xxii, 212 p.
96-002487   155.9/37   0300063490
   Terminally ill. Death -- Psychological aspects. Death -- Religious aspects.

R726.8.L586 1997
   Living with grief when illness is prolonged / edited by Kenneth J. Doka, with Joyce Davidson. Washington, D.C. : Hospice Foundation of America ; c1997. xii, 220 p. ;
97-006211   155.9/37   1560327030
   Terminal illness -- Psychological aspects. Terminally ill -- Family relationships. Bereavement -- Psychological aspects.

R726.8.P65 2001
Poor, Belinda.
   End of life nursing care / Belinda Poor, Gail P. Poirrier. Boston : Jones and Bartlett, c2001. xvi, 471 p. :
          362.1/75   0763714216
   Terminally ill. Death. Terminal care.

R726.8.P73 2000
Preston, Thomas A.,
   Final victory : taking charge of the last stages of life, facing death on your own terms / Thomas A. Preston. Roseville, CA : Forum, c2000. xx, 252 p. ;
00-061869   362.1/75   0761528997
   Terminally ill. Death. Conduct of life.

R727.3 Medical personnel and the public. Physician and the public — General works

R727.3.A53 2001
   American Medical Association guide to talking to your doctor / American Medical Association ; Angela Perry, medical editor. New York : Wiley, c2001. xi, 244 p. :
          610.69/6   0471414107
   Physician and patient. Interpersonal communication. Patient participation.

R727.3.C63 1989
   Communicating with medical patients / edited by Moira Stewart, Debra Roter. Newbury Park : Sage Publications, c1989. 286 p. :
88-036593   610.69/52   0803932162
   Physician and patient. Interpersonal communication. Confidential communications -- Physicians.

R727.3.E96 2000

Explaining illness : research, theory, and strategies / edited by Bryan B. Whaley. Mahwah, N.J. : Lawrence Erlbaum, c2000. xvi, 360 p. ;
99-032748   610.69/6   0805831118
Physician and patient. Communication in medicine. Interpersonal relations.

R727.3.F53 2002

First, do no harm :power, oppression, and violence in healthcare / Nancy L. Diekelmann, volume editor. Madison, Wis. : University of Wisconsin Press, c2002. p. ;
         610.69/6   029917784X
Medical personnel and patient. Quality of life. Patients--Legal status, laws, etc.

R727.3.G63 1995
Gordon, Thomas,

Making the patient your partner : communication skills for doctors and other caregivers / Thomas Gordon, W. Sterling Edwards. Westport, Conn. : Auburn House, 1995. xix, 213 p. :
94-042698   610.69/6   0865692556
Medical personnel and patient. Interpersonal communication. Communication in medicine.

R727.3.L565 1995
Little, J. M.

Humane medicine / Miles Little. Cambridge, UK ; Cambridge University Press , 1995. xi, 195 p. ;
94-047274   610.69/6   052149513X
Physician and patient. Medicine -- Philosophy. Medical ethics.

R727.3.L68 1997
Lowenstein, Jerome.

The midnight meal and other essays about doctors, patients, and medicine / Jerome Lowenstein. New Haven : Yale University Press, c1997. xv, 128 p. ;
96-026159   610   0300068166
Physician and patient. Medicine -- Philosophy. Physicians -- Attitudes.

R727.4 Medical personnel and the public. Physician and the public — Medical personnel and the patient. Physician and the patient — Patient education and health counseling

R727.4.R43 1999
Redman, Barbara Klug.

Women's health needs in patient education / Barbara K. Redman. New York : Springer Pub. Co., c1999. xv, 171 p. ;
99-027854   615.5/071/082   0826112641
Patient education. Women -- Health and hygiene. Women's Health.

R727.47 Medical personnel and the public. Physician and the public — Medical personnel and the patient's family. Medical personnel-caregiver relationships

R727.47.A24 2000
Abel, Emily K.

Hearts of wisdom : American women caring for kin, 1850-1940 / Emily K. Abel. Cambridge, Mass. : Harvard University Press 2000. ix, 326 p. ;
00-033596   362.1/082/0973   0674003144
Caregivers -- United States -- History -- 19th century. Caregivers -- United States -- History -- 20th century. Medical personnel-caregiver relationships -- United States -- History -- 19th century.

R729.5 Types of medical practice — Special types, A-Z

R729.5.G4.D54 1999
Digby, Anne.

The evolution of British general practice 1850-1948 / Anne Digby. Oxford ; Oxford University Press, 1999. xii, 376 376
98-051327   362.1/0941   0198205139
Physicians (General practice) -- Great Britain -- History -- 19th century. Physicians (General practice) -- Great Britain -- History -- 20th century. Family medicine -- Great Britain -- History -- 19th century.

R729.5.G4H55 1998
Hilfiker, David.

Healing the wounds : a physician looks at his work / David Hilfiker. Omaha, Neb. : Creighton University Press, c1998. xvii, 163 p. ;
         610.69/52   1881871231
Hilfiker, David. Family medicine. Medicine, Rural. Physicians--Psychology.

R730 Quackery

R730.B373 1994
Barrett, Stephen,

The vitamin pushers : how the "health food" industry is selling America a bill of goods / Stephen Barrett, Victor Herbert ; foreword by Gabe Mirkin. Amherst, N.Y. : Prometheus Books, 1994. xii, 536 p. :
94-021714   363.19/2   0879759097
Quacks and quackery -- United States. Natural foods industry -- United States.

R730.M44 2000
McCoy, Bob,

Quack! : tales of medical fraud from the Museum of Questionable Medical Devices / by Bob McCoy. Santa Monica, CA : Santa Monica Press, c2000. 235 p. :
99-059928   610   1891661108
Quacks and quackery -- United States. Consumer protection -- United States.

R730.Y68
Young, James Harvey.
The medical messiahs ; a social history of health quackery in twentieth-century America.   Princeton, N.J., Princeton University Press, 1967. xiv, 460 p.
           615/.856/0973
Quacks and quackery--United States.

R733 Special theories and systems of medicine (General). Alternative medicine. Holistic medicine

R733.A24513 2000
Abgrall, Jean-Marie.
Healing or stealing : medical charlatans in the new age / by Jean-Marie Abgrall. New York : Algora Pub., 2000. p. ;
00-011923   615.8/56   1892941511
Alternative medicine. Quacks and quackery. Alternative Medicine.

R733.A56 2001
Anderson, Robert A.
Clinician's guide to holistic medicine / Robert A. Anderson. New York : McGraw-Hill, Medical Pub. Division, c2001. xiii, 421 p. ;
           615.5   0071347143
Holistic medicine. Alternative medicine. Holistic Health.

R733.B255 1999
Ballentine, Rudolph,
Radical healing : integrating the world's great therapy traditions to create a new transformative medicine / by Rudolph M. Ballentine. New York : Harmony Books, c1999. p. cm.
98-028802   615.5   0609601377
Holistic medicine.

R733.C65 1996
Collinge, William.
The American Holistic Health Association Complete guide to alternative medicine / William Collinge ; introduction by Len Duhl. New York, N.Y. : Warner Books, 1996. xxi, 361 p. ;
95-010201   615.5   0446672580
Alternative medicine.

R733.C656 1997
Complementary therapies in rehabilitation : holistic approaches for prevention and wellness / edited by Carol M. Davis. Thorofare, NJ : Slack Inc., c1997. xlv, 296 p. :
96-044699   615.5   1556422814
Alternative medicine. Rehabilitation. Rehabilitation -- methods.

R733.C66 2001
Rees, Alan M.
The complementary and alternative medicine information source book / Alan M. Rees. [Phoenix, Ariz.] : Oryx Press, 2000. p. ;
00-012830   615.5   1573563889
Alternative medicine -- Popular works. Alternative Medicine -- Popular Works. Alternative Medicine -- Resource Guides.

R733.D38 1998
Davis-Floyd, Robbie.
From doctor to healer : the transformative journey / Robbie Davis-Floyd and Gloria St. John. New Brunswick, NJ : Rutgers University Press, c1998. xi, 308 p. ;
97-039343   610/.1   0813525195
Holistic medicine -- Social aspects. Medicine -- Philosophy.

R733.D59D59 1999
Directory of schools for alternative and complementary health care / edited by Karen Rappaport. 2nd ed. Phoenix, Ariz. : Oryx Press, 1999. xix, 330 p. ;
           615.5/071/173   1573562947
Alternative medicine--Study and teaching--United States-- Directories. Alternative medicine--Study and teaching--Canada-- Directories.

R733.D59 1998
Directory of schools for alternative and complementary health care / edited by Karen Rappaport ; [foreword by Andrew Weil]. Phoenix, Ariz. : Oryx Press, 1998. xxi, 250 p. ;
97-042687   610   157356110X
Alternative medicine -- Study and teaching -- United States -- Directories. Alternative medicine -- Study and teaching -- Canada -- Directories. Alternative Medicine -- education -- United States -- directories.

R733.E525 1999
Encyclopedia of complementary health practice / Carolyn Chambers Clark, editor in chief ; Rena J. Gordon, contributing editor ; Barbara Harris, Carl O. Helvie, advisory contributing editors. New York : Springer Pub. Co., c1999. xxi, 638 p. :
99-025832   615.5/03   0826112390
Alternative medicine -- Encyclopedias. Alternative Medicine -- Encyclopedias -- English.

R733.F48 1997
Feuerman, Francine.
Alternative medicine resource guide / Francine Feuerman and Marsha J. Handel. Lanham, Md. : Medical Library Ass., 1997. p. cm.
96-049534   615.5   0810832844
Alternative medicine -- Information resources. Alternative medicine -- Bibliography.

R733.F79 1992
Frohock, Fred M.
Healing powers : alternative medicine, spiritual communities, and the state / Fred M. Frohock. Chicago : University of Chicago Press, c1992. x, 340 p. ;
91-036941   362.1/042   0226265846
Alternative medicine. Alternative medicine -- Social aspects. Medicine, State.

R733.G34 2001
The Gale encyclopedia of alternative medicine / Kristine Krapp and Jacqueline L. Longe, editors. Detroit : Gale Group, c2001. 4 v. :
           615.5/03   078765003X
Alternative medicine--Encyclopedias.

R733.G35 1997
Galland, Leo.
 The four pillars of healing : how the new integrated medicine-- the best of conventional and alternative approaches-- can cure you / Leo Galland. New York : Random House, c1997. xix, 330 p. ;
96-049729　　　　　610　　　　0679448888
 Holistic medicine. Medicine -- Philosophy.

R733.G724 1999
Graham, Helen,
 Complementary therapies in context : the psychology of healing / Helen Graham. London ; Jessica Kingsley Publishers, c1999. 350 p. :
00-500801　　　　　615.5　　　1853026409
 Alternative medicine. Psychiatry. Healing.

R733.I57 2001
 Integrating complementary medicine into health systems / edited by Nancy Faass. Gaithersburg, Md. : Aspen Publishers, 2001. xliii, 763 p. :
　　　　　　362.1　　　0834212161
 Alternative medicine. Integrated delivery of health care. Alternative Medicine--organization & administration.

R733.K54 2000
Kilham, Christopher.
 Tales from the medicine trail :tracking down the health secrets of shamans, herbalists, mystics, yogis, and other healers / Chris Kilham. [Emmaus, Pa.] : Rodale, c2000. xi, 292 p. :
　　　　　615.88　　　1579541852
 Alternative medicine. Healers. Shamans.

R733.M38 1998
Marti, James.
 The alternative health & medicine encyclopedia./ James Marti with Andrea Hine ; foreword by Dr. Michael T. Murray. 2nd ed. Detroit, MI. : Gale Research, c1998. xxiii, 462 p. ;
　　　　　615.5/3/03　　　0787600733
 Alternative medicine--Encyclopedias.

R733.M535 2001
Milburn, Michael Peter.
 The future of healing :exploring the parallels of Eastern and Western medicine / by Michael Peter Milburn. Freedom, Calif. : Crossing Press, c2001. p. cm.
　　　　　610　　　1580910653
 Holistic medicine. Medicine, Chinese.

R733.N87 2003
 Nurse's handbook of alternative & complementary therapies. 2nd ed. Springhouse, PA : Lippincott Williams & Wilkins, c2003. p. ;
　　　　　615.5　　　1582551669
 Alternative medicine--Handbooks, manuals, etc. Nursing--Handbooks, manuals, etc. Holistic nursing--Handbooks, manuals, etc.

R733.R4 1993
 Reader's guide to alternative health methods / John F. Zwicky ... [et al.]. Chicago, Ill. : American Medical Association, c1993. x, 348 p. ;
92-031144　　　　615.5　　　0899705251
 Alternative medicine -- Evaluation. Alternative medicine -- Bibliography.

R733.S56 1992
Sinclair, Brett Jason.
 Alternative health care resources : a directory and guide / Brett Jason Sinclair ; foreword by Marshall Mandell. West Nyack, N.Y. : Parker Pub. Co., c1992. xii, 498 p. :
92-028096　　　362.1/025/73　　　0131565222
 Alternative medicine -- United States -- Directories. Alternative medicine -- Information services -- United States -- Directories.

R733.T755 2001
Trivieri, Larry,
 The American Holistic Medical Association guide to holistic health : he American Holistic Medical Association ; foreword by Robert S. Ivker. New York : J. Wiley, c2001. ix, 438 p. ;
　　　　　615.5　　　0471327433
 Holistic medicine. Alternative medicine. Alternative Medicine.

R735.A4 Medical education. Medical schools — Directories

R735.A4.D68 1999
Doughty, Harold.
 The Penguin guide to American medical and dental schools / Harold R. Doughty. New York, N.Y. : Penguin Books, 1999. 312 p. :
98-045438　　　610/.71/173　　　0140275150
 Medical colleges -- United States -- Directories.

R735.B66 Medical education. Medical schools — General works

R735.B66 1995
Bonner, Thomas Neville.
 Becoming a physician : medical education in Britain, France, Germany, and the United States, 1750-1945 / Thomas Neville Bonner. New York : Oxford University Press, 1995. xii, 412 p. ;
94-042800　　　610/.71/1　　　0195062981
 Medical education -- History.

R737 Medical education. Medical schools — General special

R737.H78 1991
Hunter, Kathryn Montgomery,
 Doctors' stories : the narrative structure of medical knowledge / Kathryn Montgomery Hunter. Princeton, N.J. : Princeton University Press, c1991. xxiii, 205 p.
90-009072　　　610/.1　　　0691068887
 Communication in medicine. Physician and patient.

R737.I54 1994

International handbook of medical education / edited by Abdul W. Sajid ... [et al.] ; foreword by George E. Miller. Westport, Conn. : Greenwood Press, 1994. xvii, 519 p.
93-037854   610/.71/1   0313284237
Medical education policy -- Handbooks, manuals, etc. Medical education -- Handbooks, manuals, etc. Education, Medical.

R737.U55 2000

Understanding cultural diversity : culture, curriculum, and community in nursing / [edited by] Mary Lebreck Kelley, Virginia Macken Fitzsimons. Sudbury, Mass. : Jones and Bartlett, c2000. xvii, 352 p.
99-029470   610/.71/1   0763711063
Medical education -- Philosophy. Medical personnel -- Study and teaching. Interdisciplinary approach in education.

R745-749 Medical education. Medical schools — By region or country — North America

R745.F57 1972
Flexner, Abraham,

Medical education in the United States and Canada; a report to the Carnegie Foundation for the Advancement of Teaching. New York, Arno Press, 1972 [c1910] xvii, 346 p.
78-180575   610/.7/117   0405039522
Medical education -- United States. Medical education -- Canada.

R745.L843 1999
Ludmerer, Kenneth M.

Time to heal : American medical education from the turn of the century to the era of managed care / Kenneth M. Ludmerer. Oxford ; Oxford University Press, 1999. xxvi, 514 p.
98-055496   610/.71/1730904   0195118375
Medical education -- United States -- History -- 20th century. Education, Medical -- history -- United States. History of Medicine, 20th Cent. -- United States.

R747.H23.R64 1998
Rogers, Naomi,

An alternative path : the making and remaking of Hahnemann Medical College and Hospital of Philadelphia / Naomi Rogers. New Brunswick, N.J. : Rutgers University Press, c1998. xi, 348 p. :
97-043595   615.5/32/071174811
0813525357
Medical colleges -- Pennsylvania -- Philadelphia -- History. Homeopathy -- Study and teaching -- Pennsylvania -- Philadelphia -- History.

R749.M42.H36 1996
Hanaway, Joseph,

McGill Medicine / Joseph Hanaway, Richard Cruess. Montreal ; McGill-Queen's University Press, c1996- v. 1 :
97-114151   610/.71/171428   0773513248

R834 Medical education. Medical schools — Teaching techniques — General works

R834.H3
Hammond, Kenneth R.

Teaching comprehensive medical care; a psychological study of a change in medical education [by] Kenneth R. Hammond and Fred Kern, Jr. [with] Wayman J. Crow [and others] Cambridge, Published for the Commonwealth Fund by Harvard U 1959. xxii, 642 p.
59-011518   610.7
Medical care. Medical education.

R836 Medical education. Medical schools — Teaching techniques — Medical illustration

R836.M3
McLarty, Margaret C.

Illustrating medicine and surgery. With a foreword by Robert Macintosh. Baltimore, Williams and Wilkins Co., 1960. 158 p.
61004124   616.084
Medical illustration.

R836.R63 1990
Roberts, K. B.

The fabric of the body : European traditions of anatomical illustrations / K.B. Roberts and J.D.W. Tomlinson. Oxford ; Clarendon Press, c1992. xx, 638 p. :
90-007650   611/.0022/2   0192611984
Medical illustration -- History.

R850 Research. Experimentation — General works

R850.C5 1959

Ciba Foundation Tenth Anniversary Symposium on Significant Trends in Medical Research. Editors for the Ciba Foundation: G. E. W. Wolstenholme, Cecilia M. O'Connor [and] Maeve O'Connor. Boston, Little, Brown [1960,c1959] xii, 356 p.
60010637   610.72
Medicine -- Research -- Congresses.

R850.W45 1991
Weisse, Allen B.

Medical odysseys : the different and sometimes unexpected pathways to twentieth-century medical discoveries / Allen B. Weisse. New Brunswick, N.J. : Rutgers University Press, c1991. viii, 250 p.
90-008387   610/.9   0813516161
Medical innovations -- History. Medicine -- Research -- History. History of Medicine.

R852 Research. Experimentation — General special

R852.S32 1993
Schaffner, Kenneth F.
Discovery and explanation in biology and medicine / Kenneth F. Schaffner. Chicago : University of Chicago Press, 1993. xxvi, 617 p.
93-021826   610/.72   0226735915
Medicine -- Research -- Philosophy. Biology -- Research -- Philosophy.

R853 Research. Experimentation — Special topics, A-Z

R853.A53.G76 1997
Groves, Julian McAllister.
Hearts and minds : the controversy over laboratory animals / Julian McAllister Groves. Philadelphia : Temple University Press, 1997. viii, 230 p.
96-007619   174/.28   1566394759
Animal experimentation -- Moral and ethical aspects. Animal experimentation -- Social aspects. Animal rights.

R853.H8.E87 1996
Evans, Donald,
A decent proposal : ethical review of clinical research / Donald Evans and Martyn Evans. New York, N.Y. : Wiley, 1996. xii, 218 p. :
95-046949   174/.28   0471963348
Human experimentation in medicine -- Moral and ethical aspects. Peer review of research grant proposals. Research -- Moral and ethical aspects.

R853.H8.H67 1998
Hornblum, Allen M.
Acres of skin : human experiments at Holmesburg Prison : a story of abuse and exploitation in the name of medical science / Allen M. Hornblum. New York : Routledge, 1998. xxii, 297 p.
97-041755   174/.28   0415919908
Human experimentation in medicine -- Pennsylvania -- Philadelphia. Prisoners -- Medical care -- Pennsylvania -- Philadelphia. Convict labor -- Pennsylvania -- Philadelphia.

R853.H8.M66 1999
Moreno, Jonathan D.
Undue risk : secret state experiments on humans from the Second World War to Iraq and beyond / by Jonathan D. Moreno. New York : W.H. Freeman, 1999. p. cm.
99-016928   174/.28   0716731428
Human experimentation in medicine -- United States. Medical ethics -- United States.

R853.H8.T87 2000
Tuskegee's truths : rethinking the Tuskegee syphilis study / edited by Susan M. Reverby ; [foreword by James H. Jones]. Chapel Hill, NC : University of North Carolina Press, c2000. xviii, 630 p.
99-056379   174/.28/0976149   0807825395
Tuskegee Syphilis Study.   Human experimentation in medicine -- Alabama -- Macon County -- History. Afro-American men -- Diseases -- Alabama -- Macon County -- History. Syphilis -- Research -- Alabama -- Macon County -- History.

R853.H8.W66 1994
Women and health research : ethical and legal issues of including women in clinical studies / Anna C. Mastroianni, Ruth Faden, and Daniel Federman, editors ; Committee on the Ethical and Legal Issues Relating to the Inclusion of Women in Clinical Studies, Division of Health Sciences Policy, Institute of Medicine. Washington, D.C. : National Academy Press, 1994.. 2 v. :
93-050549   174/.28   030904992X
Human experimentation in medicine -- Moral and ethical aspects. Human experimentation in medicine -- Law and legislation. Women -- Health and hygiene -- Research -- Moral and ethical aspects.

R853.M3.F67 1996
Fractal geometry in biological systems : an analytical approach / edited by Philip M. Iannaccone and Mustafa Khokha. Boca Raton, FL : CRC Press, c1996. 360 p. :
96-013895   574/.01/51474   084937636X
Medicine -- Mathematics. Biomathematics. Fractals.

R853.M3.W38 1996
Wavelets in medicine and biology / edited by Akram Aldroubi, Michael Unser. Boca Raton : CRC Press, c1996. 616 p. :
95-046327   610/.28   084939483X
Wavelets (Mathematics) Signal processing. Diagnostic imaging.

R853.R46.B76 1999
Brown, Sarah Jo
Knowledge for health care practice : a guide to using research evidence / Sarah Jo Brown. Philadelphia : W.B. Saunders, c1999. xiv, 256 p. :
98-027551   610/.72   0721678033
Evidence-based medicine -- Handbooks, manuals, etc. Medicine -- Research -- Evaluation -- Handbooks, manuals, etc. Medical care -- Decision making -- Handbooks, manuals, etc.

R853.S7.I59 1995
Forthofer, Ron N.,
Introduction to biostatistics : a guide to design, analysis, and discovery / Ronald N. Forthofer, Eun Sul Lee. San Diego : Academic Press, c1995. xviii, 567 p.
94-024912   574/.01/5195   0122622707
Medicine -- Research -- Statistical methods. Biometry.

R855.5 Medical technology — By region or country, A-Z

R855.5.U6.E44 1992
Emerging issues in biomedical policy / edited by Robert H. Blank, Andrea L. Bonnicksen. New York : Columbia University Press, c1992- v. ;
91040654   362.1/0973   0231074107
Medical policy -- United States. Delivery of Health Care -- United States. Genetic Engineering -- trends -- United States.

R856.A5 Biomedical engineering. Electronics. Instrumentation — History

R856.A5.D38
Davis, Audrey B.
Medicine and its technology : an introduction to the history of medical instrumentation / Audrey B. Davis. Westport, Conn. : Greenwood Press, 1981. xiv, 285 p. :
80-025202   610/.28   0313228078
Medical instruments and apparatus -- History. Medical technology -- History. Equipment and supplies -- History.

R856.I47-P76 Biomedical engineering. Electronics. Instrumentation — General works

R856.I47 2000
Introduction to biomedical engineering / [editors] John D. Enderle, Susan M. Blanchard, Joseph D. Bronzino. San Diego : Academic Press, c2000. xvii, 1062 p. :
          610/.28   0122386604
Biomedical engineering.

R856.M376 1998
Medical instrumentation :application and design / John G. Webster, editor ; contributing authors, John W. Clark, Jr. ... [et al.]. 3rd ed. New York : Wiley, c1998. xix, 691 p. :
          610/.28   0471153680
Medical instruments and apparatus. Physiological apparatus. Equipment and Supplies.

R856.P76 1993
Profio, A. Edward,
Biomedical engineering / A. Edward Profio. New York : Wiley, c1993. xii, 280 p. :
92-027830   610/.28   0471577685
Biomedical engineering.

R857 Biomedical engineering. Electronics. Instrumentation — Other special topics, A-Z

R857.B54.E35 1996
Eggins, Brian R.
Biosensors : an introduction / Brian R. Eggins. Chichester ; Wiley-Teubner, c1996. xi, 212 p. :
95-040660   681/.2   0471962856
Biosensors.

R857.M3.C64 1990
Concise encyclopedia of medical & dental materials / editor, David Williams ; executive editor, Robert W. Cahn ; senior advisory editor, Michael B. Bever. Oxford, England ; Pergamon Press ; 1990. xx, 412 p. :
90-007505   610/.28   0080361943
Biomedical materials -- Encyclopedias. Dental materials -- Encyclopedias. Biocompatible Materials -- encyclopedias.

R858 Computer applications to medicine. Medical informatics

R858.F87 1995
Future health / edited by Clifford A. Pickover. New York : St. Martin's Press, 1995. xxii, 184 p.
95-024987   610/.285   0312126026
Medicine -- Data processing -- Technological innovations. Medicine -- Data processing -- Forecasting.

R858.H35 2001
Health information :management of a strategic resource / managing editor, Mervat Abdelhak ; editors, Sara Grostick, Mary Alice Hanken, Ellen Jacobs. 2nd ed. Philadelphia : W.B. Saunders, c2001. xxiv, 847 p. :
          362.1/068/4   0721686478
Medical informatics. Information resources management.

R858.S556 1997
Slack, Warner V.,
Cybermedicine : how computing empowers doctors and patients for better health care / Warner V. Slack. ; foreword by Ralph Nader. San Francisco : Jossey-Bass Publishers, c1997. xvii, 214 p.
97-003821   610/.285   0787903434
Medical informatics. Physician and patient. Computers.

R858.W65 1993
World databases in medicine / edited by C.J. Armstrong. London ; Bowker Saur, c1993. 2 v. (x, 1646
93-024073   025.06/61   0862916135
Medical informatics -- Directories. Medicine -- Information services -- Directories. Databases -- Directories.

R859.7 Computer applications to medicinie. Medical informatics — Special topics, A-Z

R859.7.A78.H84 2000
Hudson, D. L.
   Neural networks and artificial intelligence for biomedical engineering / Donna L. Hudson, Maurice E. Cohen. New York : Institute of Electrical and Electronics Engineer c2000. xxiii, 306 p.
99-030757   610/.285/63   0780334043
   Artificial intelligence -- Medical applications. Neural networks (Computer science) Expert systems (Computer science)

R859.7.D36.G75 1999
Griffin, Attrices Dean.
   Directory of Internet sources for health professionals / Attrices Dean Griffin. Albany, N.Y. : Delmar Publishers, c1999. xxxiv, 437 p.
98-030169   025.06/61   0766804852
   Medicine -- Computer network resources -- Directories. Internet (Computer network) -- Directories. Computer Communication Networks -- directories.

R859.7.D36.S54 2002
Smith, Roger P.
   The Internet for physicians :with 93 illustrations / Roger P. Smith. 3rd ed. New York : Springer, c2002. xi, 288 p. :
                    004.67/8/02461   0387953124
   Medicine--Computer network resources. Internet. Internet.

R859.7.E43
   The internet and health communication : experiences and expectations / Ronald E. Rice, James E. Katz, editors. Thousand Oaks, Calif. : Sage Publications, c2001. xvi, 459 p. :
00-010038   025.06/3621   0761922326
   Health -- Computer network resources. Internet. Medical telematics.

RA Public Aspects of Medicine

RA7.5 Medicine and the state — Directories of sanitary authorities, boards of health, etc. — United States

RA7.5.N37
National health directory. [Washington, Science and Health Publications] v.
77-647206   353.008/41/02573
Public health administration -- United States -- Directories. Government Agencies -- United States -- directories Public Health Administration -- United States -- directories

RA8 Medicine and the state — World Health Organization — Official publications

RA8.A265
The world health report :report of the Director-General. Geneva : World Health Organization, 1995- v. :
          614.4/05
World health--Periodicals. World health--Statistics--Periodicals. Communicable Disease Control--Periodicals.

RA11 Medicine and the state — Government health agencies (General) — By region or country

RA11.D6.H37 1986
Harden, Victoria Angela.
Inventing the NIH : federal biomedical research policy, 1887-1937 / Victoria A. Harden. Baltimore, Md. : Johns Hopkins University Press, c1986. xiii, 274 p.
85-024070   353.0084   0801830710
Medicine -- Research -- Government policy -- United States -- History. Public health -- Research -- Government policy -- United States -- History. Federal aid to medical research -- United States -- History.

RA390 Medicine and the state — Medical missions. Medical assistance

RA390.U5.D583
Dooley, Thomas A.
Dr. Tom Dooley's three great books: Deliver us from evil, The edge of tomorrow [and] The night they burned the mountain. New York, Farrar, Straus & Cudahy [1960] 383 p.
60-051236   926.1
Missions, Medical -- Laos. Refugees -- Vietnam. Laos -- Description and travel.

RA393 Medicine and the state — General works

RA393.B48 1991
Biomedical politics / Kathi E. Hanna, editor ; Division of Health Sciences Policy, Committee to Study Biomedical Decision Making, Institute of Medicine. Washington, D.C. : National Academy Press, 1991. viii, 352 p.
91-018394   362.1   0309044863
Medical policy -- Case studies. Health planning -- Case studies. Decision Making.

RA393.I58 1988
The International handbook of health-care systems / edited by Richard B. Saltman. New York : Greenwood Press, 1988. vi, 403 p. :
87-017797   362.1   0313241112
Medical care. Social medicine. Medical policy.

RA393.L328 1997
Lassey, Marie L.
Health care systems around the world :characteristics, issues, reforms / Marie L. Lassey, William R. Lassey, Martin J. Jinks. Upper Saddle River, N.J. : Prentice Hall, c1997. xiii, 370 p. :
          362.1   0131042335
Medical policy--Cross-cultural studies. Medical care--Cross-cultural studies.

RA393.R593 1991
Roemer, Milton Irwin,
National health systems of the world / Milton I. Roemer. New York : Oxford University Press, 1991-1993. 2 v. ;
90-007336   362.1   0195053206
Medical policy. Medical care. Public health.

RA394 Medicine and the state — General special

RA394.H4
Health care in big cities / edited by Leslie H. W. Paine. New York : St. Martin's Press, 1978. 368 p. ;
78-007783   362.1/09173/2   0312365233
Health services administration. Medical care. Metropolitan areas.

RA395 Medicine and the state — By region or country

RA395.A3.A523 2000
American health care : government, market processes, and the public interest / edited by Roger D. Feldman ; foreword by Mark V. Pauly. New Brunswick, N.J. : Transaction Publishers, 2000. xi, 444 p. :
00-020662   362.1/0973   1560004304
Medical policy -- United States. Medical economics -- United States.

RA395.A3.F337 1999
Falk, Gerhard,
   Hippocrates assailed : the American health delivery system / Gerhard Falk. Lanham, Md. : University Press of America, c1999. xiii, 380 p.
99-030669   362.1/0973   0761814337
   Medicine -- United States. Medical care -- United States. Medicine -- United States -- History -- 20th century.

RA395.A3G54 1997
Glied, Sherry.
   Chronic condition :why health reform fails / Sherry Glied. Cambridge, Mass. : Harvard Unviersity Press, 1997. xiii, 279 p. :
              362.1/0973   0674128931
   Health care reform--Political aspects--United States. Health care reform--Economic aspects--United States.

RA395.A3.H4135 1997
   Health care policy in contemporary America / edited by Alan I. Marcus and Hamilton Cravens. University Park : Pennsylvania State University Press, c1997. viii, 156 p.
97-013457   362.1/0973   0271017406
   Medical policy -- United States.

RA395.A3.H44 1998
Heirich, Max.
   Rethinking health care : innovation and change in America / Max Heirich. Boulder, Colo. : Westview Press, c1998. xi, 452 p. ;
97-042611   362.1/0973   0813334543
   Medical care -- United States. Medical policy -- United States. Health care reform -- United States.

RA395.A3.H685 1992
   How to resolve the health care crisis : affordable protection for all Americans / the editors of Consumer reports. Yonkers, N.Y. : Consumer Reports Books, c1992. xii, 270 p. :
92-082813   368.3/82/00973   0890436266
   Insurance, Health -- United States. Medical care, Cost of -- United States. Consumer education.

RA395.A3I5557 2001
   Crossing the quality chasm :a new health system for the 21st century / Committee on Quality Health Care in America, Institute of Medicine. Washington, D.C. : National Academy Press, c2001. xx, 337 p. :
              362.1/0973   0309072808
   Medical care--United States. Health care reform--United States. Medical care--United States--Quality control.

RA395.A3.K35 1993
Kaplan, Robert M.
   The Hippocratic predicament : affordability, access, and accountability in American medicine / Robert M. Kaplan. San Diego : Academic Press, c1993. x, 275 p. :
92-011085   362.1/0973   0123973708
   Medical care -- United States. Medical care, Cost of -- United States. Medical policy -- United States.

RA395.A3.K757 1997
Kronenfeld, Jennie J.
   The changing federal role in U.S. health care policy / Jennie Jacobs Kronenfeld. Westport, Conn. : Praeger, 1997. vii, 187 p. :
97-019036   362.1/0973   0275950247
   Medical policy -- United States. Medical care -- United States. Medical care -- Law and legislation -- United States.

RA395.A3.L339 1996
Laham, Nicholas.
   A lost cause : Bill Clinton's campaign for national health insurance / Nicholas Laham. Westport, Conn. : Praeger, 1996. xiv, 251 p. ;
96-002197   368.4/2/00973   0275956113
   National health insurance -- United States. National health insurance -- Law and legislation -- United States. Health care reform -- United States.

RA395.A3.M46 1990
Menzel, Paul T.,
   Strong medicine : the ethical rationing of health care / Paul T. Menzel. New York : Oxford University Press, 1990. xv, 234 p. ;
89-016007   174/.2   0195057104
   Health planning -- Moral and ethical aspects -- United States. Medical economics -- Moral and ethical aspects. Health care rationing -- United States.

RA395.A3.N47 2001
   The new politics of state health care policy / edited by Robert B. Hackey and David A. Rochefort. Lawrence : University Press of Kansas, 2001. p. cm.
01-017546   362.1/0973   0700610847
   Medical policy -- United States -- States. Medical care -- United States -- States.

RA395.A3.O28 1999
O'Brien, Lawrence J.
   Bad medicine : how the American medical establishment is ruining our healthcare system / Lawrence J. O'Brien. Amherst, N.Y. : Prometheus Books, c1999. 283 p. ;
98-048718   362.1/0973   1573922609
   Medical care -- United States. Medical economics -- United States. Health care reform -- United States.

RA395.A3.R685 2000
Rovner, Julie.
   Health care policy and politics A to Z / Julie Rovner. Washington, DC : CQ Press, c2000. xii, 244 p. :
99-040972   362.1/0973   1568024371
   Medical policy -- United States. Medical care -- Political aspects -- United States. Public health -- Political aspects -- United States.

RA395.A3.W445 1997
Weiss, Lawrence David.
   Private medicine and public health : profit, politics, and prejudice in the American health care enterprise / Lawrence D. Weiss. Boulder, Colo. : Westview Press, 1997. xx, 220 p. ;
96-040916   362.1/0973   0813333504
   Medical policy -- United States. Medical economics -- United States.

RA395.A3.W45 1996
Weissert, Carol S.
Governing health : the politics of health policy / Carol S. Weissert and William G. Weissert. Baltimore, MD : Johns Hopkins University Press, c1996. vii, 361 p. ;
95-044487   362.1/0973   080185265X
Medical policy -- United States.

RA395.C3.C37 1992
Canadian health care and the state : a century of evolution / edited by C. David Naylor. Montreal : McGill-Queen's University Press, c1992. vi, 241 p. ;
93-189402   362.1/0971   0773509348
Medical care -- Canada -- History -- 20th century. Medical policy -- Canada -- History -- 20th century. Insurance, Health -- Canada -- History.

RA395.D44.G74 1992
Green, Andrew,
An introduction to health planning in developing countries / Andrew Green. Oxford [England] ; Oxford University Press, 1992. xvi, 351 p. :
92-018729   362.1/09172/4   019262301X
Health planning -- Developing countries. Medicine, State -- Developing countries. Health Planning -- organization & administration. Developing Countries.

RA395.G6.F68 1986
Fox, Daniel M.
Health policies, health politics : the British and American experience, 1911-1965 / Daniel M. Fox. Princeton, N.J. : Princeton University Press, c1986. xi, 234 p. ;
85-043279   362.1/0941   0691047332
Medical policy -- Great Britain -- History -- 20th century. Medical policy -- Political aspects -- Great Britain -- History -- 20th century. Medical policy -- United States -- History -- 20th century.

RA401 Medicine and the state — Pharmaceutical policy

RA401.A3.M55 2000
Miller, Henry I.
To America's health : a proposal to reform the Food and Drug Administration / Henry I. Miller. Stanford, Calif. : Hoover Institution Press, 2000. p. cm.
00-031937   353.9/98/0973   0817999027
Pharmaceutical policy -- United States. Drugs -- Law and legislation -- United States. Pharmaceutical industry -- United States.

RA401.A3.S93 1992
Szasz, Thomas Stephen,
Our right to drugs : the case for a free market / Thomas Szasz. New York : Praeger, 1992. xvii, 199 p.
91-030378   362.29   0275942163
Pharmaceutical policy -- United States. Narcotics, Control of -- Moral and ethical aspects. Narcotics, Control of -- United States.

RA407 Medicine and the state — Health status indicators. Medical statistics and surveys

RA407.P65 2001
Pol, Louis G.
The demography of health and health care / Louis G. Pol and Richard K. Thomas. 2nd ed. New York : Kluwer Academic/Plenum Publishers, c2001. xiv, 374 p. :
362.1/042   0306463377
Medical statistics. Demography. Social medicine.

RA407.3 Medicine and the state — Health status indicators. Medical statistics and surveys — By region or country

RA407.3.H423
Health care state rankings. Lawrence, KS : Morgan Quitno Corp., c1993- v. ;
93-648785   362.1/0973
Health status indicators -- United States -- States -- Periodicals. Medical care -- United States -- States -- Statistics -- Periodicals. Delivery of Health Care -- United States -- statistics. United States -- Statistics, Medical -- Periodicals.

RA407.3.S732
Statistical record of health & medicine. Detroit, MI : Gale Research Inc., c1995- v. ;
95-643957   362.1/0973/021
Medical care -- United States -- Statistics -- Periodicals. Public health -- United States -- Statistics -- Periodicals. Delivery of Health Care -- statistics. United States -- Statistics, Medical -- Periodicals.

RA408 Medicine and the state — Health status indicators. Medical statistics and surveys — Special groups, A-Z

RA408.A3.N37 1988
National Research Council (U.S.).
The aging population in the twenty-first century : statistics for health policy / Dorothy M. Gilford, editor ; Panel on Statistics for an Aging Population, Committee on National Sciences and Education, National Research Council. Washington, D.C. : National Academy Press, 1988. xv, 323 p. :
88-015151   362.1/9897/00973021   0309038812
Aged -- Diseases -- United States -- Statistics. Aged -- Medical care -- United States -- Statistics. Aged -- Diseases -- United States -- Forecasting.

RA408.I49.Y68 1994
Young, T. Kue.
The health of Native Americans : toward a biocultural epidemiology / T. Kue Young. New York : Oxford University Press, 1994. ix, 275 p. :
93-020705   614.4/2/08997   0195073398
Indians of North America -- Health and hygiene -- Statistics. Indians of North America -- Health and hygiene -- Social aspects. Indians, North American -- United States.

RA408.5 Medicine and the state — Health status indicators. Medical statistics and surveys — Health survey methods

RA408.5.M43 1992

Measuring functioning and well-being : the medical outcomes study approach / Anita L. Stewart & John E. Ware, Jr., editors ; with a foreword by Alvin R. Tarlov. Durham : Duke University Press, 1992. xxiii, 449 p.
91-034579　　　　362.1/021　　　　0822312123
Health surveys -- Statistical methods. Medical care -- Evaluation. Health status indicators.

RA409 Medicine and the state — Health status indicators. Medical statistics and surveys — Statistical methods

RA409.E53 1998

Encyclopedia of biostatistics / editors-in-chief, Peter Armitage, Theodore Colton. Chichester ; J. Wiley, c1998. 6 v. (lxii, 4
98-010160　　　　610/.2/1　　　　0471975761
Medical statistics -- Encyclopedias. Biometry -- Encyclopedias.

RA409.L33 2000
Lachin, John M.,

Biostatistical methods :the assessment of relative risks / John M. Lachin. New York : Wiley, 2000. xvii, 529 p. ;
　　　　　610/.7/27　　　　0471369969
Medical statistics. Health risk assessment--Statistical methods. Medicine--Research--Statistical methods.

RA409.L357 1997
Lang, Thomas A.

How to report statistics in medicine : annotated guidelines for authors, editors, and reviewers / Thomas A. Lang, Michelle Secic ; with a foreword by Edward J. Huth. Philadelphia, Pa. : American College of Physicians, c1997. xxv, 367 p. :
96-030333　　　　610/.72　　　　0943126444
Medical statistics. Medical writing.

RA410.5-410.53 Medicine and the state — Medical economics. Economics of medical care

RA410.5.U23 1999
Ubel, Peter A.

Pricing life : why it's time for health care rationing / Peter A. Ubel. Cambridge, MA : MIT Press, 1999. xix, 208 p. ;
99-020664　　　　362.1　　　　0262210169
Health care rationing. Medical care -- Cost effectiveness.

RA410.5.V344 1995

Valuing health care : costs, benefits, and effectiveness of pharmaceuticals and other medical technologies / edited by Frank A. Sloan. Cambridge ; Cambridge University Press, 1995. xi, 273 p. :
94-009554　　　　338.4/33621　　　　052147020X
Medical care -- Cost effectiveness -- Research -- Methodology. Drugs -- Cost effectiveness -- Research -- Methodology. Cost-Benefit Analysis -- methods.

RA410.53.G73 1991
Gray, Bradford H.,

The profit motive and patient care : the changing accountability of doctors and hospitals / Bradford H. Gray. Cambridge, Mass. : Harvard University Press, 1991. xv, 440 p. ;
90-005119　　　　338.4/73621/0973
0674713370
Medical economics -- United States. Hospitals -- United States -- Business management. Medical care -- United States.

RA410.53.K55 1994
Kissick, William L.

Medicine's dilemmas : infinite needs versus finite resources / William L. Kissick. New Haven : Yale University Press, c1994. xix, 185 p. :
94-001137　　　　338.4/73621/0973
0300059647
Medical care -- United States -- Cost control. Medical policy -- United States. Medical economics -- United States.

RA410.53.N52 1993
Newhouse, Joseph P.

Free for all? : lessons from the Rand Health Insurance Experiment / Joseph P. Newhouse and the Insurance Experiment Group. Cambridge, Mass. : Harvard University Press, 1993. x, 489 p. :
93-001356　　　　368.3/82/00973　　　　0674318463
Medical care -- United States -- Utilization. Insurance, Health -- Research -- United States. Insurance, Health -- United States -- Coinsurance.

RA410.53.P675 2001

Portrait of health in the United States / editors, Daniel Melnick, Beatrice Rouse. 1st ed., 2001. Lanham, MD : Bernan , c2001. xxi, 376 p. :
　　　　　614.4/273　　　　089059189X
Medical statistics. Health status indicators--United States--Statistics. Health care--United States--Statistics.

RA411 Medicine and the state — Provisions for personal medical care — General works

RA411.G68 1999
Graig, Laurene A.

Health of nations :an international perspective on U.S. health care reform / Laurene A. Graig; [foreword by John D. Rockefeller IV]. 3rd ed. Washington, D.C. Congressional Quarterly, c1999. xv, 222 p. :
　　　　　338.4/33621　　　　156802360X
Medical care--Finance--Case studies. Medical care--United States--Finance. Insurance, Health--Government policy--Case studies.

RA412.5 Medicine and the state — Provisions for personal medical care — State medical care plans. Socialized medicine. National health insurance. Compulsory health insurance

RA412.5.U6.M427 1998
Medicaid reform and the American States : case studies on the politics of managed care / edited by Mark R. Daniels. Westport, Conn. : Auburn House, 1998. xii, 308 p. :
97-023657   368.4/2/00973   0865692637
Medicaid. Managed care plans (Medical care) -- United States.

RA413-413.5 Medicine and the state — Provisions for personal medical care — Private medical care plans

RA413.W48 1998
Winegar, Norman.
Guidebook to managed care and practice management terminology / Norman Winegar, L. Michelle Hayter. New York : Haworth Press, c1998. ix, 86 p. ;
98-012222   362.1/04258/014   078900447X
Managed care plans (Medical care) -- Terminology.

RA413.5.U5.A55 1996
Anders, George,
Health against wealth : HMOs and the breakdown of medical trust / George Anders. Boston : Houghton Mifflin, 1996. xvi, 299 p. ;
96-024869   362.1/0425   0395822823
Health maintenance organizations -- United States.

RA413.5.U5.B495 1997
Birenbaum, Arnold.
Managed care : made in America / Arnold Birenbaum. Westport, Conn. : Praeger, 1997. xv, 193 p. ;
97-005578   362.1/04258/0973
0275959163
Managed care plans (Medical care) -- United States.

RA413.5.U5C66 1997
Competitive managed care :the emerging health care system / John D. Wilkerson, Kelly J. Devers, Ruth S. Given, editors. San Francisco : Jossey-Bass Publishers, c1997. xv, 405 p. :
      362.1/0973   0787903094
Managed care plans (Medical care)--Economic aspects--United States. Managed Care Programs--economics--United States. Economic Competition.

RA413.5.U5.C68 1999
Court, Jamie,
Making a killing : HMOs and the threat to your health / Jamie Court, Francis Smith. Monroe, Me : Common Courage Press, 1999. p. cm.
99-037783   362.1/04258   1567511694
Managed care plans (Medical care) -- United States. Health care rationing -- United States. Medical care -- United States -- Cost control.

RA413.5.U5.Z44 1998
Zelman, Walter A.
The managed care blues and how to cure them / Walter A. Zelman, Robert A. Berenson. Washington, D.C. : Georgetown University Press, c1998. xvi, 224 p. :
98-016018   362.1/04258/0973
0878406808
Managed care plans (Medical care) -- United States. Insurance, Health -- United States.

RA413.7 Medicine and the state — Provisions for personal medical care — Special groups, A-Z

RA413.7.M55.K73 1997
Krajcinovic, Ivana,
From company doctors to managed care : the United Mine Workers' noble experiment / Ivana Krajcinovic. Ithaca, NY : ILR Press, 1997. xiv, 212 p. :
97-015098   362.1/088/622   0801433924
Miners -- Medical care -- United States. Insurance, Health -- United States. Collective bargaining -- Mining industry -- United States.

RA418 Medicine and the state — Medicine and society. Social medicine. Medical sociology — General works

RA418.B5736 2001
The Blackwell companion to medical sociology / edited by William C. Cockerham. Oxford, UK ; Blackwell, 2001. xiii, 528 p.
00-033714   306.4/61   0631217037
Social medicine -- Miscellanea.

RA418.C655 1997
Cockerham, William C.
Dictionary of medical sociology / William C. Cockerham and Ferris J. Ritchey. Westport, Conn. : Greenwood Press, 1997. xxvi, 169 p.
96-036575   306.4/61/03   0313292698
Social medicine -- Dictionaries. Sociology, Medical -- dictionaries.

RA418.C664 1989
Cohen, Mark Nathan.
Health and the rise of civilization / Mark Nathan Cohen. New Haven : Yale University Press, c1989. x, 285 p. ;
      614.4   0300040067
Social medicine. Health. Civilization.

RA418.C673 2001
Coreil, Jeannine.
Social and behavioral foundations of public health / Jeannine Coreil, Carol A. Bryant, J. Neil Henderson ; with contributions from Melinda S. Forthofer and Gwendolyn P. Quinn. Thousand Oaks : Sage Publications, c2001. xvi, 360 p. :
      362.1   0761917446
Public health--Social aspects. Public health--Psychological aspects. Social medicine.

RA418.G56 2001
Goldstein, Myrna Chandler,
   Controversies in the practice of medicine / by Myrna Chandler Goldstein and Mark A. Goldstein. Westport, Conn. : Greenwood Press, 2001. xvi, 349 p. :
               362.1   0313311315
   Social medicine. Medical ethics.

RA418.H27 1999
   Handbook of gender, culture, and health / edited by Richard M. Eisler, Michel Hersen. Mahwah, N.J. : Lawrence Erlbaum Associates, 2000. x, 531 p. ;
99-030953   613/.042   0805826386
   Health -- Sex differences -- Handbooks, manuals, etc. Health -- Social aspects -- Handbooks, manuals, etc. Medical care -- Social aspects -- Handbooks, manuals, etc.

RA418.M68 1998
Morris, David B.
   Illness and culture in the postmodern age / David B. Morris. Berkeley, Calif. : University of California Press, 1998. p. cm.
98-007092   306.4/61   0520208692
   Diseases -- Social aspects. Social medicine -- Philosophy. Postmodernism.

RA418.N36 2000
   Narrative and the cultural construction of illness and healing / edited by Cheryl Mattingly and Linda C. Garro. Berkeley : University of California Press, 2000. ix, 279 p. ;
00-031629   306.4/61   0520218248
   Social medicine. Medical anthropology. Discourse analysis, Narrative.

RA418.T915 1989
Turshen, Meredeth,
   The politics of public health / Meredeth Turshen. New Brunswick : Rutgers University Press, c1989. x, 319 p. :
88-036976   362.1   0813514215
   Social medicine. Public health.

RA418.W347 1991
Waitzkin, Howard.
   The politics of medical encounters : how patients and doctors deal with social problems / Howard Waitzkin. New Haven : Yale University Press, c1991. xvi, 311 p. :
90-045611   610.69/6   0300049498
   Social medicine. Physician and patient.

RA418.3 Medicine and the state — Medicine and society. Social medicine. Medical sociology — By region or country, A-Z

RA418.3.A35.S63 1992
   The Social basis of health and healing in Africa / edited by Steven Feierman and John M. Janzen ; sponsored by the Joint Committee on African Studies of the American Council of Learned Societies and the Social Science Research Council. Berkeley : University of California Press, c1992. xviii, 487 p.
90-044243   362.1/096   0520066804
   Social medicine -- Africa. Healing -- Africa. Medical anthropology -- Africa.

RA418.3.A78H43 2000
   Healing powers and modernity :traditional medicine, shamanism, and science in Asian societies / edited by Linda H. Connor and Geoffrey Samuel. Westport, CT : Bergin & Garvey, 2000. x, 283 p. :
          615.5/095   0897897153
   Healing--Asia. Social medicine--Asia. Traditional medicine--Asia.

RA418.3.U6.B34 2001
Baer, Hans A.,
   Biomedicine and alternative healing systems in America : issues of class, race, ethnicity, and gender / Hans A. Baer. Madison, Wisconsin : The University of Wisconsin Press, c2001. xii, 222 p. ;
00-012733   306.4/61/0973   0299166902
   Social medicine -- United States. Medical anthropology -- United States. Alternative medicine -- United States.

RA418.3.U6.S74 1990
Stein, Howard F.
   American medicine as culture / Howard F. Stein ; with the editorial assistance of Margaret A. Stein. Boulder : Westview Press, 1990. xxii, 281 p.
89-022711   306.4/61/0973   0813307376
   Social medicine -- United States. Medicine -- United States -- Philosophy. Anthropology, Cultural.

RA418.3.U6S936 2001
Szasz, Thomas Stephen,
   Pharmacracy :medicine and politics in America / Thomas Szasz. Westport, Conn. : Praeger, 2001. xxiv, 212 p. ;
          362.1/0973   0275971961
   Social medicine--United States--Miscellanea. Medical care--Political aspects--United States. Medical ethics--United States.

RA418.5 Medicine and society. Social medicine. Medical sociology — Special aspects, A-Z

RA418.5.M4
   Beyond managed care : how consumers and technology are changing the future of health care / Dean C. Coddington ... [et al.]. San Francisco : Jossey-Bass, c2000. xxvii, 335 p.
00-008789   362.1   0787953830
   Medical innovations. Medical care -- Forecasting.

RA418.5.P6.A3 2001
Aday, Lu Ann.
   At risk in America : the health and health care needs of vulnerable populations in the United States / Lu Ann Aday. San Francisco : Jossey-Bass Publishers, c2001. xxiii, 372 p.
00-048758   362.1/0425/0973   0787949868
   Poor -- Medical care -- United States. Poor -- Medical care -- Government policy -- United States. Socially handicapped -- Medical care -- United States.

RA418.5.T73H65 1999

Honoring patient preferences :a guide to complying with multicultural patient requirements / editors, Anne Knights Rundle, Maria Carvalho, and Mary Robinson. 1st ed. San Francisco : Jossey-Bass, c1999. xxv, 235 p. ;
        362.1   0787946508
   Transcultural medical care--Handbooks, manuals, etc.

RA418.5.T73.L37 1995
Lassiter, Sybil M.

Multicultural clients : a professional handbook for health care providers and social workers / Sybil M. Lassiter. Westport, Conn. : Greenwood Press, 1995. xvii, 197 p.
94-030927   362.1/0973   0313291403
   Transcultural medical care -- United States. Social work with minorities -- United States. Minorities -- United States -- Social life and customs.

RA418.5.T73S64 2000
Spector, Rachel E.,

Cultural diversity in health & illness / Rachel E. Spector. 5th ed. Upper Saddle River, N.J. : Prentice Hall Health, c2000. xvi, 349 p. :
     362.1/0425   0838515363
   Transcultural medical care--United States. Health attitudes-- United States. Transcultural nursing--United States.

RA423.2 Public health. Hygiene. Preventive medicine — Communication in public health

RA423.2.H42 2001

Health communication :a multicultural perspective / edited by Snehendu B. Kar, Rina Alcalay, with Shana Alex. Thousand Oaks, Calif. : Sage Publications, c2001. xxi, 380 p. ;
     613/.089   0803973675
   Health--Social aspects--United States--Cross-cultural studies. Health promotion--United States--Cross-cultural studies. Medical care--United States--Cross-cultural studies.

RA425 Public health. Hygiene. Preventive medicine — General works — 1901-

RA425.F25 1998
Fairbanks, Jo.

The public health primer / Jo Fairbanks, William H. Wiese. Thousand Oaks, CA : Sage Publications, c1998. viii, 167 p.
97-021134   362.1   0761906525
   Public health.

RA425.M382 1998

Maxcy-Rosenau-Last public health & preventive medicine / editor, Robert B. Wallace. 14th ed. Stamford, Conn. : Appleton & Lange, c1998. xxviii, 1291 p. :
     614.4/4   0838561853
   Public health. Medicine, Preventive. Public Health

RA425.O9 2002

Oxford textbook of public health / edited by Roger Detels ... [et al.]. 4th ed. Oxford ; Oxford University Press, c2002. 3 v. :
     362.1   0192630415
   Public health.

RA425.P38 2001
Petersen, Donna J.

Needs assessment in public health :a practical guide for students and professionals / Donna J. Petersen and Greg R. Alexander. New York : Kluwer Academic, c2001. xi, 139 p. :
     362.1   0306465302
   Public health. Needs assessment. Community health services.

RA425.S28 2000
Schneider, Mary-Jane,

Introduction to public health / Mary-Jane Schneider ; drawings by Henry Schneider. Gaithersburg, Md. : Aspen Publishers, 2000. xxxi, 496 p.
99-039202   362.1   0834208393
   Public health.

RA425.T85 2000
Tulchinsky, Theodore H.

The new public health : an introduction for the 21st century / Theodore H. Tulchinsky, Elena A. Varavikova. San Diego : Academic Press, c2000. xxi, 882 p. :
99-066055   0127033505
   Public health.

RA427 Public health. Hygiene. Preventive medicine — General special

RA427.C56 2001
Coddington, Dean C.

Strategies for the new health care marketplace :managing the convergence of consumerism and technology / Dean C. Coddington, Elizabeth A. Fischer, Keith D. Moore. San Francisco : Jossey-Bass, c2001. xxviii, 418 p. :
     362.1   0787955930
   Medical care--Forecasting. Medical innovations. Consumers.

RA427.I54 1996

International handbook of public health / edited by Klaus Hurrelmann and Ulrich Laaser. Westport, Conn, : Greenwood Press, 1996. xviii, 474 p.
95-046131   362.1   031329500X
   Public health. World health.

RA427.W49 1994

Why are some people healthy and others not? : the determinants of health of populations / Robert G. Evans, Morris L. Barer, and Theodore R. Marmor, editors. New York : A. de Gruyter, c1994. xix, 378 p. :
94-016155   614.4/2   0202304892
   Public health. Social medicine. Medical policy.

RA427.25 Public health. Hygiene. Preventive medicine — Moral and ethical aspects

RA427.25.M67 1997
   Morality and health / edited by Allan M. Brandt and Paul Rozin. New York : Routledge, 1997. ix, 416 p. ;
96-052813   306.4/61   0415915813
   Health behavior -- Moral and ethical aspects. Health attitudes.

RA427.3 Public health. Hygiene. Preventive medicine — Health risk assessment

RA427.3.C68 1993
Covello, Vincent T.
   Risk assessment methods : approaches for assessing health and environmental risks / Vincent T. Covello, Miley W. Merkhofer. New York : Plenum Press, c1993. xiv, 319 p. :
93-023209   614.4   0306443821
   Health risk assessment -- Methodology. Health risk assessment -- Evaluation.

RA427.3.R58 1995
   Risk versus risk : tradeoffs in protecting health and the environment / edited John D. Graham and Jonathan Baert Wiener. Cambridge, Mass. : Harvard University Press, 1995. xiii, 337 p.
95-010457   362.1/042   0674773047
   Health risk assessment. Health behavior -- Decision making. Environmental health -- Decision making.

RA427.5 Public health. Hygiene. Preventive medicine — Medical screening — General works

RA427.5.N45 1989
Nelkin, Dorothy.
   Dangerous diagnostics : the social power of biological information / Dorothy Nelkin, Laurence Tancredi. New York : Basic Books, c1989. x, 207 p. :
89-042509   306.4/61   0465084141
   Medical screening -- Social aspects. Human chromosome abnormalities -- Diagnosis -- Social aspects. Neuropsychological tests -- Social aspects.

RA427.8 Public health. Hygiene. Preventive medicine — Health promotion

RA427.8.H36 1999
   Handbook of health promotion and disease prevention / edited by James M. Raczynski and Ralph J. DiClemente. New York : Kluwer Academic/Plenum Publishers, c1999. xvi, 669 p. :
99-037316   613   0306461404
   Health promotion -- Handbooks, manuals, etc. Medicine, Preventive -- Handbooks, manuals, etc. Preventive Medicine.

RA427.8.L45 1991
Leichter, Howard M.
   Free to be foolish : politics and health promotion in the United States and Great Britain / Howard M. Leichter. Princeton, N.J. : Princeton University Press, c1991. xv, 281 p. ;
90-038310   613/.0941   069107867X
   Health promotion -- Political aspects -- United States. Health promotion -- Political aspects -- Great Britain. Health promotion -- Government policy -- United States.

RA427.8.L54 1999
   Life-span perspectives on health and illness / edited by Thomas L. Whitman, Thomas V. Merluzzi, Robert D. White. Mahwah, N.J. : Lawrence Erlbaum Associates, 1999. x, 313 p. :
98-021788   613   0805827714
   Human Development. Life Change Events. Health promotion.

RA427.8.P766 2000
   Promoting healthy behavior : how much freedom? whose responsibility? / edited by Daniel Callahan. Washington, D.C. : Georgetown University Press, c2000. xi, 186 p. ;
99-038856   613   0878407626
   Health promotion -- Social aspects. Health promotion -- Moral and ethical aspects.

RA427.8.P7665 2000
   Promoting human wellness : new frontiers for research, practice, and policy / edited by Margaret Schneider Jamner and Daniel Stokols. Berkeley : University of California Press, c2000. xii, 737 p. :
99-087690   613   0520226089
   Health promotion. Health promotion -- Social aspects.

RA431 Public health. Hygiene. Preventive medicine — Popular works

RA431.I46 1985
Imperato, Pascal James.
   Acceptable risks / Pascal James Imperato, Greg Mitchell. New York, N.Y. : Viking, 1985. xix, 286 p. ;
83-040634   613   0670102059
   Medicine, Preventive. Safety education. Health.

RA440.5 Public health. Hygiene. Preventive medicine — Study and teaching — Health and education of the public

RA440.5.D46 1995
   Designing health messages : approaches from communication theory and public health practice / Edward Maibach, Roxanne Louiselle Parrott, editors. Thousand Oaks, Calif. : Sage Publications, c1995. xiii, 304 p.
94-040646   362.1/014   0803953976
   Mass media in health education. Health promotion.

RA440.55 Public health. Hygiene. Preventive medicine — Study and teaching — Audiovisual aids

RA440.55.B33 1992
Backer, Thomas E.
   Designing health communication campaigns : what works? / Thomas E. Backer, Everett M. Rogers, Pradeep Sopory. Newbury Park, Calif. : Sage, c1992. xv, 181 p. :
92-006165   362.1/014   0803943318
   Mass media in health education. Communication in medicine.

RA441 Public health. Hygiene. Preventive medicine — World health. International cooperation

RA441.B38 1999
Basch, Paul F.,
   Textbook of international health / Paul F. Basch. 2nd ed. New York : Oxford University Press, 1999. xv, 555 p. ;
            362.1   0195132041
   World health.

RA441.C75 2001
   Critical issues in global health / C. Everett Koop, Clarence E. Pearson, M. Roy Schwarz [editors] ; foreword by Jimmy Carter. San Francisco : Jossey-Bass, c2001. xxvi, 472 p.
00-055498   362.1   0787948241
   World health. World health -- Case studies. Medical geography.

RA441.G37 2001
Garrett, Laurie.
   Betrayal of trust : the collapse of global health / Laurie Garrett. Oxford ; Oxford University Press, 2001. xi, 477 p. ;
            362.1   0198509952
   World health. Public health--Cross-cultural studies. Epidemiology.

RA441.M43 2001
McMurray, Christine.
   Diseases of globalization : socioeconomic transitions and health / Christine McMurray and Roy Smith. Sterling, VA : Earthscan Publications, 2001. p. cm.
00-050402   362.1   1853837105
   Health transition. World health. Globalization -- Health aspects.

RA441.W68 2000
   Worldwide health sourcebook : basic information about global health issues, including malnutrition, reproductive health, disease dispersion and prevention ... / edited by Joyce Brennfleck Shannon. Detroit, MI : Omnigraphics, 2000. xiii, 614 p.
00-052463   362.1   0780803302
   World health.

RA441.5 Public health. Hygiene. Preventive medicine — Developing countries

RA441.5.E43 2001
Elder, John P.
   Behavior change & public health in the developing world / John P. Elder. Thousand Oaks, Calif. : Sage Publications, c2001. xviii, 171 p.
00-009852   614.4/4   0761917780
   Public health -- Developing countries -- Psychological aspects. Medicine, Preventive -- Developing countries. Health behavior -- Developing countries.

RA445–448.5 Public health. Hygiene. Preventive medicine — By region or country — America

RA445.D84 1990
Duffy, John,
   The sanitarians : a history of American public health / John Duffy. Urbana : University of Illinois Press, c1990. 330 p. ;
89-005107   614.4/4/097309   0252016637
   Public health -- United States -- History.

RA445.H3483 1990
   Healthy people 2000 : citizens chart the course / Michael A. Stoto, Ruth Behrens, Connie Rosemont, editors. Washington, D.C. : National Academy Press, 1990. xiv, 228 p. ;
90-062772   362.1/0973   0309043409
   Public health -- United States. Health planning -- United States.

RA445.L45
Lerner, Monroe.
   Health progress in the United States, 1900-1960; a report of Health Information Foundation [by] Monroe Lerner [and] Odin W. Anderson. Chicago, University of Chicago Press [1963] xv, 354 p.
63-018854   614.0973
   Public health -- United States -- History.

RA445.M36 2000
Mays, Glen P.
   Local public health practice : trends & models / Glen P. Mays, C. Arden Miller, Paul K. Halverson. Washington, DC : American Public Health Association, c2000. x, 292 p. :
99-073691   362.1/2/0973   0875532438
   Community health services -- United States. Community health services -- United States -- Case studies.

RA448.N5.H54 1995
   Hives of sickness : public health and epidemics in New York City / edited by David Rosner. New Brunswick, N.J. : Published for the Museum of the City of New York c1995. 223 p. :
94-029784   614.4/9747/1   0813521580
   Public health -- New York (State) -- New York -- History. Communicable diseases -- New York (State) -- New York. Disease Outbreaks -- history -- New York City.

RA448.4.L68 1999
Loue, Sana.
Gender, ethnicity, and health research / Sana Loue. New York : Kluwer Academic/Plenum Publishers, c1999. xiii, 195 p.
99-033678   362.1/089   0306461722
Minorities -- Medical care. Health -- Research -- Cross-cultural studies. Social medicine.

RA448.4.M566 2000
Minority health in America : findings and policy implications from the Commonwealth Fund minority health survey / edited by Carol J.R. Hogue, Martha A. Hargraves, Karen Scott Collins. Baltimore, MD : Johns Hopkins University Press, c2000. xviii, 326 p.
99-030914   362.1/089/00973   0801862981
Minorities -- Health and hygiene -- United States. Health surveys -- United States.

RA448.4.P76 1999
Promoting health in multicultural populations : a handbook for practitioners / [edited by] Robert M. Huff, Michael V. Kline. Thousand Oaks, Calif. : Sage Publications, c1999. xvii, 554 p.
98-025455   362.1/089/00973   0761901825
Minorities -- Medical care -- United States. Health promotion -- United States. Transcultural medical care -- United States.

RA448.5.H57H395 2001
Health issues in the Latino community / Marilyn Aguirre-Molina, Carlos W. Molina, Ruth Enid Zambrana, editors. San Francisco : Jossey Bass Publishers 2001. xxxiv, 492 p. :
                362.1/089/68073   0787953156
Hispanic Americans--Medical care. Hispanic Americans--Health and hygiene.

RA448.5.I44H36 1998
Handbook of immigrant health / edited by Sana Loue. New York : Plenum Press, c1998. xii, 654 p. :
                362.1/086/91   0306459590
Immigrants--Health and hygiene--United States--Handbooks, manuals, Minorities--Health and hygiene--United States--Handbooks, manuals, Medical care--United States--Cross-cultural studies--Handbooks,

RA448.5.I44.K73 1994
Kraut, Alan M.
Silent travelers : germs, genes, and the "immigrant menace" / Alan M. Kraut. New York, NY : BasicBooks, c1994. xiv, 369 p. :
93-034572   614.4/08/69   0465078230
Immigrants -- Health and hygiene -- Government policy -- United States. Medical policy -- United States. Immigrants -- Medical examinations -- United States. United States -- Emigration and immigration -- Government policy.

RA448.5.I5.L36 1998
Lambert Colomeda, Lorelei Anne.
Keepers of the central fire : issues in ecology for indigenous peoples / Lorelei (Lori) A. Lambert Colomeda. Sudbury, Mass. : Jones & Bartlett, c1998. p. cm.
97-051179   613/.089/97   0763709239
Indians of North America -- Health and hygiene. Ecology -- Environmental aspects. Environmental Health.

RA448.5.N4.B73 2000
Braithwaite, Ronald L.,
Building health coalitions in the Black community / Ronald L. Braithwaite, Sandra E. Taylor, John N. Austin. Thousand Oaks, Calif. : Sage Publications, c2000. ix, 194 p. :
99-006715   362.1/089/96073   0803973098
Afro-Americans -- Health and hygiene. Public health -- United States -- Citizen participation. Health promotion -- United States -- Citizen participation.

RA448.5.N4.B97 2000
Byrd, W. Michael.
An American health dilemma : the medical history of African Americans and the problem of race / W. Michael Byrd, Linda A. Clayton. New York : Routledge, 2000- v. 1   :
99-027882   362.1/089/96073   0415924499
African Americans -- Health and hygiene -- History. African Americans -- Medical care -- History.

RA448.5.N4.H385 2000
Health care in the Black community : empowerment, knowledge, skills, and collectivism / Sadye L. Logan, Edith M. Freeman, editors. New York : Haworth Press, 2000. xix, 276 p. :
00-038882   362.1/089/96073   0789004577
African Americans -- Health and hygiene. African Americans -- Medical care. Health services accessibility -- United States.

RA448.5.N4.R52 1990
Rice, Mitchell F.
Health of Black Americans from post reconstruction to integration, 1871-1960 : an annotated bibliography of contemporary sources / compiled by Mitchell F. Rice and Woodrow Jones, Jr. New York : Greenwood Press, 1990. xxiii, 206 p.
89-078161   016.3621/08996073
0313263140
Afro-Americans -- Diseases -- History -- 19th century -- Abstracts. Afro-Americans -- Diseases -- History -- 20th century -- Abstracts. Afro-Americans -- Medical care -- History -- 19th century -- Abstracts.

RA448.5.N4.S65 1995
Smith, Susan Lynn,
Sick and tired of being sick and tired : Black women's health activism in America, 1890-1950 / Susan L. Smith. Philadelphia : University of Pennsylvania Press, c1995. xi, 247 p. :
95-011310   362.1/089/96073   0812232372
Afro-American women health reformers -- Southern States -- History. Afro-Americans -- Medical care -- Southern States -- History. Health care reform -- Southern States -- History.

RA448.5.P83.P84 1994
Puerto Rican women and children : issues in health, growth, and development / edited by Gontran Lamberty and Cynthia Garcia Coll. New York : Plenum Press, c1994. xix, 285 p. :
93-049633   362.1/089687295073
0306446154
Puerto Rican women -- Health and hygiene -- Congresses. Puerto Rican children -- Health and hygiene -- United States -- Congresses. Child Welfare.

RA563 Public health. Hygiene. Preventive medicine — By ethnic group, etc. — Blacks

RA563.M56.E838 2001
Ethnic diseases sourcebook / edited by Joyce Brennfleck Shannon. Detroit, MI : Omnigraphics, c2001. xiii, 664 p.
00-052853   362.1/089/00973   0780803361
Minorities -- Health and hygiene -- United States. Minorities -- Diseases -- United States. Genetic disorders -- United States.

RA564 Public health. Hygiene. Preventive medicine — By age group, class, etc.

RA564.H45 1997
Heggenhougen, Kris.
Reaching new highs : alternative therapies for drug addicts / H.K. Heggenhougen. Northvale, N.J. : Jason Aronson, c1997. 208 p. ;
96-035037   616.86/06   0765700360
Substance abuse -- Alternative treatment. Narcotic addicts -- Rehabilitation. Alcoholics -- Rehabilitation.

RA564.7-564.8 Public health. Hygiene. Preventive medicine — By age group, class, etc. — Adults

RA564.7.S73 1990
The Legacy of longevity : health and health care in later life / edited by Sidney M. Stahl. Newbury Park, Calif. : Sage Publications, c1990. 342 p. :
90038946   362.1/9897   0803940017
Aged -- Health and hygiene.

RA564.8.A389 1989
Aging and health : perspectives on gender, race, ethnicity, and class / edited by Kyriakos S. Markides. Newbury Park, Calif. : Sage Publications, c1989. 255 p. ;
88-035932   362.1/9897/00973
0803932065
Aged -- Health and hygiene -- United States. Aging -- United States.

RA564.8.C465 1996
Choosing who's to live : ethics and aging / edited by James W. Walters. Urbana : University of Illinois Press, c1996. xiii, 165 p.
95-041785   174/.24   0252022408
Aged -- Medical care -- Moral and ethical aspects. Health care rationing. Aged -- Medical care -- Economic aspects.

RA564.8.H4293 2001
Health promotion and disease prevention in the older adult : Tripp-Reimer, and Kathleen Buckwalter, editors. New York : Springer, c2001. xviii, 270 p. ;
613.7/0446   0826113761
Geriatric nursing--United States. Aged--Health and hygiene--United States. Aged--Medical care--United States.

RA564.8.I57 1990
Institute of Medicine (U.S.).
The second fifty years : promoting health and preventing disability / Robert L. Berg and Joseph S. Cassells, editors ; Institute of Medicine, Division of Health Promotion and Disease Prevention. Washington, D.C. : National Academy Press, 1990. x, 332 p. :
90-013385   613/.0438/0973   0309043395
Aged -- Health and hygiene. Aged -- Diseases -- Prevention. Aged -- Services for -- United States.

RA564.8.N5 1999
New ways to care for older people : building systems based on evidence / Evan Calkins ... [et al.], editors. New York : Springer Pub., c1999. xix, 260 p. :
98-038606   362.1/9897   082611220X
Aged -- Medical care. Aged -- Medical care -- United States.

RA564.8.P4 1998
Peake, Tom H.
Healthy aging, healthy treatment : the impact of telling stories / Thomas H. Peake. Westport, Conn. : Praeger, 1998. viii, 153 p.
97-033704   362.1/9897   0275959228
Aged -- Medical care. Aging -- Psychological aspects. Aging -- Religious aspects.

RA564.85-564.86 Public health. Hygiene. Preventive medicine — By age group, class, etc. — Women

RA564.85.D38 2001
Davis, Cortney,
I knew a woman :the experience of the female body / Cortney Davis. 1st ed. New York : Random House, c2001. xvi, 263 p. ;
613/.04244   0375504184
Women--Health and hygiene--Case studies. Women--Medical care--Case studies.

RA564.85.G4653 2000
Gender inequalities in health / edited by Ellen Annandale and Kate Hunt. Buckingham ; Open University Press, 2000. ix, 214 p. :
99-030442   362.1   0335203655
Health -- Sex differences. Medical care -- Utilization -- Sex differences. Sex discrimination in medicine.

RA564.85.M36 1996

Man-made medicine : women's health, public policy, and reform / Kary L. Moss , editor. Durham : Duke University Press, 1996. 288 p. ;

96-021855   362.1/082   0822318113

Women's health services -- Government policy -- United States. Sexism in medicine -- United States. Sex discrimination in medicine -- United States.

RA564.86.B38 1996

Race, gender, and health / Marcia Bayne-Smith, editor. Thousand Oaks : Sage Publications, c1996. xvii, 210 p.

95-035483   362.1/08/693   0803955049

Minority women -- Health and hygiene -- United States. Minority women -- Medical care -- United States. Minority women -- United States -- Social conditions.

RA565 Public health. Hygiene. Preventive medicine — Environmental health — General works

RA565.M64 1997
Moeller, D. W.

Environmental health / Dade W. Moeller. Cambridge, Mass. : Harvard University Press, 1997. xv, 480 p. :

96-043287   616.9/8   0674258592

Environmental health.

RA565.P48 1995
Philp, Richard B.

Environmental hazards & human health / Richard B. Philp. Boca Raton : Lewis Publishers, c1995. 306 p. :

94-038920   615.9/02   1566701333

Environmental health.

RA565.W67 2000

World resources, 2000-2001 : people and ecosystems, the fraying web of life.   Washington,D.C. : World Resources Institute, c2000. ix, 389 p. :

00-691108   1569734437

Natural resources -- Health aspects. Environmental health. Environmental degradation -- Health aspects.

RA566 Public health. Hygiene. Preventive medicine — Environmental health — General special

RA566.K465 2001
Kerns, Thomas A.,

Environmentally induced illnesses :ethics, risk assessment, and human   rights / Thomas Kerns. Jefferson, N.C. : McFarland, c2001. ix, 294 p. ;

              615.9/02   0786408278

Environmentally induced diseases. Environmentally induced diseases--Moral and ethical aspects. Environmental health--Moral and ethical aspects.

RA566.N87 1995

Nursing, health & the environment : strengthening the relationship to improve the public's health / Andrew M. Pope, Meta A. Snyder, and Lillian H. Mood, editors ; Committee on Enhancing Environmental Health Content in Nursing Practice, Division of Health Promotion and Disease Prevention, Institute of Medicine. Washington, D.C. : National Academy Press, 1995. xii, 288 p. :

95-039601   610.73   030905298X

Environmental health. Nursing. Industrial nursing.

RA566.5 Public health. Hygiene. Preventive medicine — Environmental health — By region or country

RA566.5.N7.S48 1993
Setterberg, Fred.

Toxic nation : the fight to save our communities from chemical contamination / Fred Setterberg, Lonny Shavelson ; photographs by Lonny Shavelson. New York : J. Wiley, c1993. xiii, 301 p.

93-008010   363.73/8/0973   0471575453

Environmental health -- North America. Pollution -- Social aspects -- North America.

RA566.5.S65.F47 1992
Feshbach, Murray,

Ecocide in the USSR : health and nature under siege / Murray Feshbach and Alfred Friendly, Jr. ; foreword by Lester Brown. New York, NY : BasicBooks, c1992. xvii, 376 p.

91-055456   615.9/02/0947

Environmental health -- Soviet Union.

RA569 Public health. Hygiene. Preventive medicine — Environmental health — Radioactive substances and ionizing radiation

RA569.E55 1996
Gould, Jay M.

The enemy within : the high cost of living near nuclear reactors : breast cancer, AIDS, low birthweights, and other radiation-induced immune deficiency effects / by Jay M. Gould, with members of the Radiation and Public Health Project, Ernest J. Sternglass, Joseph J. Mangano, William McDonnell. New York : Four Walls Eight Windows ; c1996. v, 346 p. :

96000789   616.9/897   1568580665

Immunosuppression -- Risk factors. Immunodeficiency -- Complications. Nuclear reactors -- Health aspects.

RA569.M36 1999
Mangano, Joseph J.,

Low-level radiation and immune system damage : an atomic era legacy / Joseph J. Mangano. Boca Raton : Lewis Publishers, c1999. 227 p. :

98-018138   616.9/897   1566703344

Low-level radiation -- Health aspects -- United States. Immunosuppression -- United States.

RA569.M43 1996
Medical consequences of the Chernobyl nuclear accident / edited by P.V. Ramzaev. New York : Nova Science Publisher, c1996. vi, 135 p. :
93-022794   616.9/897/00947714
1560721111
Chernobyl Nuclear Accident, Chornobyl, Ukraine, 1986 -- Health aspects.

RA569.R33 1995
Radiation and public perception : benefits and risks / Jack P. Young, editor, Rosalyn S. Yalow, editor. Washington, DC : American Chemical Society, 1995. xiii, 346 p.
94-035190   363.17/99   0841229325
Radiation -- Health aspects.

RA569.3 Public health. Hygiene. Preventive medicine — Environmental health — Noniodizing radiation in relation to public health

RA569.3.B46 1994
Bennett, William Ralph,
Health and low-frequency electromagnetic fields / William Ralph Bennett, Jr. New Haven, CT : Yale University Press, c1994. viii, 189 p.
93-040340   616.9/89   0300057636
ELF electromagnetic fields -- Health aspects. Electromagnetic fields -- Health aspects.

RA569.3.S24 1996
Sagan, Leonard A.
Electric and magnetic fields : invisible risks? / Leonard A. Sagan. Amsterdam, Netherlands : Gordon and Breach Publishers, c1996. xxiv, 214 p.
99-460420   363.18/9   2884492178
Electromagnetic fields -- Health aspects. Electromagnetic Fields -- adverse effects. Environmental Exposure -- adverse effects.

RA577-578 Public health. Hygiene. Preventive medicine — Environmental health — Air

RA577.D8.A48 2000
Amato, Joseph Anthony.
Dust : a history of the small and the invisible / Joseph A. Amato ; illustrations by Abigail Rorer. Berkeley, Calif. : University of California Press, 2000. xii, 250 p. :
99-027115   551.51/13   0520218752
Dust -- Social aspects -- History. Size perception. Science -- Philosophy.

RA577.5.G63 1995
Godish, Thad.
Sick buildings : definition, diagnosis, and mitigation / Thad Godish. Boca Raton : Lewis Publishers, c1995. 398 p. :
94-017544   613/.5   087371346X
Sick building syndrome. Indoor air pollution.

RA578.H38.H38 1999
Hazardous waste incineration : evaluating the human health and environmental risks / edited by Stephen M. Roberts, Christopher M. Teaf, Judy A. Bean. Boca Raton : Lewis Publishers, c1999. xii, 351 p. :
98-028649   363.72/8   156670250X
Hazardous wastes -- Incineration -- Health aspects -- United States. Hazardous wastes -- Incineration -- Environmental aspects -- United States. Incineration -- Waste disposal -- Environmental aspects -- United States.

RA591-591.5 Public health. Hygiene. Preventive medicine — Environmental health — Water supply in relation to public health. Water pollution

RA591.M54 1995
Millichap, J. Gordon.
Is our water safe to drink? : a guide to drinking water : hazards and health risks / J. Gordon Millichap. Chicago : PNB Publishers, c1995. viii, 212 p.
95-067490   0962911550
Drinking water -- Health aspects.

RA591.5.E97 1999
Exposure to contaminants in drinking water : estimating uptake through the skin and by inhalation / edited by Stephen S. Olin. Boca Raton : CRC Press ; c1999. 232 p. :
98-041145   615.9/02   0849328047
Drinking water -- Contamination. Biological exposure indices (Industrial toxicology)

RA600 Public health. Hygiene. Preventive medicine — Environmental health — Seawater. Ocean

RA600.F76 1999
From monsoons to microbes : understanding the ocean's role in human health / Committee on the Ocean's Role in Human Health, Ocean Studies Board, Commission on Geosciences, Environment, and Resources, National Research Council. Washington, D.C. : National Academy Press, 1999. xii, 132 p. :
99-006094   616.9/8   0309065690
Marine pollution -- Health aspects. Marine microbiology. Marine pharmacology.

RA601.5 Public health. Hygiene. Preventive medicine — Food and food supply in relation to public health — Foodborne diseases

RA601.5.F68 1997
Fox, Nicols.
Spoiled : the dangerous truth about a food chain gone haywire / Nicols Fox. New York : BasicBooks, c1997. xiv, 434 p. ;
97-001239   615.9/54   0465019803
Foodborne diseases -- Popular works.

RA619 Public health. Hygiene. Preventive medicine — Disposal of the dead

RA619.S37 2001
Sappol, Michael.
  A traffic of dead bodies :anatomy and embodied social identity in nineteenth-century America / Michael Sappol. Princeton, N.J. : Princeton University Press, 2001. p. cm.
         069105925X
  Dead--Social aspects--United States--History--19th century. Human anatomy--United States--History--19th century. Human dissection--United States--History--19th century.

RA639-639.5 Public health. Hygiene. Preventive medicine — Transmission of disease — Transmission by animals. Zoonoses

RA639.F53
T-W-Fiennes, Richard N.
  Zoonoses and the origins and ecology of human disease / by Richard N. T-W-Fiennes. London ; Academic Press, 1978. xv, 196 p. :
77-093212   614.5/6   0122560507
  Zoonoses. Epidemiology.

RA639.5.B56 1996
  The biology of disease vectors / edited by Barry J. Beaty and William C. Marquardt. Niwot, Colo. : University Press of Colorado, c1996. xv, 632 p. :
95-032509   614.4/32   0870814117
  Insects as carriers of disease. Insects -- Molecular aspects.

RA639.5.M435 2000
  Medical entomology :a textbook on public health and veterinary problems caused by arthropods / edited by Bruce F. Eldridge and John D. Edman. Dordrecht ; Kluwer Academic Publishers, c2000. x, 659 p. :
         614.4/32   0792363205
  Insects as carriers of disease. Arthropoda. Medical parasitology.

RA643 Public health. Hygiene. Preventive medicine — Communicable diseases and public health — General works

RA643.W37 1996
Webber, Roger.
  Communicable disease epidemiology and control / Roger Webber. Wallingford, Oxon, UK : CAB International, c1996. xiv, 352 p. :
97-142322   614.5   0851991386
  Communicable diseases -- Epidemiology. Communicable diseases -- Prevention. Communicable Diseases -- epidemiology.

RA643.7-643.86 Public health. Hygiene. Preventive medicine — Communicable diseases and public health — By region or country

RA643.7.G7.H37 1993
Hardy, Anne,
  The epidemic streets : infectious disease and the rise of preventive medicine, 1856-1900 / Anne Hardy. Oxford : Clarendon Press ; 1993. xii, 325 p. :
93-028155   614.4/4212/09034
0198203772
  Communicable diseases -- England -- London -- History -- 19th century. Medicine, Preventive -- England -- London -- History -- 19th century. Epidemiology -- England -- London.

RA643.83.N6 2001
  No time to lose :getting more from HIV prevention / Committee on HIV Prevention Strategies in the United States, Division of Health Promotion and   Disease Prevention, Institute of Medicine ; Monica S. Ruiz ... [et al.] editors. Washington, D.C. : National Academy Press, c2001. xxiii, 227 p. :
         362.1/969792/00973   0309071372
  AIDS (Disease)--United States--Prevention.

RA643.86.A35A35 2002
  AIDS in Africa / edited by Max Essex ... [et al.]. 2nd ed. New York : Kluwer Academic/Plenum Publishers, c2002. xx, 724 p. :
         362.1/969792/0096   0306466996
  AIDS (Disease)--Africa.

RA644 Public health. Hygiene. Preventive medicine — Communicable diseases and public health — Individual diseases or groups of diseases, A-Z

RA644.A25.A362 1988
  AIDS : ethics and public policy / [edited by] Christine Pierce, Donald VanDeVeer. Belmont, Calif. : Wadsworth Pub. Co., c1988. x, 241 p. ;
87-010695   362.1/969792/00973
0534082866
  AIDS (Disease) -- Moral and ethical aspects -- United States -- Prevention. AIDS (Disease) -- Government policy -- United States. AIDS (Disease) -- Patients -- United States -- Social conditions.

RA644.A25.A36358 1992
  AIDS in the world / The Global AIDS Policy Coalition, Jonathan Mann, general editor ; Daniel J.M. Tarantola, scientific editor ; Thomas W. Netter, managing editor. Cambridge, Mass. : Harvard University Press, c1992. xiv, 1037 p.
92-001545   614.5/993   0674012666
  AIDS (Disease) -- Epidemiology. World health. Acquired Immunodeficiency Syndrome.

RA644.A25A363582 1996

AIDS in the world II :global dimensions, social roots, and responses / the Global AIDS Policy Coalition ; edited by Jonathan M. Mann and Daniel J.M. Tarantola. New York : Oxford University Press, 1996. xxxiv, 616 p. :

362.1/969792   0195090977

AIDS (Disease)--Epidemiology. AIDS (Disease)--Government policy. AIDS (Disease)--International cooperation.

RA644.A25.B358 1999
Bastos, Cristiana.

Global responses to AIDS : science in emergency / Cristiana Bastos. Bloomington : Indiana University Press, c1999. xvii, 225 p.

99-032161   362.1/969792   0253335906

AIDS (Disease) -- Social aspects. AIDS (Disease) -- Brazil -- Rio de Janeiro.

RA644.A25.B387 2000
Bayer, Ronald.

AIDS doctors : voices from the epidemic / Ronald Bayer, Gerald M. Oppenheimer. Oxford ; Oxford University Press, 2000. x, 310 p. ;

00-020913   616.97/92/00973   0195126815

AIDS (Disease) -- United States -- History. Oral history. AIDS (Disease) -- United States -- Biography.

RA644.A25.B745 1997
Brody, Stuart.

Sex at risk : lifetime number of partners, frequency of intercourse, and the low AIDS risk of vaginal intercourse / Stuart Brody. New Brunswick, N.J. : Transaction Publishers, c1997. ix, 222 p. :

97-012110   616.97/92   156000309X

AIDS (Disease) -- Transmission. AIDS (Disease) -- Risk factors. Heterosexuals -- Diseases -- Transmission.

RA644.A25.E68 1996
Epstein, Steven.

Impure science : AIDS, activism, and the politics of knowledge / Steven Epstein. Berkeley : University of California Press, c1996. xiii, 466 p.

96-016805   362.1/969792/00973

0520202333

AIDS (Disease) -- Research -- Social aspects -- United States.

RA644.A25.F47 1993
Fernando, M. Daniel.

AIDS and intravenous drug use : the influence of morality, politics, social science, and race in the making of a tragedy / M. Daniel Fernando. Westport, Conn. : Praeger, 1993. x, 167 p. ;

92-046557   614.5/993   0275942457

AIDS (Disease) -- Prevention -- Government policy -- United States. AIDS (Disease) -- Social aspects -- United States. Intravenous drug abuse -- United States.

RA644.A25G386 1996
Garrett, Laurie.

Microbes versus mankind :the coming plague / by Laurie Garrett. New York : Foreign Policy Association, 1996. 72 p. :

362.1/969792   0871241692

AIDS (Disease)--Epidemiology. Communicable diseases--Popular works. AIDS (Disease)--Popular works.

RA644.A25.H365 2000

Handbook of HIV prevention / edited by John L. Peterson and Ralph J. DiClemente. New York : Kluwer/Plenum, 2000. xvi, 337 p. ;

99-053994   616.97/9205   0306462230

AIDS (Disease) -- Prevention -- Handbooks, manuals, etc.

RA644.A25.N656 1997

No place for borders : the HIV/AIDS epidemic and development in Asia and the Pacific / edited by Godfrey Linge and Doug Porter. New York : St. Martin's Press, 1997. xxii, 191 p.

96-052306   362.1/969792/0095

0312173547

AIDS (Disease) -- Asia.

RA644.A25.P43 2001
Perloff, Richard M.

Persuading people to have safer sex : applications of social science to the AIDS crisis / Richard M. Perloff. Mahwah, N.J. : Lawrence Erlbaum Associates, 2001. ix, 159 p. :

00-058759   362.1/969792   0805833803

Safe sex in AIDS prevention. AIDS (Disease) -- Prevention -- Social aspects. Health behavior.

RA644.A25.S564 1998
Slack, James D.,

HIV/AIDS and the public workplace : local government preparedness in the 1990s / James D. Slack ; with a foreword by Chester A. Newland. Tuscaloosa : University of Alabama Press, c1998. xix, 162 p. :

97-040918   362.1/969792/00973

0817308636

AIDS (Disease) -- United States. Municipal officials and employees -- Health and hygiene -- United States.

RA644.A25T736 2001

Transgender and HIV :risks, prevention, and care / Walter Bockting, Sheila Kirk, editors. New York : Haworth Press, c2001. xxiv, 181 p. ;

616.97/92/00866   0789012685

AIDS (Disease) Transsexuals--Diseases.

RA644.A25.W646 1998

Women and AIDS : negotiating safer practices, care, and representation / Nancy L. Roth, Linda K. Fuller, editors. Binghamton, NY : Harrington Park Press, c1998. xvi, 330 p. ;

97-016980   616.97/9205/082   0789060140

AIDS (Disease) -- Prevention. Women -- Diseases -- Prevention. Women -- Health and hygiene.

RA644.C26.B37 1998
Bastien, Joseph William,
The kiss of death : Chaga's disease in the Americas / Joseph William Bastien. Salt Lake City : University of Utah Press, c1998. xxiv, 301 p.
98-018279   614.5/33   0874805597
Chagas' disease -- Bolivia -- Epidemiology. Chagas' disease -- Latin America -- Epidemiology. Chagas' disease -- Social aspects -- Bolivia.

RA644.C74.R35 1997
Rampton, Sheldon,
Mad cow U.S.A. : could the nightmare happen here? / Sheldon Rampton and John Stauber. Monroe, Me : Common Courage Press, c1997. 246 p. :
97-022500   616.8/3   1567511112
Creutzfeldt-Jakob disease -- United States. Bovine spongiform encephalopathy -- United States. Beef industry -- United States.

RA644.D6.H36 1999
Hammonds, Evelynn Maxine.
Childhood's deadly scourge : the campaign a control diphtheria in New York City, 1880-1930 / Evelynn Maxine Hammonds. Baltimore, Md. : Johns Hopkins University Press, 1999. p. cm.
98-038209   614.5/123/097471
0801859786
Diphtheria -- New York (State) -- New York -- History -- 19th century. Diphtheria -- New York (State) -- New York -- History -- 20th century.

RA644.H32.H37 1999
Harper, David.
Of mice, men, and microbes : hantavirus / David R. Harper, Andrea S. Meyer. San Diego : Academic Press, c1999. xv, 278 p. :
99-060590   616.9/25   012326460X
Hantavirus infections -- Four Corners Region.

RA644.H4.M87 1995
Muraskin, William A.
The war against hepatitis B : a history of the International Task Force on Hepatitis B Immunization / William Muraskin. Philadelphia : University of Pennsylvania Press, c1995. 248 p. :
94-043276   614.5/9362   0812232674
Hepatitis B -- Vaccination -- History. Hepatitis B -- history. Hepatitis B -- prevention & control.

RA644.I6.S54
Silverstein, Arthur M.
Pure politics and impure science : the swine flu affair / Arthur M. Silverstein. Baltimore : Johns Hopkins University Press, c1981. xv, 176 p. :
81-047590   614.5/18   0801826322
Swine influenza -- Vaccination -- Political aspects -- United States. Swine influenza -- Vaccination -- United States. Medical policy -- United States.

RA644.L23.F74 1996
Freije, Matthew R.
Legionellae control in health care facilities : a guide for minimizing risk / Matthew R. Freije ; [James M. Barbaree, technical editor ; foreword by Alfred P. Dufour]. Indianapolis, IN : HC Information Resources, c1996. xi, 131 p. :
95-082252   616.2/41   0964992647
Legionnaires' disease. Legionella penumophila.

RA644.L3.G878 1989
Gussow, Zachary,
Leprosy, racism, and public health : social policy in chronic disease control / Zachary Gussow. Boulder : Westview Press, 1989. xiv, 265 p. ;
88-005567   362.1/96998/00973
0813306744
Leprosy -- Social aspects -- United States -- History. Leprosy -- Government policy -- United States -- History. Racism -- United States -- History.

RA644.L94.E26 1993
Ecology and environmental management of lyme disease / edited by Howard S. Ginsberg. New Brunswick, N.J. : Rutgers University Press, c1993. viii, 224 p.
92-024221   614.5/7   0813519284
Lyme disease. Lyme disease -- Environmental aspects. Borrelia burgdorferi.

RA644.P7S65 1990
Slack, Paul.
The impact of plague in Tudor and Stuart England / Paul Slack. Oxford : Clarendon Press ; xvi, 443 p. :
     942.05   019820213X
Plague--England--History. Plague--England--Case studies. Plague--Social aspects--England.

RA644.P9.S553 1990
Smith, Jane S.
Patenting the sun : polio and the Salk vaccine / Jane S. Smith. New York : W. Morrow, c1990. 413 p., [16]
89-013802   616.8/35/009   0688094945
Poliomyelitis -- United States -- History. Poliomyelitis -- Vaccination -- History. Poliomyelitis vaccine -- History.

RA644.P93.K57 1998
Klitzman, Robert.
The trembling mountain : a personal account of kuru, cannibals, and mad cow disease / Robert Klitzman. New York : Plenum Trade, c1998. ix, 333 p. :
98-014386   616.8   030645792X
Prion diseases. Kuru -- Papua New Guinea. Bovine spongiform encephalopathy.

RA644.P93.M33 1998
The mad cow crisis : health and the public good / edited by Scott C. Ratzan. Washington Square, N.Y. : New York University Press, c1998. xii, 247 p. :
97-038913   362.1/9683   0814775101
Bovine spongiform encephalopathy -- Social aspects. Bovine spongiform encephalopathy -- Political aspects. Mass media in health education.

RA644.R3.F54 1998
Finley, Don,
   Mad dogs : the new rabies plague / Don Finley. College Station : Texas A&M University Press, c1998. xiv, 215 p. :
97-034672   614.5/63/09764   0890968047
   Rabies -- Texas -- Epidemiology. Rabies vaccines.

RA644.T8.L43 1996
Leavitt, Judith Walzer.
   Typhoid Mary : captive to the public's health / Judith Walzer Leavitt. Boston : Beacon Press, c1996. xviii, 331 p.
95-043486   614.5/112/097471
0807021024
Typhoid Mary, -- d. 1938.   Typhoid fever -- New York (State) -- New York -- History. Quarantine -- New York (State) -- New York -- History.

RA644.V4.A45 2000
Allen, Peter L.,
   The wages of sin : sex and disease, past and present / Peter Lewis Allen. Chicago : University of Chicago Press, 2000. xxiii, 202 p.
99-048603   306.4/61   0226014606
   Sexually transmitted diseases -- Social aspects. Sexually transmitted diseases -- Moral and ethical aspects. Sexually transmitted diseases -- History.

RA644.V4.I495 1997
Institute of Medicine (U.S.).
   The hidden epidemic : confronting sexually transmitted diseases / Thomas R. Eng and William T. Butler, editors ; Committee on Prevention and Control of Sexually Transmitted Diseases, Institute of Medicine, Division of Health Promotion and Disease Prevention. Washington, D.C. : National Academy Press, 1997. xii, 432 p. :
97-004218   614.5/47/0973   0309054958
   Sexually transmitted diseases -- United States. Sexually Transmitted Diseases -- prevention & control -- United States. Sexually Transmitted Diseases -- epidemiology -- United States.

RA644.V55.S63 2001
Society for General Microbiology.
   New challenges to health : the threat of virus infection / edited by G.L. Smith ... [et al.] Cambridge ; Cambridge University Press, 2001. ix, 347 p. :
00-1269896   616/.0194   0521806143
   Virus diseases -- Congresses. Medical virology -- Congresses. Infection -- Congresses.

RA644.Y4.E44 1992
Ellis, John H.
   Yellow fever & public health in the New South / John H. Ellis. Lexington, Ky. : University Press of Kentucky, c1992. xii, 233 p. :
91-035692   614.5/41/097609034
081311781X
   Yellow fever -- Southern States -- History -- 19th century. Public health -- Southern States -- History -- 19th century. Public Health -- history -- Southeastern United States.

RA644.5 Public health. Hygiene. Preventive medicine — Chronic and noninfectious diseases and public health — General works

RA644.5.R69 1998
Royer, Ariela.
   Life with chronic illness : social and psychological dimensions / Ariela Royer. Westport, Conn. : Praeger, 1998. xiv, 211 p. ;
98-011133   616/.001/9   0275961230
   Chronic diseases -- Social aspects. Chronic diseases -- Psychological aspects.

RA644.6 Public health. Hygiene. Preventive medicine — Chronic and noninfectious diseases and public health — By region or country

RA644.6.I53 1997
   Indicators of chronic health conditions : monitoring community-level delivery systems / edited by Robert J. Newcomer, A.E. Benjamin. Baltimore : Johns Hopkins University Press, 1997. xiv, 377 p. :
96-042207   362.1/2/0973   0801854911
   Chronic diseases -- United States -- Epidemiology -- Statistical methods. Health status indicators -- United States. Community health services -- United States -- Evaluation.

RA644.6.I58 1991
Institute of Medicine (U.S.).
   Disability in America : toward a national agenda for prevention / Andrew M. Pope and Alvin R. Tarlov, editors ; Committee on a National Agenda for the Prevention of Disabilites, Division of Health Promotion and Disease Prevention, Institute of Medicine. Washington, D.C. : National Academy Press, 1991. xii, 362 p. :
91-015496   614.5/99   0309043786
   Chronic diseases -- United States -- Prevention. Handicapped -- United States. Handicapped.

RA644.6.P8 1998
   Public and private responsibilities in long-term care : finding the balance / edited by Leslie C. Walker, Elizabeth H. Bradley, and Terrie Wetle. Baltimore : Johns Hopkins University Press, 1998. xv, 206 p. ;
98-003335   362.1/6/0973   0801859018
   Long-term care of the sick -- United States -- Finance. Long-term care of the sick -- Government policy -- United States. Insurance, Long-term care -- United States.

RA645 Public health. Hygiene. Preventive medicine — Chronic and noninfectious diseases and public health — Individual diseases or groups of diseases, A-Z

RA645.C3.C32 1997
   Cancer, AIDS, and quality of life / edited by Jay A. Levy, Claude Jasmin, and Gabriel Bez. New York : Plenum Press, c1997. xiii, 198 p.
97-005782   362.1/969792   030645517X
   Cancer -- Patients -- Care -- Congresses. AIDS (Disease) -- Patients -- Care -- Congresses. Quality of life -- Congresses.

RA645.N87.W469 1994
Western diseases : their dietary prevention and reversibility / edited by Norman J. Temple and Denis P. Burkitt ; foreword by Sir Richard Doll. Totowa, N.J. : Humana Press, c1994. xiii, 453 p.
94-014051   614.5939   0896032647
Nutritionally induced diseases -- Epidemiology. Chronic diseases -- Epidemiology. Medical geography.

RA645.O23.I55 1999
Interpreting weight : the social management of fatness and thinness / Jeffery Sobal and Donna Maurer, editors. New York : Aldine de Gruyter, c1999. x, 264 p. :
99-013617   306.4/61   0202305775
Obesity -- Social aspects. Food -- Social aspects. Nutrition -- Social aspects.

RA645.O23.W45 1999
Weighty issues : fatness and thinness as social problems / Jeffery Sobal and Donna Maurer, editors. Hawthorne, N.Y. : Aldine de Gruyter, c1999. xii, 260 p. ;
99-013616   306.4/61   0202305791
Obesity -- Social aspects. Food -- Social aspects. Nutrition -- Social aspects.

RA645.R35.P55 1986
Plough, Alonzo L.
Borrowed time : artificial organs and the politics of extending lives / Alonzo L. Plough. Philadelphia : Temple University Press, 1986. ix, 214 p. :
85-026196   362.1/97461   0877224153
Chronic renal failure -- Treatment -- Government policy -- United States. Chronic renal failure -- Treatment -- Social aspects -- United States. Medical technology -- United States -- Evaluation.

RA645.S53.W35 2001
Wailoo, Keith.
Dying in the city of the blues : sickle cell anemia and the politics of race and health / Keith Wailoo. Chapel Hill : University of North Carolina Press, c2001. ix, 338 p. :
00-062865   362.1/961527/00976819
0807825840
Sickle cell anemia -- Tennessee -- Memphis -- History.

RA645.S68.E65 1996
Epidemiology of sports injuries / Dennis J. Caine, Caroline G. Caine, Koenraad J. Lindner, editors. Champaign, IL : Human Kinetics, c1996. xiv, 455 p. :
95-039000   617.1/027   0873224663
Sports injuries -- Epidemiology.

RA645.35.M37 2001
Marrelli, T. M.
Handbook of home health standards & documentation guidelines for reimbursement / T.M. Marrelli.4th ed. St. Louis : Mosby, c2001. xxiii, 680 p. :
          362.1/4/021873   20 032
Home care services--Standards--United States--Handbooks, manuals, etc. Home care services--United States--Medical records--Handbooks, manuals, Insurance, Health--United States--Handbooks, manuals, etc.

RA648.3 Public health. Hygiene. Preventive medicine — War and public health — Nuclear warfare

RA648.3.S38 1995
Schull, William J.
Effects of atomic radiation : a half-century of studies from Hiroshima and Nagasaki / William J. Schull. New York : Wiley-Liss, c1995. xiii, 397 p.
95-014938   616.9/897   0471125245
Atomic bomb victims -- Health and hygiene -- Japan. Ionizing radiation -- Health aspects. Atomic bomb victims -- Health and hygiene -- Japan -- Research.

RA649 Public health. Hygiene. Preventive medicine — Epidemics. Epidemiology — History

RA649.E53 2001
Encyclopedia of plague and pestilence :from ancient times to the present / George Childs Kohn, editor ; [foreword by Mary-Louise Scully]. Rev. ed. New York : Facts on File, c2001. x, 459 p. ;
          614.4/9/03   0816042632
Epidemics--History--Encyclopedias.

RA649.H29 1998
Hays, J. N.
The burdens of disease : epidemics and human response in western history / J.N. Hays. New Brunswick, N.J. : Rutgers University Press, c1998. xi, 361 p. ;
97-039328   614.4/9   0813525276
Epidemics -- America -- History.

RA650.5 Public health. Hygiene. Preventive medicine — Epidemics. Epidermiology — By region or country

RA650.5.D8 1972
Duffy, John,
Epidemics in colonial America. Port Washington, N.Y., Kennikat Press [1972, c1953] xi, 274 p.
71-159070   614.4/9/73   0804616647
Epidemics -- United States.

RA650.5.E84 1991
Etheridge, Elizabeth W.
Sentinel for health : a history of the Centers for Disease Control / Elizabeth W. Etheridge. Berkeley : University of California Press, c1992. xix, 414 p. :
90-024679   614.4/273   0520071077
Epidemiology -- United States -- History.

RA650.5.K75 1992
Krieg, Joann P.
Epidemics in the modern world / Joann P. Krieg. New York : Twayne Publishers ; c1992. xiii, 172 p.
92-014090   614.4/973   0805788522
Epidemiology -- United States. Social medicine. Literature and medicine.

RA650.6-652.2 Public health. Hygiene. Preventive medicine — Quarantine (Land, maritime, and air) — By region or country

RA650.6.A1.S36 2001
Scott, Susan,
 Biology of plagues : evidence from historical populations / Susan Scott and Christopher J. Duncan. Cambridge ; Cambridge University Press, 2001. xiv, 420 p. :
00-063066   614.4/94   0521801508
 Epidemics. Epidemics -- Europe -- History -- 16th century. Epidemics -- Europe -- History -- 17th century.

RA651.B53
 Biocultural aspects of disease / edited by Henry Rothschild ; coordinating editor Charles F. Chapman. New York : Academic Press, 1981. xix, 653 p. :
81-012714   616.07/1   012598720X
 Epidemiology. Health and race. Medical anthropology.

RA651.G37 1994
Garrett, Laurie.
 The coming plague : newly emerging diseases in a world out of balance / Laurie Garrett. New York : Farrar, Straus and Giroux, c1994. xiii, 750 p.
94-026285   614.4   0374126461
 Epidemiology -- Popular works. Communicable diseases -- Popular works.

RA651.S75 1995
Stolley, Paul D.
 Investigating disease patterns : the science of epidemiology / Paul D. Stolley, Tamar Lasky. New York : Scientific American Library : c1995. x, 242 p. :
95-014250   614.4   0716750589
 Epidemiology. Epidemiology. Epidemiologic Methods.

RA652.N49 1999
 New ethics for the public's health / edited by Dan E. Beauchamp, Bonnie Steinbock. New York : Oxford University Press, 1999. xv, 382 p. :
99-023617   174/.2   0195124383
 Public health -- Moral and ethical aspects. Medical policy -- Moral and ethical aspects.

RA652.W43 2000
Weindling, Paul.
 Epidemics and genocide in eastern Europe, 1890-1945 / Paul Julian Weindling. Oxford ; Oxford University Press, 2000. xxi, 463 p. :
99-034520   614.4/943/09041   0198206917
 Epidemics -- Europe, Eastern -- History -- 19th century. Epidemics -- Europe, Eastern -- History -- 20th century. Bacteriology -- Germany -- History -- 19th century.

RA652.2.C55W45 1996
Weiss, Noel S.,
 Clinical epidemiology :the study of the outcome of illness / Noel S. Weiss. 2nd ed. New York : Oxford University Press, 1996. viii, 163 p. :
614.4   0195110269
 Clinical epidemiology. Epidemiologic Methods. Treatment Outcome.

RA652.2.M3.D34 1999
Daley, Daryl J.
 Epidemic modelling : an introduction / D.J. Daley and J. Gani. Cambridge ; Cambridge University Press, 1999. xii, 213 p. :
98-044051   614.4/01/5   0521640792
 Epidemiology -- Mathematical models. Epidemiology -- Statistical methods.

RA761 Public health. Hygiene. Preventive medicine — Disinfection. Fumigation. Sterilization. Decontamination — General works

RA761.L33 2001
 Disinfection, sterilization, and preservation / editor, Seymour S. Block. 5th ed. Philadelphia, PA : Lippincott Williams & Wilkins, 2001. xxii, 1481 p. :
614.4/8   0683307401
 Disinfection and disinfectants. Antiseptics. Sterilization.

RA770 Public health. Hygiene. Preventive medicine — Housing and public health

RA770.H43 1985
 Health care of homeless people / Philip W. Brickner ... [et al.], editors. New York : Springer Pub. Co., c1985. xiii, 349 p.
84-023625   362.1/0425   0826149901
 Homelessness -- Health aspects -- United States. Homeless persons -- Diseases -- United States. Homeless persons -- Medical care -- United States.

RA771 Public health. Hygiene. Preventive medicine — Rural health and hygiene. Rural health services — General works

RA771.H26 2001
 Handbook of rural health / edited by Sana Loue and Beth E. Quill. New York : Kluwer Academic, c2001. x, 370 p. :
00-062191   362.1/04257   0306464799
 Rural health -- Handbooks, manuals, etc. Public health -- Handbooks, manuals, etc. Rural health services -- Handbooks, manuals, etc.

RA771.5 Public health. Hygiene. Preventive medicine — Rural health and hygiene. Rural health services — By region or country

RA771.5.R86 1992
Rural health nursing : stories of creativity, commitment, and connectedness / edited by Patricia Winstead-Fry, Julia Churchill Tiffany, Raelene V. Shippee-Rice. New York : National League for Nursing Press, c1992. xvi, 406 p. :
92-150302   362.1/0425   0887375243
Rural health services -- United States. Community health nursing -- United States.

RA773.6 Public health. Hygiene. Preventive medicine — Personal health and hygiene — Communication in health

RA773.6.M39 1998
Maxwell, Bruce,
How to find health information on the Internet / Bruce Maxwell. Washington, D.C. : Congressional Quarterly, c1998. xviii, 332 p.
98-020101   025.06/61   1568022719
Medical care -- Computer network resources -- Directories. Medicine -- Computer network resources -- Directories. Health -- Computer network resources -- Directories.

RA776.75 Public health. Hygiene. Preventive medicine — Personal health and hygiene — Longevity. Rejuvenation. Youth extension

RA776.75.G646 1998
Golczewski, James A.,
Aging : strategies for maintaining good health and extending life / by James A. Golczewski. Jefferson, NC : McFarland & Co., 1998. vii, 203 p. ;
98-010801   613   0786404124
Longevity. Aging. Medicine, Preventive.

RA777.6-778 Public health. Hygiene. Preventive medicine — Personal health and hygiene — Personal health and grooming guides for classes of people

RA777.6.M39 2001
Mayo Clinic on healthy aging / Edward T. Creagan, editor in chief.1st ed. Rochester, Minn. : Mayo Clinic ; viii, 244 p. :
613/.0438   1893005070
Aging. Aging--Prevention.

RA777.8.A46 2001
American Medical Association complete guide to men's health / American Medical Association ; Angela Perry, medical editor. New York : J. Wiley, c2001. ix, 502 p. :
613/.04234   0471414115
Men--Health and hygiene. Self-care, Health.

RA778.C2163 1996
Carlson, Karen J.
The Harvard guide to women's health / Karen J. Carlson, Stephanie A. Eisenstat, Terra Ziporyn. Cambridge, Mass. : Harvard University Press, 1996. xiii, 718 p.
95-050876   616/.0082   0674367693
Women -- Health and hygiene. Women -- Diseases. Medicine, Popular.

RA778.G39 2002
Gay, Kathlyn.
Encyclopedia of women's health issues / Kathlyn Gay. Westport, CT : Oryx Press, 2002. xvii, 300 p. :
613/.04244/03   157356303X
Women--Health and hygiene--Encyclopedias. Women--Diseases--Encyclopedias.

RA778.H225 2001
Handbook of women's health : an evidence-based approach / edited by Jo Ann Rosenfeld. Cambridge ; Cambridge University Press, 2001. xi, 613 p. :
613/.04244   0521788331
Women--Health and hygiene--Handbooks, manuals, etc. Evidence-based medicine--Handbooks, manuals, etc. Women's Health--Handbooks.

RA778.N49 1998
Our bodies, ourselves for the new century : a book by and for women / the Boston Women's Health Book Collective.Newly revised and updated New York : Simon & Schuster, 1998. 780 p. :
613/.04244   0684842319
Women--Health and hygiene. Women--Diseases. Women--Psychology.

RA780 Public health. Hygiene. Preventive medicine — Personal health and hygiene — Cleanliness. Bathing

RA780.H69 1995
Hoy, Suellen M.
Chasing dirt : the American pursuit of cleanliness / Suellen Hoy. New York : Oxford University Press, 1995. xiv, 258 p. :
94-027129   614/.4/0973   0195094204
Hygiene -- United States -- History. Sanitation -- United States -- History.

RA780.5 Public health. Hygiene. Preventive medicine — Personal health and hygiene — Massage

RA780.5.L53 2001
Lidell, Lucy.
The book of massage : the complete step-by-step guide to Eastern and Western techniques / by Lucinda Lidell ... [et al.] ; photography by Faurso Dorelli ; foreword by Clare Maxwell-Hudson. 1st Fireside ed. New York : Simon & Schuster, 2001. 192 p. :
615.8/22   0743203909
Massage. Mind and body. Holistic medicine.

RA781-784 Public health. Hygiene. Preventive medicine — Personal health and hygiene — Exercise for health

RA781.A196 2001
Active living every day / Steven N. Blair ... [et al.]. Champaign, IL : Human Kinetics, c2001. xiii, 194 p. :
      613.7   0736037012
Exercise. Physical fitness. Health.

RA781.F683 2000
Free radicals in exercise and aging / Zsolt Radak, editor. Champaign, IL : Human Kinetics, c2000. xiii, 265 p.
00-044938   612/.015   0880118814
Exercise -- Molecular aspects. Aging -- Molecular aspects. Free radicals (Chemistry) -- Physiological effect.

RA784.D534 1999
Diet and nutrition sourcebook : basic consumer health information about dietary guidelines-- / edited by Karen Bellenir. 2nd ed. Detroit, MI : Omnigraphics, c1999. xiii, 650 p. :
      613.2   0780802284
Nutrition.

RA784.W635 2001
Willett, Walter C.
Eat, drink, and be healthy : the Harvard Medical School guide to healthy eating / Walter C. Willett with P.J. Skerrett ; contributions by Edward L. Giovannucci ; recipes by Maureen Callahan. New York : Simon & Schuster Source, 2001. 299 p.
      613.2   0684863375
Nutrition--Popular works.

RA790.5 Public health. Hygiene. Preventive medicine — Mental health. Mental illness prevention — General special

RA790.5.E53 1998
Encyclopedia of mental health / editor-in-chief, Howard S. Friedman. San Diego : Academic Press, c1998. 3 v. :
98-084208   616.89/003   0122266757
Mental health -- Dictionaries. Psychology -- Dictionaries. Mental illness -- Dictionaries.

RA790.5.S64 1998
Speer, David C.
Mental health outcome evaluation / David C. Speer. San Diego : Academic Press, c1998. xii, 121 p. :
97-080314   362.2   0126565759
Mental health services -- Evaluation. Outcome assessment (Medical care) Mental Health Services -- organization & administration.

RA790.55 Public health. Hygiene. Preventive medicine — Mental health. Mental illness prevention — Community psychology

RA790.55.H36 2000
Handbook of community psychology / edited by Julian Rappaport and Edward Seidman. New York : Kluwer Academic/Plenum, c2000. xxi, 1011 p ;
99-049482   362.2   0306461609
Community psychology -- Handbooks, manuals, etc.

RA790.6-790.7 Public health. Hygiene. Preventive medicine — Mental health. Mental illness prevention — By region or country

RA790.6.B78 1985
Brown, Phil.
The transfer of care : psychiatric deinstitutionalization and its aftermath / Phil Brown. Boston : Routledge & Kegan Paul, 1985. xiii, 275 p.
84-009797   362.2/0973   0710099002
Mentally ill -- Deinstitutionalization -- United States. Mentally ill -- Care -- United States. Mental health services -- United States.

RA790.6.G76 1991
Grob, Gerald N.,
From asylum to community : mental health policy in modern America / Gerald N. Grob. Princeton, N.J. : Princeton University Press, c1991. xv, 406 p., [
90-009178   362.2/0973   0691047901
Mental health policy -- United States -- History -- 20th century. Health Policy -- history -- United States. Mental Health Services -- history -- United States.

RA790.7.G7.J658 1993
Jones, Kathleen,
Asylums and after : a revised history of the mental health services : from the early 18th century to the 1990s / Kathleen Jones. London ; Athlone Press, 1993. 306 p. ;
93-031413   362.2/0942   0485114291
Mental health services -- England -- History.

RA792 Medical geography. Climatology. Meteorology — Medical geography (General) — General works

RA792.G38 2002
Gatrell, Anthony C.
Geographies of health: an introduction / Anthony C. Gatrell. Oxford : Blackwell, 2002. p. cm.
      614.4/2   0631219854
Medical geography. Environmental health.

RA792.G486 2001
Gesler, Wilbert M.,
Culture/place/health / Wilbert M. Gesler and Robin A. Kearns. New York : Routledge, 2001. p. cm.
      614.4/2   0415190665
Medical geography. Social medicine. Medical care--Social aspects.

RA792.5 Medical geography. Climatology. Meteorology — Medical geography (General) — Cartography. Mapping

RA792.5.H34 2000
Haggett, Peter.
The geographical structure of epidemics / Peter Haggett. Oxford ; Clarendon Press, 2000. xiv, 149 p. :
00-031359   614.4/2   0198233639
Medical geography. Epidemics. Epidemiology.

RA793 Medical geography. Climatology. Meteorology — Medical climatology and meteorology

RA793.U53 2001
Under the weather : climate, ecosystems, and infectious disease / National Research Council Division on Earth and Life Studies Board on Atmospheric Sciences and Climate Committee on Climate, Ecosystems, Infectious Disease, and Human Health. Washington, D.C. : National Academy Press, c2001. xiv, 146 p. :
              616.9/88   0309072786
Medical climatology. Epidemiology. Communicable diseases.

RA804 Medical geography. Climatology. Meteorology — By region or country — United States

RA804.S54 1993
Shannon, Gary William.
Disease and medical care in the United States : a medical atlas of the twentieth century / Gary W. Shannon, Gerald F. Pyle. New York : Macmillan Pub. Co. ; c1993. vii, 150 p. :
93-018364   614.4/273   0028973712
Medical geography -- United States -- Atlases. Epidemiology -- United States -- Atlases. Morbidity -- United States.

RA964 Medical centers. Hospitals. Dispensaries. Clinics — History

RA964.R57 1999
Risse, Guenter B.,
Mending bodies, saving souls : a history of hospitals / Guenter B. Risse. New York : Oxford University Press, 1999. xx, 716 p. :
98-040966   362.1/1/09   0195055233
Hospitals -- History. Hospital care -- History. Hospitals -- history.

RA965.3 Medical centers. Hospitals. Dispensaries. Clinics — Psychological aspects

RA965.3.M55 1994
Milstein, Linda Breiner.
Giving comfort : what you can do when someone you love is ill / Linda Breiner Milstein. New York : Penguin Books, 1994. xxi, 132 p. ;
93-032169   610.73   0140235388:
Hospital care -- Psychological aspects. Hospital patients -- Psychology. Caregivers.

RA965.5 Medical centers. Hospitals. Dispensaries. Clinics — Public relations. Hospital and community

RA965.5.A43 1989
The American general hospital : communities and social contexts / Diana Elizabeth Long and Janet Golden, editors. Ithaca : Cornell University Press, 1989. xvi, 217 p. :
89-007264   362.1/097309   080142349X
Hospital and community -- United States -- History. Hospitals, Community -- history -- United States. Hospitals, General -- history -- United States.

RA965.6 Medical centers. Hospitals. Dispensaries. Clinics — Hospital patients. Hospital-patient relations

RA965.6.C76 1997
Cromer, Mark,
Health care handbook : a consumer's guide to the American health care system / Mark Cromer. Santa Monica, Calif. : Santa Monica Press, c1997. xvii, 236 p.
97-015262   362.1/0973   0963994670
Hospital care. Medical care. Consumer education.

RA971.38 Medical centers. Hospitals. Dispensaries. Clinics — Hospital and health facility administration — Risk management

RA971.38.R58 2001
Risk management handbook for health care organizations / American Society for Healthcare Risk Management ; Roberta Carroll, editor. 3rd ed. San Francisco : Jossey-Bass ; c2001. xxxi, 938 p. :
              362.1/1/068   0787955531
Health facilities--Risk management. Health Facilities--economics. Health Facilities--organization & administration.

RA975.5 Medical centers. Hospitals. Dispensaries. Clinics — Other special services and departments, A-Z

RA975.5.D47.H68 1995
Howell, Joel D.
Technology in the hospital : transforming patient care in the early twentieth century / Joel D. Howell. Baltimore : Johns Hopkins University Press, c1995. xv, 341 p. :
94-038601   610/.28   0801850207
Hospitals -- United States -- Diagnostic services -- History -- 20th century. Medical technology -- United States -- History -- 20th century. Hospital care -- United States -- History -- 20th century.

RA981 Medical centers. Hospitals. Dispensaries. Clinics — By region or country — America

RA981.A2.G495 1996
Ginzberg, Eli,
Tomorrow's hospital : a look to the twenty-first century / Eli Ginzberg. New Haven : Yale Univerity Press, c1996. ix, 165 p.
95-039952   362.1/1/0973   0300065744
Hospitals -- Economic aspects -- United States. Hospitals -- United States -- Forecasting. Hospitals -- trends -- United States.

RA981.A2.G56 2000
Ginzberg, Eli,
Teaching hospitals and the urban poor / Eli Ginzberg ; with the assistance of Howard Berliner ... [et al.]. New Haven : Yale University Press, c2000. x, 129 p. ;
00-028294   362.1/1/0973   0300082320
Academic medical centers -- United States. Urban poor -- Medical care -- United States. Medical care -- United States -- Finance.

RA981.A2.H27 1998
Hackey, Robert B.
Rethinking health care policy : the new politics of state regulation / Robert B. Hackey. Washington, D.C. : Georgetown University Press, c1998. xi, 253 p. ;
97-037198   362.1/1/0973   0878406689
Hospital care -- Cost control -- Government policy -- United States -- States.

RA981.A2.S86 1995
Wright, John W.,
The best hospitals in America / John W. Wright & Linda Sunshine. New York : Gale Research, c1995. xx, 609 p. ;
94-037062   362.1/025/73   0810398745
Hospitals -- United States -- Directories. Medicine -- Specialties and specialists -- United States -- Directories. Medicine -- Research -- United States -- Directories.

RA997 Medical centers. Hospitals. Dispensaries. Clinics — Nursing homes. Long-term care facilities — By region or country

RA997.C85 1995
The Culture of long term care : nursing home ethnography / edited by J. Neil Henderson and Maria D. Vesperi ; foreword by Philip B. Stafford. Westport, Conn. : Bergin & Garvey, 1995. x, 251 p. ;
94-042151   362.1/6   0897894227
Nursing homes -- Anthropological aspects. Nursing homes -- Sociological aspects. Nursing home patients -- Social conditions.

RA997.F87 1996
The future of long-term care : social and policy issues / edited by Robert H. Binstock, Leighton E. Cluff, and Otto von Mering. Baltimore : Johns Hopkins University Press, c1996. xviii, 300 p.
96-002146   362.1/6/0973   0801853206
Long-term care of the sick -- United States. Aged -- Long-term care -- United States.

RA1025 Forensic medicine. Medical jurisprudence. Legal medicine — Biography

RA1025.H4.A3 1977
Helpern, Milton,
Autopsy : the memoirs of Milton Helpern, the world's greatest medical detective / by Milton Helpern, with Bernard Knight. New York : St. Martin's Press, c1977. 273 p., [8] l
77-076639   614/.19/0924   0312062117
Helpern, Milton, -- 1902-   Medical examiners (Law) -- New York (State) -- New York -- Biography. Autopsy. Forensic medicine.

RA1053 Forensic medicine. Medical jurisprudence — General special

RA1053.F67 1999
Forensic medicine sourcebook : basic consumer information for the layperson about forensic medicine ... / edited by Annemarie S. Muth. Detroit, MI : Omnigraphics, c1999. xiii, 574 p.
99-026967   614/.1   0780802322
Medical jurisprudence -- Popular works.

RA1055.5 Forensic medicine. Medical jurisprudence. Legal medicine — Disability evaluation

RA1055.5.G85 2001
Guides to the evaluation of permanent impairment / Linda Cocchiarella, Gunnar B.J. Anderson, [editors]. 5th ed. [Chicago] : American Medical Association, c2001. xxii, 613 p. :
          614/.1   1579470858
Disability evaluation--Handbooks, manuals, etc. Medical jurisprudence--Handbooks, manuals, etc.

RA1057.5 Forensic medicine. Medical jurisprudence. Legal medicine — Forensic genetics

RA1057.5.E94 1996
The evaluation of forensic DNA evidence / Committee on DNA Forensic Science: an Update, Commission on DNA Forensic Science: an Update, National Research Council. Washington, D.C. : National Academy Press, 1996. xv, 254 p. :
96-025364   614/.1   0309053951
Forensic genetics.

RA1057.5.E945 1998
Evett, Ian.
Interpreting DNA evidence : statistical genetics for forensic scientists / Ian W. Evett, Bruce S. Weir. Sunderland, Mass. : Sinauer Associates, c1998. xv, 278 p. :
98-004081   614/.1   0878931554
Forensic genetics. Forensic genetics -- Statistical methods. Population genetics -- Statistical methods.

RA1063-1063.45 Forensic medicine. Medical jurisprudence. Legal medicine — Forensic medicine. Medical jurisprudence. Legal medicine — Death determination and certification

RA1063.D44 1999
The definition of death : contemporary controversies / edited by Stuart J. Youngner, Robert M. Arnold, and Renie Schapiro. Baltimore : Johns Hopkins University Press, 1999. xx, 346 p. ;
98-020216   614/.1   0801859859
Death -- Proof and certification. Brain death.

RA1063.45.G64 2000
Goff, M. Lee
A fly for the prosecution : how insect evidence helps solve crimes / M. Lee Goff. Cambridge, Mass. : Harvard University Press, 2000. 225 p. :
99-058194   614/.1   0674002202
Forensic entomology.

RA1122.5 Forensic medicine. Medical jurisprudence. Legal medicine — Assault and battery — Battered child syndrome

RA1122.5.R44 2002
Recognition of child abuse for the mandated reporter / [edited by] Angelo P. Giardino, Eileen R. Giardino. 3rd ed. St. Louis, Mo. : G. W. Medical Pub., 2002. xxv, 440 p. :
      618.92/858223   187806052X
Battered child syndrome. Child abuse.

RA1151 Forensic medicine. Medical jurisprudence. Legal medicine — Forensic psychiatry — General works

RA1151.B935 2001
Bursten, Ben.
Psychiatry on trial :fact and fantasy in the courtroom / by Ben Bursten. Jefferson, NC : McFarland & Co., 2001. vi, 210 p. ;
      614/.1   0786410787
Forensic psychiatry.

RA1193 Toxicology — Dictionaries and encyclopedias

RA1193.L48 1996
Lewis, Robert A.
Lewis dictionary of toxicology / Robert A. Lewis. Boca Raton, Fla. : Lewis Publishers, 1996. 1127 p. ;
96-035759   615.9/003   1566702232
Toxicology -- Dictionaries.

RA1193.3 Toxicology — Communication in toxicology — General works

RA1193.3.I54 2000
Information resources in toxicology / editor-in-chief Philip Wexler ; associate editors, P.J. (Bert) Hakkinen, Gerald L. Kennedy, Jr., Frederick W. Stoss. San Diego : Academic Press, c2000. xxviii, 921 p
99-066137   0127447709
Toxicology -- Information resources.

RA1199 Toxicology — Research. Experimentation — General works

RA1199.C648 1997
Comprehensive toxicology / editors-in-chief, I. Glenn Sipes, Charlene A. McQueen, A. Jay Gandolfi. New York : Pergamon, 1997. 13 v. :
96-033052   615.9   0080423019
Toxicology. Poisons. Poisoning.

RA1199.N375 1984
National Research Council (U.S.).
Toxicity testing : strategies to determine needs and priorities / Steering Committee on Identification of Toxic and Potentially Toxic Chemicals for Consideration by the National Toxicology Program, Board on Toxicology and Environmental Health Hazards, Commission on Life Sciences, National Research Council. Washington, D.C. : National Academy Press, 1984. xiii, 382 p.
84-060095   615.9/07   0309034337
Toxicity testing. Toxicity testing -- United States.

RA1211 Toxicology — General works — 1901-

RA1211.H28 1993
Handbook of hazardous materials / edited by Morton Corn.
San Diego : Academic Press, c1993. xv, 772 P. :
93-002111   615.9/02   012189410X
Toxicology. Environmental health. Hazardous Substances -- toxicity.

RA1213 Toxicology — Popular works

RA1213.E47 1994
Emsley, John.
The consumer's good chemical guide : a jargon-free guide to the chemicals of everyday life / John Emsley. Oxford ; W.H. Freeman, [1994] xi, 347 p. :
94-008286   615.9   0716745054
Toxicology -- Popular works. Medical misconceptions.

RA1213.S73 2000
Stelljes, Mark E.,
Toxicology for non-toxicologists / Mark E. Stelljes. Rockville, Md. : ABS Group, Government Institutes Division, c2000. xiii, 168 p.
99-051974   615.9   0865876118
Toxicology -- Popular works.

RA1213.T76 1991
Toxics A to Z : a guide to everyday pollution hazards / John Harte ... [et al.]. Berkeley : University of California Press, c1991. xviii, 479 p.
90-025860   615.9   0520072235
Toxicology -- Popular works. Environmental health -- Popular works. Consumer education.

RA1215 Toxicology — Handbooks, manuals, etc.

RA1215.C37 2001
Casarett and Doull's toxicology :the basic science of poisons / editor, Curtis D. Klaassen. 6th ed. New York : McGraw-Hill Medical Pub. Division, c2001. xix, 1236 p. :
          615.9   0071347216
Toxicology--Handbooks, manuals, etc. Poisoning. Poisons.

RA1215.C483 2000
Cheremisinoff, Nicholas P.
Handbook of hazardous chemical properties / Nicholas P. Cheremisinoff. Boston : Butterworth-Heinemann, c2000. x, 433 p. ;
00-501885   615.9   0750672099
Toxicology -- Handbooks, manuals, etc. Chemicals -- Safety measures -- Handbooks, manuals, etc. Hazardous substances -- Handbooks, manuals, etc.

RA1215.N37
Registry of toxic effects of chemical substances. Cincinnati, Ohio : U.S. Dept. of Health and Human Services, Public v. ;
75-649213   615.9/02/0212
Poisons -- Tables -- Periodicals. Industrial toxicology -- Periodicals. Toxicology -- nomenclature

RA1224.2 Toxicology — Reproductive toxicology

RA1224.2.C65 1997
Colborn, Theo.
Our stolen future : are we threatening our fertility, intelligence, and survival? : a scientific detective story : with a new epilogue by the authors / Theo Colborn, Dianne Dumanoski, and John Peterson Myers. New York : Penguin Group, c1997. xx, 316 p. :
          615.9/02   0525939822
Reproductive toxicology. Environmental health.

RA1224.2.R466 1998
Reproductive hazards of the workplace / [edited by] Linda M. Frazier, Marvin L. Hage. New York : Van Nostrand Reinhold, c1998. xviii, 572 p.
97-005940   616.9/803   0442020422
Reproductive toxicology. Occupational diseases.

RA1224.5 Toxicology — Toxicological emergencies

RA1224.5.T873 1999
Turkington, Carol.
The poisons and antidotes sourcebook / Carol Turkington ; foreword by Shirley K. Osterhout. 2nd ed. New York, NY : Facts On File, c1999. viii, 408 p. :
          615.9   0816039607
Toxicological emergencies--Handbooks, manuals, etc. Poisoning--Handbooks, manuals, etc.

RA1226 Toxicology — Environmental toxicology

RA1226.C76 1998
Crosby, Donald G.
Environmental toxicology and chemistry / Donald G. Crosby. New York : Oxford University Press, 1998. xiv, 336 p. :
97-022438   615.9/02   0195117131
Environmental toxicology. Environmental chemistry.

RA1226.P64 1997
Pohanish, Richard P.
Rapid guide to hazardous chemicals in the environment / Richard P. Pohanish. New York : Van Nostrand Reinhold, c1997. xix, 519 p. ;
97-014013   615.9/02   0442025270
Environmental toxicology -- Handbooks, manuals, etc.

RA1229 Toxicology — Industrial toxicology — General works

RA1229.P76 1996
Proctor, Nick H.
   Proctor and Hughes' Chemical hazards of the workplace / [edited by] Gloria J. Hathaway ; [by] Nick H. Proctor, James P. Hughes. New York : Van Nostrand Reinhold, 1996. ix, 704 p. ;
96-018126   615.9/02   0442020503
   Industrial toxicology. Industrial hygiene.

RA1229.3 Toxicology — Industrial toxicology — Handbooks, manuals, etc.

RA1229.3.C48 1995
   Chemical information manual. Rockville, MD : Government Institutes, c1995. xi, 341 p. ;
95-077857   615.9/02   0865874697
   Industrial toxicology -- Handbooks, manuals, etc.

RA1231 Toxicology — Special poisons and groups of poisons — Inorganic poisons

RA1231.L4.W37 2000
Warren, Christian.
   Brush with death : a social history of lead poisoning / Christian Warren. Baltimore, MD : Johns Hopkins University Press, c2000. xiv, 362 p. :
99-046329   615.9/25688/0973
0801862892
   Lead poisoning -- United States -- History.

RA1231.R2.L497 1994
Lindee, M. Susan.
   Suffering made real : American science and the survivors at Hiroshima / M. Susan Lindee. Chicago : University of Chicago Press, c1994. xi, 287 p. :
94-001832   363.17/99   0226482375
   Radiation -- Physiological effect -- Research -- Social aspects. Atomic bomb victims -- Japan -- Hiroshima-shi. Children of atomic bomb victims -- Japan -- Hiroshima-shi. Hiroshima-shi (Japan) -- History -- Bombardment, 1945.

RA1231.R2.W45 1999
Welsome, Eileen.
   The plutonium files : America's secret medical experiments in the Cold War / Eileen Welsome. New York, N.Y. : Dial Press, c1999. ix, 580 p. :
99-010991   616.9/897/00973   0385314027
   Radiation -- Toxicology -- Research -- United States. Human experimentation in medicine -- United States. Radiation victims -- United States.

RA1242 Toxicology — Special poisons and groups of poisons — Organic poisons

RA1242.C436.T48 2000
Thornton, Joe.
   Pandora's poison : chlorine, health, and a new environmental strategy / Joe Thornton. Cambridge, Mass. : MIT Press, c2000. xii, 599 p. :
99-057011   615.9/51   0262201240
   Organochlorine compounds -- Toxicology. Organochlorine compounds -- Environmental aspects. Environmental policy.

RA1242.D48.A64 1984
Apfel, Roberta J.,
   To do no harm : DES and the dilemmas of modern medicine / Roberta J. Apfel, Susan M. Fisher. New Haven : Yale University Press, c1984. x, 199 p. ;
84-005089   363.1/94   0300031920
   Diethylstilbestrol -- Toxicology. Vagina -- Cancer -- Psychological aspects. Physician and patient.

RA1242.D55.G53 1995
Gibbs, Lois Marie.
   Dying from dioxin : a citizen's guide to reclaiming our health and rebuilding democracy / by Lois Marie Gibbs and the Citizens Clearinghouse for Hazardous Waste. Boston, MA : South End Press, c1995. xxxii, 361 p.
95-023589   363.17/91   0896085260
   Dioxins -- Health aspects. Dioxins -- Environmental aspects.

RA1242.T5.G56 2000
Stephens, Trent D.
   Dark remedy : the impact of thalidomide and its revival as a vital medicine / Trent Stephens and Rock Brynner. Cambridge, Mass. : Perseus Pub., c2001. xii, 228 p. ;
                            0738204048
   Thalidomide. Thalidomide -- Side effects. Thalidomide -- Research.

RA1242.T6.D68 1990
Douville, Judith A.
   Active and passive smoking hazards in the workplace / Judith A. Douville. New York, N.Y. : Van Nostrand Reinhold, c1990. xii, 221 p. ;
89-024999   616.86/5   0442001673
   Smoking -- Health aspects. Passive smoking -- Health aspects. Industrial hygiene.

RA1242.T6.N34 1996
Napier, Kristine M.
   Cigarettes-- what the warning label doesn't tell you : the first comprehensive guide to the health consequences of smoking / Kristine Napier, writer ; William M. London, Elizabeth M. Whelan, Andrea Golaine Case, editor ; drawings by Friederike Paetzold. New York : American Council on Science and Health, c1996. xxii, 186 p.
96-086418   616.86/507
   Tobacco -- Toxicology. Cigarette habit -- Health aspects.

RA1250 Toxicology — Special poisons and groups of poisons — Vegetable poisons (General)

RA1250.D53 1996
Dictionary of plant toxins / editor, J.B. Harborne ; executive editor, H. Baxter. Chichester [England] ; Wiley, 1996- p. cm.
96-011164   615.9/52/03   0471951072
  Plant toxins -- Dictionaries.

RA1250.L27 1985
Lampe, Kenneth F.
  AMA handbook of poisonous and injurious plants / Kenneth F. Lampe, Mary Ann McCann. Chicago, Ill. : American Medical Association : c1985. xi, 432 p. :
84-028532   615.9/52   0899701833
  Poisonous plants -- Toxicology -- Handbooks, manuals, etc. Skin -- Inflammation -- Handbooks, manuals, etc. Poisonous plants -- United States -- Identification.

RA1258 Toxicology — Special poisons and groups of poisons — Food poisons

RA1258.E48 1999
Emsley, John.
  Was it something you ate? : food intolerance, what causes it and how to avoid it / John Emsley and Peter Fell. Oxford ; Oxford University Press, 1999. 184 p. ;
99-015702   615.9/54   0198504438
  Food -- Toxicology. Nutritionally induced diseases.

RA1270 Toxicology — Special poisons and groups of poisons — Other poisons and groups of poisons, A-Z

RA1270.F4.M37 1994
Marcus, Alan I,
  Cancer from beef : DES, federal food regulation, and consumer confidence / Alan I Marcus. Baltimore : Johns Hopkins University Press, 1994. x, 235 p. ;
93-021505   615.9/54   0801847001
  Feed additives -- Toxicology. Diethylstilbestrol -- Carcinogenicity. Meat -- Contamination.

RA1270.P4.B73 1992
Briggs, Shirley A.
  Basic guide to pesticides : their characteristics and hazards / Shirley A. Briggs and the staff of Rachel Carson Council. Washington : Hemisphere Pub. Corp., c1992. xvii, 283 p.
92-007024   363.17/92   1560322535
  Pesticides -- Toxicology.

RA1270.P4.H36 2001
  Handbook of pesticide toxicology / edited by Robert I. Krieger. 2nd ed. San Diego : Academic Press, c2001. 2 v. (xxxiv, 1908) :
          615.9/51   0124262627
  Pesticides--Toxicology.

RB Pathology

RB25 Pathological anatomy and histology — General works — 1901-

RB25.M36 1987
Maulitz, Russell Charles,
Morbid appearances : the anatomy of pathology in the early nineteenth century / Russell C. Maulitz. Cambridge ; Cambridge University Press, 1987. ix, 277 p. :
86-034347   616.07/09034   0521328284
Anatomy, Pathological -- France -- History -- 19th century. Anatomy, Pathological -- Great Britain -- History -- 19th century. Pathology -- history -- France.

RB36.2.L33 1995
Laboratory instrumentation / edited by Mary C. Haven, Gregory A. Tetrault, Jerald R. Schenken. 4th ed. New York : Van Nostrand Reinhold, c1995. xix, 492 p. :
          616.07/54/028   0442015208
Medical laboratories--Equipment and supplies.

RB37 Clinical pathology. Laboratory technique — Societies. Serials

RB37.C54 2001
Clinical diagnosis and management by laboratory methods / [edited by] John Bernard Henry. 20th ed. Philadelphia : W.B. Saunders, c2001. xxiv, 1512 p. :
          616.07/56   0721688640
Diagnosis, Laboratory. Laboratory Techniques and Procedures.

RB37.L2755 1992
The Laboratory revolution in medicine / edited by Andrew Cunningham and Perry Williams. Cambridge ; Cambridge University Press, 1992. xi, 347 p. :
91-036254   616.07/56/09034   0521404843
Diagnosis, Laboratory -- History -- 19th century. Medicine -- Research -- History -- 19th century. History of Medicine, 19th Cent. -- Europe.

RB37.L2758 2001
Jacobs & DeMott laboratory test handbook / David S. Jacobs, Dwight K. Oxley, co-editor-in-chief ; Wayne R. DeMott.5th ed. with key word index. Hudson [Ohio] : Lexi-Comp., c2001. 1031 p. :
          616.07/56   1930598424
Diagnosis, Laboratory--Handbooks, manuals, etc.

RB37.L276 1986
Laboratory tests : implications for nursing care / C. Judith Byrne ... [et al.]. Menlo Park, Calif. : Addison-Wesley Pub. Co., Health Sciences Divisio c1986. xxi, 756 p. ;
85-013555   616.07/5   0201126702
Diagnosis, Laboratory. Nursing. Diagnosis, Laboratory -- nurses' instruction.

RB37.W42 1998
Wedding, Mary Ellen.
Medical laboratory procedures / Mary Ellen Wedding, Sally A. Toenjes. 2nd ed. Phildadelphia : F.A. Davis, c1998. xii, 427 p. :
          616.07/5/078   0803600526
Diagnosis, Laboratory. Physicians' assistants. Diagnosis, Laboratory--programmed instruction.

RB37.5 Clinical pathology. Laboratory technique — Study and teaching

RB37.5.W35 1998
Wallace, M. Ann.
Clinical laboratory science education & management / M. Ann Wallace, Deanna D. Klosinski. Philadelphia : W.B. Saunders, c1998. xii, 420 p. :
96-049581   616.07/068   0721645437
Medical laboratory technology -- Study and teaching. Pathological laboratories -- Management.

RB38.2 Clinical pathology. Laboratory technique — Handbooks, manuals, etc.

RB38.2.L33 2001
Laboratory tests and diagnostic procedures / edited by Cynthia C. Chernecky, Barbara J. Berger. 3rd ed. Philadelpha : W.B. Saunders, c2001. xix, 1114 p. :
          616.07/56   0721686095
Diagnosis, Laboratory--Handbooks, manuals, etc. Diagnosis, Laboratory--Encyclopedias. Laboratory Techniques and Procedures--Handbooks.

RB38.2.P34 2002
Pagana, Kathleen Deska,
Mosby's manual of diagnostic and laboratory tests / Kathleen Deska Pagana, Timothy J. Pagana. 2nd ed. St. Louis : Mosby, c2002. xi, 1166 p. :
          616.07/56   032301609X
Diagnosis, Laboratory--Handbooks, manuals, etc. Diagnosis, Radioscopic--Handbooks, manuals, etc. Reference values (Medicine)--Handbooks, manuals, etc.

RB40 Clinical pathology. Laboratory technique — Chemical examination

RB40.F84 2001
Tietz fundamentals of clinical chemistry / [edited by] Carl A. Burtis, Edward R. Ashwood ; consulting editor, Barbara Border. Philadelphia : W.B. Saunders, c2001. xxv, 1091 p.
00-061891   616.07/56   0721686346
Clinical chemistry. Chemistry, Clinical.

RB40.M32 1989
Meites, Samuel,
  Otto Folin : America's first clinical biochemist / Samuel
Meites. [Washington, D.C.] : American Association for
Clinical Chemistry, c1989. xx, 428 p., [
  88-007418   616.07/56/0924   0915274485
*Folin, Otto, -- 1867-1934. Folin, Otto, -- 1867-1934. Clinical
chemists -- United States -- Biography. Chemistry, Clinical --
biography.*

RB43.7 Clinical pathology. Laboratory technique — Molecular diagnosis — General works

RB43.7.M646 2001
  Molecular pathology protocols / edited by Anthony A.
Killeen. Totowa, N.J. : Humana Press, 2001. xiv, 491 p. :
        616.07/5   0896036812
  *Molecular diagnosis--Laboratory manuals. Pathology, Molecular-
-Laboratory manuals. Pathology, Clinical--methods--Laboratory
Manuals.*

RB43.8 Clinical pathology. Laboratory technique — Molecular diagnosis — Special methods, A-Z

RB43.8.P64N86 1997
Nuovo, Gerard J.
  PCR in situ hybridization : protocols and applications /
Gerard J. Nuovo. 3rd ed. Philadelphia : Lippincott-Raven
Publishers, c1997. xi, 497 p. :
        616.07/582   039758749X
  Polymerase chain reaction. In situ hybridization. Cytodiagnosis.

RB44 Clinical pathology. Laboratory technique — Examination of chromosomes

RB44.G7613 1984
Grouchy, Jean de.
  Clinical atlas of human chromosomes / Jean de Grouchy,
Catherine Turleau ; foreword by Victor McKusick. New York :
Wiley, c1984. xx, 487 p. :
  83-016839   616/.042   047189205X
  *Human chromosome abnormalities -- Atlases. Human cytogenetics
-- Atlases. Medical genetics -- Atlases.*

RB45.15 Clinical pathology. Laboratory technique — Examination of the blood — Phlebotomy. Blood collection

RB45.15.D525 2001
Di Lorenzo, Marjorie Schaub,
  Blood collection in healthcare / Marjorie Schaub Di
Lorenzo, Susan King Strasinger. Philadelphia, PA : F.A. Davis
Co., c2001. xiii, 98 p. :
        616.07/561   0803608489
  Blood--Collection and preservation. Phlebotomy.

RB45.15.E76 2001
Ernst, Dennis J.
  Phlebotomy for nurses and nursing personnel : what every
nurse and nursing assistant must know about blood specimen
collection / Dennis J. Ernst, Catherine Ernst. Ramsey, Ind. :
HealthStar Press, c2001. 182 p. :
        616.07/561   0970058896
  *Phlebotomy--Handbooks, manuals, etc. Nurses--Handbooks,
manuals, etc.*

RB45.15.G37 1989 Suppl.
Becan-McBride, Kathleen,
  Phlebotomy examination review / Kathleen Becan-McBride,
Diana Garza. Norwalk, Conn. : Appleton & Lange, c1991. ix,
185 p. :
  91-004533   616.07/561/076   0838578292
  *Phlebotomy -- Examinations, questions, etc. Blood Specimen
Collection -- examination questions. Bloodletting -- examination
questions.*

RB56 Clinical pathology. Laboratory technique — Examination for drugs — General works

RB56.C48 1995
Chamberlain, Joseph.
  The analysis of drugs in biological fluids / Joseph
Chamberlain. Boca Raton : CRC Press, c1995. vii, 351 p. :
  95-019022   615/.1901   0849324920
  Drugs -- Analysis. Body fluids -- Analysis.

RB111 General pathology — General works — 1901-

RB111.A5 1980
Anderson, W. A. D.
  Synopsis of pathology / W. A. D. Anderson, Thomas M.
Scotti. 10th ed. St. Louis : Mosby, 1980. ix, 804 p. :
        616.07   0801602319
  Pathology. Pathology.

RB111.K45 1998
Kent, Thomas H.
  Introduction to human disease / Thomas H. Kent, Michael
Noel Hart. 4th ed. Stamford, Conn. : Appleton & Lange,
c1998. vii, 656 p. :
        616.07   0838540708
  Pathology. Allied health personnel. Pathology.

RB111.K895 2002
  Robbins basic pathology / [edited by] Vinay Kumar, Ramzi
S. Cotran, Stanley L. Robbins ; with illustrations by James A.
Perkins. 7th ed. Philadelphia, PA : Saunders, 2002. p. cm.
        616.07   0721692745
  Pathology.

RB111.R62 1999
Cotran, Ramzi S.,
  Robbins pathologic basis of disease. 6th ed. / Ramzi S.
Cotran, Vinay Kumar, Tucker Collins. Philadelphia : Saunders,
c1999. xv, 1424 p. :
        616.07   072167335X
  Pathology. Pathology.

RB111.S445 1992
Boyd, William,
Boyd's introduction to the study of disease. 11th ed. / Huntington Sheldon. Philadelphia : Lea & Febiger, 1992. vii, 606 p. :
      616   0812115619
Pathology. Pathology.

RB112 General pathology — General special

RB112.C76 2001
Crowley, Leonard V.,
An introduction to human disease : pathology and pathophysiology correlations / Leonard V. Crowley. 5th ed. Sudbury, Mass. : Jones and Bartlett Publishers, c2001. xvii, 790 p. :
      616.07   0763714348
Pathology. Diseases--Causes and theories of causation. Disease.

RB112.5 General pathology — Clinical biochemistry

RB112.5.A84 2000
Ashcroft, Frances M.
Ion channels and disease : channelopathies / Frances M. Ashcroft. San Diego : Academic Press, c2000. xxi, 481 p. :
98-085618   616.07   0120653109
Ion channels. Pathology, Molecular.

RB113 General pathology — Physiological pathology. Clinical physiology

RB113.C785 1996
Corwin, Elizabeth J.
Handbook of pathophysiology / Elizabeth J. Corwin. Philadelphia : Lippincott, c1996. xxx, 705 p. :
95-038026   616.07   0397552130
Physiology, Pathological -- Handbooks, manuals, etc. Pathology - - handbooks. Physiology -- handbooks.

RB113.H24 2001
Handbook of pathophysiology. Springhouse, Pa. : Springhouse Corp., c2001. 1 v. (various pagings) :
      616.07   1582550468
Physiology, Pathological--Handbooks, manuals, etc. Pathology-- Handbooks. Physiology--Handbooks.

RB113.L322 1999
Langer, Glenn A.,
Understanding disease / G.A. Langer. Fort Bragg, Calif. : QED Press, 1999- v. 1 :
99-024762   616.07   0936609400
Physiology, Pathological -- Popular works. Physiology, Pathological -- Case studies.

RB113.M35 2002
Pathophysiology : the biologic basis for disease in adults & children / [edited by] Kathryn L. McCance, Sue E. Huether. 4th ed. St. Louis : Mosby, c2002. xxvi, 1616 p. :
      616.07   0323014380
Physiology, Pathological. Nursing. Pathology--Nurses' Instruction.

RB113.M5854 1997
Molecular biology in medicine / edited by Timothy M. Cox, John Sinclair. Oxford [England] ; Blackwell Science, 1997. x, 340 p., [1
96-021997   616/.042   0865427925
Pathology, Molecular. Genetics, Medical. Transcription, Genetic.

RB113.P45 2000
Copstead, Lee Ellen.
Pathophysiology : biological and behavioral perspectives / Lee-Ellen C. Copstead, Jacquelyn L. Banasik. Philadelphia : Saunders, c2000. xxi, 1337 p.
98-053145   616.07   0721671780
Physiology, Pathological. Pathology. Physiology.

RB121 General pathology — Addresses, essays, lectures

RB121.B86
Busch, Harris.
Biochemical frontiers in medicine, by five authors. Boston, Little, Brown [1963] 364 p.
63016148   612.015
Biochemistry Physiology, Pathological

RB127 Manifestations of disease — Pain

RB127.C4753 1990
Chronic pain / edited by Thomas W. Miller. Madison, Conn. : International Universities Press, c1990. 2 v. :
90-004262   616/.0472   0823608506
Chronic pain. Chronic Disease. Pain.

RB127.C5 1990
Chronic pain : psychosocial factors in rehabilitation / edited by Eldon Tunks, Anthony Bellissimo, Ranjan Roy. Malabar, Fla. : R.E. Krieger Pub. Co., 1990. x, 293 p. :
88-013252   616/.0472   0894642219
Chronic pain -- Treatment. Psychotherapy. Chronic pain -- Psychological aspects.

RB127.G745 2001
Greenhalgh, Susan.
Under the medical gaze :facts and fictions of chronic pain / Susan Greenhalgh. Berkeley: University of California Press, c2001. xii, 371 p. :
      616/.0472/092   0520223985
Greenhalgh, Susan--Health.   Chronic pain--Patients--United States- -Biography. Arthritis--Patients--United States--Biography. Fibromyalgia--Patients--United States--Biography.

RB127.M346 1999

Managing pain. Pleasantiville, NY : Reader's Digest Association, 1999. p. cm.

    616/.0472   076210144X

Pain--Popular works. Analgesia--Popular works.

RB127.M67 1991
Morris, David B.

The culture of pain / David B. Morris. Berkeley : University of California Press, c1991. xii, 342 p. :

90-011305   306.4/61   0520072669

Pain -- Social aspects. Pain -- Psychological aspects. Medicine in Art.

RB127.P346 1998

Pain sourcebook / edited by Allan R. Cook. Detroit, Mich. : Omnigraphics, c1998. xi, 667 p. :

97-037833   616/.0472   0780802136

Pain.

RB127.R4913 1995
Rey, Roselyne.

The history of pain / Roselyne Rey ; translated by Louise Elliott Wallace, J.A. Cadden, and S.W. Cadden. Cambridge, Mass. : Harvard University Press, 1995. 394 p. ;

94-031948   616/.0472/09   0674399676

Pain -- History. Pain -- history. History of Medicine.

RB127.R675 1992
Roy, R.

The social context of the chronic pain sufferer / Ranjan Roy. Toronto ; University of Toronto Press, c1992. xvi, 183 p. ;

93-108368   616/.0472   0802028608

Chronic pain -- Social aspects. Chronic pain -- Psychological aspects.

RB127.V47 2000
Vertosick, Frank T.

Why we hurt : the natural history of pain / Frank T. Vertosick, Jr. New York : Harcourt, 2000. p. cm.

99-045848   616/.0472   0151003777

Pain -- Popular works. Pain -- History.

RB127.W355 2000
Wall, Patrick D.

Pain : the science of suffering / Patrick Wall. New York : Columbia University Press, c2000. viii, 184 p.

00-023889   616/.0472   0231120060

Pain.

RB127.Z2
Zborowski, Mark.

People in pain. Foreword by Margaret Mead. San Francisco, Jossey-Bass, 1969. xviii, 274 p.

70-092888   616   0875890466

Pain. Ethnopsychology.

RB135 Manifestations of disease — Atrophy

RB135.S73
Steinberg, Franz U.,

The immobilized patient : functional pathology and management / Franz U. Steinberg. New York : Plenum Medical Book Co., c1980. ix, 156 p. :

79-025903   616.7   0306403722

Hypokinesia. Hypokinesia -- Physiological aspects. Immobilization.

RB145 Manifestations of disease — Pathology of the blood

RB145.T79 1999
Turgeon, Mary Louise.

Clinical hematology :theory and procedures / Mary L. Turgeon. 3rd ed. Philadelphia : Lippincott, c1999. xii, 480 p. :

    616.1/5   0316856231

Hematology. Hematologic Diseases. Hematology--methods.

RB150 Manifestations of disease — Other manifestations of disease, A-Z

RB150.C6.L39 1997
Lawrence, Madelaine.

In a world of their own : experiencing unconsciousness / Madelaine Lawrence. Westport, Conn. : Praeger, 1997. viii, 186 p.

96-025076   616.8/49   0275953238

Coma. Loss of consciousness. Subconsciousness.

RB150.F37.C47 1993

Chronic fatigue syndrome / edited by David M. Dawson, Thomas D. Sabin. Boston : Little, Brown, c1993. xii, 218 p. :

92-049249   616/.047   0316177482

Chronic fatigue syndrome. Fatigue Syndrome, Chronic.

RB150.F37.C474 1996

Chronic fatigue syndrome : an integrative approach to evaluation and treatment / edited by Mark A. Demitrack, Susan E. Abbey ; foreword by Stephen E. Straus. New York : Guilford Press, c1996. xviii, 317 p.

95-026739   616/.047   1572300388

Chronic fatigue syndrome -- Psychological aspects. Psychotherapy. Fatigue Syndrome, Chronic -- psychology.

RB150.F37.F753 1998
Friedberg, Fred.
   Understanding chronic fatigue syndrome : an empirical guide to assessment and treatment / Fred Friedberg, Leonard A. Jason. Washington, DC : American Psychological Association, c1998. xvii, 266 p.
98-021293   616/.0478   1557985111
   Chronic fatigue syndrome. Fatigue Syndrome, Chronic -- diagnosis. Fatigue Syndrome, Chronic -- therapy.

RB150.F37.J64 1996
Johnson, Hillary.
   Osler's web : inside the labyrinth of the chronic fatigue syndrome epidemic / Hillary Johnson. New York : Crown Publishers, c1996. xi, 720 p. ;
95-031149   616/.047   051770353X
   Chronic fatigue syndrome -- Popular works.

RB150.S5.B6 1980
Bordicks, Katherine J.
   Patterns of shock : implications for nursing care / Katherine J. Bordicks. New York : Macmillan, c1980. xx, 279 p. :
79-009824   617/.21   0023124504
   Shock. Shock -- Nursing.

RB151 Theories of disease. Etiology. Pathogenesis — General works

RB151.K5
King, Lester S.
   The growth of medical thought. [Chicago] Univ. of Chicago Press [c1963] xi, 254 p.
63009729   616.09
   History of Medicine. Philosophy, Medical -- history. Diseases -- Causes and theories of causation.

RB151.M28 1988
McKeown, Thomas.
   The origins of human disease / Thomas McKeown. Oxford, UK : B. Blackwell, 1988. vi, 233 p. :
88-014449   616.07/1   0631155058
   Diseases -- Causes and theories of causation.

RB152 Theories of disease. Etiology. Pathogenesis — General special

RB152.K76 1997
Kroll-Smith, J. Stephen,
   Bodies in protest : environmental illness and the struggle over medical knowledge / Steve Kroll-Smith and H. Hugh Floyd. New York : New York University Press, c1997. xiii, 223 p.
97-004665   616.9/8   0814746624
   Environmentally induced diseases. Allergy.

RB152.L37 1995
Lappe, Marc.
   Breakout : the evolving threat of drug-resistant disease / Marc Lappe. San Francisco, CA : Sierra Club Books, 1995. xi, 255 p. :
95012016   616.07/1/01   0871563827
   Environmental health. Human evolution. Drug resistance in microorganisms.

RB152.M37 1992
Matthews, Bonnye L.,
   Chemical sensitivity : a guide to coping with hypersensitivity syndrome, sick building syndrome, and other environmental illnesses / by Bonnye L. Matthews. Jefferson, N.C. : McFarland, c1992. xvi, 275 p. :
92-054089   616.9/8   089950731X
   Environmentally induced diseases. Sick building syndrome. Allergy.

RB152.M85 1992
   Multiple chemical sensitivities : addendum to Biologic markers in immunotoxicology / Board on Environmental Studies and Toxicology, Commission on Life Sciences, National Research Council. Washington, D.C. : National Academy Press, 1992. iii, 195 p. :
92-080854   615.9/07   0309047366
   Multiple chemical sensitivity. Chemicals -- Health aspects.

RB152.R38 1992
Rea, William J.
   Chemical sensitivity / William J. Rea. Boca Raton [Fla.] : Lewis Publishers, c1992-1997. 4 v. :
92-009436   616.9/8   0873715411
   Environmentally induced diseases. Chemicals -- Health aspects. Toxicology.

RB152.W49 1993
Wilson, Cynthia,
   Chemical exposure and human health : a reference to 314 chemicals with a guide to symptoms and a directory of organizations / by Cynthia Wilson. Jefferson, N.C. : McFarland & Co., c1993. xii, 339 p. ;
92-051010   615.9/02   0899508103
   Environmentally induced diseases. Environmental health. Toxicology.

RB152.6 Theories of disease. Etiology. Pathogenesis — Environmental induced diseases — Multiple chemical sensitivity

RB152.6.A84 1998
Ashford, Nicholas Askounes.
   Chemical exposures : low levels and high stakes / Nicholas A. Ashford, Claudia S. Miller. New York : Van Nostrand Reinhold, c1998. xxiii, 440 p.
97-019690   615.9/02   0471292400
   Multiple chemical sensitivity.

RB152.6.B37 1998
Barrett, Stephen,
  Chemical sensitivity : the truth about environmental illness / Stephen Barrett, Ronald E. Gots. Amherst, N.Y. : Prometheus Books, 1998. viii, 212 p.
97-053181   615.9/02   1573921955
  Multiple chemical sensitivity. Environmentally induced diseases. Medical misconceptions.

RB155 Theories of disease. Etiology. Pathogenesis — Heredity. Medical genetics

RB155.A76 1994
  Assessing genetic risks : implications for health and social policy / Lori B. Andrews ... [et al.], editors. Washington, D.C. : National Academy Press, 1994. xi, 338 p. :
93-047973   616/.042   0309047986
  Medical genetics -- Social aspects. Human chromosome abnormalities -- Diagnosis -- Social aspects. Medical policy -- United States.

RB155.C496 1999
Childs, Barton.
  Genetic medicine : a logic of disease / Barton Childs. Baltimore : Johns Hopkins University Press, c1999. xii, 326 p. :
99-012783   616/.042   0801861306
  Medical genetics. Medicine -- Philosophy. Human evolution.

RB155.C575 1992
  The Code of codes : scientific and social issues in the Human Genome Project / edited by Daniel J. Kevles and Leroy Hood. Cambridge, Mass. : Harvard University Press, 1992. x, 397 p. :
91-038477   174/.25   0674136454
  Human gene mapping -- Moral and ethical aspects. Human gene mapping -- Social aspects.

RB155.D76 1994
Drlica, Karl.
  Double-edged sword : the promises and risks of the genetic revolution / Karl A. Drlica. Reading, Mass. : Addison-Wesley, c1994. ix, 242 p. :
94-014033   616/.042   0201408384
  Medical genetics -- Social aspects. Genetic engineering -- Social aspects.

RB155.E56 1999
  Engineering the human germline : an exploration of the science and ethics of altering the genes we pass to our children / edited by Gregory Stock and John Campbell. New York : Oxford University Press, 2000. xvi, 169 p. ;
99-015224   174/.25   0195133021
  Medical genetics. Medical genetics -- Moral and ethical aspects. Genetic engineering.

RB155.G3585 1992
  Gene mapping : using law and ethics as guides / edited by George J. Annas, Sherman Elias. New York : Oxford University Press, 1992. xxii, 291 p.
91-046283   174/.25   0195073037
  Human gene mapping -- Moral and ethical aspects. Human gene mapping -- Law and legislation. Chromosome Mapping -- methods.

RB155.G3854 1994
  The genetic frontier : ethics, law, and policy / Mark S. Frankel and Albert H. Teich, editors. Washington, D.C. : American Association for the Advancement of Scie c1994. xix, 240 p. :
93-037230   174/.2   0871685264
  Medical genetics -- Moral and ethical aspects. Medical ethics -- Law and legislation. Medical genetics -- Social aspects.

RB155.G398 1997
  Genetic secrets : protecting privacy and confidentiality in the genetic era / edited by Mark A. Rothstein. New Haven : Yale University Press, c1997. xvi, 511 p. :
97-028439   323.44/8   0300072511
  Medical genetics -- Moral and ethical aspects. Medical genetics -- Law and legislation. Medical records -- Law and legislation.

RB155.H59 1989
Holtzman, Neil A.
  Proceed with caution : predicting genetic risks in the recombinant DNA era / Neil A. Holtzman. Baltimore : John Hopkins University Press, c1989. xiii, 303 p.
88-029658   616/.042   0801837308
  Medical genetics. Genetic counseling. Genetic disorders -- Diagnosis -- Social aspects.

RB155.H8 1999
Hubbard, Ruth,
  Exploding the gene myth : how genetic information is produced and manipulated by scientists, physicians, employers, insurance companies, educators, and law enforcers / Ruth Hubbard and Elijah Wald ; with a new preface. Boston, Mass : Beacon Press, c1999. xxiii, 225 p. :
          616/.042   0807004316
  Medical genetics--Moral and ethical aspects. Medical genetics--Social aspects.

RB155.K36 2000
Kaplan, Jonathan Michael.
  The limits and lies of human genetic research : dangers for social policy / Jonathan Michael Kaplan. New YorK : Routledge, 2000. xi, 224 p. :
99-044899   174/.28   0415926378
  Medical genetics -- Moral and ethical aspects. Human genetics -- Research -- Moral and ethical aspects. Human genetics -- Research -- Social aspects.

RB155.L37 1998
Lashley, Felissa R.,
  Clinical genetics in nursing practice / by Felissa R. (Cohen) Lashley. New York : Springer, c1998. xvi, 543 p. :
98-012409   616/.042/024613   0826111777
  Medical genetics. Nursing. Genetics, Medical -- nurses' instruction.

RB155.M3135 2000
Mahowald, Mary Briody.
  Genes, women, equality / Mary Briody Mahowald. New York : Oxford University Press, 2000. xvii, 314 p.
99-014296   616/.042/082   0195121104
  Medical genetics -- Moral and ethical aspects. Medical genetics -- Social aspects. Women -- Health and hygiene -- Sociological aspects.

RB155.M56 1991
Miringoff, Marque-Luisa,
  The social costs of genetic welfare / Marque-Luisa Miringoff. New Brunswick, N.J. : Rutgers University Press, c1991. xvii, 210 p.
91-016793   174/.25   0813517060
  Genetic engineering -- Moral and ethical aspects. Human reproductive technology -- Moral and ethical aspects. Handicapped -- Public opinion.

RB155.N44 1994
Neel, James V.
  Physician to the gene pool : genetic lessons and other stories / James V. Neel. New York : J. Wiley, c1994. ix, 457 p. :
93-036614   575.1/092   0471308447
  Neel, James V. -- (James Van Gundia), -- 1915-   Geneticists -- United States -- Biography. Medical genetics -- United States -- Biography.

RB155.R77
Rosenthal, David,
  Genetic theory and abnormal behavior.   New York, McGraw-Hill [1970] xvii, 318 p.
79-104739   616.89/042
  Medical genetics.

RB155.R87 1994
Rushton, Alan R.
  Genetics and medicine in the United States, 1800 to 1922 / Alan R. Rushton. Baltimore : The Johns Hopkins University Press, c1994. xi, 209 p. ;
93-035943   616/.042/0973   0801847818
  Medical genetics -- United States -- History. Human genetics -- United States -- History. Genetics, Medical -- history -- United States.

RB155.W35 1993
Weiss, Kenneth M.
  Genetic variation and human disease : principles and evolutionary approaches / Kenneth M. Weiss. Cambridge ; Cambridge University Press, 1993. xxiv, 354 p.
92-049275   573.2/1   0521334217
  Medical genetics. Human genetics. Genetic epidemiology.

RB155.W54 1991
Wills, Christopher.
  Exons, introns, and talking genes : the science behind the Human Genome Project / Christopher Wills. [New York] : BasicBooks, c1991. xvi, 368 p. :
91-070062   616/.042   0465050204
  Medical genetics -- Popular works. Molecular genetics -- Popular works. Exons (Genetics) -- Popular works.

RB155.5-155.8 Theories of disease. Etiology. Pathogenesis — Heredity, Medical genetics — Genetic disorders. Human chromosome abnormalities

RB155.5.A67 1998
  Approaches to gene mapping in complex human diseases / edited by Jonathan L. Haines, Margaret A. Pericak-Vance. New York : Wiley-Liss, c1998. xxii, 434 p.
97-042666   616/.042   0471171956
  Genetic disorders. Human gene mapping. Hereditary Diseases -- genetics.

RB155.5.G455 2000
  Genetic disorders sourcebook : basic consumer information about hereditary diseases and disorders, including cystic fibrosis, Down syndrome ... / edited by Kathy Massimini. Detroit, MI : Omnigraphics, c2000. xiv, 768 p. :
00-063715   616/.042   0780802411
  Human chromosome abnormalities -- Popular works.

RB155.5.W96 2000
Wynbrandt, James.
  The encyclopedia of genetic disorders and birth defects / James Wynbrandt and Mark D. Ludman. New York, NY : Facts on File, c2000. xx, 474 p. :
98-053568   616/.042/03   0816038090
  Genetic disorders -- Encyclopedias. Abnormalities, Human -- Encyclopedias.

RB155.6.D73 1991
Draper, Elaine.
  Risky business : genetic testing and exclusionary practices in the hazardous workplace / Elaine Draper. Cambridge [England] ; Cambridge University Press, 1991. xv, 315 p. ;
90-028112   363.11   0521370272
  Human chromosome abnormalities -- Diagnosis -- Social aspects. Occupational diseases -- Diagnosis -- Social aspects. Medical screening -- Social aspects.

RB155.65.A53 2001
Andrews, Lori B.,
  Future perfect : confronting decisions about genetics / Lori B. Adrews. New York : Columbia University Press, c2001. ix, 264 p. ;
00-059657   616/.042   0231121628
  Genetic screening -- Social aspects.

RB155.65.G465 2000
  Genetics and public health in the 21st century :using genetic information to improve health and prevent disease / edited by Muin J. Khoury, Wylie Burke, Elizabeth J. Thomson. Oxford ; Oxford University Press, 2000. xx, 639 p. ;
          616/.042   0195128303
  Genetic screening. Public health. Medical genetics.

RB155.7.C85 1996

Cultural and ethnic diversity : a guide for genetics professionals / edited by Nancy L. Fisher. Baltimore : Johns Hopkins University Press, 1996. xxi, 246 p. ;
96-013763   616/.042   080185346X
Genetic counseling -- United States. Cross-cultural counseling -- United States.

RB155.8.C53 1997
Clark, William R.,

The new healers : the promise and problems of molecular medicine in the twenty-first century / William R. Clark. New York : Oxford University Press, 1997. ix, 245 p. :
97-009086   616/.042   0195117301
Gene therapy -- Popular works.

RB155.8.L96 1995
Lyon, Jeff.

Altered fates : gene therapy and the retooling of human life / Jeff Lyon and Peter Gorner. New York : Norton, c1995. 636 p. ;
95-179610   0393035964
Gene therapy. Genetic engineering -- Research. Gene Therapy -- history

RB155.8.T48 1994
Thompson, Larry.

Correcting the code : inventing the genetic cure for the human body / Larry Thompson. New York : Simon & Schuster, c1994. 378 p. :
93-042299   616/.042   0671770829
Anderson, W. French, -- 1936-   Gene therapy.

RB170 Theories of disease. Etiology. Pathogenesis — Oxidation. Free radicals

RB170.A58 1997

Antioxidants and disease prevention / edited by Harinder S. Garewal. Boca Raton : CRC Press, c1997. 186 p. :
96-045089   616.07   0849385091
Antioxidants -- Therapeutic use. Medicine, Preventive. Free radicals (Chemistry) -- Pathophysiology.

RB170.S69 1998
Smythies, John R.

Every person's guide to antioxidants / John R. Smythies. New Brunswick, N.J. : Rutgers University Press, c1998. 140 p. ;
98-006810   616.07   0813525748
Oxidation, Physiological. Antioxidants -- Health aspects. Free radicals (Chemistry) -- Pathophysiology.

RB212 Theories of disease. Etiology. Pathogenesis — Special factors in the production of disease — Influence of sex

RB212.E96 1998

Sex and gender in paleopathological perspective / edited by Anne L. Grauer, Patricia Stuart-Macadam. Cambridge, UK ; Cambridge University Press, 1998. xi, 192 p. :
98-026485   616.07   0521620902
Sex factors in disease. Sex differences. Paleopathology.

RC Internal Medicine

RC41 Collected works (nonserial) — Dictionaries and encyclopedias

RC41.G35 2001
Gale encyclopedia of medicine / Jacqueline L. Longe, editor ; Deirdre S. Blanchfield, associate editor. 2nd ed. Detroit, MI : Gale Group, 2001. p. cm.
     616/.003   0787654949
Internal medicine--Encyclopedias.

RC41.M34 2002
Magill's medical guide / medical consultants, Karen E. Kalumuck, Nancy A. Piotrowski, Connie Rizzo ; project editor, Tracy Irons-Georges. 2nd rev. ed. Pasadena, Calif. : Salem Press, c2002. 3 v. (xviii, 2576, cxcv p.) :
     610/.3   20   058
Medicine--Encyclopedias.

RC46 General works

RC46.C423 2000
Cecil textbook of medicine / edited by Lee Goldman, J. Claude Bennett. 21st ed. Philadelphia : W.B. Saunders, c2000 xli, 2308, clxx p., [18] p. of plates :
     616   072167996X
Internal medicine. Medicine.

RC46.H333 2001
Harrison's principles of internal medicine. 15th ed. / editors, Eugene Braunwald ... [et al.]. New York : McGraw-Hill, c2001. 2 v. :
     616   0070072744
Internal medicine.

RC46.O8 1967
Osler, William,
Osler's textbook revisited; reprint of selected sections with commentaries. Edited by A. McGehee Harvey and Victor A. McKusick. New York Appleton-Century-Crofts [1967] xi, 361 p.
66-029265   616
Internal medicine.

RC46.P89 1996
The principles and practice of medicine. 23rd ed. / edited by John D. Stobo ... [et al.]. Stamford, Conn. : Appleton & Lange, c1996. xv, 1046 p. :
     616   0838579639
Internal medicine. Medicine. Internal medicine.

RC49 Psychosomatic medicine — General works

RC49.D2613 1993
Dantzer, Robert.
The psychosomatic delusion : why the mind is not the source of all our ills / Robert Dantzer. New York : Free Press ; c1993. xvii, 247 p.
93-019682   616.08   0029069378
Medicine, Psychosomatic

RC49.F58 1991
Fletcher, Ben
Work, stress, disease, and life expectancy / Ben (C) Fletcher. Chichester ; Wiley, c1991. xi, 255 p. :
91-000166   616.9/8   0471919705
Medicine, Psychosomatic. Stress (Psychology) Job stress.

RC49.M522 1996
Mind/body health : the effects of attitudes, emotions, and relationships / Brent Q. Hafen ... [et al.]. Boston : Allyn and Bacon, 1996. xvii, 634 p.
95-013437   616/.001/9   0205172113
Medicine, Psychosomatic. Emotions -- Health aspects. Psychoneuroimmunology.

RC49.N493 1991
Newberry, Benjamin H.
A holistic conceptualization of stress and disease / Benjamin H. Newberry, Janet E. Jaikins-Madden, Thomas J. Gerstenberger. New York : AMS Press, 1991. p.
86-082021   616.08   0404632580
Medicine, Psychosomatic. Holistic medicine. Stress (Psychology)

RC49.S354 1994
Shorter, Edward.
From the mind into the body : the cultural origins of psychosomatic symptoms / Edward Shorter. New York : Free Press ; c1994. ix, 268 p. ;
93-005430   616/.001/9   0029286662
Medicine, Psychosomatic -- Cross-cultural studies -- History.

RC49.W65 1988
Wolman, Benjamin B.
Psychosomatic disorders / Benjamin B. Wolman. New York : Plenum Medical Book Co., c1988. xiv, 312 p. ;
88-022555   616.08   0306429454
Medicine, Psychosomatic. Psychophysiologic Disorders.

RC69 Semiology. Symptomatology

RC69.M33 1997
Magalini, Sergio I.
Dictionary of medical syndromes / Sergio I. Magalini, Sabina C. Magalini. 4th ed. Philadelphia : Lippincott-Raven, c1997. vii, 960 p. ;
     616/.003   0397584180
Syndromes--Dictionaries. Dictionaries, Medical. Syndrome--dictionaries.

RC71 Examination. Diagnosis — Societies. Serials

RC71.P38 1997

The patient's guide to medical tests / by faculty members at the Yale University School of Medicine ; Barry L. Zaret, senior editor ... [et al.]. Boston : Houghton Mifflin Co., 1997. xx, 620 p. :
96-053904   616.07/5   0395765366
Diagnosis. Medicine, Popular.

RC71.3 Examination. Diagnosis — Collected works (nonserial) — General special

RC71.3.M45 1999

Medical tests sourcebook : basic consumer health information about medical tests, including periodic health exams, general screening tests, tests you can do at home, findings of the U.S. Preventive edited by Joyce Brennfleck Shannon. Detroit, MI : Omnigraphics, 1999. p. cm.
99-035456   616.07/5   0780802438
Diagnosis -- Popular works. Diagnosis, Laboratory -- Popular works. Medicine, Popular.

RC71.3.S424 2002
Segen, J. C.

The patient's guide to medical tests :everything you need to know about the tests your doctor orders / Joseph C. Segen and Josie Wade. 2nd ed. New York : Facts on File, 2002. p. cm.
             616.07/5   0816046522
Diagnosis--Popular works. Diagnosis, Laboratory--Popular works.

RC76 Examination. Diagnosis — Physical diagnosis — General works

RC76.B37 2002
Bickley, Lynn S.

Bates' guide to physical examination and history taking. 8th ed. / Lynn S. Bickley, Robert A. Hoekelman. Philadelphia : Lippincott, c2002. xxii, 789 p. :
             616.07/54   0781735114
Physical diagnosis. Medical history taking. Physical Examination--methods.

RC76.M63 1999

Mosby's guide to physical examination / Henry M. Seidel ... [et al.].4th ed. St. Louis, Mo. : Mosby, c1999. xxv, 998 p. :
             616.07/54   0323001785
Physical diagnosis. Physical Examination--methods.

RC78.7 Examination. Diagnosis — Other special, A-Z

RC78.7.D53.C48 1993
Cho, Z.-H.

Foundations of medical imaging / Z.H. Cho, Joie P. Jones, Manbir Singh. New York : Wiley, c1993. xiii, 586 p.
92-026906   616.07/54   0471545732
Diagnostic imaging.

RC78.7.D53.K48 1997
Kevles, Bettyann.

Naked to the bone : medical imaging in the twentieth century / Bettyann Holtzmann Kevles. New Brunswick, N.J. : Rutgers University Press, c1997. xiv, 378 p. :
96-002844   616.07/54/0904   0813523583
Diagnostic imaging -- History. Radiography, Medical -- History.

RC78.7.D53.W48 1999
Whitley, A. Stewart.

Clark's special procedures in diagnostic imaging / A. Stewart Whitley, Chrissie W. Alsop, Adrian D. Moore ; with contributions from Michael J. Wright. Oxford [England] ; Butterworth-Heinemann, 1999. x, 415 p. :
98-020552   616.07/54   0750617152
Diagnostic imaging. Diagnostic Imaging -- methods. Technology, Radiologic -- methods.

RC78.7.N83M9385 2000

MRI for technologists / author [i.e., editor], Peggy Woodward. 2nd ed. New York : McGraw-Hill Medical Publishing Division, c2000. p. ;
             616.07/548   0071353186
Magnetic resonance imaging. Radiologic technologists. Magnetic Resonance Imaging.

RC78.7.U4T46 1999
Tempkin, Betty Bates.

Ultrasound scanning :principles and protocols / Betty BatesTempkin. 2nd ed. Philadelphia : W.B. Saunders Co., c1999. xx, 475 p. :
             616.07/543   0721668798
Diagnosis, Ultrasonic. Ultrasonography--methods. Ultrasonography--standards.

RC80 Examination. Diagnosis — Prognosis

RC80.C48 1999
Christakis, Nicholas A.

Death foretold : prophecy and prognosis in medical care / Nicholas A. Christakis. Chicago : University of Chicago, c1999. xxii, 328 p.
99-016442   362.1   0226104702
Prognosis.

RC81 Examination. Diagnosis — Popular medicine

RC81.A2.A52 1989

The American Medical Association encyclopedia of medicine / medical editor, Charles B. Clayman. New York, NY : Random House, c1989. 1184 p. :
88-029693   610/.3/21   0394565282
Medicine, Popular -- Dictionaries.

RC81.A2C56 2001

The complete family health book / Donna Shelley ... [et al.]. 1st ed. New York : St. Martin's Press, 2001. xii, 755 p. :
             610   0312253087
Medicine, Popular. Health. Family--Health and hygiene.

RC81.C725 1995

Consumer health USA : essential information from the federal health network / edited by Alan M. Rees. Phoenix, Ariz. : Oryx Press, 1995-1997. 2 v. :
94-037594   616   0897748891
Medicine, Popular. Consumer education.

RC81.F865 1994

Freed, Melvyn N.
The patient's desk reference : where to find answers to medical questions / Melvyn N. Freed, Karen J. Graves. New York ; Macmillan Pub. Co. ; c1994. xi, 388 p. ;
93-010267   610   0028971531
Medicine, Popular. Medicine -- Information services. Medicine -- Bibliography.

RC81.V5 2001

Vickery, Donald M.
Take care of yourself : the complete illustrated guide to medical self-care / Donald M. Vickery, James F. Fries. 7th ed. Cambridge, Mass. : Perseus Books, c2001. xxvi, 342 p. :
          616.02/4   0738203068
Self-care, Health. Medicine, Popular.

RC86.7 Medical emergencies. Critical care. Intensive care. First aid — General works

RC86.7.B376 2001

The basic EMT :comprehensive prehospital patient care. 2nd ed. / [edited by] Norman E. McSwain, Jr., James L. Paturas. St. Louis, MO : Mosby, c2001. xxix, 926 p. :
          616.02/5   0323011160
Medical emergencies. Emergency medical technicians.

RC86.7.B464 2002

Bennett, Jeffrey,
Medical emergencies in dentristy / Jeffrey Bennett, Morton Rosenberg. Philadelphia, PA : W.B. Saunders, c2002. p. ;
          616.02/5/0246176   0721684815
Medical emergencies. Dental emergencies. Emergencies.

RC86.8 Medical emergencies. Critical care. Intensive care. First aid — Handbooks, manuals, etc.

RC86.8.F64 1993

Foden, Charles R.
Household chemicals and emergency first aid / Charles R. Foden and Jack L. Weddell. Boca Raton : Lewis Publishers, c1993. 432 p. ;
92-026703   615.9/08   0873719018
First aid in illness and injury -- Handbooks, manuals, etc. Household products -- Toxicology -- Handbooks, manuals, etc. Household products -- Safety measures -- Handbooks, manuals, etc.

RC86.95 Medical emergencies. Critical care. Intensive care. First aid — Moral and ethical aspects

RC86.95.H86 1986

Human values in critical care medicine / edited by Stuart J. Youngner. New York : Praeger, 1986. v, 192 p. ;
86-022569   174/.24   0275922642
Critical care medicine -- Moral and ethical aspects. Critical care medicine -- Social aspects. Long-term care of the sick -- Moral and ethical aspects.

RC86.95.S54 1988

Sherlock, Richard.
Families and the gravely ill : roles, rules, and rights / Richard Sherlock and C. Mary Dingus. New York : Greenwood Press, 1988. xxi, 180 p. ;
87-032264   174/.2   0313256152
Critically ill -- Family relationships. Medical ethics.

RC87.9 Medical emergencies. Critical care. Intensive care. First aid — Artificial respiration. CPR

RC87.9.E37 1997

Eisenberg, Mickey S.
Life in the balance : emergency medicine and the quest to reverse sudden death / Mickey S. Eisenberg. New York : Oxford University Press, 1997. xv, 304 p. :
96-036114   615.8/043   0195101790
Resuscitation -- Popular works. Sudden death -- Popular works.

RC87.9.T56 1999

Timmermans, Stefan,
Sudden death and the myth of CPR / Stefan Timmermans ; foreword by Bern Shen. Philadelphia : Temple University Press, 1999. xvii, 256 p.
99-017282   616.1/025   1566397154
CPR (First aid) -- Social aspects -- United States. Cardiac arrest -- Treatment -- Social aspects -- United States. Sudden death -- Social aspects -- United States.

RC88.9 Medical emergencies. Critical care. Intensive care. First aid — By activity or environment, A-Z

RC88.9.O95A938 1999

Auerbach, Paul S.
Field guide to wilderness medicine / Paul S. Auerbach, Howard J. Donner, Eric A. Weiss ; art by Christine Gralapp. 1st ed. St. Louis : Mosby, c1999. x, 549 p. :
          616.02/5   0815109261
Outdoor medical emergencies--Handbooks, manuals, etc. Emergencies--handbooks. Wounds and Injuries--therapy--handbooks.

RC88.9.O95M36 2001
Wilderness medicine / [edited by] Paul S. Auerbach. 4th ed. St. Louis : Mosby, c2001. xxiii, 1910 p. :
616.9/8   0323009506
Outdoor medical emergencies. Mountaineering injuries. Environmentally induced diseases.

RC95 Diseases due to physical and chemical agents — Diseases due to radioactive substances

RC95.A42.H43 1988
Health risks of radon and other internally deposited alpha-emitters / Committee on the Biological Effects of Ionizing Radiations, Board on Radiation Effects Research, Commission on Life Sciences, National Research Council. Washington, D.C. : National Academy Press, 1988. xvi, 602 p. :
87-031280   616.9/897   0309037891
Alpha rays -- Health aspects. Radioisotopes in the body -- Health aspects. Radon -- Health aspects.

RC108 Chronic diseases

RC108.B54 1991
Biegel, David E.
Family caregiving in chronic illness : Alzheimer's disease, cancer, heart disease, mental illness, and stroke / David E. Biegel, Esther Sales, Richard Schulz. Newbury Park, Calif. : Sage Publications, c1991. 332 p. ;
90-043952   362.1   0803932138
Chronically ill -- Home care. Caregivers. Chronically ill -- Family relationships.

RC108.C67 1988
Corbin, Juliet M.,
Unending work and care : managing chronic illness at home / Juliet M. Corbin, Anselm Strauss. San Francisco : Jossey-Bass Publishers, 1988. xviii, 358 p.
87-046343   649.8   1555420826
Chronic diseases -- Social aspects. Chronic diseases -- Psychological aspects. Chronically ill -- Home care -- Psychological aspects.

RC108.F35 1999
Falvo, Donna R.
Medical and psychosocial aspects of chronic illness and disability / Donna R. Falvo. 2nd ed. Gaithersburg, Md. : Aspen Publishers, 1999. xxi, 464 p. :
616/.044   083421198X
Chronic diseases. Chronically ill--Rehabilitation. Chronic diseases--Social aspects.

RC108.N38 1989
National Research Council (U.S.).
Diet and health : implications for reducing chronic disease risk / Committee on Diet and Health, Food and Nutrition Board, Commission on Life Sciences, National Research Council. Washington, D.C. : National Academy Press, 1989. xiv, 749 p. :
89-003261   613.2   0309039940
Chronic diseases -- Nutritional aspects. Chronic Disease. Diet.

RC108.S38 1988
Schover, Leslie R.
Sexuality and chronic illness : a comprehensive approach / Leslie R. Schover, Soren Buus Jensen. New York : Guilford Press, c1988. ix, 357 p. :
87-023640   616.85/83   089862715X
Chronically ill -- Sexual behavior. Sexual disorders. Chronic Disease.

RC111 Infectious and parasitic diseases — General works

RC111.C47 1987
Christie, A. B.
Infectious diseases : epidemiology and clinical practice / A.B. Christie. 4th ed. Edinburgh ; Churchill Livingstone, 1987. 2 v. (xix, 1317, 51 p., [16] p. of plates) :
616.9   0443035857
Communicable diseases. Communicable Diseases.

RC111.P78 2000
Mandell, Douglas, and Bennett's principles and practice of infectious diseases / edited by Gerald L. Mandell, John E. Bennett, Raphael Dolin. 5th ed. Philadelphia : Churchill Livingstone, c2000. 2 v. :
616.9   044307593X
Communicable diseases. Communicable Diseases.

RC119 Infectious and parasitic diseases — Parasitic diseases — General works

RC119.M3 1999
Markell, Edward K.
Markell and Voge's medical parasitology / Edward K. Markell, David T. John, Wojciech A. Krotoski. 8th ed. Philadelphia : Saunders, c1999. viii, 501 p. :
616.9/6   0721676340
Medical parasitology. Parasites. Parasitic Diseases.

RC119.P3494 1988
Parasitology in focus : facts and trends / Heinz Mehlhorn, ed. ; with contributions by Bunnag, D. ... [et al.]. Berlin ; Springer-Verlag, c1988. xvii, 924 p.
88-004523   616.9/6   0387178384
Medical parasitology. Veterinary parasitology.

RC133 Infectious and parasitic diseases — Individual diseases — Cholera

RC133.F9.P33 1986
Delaporte, Francois,
Disease and civilization : the cholera in Paris, 1832 / Francois Delaporte ; translated by Arthur Goldhammer ; foreword by Paul Rabinow. Cambridge, Mass. : MIT Press, c1986. xiii, 250 p.
85-018232   944/.36/063   0262040840
Cholera -- France -- Paris -- History -- 19th century. Cholera -- history -- Paris. Civilization -- history -- Paris.

RC133.F9.P334 1996
Kudlick, Catherine Jean.
  Cholera in post-revolutionary Paris : a cultural history / Catherine J. Kudlick. Berkeley : University of California Press, c1996. xiv, 293 p. :
95-025418   614.5/14/09443609034
0520202732
  Cholera -- France -- Paris -- History -- 19th century.

RC143 Infectious and parasitic diseases — Individual diseases — Food poisoning (Infection and intoxication)

RC143.F655 1995
  Food and animal borne diseases sourcebook : basic information about diseases that can be spread to humans through the ingestion of contaminated food or water or by contact with infected animals and edited by Karen Bellenir and Peter D. Dresser. Detroit, MI : Omnigraphics, c1995. x, 535 p. :
95-021240   616.9   0780800338
  Foodborne diseases. Waterborne infection. Zoonoses.

RC150.4-150.5 Infectious and parasitic diseases — Individual diseases — Influenza

RC150.4.C64 1996
Collier, Richard,
  The plague of the Spanish lady : the influenza pandemic of 1918-1919 / Richard Collier. 1st American ed. London : Allison & Busby, 1996, c1974. 376 p., [8] p. of plates :
          614.5/18/09041   0749002468
  Influenza--History.

RC150.4.K64 1999
Kolata, Gina Bari,
  Flu : the story of the great influenza pandemic of 1918 and the search for the virus that caused it / Gina Kolata. New York : Farrar, Straus and Giroux, 1999. xi, 330 p. :
99-039665   614.5/18/09041   0374157065
  Influenza -- History -- 20th century.

RC150.5.A2.I494 2000
Iezzoni, Lynette.
  Influenza 1918 : the worst epidemic in American history / Lynette Iezzoni ; foreword by David McCullough. New York : TV Books, 2000. p. cm.
00-041197   614.5/18/097309041
1575001837
  Influenza -- United States -- History -- 20th century.

RC154.1-154.8 Infectious and parasitic diseases — Individual diseases — Leprosy. Hansen's disease

RC154.1.B76
Brody, Saul Nathaniel.
  The disease of the soul; leprosy in medieval literature. Ithaca [N.Y.] Cornell University Press [1974] 223 p.
73-008407   616.9/98/00902   0801408040
  Leprosy -- History -- To 1500. Literature, Medieval -- History and criticism. Medicine, Medieval, in literature.

RC154.8.M42.S56 1998
Silla, Eric.
  People are not the same : leprosy and identity in twentieth-century Mali / Eric Silla. Portsmouth, NH : Heinemann ; 1998. xi, 220 p. :
97-039954   362.1/96998/0096623
0325000050
  Leprosy -- Mali -- History.

RC178-179 Plague. Bubonic plague. Black death

RC178.A1.B58 1994
  The Black death / translated and edited by Rosemary Horrox. Manchester ; Manchester University Press ; c1994. xiv, 364 p. ;
93-050558   614.4/94   0719034973
  Black death -- Europe -- History. Medicine, Medieval.

RC178.A1.M37 1996
Martin, A. Lynn.
  Plague? : Jesuit accounts of epidemic disease in the 16th century / A. Lynn Martin. Kirksville, Mo., USA : Sixteenth Century Journal Publishers, 1996. xiv, 268 p. :
94-021215   614.4/94/09031   0940474301
  Plague -- Europe -- History -- 16th century. Plague -- history -- Europe. Plague -- epidemiology -- Europe.

RC179.C6.B46 1996
Benedict, Carol
  Bubonic plague in nineteenth-century China / Carol Benedict. Stanford, Calif. : Stanford University Press, c1996. xx, 256 p. ;
96-005157   614.5/732/0095109034
0804726612
  Plague -- China -- History -- 19th century.

RC179.G7.P56 1996
Platt, Colin.
  King Death : the Black Death and its aftermath in late-medieval England / Colin Platt. Toronto ; University of Toronto Press, c1996. viii, 262 p.
96-166991   614.5/732/00942   0802009301
  Black death -- Social aspects -- England. Black death -- England -- History. Social history -- Medieval, 500-1500. England -- Social conditions -- 1066-1485.

RC180.1-181 Infectious and parasitic diseases — Individual diseases — Poliomyelitis

RC180.1.S56 2001
Silver, J. K.
  Post-polio syndrome :a guide for polio survivors and their families / Julie K. Silver ; foreword by Lauro S. Halstead. New Haven : Yale University Press, c2001. xvi, 280 p. :
          616.8/35   0300088086
  Postpoliomyelitis syndrome.

RC180.9.G68 1995
Gould, Tony.
A summer plague : polio and its survivors / Tony Gould. New Haven : Yale University Press, 1995. xvi, 366 p.,
94-047253   616.8/35/009   0300062923
Poliomyelitis -- History.

RC181.U5.P65 1996
Polio's legacy : an oral history / [edited by] Edmund J. Sass with George Gottfried, Anthony Sorem ; foreword by Richard Owen. Lanham [Md.] : University Press of America, c1996. xviii, 278 p.
95-045236   616.8/35   076180143X
Poliomyelitis -- United States -- Biography.

RC181.U6.A63 1996
Black, Kathryn.
In the shadow of polio : a personal and social history / Kathryn Black. Reading, Mass. : Addison-Wesley Pub., c1996. ix, 307 p. :
95-043963   362.1/96835/0092
0201407396
Black, Virginia, -- d. 1956 -- Health.   Poliomyelitis -- Patients -- Arizona -- Biography.

RC182 Infectious and parasitic diseases — Individual diseases — Rocky Mountain spotted fever. Tick fever

RC182.R6.H37 1990
Harden, Victoria Angela.
Rocky Mountain spotted fever : history of a twentieth-century disease / Victoria A. Harden. Baltimore : Johns Hopkins University Press, c1990. xvi, 375 p. :
89-048033   616.9/223   080183905X
Rocky Mountain spotted fever -- History.

RC183.1 Infectious and parasitic diseases — Individual diseases — Smallpox

RC183.1.H66 2002
Hopkins, Donald R.
The greatest killer : smallpox in history, with a new introduction / Donald R. Hopkins. Chicago : University of Chicago Press, c2002 xviii, 380 p. :
          614.5/21/09   0226351688
Smallpox--History.

RC199.1 Infectious and parasitic diseases — Individual diseases — Typhus

RC199.1.Z54 1996
Zinsser, Hans,
Rats, lice, and history :being a study in biography, which, after twelve preliminary chapters indispensable for the preparation of the lay reader, deals with the life history of typhus fever ... / by Hans Zinsser. New York, NY : Black Dog & Leventhal Publishers : xii, 301 p. ;
          616.9/222/009   1884822479
Typhus fever--History. Rats as carriers of disease--History. Lice as carriers of disease--History.

RC200-201.6 Infectious and parasitic diseases — Individual diseases — Sexually transmitted diseases. Venereal diseases

RC200.S52 1997
Sexually transmitted diseases sourcebook : basic information about herpes, chlamydia, gonorrhea, hepatitis, nongonoccocal urethritis, pelvic inflammatory disease, syphilis, AIDS, and more. edited by Linda M. Ross. Detroit, MI : Omnigraphics, c1997. xiii, 550 p.
97-017036   616.95/1   0780802179
Sexually transmitted diseases.

RC201.4.Q4813 1990
Quetel, Claude,
History of syphilis / Claude Quetel ; translated by Judith Braddock and Brian Pike. Baltimore : Johns Hopkins University Press, 1990. 342 p. :
90004267   614.5/472/09   0801840899
Syphilis -- History.

RC201.6.A1.A77 1997
Arrizabalaga, Jon.
The great pox : the French disease in Renaissance Europe / Jon Arrizabalaga, John Henderson, and Roger French. New Haven : Yale University Press, c1997. xv, 352 p. :
96-023453   614.5/472/09409031
0300069340
Syphilis -- Europe -- History -- 16th century.

RC210-211 Infectious and parasitic diseases — Individual diseases — Yellow fever

RC210.D4513 1991
Delaporte, Francois,
The history of yellow fever : an essay on the birth of tropical medicine / Francois Delaporte ; foreword by Georges Canguilhem ; translated by Arthur Goldhammer. Cambridge, Mass. : MIT Press, c1991. xi, 181 p. :
90-006086   616.9/28/009   026204112X
Yellow fever -- History. Tropical medicine -- History. Yellow Fever -- history.

RC211.P5.M44 1997
A melancholy scene of devastation : the public response to the 1793 Philadelphia yellow fever epidemic / edited by J. Worth Estes and Billy G. Smith. Canton, MA : Published for the College of Physicians of Phila 1997. xii, 211 p. :
96-054741   614.5/41/097481109033
088135192X
Yellow fever -- Pennsylvania -- Philadelphia -- History -- 18th century. Afro-Americans -- Diseases -- Pennxylvania -- Philadelphia -- History -- 18th century.

RC211.S85H85 1999
Humphreys, Margaret,
Yellow fever and the South / Margaret Humphreys. Baltimore, Md. : Johns Hopkins University Press, [1999] x, 226 p. :
          614.5/41/097509034   0801861969
Yellow fever--Southern States--History.

RC254.5 Neoplasms. Tumors. Oncology — General special

RC254.5.G353 2001
The Gale encyclopedia of cancer / Ellen Thackery. Detroit : Gale Group, 2001. p. cm.
       616.99/4/003   0787656097
Cancer--Encyclopedias. Oncology--Encyclopedias.

RC261 Neoplasms. Tumors. Oncology — Cancer and other malignant neoplasms — General works

RC261.A1C386
Cancer, principles and practice of oncology. Philadelphia : Lippincott Co., c1982- v. :
       616
Cancer--Periodicals. Oncology--Periodicals.

RC261.M436 1998
McKinnell, Robert Gilmore.
The biological basis of cancer / Robert G. McKinnell ... [et al.]. Cambridge ; Cambridge University Press, 1998. xix, 378 p. :
97-042369   616.99/4   0521592984
Cancer. Carcinogenesis. Cancer cells.

RC261.N48 1996
The new cancer sourcebook : basic information about major forms and stages of cancer ... / edited by Alan R. Cook. Detroit, MI : Omnigraphics, c1996. xi, 1313 p. :
95-033730   616.99/4   0780800419
Cancer -- Popular works.

RC261.P74 2001
Progress in oncology 2001 / edited by Vincent T. DeVita, Jr., Samuel Hellman, Steven A. Rosenberg. Boston : Jones and Bartlett, c2001. 362 p.
       616.99/4   0763715891
Cancer. Cancer--Treatment. Neoplasms--therapy.

RC262 Neoplasms. Tumors. Oncology — Cancer and other malignant neoplasms — General special

RC262.A39 2000
Altman, Roberta.
The cancer dictionary / Roberta Altman, Michael J. Sarg. New York, NY : Facts on File, 2000. xi, 387 p. :
99-021201   616.99/4/003   0816039534
Cancer -- Dictionaries.

RC262.A645 2001
American Cancer Society's guide to pain control :powerful methods to overcome cancer pain. Atlanta, GA : American Cancer Society, c2001. x, 358 p. :
       616/.0472   0944235336
Cancer pain.

RC262.C291196 2001
The cancer pain sourcebook / Roger S. Cicala [editor]. Los Angeles : Contemporary, 2001. xviii, 301 p. :
       616.99/4   0737304235
Cancer pain.

RC262.E558 2002
Encyclopedia of cancer / editor-in-chief, Joseph R. Bertino. 2nd ed. San Diego, Calif. : Academic Press, c2002. 4 v. :
       616.99/4/003   0122275594
Cancer--Encyclopedias.

RC262.G736 1992
Greenwald, Howard P.
Who survives cancer? / Howard P. Greenwald. Berkeley : University of California Press, c1992. xxi, 280 p. :
91-036909   362.1/96994   0520077253
Cancer -- Prognosis. Cancer -- Social aspects. Cancer -- Psychological aspects.

RC262.O47 1989
Olson, James Stuart,
The history of cancer : an annotated bibliography / compiled by James S. Olson. New York : Greenwood Press, 1989. viii, 426 p.
89-002174   616.99/4/009   0313258899
Cancer -- History -- Abstracts. Cancer -- History -- Bibliography. Neoplasms -- history -- abstracts.

RC263 Neoplasms. Tumors. Oncology — Cancer and other malignant neoplasms — Popular works

RC263.A37 1996
Aigotti, Ronald E.
The people's cancer guide book / by Ronald E. Aigotti. South Bend, IN : Ronald E. Aigotti, 1995, c1996. v, ii, 425 p.
95-076465   616.99/4   0897541065
Cancer -- Popular works.

RC263.M574 2001
Moore, Katen,
Living well with cancer :a nurse tells you everything you need to know about managing the side effects of your treatment / Katen Moore and Libby Schmais. New York : Putnam's, c2001. xxii, 297 p. ;
       362.1/96994   0399146873
Cancer--Popular works. Cancer--Treatment--Complications--Treatment. Cancer--Alternative treatment.

RC266 Neoplasms. Tumors. Oncology — Cancer and other malignant neoplasms — Nursing

RC266.C356 2000
Cancer nursing :principles and practice / edited by Connie Henke Yarbro ... [et al.]. 5th ed. Sudbury, Mass. : Jones and Bartlett, c2000. xxxiv, 1911 p. :
       610.73/698   0763711640
Cancer--Nursing. Neoplasms--nursing.

RC266.O53 2001

Oncology nursing / [edited by] Shirley E. Otto. 4th ed. St. Louis : Mosby, c1997. xxv, 901 p. :

610.73/698   0323012175

Cancer--Nursing. Neoplasms--nursing. Neoplasms--therapy.

RC267 Neoplasms. Tumors. Oncology — Cancer and other malignant neoplasms — Research. Experimentation

RC267.W45 1996
Weinberg, Robert A.

Racing to the beginning of the road : the search for the origin of cancer / Robert A. Weinberg. New York : Harmony Books, c1996. xiii, 270 p.

96-004109   616.99/4/0072   0517591189

Cancer -- Research -- History.

RC268 Neoplasms. Tumors. Oncology — Cancer and other malignant neoplasms — Prevention

RC268.P77 1999
Proctor, Robert,

The Nazi war on cancer / Robert N. Proctor. Princeton, N.J. : Princeton University Press, 1999. p. cm.

98-049405   362.1/96994/0094309043
0691001960

Cancer -- Prevention -- Government policy -- Germany -- History -- 20th century. Public health -- Germany -- History -- 20th century. Health care reform -- Germany -- History -- 20th century.

RC268.W528 1994
Whelan, Elizabeth M.

The complete guide to preventing cancer : how you can reduce your risks / Elizabeth Whelan. Amherst, N.Y. : Prometheus Books, 1994. 385 p. ;

94-011606   616.99/4052   0879758902

Cancer -- Prevention. Cancer -- Popular works.

RC268.25 Neoplasms. Tumors. Oncology — Cancer and other malignant neoplasms — Environmental aspects

RC268.25.S74 1997
Steingraber, Sandra.

Living downstream : an ecologist looks at cancer and the environment / Sandra Steingraber. Reading, Mass. : Addison-Wesley Publishing, c1997. xvi, 357 p. :

97-008164   616.99/4071   0201483033

Cancer -- Environmental aspects. Environmental toxicology.

RC268.415 Neoplasms. Tumors. Oncology — Cancer and other malignant neoplasms — Genetic aspects

RC268.415.F84 1996
Fujimura, Joan H.

Crafting science : a sociohistory of the quest for the genetics of cancer / Joan H. Fujimura. Cambridge, Mass. : Harvard University Press, 1996. x, 322 p. :

96-032222   616.99/4042   0674175530

Proto-oncogenes -- Research -- History. Cancer -- Genetic aspects -- Research -- History. Science -- Social aspects.

RC268.48 Neoplasms. Tumors. Oncology — Cancer and other malignant neoplasms — Etiology

RC268.48.C36 1990

Cancer : causes, occurrence, and control / editor-in-chief, L. Tomatis ; co-editors, A. Aitio ... [et al.]. Lyon : International Agency for Research on Cancer ; 1990. xvi, 352 p. :

91-109496   616.99/4   9283201108

Cancer -- Etiology. Cancer -- Epidemiology. Cancer -- Prevention.

RC268.48.G74 2000
Greaves, M. F.

Cancer : the evolutionary legacy / Mel Greaves. Oxford ; Oxford University Press, 2000. x, 276 p. :

99-053972   616.99/4071   0192628356

Cancer -- Etiology. Cancer -- Genetic aspects. Human evolution.

RC268.48.W45 1998
Weinberg, Robert A.

One renegade cell : how cancer begins / Robert A. Weinberg. New York, NY : Basic Books, c1998. v, 170 p. :

98-041277   616.99/4071   0465072755

Cancer -- Etiology. Cancer -- Research -- History. Carcinogenesis.

RC268.5-268.6 Neoplasms. Tumors. Oncology — Cancer and other malignant neoplasms — Carcinogenesis

RC268.5.H47 1997
Hess, David J.

Can bacteria cause cancer? : alternative medicine confronts big science / David J. Hess. New York : New York University Press, 1997. vii, 233 p. ;

97-004910   616.99/4071   0814735614

Carcinogenesis. Cocarcinogenesis. Bacterial diseases.

RC268.55.G63 1990
Gofman, John W.

Radiation-induced cancer from low-dose exposure : an independent analysis / John W. Gofman ; edited by Egan O'Connor. San Francisco, Calif. : Committee for Nuclear Responsibility, 1990. 1 v. (various

89-062431   616.99/4071   0932682898

Radiation carcinogenesis. Ionizing radiation -- Dose-response relationship.

RC268.6.C363 1996

Carcinogens and anticarcinogens in the human diet : a comparison of naturally occurring and synthetic substances / Committee on Comparative Toxicity of Naturally Occuring Carcinogens, Board on Environmental Studies and Toxicology, Commission on Life Sciences, National Research Council. Washington, D.C. : National Academy Press, 1996. xv, 417 p. :

95-073149   616.99/4071   0309053919
Carcinogens. Food -- Toxicology.

RC268.6.G73 1988
Graham, John D.

In search of safety : chemicals and cancer risk / John D. Graham, Laura C. Green, and Marc J. Roberts. Cambridge, Mass. : Harvard University Press, 1988. xiii, 260 p.
88-011011   363.1/79   0674446356
Carcinogens -- Safety regulations -- United States. Carcinogens -- Government policy -- United States. Benzene -- Health aspects.

RC270.8 Neoplasms. Tumors. Oncology — Cancer and other malignant neoplasms — Therapeutics

RC270.8.C38 2001

Cancer treatment / [edited by] Charles M. Haskell ; with 127 contributors ; Jonathan S. Berek, section editor for gynecologic neoplasms. 5th ed. Philadelphia : W.B. Saunders, c2001. xxiv, 1229 p. :
          616.99/406   0721678335
Cancer--Treatment. Neoplasms--therapy.

RC271 Neoplasms. Tumors. Oncology — Cancer and other malignant neoplasms — Therapeutics

RC271.D52V37 2001
Varona, Verne.

Nature's cancer-fighting foods :prevent and reverse the most common forms of cancer using the proven power of great food and easy recipes / Verne Varona. Paramus, NJ : Reward Books, c2001. xxiv, 368 p. :
          616.99/40654   0130170879
Cancer--Diet therapy. Cancer--Prevention.

RC271.N46
Cooke, Robert,

Dr. Folkman's war : angiogenesis and the struggle to defeat cancer / Robert Cooke. New York : Random House , c2001. xiv, 366 p. :
00-034165   616.99/4061   0375502440
Folkman, M. Judah.   Cancer -- Chemotherapy. Neovascularization inhibitors -- Therapeutic use. Cancer -- Research.

RC271.P27G66 2001
Goodman, Jordan.

The story of taxol :nature and politics in the pursuit of an anti-cancer drug / Jordan Goodman, Vivien Walsh. Cambridge ; Cambridge University Press, 2001. xiii, 282 p. :
          616.99/406   052156123X
Paclitaxel--Research--Political aspects--United States. Paclitaxel--Research--Economic aspects--United States. Cancer--Treatment--Research--Political aspects--United States.

RC271.V58P73 2001
Prasad, Kedar N.

Fight cancer with vitamins and supplements :a guide to prevention and   treatment / Kedar N. Prasad and K. Che Prasad. Rochester, Vt. : Healing Arts Press, c2001. xii, 178 p. ;
          616.99/40654   0892819499
Cancer--Diet therapy. Vitamin therapy. Dietary supplements.

RC276 Neoplasms. Tumors. Oncology — By region or country — United States

RC276.P76 1995
Proctor, Robert,

Cancer wars : how politics shapes what we know and don't know about cancer / Robert N. Proctor. New York : BasicBooks, c1995. viii, 356 p.
94-038792   616.99/4   0465027563
Cancer -- Political aspects -- United States. Cancer -- Social aspects -- United States. Carcinogenesis.

RC276.R67 1987
Ross, Walter Sanford,

Crusade : the official history of the American Cancer Society / Walter S. Ross. New York : Arbor House, c1987. xx, 283 p. ;
86-028701   616.99/4/006073   0877958114
Cancer -- Research -- United States -- History.

RC280 Neoplasms. Tumors. Oncology — By region, system, or organ of the body, or type of tumor, A-Z

RC280.B7.T63 1994
Todd, Alexandra Dundas.

Double vision : an East-West collaboration for coping with cancer / Alexandra Dundas Todd. Hanover : Published by University Press of New England [fo c1994. xv, 188 p. ;
94-008013   362.1/96994/0092
0819552798
Todd, John Andrew -- Health. Todd, John Andrew.   Cancer -- Alternative treatment. Brain -- Cancer -- Patients -- United States -- Biography. Neoplasms -- therapy -- popular works.

RC280.B8.A444 1996
Altman, Roberta.

Waking up, fighting back : the politics of breast cancer / Roberta Altman. Boston : Little, Brown, 1996. x, 421 p. ;
95-025211   362.1/9699449   0316035327
Breast -- Cancer -- Social aspects -- United States.

RC280.B8B66554 1999

Breast cancer / [edited by] Daniel F. Roses. New York : Churchill Livingstone, c1999. xiii, 688 p. :
          616.99/449   0443055815
Breast--Cancer. Breast Neoplasms.

RC280.B8.B6887 2001

Breast cancer sourcebook :Basic consumer health information about breast cancer, including diagnostic methods ... / edited by Edward J. Prucha and Karen Bellenir. 1st ed. Detroit, MI : Omnigraphics, c2001. xiii, 580 p. :

      616.99/449   0780802446

Breast--Cancer--Popular works.

RC280.B8.D425 2001
Dervan, Peter A.,

Understanding breast cancer / by Peter A. Dervan. Jefferson, N.C. : McFarland, c2001. viii, 189 p.

00-054808   616.99/449   0786410043

Breast -- Cancer -- Popular works.

RC280.B8.I34 1999

Ideologies of breast cancer : feminist perspectives / edited by Laura K. Potts. New York : St. Martin's Press, 1999. p. cm.

99-037438   616.99/449   0312228511

Breast -- Cancer. Breast -- Cancer -- Social aspects. Feminism.

RC280.B8L375 2001
Lerner, Barron H.

The breast cancer wars :hope, fear, and the pursuit of a cure in twentieth-century America / Barron H. Lerner. New York : Oxford University Press, 2001. xvi, 383 p. :

      616.99/449/00973   0195142616

Breast--Cancer--United States--History--20th century. Breast Neoplasms--history--United States. Breast Neoplasms--surgery--United States.

RC280.B8.P34 1995
Pederson, Lucille M.

Breast cancer : a family survival guide / Lucille M. Pederson and Janet M. Trigg. Westport, Conn. : Bergin & Garvey, 1995. xiv, 282 p. ;

94-037836   616.99/449   0897892933

Breast -- Cancer -- Popular works. Breast Neoplasms -- therapy. Breast Neoplasms -- psychology.

RC280.B8R64 2000
Rollin, Betty.

First, you cry / Betty Rollin. New York : Quill , 2000. xi, 222 p. ;

      362.1/9699449/0092   0060956305

Rollin, Betty--Health. Breast--Cancer--Patients--United States--Biography.

RC280.B8.W665 1998

Women confront cancer : making medical history by choosing alternative and complementary therapies / [edited by] Margaret J. Wooddell and David J. Hess ; foreword by Barbara Joseph. New York : New York University Press, c1998. xi, 258 p. ;

98-019752   616.99/44906   081473586X

Breast -- Cancer -- Alternative treatment -- Case studies.

RC280.G5.C34 2002

Cancer sourcebook for women : basic consumer health information about gynecologic cancers and related concerns ... / edited by Karen Bellenir. 2nd ed. Detroit, MI : Omnigraphics, c2002. xiv, 604 p. :

      616.99/4/0082   0780802268

Generative organs, Female--Popular works. Cancer in women--Popular works.

RC280.L8.H34 1990

Indoor radon and lung cancer, reality or myth? : twenty-ninth Hanford Symposium on Health and the Environment, October 15-19, 1990 / edited by Fredrick T. Cross. Columbus, Ohio : Battelle Press, c1992. 2 v. (xv, 114

92-037686   616.99/424071   0935470697

Lungs -- Cancer -- Epidemiology -- Congresses. Radon -- Carcinogenicity -- Congresses.

RC280.M6O67 1998

Oral cancer / American Cancer Society ; [edited by] Sol Silverman, Jr. 4th ed. Hamilton, ON ; B.C. Decker ; xvi, 174 p. :

      616.99/431   155009050X

Mouth--Cancer. Head and Neck Neoplasms. Mouth Neoplasms.

RC280.O8.P576 1996
Piver, M. Steven.

Gilda's disease : sharing personal experiences and a medical perspective on ovarian cancer / M. Steven Piver with Gene Wilder. Amherst, N.Y. : Prometheus Books, 1996. 184 p., [8] p

96-022847   616.99/465   1573920894

Ovaries -- Cancer -- Popular works.

RC280.P7.K67 1996
Korda, Michael,

Man to man : surviving prostate cancer / Michael Korda. New York : Random House, c1996. 254 p. ;

95-053314   362.1/9699463   0679448446

Korda, Michael, -- 1933- -- Health. Prostate -- Cancer -- Patients -- United States -- Biography.

RC281 Neoplasms. Tumors. Oncology — By age group, class, etc.

RC281.C4.K64
Koocher, Gerald P.

The Damocles syndrome : psychosocial consequences of surviving childhood cancer / Gerald P. Koocher and John E. O'Malley. New York : McGraw-Hill, c1981. xx, 219 p. ;

80-022462   362.1/9892/994   0070353409

Tumors in children -- Psychological aspects. Tumors in children -- Social aspects. Neoplasms -- In infancy and childhood.

RC281.W65.F35 1998
Falco, Kristine L.

Reclaiming our lives after breast and gynecologic cancer / Kristine Falco. Northvale, N.J. : Jason Aronson, c1998. viii, 239 p.

97-016795   155.9/16/082   0765700999

Cancer -- Psychological aspects. Women -- Diseases -- Psychological aspects.

RC309 Tuberculosis — Hospitals, clinics, etc.

RC309.N7.C64 2000
Coker, Richard J.,
From chaos to coercion : detention and the control of tuberculosis / Richard Coker. New York : St. Martin's Press, 2000. xviii, 261 p.
99-030119   362.1/96995/009747
0312222505
Tuberculosis -- New York (State) -- New York. Patient compliance -- New York (State) -- New York. Detention of persons -- New York (State) -- New York.

RC309.P4.B38 1992
Bates, Barbara,
Bargaining for life : a social history of tuberculosis, 1876-1938 / Barbara Bates. Philadelphia : University of Pennsylvania Press, c1992. x, 435 p. :
91-040040   614.5/42/09748   0812231201
Tuberculosis -- Pennsylvania -- History. Tuberculosis -- history -- United States.

RC310 Tuberculosis — History

RC310.D36 2000
Daniel, Thomas M.
Pioneers of medicine and their impact on tuberculosis / Thomas M. Daniel. Rochester, NY : University of Rochester Press, 2000. xiii, 255 p.
00-062850   616.9/95/009   1580460674
Tuberculosis -- History. Medical scientists -- Biography.

RC310.F76 1994
From consumption to tuberculosis : a documentary history / edited by Barbara Gutmann Rosenkrantz. New York : Garland Pub., 1994. xxii, 623 p.
93-023171   616.9/95/009   0815306083
Tuberculosis -- History -- Sources. Tuberculosis.

RC310.R68 1994
Rothman, Sheila M.
Living in the shadow of death : tuberculosis and the social experience of illness in American history / Sheila M. Rothman. New York : BasicBooks, c1994. xi, 319 p. ;
91-059017   616.9/95/00973   0465030025
Tuberculosis -- United States -- History.

RC310.R9 1993
Ryan, Frank,
The forgotten plague : how the battle against tuberculosis was won--and lost / Frank Ryan. Boston : Little, Brown, c1993. xix, 460 p.,
92-046893   614.5/42/09   0316763802
Tuberculosis -- History.

RC310.5 Tuberculosis — General works — Through 1900

RC310.5.F45 1995
Feldberg, Georgina D.,
Disease and class : tuberculosis and the shaping of modern North American society / Georgina D. Feldberg. New Brunswick, N.J. : Rutgers University Press, c1995. xiii, 274 p.
95-015169   614.5/42/0973   081352217X
Tuberculosis -- Government policy -- United States -- History. Tuberculosis -- Government policy -- Canada -- History. Tuberculosis -- history -- North America.

RC311 Tuberculosis — General works — 1901-

RC311.D25 1997
Daniel, Thomas M.
Captain of death : the story of tuberculosis / Thomas M. Daniel. Rochester, NY, USA : University of Rochester Press, 1997. viii, 296 p.
97-029886   616.9/95/009   1878822969
Tuberculosis -- History. Tuberculosis -- history.

RC311.D67 2000
Dormandy, Thomas.
The white death : a history of tuberculosis / Thomas Dormandy. New York : New York University Press, 2000. xiv, 433 p. :
99-032169   616.9/95/009   0814719279
Tuberculosis -- History.

RC334 Neurosciences. Biological psychiatry. Neuropsychiatry — Dictionaries and encyclopedias

RC334.E53 1999
Encyclopedia of neuroscience / edited by George Adelman, Barry H. Smith ; foreword by Theodore H. Bullock. 2nd enlarged & rev. ed. Amsterdam ; Elsevier, 1999. 2 v. (lvi, 2213 p.) :
          612.8/03   0444816127
Neurosciences--Encyclopedias. Neurosciences--Encyclopedias--English.

RC334.P79 1995
Pryse-Phillips, William.
Companion to clinical neurology / William Pryse-Phillips. Boston : Little, Brown, c1995. x, 1009 p. ;
          616.8/03   0316720410
Neurology--Dictionaries. Neurology--dictionaries. Nervous System Diseases--dictionaries.

RC336 Neurosciences. Biological psychiatry. Neuropsychiatry — Study and teaching

RC336.L78 2000
Luhrmann, T. M.
Of two minds : the growing disorder in American psychiatry / T.M. Luhrmann. New York : Knopf, 2000. ix, 337 p. ;
99-040732   616.89/0071/173   0679421912
Psychiatry -- Study and teaching. Psychiatry.

RC337 Neurosciences. Biological psychiatry. Neuropsychiatry — Research. Experimentation

RC337.B75 1998
Brockman, Richard.
A map of the mind : toward a science of psychotherapy / Richard Brockman. Madison, Conn. : Psychosocial Press, c1998. xiv, 297 p. :
98-011890   616.89/14   1887841148
Psychotherapy -- Research -- Methodology. Psychotherapy -- Research -- Methodology.

RC338 Neurosciences. Biological psychiatry. Neuropsychiatry — History — General works

RC338.R5
Riese, Walther,
A history of neurology. Foreword by Felix Marti-lbanez. New York, MD Publications, [1959] 223 p.
58010645   616.809
Neurology -- History. Neurology -- history

RC339.52 Neurosciences. Biological psychiatry. Neuropsychiatry — Biography — Individual, A-Z

RC339.52.B48.S74 1992
Stewart, Ian,
Eric Berne / Ian Stewart. London ; Sage Publications, 1992. xiv, 161 p. ;
91-051204   616.89/14/092   0803984669
Berne, Eric. Counseling -- History. Psychotherapy -- History.

RC339.52.F733.D55 1990
Diller, Jerry V.
Freud's Jewish identity : a case study in the impact of ethnicity / Jerry Victor Diller. Rutherford, NJ : Fairleigh Dickinson University Press ; c1991. 243 p. ;
89-045621   150.19/52   0838633749
Freud, Sigmund, -- 1856-1939. Psychoanalysts -- Austria -- Vienna -- Biography. Ethnicity -- Austria -- Vienna -- Psychological aspects. Jews -- Cultural assimilation -- Austria -- Vienna Vienna (Austria) -- Ethnic relations.

RC339.52.H67.R8
Rubins, Jack L.
Karen Horney : gentle rebel of psychoanalysis / Jack L. Rubins. New York : Dial Press, c1978. xviii, 362 p.
78-009339   616.8/917/0924   0803744250
Horney, Karen, -- 1885-1952. Psychoanalysts -- Biography.

RC339.52.L34.E9 1976
Evans, Richard I.
R. D. Laing, the man and his ideas / Richard I. Evans. New York : Dutton, 1976. lxxv, 170 p.
75-014294   616.8/9/00924   0525187650
Laing, R. D. -- (Ronald David), -- 1927- Psychiatrists -- England -- Biography. Psychiatry. Psychology.

RC339.52.L87
Alexander Romanovich Luria : a scientific biography / Evgenia D. Homskaya ; edited, with a foreword by David E. Tupper ; translated by Daria Krotova. New York : Kluwer Academic/Plenum Publishers, c2001. xvi, 184 p. :
00-062190   153/.092   0306464942
Luriia, A. R. -- (Aleksandr Romanovich), -- 1902- Neurologists -- Russia -- Biography. Psychologists -- Russia -- Biography.

RC339.52.R64.T48 1992
Thorne, Brian,
Carl Rogers / Brian Thorne. London ; Sage Publications, 1992. ix, 118 p. ;
91-051203   616.89/14/092   0803984626
Rogers, Carl R. -- (Carl Ransom), -- 1902- Counseling -- History. Psychotherapy -- History.

RC339.52.S87P37
Perry, Helen Swick.
Psychiatrist of America, the life of Harry Stack Sullivan / Helen Swick Perry. Cambridge, Mass. : Belknap Press, c1982. 462 p., [16] p. of plates :
616.89/0092/4   0674720768
Sullivan, Harry Stack, 1892-1949. Psychiatrists--United States--Biography. Psychologists--United States--Biography. Sociologists--United States--Biography.

RC341 Neurosciences. Biological psychiatry. Neuropsychiatry — General works — 1901-

RC341.B33 1993
Barondes, Samuel H.,
Molecules and mental illness / Samuel H. Barondes. New York : Scientific American Library, c1993. vi, 215 p. :
92-035150   616.89   0716750414
Biological psychiatry.

RC341.H96 1993
Hyman, Steven E.
The molecular foundations of psychiatry / Steven E. Hyman, Eric J. Nestler. Washington, D.C. : American Psychiatric Press, c1993. xix, 239 p. :
92-007017   616.8   0880483539
Neuropsychiatry. Neuropsychopharmacology. Mental illness -- Molecular aspects.

RC343 Neurosciences. Biological psychiatry. Neuropsychiatry — General special

RC343.B59 1945
Bochner, Ruth (Rothenberg)
The clinical application of the Rorschach test, by Ruth Bochner and Florence Halpern. New York, Grune & Stratton, 1945. xi, 331 p.
47-001460
Rorschach test.

RC343.D57 1998
Disorders of brain and mind / edited by Maria A. Ron and Anthony S. David. Cambridge ; Cambridge University Press, 1998. xiv, 373 p. :
616.8   0521473063
Neuropsychiatry. Brain--Diseases. Psychology, Pathological.

RC343.F75
Freud, Sigmund,
The history of the psychoanalytic movement, by Prof. Dr. Sigmund Freud ... authorized English translation by A. A. Brill ... New York, The Nervous and Mental Disease Publishing Compan 1917. 2 p.l., 58 p.
17-007058
Psychoanalysis -- History.

RC343.G56513 1995
Goldstein, Kurt,
The organism : a holistic approach to biology derived from pathological data in man / Kurt Goldstein ; with a foreword by Oliver Sacks. New York : Zone Books, c1995. 422 p. ;
94-040858   612.8/2/01   0942299965
Neurology -- Philosophy. Neuropsychology -- Philosophy. Holistic medicine.

RC343.H636 1999
Horgan, John,
The undiscovered mind : how the human brain defies replication, medication, and explanation / John Horgan. New York : Free Press, c1999. 325 p. ;
99-031051   612.8/2   0684850753
Neurosciences -- Popular works.

RC343.H65
Horney, Karen,
The neurotic personality of our time, by Dr. Karen Horney. New York, W. W. Norton & company, inc. [c1937] xii, 13-299 p
37-003732   616.8
Neuroses. Psychoanalysis. Personality.

RC343.M44 1994
Mender, Donald.
The myth of neuropsychiatry : a look at paradoxes, physics, and the human brain / Donald Mender. New York : Plenum Press, c1994. 280 p. ;
94-002840   616.8   0306446529
Neuropsychiatry -- Philosophy. Psychiatry -- Philosophy. Mind-brain identity theory.

RC344 Neurosciences. Biological psychiatry. Neuropsychiatry — Addresses, essays, lectures

RC344.C55
Classics of neurology (from Emerson C. Kelly's "Medical classics") Huntington, N.Y., R. E. Krieger Pub. Co., 1971. v, 377 p.
78-158127   616.8/08
Neurology. Neurologists.

RC346 Neurosciences. Biological psychiatry. Neuropsychiatry — Neurology. Diseases of the nervous system — General works

RC346.A3 2001
Victor, Maurice,
Adams and Victor's principles of neurology / Maurice Victor, Allan H. Ropper. 7th ed. New York : Medical Pub. Division, McGraw-Hill, c2001. xi, 1692 p. :
616.8   0071163336
Nervous system--Diseases. Neuropsychiatry. Nervous System Diseases.

RC346.B86
Burr, Harold Saxton,
Classics in neurology; selected by Richard Sherman Lyman. Springfield, Ill., Thomas [1963] 176 p.
63009636   616.8
Neurology -- Cases, clinical reports, statistics. Neurologic manifestations Neurology.

RC346.M4 2000
Merritt's neurology. 10th ed. / editor, Lewis P. Rowland. Philadelphia : Lippincott Williams & Wilkins, c2000. xx, 1002 p. :
616.8   0683304747
Nervous system--Diseases. Neurology. Nervous System Diseases.

RC347.5 Neurosciences. Biological psychiatry. Neuropsychiatry — Neurology. Diseases of the nervous system — Neurotoxicology

RC347.5.H86 1991
Human lead exposure / editor, Herbert L. Needleman. Boca Raton : CRC Press, c1992. 290 p. :
91-020525   615.9/25688   084936034X
Neurotoxicology. Lead -- Toxicology. Environmental Exposure.

RC351 Neurosciences. Biological psychiatry. Neuropsychiatry — Neurology. Diseases of the nervous system — Popular works

RC351.R24 1998
Ramachandran, V. S.
  Phantoms in the brain : probing the mysteries of the human mind / V.S. Ramachandran, and Sandra Blakeslee. New York : William Morrow, c1998. xix, 328 p. :
98-003953   612.8/2   0688152473
  Neurology -- Popular works. Brain -- Popular works. Neurosciences -- Popular works.

RC372-394 Neurosciences. Biological psychiatry. Neuropsychiatry — Neurology. Diseases of the nervous system — Diseases of the central nervous system

RC372.S576 2000
Slater, Lauren.
  Lying : a metaphorical memoir / Lauren Slater. New York : Random House, c2000. 221 p. ;
99-056284   361.1/96853/0092
0375501126
  Slater, Lauren -- Health.   Epilepsy -- Patients -- United States -- Biography.

RC372.T45 1971
Temkin, Owsei,
  The falling sickness; a history of epilepsy from the Greeks to the beginnings of modern neurology.   Baltimore, Johns Hopkins Press [1971] xv, 467 p.
70-139522   616.85/3/009   0801812119
  Epilepsy -- History.

RC377.S583 2001
  Multiple sclerosis :the guide to treatment and management / Chris H. Polman ... [et al.] 5th ed. New York : Demos, c2001. xiv, 137 p. ;
          616.8/3406   1888799544
  Multiple sclerosis. Multiple sclerosis--Treatment. Multiple Sclerosis--therapy.

RC386.B72 1995
Bradshaw, John L.,
  Clinical neuropsychology : behavioral and brain science / John L. Bradshaw & Jason B. Mattingley. San Diego : Academic Press, c1995. xv, 458 p. :
94-049187   616.8   0121245454
  Clinical neuropsychology. Neuropsychiatry. Nervous System Diseases.

RC386.S73 1992
Strange, P. G.
  Brain biochemistry and brain disorders / Philip G. Strange. Oxford ; Oxford University Press, 1992. xi, 342 p. :
91-046384   616.8/047   0198542593
  Brain -- Pathophysiology. Brain -- Physiology. Neuroanatomy.

RC386.2.I5 1997
  Injured brains of medical minds : views from within / compiled and edited by Narinder Kapur. Oxford [England] ; Oxford University Press, 1997. xvi, 426 p. :
96-025724   616.8/049   0198521448
  Brain -- Diseases -- Case studies. Neurologists -- Diseases -- Case studies. Brain Diseases -- personal narratives.

RC386.6.M34B895 2002
Buxton, Richard B.,
  Introduction to functional magnetic resonance imaging :principles and techniques / Richard B. Buxton. Cambridge, UK ; Cambridge University Press, c2002. xi, 523 p. :
          616/.047548   0521581133
  Brain--Magnetic resonance imaging. Magnetic resonance imaging.

RC386.6.N48.N492 1998
  Neuropsychology / edited by Gerald Goldstein, Paul David Nussbaum, and Sue R. Beers. New York : Plenum Press, c1998. xvi, 497 p. ;
97-042120   616.8   030645646X
  Clinical neuropsychology. Neuropsychological tests. Neuropsychology.

RC386.6.N48S67 1998
Spreen, Otfried.
  A compendium of neuropsychological tests : administration, norms, and commentary / Otfried Spreen, Esther Strauss. 2nd ed. New York : Oxford University Press, 1998. xvi, 736 p. :
          152   0195100190
  Neuropsychological tests--Handbooks, manuals, etc.

RC387.5.B713 1995
Stein, Donald G.
  Brain repair / Donald G. Stein, Simon Brailowsky, Bruno Will. New York : Oxford University Press, 1995. x, 156 p. ;
94-016517   616.8   0195076427
  Brain damage. Brain -- Regeneration. Neuroplasticity.

RC387.5.C648 1999
  Communication disorders following traumatic brain injury / edited by Skye McDonald, Leanne Togher, Chris Code. Hove, East Sussex, UK : Psychology Press, c1999. xiv, 338 p. ;
00-361287   616.8/043   0863777244
  Brain damage -- Patients -- Rehabilitation. Communicative disorders.

RC387.5.G34
Macmillan, Malcolm,
  An odd kind of fame : stories of Phineas Gage / Malcolm Macmillan. Cambridge, Mass., MIT Press, c2000. xiii, 562 p.
99-056640   617.4/81044/092   0262133636
  Gage, Phineas -- Health.   Brain damage -- Patients -- United States -- Biography. Split brain -- History. Psychosurgery -- History.

RC388.5.M28 1998
McCrum, Robert.
My year off / Robert McCrum. New York : W. W. Norton, 1998. 231 p. ;
98-029629   362.1/9681   0393046567
McCrum, Robert -- Health.   Cerebrovascular disease -- Patients -- Great Britain -- Biography. Book editors -- Great Britain -- Biography. Authors, English -- 20th century -- Biography.

RC394.A85.F57 1998
Fisher, Barbara C.
Attention deficit disorder : practical coping methods / Barbara C. Fisher, Ross A. Beckley. Boca Raton : CRC Press, 1998. 380 p. ;
98-007960   616.85/89   0849318998
Attention-deficit hyperactivity disorder. Adjustment (Psychology) Biological psychiatry.

RC394.H85.W49 1995
Wexler, Alice,
Mapping fate : a memoir of family, risk, and genetic research / Alice Wexler. New York : Times Books : c1995. xxv, 294 p. :
94-025295   362.1/96851/0092
0812917103
Wexler, Alice, -- 1942-   Huntington's chorea -- Research -- United States -- History. Huntington's chorea -- Patients -- United States -- Family relationships.

RC394.S93
Harrison, John E.
Synaesthesia : the strangest thing / John Harrison. Oxford ; Oxford University Press, 2001. xii, 277 p. :
00-067603   616.8   0192632450
Synesthesia.

RC423-428.8 Neurosciences. Biological psychiatry. Neuropsychiatry — Neurology. Diseases of the nervous system — Speech and language disorders

RC423.B28 2000
Baken, R. J.
Clinical measurement of speech and voice / R.J. Baken, Robert F. Orlikoff. San Diego : Singular Thomson Learning, c2000. xii, 610 p. :
99-024709   616.85/5075   1565938690
Speech disorders -- Diagnosis. Voice disorders -- Diagnosis. Speech -- Measurement.

RC423.B3 1960
Barbara, Dominick A.
Psychological and psychiatric aspects of speech and hearing. Springfield, Ill., Thomas [1960] 756 p.
60009307   616.855
Speech Voice Speech therapy

RC423.B74 2003
Brookshire, Robert H.
Introduction to neurogenic communication disorders / Robert H. Brookshire.6th ed. St. Louis, Mo. : Mosby, c2003. xiv, 658 p. :
          616.85/52   0323016863
Communicative disorders.

RC423.C66 1997
Contested words, contested science : unraveling the facilitated communication controversy / edited by Douglas Biklen and Donald N. Cardinal. New York : Teachers College Press, c1997. vii, 245 p. ;
96-052240   616.85/503   0807736023
Communicative disorders -- Patients -- Rehabilitation. Communication devices for the disabled. Handicapped -- Means of communication.

RC423.D473 2000
Diagnosis in speech-language pathology / edited by J. Bruce Tomblin, Hughlett L. Morris, D.C. Spriestersbach; assistant to the editors, Juanita C. Limas. 2nd ed. San Diego : Singular, c2000. xxi, 513 p. :
          616.85/5075   0769300502
Speech disorders--Diagnosis. Language Disorders. Speech Disorders.

RC423.N52 1996
Nicolosi, Lucille.
Terminology of communication disorders :speech-language-hearing / Lucille Nicolosi, Elizabeth Harryman, Janet Kresheck.4th ed. Baltimore : Williams & Wilkins, c1996. xx, 369 p. :
          616.85/5/003   068306505X
Communicative disorders--Dictionaries. Communicative Disorders--dictionaries.

RC423.R65 2000
Rollin, Walter J.,
Counseling individuals with communication disorders : psychodynamic and family aspects / Walter J. Rollin ; foreword by Audrey L. Holland. Boston : Butterworth-Heinemann, c2000. xvii, 262 p.
99-461973   616.85/50651   0750671785
Communicative disorders -- Psychological aspects. Communicative disorders -- Patients -- Family relationships. Communicative disorders -- Patients -- Counseling of.

RC423.V35 1996
Van Riper, Charles,
Speech correction : an introduction to speech pathology and audiology / Charles Van Riper, Robert L. Erickson. 9th ed. Boston : Allyn and Bacon, c1996. xii, 532 p. :
          616.85/5   0138251428
Speech disorders. Speech therapy. Audiology.

RC424.S768 1998
Stuttering and related disorders of fluency / editor, Richard F. Curlee. 2nd ed. New York : Thieme Medical Publishers, 1998. p. cm.
          616.85/54   0865777640
Stuttering. Stuttering--therapy. Speech Therapy--methods.

RC424.7.B47 1998
Articulation and phonological disorders / [edited by] John E. Bernthal, Nicholas W. Bankson. 4th ed. Boston : Allyn and Bacon, c1998. xii, 432 p. :
          616.85/5   0205196934
Articulation disorders. Articulation Disorders. Voice Disorders.

RC425.A615 1997
Aphasia and related neurogenic language disorders / [edited by] Leonard L. LaPointe. 2nd ed. Stuttgart ; Thieme, 1997. xiv, 298 p. ;
          616.85/52   3137477026
Aphasia. Language disorders. Central nervous system--Diseases--Complications.

RC425.S675 2003
Spreen, Otfried.
Assessment of aphasia / Otfried Spreen, Anthony H. Risser. New York, N.Y. : Oxford University Press, 2003. p. ;
          616.85/52075   0195140753
Aphasia--Diagnosis. Aphasia--diagnosis.

RC428.8.G65 2000
Goldstein, Brian.
Resource guide on cultural and linguistic diversity / Brian Goldstein. San Diego, Calif. : Singular Pub. Group, c2000. xvii, 179 p.
99-037152   616.85/506   0769300316
Speech therapy. Transcultural medical care. Language Development Disorders -- rehabilitation.

RC435 Neurosciences. Biological psychiatry. Neuropsychiatry — Psychiatry — Collected works (nonserial)

RC435.A562
American handbook of psychiatry. Silvano Arieti, editor-in-chief. New York, Basic Books [1974-c1986 v. 1-8   ;
73-078893   616.8/9/008   0465001475
Psychiatry. Mental disorders.

RC437 Neurosciences. Biological psychiatry. Neuropsychiatry — Psychiatry — Dictionaries and encyclopedias

RC437.E49 1996
The encyclopedia of psychiatry, psychology, and psychoanalysis / Benjamin B. Wolman, editor in chief. New York : Henry Holt, c1996. xx, 649 p. ;
95-041116   616.89/003   0805022341
Psychiatry -- Encyclopedias. Psychology -- Encyclopedias. Psychoanalysis -- Encyclopedias.

RC437.K34 1993
Kahn, Ada P.
The encyclopedia of mental health / Ada P. Kahn and Jan Fawcett. New York, NY, USA : Facts on File, c1993. xi, 464 p. ;
92-035148   616.89/003   0816026947
Psychiatry -- Encyclopedias. Mental health -- Encyclopedias.

RC437.P795 2001
Psychology and mental health / edited by Jaclyn Rodriguez ; project editor, Tracy Irons-Georges. Pasadena, Calif. : Salem Press, c2001. 2 v. (xx, 729
00-046312   616.89/003   0893560669
Psychology, Pathological -- Encyclopedias. Mental illness -- Encyclopedias. Mental health -- Encyclopedias.

RC437.S76 1994
American psychiatric glossary / edited by Jane E. Edgerton, Robert J. Campbell, III. 7th ed. Washington, D.C. : American Psychiatric Press, c1994. ix, 182 p. ;
          616.89/003   0880485086
Psychiatry--Dictionaries.

RC437.5 Neurosciences. Biological psychiatry. Neuropsychiatry — Psychiatry — Philosophy. Methodology

RC437.5.B468 1996
Berrios, G. E.
The history of mental symptoms : descriptive psychopathology since the nineteenth century / German E. Berrios. Cambridge [England] ; Cambridge University Press, 1996. xiv, 565 p. ;
95-020315   616.89/001   0521431352
Psychology, Pathological -- Philosophy. Descriptive psychology. Psychology, Pathological -- History.

RC437.5.C48 1992
Chessick, Richard D.,
What constitutes the patient in psychotherapy : alternative approaches to understanding humans / Richard D. Chessick. Northvale, N.J. : Jason Aronson, c1992. xxi, 220 p. ;
91-041341   616.89/14/01   0876685491
Psychotherapy -- Philosophy. Psychology and philosophy -- History -- 20th century. Philosophical anthropology -- History -- 20th century.

RC437.5.F335 1995
Fancher, Robert T.
Cultures of healing : correcting the image of American mental health care / Robert T. Fancher. New York : W.H. Freeman, c1995. xi, 355 p. ;
94-041495   616.89/001   0716723832
Psychiatry -- Philosophy. Cultural psychiatry. Psychotherapy -- Social aspects.

RC437.5.F35 1993
Farber, Seth,
Madness, heresy, and the rumor of angels : the revolt against the mental health system / Seth Farber. Chicago, Ill. : Open Court, c1993. xviii, 266 p.
93-001276   616.89   0812691997
Antipsychiatry. Psychotherapy patients -- Abuse of. Ex-mental patients -- Case studies.

RC437.5.G75
Gross, Martin L.

The psychological society : a critical analysis of psychiatry, psychotherapy, psychoanalysis and the psychological revolution / Martin L. Gross. New York : Random House, c1978. 369 p. ;
77-090288   616.8/9/001   0394462335
Psychiatry -- Philosophy. Psychology -- Philosophy. Civilization, Modern -- 20th century.

RC437.5.S89 1992
Szasz, Thomas Stephen,

A lexicon of lunacy : metaphoric malady, moral responsibility, and psychiatry / Thomas Szasz. New Brunswick, U.S.A. : Transaction Publishers, c1993. xi, 202 p. ;
92-005866   616.89/001   1560000651
Antipsychiatry. Mental health personnel -- Language. Mental illness -- Terminology.

RC437.5.S927 1984
Szasz, Thomas Stephen,

The therapeutic state : psychiatry in the mirror of current events / Thomas Szasz. Buffalo, N.Y. : Prometheus Books, 1984. 360 p. ;
83-063057   616.89   0879752394
Psychiatry -- United States -- Methodology. Mental illness -- Social aspects.

RC437.5.W46 1998
Weissmark, Mona Sue.

Doing psychotherapy effectively / Mona Sue Weissmark & Daniel A. Giacomo. Chicago : University of Chicago Press, c1998. x, 177 p. ;
97-025027   616.89/14   0226891674
Psychotherapy -- Philosophy. Psychotherapy -- Evaluation. Psychotherapist and patient.

RC438 Neurosciences. Biological psychiatry. Neuropsychiatry — Psychiatry — History

RC438.A253
Ackerknecht, Erwin Heinz,

A short history of psychiatry. Translated from the German by Sulammith Wolff. New York, Hafner Pub. Co., 1959. vi, 98 p.
59-002551   616.8909
Psychiatry -- History.

RC438.A39
Alexander, Franz,

The history of psychiatry; an evaluation of psychiatric thought and practice from prehistoric times to the present, by Franz G. Alexander and Sheldon T. Selesnick. New York, Harper & Row [1966] xvi, 471 p.
64-018048   616.89009
Psychiatry -- History.

RC438.G54 1988
Gilman, Sander L.

Disease and representation : images of illness from madness to AIDS / Sander L. Gilman. Ithaca : Cornell University Press, 1988. xiv, 320 p. :
87-032968   306/.46   0801494761
Mental illness -- History. Mental illness in art. Diseases in art.

RC438.H84
Hunter, Richard Alfred,

Three hundred years of psychiatry, 1535-1860; a history presented in selected English texts [by] Richard Hunter [and] Ida Macalpine. London, Oxford University Press, 1963. xxvi, 1107 p.
63-002062   616.89/00941
Psychiatry -- Great Britain -- History. Psychiatry -- History. Psychiatry.

RC438.M27
MacDonald, Michael,

Mystical Bedlam : madness, anxiety, and healing in seventeenth-century England / Michael MacDonald. Cambridge ; Cambridge University Press, 1981. xvi, 323 p. :
80-025787   362.2/0942   0521231701
Psychiatry -- History -- 17th century. Mental illness -- Great Britain -- Public opinion -- History -- 17th century. Mental illness -- Great Britain -- History -- 17th century.

RC438.S54 1997
Shorter, Edward.

A history of psychiatry : from the era of the asylum to the age of Prozac / by Edward Shorter. New York : John Wiley & Sons, c1997. xii, 436 p. :
96-015292   616.89/009   047115749X
Psychiatry -- History. Psychiatry -- history. Psychoanalysis -- history.

RC438.6 Neurosciences. Biological psychiatry. Neuropsychiatry — Psychiatry — Biography

RC438.6.B48.S8813 1996
Sutton, Nina.

Bettelheim, a life and a legacy / Nina Sutton ; translated from the French by David Sharp, in collaboration with the author. New York : BasicBooks, c1996. xvii, 606 p.,
95-044421   618.92/89/0092   0465006353
Bettelheim, Bruno. Psychoanalysts -- United States -- Biography.

RC438.6.E45.W54 1988
Wiener, Daniel N.

Albert Ellis : passionate skeptic / Daniel N. Wiener. New York : Praeger, 1988. xix, 201 p.,
87-022495   150/.92/4   0275927512
Ellis, Albert. Clinical psychologists -- United States -- Biography. Rational-emotive psychotherapy -- History.

RC438.6.K64.A4 1994
Kohut, Heinz.
The curve of life : correspondence of Heinz Kohut, 1923-1981 / edited by Geoffrey Cocks. Chicago : University of Chicago Press, 1994. xv, 443 p. :
93-040922   150.19/5/092   0226111709
Kohut, Heinz -- Correspondence.   Psychoanalysts -- Correspondence.

RC438.6.M46.A4 1995
Menninger, Karl A.
The selected correspondence of Karl A. Menninger, 1946-1965 / edited with an introduction by Howard J. Faulkner and Virginia D. Pruitt. Columbia : University of Missouri Press, c1995. xi, 278 p. :
95-008760   616.89   082620998X
Menninger, Karl A. -- (Karl Augustus), -- 1893- -- Correspondence. Psychiatrists -- United States -- Correspondence.

RC438.6.W56.A27 1997
Abram, Jan.
The language of Winnicott : a dictionary and guide to understanding his work / Jan Abram ; bibliography compiled by Harry Karnac. Northvale, N.J. : J. Aronson, 1997. xx, 378 p. ;
96-050065   616.89/17   1568217005
Winnicott, D. W. -- (Donald Woods), -- 1896-1971. Winnicott, D. W. -- (Donald Woods), -- 1896-1971 -- Bibliography.   Psychoanalysis.

RC439 Neurosciences. Biological psychiatry. Neuropsychiatry — Psychiatry — Hospitals and hospital treatment

RC439.B4 1953
Beers, Clifford Whittingham,
A mind that found itself; an autobiography. Garden City, N.Y., Doubleday, 1953. 394 p.
      362.2/092/4
Beers, Clifford Whittingham, --1876-1943.   Mentally ill--United States--Biography. Mentally ill--Care.

RC439.G2813 1999
Gauchet, Marcel.
Madness and democracy : the modern psychiatric universe / Marcel Gauchet and Gladys Swain ; translated by Catherine Porter, with a foreword by Jerrold Seigel. Princeton, NJ : Princeton University Press, c1999. xxvi, 323 p.
98-045014   362.2/1   0691033722
Psychiatric hospital care. Power (Social sciences) Mental illness -- Social aspects.

RC439.W65 1994
Woodson, Marle,
Behind the door of delusion / by "Inmate Ward 8" ; edited, with an introduction and afterword by William W. Savage and James H. Lazalier. Niwot, Colo. : University Press of Colorado, c1994. xiv, 178 p. ;
94-008412   362.2/1   0870813145
Psychiatric hospitals -- Sociological aspects -- Case studies. Psychiatric hospital patients -- Case studies. Psychiatric hospital care -- Case studies.

RC439.5 Neurosciences. Biological psychiatry. Neuropsychiatry — Psychiatry — Aftercare of hospitalized patients. Rehabilitation. Home care

RC439.5.B8
Budson, Richard D.
The psychiatric halfway house : a handbook of theory and practice / Richard D. Budson. Pittsburgh : University of Pittsburgh Press, c1978. xix, 278 p. :
77-074548   362.2/2   0822933500
Mentally ill -- Rehabilitation. Halfway houses. Halfway houses -- Handbooks.

RC439.5.C37 1995
Carling, Paul J.
Return to community : building support systems for people with psychiatric disabilities / Paul J. Carling ; foreword by Jacqueline Parrish. New York : Guilford Press, c1995. xx, 348 p. ;
94-029724   362.2/2   0898622999
Mentally ill -- Deinstitutionalization. Community mental health services.

RC439.5.E84
Estroff, Sue E.
Making it crazy : an ethnography of psychiatric clients in an American community / Sue E. Estroff ; foreword by H. Richard Lamb. Berkeley : University of California Press, c1981. xxi, 328 p. :
79-064660   362.2/2/0973   0520039637
Mentally ill -- Rehabilitation -- United States. Community mental health services -- United States. Sheltered workshops -- United States.

RC439.5.I78 1990
Isaac, Rael Jean.
Madness in the streets : how psychiatry and the law abandoned the mentally ill / Rael Jean Isaac, Virginia C. Armat. New York : Free Press ; c1990. ix, 436 p. ;
90-037735   362.2/08/6942   0029153808
Mentally ill -- Deinstitutionalization -- United States. Ex-mental patients -- Mental health services -- United States. Community mental health services -- United States.

RC439.5.L44 1996
Lefley, Harriet P.
Family caregiving in mental illness / Harriet P. Lefley. Thousand Oaks : Sage Publications, c1996. x, 261 p. :
95-041722   362.2/042   0803957203
Mentally ill -- Home care. Mentally ill -- Family relationships. Caregivers.

RC439.5.N46 1999
Neugeboren, Jay.
Transforming madness : new lives for people living with mental illness / Jay Neugeboren. New York : William Morrow & Company, c1999. 390 p. ;
98-050056   616.89   068815655X
Mentally ill -- Rehabilitation. Mental illness -- Treatment. Mentally ill -- Rehabilitation -- United States -- Case studies.

RC440 Neurosciences. Biological psychiatry. Neuropsychiatry — Psychiatry — Psychiatric nursing

RC440.B353 2000
Bauer, Barbara B.
Mental health nursing : an introductory text / Barbara B. Bauer, Signe S. Hill. Philadelphia, Pa. : W.B. Saunders, c2000. xvi, 382 p. :
99-029020   610.73/68   0721677533
Psychiatric nursing. Mental Disorders -- nursing. Mental Disorders -- therapy -- Nurses' Instruction.

RC440.G659 2002
Gorman, Linda M.
Psychosocial nursing for general patient care / Linda M. Gorman, Marica L. Raines, Donna F. Sultan. 2nd ed. Philadelphia : F.A. Davis Co., c2002. xiii, 423 p. :
          610.73/68   0803608020
Psychiatric nursing--Handbooks, manuals, etc. Nursing--Social aspects--Handbooks, manuals, etc.

RC440.M325 1999
McFarland-Icke, Bronwyn Rebekah,
Nurses in Nazi Germany : moral choice in history / Bronwyn Rebekah McFarland-Icke. Princeton, N.J. : Princeton University Press, c1999. xv, 343 p. ;
99-018151   610.73/0943/0904
0691006652
Psychiatric nursing -- Moral and ethical aspects -- Germany -- History -- 20th century. Nursing ethics -- Germany -- History -- 20th century. Medical policy -- Germany -- History -- 20th century.

RC440.M3544 1997
Mental health nursing in the community / [edited by] Nancy K. Worley. St. Louis, MO : Mosby, c1997. xxiv, 468 p.
96-025537   610.73/68   0815194293
Psychiatric nursing. Community mental health services. Community health nursing.

RC440.P7338 2000
Psychiatric mental health nursing / [edited by] Katherine M. Fortinash, Patricia A. Holoday-Worret. St. Louis : Mosby, c2000. xxv, 854 p. :
99-043208   610.73/68   0323006485
Psychiatric nursing. Psychiatric Nursing. Mental Disorders -- nursing.

RC440.S795 2001
Principles and practice of psychiatric nursing / Gail W. Stuart, Michele T. Laraia. 7th ed. St. Louis : Mosby, c2001. xxv, 915 p. :
          610.73/68   032301254X
Psychiatric nursing. Psychiatric Nursing--methods. Mental Disorders--nursing.

RC440.9 Neurosciences. Biological psychiatry. Neuropsychiatry — Psychiatry — Psychiatric as a profession

RC440.9.M37 1989
Martin, Daniel R.
A directory of credentials in counseling and psychotherapy / Daniel R. Martin and J. Richard Cookerly. Boston, Mass. : G.K. Hall, c1989. x, 219 p. ;
89-019787   362.2/025/73   0816190623
Psychotherapists -- Certification -- United States -- Directories. Counselors -- Certification -- United States -- Directories. Social workers -- Certification -- United States -- Directories.

RC443-451 Neurosciences. Biological psychiatry. Neuropsychiatry — Psychiatry — By region or country

RC443.C33 1998
Caplan, Eric,
Mind games : American culture and the birth of psychotherapy / Eric Caplan. Berkeley, Calif. : University of California Press, c1998. xiii, 242 p.
98-016999   616.89/00973   0520211693
Psychotherapy -- United States -- History -- 19th century. Psychotherapy -- Social aspects -- United States. Mental healing -- United States -- History -- 19th century.

RC443.C84 1995
Cushman, Philip.
Constructing the self, constructing America : a cultural history of psychotherapy / Philip Cushman. Boston, Mass. : Addison-Wesley Pub., c1995. xiii, 430 p.
94-033066   616.89/14/0973   0201626438
Psychotherapy -- Social aspects -- United States. Psychotherapy -- Moral and ethical aspects. Identity (Psychology) -- United States. United States -- Civilization -- Psychological aspects.

RC443.G35 1995
Gamwell, Lynn,
Madness in America : cultural and medical perceptions of mental illness before 1914 / Lynn Gamwell, Nancy Tomes. Ithaca, N.Y. : Cornell University Press ; 1995. 182 p. :
94-046520   362.2/0973   0801431611
Psychiatry -- United States -- History. Mental illness -- United States -- Public opinion. Social psychiatry -- United States -- History.

RC443.G747 1994
Grob, Gerald N.,
The mad among us : a history of the care of America's mentally ill / Gerald N. Grob. New York : Free Press ; c1994. xi, 386 p. :
93-040806   362.2/0973   0029126959
Mentally ill -- Care -- United States -- History. Psychiatry -- United States -- History. Mentally ill -- United States -- Public opinion.

RC443.H57 1992
History of psychotherapy : a century of change / edited by Donald K. Freedheim ; associate editors, Herbert J. Freudenberger ... [et al.]. Washington, D.C. : American Psychological Association, 1992. xxxiii, 930 p
91-043409   616.89/14/0973   1557981493
Psychotherapy -- United States -- History. Psychotherapy -- History.

RC443.S26 1994
Sareyan, Alex,
The turning point : how men of conscience brought about major change in the care of America's mentally ill / Alex Sareyan. Washington, DC : American Psychiatric Press, c1994. xviii, 309 p.
93-009227   362.2/1/097309044
0880485604
World War, 1939-1945 -- Conscientious objectors -- United States. Mentally handicapped -- Institutional care -- United States -- History -- 20th century. Psychiatric hospital patients -- United States -- Abuse of.

RC445.K3.T626 1990
Friedman, Lawrence Jacob,
Menninger : the family and the clinic / Lawrence J. Friedman. New York : Knopf, 1990. xix, 472 p.,
89-015498   362.2/1/0978163   0394535693
Menninger family.

RC445.M4.B448 1994
Berger, Lisa.
Under observation : life inside a psychiatric hospital / Lisa Berger and Alexander Vuckovic. New York : Ticknor & Fields, 1994. xvi, 269 p. ;
94-005051   362.2/1/097444   039563413X
Psychiatric hospital care. Mental illness -- Popular works. Belmont (Mass.).

RC450.G3.C64 1998
Cocks, Geoffrey,
Treating mind & body : essays in the history of science, professions, and society under extreme conditions / Geoffrey Cocks ; with a foreword by Peter J. Loewenberg. New Brunswick, N.J., U.S.A. : Transaction Publishers, c1998. xvii, 219 p.
97-020184   616.89/00943/09043
1560003103
Psychotherapy -- Political aspects -- Germany. Psychoanalysis -- Political aspects -- Germany. National socialism and medicine. Germany -- History -- 1933-1945.

RC450.G3.M53 1994
Midelfort, H. C. Erik.
Mad princes of renaissance Germany / H.C. Erik Midelfort. Charlottesville : University Press of Virginia, 1994. xii, 204 p. :
93-039116   616.89/00943/09031
0813914868
Psychiatry -- Germany -- History -- 16th century. Princes -- Mental health -- Germany. Princes -- Germany -- History -- 16th century. Germany -- History -- Maximilian I, 1493-1519. Germany -- History -- 1517-1648.

RC450.G4.G64 1999
Goldberg, Ann.
Sex, religion, and the making of modern madness : the Eberbach Asylum and Germany society, 1815-1849 / Ann Goldberg. New York : Oxford University Press, 1999. x, 236 p. :
98-013682   616.89/00943/09034
0195125819
Mental illness -- Germany -- History -- 19th century. Psychiatry -- Germany -- History -- 19th century. Psychiatric hospitals -- Germany -- Sociological aspects.

RC450.G7.C48 1989
Cherry, Charles L.,
A quiet haven : Quakers, moral treatment, and asylum reform / Charles L. Cherry. Rutherford : Fairleigh Dickinson University Press, c1989. 237 p. ;
88-048019   362.2/1/088286   0838633412
Mentally ill -- Care -- Great Britain -- History. Mentally ill -- Care -- United States -- History. Quakers -- Charitable contributions -- History.

RC450.G7.S284 1996
Scull, Andrew T.
Masters of Bedlam : the transformation of the mad-doctoring trade / Andrew Scull, Charlotte MacKenzie, Nicholas Hervey. Princeton, N.J. : Princeton University Press, c1996. x, 363 p. :
96-012051   616.89/00941/09034
0691034117
Psychiatrists -- Great Britain -- Biography. Psychiatry -- Great Britain -- History -- 19th century.

RC451.S65.C35 1993
Calloway, Paul.
Russian/Soviet and Western psychiatry : a contemporary comparative study / Paul Calloway. New York : Wiley, c1993. xxii, 266 p.
93-019938   616.89/00947   0471595748
Psychiatry -- Soviet Union. Mental Disorders. Cross-Cultural Comparison.

RC451.4 Neurosciences. Biological psychiatry. Neuropsychiatry — Psychiatry — By age group, professions, etc.

RC451.4.A5.B5 1993
Billig, Nathan.
Growing older and wiser : coping with expectations, challenges, and change in the later years / Nathan Billig. New York : Lexington Books ; c1993. xii, 230 p. :
92-024310   613/.043   0669276782
Aged -- Mental health. Aging -- Psychological aspects. Life change events in old age.

RC451.4.A5B56 1998
Blazer, Dan G.
Emotional problems in later life : intervention strategies for professional caregivers / Dan Blazer.2nd ed. New York : Springer Pub. Co., c1998. ix, 270 p. ;
      618.97/689   0826175619
Affective disorders--Treatment. Geriatric psychiatry.

RC451.4.A5.H39 1997
Handbook of neuropsychology and aging / edited by Paul David Nussbaum. New York : Plenum Press, c1997. xvii, 559 p.
97-012001   618.97/68   0306454602
   Geriatric neuropsychiatry. Geriatric neurology. Clinical neuropsychology.

RC451.4.A5.P735 2000
Professional psychology in long term care : a comprehensive guide / edited by Victor Molinari. New York : Hatherleigh Press, c2000. xxxi, 495 p.
99-037326   618.97/689   1578260353
   Geriatric psychiatry. Aged -- Long-term care. Aged -- Mental health.

RC451.4.A5S66 1999
Smyer, Michael A.
Aging and mental health / Michael A. Smyer and Sarah H. Qualls. Malden, Mass. : Blackwell Publishers, 1999. xxiv, 335 p. :
               618.97/689   1557865574
   Aged--Mental health. Geriatric psychiatry.

RC451.4.A5.Z374 1998
Zarit, Steven H.
Mental disorders in older adults : fundamentals of assessment and treatment / Steven H. Zarit, Judy M. Zarit. New York : Guilford Press, c1998. ix, 418 p. ;
98-022968   618.97/689   1572303689
   Aged -- Mental health. Aged -- Psychology. Mentally ill aged.

RC451.4.A83.S66 1995
Sport psychology interventions / Shane M. Murphy, editor. Champaign, IL : Human Kinetics, c1995. ix, 389 p. :
94-010390   616.89/008/8796   0873226593
   Athletes -- Mental health. Athletes -- Mental health services. Athletes -- Counseling of.

RC451.4.D57.P79 1989
Psychosocial aspects of disaster / edited by Richard Gist, Bernard Lubin. New York : Wiley, c1989. xiv, 357 p. :
88-033898   362.2   0471848948
   Disaster victims -- Mental health. Disasters -- Social aspects.

RC451.4.G39.C64 2000
Cohler, Bertram J.
The course of gay and lesbian lives : social and psychoanalytic perspectives / Bertram J. Cohler and Robert M. Galatzer-Levy. Chicago : University of Chicago Press, 2000. xviii, 537 p.
99-087700   306.76/6   0226113035
   Homosexuality -- Psychological aspects. Homosexuality -- Social aspects. Psychoanalysis and homosexuality.

RC451.4.H62.K47 1996
Kestenberg, Judith S.
The last witness : the child survivor of the Holocaust / by Judith S. Kestenberg and Ira Brenner. Washington, DC : American Psychiatric Press, c1996. xxii, 238 p.;
95-026268   616.85/21   0880486627
   Stress Disorders, Post-Traumatic. Holocaust -- psychology. Concentration Camps.

RC451.4.H62.W48 1993
Whiteman, Dorit Bader.
The uprooted : a Hitler legacy : voices of those who escaped before the "final solution" / Dorit Bader Whiteman ; foreword by William B. Helmreich. New York : Insight Books, c1993. xv, 446 p. ;
92-048291   155.9/3   0306444674
   Holocaust survivors -- Mental health. Holocaust, Jewish (1939-1945) -- Psychological aspects. Holocaust, Jewish (1939-1945) -- Personal narratives.

RC451.4.M45.F56 1988
Fine, Reuben,
Troubled men : the psychology, emotional conflicts, and therapy of men / Reuben Fine. San Francisco : Jossey-Bass Publishers, 1988. xv, 348 p. ;
88-042788   155.6/32   1555421059
   Men -- Mental health. Men -- Psychology. Psychotherapy.

RC451.4.M45.G66 1991
Gomez, Joan.
Psychological and psychiatric problems in men / Joan Gomez. London ; Routledge, 1991. v, 131 p. ;
90-008718   155.6/32   041502336X
   Men -- Mental health. Men -- Psychology.

RC451.4.M47.C486 1999
Challenging behavior of persons with mental health disorders and severe developmental disabilities / edited by Norman A. Wieseler and Ronald H. Hanson ; Gary Siperstein, editor. Washington, DC : American Association on Mental Retardation, 1999. p. cm.
99-033488   616.89   0940898667
   Mentally handicapped -- Mental health. Mentally handicapped -- Behavior modification. Self-injurious behavior -- Prevention.

RC451.4.M47.M48 1989
Mental retardation and mental illness : assessment, treatment, and service for the dually diagnosed / edited by Robert J. Fletcher, Frank J. Menolascino. Lexington, Mass. : Lexington Books, c1989. x, 300 p. :
89-008315   616.85/88   0669212113
   Mental retardation -- Complications. Mental illness. Mental Disorders.

RC451.4.M54.G65 1986
Golan, Naomi.
The perilous bridge : helping clients through mid-life transitions / Naomi Golan. New York : Free Press ; c1986. xiii, 255 p.
85-020522   616.89/14   002912090X
   Middle age -- Psychological aspects. Middle aged persons -- Psychology. Psychotherapy.

RC451.4.N87.L53 1994
Lichtenberg, Peter A.
 A guide to psychological practice in geriatric long-term care / Peter A. Lichtenberg. New York : Haworth Press, c1994. xv, 209 p. ;
92-048389   362.1/6   1560244100
 Nursing home patients -- Mental health services. Aged -- Long-term care -- Psychological aspects. Behavior therapy for the aged.

RC451.4.P68.T74 1998
 Treatment of offenders with mental disorders / edited by Robert M. Wettstein. New York : Guilford Press, c1998. ix, 438 p. ;
97-042397   362.2/086/927   1572302712
 Criminals -- Mental health services. Prisoners -- Mental health services. Forensic psychiatry.

RC451.4.P79.P47 1995
 A perilous calling : the hazards of psychotherapy practice / Michael B. Sussman, editor. New York : Wiley, c1995. xix, 332 p. :
94-034135   616.89/023   047105657X
 Psychotherapists -- Job stress. Psychotherapists -- Mental health.

RC451.4.W6.B469 1993
Bernstein, Anne E.
 The psychodynamic treatment of women / Anne E. Bernstein, Sharyn A. Lenhart. Washington, DC : American Psychiatric Press, c1993. xviii, 670 p.
92-048733   616.89/0082   0880483687
 Women -- Mental health. Psychodynamic psychotherapy. Psychoanalytic Therapy.

RC451.4.W6.M55 1988
Miles, Agnes.
 The neurotic woman : the role of gender in psychiatric illness / Agnes Miles. New York : New York University Press, 1988. viii, 168 p.
87-035682   616.85/2/0088042
0814754414
 Women -- Mental health. Neuroses -- Social aspects.

RC451.4.W6.R87 1994
Russell, Denise.
 Women, madness, and medicine / Denise Russell. Cambridge, Mass. : Polity Press, 1994. p. cm.
94-038395   616.89/0082   0745612601
 Women -- Mental health -- Sociological aspects.

RC451.4.W6.U87 1992
Ussher, Jane M.,
 Women's madness : misogyny or mental illness? / Jane M. Ussher. Amherst : University of Massachusetts Press, 1992. ix, 341 p. ;
91-032410   616.89/0082   0870237861
 Women -- Mental health -- Social aspects. Women -- Mental health -- Sociological aspects. Misogyny.

RC451.4.W6.W6665 1998
 Women's mental health services : a public health perspective / edited by Bruce Lubotsky Levin, Andrea K. Blanch, Ann Jennings. Thousand Oaks, Calif. : Sage Publications, c1998. xix, 428 p. :
97-045341   362.2/082   0761905081
 Women -- Mental health. Women -- Mental health services.

RC451.5 Neurosciences. Biological psychiatry. Neuropsychiatry — Psychiatry — By ethnic group, A-Z

RC451.5.A2.A46 1994
American Psychiatric Association.
 Ethnic minority elderly : a task force report of the American Psychiatric Association / [the American Psychiatric Association Task Force on Ethnic Minority Elderly]. Washington, DC : American Psychiatric Association, c1994. 190 p. ;
93-027940   362.2/08/693   0890422478
 Minority aged -- Mental health services -- United States -- Evaluation. Minority aged -- Mental health services -- United States -- Planning. Minority aged -- Mental health services -- United States -- Abstracts.

RC451.5.A2.E83 1996
 Ethnicity and family therapy / edited by Monica McGoldrick, Joe Giordano, John K. Pearce. New York : Guilford Press, c1996. xviii, 717 p.
96-007923   616.89/156   0898629594
 Minorities -- Mental health services -- United States. Family psychotherapy -- United States. Minorities -- United States -- Family relationships.

RC451.5.A2.M465 1995
 Mental health in a multi-ethnic society : a multi-disciplinary handbook / edited by Suman Fernando. London ; Routledge, 1995. xiii, 235 p.
95-008129   362.2/08/693   0415105366
 Minorities -- Mental health services -- Great Britain. Social psychiatry -- Great Britain. Community mental health services -- Great Britain.

RC451.5.A2.P79 1995
 Psychological interventions and cultural diversity / edited by Joseph F. Aponte, Robin Young Rivers, Julian Wohl. Boston : Allyn and Bacon, c1995. xviii, 333 p.
94-044704   362.2/08/693   0205146686
 Minorities -- Mental health services -- United States. Cultural psychiatry -- United States. Psychiatry, Transcultural -- United States.

RC451.5.A75.S93 1982
Sue, Stanley.
 The mental health of Asian Americans / Stanley Sue, James K. Morishima. San Francisco : Jossey-Bass, 1982. xvi, 222 p. :
82-048060   362.2/08995073   0875895352
 Asian Americans -- Mental health. Asian Americans -- Mental health services. Mental health services -- United States.

RC451.5.H57F35 1998
Falicov, Celia Jaes.
   Latino families in therapy : a guide to multicultural practice / Celia Jaes Falicov. New York : Gulford Press, c1998. xv, 303 p. ;
                616.89/0089/68073   1572303646
Hispanic Americans--Mental health. Family psychotherapy--United States. Minorities--United States--Family relationships.

RC451.5.H57.R64 1989
Rogler, Lloyd H.
   Hispanics and mental health : a framework for research / Lloyd H. Rogler, Robert G. Malgady, Orlando Rodriguez. Malabar, Fla. : R.E. Krieger Pub. Co., 1989. 163 p. ;
88-037203   362.2/08968073   0894642480
   Hispanic Americans -- Mental health. Hispanic Americans -- Mental health services. Hispanic Americans -- Mental health -- Research.

RC451.5.N4.B69 1989
Boyd-Franklin, Nancy.
   Black families in therapy : a multisystems approach / Nancy Boyd-Franklin. New York : Guilford Press, c1989. xiv, 274 p. :
88-024416   616.89/156/08996073
0898627354
   Afro-American families -- Mental health. Afro-Americans -- Social conditions. Family psychotherapy.

RC451.5.N4.H36 1990
   Handbook of mental health and mental disorder among Black Americans / edited by Dorothy S. Ruiz ; foreword by James P. Comer. New York : Greenwood Press, 1990. xxiii, 328 p.
89-071401   362.2/089/96073   0313263302
   Afro-Americans -- Mental health. Cultural psychiatry -- United States.

RC454 Neurosciences. Biological psychiatry. Neuropsychiatry — Psychiatry — General works

RC454.C2745 2001
Carr, Alan,
   Abnormal psychology / Alan Carr. Philadelphia : Psychology Press, 2001. p. cm.
                616.89   1841692425
Psychology, Pathological.

RC454.C637 2000
   Kaplan & Sadock's comprehensive textbook of psychiatry / editors, Benjamin J. Sadock, Virginia A. Sadock. 7th ed. Philadelphia : Lippincott Williams & Wilkins, c2000. 2 v. (lxiv, 3344 p). :
                616.89   0683301284
Psychiatry. Mental Disorders. Psychiatry.

RC454.C655 1995
   Core readings in psychiatry : an annotated guide to the literature / edited by Michael H. Sacks, William H. Sledge, Catherine Warren. Washington, D.C. : American Psychiatric Press, c1995. xxv, 944 p. ;
95-010613   616.89   0880485590
   Psychiatry -- Abstracts. Psychology, Pathological -- Abstracts. Psychotherapy -- Abstracts.

RC454.L456 1996
Lemma, Alessandra.
   Introduction to psychopathology / Alessandra Lemma. London ; Sage Publications, 1996. xii, 226 p. ;
96-068912   616.89   0803974701
   Psychology, Pathological.

RC454.L48 1981
Lewis, Helen Block.
   Freud and modern psychology / Helen Block Lewis. New York : Plenum Press, c1981-c1983. 2 v. ;
80-020937   616.89/001/9   0306405253
Freud, Sigmund, -- 1856-1939.   Psychology, Pathological. Emotions. Interpersonal relations.

RC454.M38 1977
Menninger, Karl A.
   The vital balance : the life process in mental health and illness / Karl Menninger, with Martin Mayman and Paul Pruyser. New York : Penguin Books, 1977, c1963. 531 p. ;
                616.8/9   0140045309
   Psychiatry.

RC454.N47 1988
   The New Harvard guide to psychiatry / edited by Armand M. Nicholi, Jr. Cambridge, Mass. : Belknap Press of Harvard University Press, 1988. xiv, 865 p. ;
87-024115   616.89   0674615409
   Psychiatry. Psychiatry.

RC454.P787 2000
   Psychopathology in adulthood / edited by Michel Hersen, Alan S. Bellack. 2nd ed. Boston : Allyn and Bacon, c2000. xiii, 481 p. :
                616.89   0205200273
   Psychology, Pathological. Psychopathology. Mental Disorders.

RC454.4 Neurosciences. Biological psychiatry. Neuropsychiatry — Psychiatry — General special

RC454.4.B372 2002
Barry, Patricia D.
  Mental health & mental illness / Patricia D. Barry ; consultant and contributor, Suzette Farmer. 7th ed. Philadelphia : Lippincott, Williams & Wilkins, c2002 xvi, 512 p. ;
                616.89   0781731380
  Psychiatry. Mental health. Psychiatric nursing.

RC454.4.G54 1992
Gilbert, Paul.
  Human nature and suffering / Paul Gilbert. New York : Guilford Press, 1992. xiv, 406 p. :
92-001446   616.89   0898620287
  Mental illness -- Etiology. Psychobiology. Sociobiology.

RC454.4.H625 2001
Hobson, J. Allan,
  Out of its mind : psychiatry in crisis : a call for reform / J. Allan Hobson, Jonathan A. Leonard. Cambridge, Mass. : Perseus Pub., c2001. xii, 292 p. :
                          0738202517
  Neurosciences. Psychiatry.

RC454.4.M458 1999
  Mental health disorders sourcebook : basic consumer health information about anxiety disorders, depression, and other mood disorders ... / edited by Karen Bellenir. Detroit, MI : Omnigraphics, 1999. xiii, 605 p.
99-049596   616.89   0780802403
  Mental illness. Psychiatry.

RC454.4.M4595 2001
  The mental health resource guide. Lexington, Mass. : Resources for Rehabilitation, c2001. 224 p. ;
00-062632   362.2/0973   0929718275
  Mental illness -- United States -- Popular works. Mental health -- United States -- Popular works. Mental health laws -- United States -- Popular works.

RC454.4.P37
Park, Clara Claiborne.
  You are not alone : understanding and dealing with mental illness : a guide for patients, families, doctors, and other professionals / by Clara Claiborne Park, with Leon N. Shapiro. Boston : Little, Brown, c1976. xiii, 496 p.
76-003423   362.2   0316690732
  Psychiatry. Mental health services. Mental health laws.

RC455 Neurosciences. Biological psychiatry. Neuropsychiatry — Psychiatry — Social psychiatry. Community psychiatry

RC455.S93
Szasz, Thomas Stephen,
  The myth of mental illness; foundations of a theory of personal conduct. [New York] Hoeber-Harper [1961] 337 p.
61-009714   132.1
  Psychiatry. Mental illness. Hysteria.

RC455.2 Neurosciences. Biological psychiatry. Neuropsychiatry — Psychiatry — Special aspects of the subject as a whole

RC455.2.C4D536 2000
  Diagnostic and statistical manual of mental disorders :DSM-IV-TR. 4th ed., text revision. Washington, DC : American Psychiatric Association, c2000. xxxvii, 943 p. ;
                616.89/075   0890420254
  Mental illness--Classification--Handbooks, manuals, etc. Mental illness--Diagnosis--Handbooks, manuals, etc. Mental Disorders--classification.

RC455.2.C4H57 1995
  A history of clinical psychiatry :the origin and history of psychiatric disorders / edited by German E. Berrios & Roy Porter. New York : New York University Press, 1995. xx, 684 p. ;
                616.89/0012   0814712592
  Mental illness--Classification--History. Neurobehavioral disorders--Classification--History. Psychology, Pathological--History.

RC455.2.C4.M86 2001
Munson, Carlton E.
  The mental health diagnostic desk reference : visual guides and more for learning to use the Diagnostic and statistical manual (DSM-IV-TR) / Carlton E. Munson. Binghamton, NY : Haworth Press, c2001. xxvii, 337 p.
00-047282   616.89/001/2   0789014645
  Mental illness -- Classification -- Handbooks, manuals, etc. Mental illness -- Diagnosis -- Handbooks, manuals, etc.

RC455.2.C4.R47 1987
Reznek, Lawrie.
  The nature of disease / Lawrie Reznek. London ; Routledge & Kegan Paul, 1987. x, 227 p. ;
87-009861   616/.0012   0710210825
  Mental illness -- Classification. Psychiatric ethics. Nosology -- Philosophy.

RC455.2.D42.G37 1998
Garb, Howard N.
  Studying the clinician : judgment research and psychological assessment / Howard N. Garb. Washington, DC : American Psychological Association, 1998. x, 333 p. ;
97-047679   616.89   1557984832
  Psychiatry -- Decision making. Clinical psychology -- Decision making. Psychodiagnostics.

RC455.2.E8.L35 1988
Lakin, Martin.
 Ethical issues in the psychotherapies / Martin Lakin. New York : Oxford University Press, 1988. ix, 174 p. ;
87-007663   174/.2   0195044460
 Psychotherapy -- Moral and ethical aspects. Ethics, Professional. Professional-Patient Relations.

RC455.2.F35.C35 1998
Campbell, Terence W.
 Smoke and mirrors : the devastating effect of false sexual abuse claims / Terence W. Campbell. New York : Insight Books, c1998. xiv, 338 p. ;
98-012417   616.85/836   0306459841
 False memory syndrome. Child sexual abuse -- Investigation. False testimony.

RC455.2.F35.P46 1995
Pendergrast, Mark.
 Victims of memory : incest accusations and shattered lives / by Mark Pendergrast. Hinesburg, Vt. : Upper Access, 1995. 603 p. ;
94-034855   616.85/8369   0942679164
 False memory syndrome. Recovered memory. Adult child sexual abuse victims.

RC455.2.F35.R426 1997
 Recovered memories and false memories / edited by Martin A. Conway. Oxford ; Oxford University Press, 1997. xi, 301 p. :
97-175116   616.89/14   0198523874
 False memory syndrome. Recovered memory.

RC455.2.F35R43 1996
 The recovered memory/false memory debate / edited by Kathy Pezdek, William P. Banks. San Diego : Academic Press, c1996. xv, 394 p. :
     616.85/8369   0125529759
 False memory syndrome. Recovered memory in children. Memory in children.

RC455.2.F35.S67 1996
Spanos, Nicholas P.
 Multiple identities & false memories : a sociocognitive perspective / Nicholas P. Spanos. Washington, DC : American Psychological Association, c1996. xiii, 371 p.
96-009772   616.85/236   1557983402
 False memory syndrome. Multiple Personality.

RC455.2.F35.T78 1998
 Truth in memory / edited by Steven Jay Lynn, Kevin M. McConkey. New York : Guilford Press, c1998. xix, 508 p. :
98-006870   616.85/822390651
157230345X
 False memory syndrome. Recovered memory. Autobiographical memory.

RC455.2.F35.W37 1995
Wassil-Grimm, Claudette.
 Diagnosis for disaster : the devastating truth about false memory syndrome and its impact on accusers and families / Claudette Wassil-Grimm. Woodstock, N.Y. : Overlook Press, 1995. 381 p. ;
94-036787   616.85/83690651
0879515724
 False memory syndrome. Recovered memory.

RC455.4 Neurosciences. Biological psychiatry. Neuropsychiatry — Psychiatry — Special aspects of mental illness, A-Z

RC455.4.A77.M33 1989
MacGregor, John M.
 The discovery of the art of the insane / John M. MacGregor. Princeton, N.J. : Princeton University Press, c1989. xix, 390 p.,
88-037986   616.89   0691040710
 Art and mental illness -- History.

RC455.4.B5.M43 1986
 Medical mimics of psychiatric disorders / edited by Irl Extein and Mark S. Gold. Washington, DC : American Psychiatric Press, c1986. x, 198 p. :
86-008012   616/.047   0880480920
 Mental illness -- Physiological aspects. Psychological manifestations of general diseases. Diagnosis, Differential.

RC455.4.B5.W35 1996
Walker, Sydney.
 A dose of sanity : mind, medicine, and misdiagnosis / Sydney Walker III. New York : Wiley & Sons, c1996. xi, 260 p. ;
95-046671   616.89/075   0471141364
 Psychological manifestations of general diseases. Mental illness -- Physiological aspects. Diagnostic errors.

RC455.4.E46.S74 1991
Stein, Ruth E. K.
 Psychoanalytic theories of affect / Ruth Stein ; foreword by Joseph Sandler. New York : Praeger, 1991. xiv, 220 p. ;
91-002762   616.85/27   0275939847
 Affect (Psychology) Psychoanalysis. Affective Disorders.

RC455.4.E8.B367 2000
Bartholomew, Robert E.
 Exotic deviance : medicalizing cultural idioms--from strangeness to illness / Robert E. Bartholomew. Boulder : University Press of Colorado, c2000. xviii, 280 p.
00-051878   616.85/8   9639116998
 Psychiatry, Transcultural. Ethnopsychology. Ethnocentrism.

RC455.4.E8.C795 2001
 Cultural cognition and psychopathology / edited by John F. Schumaker and Tony Ward. Westport, Conn. : Praeger, c2001. xxiii, 276 p.
00-022888   616.89   0275966046
 Cultural psychiatry. Cognition and culture.

RC455.4.E8F468 2002
Fernando, Suman.
   Mental health, race, and culture / Suman Fernando ; consultant editor, Jo Campling. 2nd ed. New York : Palgrave, 2002. ix, 246 p. :
                  616.89   0333960262
   Psychiatry, Transcultural.

RC455.4.E8.F47 1988
Fernando, Suman.
   Race and culture in psychiatry / Suman Fernando. London : Croom Helm, c1988. xviii, 216 p.
87-032970   616.89   070994912X
   Cultural psychiatry. Psychiatrists -- Attitudes. Psychiatry, Transcultural.

RC455.4.F3.H35 1994
   Handbook of developmental family psychology and psychopathology / Luciano L'Abate, editor. New York : Wiley, c1994. xiii, 462 p.
93-017725   306.85   0471535273
   Family -- Mental health. Family -- Psychological aspects. Problem families.

RC455.4.F3.H354 1998
   Family psychopathology : the relational roots of dysfunctional behavior / edited by Luciano L'Abate. New York, NY : The Guilford Press, c1998. xii, 528 p. ;
98-013462   616.89/156   1572303697
   Family -- Mental health. Family psychotherapy.

RC455.4.F3.L53 1992
Lidz, Theodore.
   The relevance of the family to psychoanalytic theory / Theodore Lidz. Madison, Conn. : International Universities Press, Inc., c1992. ix, 256 p. ;
92-001477   150.19/5   0823657841
   Family -- Psychological aspects Psychoanalysis. Family

RC455.4.F3.T46 2000
Tessler, Richard C.
   Family experiences with mental illness / Richard Tessler and Gail Gamache. Westport, Conn. : Auburn House, 2000. xviii, 187 p.
99-045816   362.2/0422   0865692513
   Mentally ill -- Family relationships. Mental illness.

RC455.4.F3.W335 1996
Wallace, Barbara C.
   Adult children of dysfunctional families : prevention, intervention, and treatment for community mental health promotion / Barbara C. Wallace. Westport, Conn. : Praeger, 1996. xv, 312 p. :
95-045415   616.89   0275944751
   Adult children of dysfunctional families. Problem families. Family counseling.

RC455.4.G4.A53 2001
Andreasen, Nancy C.
   Brave new brain : conquering mental illness in the era of the genome / Nancy C. Andreasen. Oxford ; Oxford University Press, 2001. xii, 368 p.,
00-050141   616.89/042   0195145097
   Mental illness. Mental illness -- Genetic aspects. Human genome.

RC455.4.L53.C55 1997
   Clinical disorders and stressful life events / edited by Thomas W. Miller. Madison, Conn. : International Universities Press, c1997. xxx, 416 p. :
96-039360   616.85/21   0823609103
   Life change events -- Psychological aspects. Post-traumatic stress disorder. Psychic trauma.

RC455.4.L67.B87 1989
Burnell, George M.
   Clinical management of bereavement : a handbook for healthcare professionals / George M. Burnell, Adrienne L. Burnell. New York, N.Y. : Human Sciences Press, c1989. 226 p. ;
87-035613   616.85/2   0898854245
   Bereavement -- Psychological aspects. Death -- Psychological aspects. Consolation.

RC455.4.L67.D36 1992
Dane, Barbara O.
   AIDS : intervening with hidden grievers / Barbara O. Dane and Samuel O. Miller ; foreword by George Getzel. New York : Auburn House, 1992. viii, 225 p.
92-010959   362.1/969792   0865690286
   Bereavement -- Psychological aspects. AIDS (Disease) -- Psychological aspects. AIDS (Disease) -- Patients -- Family relationships.

RC455.4.R4.P755 2000
   Psychiatry and religion : the convergence of mind and spirit / edited by James K. Boehnlein. Washington, DC : American Psychiatric Press, c2000. xx, 196 p. :
99-040826   616.89   0880489200
   Psychiatry and religion. Religion and Psychology. Mental Disorders -- therapy.

RC455.4.S43.B47 1993
Berglas, Steven.
   Your own worst enemy : understanding the paradox of self-defeating behavior / Steven Berglas and Roy F. Baumeister. New York, NY : BasicBooks, c1993. 216 p. ;
92-053238   616.85/82   0465076807
   Self-defeating behavior.

RC455.4.S53.G65 1991
Goldberg, Carl.
   Understanding shame / Carl Goldberg. Northvale, N.J. : J. Aronson, c1991. xix, 307 p. ;
91-013935   152.4   0876685416
   Shame. Psychotherapy. Psychoanalytic Theory.

RC455.4.S53.K38 1989
Kaufman, Gershen.
The psychology of shame : theory and treatment of shame-based syndromes / Gershen Kaufman. New York : Springer Pub. Co., c1989. xvi, 299 p. ;
88-039380   616.85/2   0826166709
Shame. Self. Affect (Psychology)

RC455.4.S87H67 2002
Horowitz, Mardi Jon,
Treatment of stress response syndromes / Mardi J. Horowitz. Washington, DC : American Psychiatric Pub., c2002. p. ;
          155.9/042   1585621072
Stress (Psychology) Stress management. Post-traumatic stress disorder--Treatment.

RC456 Neurosciences. Biological psychiatry. Neuropsychiatry — Psychiatry — Handbooks, manuals, etc.

RC456.H38 1996
The Hatherleigh guides series. New York : Hatherleigh Press, c1996-1997. 10 v. :
96-102294   616.89   1886330050
Psychiatry -- Handbooks, manuals, etc. Mental Disorders.

RC460 Neurosciences. Biological psychiatry. Neuropsychiatry — Psychiatry — Popular works

RC460.B694 1993
Bruno, Frank Joe,
Psychological symptoms / Frank J. Bruno. New York : John Wiley & Sons, c1993. xii, 276 p. ;
92-028510   616.89   047155281X
Psychiatry -- Popular works. Mental illness.

RC460.H47 1991
Heston, Leonard L.
Mending minds : a guide to the new psychiatry of depression, anxiety, and other serious mental disorders / Leonard L. Heston. New York : W.H. Freeman, c1992. xi, 233 p. ;
91-025061   616.85/27   0716721589
Psychiatry -- Popular works. Depression, Mental -- Popular works. Anxiety -- Popular works.

RC463-464 Neurosciences. Biological psychiatry. Neuropsychiatry — Psychiatry — Biography

RC463.P4 1974
Perceval, John,
Perceval's narrative : a patient's account of his psychosis, 1830-1832 / edited by Gregory Bateson. New York : Morrow, 1974, c1961. xxii, 331 p. ;
          616.8/982/00924   0688078834
Mental illness--Personal narratives.

RC464.A1.P67 1988
Porter, Roy,
A social history of madness : the world through the eyes of the insane / Roy Porter. New York : Weidenfeld & Nicolson, 1988, c1987. 261 p. ;
87-033979   362.2/092/2   1555841856
Mentally ill -- Biography. Mental illness -- Case studies.

RC464.I87.A3 1990
Israeloff, Roberta,
In confidence : four years of therapy / Roberta Israeloff. Boston : Houghton Mifflin, 1990. p. cm.
89-035545   616.89/14/092   039547101X
Israeloff, Roberta, -- 1952- -- Mental health.   Psychotherapy patients -- United States -- Biography.

RC464.S5.A4 1993
The Letters of a Victorian madwoman / edited by John S. Hughes. Columbia, S.C. : University of South Carolina, c1993. xiii, 260 p.
92-027442   362.2/1/092   0872498409
Sheffield, Andrew M., -- d. 1920 -- Correspondence.   Psychiatric hospital patients -- Alabama -- Tuscaloosa -- Correspondence.

RC465 Neurosciences. Biological psychiatry. Neuropsychiatry — Psychiatry — Clinical cases

RC465.T45 1990
Tejirian, Edward J.,
Sexuality and the devil : symbols of love, power, and fear in male psychology / Edward J. Tejirian. New York : Routledge, 1990. xiv, 254 p. ;
89-028929   616.89/17   0415902053
Psychotherapy -- Case studies. Demoniac possession -- Case studies. Cultural psychiatry -- Case studies.

RC467-467.95 Neurosciences. Biological psychiatry. Neuropsychiatry — Psychiatry — Clinical psychology

RC467.C597 1998
Comprehensive clinical psychology / editors-in-chief, Alan S. Bellack, Michel Hersen. Amsterdam ; Pergamon, 1998. 11 v. :
97-050185   616.89   0080427073
Clinical psychology. Psychology, Clinical.

RC467.G46 1992
Gender issues in clinical psychology / edited by Jane M. Ussher and Paula Nicholson. London ; Routledge, 1992. x, 245 p. ;
91-025284   616.89/023   0415054850
Clinical psychology. Feminist psychology. Women psychologists.

RC467.H29 1990
Handbook of social and clinical psychology : the health perspective / [edited by] C.R. Snyder, Donelson R. Forsyth. New York : Pergamon Press, c1991. xxii, 878 p.
89-072133   616.89   0080361285
Clinical psychology. Social psychology. Psychology, Clinical.

RC467.R4 1976
Reisman, John M.
A history of clinical psychology / by John M. Reisman. New York : Irvington Publishers : distributed by Halsted Pr c1976. ix, 420 p. ;
75-040102   616.89/009   047015229X
Clinical psychology -- History. Psychology -- History.

RC467.8.T74 1998
Trierweiler, Steven J.
The scientific practice of professional psychology / Steven J. Trierweiler, George Stricker. New York : Plenum Press, c1998. xi, 312 p. :
97-034813   616.89   0306456540
Clinical psychology -- Research. Clinical psychology -- Methodology. Psychology, Clinical.

RC467.95.W66 1988
Woody, Robert Henley.
Becoming a clinical psychologist / Robert Henley Woody and Malcolm Robertson. Madison, Conn. : International Universities Press, c1988. x, 333 p. ;
88-012890   157/.9/023   0823604918
Clinical psychology -- Practice. Clinical psychology -- Vocational guidance.

RC467.95.W663 1997
Woody, Robert Henley.
A career in clinical psychology : from training to employment / Robert Henley Woody and Malcolm Higgins Robertson. Madison, Conn. : International Universities Press, c1997. xiii, 241 p.
96-025086   616.89/023   082360652X
Clinical psychology -- Vocational guidance.

RC469–473 Neurosciences. Biological psychiatry. Neuropsychiatry — Psychiatry — Examination. Diagnosis

RC469.D3
Dahlstrom, W. Grant
An MMPI handbook; a guide to use in clinical practice and research, by W. Grant Dahlstrom and George Schlager Welsh. Minneapolis, Univ. of Minnesota Press [c1960] xviii, 559 p.
60009598   137.82
MMPI.

RC473.M5.B87 1990
Butcher, James Neal,
MMPI-2 in psychological treatment / James Neal Butcher. New York : Oxford University Press, 1990. ix, 195 p. :
89-078535   616.89/075   0195063449
Minnesota Multiphasic Personality Inventory.

RC473.M5.F75 1989
Friedman, Alan F.
Psychological assessment with the MMPI / Alan F. Friedman, James T. Webb, Richard Lewak. Hillsdale, N.J. : L. Erlbaum Associates, 1989. xx, 411 p. :
89-011662   155.2/83   0805803106
Minnesota Multiphasic Personality Inventory.

RC473.M5P79 2000
Psychological assessment with the MMPI-2 / Alan F. Friedman ... [et al.]. Mahwah, N.J. : L. Erlbaum Associates, 2001. xxxiii, 688 p. :
155.2/83   0805814442
Minnesota Multiphasic Personality Inventory.

RC473.R6.L468 1998
Lerner, Paul M.
Psychoanalytic perspectives on the Rorschach / Paul M. Lerner. Hillsdale, NJ : Analytic Press, 1998. xvi, 494 p. ;
97-051640   155.2/842   0881632341
Rorschach Test. Psychoanalysis.

RC475.7–489 Neurosciences. Biological psychiatry. Neuropsychiatry — Psychiatry — Therapeutics. Psychotherapy

RC475.7.C48 1993
Chessick, Richard D.,
A dictionary for psychotherapists : dynamic concepts in psychotherapy / Richard D. Chessick. Northvale, N.J. : Aronson, c1993. xvii, 405 p.
92-023967   616.89/14/03   0876683383
Psychotherapy -- Dictionaries. Psychotherapy -- Encyclopedias. Psychotherapy -- dictionaries.

RC475.7.W35 1986
Walrond-Skinner, Sue.
A dictionary of psychotherapy / Sue Walrond-Skinner. London ; Routledge & Kegan Paul, 1986. 379 p. ;
616.89/14/0321   0710099789
Psychotherapy--Dictionaries. Psychotherapy--encyclopedias.

RC480.H286 1994
Handbook of psychotherapy and behavior change / editors, Allen E. Bergin, Sol L. Garfield. 4th ed. New York : J. Wiley, c1994. xvi, 864 p. :
616.89/14   0471545139
Psychotherapy. Psychotherapy--Research. Psychotherapy.

RC480.K28513 1992
Kast, Verena,
The dynamics of symbols : fundamentals of Jungian psychotherapy / Verena Kast ; translated by Susan A. Schwarz. New York : Fromm International Pub. Corp., c1992. x, 220 p. :
91-037673   616.89/14   0880642009
Jung, C. G. -- (Carl Gustav), -- 1875-1961. Psychotherapy. Symbolism (Psychology)

RC480.T442 1997
Theories of psychotherapy : origins and evolution / edited by Paul L. Wachtel and Stanley B. Messer. Washington, DC : American Psychological Association, c1997. x, 310 p. :
97-020793   616.89/14   1557984352
Psychotherapy. Psychotherapy -- Philosophy.

RC480.T69 2001
Treatments of psychiatric disorders / Glen O. Gabbard, editor-in-chief. 3rd ed. Washington, DC : American Psychiatric Press, c2001. 2 v. :
        616.89/1   0880489111
Mental illness--Treatment. Mental Disorders--therapy.

RC480.5.B725 1997
Braslow, Joel T.,
Mental ills and bodily cures : psychiatric treatment in the first half of the twentieth century / Joel Braslow. Berkeley : University of California Press, c1997. xiv, 240 p. ;
96-039469   616.89/1   0520205472
Mental illness -- Treatment -- United States -- History -- 20th century. Mental illness -- Physical therapy -- United States -- History -- 20th century. Mind and body.

RC480.5.D38 1994
Dawes, Robyn M.,
House of cards : psychology and psychotherapy built on myth / Robyn M. Dawes. New York : Free Press ; c1994. xi, 338 p. ;
93-027312   616.89/14/01   0029072050
Psychotherapy -- Philosophy. Clinical psychology -- Philosophy. Psychotherapists.

RC480.5.G476 1996
The therapist as a person : life crises, life choices, life experiences, and their effects on treatment / edited by Barbara Gerson. Hillsdale, N.J. : Analytic Press, 1996. xxiii, 302 p.
96-027077   616.89/14/023   0881631787
Psychotherapists -- Psychology. Psychotherapist and patient.

RC480.5.G76 1988
Grof, Stanislav,
The adventure of self-discovery / Stanislav Grof. Albany : State University of New York Press, c1988. xvii, 321 p.
87-017967   616.89/14   0887065406
Psychotherapy. Hallucinogenic drugs. Consciousness -- Research.

RC480.5.G85 1998
A guide to treatments that work / edited by Peter E. Nathan, Jack M. Gorman. New York : Oxford University Press, 1998. xxx, 594 p. :
97-036492   616.89/1   0195102274
Mental illness -- Treatment -- Evaluation.

RC480.5.H32
Harris, Thomas Anthony,
I'm OK, you're OK; a practical guide to transactional analysis, by Thomas A. Harris. New York, Harper & Row [1969] xix, 278 p.
69-013495   616.89/1
Transactional analysis.

RC480.5.H54
The History of psychotherapy : from healing magic to encounter / edited by Jan Ehrenwald. New York : J. Aronson, c1976. 589 p. ;
76-026565   616.8/914/09   0876682808
Psychotherapy -- History. Psychotherapy. Psychotherapy -- History.

RC480.5.H54 1991
The History of psychotherapy / edited by Jan Ehrenwald. Northvale, N.J. : J. Aronson, c1991. 589 p. ;
        616.89/14/09   0876682808
Psychotherapy--History. Psychotherapy.

RC480.5.J28 1970
Janov, Arthur.
The primal scream; primal therapy: the cure for neurosis. New York, Putnam [1970] 446 p.
74-097084   616.89/1
Primal therapy.

RC480.5.M325 1997
Managing managed care : quality improvements in behavioral health / Margaret Edmunds ... [et al.], editors ; Committee on Quality Assurance and Accreditation Guidelines for Managed Behavioral Health Care, Division of Neuroscience and Behavioral Health [and] Division of Health Care Services, Institute of Medicine. Washington, D.C. : National Academy Press, 1997. xxi, 370 p. :
97-002004   362.2/0973   030905642X
Managed mental health care -- United States -- Quality control. Managed mental health care -- Accreditation -- United States. Mental Health Services -- organization & administration -- United States.

RC480.5.R39
Reynolds, David K.
The quiet therapies : Japanese pathways to personal growth / David K. Reynolds ; afterword by George DeVos. Honolulu : University Press of Hawaii, c1980. viii, 135 p.
80-017611   616.89/14/0952   0824806905
Psychotherapy. Psychotherapy -- Japan.

RC480.5.R62
Rogers, Carl R.
On becoming a person; a therapist's view of psychotherapy. Boston, Houghton Mifflin [1961] 420 p.
61-004718   131.322
Client-centered psychotherapy.

RC480.5.S675 1999
Steinberg, Frances E.,
Whispers from the East : applying the principles of eastern healing to psychotherapy / Frances E. Steinberg and Richard G. Whiteside. Phoenix, Ariz. : Zeig, Tucker & Co., c1999. 178 p. :
98-038991   616.89/14   1891944045
Psychotherapy. Medicine, Chinese. Mind and body therapies.

RC480.5.T747 1993
Treatment of mental disorders : a review of effectiveness / edited by Norman Sartorius ... [et al.]. Washington, DC : Published on behalf of The World Health Organiza 1993. xx, 501 p. :
93-002989　　　　616.89/1　　　　0880489758
Mental illness -- Treatment. Mental Disorders -- therapy.

RC480.5.W49 1987
Wilmer, Harry A.,
Practical Jung : nuts and bolts of Jungian psychotherapy / Harry A. Wilmer. Wilmette, Ill. : Chiron Publications, c1987. xiii, 279 p.
87-018233　　　　150.19/54　　　　0933029241
Jung, C. G. -- (Carl Gustav), -- 1875-1961. Psychotherapy.

RC480.515.N38 1999
Nathan, Peter E.
Treating mental disorders : a guide to what works / Peter E. Nathan, Jack M. Gorman, Neil J. Salkind. New York : Oxford University Press, 1999. xxvii, 208 p.
98-049355　　　　616.89　　　　0195102282
Mental illness -- Popular works. Mental illness -- Treatment -- Evaluation -- Miscellanea. Consumer education.

RC480.52.A78 1995
The art and science of assessment in psychotherapy / edited by Chris Mace. London ; Routledge, 1995. x, 222 p. :
94-046785　　　　616.89/075　　　　0415105382
Psychiatry -- Differential therapeutics. Psychotherapy -- Decision making. Psychotherapy.

RC480.8.B384 1997
Baur, Susan.
The intimate hour : love and sex in psychotherapy / Susan Baur. Boston : Houghton Mifflin Co., 1997. viii, 309 p.
96-031380　　　　616.89/14　　　　039582284X
Psychotherapists -- Sexual behavior. Psychotherapy patients -- Sexual behavior.

RC480.8.H36 1982
Handbook of interpersonal psychotherapy / edited by Jack C. Anchin, Donald J. Kiesler. New York : Pergamon Press, c1982. xxi, 346 p. :
81-008499　　　　616.89/14　　　　0080259596
Psychotherapist and patient. Psychotherapy. Physician-patient relations.

RC480.8.L49 1996
Lewin, Roger A.
Compassion. : the core value that animates psychotherapy / Roger A. Lewin. Northvale, N.J. : J. Aronson, c1996. xii, 348 p. ;
95-023012　　　　616.89/14　　　　1568216785
Psychotherapist and patient. Psychotherapy -- Moral and ethical aspects. Psychotherapists -- Professional ethics.

RC481.R59
Rogers, Carl R.
Counseling and psychotherapy; newer concepts in practice, by Carl R. Rogers. Boston, Houghton Mifflin company [1942] xiv, 450 p.
42-024693　　　　616.89/17
Client-centered psychotherapy.

RC481.R6
Rogers, Carl R.
Person to person: the problem of being human; a new trend in psychology [by] Carl R. Rogers and Barry Stevens. With contributions from: Eugene T. Gendlin, John M. Shlien [and] Wilson Van Dusen. [Walnut Creek, Calif., Real People Press, 1967] 276 p.
67-026674　　　　616.89/1
Client-centered psychotherapy -- Addresses, essays, lectures. Psychology -- Addresses, essays, lectures.

RC483.E86 2001
Essentials of clinical psychopharmacology / edited by Alan F. Schatzberg, Charles B. Nemeroff. Washington, DC : American Psychiatric Pub., c2001. xx, 780 p. :
　　　　616.89/18　　　　1585620173
Mental illness--Chemotherapy. Psychotropic drugs. Psychopharmacology.

RC483.K44 1998
Keen, Ernest,
Drugs, therapy, and professional power : problems and pills / Ernest Keen. Westport, Conn. : Praeger, 1998. xvi, 227 p. :
97-041933　　　　616.89/18　　　　0275962008
Mental illness -- Chemotherapy -- Moral and ethical aspects. Mental illness -- Chemotherapy -- Social aspects. Mental illness -- Treatment -- Philosophy.

RC483.L38
Legal and ethical issues in human research and treatment : psychopharmacologic considerations / edited by Donald M. Gallant and Robert Force. Jamaica, N.Y. : Spectrum Publications ; c1978. 186 p. ;
77-012628　　　　615/.78/072　　　　0893350397.
Psychopharmacology -- Congresses. Psychiatric ethics -- Congresses. Psychiatry -- Research -- United States -- Congresses.

RC483.S65 2001
Spinella, Marcello.
The psychopharmacology of herbal medicine : plant drugs that alter mind, brain, and behavior / Marcello Spinella. Cambridge, Mass. : MIT Press, c2001. viii, 578 p. :
　　　　615/.788　　　　0262692651
Psychotropic drugs. Herbs--Therapeutic use. Psychopharmacology.

RC483.5.F55.K7 1993
Kramer, Peter D.
Listening to Prozac / Peter D. Kramer. New York, N.Y., U.S.A. : Viking, 1993. xix, 409 p. ;
92-050733　　　　616.85/27061　　　　0670841838
Fluoxetine -- Moral and ethical aspects. Fluoxetine -- Social aspects. Fluoxetine -- Psychotropic effects.

RC488.B43
Berne, Eric.
 Transactional analysis in psychotherapy; a systematic individual and social psychiatry. New York, Grove Press [1961] 270 p.
60-013795   616.8915
 Transactional analysis. Group psychotherapy. Psychotherapy -- Cases studies.

RC488.H35 1992
 Handbook of contemporary group psychotherapy : contributions from object relations, self psychology, and social systems theories / edited by Robert H. Klein, Harold S. Bernard, David L. Singer. Madison, Conn. : International Universities Press, c1992. xiii, 432 p.
92-001472   616.89/152   0823622851
 Group psychotherapy. Object relations (Psychoanalysis) Self psychology.

RC488.J36 1982
Janosik, Ellen Hastings.
 Life cycle group work in nursing / Ellen Hastings Janosik, Lenore Bolling Phipps. Monterey, Calif. : Wadsworth Health Sciences Division, c1982. xviii, 394 p.
80-071075   616.89/152   0534010970
 Group psychotherapy. Psychiatric nursing. Team nursing.

RC488.5.A56 1994
Annunziata, Jane.
 Solving your problems together : family therapy for the whole family / Jane Annunziata, Phyllis Jacobson-Kram ; illustrated by Elizabeth Wolf. Washington, DC : American Psychological Association, c1994. 37 p. :
94-029708   616.89/156   1557982686
 Family psychotherapy -- Popular works.

RC488.5.B3798 1990
Beavers, W. Robert,
 Successful families : assessment and intervention / W. Robert Beavers, Robert B. Hampson. New York : Norton, c1990. xiv, 237 p. ;
90-006902   616.89/156   0393700917
 Family psychotherapy. Family assessment. Family Therapy -- methods.

RC488.5.B85 1997
Butz, Michael R.
 Strange attractors : chaos, complexity, and the art of family therapy / Michael R. Butz, Linda L. Chamberlain, William G. McCown. New York : Wiley, c1997. xvii, 267 p.
96016000   616.89/156   0471079510
 Family psychotherapy. Chaotic behavior in systems.

RC488.5.C6435 2000
 Couples on the fault line : new directions for therapists / edited by Peggy Papp. New York, NY : Guilford Press, 2000. xv, 344 p. ;
99-086313   616.89/156   1572305363
 Marital psychotherapy.

RC488.5.D525 1993
 The Dictionary of family psychology and family therapy / S. Richard Sauber ... [et al.]. Newbury Park, Calif. : Sage Publications, c1993. xix, 468 p. ;
93-001588   616.89/156/03   0803953321
 Family psychotherapy -- Dictionaries. Family -- Psychological aspects -- Dictionaries.

RC488.5.D59 1998
 The disordered couple / edited by Jon Carlson and Len Sperry. Bristol, Pa. : Brunner/Mazel, c1998. xxiii, 342 p.
97-024085   616.89/156   0876308159
 Marital psychotherapy. Mentally ill -- Family relationships.

RC488.5.F3
 Families of the slums; an exploration of their structure and treatment [by] Salvador Minuchin [and others] New York, Basic Books [1967] xiv, 460 p.
67-028507   362.8/2
 Family psychotherapy. Problem families.

RC488.5.F73 1987
Fredman, Norman,
 Handbook of measurements for marriage and family therapy / by Norman Fredman & Robert Sherman. New York : Brunner/Mazel, c1987. xviii, 218 p.
87-009417   616.89/16   0876304668
 Family psychotherapy. Marital psychotherapy. Psychological tests.

RC488.5.H47 1990
Henggeler, Scott W.,
 Family therapy and beyond : a multisystemic approach to treating the behavior problems of children and adolescents / Scott W. Henggeler, Charles M. Borduin. Pacific Grove, Calif. : Brooks/Cole, c1990. xiii, 354 p.
89-022165   616.89/156   0534124321
 Family psychotherapy. Child psychotherapy.

RC488.5.M5313 1995
Miermont, Jacques.
 A dictionary of family therapy / Jacques Miermont ; edited, expanded, and revised by Hugh Jenkins ; translated by Chris Turner. Oxford, OX, UK ; Blackwell Reference, 1995. xliii, 492 p.
93-044716   616.89/156/03   0631170480
 Family psychotherapy -- Dictionaries.

RC488.5.M56
Minuchin, Salvador.
 Family therapy techniques / Salvador Minuchin, H. Charles Fishman. Cambridge, Mass. : Harvard University Press, 1981. 303 p. ;
80-025392   616.89/156   0674294106
 Family psychotherapy.

RC488.5.P786 1990
The Psychology of marriage : basic issues and applications / edited by Frank D. Fincham, Thomas N. Bradbury ; foreword by John Mordechai Gottman. New York : Guilford Press, c1990. xvi, 432 p. ;
90-003038   616.89/156   0898624339
Marital psychotherapy. Marriage -- Psychological aspects. Marital Therapy.

RC488.5.S28 1995
Scarf, Maggie,
Intimate worlds : life inside the family / Maggie Scarf. New York : Random House, c1995. xxxviii, 466
95-000827   616.89/156   0394565436
Family psychotherapy. Family -- Mental health. Family -- Psychological aspects.

RC488.5.S384 1994
Schwebel, Andrew I.
Understanding and helping families : a cognitive-behavioral approach / Andrew I. Schwebel, Mark A. Fine. Hillsdale, N.J. : Erlbaum, 1994. ix, 215 p. :
93-032023   616.89/156   0805812253
Family psychotherapy. Cognitive therapy. Family -- Psychological aspects.

RC488.5.T79 1991
Tseng, Wen-Shing,
Culture and family : problems and therapy / Wen-Shing Tseng and Jing Hsu. New York : Haworth Press, c1991. xv, 255 p. ;
90-021961   616.89/156   156024058X
Family -- Mental health. Family psychotherapy. Cultural psychiatry.

RC488.5.V56 1988
Visher, Emily B.,
Old loyalties, new ties : therapeutic strategies with stepfamilies / by Emily B. Visher and John S. Visher. New York : Brunner/Mazel, c1988. ix, 261 p. :
87-023899   616.89/156   0876304897
Family psychotherapy. Stepparents -- Psychology. Stepchildren -- Psychology.

RC489.A7.F43
Feder, Elaine.
The expressive arts therapies / Elaine & Bernard Feder. Englewood Cliffs, N.J. : Prentice-Hall, c1981. vi, 249 p. :
80-023887   616.89/165   0132980428
Art therapy. Music therapy. Dance therapy.

RC489.A7I45 1987
Images of art therapy : new developments in theory and practice / Tessa Dalley ... [et al.]. London ; Tavistock Publications, 1987. xi, 221 p., [8] p. of plates :
               616.89/1656   0422603902
Art therapy.

RC489.A7.S56 1992
Simon, R. M.
The symbolism of style : art as therapy / R.M. Simon. London ; Tavistock/Routledge, 1992. xiii, 209 p.,
91-032552   615.8/5156   0415041309
Art therapy.

RC489.B4.A9
Ayllon, Teodoro,
The token economy; a motivational system for therapy and rehabilitation [by] Teodoro Ayllon [and] Nathan Azrin. New York, Appleton-Century-Crofts [1968] viii, 288 p.
69-012160   616.89/1
Token economy (Psychology)

RC489.B4.B3
Bandura, Albert,
Principles of behavior modification. New York, Holt, Rinehart and Winston [1969] ix, 677 p.
74-081173   616.89/1   0030811511
Behavior therapy. Personality change.

RC489.B4.R87 1986
Russell, Michael L.
Behavioral counseling in medicine : strategies for modifying at-risk behavior / Michael L. Russell. New York : Oxford University Press, 1986. 327 p. ;
85-029668   616.89/142   0195039904
Behavior therapy. Counseling. Medical personnel and patient.

RC489.C63.R67 1989
Rose, Sheldon D.
Working with adults in groups : integrating cognitive-behavioral and small group strategies / Sheldon D. Rose. San Francisco : Jossey-Bass Publishers, 1989. xix, 360 p. ;
89-045589   616.89/152   1555421660
Cognitive therapy. Group psychotherapy.

RC489.D3.C49 1975
Chace, Marian,
Marian Chace, her papers / edited by Harris Chaiklin. [Kensington, Md.] : American Dance Therapy Association, c1975. ix, 261 p. :
75-028984   616.8/916/5   0915126044
Chace, Marian, -- 1896-1970. Dance therapy. Psychotherapists -- Biography.

RC489.D46.G74 1997
Greenspan, Stanley I.
Developmentally based psychotherapy / Stanley I. Greenspan. Madison, Conn. : International Universities Press, c1997. vi, 462 p. ;
95-017189   616.89/14   082361199X
Developmental therapy. Personality development. Ego (Psychology)

RC489.D74.C66 1997
Conigliaro, Vincenzo.
Dreams as a tool in psychotherapy : traveling the royal road to the unconscious / Vincenzo Conigliaro. Madison, Conn. : International Universities Press, c1997. xix, 407 p. ;
96-029393   616.89/14   0823614395
Dreams. Dreams -- Therapeutic use. Dream interpretation.

RC489.D74.T73 1996
Trauma and dreams / edited by Deirdre Barrett. Cambridge, Mass. : Harvard University Press, 1996. viii, 272 p.
96-013023   616.85/21   0674905520
Dreams. Post-traumatic stress syndrome. Psychic trauma.

RC489.E45.E46 1991
Emotion, psychotherapy, and change / edited by Jeremy D. Safran, Leslie S. Greenberg. New York : Guilford Press, c1991. xii, 372 p. ;
90-014130   616.89/14   0898625564
Emotions. Psychotherapy. Emotions.

RC489.E45.P58 2000
Plutchik, Robert.
Emotions in the practice of psychotherapy : clinical implications of affect theories / Robert Plutchik. Washington, DC : American Psychological Association Press, c2000. xiii, 229 p.
00-041612   616.89/14   1557986940
Emotions. Psychotherapy.

RC489.E46.B47 1987
Berger, David M.
Clinical empathy / David M. Berger. Northvale, N.J. : Aronson, c1987. x, 294 p. ;
86-032138   616.89/14   0876689209
Empathy. Psychotherapist and patient. Empathy.

RC489.E46.E48 1997
Empathy reconsidered : new directions in psychotherapy / edited by Arthur C. Bohart and Leslie S. Greenberg. Washington, DC : American Psychological Association, c1997. xv, 477 p. ;
97-003398   616.89/14   1557984107
Empathy. Psychotherapist and patient.

RC489.E93.M68 1994
Moustakas, Clark E.
Existential psychotherapy and the interpretation of dreams / Clark Moustakas. Northvale, N.J. : J. Aronson, c1994. xii, 219 p. ;
93-040807   616.89/14   1568211805
Existential psychotherapy. Dream interpretation. Existentialism.

RC489.E93.W45 1993
Weisman, Avery D.
The vulnerable self : confronting the ultimate questions / Avery D. Weisman ; foreword by John C. Nemiah. New York : Insight Books, c1993. xxiii, 253 p.
93-002600   616.89/14   0306445018
Existential psychotherapy. Adjustment (Psychology) Psychotherapy.

RC489.E98.S53 1997
Shapiro, Francine.
EMDR : the breakthrough therapy for overcoming anxiety, stress, and trauma / Francine Shapiro and Margot Silk Forrest. New York, NY : BasicBooks, c1997. xii, 285 p. ;
96-046586   616.85/210651   0465043003
Eye movement desensitization and reprocessing -- Popular works.

RC489.F33.W34 1998
Walsh, Froma.
Strengthening family resilience / Froma Walsh. New York : Guilford Press, c1998. xiv, 338 p. ;
98-008527   616.89/156   1572304081
Family -- Mental health. Resilience (Personality trait) Problem families.

RC489.F45.F45 1988
Feminist psychotherapies : integration of therapeutic and feminist systems / edited by Mary Ann Dutton-Douglas and Lenore E.A. Walker. Norwood, N.J. : Ablex Pub. Corp., c1988. vi, 312 p. ;
88-016705   616.89/14   0893913871
Feminist therapy.

RC489.F45.W664 1994
Women in context : toward a feminist reconstruction of psychotherapy / edited by Marsha Pravder Mirkin ; forword [sic] by Monica McGoldrick. New York : Guilford Press, c1994. xxi, 502 p. ;
94-005534   616.89/14/082   0898620953
Feminist therapy. Women -- Mental health. Women -- Medical care -- Social aspects.

RC489.M96.M39 1990
May, Rollo.
The cry for myth / Rollo May. New York : Norton, c1991. 320 p. ;
90-030451   616.89/14   0393027686
Mythology -- Therapeutic use. Psychotherapy.

RC489.P7.G72
Greenberg, Ira A.,
Psychodrama: theory and therapy, edited by Ira A. Greenberg. New York, Behavioral Publications, 1974. xvi, 496 p.
73-020227   616.8/915   0877051100
Psychodrama. Psychodrama.

RC489.P72.W35 1995
Wallerstein, Robert S.
The talking cures : the psychoanalyses and the psychotherapies / Robert S. Wallerstein. New Haven : Yale University Press, c1995. xx, 587 p. ;
95-001548   616.89/17   0300061072
Psychodynamic psychotherapy. Psychoanalysis.

RC489.R3.E427 1996
Ellis, Albert.
Better, deeper, and more enduring brief therapy : the rational emotive behavior therapy approach / Albert Ellis. New York : Brunner/Mazel Publishers, c1996. xii, 301 p. :
95-044400   616.89/14   0876307926
Rational-emotive psychotherapy. Brief psychotherapy.

RC489.R3.E437 1990
Ellis, Albert.
The essential Albert Ellis : seminal writings on psychotherapy / Windy Dryden, editor. New York : Springer Pub. Co., c1990. xiv, 321 p. ;
89-026338   616.89/14   0826169406
Rational-emotive psychotherapy.

RC489.R3.H36
Handbook of rational-emotive therapy / Albert Ellis and Russell Grieger, with contributors. New York : Springer Pub. Co., c1977-c1986 v. 1-2 ;
77-021410   616.8/914   0826122000
Rational-emotive psychotherapy. Psychotherapy -- Handbooks.

RC489.R3.I55 1993
Innovations in rational-emotive therapy / [edited by] Windy Dryden, Larry K. Hill. Newbury Park, Calif. : Sage Publications, c1993. v, 297 p. :
92-049498   616.89/14   0803943008
Rational-emotive psychotherapy -- Congresses. Psychotherapy, Rational-Emotive -- congresses.

RC489.R3.N54 2001
Nielsen, Stevan L.
Counseling and psychotherapy with religious persons : a rational emotive behavior therapy approach / Stevan L. Nielsen, W. Brad Johnson, Albert Ellis Institute. Mahwah, NJ : L. Erlbaum Associates, 2001. p. cm.
01-018771   616.89/14   0805828788
Rational-emotive psychotherapy. Counseling -- Religious aspects. Psychiatry and religion.

RC489.R46.S64 1995
Smith, C. Michael.
Psychotherapy and the sacred : religious experience and religious resources in psychotherapy / C. Michael Smith. Chicago, Ill. : Center for the Scientific Study of Religion, c1995. xiii, 199 p.
92-074688   616.89   0913348287
Psychotherapy -- Religious aspects. Holy, The.

RC489.S43.L43 1991
Lee, Ronald R.
Psychotherapy after Kohut : a textbook of self psychology / Ronald R. Lee, J. Colby Martin. Hillsdale, NJ : Analytic Press, 1991. vi, 344 p. ;
91-031485   616.89/14/01   0881631299
Self psychology. Psychotherapy. Ego.

RC489.S74.P37 1994
Parry, Alan
Story re-visions : narrative therapy in the postmodern world / Alan Parry, Robert E. Doan. New York : The Guilford Press, 1994. viii, 216 p.
94-018296   616.89/14/01   0898622131
Storytelling -- Therapeutic use. Postmodernism -- Psychological aspects. Personal construct therapy.

RC489.T45.K87 1988
Kupers, Terry Allen.
Ending therapy : the meaning of termination / Terry A. Kupers. New York : New York University Press, c1988. 153 p. ;
87-035330   616.89/14   0814745946
Psychotherapy -- Termination.

RC489.T7.T69
Transactional analysis after Eric Berne : teachings and practices of three TA schools / Graham Barnes, editor ; contributors, Michael Brown ... [et al.]. New York : Harper's College Press, c1977. xv, 543 p. :
77-004754   158   0061684120
Transactional analysis.

RC495-497 Neurosciences. Biological psychiatry. Neuropsychiatry — Psychiatry — Hypnotism and hypnosis. Suggestion therapy

RC495.A48 1968
Ambrose, Gordon.
A handbook of medical hypnosis; an introduction for practitioners and students [by] Gordon Ambrose [and] George Newbold. Baltimore, Williams and Wilkins Co. [1968] xiv, 312 p.
68-005920   615/.8512   0702002311
Hypnotism -- Therapeutic use.

RC495.F74 1997
Fromm, Erika.
Psychoanalysis and hypnosis / Erika Fromm, Michael R. Nash. Madison, Conn. : International Universities Press, 1997. p. cm.
96-043561   616.89/162   0823651819
Hypnotism -- Therapeutic use. Psychoanalysis.

RC495.G464 1991
Gibson, H. B.
Hypnosis in therapy / H. B. Gibson, M. Heap. Hove ; L. Erlbaum, c1991. ix, 240 p.
90026376   616.89162   0863771556
Hypnotism -- Therapeutic use. Hypnosis Psychotherapy

RC497.F67 2000
Forrest, Derek William.
Hypnotism : a history / Derek Forrest ; foreword by Anthony Storr. London ; Penguin, 2000. xviii, 334 p. ;
          615.8/512/094   0140280405
Hypnotism--History.

RC501.4-569.5 Neurosciences. Biological psychiatry. Neuropsychiatry — Psychiatry — Psychopathology

RC501.4.P79 1990

Psychoanalytic terms and concepts / edited by Burness E. Moore and Bernard D. Fine. [New York] : American Psychoanalytic Association ; c1990. xxv, 210 p. ;
89-036223   616.89/17/03   0300045778
Psychoanalysis -- Dictionaries.

RC501.4.S65 1992
Solomon, Irving.

The encyclopedia of evolving techniques in psychodynamic therapy / Irving Solomon. Northvale, N.J. : J. Aronson, c1992. xix, 402 p. ;
92-011362   616.89/17   0876685114
Psychoanalysis -- Methodology -- Encyclopedias. Psychotherapy -- Methodology -- Encyclopedias. Psychoanalytic Therapy -- encyclopedias.

RC503.G433 1999
Gedo, John E.

The evolution of psychoanalysis : contemporary theory and practice / by John Gedo. New York, NY : Other Press, LLC , c1999. p. cm.
99-017458   616.89/17   1892746271
Psychoanalysis -- History. Psychoanalysis -- Philosophy. Psychoanalytic Theory.

RC503.G63 2001
Goggin, James E.,

Death of a "Jewish science" : psychoanalysis in the Third Reich / James E. Goggin and Eileen Brockman Goggin. West Lafayette, Ind. : Purdue University Press, c2001. xvi, 242 p. ;
99-050840   616.89/17/0943   1557531935
Psychoanalysis -- Political aspects -- Germany -- History. National socialism. Psychoanalysis -- Germany -- History.

RC504.B35 1990
Bettelheim, Bruno.

Freud's Vienna and other essays / Bruno Bettelheim. New York : Knopf : 1990. xi, 281 p. ;
89-045286   150.19/52   0394572092
Psychoanalysis.

RC504.C57 1990

Classics in psycho-analytic technique / Robert Langs, editor. Northvale, N.J. : J. Aronson, c1990. xii, 500 p. ;
90-038548   616.89/17   0876687443
Psychoanalysis. Psychotherapy.

RC504.K6613 1995
Konig, Karl,

The practice of psychoanalytic therapy / Karl Konig ; translated from German by Paul Foulkes. Northvale, N.J. : J. Aronson, c1995. xvii, 318 p.
94-029292   616.89/17   1568213530
Psychoanalysis. Psychodynamic psychotherapy. Psychoanalytic Therapy.

RC504.P754 1995

Psychoanalysis :the major concepts / edited by Burness E. Moore and Bernard D. Fine ; editorial board, Alvin Frank ... [et al.] ; consultants, Jacob A. Arlow ... [et al.]. New Haven : Yale University Press, c1995. xix, 577 p. ;
        616.89/17   0300063296
Psychoanalysis. Psychoanalysis. Psychoanalytic Therapy.

RC504.T44 1996

Textbook of psychoanalysis / edited by Edward Nersessian, Richard G. Kopff, Jr. Washington, DC : American Psychiatric Press, c1996. xv, 726 p. :
95-008218   616.89/17   0880485078
Psychoanalysis. Psychoanalytic interpretation. Psychoanalysis.

RC506.C29 1991
Cannon, Betty.

Sartre and psychoanalysis : an existentialist challenge to clinical metatheory / Betty Cannon. Lawrence, Kan. : University Press of Kansas, c1991. xvii, 397 p.
90-012993   616.89/17   0700604456
Sartre, Jean Paul, -- 1905- Psychoanalysis. Existential psychotherapy.

RC506.C56 1997

Cognitive science and the unconscious / edited by Dan J. Stein. Washington, DC : American Psychiatric Press, c1997. xv, 217 p. :
96-030885   616.89/17   0880484985
Psychoanalysis. Subconsciousness. Cognitive science.

RC506.C73 1990
Craib, Ian,

Psychoanalysis and social theory / Ian Craib. Amherst : University of Massachusetts Press, 1990, c1989. x, 206 p. ;
89-020163   150.19/5   0870237012
Psychoanalysis. Social psychology. Social sciences -- Philosophy.

RC506.F69713
Freud, Sigmund,

The Freud/Jung letters; the correspondence between Sigmund Freud and C. G. Jung. Edited by William McGuire. Translated by Ralph Manheim and R. F. C. Hull. [Princeton, N.J.] Princeton University Press [1974] xlii, 650 p.
76-166373   150.19/52   0691098905
Freud, Sigmund, -- 1856-1939. Jung, C. G. -- (Carl Gustav), -- 1875-1961. Psychoanalysts -- Europe -- Correspondence.

RC506.H66 2001

Homosexuality & psychoanalysis / edited by Tim Dean and Christopher Lane. Chicago : University of Chicago Press, 2001. x, 466 p. ;
00-046713   616.89/17/08664   0226139360
Psychoanalysis and homosexuality.

RC506.I595 1997

The inward eye : psychoanalysts reflect on their lives and work / edited by Laurie W. Raymond and Susan Rosbrow-Reich. Hillsdale, NJ : Analytic Press, 1997. p. cm.
96-012694   616.89/17   088163252X
Psychoanalysts -- Interviews. Psychoanalysis. Psychoanalysis -- interviews.

RC506.L58
Lorand, Sandor,
Adolescents; psychoanalytic approach to problems and therapy, by 19 contributors. Edited by Sandor Lorand and Henry I. Schneer. Foreword by David M. Engelhardt. [New York] P. B. Hoeber [1961] 378 p.
61-006722   131.342
Adolescent analysis. Adolescent psychiatry.

RC509.H67 1987
Horney, Karen,
Final lectures / Karen Horney ; edited by Douglas H. Ingram. New York : Norton, c1987. 128 p. :
87-020366   616.89/17   0393024857
Psychoanalysis.

RC509.K64
Klein, Melanie.
New directions in psycho-analysis; the significance of infant conflict in the pattern of adult behavior. Edited by Melanie Klein, Paula heiman [and] R. E. Money-Kyrle. With a pref. by Ernest Jones. New York, Basic Books [1957] 534 p.
56059230   131.34082
Psychonnalysis. Child study.

RC509.8.G65 2000
Goldberg, Carl.
The evil we do : the psychoanalysis of destructive people / Carl Goldberg. Amherst, N.Y. : Prometheus Books, 2000. 259 p. ;
00-042166   616.89/17   1573928399
Psychoanalysis -- Case studies. Good and evil. Social sciences and psychoanalysis.

RC512.K7
Kringlen, Einar.
Heredity and environment in the functional psychoses: an epidemiological-clinical twin study. London, Heinemann Medical [1968] [1], 201 p.
68-068828   616.89/07
Psychoses. Twins. Diseases in Twins.

RC514.B43
Bellak, Leopold,
Schizophrenia : a review of the syndrome / with the collaboration of Paul K. Benedict. New York : Logos Press, 1958. xx, 1010 p. :
58011008   616.8982
Schizophrenia.

RC514.G44 1999
Gelman, Sheldon,
Medicating schizophrenia : a history / Sheldon Gelman. New Brunswick, N.J. : Rutgers Unviversity Press, c1999. ix, 274 p. ;
98-047002   616.89/82061   0813526426
Schizophrenia -- Chemotherapy -- History. Antipsychotic drugs -- History.

RC514.G673 1991
Gottesman, Irving I.
Schizophrenia genesis : the origins of madness / Irving I. Gottesman, with the assistance of Dorothea L. Wolfgram. New York : Freeman, c1991. xiii, 296 p.
90-003840   616.89/82071   0716721457
Schizophrenia -- Etiology. Schizophrenia -- etiology.

RC514.H434 2001
Heinrichs, R. Walter,
In search of madness : schizophrenia and neuroscience / R. Walter Heinrichs. Oxford ; Oxford University Press, 2001. x, 347 p. :
00-062335   616.89/82   0195122194
Schizophrenia.

RC514.H59 1990
Hollandsworth, James G.
The physiology of psychological disorders : schizophrenia, depression, anxiety, and substance abuse / James G. Hollandsworth, Jr. New York : Plenum Press, c1990. xvii, 318 p.
89-026559   616.89/07   0306433532
Schizophrenia -- Physiological aspects. Depression, Mental -- Physiological aspects. Anxiety -- Physiological aspects.

RC514.N63 2000
Noll, Richard,
The encyclopedia of schizophrenia and other psychotic disorders / Richard Noll ; foreword by Susan Naylor. New York : Facts On File, 2000. p. cm.
99-044166   616.89/003   0816040702
Schizophrenia -- Encyclopedias. Schizophrenia -- Information services -- Directories.

RC514.P71879 1996
Psychopathology : the evolving science of mental disorder / edited by Steven Matthysse ... [et al.]. Cambridge [England] ; Cambridge University Press, 1996. xiv, 633 p. :
95-012354   616.89/82   0521444691
Schizophrenia. Schizophrenia. Psychopathology.

RC514.R383 1989
Reconstructing schizophrenia / edited by Richard P. Bentall. London ; Routledge, 1992. xvii, 308 p.
89-010209   616.89/82   041501574X
Schizophrenia. Schizophrenia.

RC514.R63
Rogers, Carl R.
The therapeutic relationship and its impact; a study of psychotherapy with schizophrenics. Edited by Carl R. Rogers with the collaboration of Eugene T.Gendlin, Donald J. Kiesler [and] Charles B. Truax. Madison, University of Wisconsin Press, 1967. xix, 625p.
67013554   616.89
Psychotherapy. Schizophrenia. Physician-patient relations.

RC514.S316 1992
Sass, Louis Arnorsson.
Madness and modernism : insanity in the light of modern art, literature, and thought / Louis A. Sass. New York, NY : BasicBooks, c1992. x, 595 p. :
91-059013   616.89/83   0465043127
Schizophrenia. Modernism (Art) Modernism (Literature)

RC514.S33625 1993
Schizophrenia : origins, processes, treatment, and outcome / edited by Rue L. Cromwell, C.R. Snyder. New York : Oxford University Press, 1993. x, 373 p. :
92-048996   616.89/82   0195069226
Schizophrenia. Schizophrenia.

RC514.S59 2001
Social cognition and schizophrenia / edited by Patrick W. Corrigan and David L. Penn. Washington, D.C. : American Psychological Association, 2001. xvii, 353 p.
00-054824   616.89/82   1557987742
Schizophrenia. Social perception.

RC514.S754 2001
Steele, Ken,
The day the voices stopped :a schizophrenic's journey from madness to hope / Ken Steele with Claire Berman. New York : Basic Books, 2001. p. cm.
          616.89/82/0092   0465082262
Steele, Ken, 1948-2000.   Schizophrenics--United States--Biography.

RC514.S88 1993
Symptoms of schizophrenia / edited by Charles G. Costello. New York : Wiley, c1993. xi, 322 p. ;
93-016759   616.89/8   0471548758
Schizophrenia. Symptoms. Schizophrenia -- diagnosis.

RC516.J36 1993
Jamison, Kay R.
Touched with fire : manic-depressive illness and the artistic temperament / Kay Redfield Jamison. New York : Free Press ; c1993. xii, 370 p. :
92-018327   616.89/5/00887   0029160308
Manic-depressive illness. Artists -- Mental health. Authors -- Mental health.

RC521.E43 1994
Edwards, Allen Jack,
When memory fails : helping the Alzheimer's and dementia patient / Allen Jack Edwards. New York : Plenum Press, c1994. xiv, 282 p. :
94-002058   616.8/3   0306446480
Dementia. Alzheimer's disease. Caregivers.

RC521.L4 1996
Le Navenec, Carole-Lynne.
One day at a time : how families manage the experience of dementia / Carole-Lynne Le Navenec and Tina Vonhof ; foreword by Otto von Mering and Leon Earle. Westport, Conn. : Auburn House, 1996. xiii, 221 p.
95-024263   649.8   0865692572
Dementia -- Patients -- Family relationships. Caregivers -- Psychology. Dementia -- Patients -- Home care -- Psychological aspects.

RC523.G78 2001
Gruetzner, Howard.
Alzheimer's : a caregiver's guide and sourcebook / Howard Gruetzner. 3rd ed. New York : Wiley, 2001. xv, 336 p. :
          362.1/96831   0471379670
Alzheimer's disease.

RC523.J67 1987
Jorm, A. F.,
A guide to the understanding of Alzheimer's disease and related disorders / Anthony F. Jorm. Washington Square, N.Y. : New York University Press, c1987. 158 p. :
87-007929   618.97/683   0814741703
Alzheimer's disease. Dementia. Alzheimer's Disease.

RC523.P67 1995
Post, Stephen Garrard,
The moral challenge of Alzheimer disease / Stephen G. Post. Baltimore, Md. : Johns Hopkins University Press, c1995. viii, 142 p.
95-013505   362.1/96831   0801851742
Alzheimer's disease -- Moral and ethical aspects.

RC523.2.D43 2000
Tanzi, Rudolph E.
Decoding darkness : the search for the genetic causes of Alzheimer's disease / Rudolph E. Tanzi, Ann B. Parsons. Cambridge, Mass. : Perseus Publishing, c2000. xviii, 281 p.
          0738201952
Alzheimer's disease. Alzheimer's disease -- Genetic aspects. Amyloid beta-protein.

RC524.D44 1992
Dementia and aging : ethics, values, and policy choices / edited by Robert H. Binstock, Stephen G. Post, Peter J. Whitehouse. Baltimore : Johns Hopkins University Press, c1992. xviii, 184 p.
92-006220   616.89/83   080184424X
Senile dementia -- Treatment -- Moral and ethical aspects. Senile dementia -- Treatment -- Government policy -- United States. Senile dementia -- Patients -- Care -- Moral and ethical aspects.

RC530.E9
Eysenck, H. J.
The causes and cures of neurosis; an introduction to modern behaviour therapy based on learning theory and the principles of conditioning, by H. J. Eysenck and S. Rachman. San Diego, Calif., R. R. Knapp [1965] xii, 318 p.
64-021700   616.85
Neuroses. Behavior therapy.

RC531.A638 1998
Anxiety sensitivity : theory, research, and treatment of the fear of anxiety / edited by Steven Taylor. Mahwah, N.J. : L. Erlbaum Associates, 1998. xii, 370 p. ;
98-023956   616.85/223   0805828656
Anxiety sensitivity.

RC531.C727 1999
Craske, Michelle Genevieve,
Anxiety disorders : psychological approaches to theory and treatment / Michelle G. Craske. Boulder, CO : Westview Press, c1999. xxi, 425 p. :
98-019027   616.85/223   0813332508
Anxiety. Anxiety Disorders -- diagnosis. Anxiety Disorders -- therapy.

RC531.P69 1990
Powell, Trevor J.,
Anxiety and stress management / Trevor J. Powell and Simon J. Enright. London ; Routledge, 1990. x, 196 p. :
89-024320   616.85/223   041504457X
Anxiety -- Treatment. Stress management.

RC532.M34 1996
Mahony, Patrick,
Freud's Dora : a psychoanalytic, historical, and textual study / Patrick J. Mahony. New Haven : Yale University Press, c1996. xviii, 170 p.
96-010372   616.85/2409   0300066228
Bauer, Ida, -- 1882-1945 -- Mental health. Freud, Sigmund, -- 1856-1939. Hysteria -- Case studies. Psychoanalysis -- Case studies.

RC532.M53 1995
Micale, Mark S.,
Approaching hysteria : disease and its interpretations / Mark S. Micale. Princeton, N.J. : Princeton University Press, c1995. xii, 327 p. ;
94-016596   616.85/24/009   0691037175
Hysteria -- History. Hysteria -- Historiography. Hysteria -- history.

RC532.S46 1997
Showalter, Elaine.
Hystories : hysterical epidemics and modern culture / Elaine Showalter. New York : Columbia University Press, c1997. x, 244 p. ;
96-044108   616.85/24   0231104588
Hysteria, Epidemic. Hysteria (Social psychology) Popular culture.

RC533.A88
Autism : a sensorimotor approach to management / editor, Ruth A. Huebner. Gaithersburg, MD : Aspen Publishers, 2001. xvii, 493 p.
00-058298   616.89/82   0834216450
Autism. Sensorimotor integration. Sensorimotor cortex -- Diseases.

RC533.F45 1990
Feminist perspectives on addictions / Nan Van Den Bergh, editor. New York : Springer Pub. Co., c1991. xv, 222 p. ;
90-010434   616.86/0082   0826173500
Compulsive behavior. Codependency. Feminism.

RC533.N49 1997
Neziroglu, Fugen A.,
Over and over again : understanding obsessive-compulsive disorder / Fugen Neziroglu, Jose A. Yaryura-Tobias. San Francisco, Calif. : Jossey-Bass Publishers, 1997. p. cm.
616.85/227   0787908762
Obsessive-compulsive disorder--Popular works.

RC533.O2745 2003
Obsessive compulsive disorder : theory, research, and treatment / edited by Ross G. Menzies and Padmal de Silva. New York : J. Wiley, c2003. p. cm.
616.85/227   0471494453
Obsessive-compulsive disorder.

RC535.D63 2000
Doctor, Ronald M.
The encyclopedia of phobias, fears, and anxieties / Ronald M. Doctor and Ada P. Kahn. 2nd ed. New York : Facts on File, c2000. viii, 568 p. :
616.85/22/003   0816039895
Phobias--Dictionaries. Fear--Dictionaries. Anxiety--Dictionaries.

RC535.G724 1998
Granet, Roger.
If you think you have panic disorder / Roger Granet and Robert Aquinas McNally. New York : Dell, c1998. 198 p. ;
616.85/223   044022540X
Panic disorders.

RC535.M396 1994
McNally, Richard J.
Panic disorder : a critical analysis / Richard J. McNally. New York : Guilford Press, c1994 xi, 276 p. ;
94-026243   616.85/223   0898622638
Panic disorders. Panic Disorder.

RC537.B497 1990
Biological rhythms, mood disorders, light therapy, and the pineal gland / edited by Mohammad Shafii, Sharon Lee Shafii. Washington, DC : American Psychiatric Press, c1990. xix, 213 p. :
89-018447   616.85/27   0880481692
Affective disorders -- Physiological aspects. Pineal gland. Melatonin.

RC537.H337 1992b
Handbook of affective disorders / edited by Eugene S. Paykel. 2nd ed. New York : Guilford Press, 1992. xii, 699 p. :
616.85/27   0898626749
Affective disorders--Handbooks, manuals, etc. Affective Disorders.

RC537.J26 1991
Jack, Dana Crowley.
    Silencing the self : women and depression / Dana Crowley Jack. Cambridge, Mass. : Harvard University Press, 1991. viii, 256 p.
91-015472   616.85/27/0082   0674808150
    Depression in women.

RC537.K367 1996
Karp, David Allen,
    Speaking of sadness : depression, disconnection, and the meanings of illness / David A. Karp. New York : Oxford University Press, 1996. vii, 240 p. ;
95-002143   616.85/27/0092   0195094867
    Depressed persons. Depression, Mental. Depressed persons -- Interviews.

RC537.N65 1990
Nolen-Hoeksema, Susan,
    Sex differences in depression / Susan Nolen-Hoeksema. Stanford, Calif. : Stanford University Press, c1990. vii, 258 p. ;
89-027303   616.85/27   0804716404
    Depression, Mental -- Sex factors. Women -- Mental health. Women -- Social conditions.

RC537.R58 1993
Robbins, Paul R.
    Understanding depression / by Paul R. Robbins. Jefferson, N.C. : McFarland & Co., c1993. xiv, 186 p. ;
92-056685   616.85/27   0899508782
    Depression, Mental -- Popular works.

RC537.R63 2001
Roesch, Roberta.
    The encyclopedia of depression / Roberta Roesch ; introduction by Ewald Horwath. 2nd ed. New York : Facts on File, 2001. ix, 278 p. :
          616.85/27/003   0816040478
    Depression, Mental--Encyclopedias. Depression, Mental--Information services--Directories. Depression--Dictionary--English.

RC537.W487 1997
Whybrow, Peter C.
    A mood apart : depression, mania, and other afflictions of the self / Peter C. Whybrow. New York, NY : BasicBooks, c1997. xx, 363 p. :
96-047974   616.89/5   0465047254
    Affective disorders. Self. Personality.

RC545.R67 1998
Rosenthal, Norman E.
    Winter blues : seasonal affective disorder : what it is and how to overcome it / Norman E.Rosenthal. Rev. and updated. New York : Guilford Press, c1998. x, 354 p. :
          616.85/27   1572303956
    Seasonal affective disorder--Research--Popular works. Seasonal affective disorder--Prevention--Popular works. Phototherapy--Popular works.

RC547.Y34 2001
Thorpy, Michael J.
    The encyclopedia of sleep and sleep disorders / Michael J. Thorpy and Jan Yager. 2nd, ed., updated and rev. New York : Facts On File, c2001. xxxvii, 314 p. ;
          616.8/498/03   0816040893
    Sleep disorders--Dictionaries. Sleep--Dictionaries.

RC552.A44.A38 1989
    Agoraphobia : current perspectives on theory and treatment / edited by Kevin Gournay. London ; Routledge, 1989. xii, 242 p. ;
88-036568   616.85/225   0415018862
    Agoraphobia -- Treatment. Behavior therapy. Phobic Disorders -- therapy.

RC552.A44.C37 1995
Capps, Lisa.
    Constructing panic : the discourse of agoraphobia / Lisa Capps and Elinor Ochs. Cambridge, Mass. : Harvard University Press, 1995. xi, 244 p. ;
95-022566   616.85/225   0674165489
    Agoraphobia -- Case studies. Personal construct theory. Discourse analysis.

RC552.A5.A37 1984
Abraham, Suzanne.
    Eating disorders : the facts / Suzanne Abraham and Derek Llewellyn-Jones. Oxford, [Oxfordshire] ; Oxford University Press, 1984. 162 p. :
84-000782   616.85/2   0192614592
    Eating disorders. Bulimia. Appetite disorders.

RC552.A5.B78
Bruch, Hilde,
    The golden cage : the enigma of anorexia nervosa / Hilde Bruch. Cambridge, Mass. : Harvard University Press, 1978. xii, 150 p. ;
77-010674   616.8/5   0674356500
    Anorexia nervosa. Anorexia nervosa. Diet, reducing -- Adverse effects.

RC552.A5.G375 1998
Garrett, Catherine,
    Beyond anorexia : narrative, spirituality, and recovery / Catherine Garrett. Cambridge, UK ; Cambridge University Press, 1998. xiii, 245 p.
98-006161   616.85/262   0521620155
    Anorexia nervosa -- Patients -- Rehabilitation. Anorexia nervosa -- Patients -- Religious life. Spiritual life.

RC552.A5.G67 1990
Gordon, Richard A.
    Anorexia and bulimia : anatomy of a social epidemic / Richard A. Gordon. Cambridge, Mass., USA : B. Blackwell, 1990. xi, 174 p. ;
89-038720   616.85/262   0631148515
    Anorexia nervosa -- Social aspects. Bulimia -- Social aspects.

RC552.A5.M33 1993
MacSween, Morag,
   Anorexic bodies : a feminist and sociological perspective on anorexia nervosa / Morag MacSween. London ; Routledge, 1993. 273 p. ;
93-007246   616.85/262   0415028469
   Anorexia nervosa -- Social aspects. Anorexia nervosa -- Etiology.

RC552.A5.M56
Minuchin, Salvador.
   Psychosomatic families : anorexia nervosa in context / Salvador Minuchin, Bernice L. Rosman, Lester Baker, with a contribution by Ronald Liebman. Cambridge, Mass. : Harvard University Press, 1978. viii, 351 p.
78-001742   616.8/5   0674722205
   Anorexia nervosa. Medicine, Psychosomatic. Family psychotherapy.

RC552.A5.P77 1992
   Psychobiology and treatment of anorexia nervosa and bulimia nervosa / [edited by] Katherine A. Halmi. Washington, D.C. : American Psychiatric Press, c1992. xiii, 356 p.
92-017984   616.85/26   088048506X
   Anorexia nervosa -- Congresses. Anorexia nervosa -- Physiological aspects -- Congresses. Bulimia -- Congresses.

RC552.A5.R63 1992
Robertson, Matra.
   Starving in the silences : an exploration of anorexia nervosa / Matra Robertson. Washington Square, N.Y. : New York University Press, 1992. xiv, 101 p. ;
92-016188   616.85/262   0814774342
   Anorexia nervosa -- Social aspects. Anorexia nervosa -- Psychological aspects. Women -- Psychology.

RC552.A5R664 2001
Ronen, Tammie,
   In and out of anorexia :the story, the client, the therapist, and recovery / Tammie Ronen and Ayelet ; foreword by Michael Mahoney. Philadelphia, PA : Jessica Kingsley Publishers, 2001. p. cm.
          616.85/262/0092   1853029904
Ayelet, 1974---Mental health.   *Anorexia nervosa--Patients-- Biography. Psychotherapist and patient.*

RC552.A5.T49 1990
Thompson, J. Kevin.
   Body image disturbance : assessment and treatment / J. Kevin Thompson. Elmsford, N.Y., U.S.A. : Pergamon Press, c1990. xvi, 140 p. :
89-039663   616.85/2   0080368220
   Anorexia nervosa. Body image disturbance. Self-acceptance.

RC552.B84.R45 2001
Reindl, Sheila M.,
   Sensing the self : women's recovery from bulimia / Sheila M. Reindl. Cambridge, Mass. : Harvard University Press, 2001. 337 p. ;
00-050582   616.85/263   0674004876
   Bulimia. Women -- Health and hygiene. Eating disorders.

RC552.C65.B56 1993
   Binge eating : nature, assessment, and treatment / Christopher G. Fairburn, G. Terence Wilson, editors. New York : Guilford Press, c1993. xii, 419 p. :
92-048235   616.85/26   0898629950
   Compulsive eating. Compulsive Behavior. Eating Disorders.

RC552.E18C37 2000
Cassell, Dana K.
   The encyclopedia of obesity and eating disorders / Dana K. Cassell and David H. Gleaves. 2nd ed. New York, N.Y. : Facts On File, c2000. xiv, 290 p. ;
          616.85/26/003   0816040427
   Eating disorders--Encyclopedias. Obesity--Encyclopedias. Obesity--Encyclopedias--English.

RC552.E18E287 2001
   Eating disorders sourcebook :basic consumer health information about eating disorders, including information about anorexia nervosa ... / edited by Dawn D. Matthews. 1st ed. Detroit, MI : Omnigraphics, c2001. xii, 322 p. ;
          616.85/26   0780803353
   Eating disorders. Consumer education.

RC552.E18.E29 1987
   Eating disorders throughout the life span / edited by Howard L. Field and Barbara B. Domangue. New York : Praeger, 1987. x, 164 p. :
87-016955   616.3/9   027592212X
   Eating disorders. Eating disorders in children. Appetite Disorders.

RC552.E18.F46 1994
   Feminist perspectives on eating disorders / edited by Patricia Fallon, Melanie A. Katzman, Susan C. Wooley. New York : Guilford Press, 1994. xix, 465 p. :
93-023951   616.85/26/0082   0898621801
   Eating disorders -- Social aspects. Feminist therapy. Women -- Psychology.

RC552.E18.H367 1997
   Handbook of treatment for eating disorders / edited by David M. Garner and Paul E. Garfinkel. New York : Guilford Press, c1997. p. cm.
97-003395   616.85/2606   1572301864
   Eating disorders -- Treatment. Eating Disorders -- therapy. Eating Disorders -- psychology.

RC552.E18.M35 1990
   Males with eating disorders / edited by Arnold E. Andersen. New York : Brunner/Mazel, c1990. x, 264 p. :
89-023909   616.85/26/0081   0876305567
   Eating disorders. Men -- Mental health. Anorexia Nervosa.

RC552.E18.M43 1996
Meadow, Rosalyn M.
   Good girls don't eat dessert : changing your relationship to food and sex / Rosalyn M. Meadow, Lillie Weiss. New York : Harmony Books, [1996] x, 195 p. ;
96-000970   616.85/26/0082   051770384X
   Eating disorders. Psychosexual disorders. Women -- Mental health.

RC552.E18.S26 1999
Sanders, Pete.
Anorexia & bulimia / by Pete Sanders and Steve Myers ; [illustrators, Mike Lacy and Liz Sawyer]. Brookfield, Conn. : Copper Beech Books, 1999. 32 p. :
98-047318   616.85/26   0761309144
Eating disorders -- Juvenile literature. Anorexia nervosa -- Juvenile literature. Bulimia -- Juvenile literature.

RC552.N5.G67 1987
Gosling, Francis G.
Before Freud : neurasthenia and the American medical community, 1870-1910 / F.G. Gosling. Urbana : University of Illinois Press, c1987. xviii, 192 p.
87-006038   616.85/28/060973
0252014065
Neurasthenia -- Treatment -- United States -- History -- 19th century. Mental illness -- Treatment -- United States -- History -- 19th century. Neurasthenia -- history -- United States.

RC552.O25.B47 2000
Berg, Francie M.
Women afraid to eat : breaking free in today's weight-obsessed world / Frances M. Berg ; edited by Kendra Rosencrans. Hettinger, ND : Healthy Weight Network, c2000. 376 p. :
                   0918532620
Eating disorders -- United States. Body image. Obesity -- Social aspects -- United States.

RC552.O25.P75 1982
Psychological aspects of obesity : a handbook / Benjamin B. Wolman, editor ; Stephen DeBerry, editorial associate. New York : Van Nostrand Reinhold, c1982. ix, 318 p. :
81-001917   616.3/98/0019   0442226098
Obesity -- Psychological aspects.

RC552.O25.T48 1997
Thone, Ruth Raymond.
Fat-- a fate worse than death : women, weight, and appearance / Ruth Raymond Thone. New York : The Haworth Press, c1997. xvi, 211 p. ;
97-004041   616.3/98/0019   0789001780
Obesity -- Psychological aspects. Obesity -- Social aspects. Overweight women.

RC552.P67.A45 1995
Allen, Jon G.
Coping with trauma : a guide to self-understanding / Jon G. Allen. Washington, DC : American Psychiatric Press, c1995. xx, 385 p. :
95-000578   616.85/21   0880487208
Psychic trauma. Post-traumatic stress disorder -- Popular works. Post-traumatic stress disorder -- Treatment.

RC552.P67.A85 1997
Assessing psychological trauma and PTSD / edited by John P. Wilson, Terence M. Keane ; foreword by Susan D. Solomon. New York : Guilford Press, c1997. xiv, 577 p. :
96-030206   616.85/21   1572301627
Post-traumatic stress disorder -- Diagnosis. Psychodiagnostics. Neuropsychological tests.

RC552.P67.B75 1997
Briere, John.
Psychological assessment of adult posttraumatic states / John Briere. Washington, DC : American Psychological Association, c1997. xv, 251 p. ;
96-052132   616.85/21   1557984034
Post-traumatic stress disorder -- Diagnosis. Stress (Psychology) -- Testing.

RC552.P67.E83 1996
Ethnocultural aspects of posttraumatic stress disorder : issues, research, and clinical applications / edited by Anthony J. Marsella ... [et al.]. Washington, DC : American Psychological Association, 1996. xxii, 576 p.
95-040252   616.85/21   1557983194
Post-traumatic stress disorder -- Cross-cultural studies. Psychiatry, Transcultural.

RC552.P67.H67 1997
Horowitz, Mardi Jon,
Stress response syndromes : PTSD, grief, and adjustment disorders / Mardi Jon Horowitz. Northvale, N.J. : J. Aronson, c1997. xx, 358 p. :
97-209669   616.85/21   0765700255
Post-traumatic stress disorder. Post-traumatic stress disorder -- Case studies.

RC552.P67.L56 1988
Lindy, Jacob D.,
Vietnam : a casebook / by Jacob D. Lindy ; in collaboration with Bonnie L. Green ... [et al.]. New York : Brunner/Mazel, c1988. xxviii, 353 p
87-015062   616.85/21209   0876304714
Post-traumatic stress disorder -- Case studies. War neuroses -- Case studies. Psychotherapy.

RC552.P67.O27 1998
O'Brien, L. Stephen,
Traumatic events and mental health / L. Stephen O'Brien. Cambridge ; Cambridge University Press, 1998. ix, 302 p. ;
97-022865   616.85/21   0521570271
Post-traumatic stress disorder.

RC552.P67.P666 1997
Posttraumatic stress disorder : acute and long-term responses to trauma and disaster / edited by Carol S. Fullerton and Robert J. Ursano. Washington, D.C. : American Psychiatric Press, c1997. xii, 296 p. :
96-024027   616.85/21   0880487518
Post-traumatic stress disorder. Stress Disorders, Post-Traumatic. Stress, Psychological -- complications.

RC552.P67.T747 1990
Trauma and the Vietnam War generation : report of findings from the National Vietnam veterans readjustment study / Richard A. Kulka ... [et al.] ; foreword by Alan Cranston. New York : Brunner/Mazel, c1990. xxix, 322 p.
89-071185   616.85/21   0876305737
Post-traumatic stress disorder. Veterans -- Mental health -- United States. Vietnamese Conflict, 1961-1975 -- Psychological aspects.

RC552.P67.T756 1995
Traumatic stress : from theory to practice / edited by John R. Freedy and Stevan E. Hobfoll. New York : Plenum Press, c1995. xvii, 402 p.
95-033370   616.85/21   0306450208
Post-traumatic stress disorder. Psychic trauma. Stress Disorders, Post-Traumatic.

RC552.P67.Y68 1995
Young, Allan,
The harmony of illusions : inventing post-traumatic stress disorder / Allan Young. Princeton, N.J. : Princeton University Press, c1995. x, 327 p. ;
95-016254   616.85/21   0691033528
Post-traumatic stress disorder -- Philosophy. Social epistemology.

RC552.R44.F44 1999
Feeney, Don J.,
Entrancing relationships : exploring the hypnotic framework of addictive relationships / Don J. Feeney, Jr. Westport, Conn. : Praeger, 1999. xii, 238 p. :
98-047747   616.86   0275964159
Relationship addiction. Hypnotism.

RC552.S4.C66 1998
Conterio, Karen,
Bodily harm : the breakthrough treatment program for self-injurers / Karen Conterio and Wendy Lader, with Jennifer Kingson Bloom. New York : Hyperion, c1998. x, 319 p. ;
98-038171   616.85/82
Self-mutilation.

RC552.S4.F36 2000
Farber, Sharon Klayman.
When the body is the target : self-harm, pain, and traumatic attachments / Sharon Klayman Farber. Northvale, N.J. : Jason Aronson, c2000. xxxiii, 580 p
99-055414   616.85/82   0765702568
Self-mutilation. Self-injurious behavior. Eating disorders.

RC552.S4.H95 1999
Hyman, Jane Wegscheider.
Women living with self-injury / Jane Wegscheider Hyman. Philadelphia : Temple University Press, 1999. x, 214 p. ;
99-017714   616.85/82/0082   1566397200
Self-mutilation. Women -- Mental health. Self-injurious behavior.

RC552.S62.B45 1998
Beidel, Deborah C.
Shy children, phobic adults : nature and treatment of social phobia / Deborah C. Beidel, Samuel M. Turner. Washington, DC : American Psychological Association, c1998. xiii, 324 p.
97-033477   616.85/225   1557984611
Social phobia.

RC552.S62.M37 1994
Marshall, John R.,
Social phobia : from shyness to stage fright / John R. Marshall ; with the assistance of Suzanne Lipsett. New York : BasicBooks, c1994. xviii, 219 p.
93-045449   616.85/22   0465072143
Social phobia.

RC552.T7.L49 2000
Leys, Ruth.
Trauma : a genealogy / Ruth Leys. Chicago : University of Chicago Press, 2000. x, 318 p. ;
99-052681   616.85/21   0226477657
Psychic trauma. Traumatic neuroses.

RC553.A84.S74 2000
Stephens, G. Lynn.
When self-consciousness breaks : alien voices and inserted thoughts / G. Lynn Stephens, George Graham. Cambridge, MA : MIT Press, 2000. xii, 198 p. ;
00-026720   154.4   0262194376
Auditory hallucinations. Thought insertion. Self.

RC553.A88A788 2000
Asperger syndrome / edited by Ami Klin, Fred R. Volkmar, Sara S. Sparrow ; foreword by Maria Asperger Felder. New York : Guilford Press, c2000. xvii, 489 p. :
                    616.89/82   1572305347
Asperger's syndrome. Autistic Disorder.

RC553.A88.G74 1995
Grandin, Temple.
Thinking in pictures : and other reports from my life with autism / Temple Grandin. New York : Doubleday, c1995. 222 p. :
95-008513   616.89/82/0092   0385477929
Grandin, Temple.   Autism -- Patients -- United States -- Biography.

RC553.A88.H36 1995
Happe, Francesca.
Autism : an introduction to psychological theory / Francesca Happe. Cambridge, Mass. : Harvard University Press, 1995. viii, 152 p.
94077278   616.89/82   0674053125
Autism.

RC553.A88H64 1997
Holmes, David L.,
Autism through the lifespan : the Eden model / David L. Holmes. Bethesda, MD : Woodbine House, 1997. xiv, 383 p. :
                    616.89/82   093314928X
Autism. Autism in children.

RC553.A88.H67 2000
Houston, R. A.
Autism in history : the case of Hugh Blair of Borgue / Rab Houston and Uta Frith. Oxford [England] ; Blackwell, 2000. ix, 207 p. :
00-036033   616.89/82/0092   0631220887
Blair, Hugh -- 1708-1765.   Autism -- Patients -- Scotland -- Biography.

RC553.A88M675 2001
Mesibov, Gary B.
Understanding Asperger syndrome and high functioning autism / Gary B. Mesibov, Victoria Shea, and Lynn W. Adams. New York : Kluwer Academic/Plenum Publishers, c2001. xi, 130 p. ;
                    616.89/82   0306466279
Asperger's syndrome. Autistic children. Autism.

RC553.A88.M97 1998
Myles, Brenda.
Asperger syndrome : a guide for educators and parents / Brenda Smith Myles and Richard L. Simpson. Austin, Tex. : Pro-Ed, c1998. viii, 140 p.
97-017269   616.89/82   0890797277
Asperger's syndrome.

RC553.A88.W55 1992
Williams, Donna,
Nobody nowhere : the extraordinary autobiography of an autistic / Donna Williams. New York : Times Books, c1992. xviii, 219 p.
92-053669   616.89/82/0092   0812920422
Williams, Donna, -- 1963- -- Mental health.   Autism -- Patients -- Biography.

RC553.F83.H33 1998
Hacking, Ian.
Mad travelers : reflections on the reality of transient mental illnesses / Ian Hacking. Charlottesville, Va. : University Press of Virginia, 1998. x, 239 p. :
98-020894   616.85/232   0813918235
Tissie, Philippe, -- 1852-1925.   Fugue (Psychology) -- Case studies. Social psychiatry. Niche (Ecology)

RC553.H3.M47 1998
Merkur, Daniel.
The ecstatic imagination : psychedelic experiences and the psychoanalysis of self-actualization / Dan Merkur. Albany : State University of New York Press, c1998. xiv, 226 p. ;
97-020414   616.89   0791436055
Hallucinations and illusions. Psychoanalysis. Self-actualization (Psychology)

RC553.H3.S57 1988
Slade, Peter D.
Sensory deception : a scientific analysis of hallucination / Peter D. Slade and Richard P. Bentall. Baltimore : Johns Hopkins University Press, c1988. x, 275 p. :
88-045398   154.3   080183760X
Hallucinations and illusions. Hallucinations.

RC553.N36.A8613 1993
Asper, Kathrin,
The abandoned child within : on losing and regaining self-worth / Kathrin Asper ; translated by Sharon E. Rooks. New York : Fromm International Pub., c1993. 360 p., [8] p
93-000321   616.85/85   0880642033
Narcissism. Emotional deprivation. Self-esteem.

RC553.N36.E77 1986
Essential papers on narcissism / Andrew P. Morrison, editor. New York : New York University Press, 1986. viii, 491 p.
85-025845   616.85/82   0814753949
Narcissism.

RC553.N36.F74 1991
Freud's "On narcissism--an introduction" / edited by Joseph Sandler, Ethel Spector Person, Peter Fonagy for the International Psychoanalytical Association. New Haven : Yale University Press, c1991. xx, 236 p. ;
91-007241   616.85/85   0300050798
Freud, Sigmund, -- 1856-1939. -- Zur Einfuhrung des Narzissmus. Freud, Sigmund, -- 1856-1939. Narcissism. Narcissism.

RC553.N36.M369 1993
Masterson, James F.
The emerging self : a developmental, self, and object relations approach to the treatment of the closet narcissistic disorder of the self / James F. Materson. New York : Brunner/Mazel, c1993. xi, 294 p. :
93-001604   616.85/85   0876307217
Narcissism. Narcissism. Borderline Personality Disorder -- etiology.

RC554.B43 1990
Beck, Aaron T.
Cognitive therapy of personality disorders / Aaron T. Beck, Arthur Freeman, and associates. New York : Guilford Press, c1990. xviii, 396 p.
90-033575   616.85/8   0898624347
Personality disorders -- Treatment. Cognitive therapy.

RC555.H35 1997
Handbook of antisocial behavior / David M. Stoff, James Breiling, and Jack D. Maser, editors. New York : J. Wiley & Sons, c1997. xxii, 600 p.
96-053445   616.85/82   0471124524
Antisocial personality disorders. Violence.

RC555.H36
Handbook of sex therapy / edited by Joseph LoPiccolo and Leslie LoPiccolo. New York : Plenum Press, c1978. xx, 531 p. :
77-018818   616.6/06   0306310740
Sex therapy -- Addresses, essays, lectures.

RC555.L95 1995
Lykken, David Thoreson.
The antisocial personalities / David T. Lykken. Hillsdale, N.J. : Lawrence Erlbaum Associates, 1995. x, 259 p. :
95-012891   616.85/82   080581941X
Antisocial personality disorders.

RC555.P77
The Psychopath : a comprehensive study of antisocial disorders and behaviors / edited by William H. Reid. New York : Brunner/Mazel, c1978. xvi, 349 p. ;
78-008629   616.8/582   0876301723
Antisocial personality disorders. Antisocial personality. Social behavior disorders.

RC555.S57 1996
Simon, Robert I.
  Bad men do what good men dream : a forensic psychiatrist illuminates the darker side of human behavior / Robert I. Simon. Washington, D.C. : American Psychiatric Press, c1996. xi, 362 p. ;
95-010723   616.85/82   0880486880
  Antisocial personality disorders. Insane, Criminal and dangerous. Psychopaths.

RC555.T5
Thigpen, Corbett H.
  The three faces of Eve, by Corbett H. Thigpen and Hervey M. Cleckley. New York, McGraw-Hill [1957] 308 p.
56-012526   616.8
  Multiple Personality.

RC556.K33
Kaplan, Helen Singer,
  The new sex therapy; active treatment of sexual dysfunctions. New York, Brunner/Mazel [1974] xvi, 544 p.
73-087724   616.6   0876300832
  Sex therapy.

RC556.M37
Masters, William H.
  Human sexual inadequacy [by] William H. Masters [and] Virginia E. Johnson. Boston, Little, Brown [1970] x, 467 p.
71-117043   616.6   070000193X
  Sexual disorders.

RC556.M665 1994
Money, John,
  Reinterpreting the unspeakable : human sexuality 2000 : the complete interviewer and clinical biographer, exigency theory, and sexology for the Third Millennium / John Money. New York : Continuum, 1994. x, 242 p. ;
93-045465   616.85/83   0826406513
  Sexual deviation. Psychosexual disorders. Sexual disorders.

RC558.H63 1991
  The homosexualities and the therapeutic process / edited by Charles W. Socarides, Vamik D. Volkan. Madison, Conn. : International Universities Press Inc., c1991. xii, 315 p. ;
91-020827   616.85/834   0823623483
  Gays -- Mental health. Psychotherapy. Psychoanalysis and homosexuality.

RC558.L49 1988
Lewes, Kenneth.
  The psychoanalytic theory of male homosexuality / Kenneth Lewes. New York : Simon and Schuster, c1988. 301 p. ;
88-023055   306.7/662   0671623915
  Homosexuality, Male -- Psychological aspects. Psychoanalysis and homosexuality.

RC558.M43 1990
McDonald, Helen B.
  Homosexuality : a practical guide to counseling lesbians, gay men, and their families / Helen Б. McDonald and Audrey I. Steinhorn ; foreword by William Van Ornum. New York : Continuum, 1990. 186 p. ;
90-030715   616.85/834   0826404693
  Homosexuality. Gay men -- Counseling of. Lesbians -- Counseling of.

RC558.N52 1993
Nicolosi, Joseph.
  Healing homosexuality : case stories of reparative therapy / by Joseph Nicolosi, with the assistance of Lucy Freeman. Northvale, N.J. : J. Aronson, c1993. x, 230 p. :
92-016501   616.85/834   0876683405
  Gay men -- Mental health -- Case studies. Psychotherapy -- Case studies. Homosexuality, Male -- Case studies.

RC560.R36.Q56 1989
Quina, Kathryn.
  Rape, incest, and sexual harassment : a guide for helping survivors / Kathryn Quina and Nancy L. Carlson. New York : Praeger, 1989. xii, 263 p. ;
89-016160   362.88/3   0275925331
  Rape victims -- Mental health. Incest victims -- Mental health. Sexual harassment -- Psychological aspects.

RC560.S43.E23 1995
Earle, Ralph
  Sex addiction : case studies and management / Ralph H. Earle and Marcus R. Earle, with Kevin Osborn. New York : Brunner/Mazel Publishers, c1995. x, 270 p. :
95-030129   616.85/83   0876307853
  Sex addiction -- Treatment. Sex addiction -- Treatment -- Case studies.

RC560.S43.G66 1998
Goodman, Aviel.
  Sexual addiction : an integrated approach / Aviel Goodman. Madison, Conn. : International Universities Press, c1998. xi, 464 p. :
97-027415   616.85/83   082366063X
  Sex addiction.

RC560.S47.S488 1999
  Sexual aggression / edited by Jon A. Shaw. Washington, DC : American Psychiatric Press, c1999. xv, 343 p. ;
98-017929   616.85/82   0880487577
  Sex crimes. Sex offenders. Child sexual abuse.

RC564.D535 2000
Diamond, Jonathan,
  Narrative means to sober ends : treating addiction and its aftermath / Jonathan Diamond ; foreword by David Treadway. New York : Guilford Press, c2000. xxviii, 386 p
00-026074   616.86/06   1572305665
  Substance abuse -- Patients -- Rehabilitation. Letter writing -- Therapeutic use. Substance abuse -- Treatment.

RC564.E3658 1990

The Effectiveness of drug abuse treatment : Dutch and American perspectives / edited by Jerome J. Platt, Charles D. Kaplan, Patricia J. McKim. Malabar, Fla. : R.E. Krieger, 1990. xiv, 330 p. ;

89-015479   362.29/38   0894642669

Drug abuse -- Treatment -- Evaluation. Drug abuse -- Treatment -- United States -- Evaluation. Drug abuse -- Treatment -- Netherlands -- Evaluation.

RC564.E785 2001

Ethnocultural factors in substance abuse treatment / edited by Shulamith Lala Ashenberg Straussner. New York : Guilford Press, c2001. xv, 447 p. ;

00-067723   616.86/06   1572306300

Substance abuse -- Treatment -- Cross-cultural studies. Drug abuse -- Treatment -- Cross-cultural studies. Cross-cultural counseling.

RC564.G66 2001
Goldstein, Avram.

Addiction : from biology to drug policy / Avram Goldstein. 2nd ed. Oxford ; Oxford University Press, 2001. xii, 353 p. :

          616.86   0195146646

Drug abuse--Physiological aspects. Drug abuse--Social aspects.

RC564.H364 1998

Harm reduction : pragmatic strategies for managing high risk behaviors / edited by G. Alan Marlatt ; foreword by David B. Abrams and David C. Lewis. New York : Guilford Press, c1998. xxiv, 390 p.

98-037938   616.86   1572303972

Substance abuse -- Complications -- Prevention. Substance abuse -- Treatment. Health behavior -- Social aspects.

RC564.I544 1997
Institute of Medicine (U.S.).

Dispelling the myths about addiction : strategies to increase understanding and strengthen research / Committee to Identify Strategies to Raise the Profile of Substance Abuse and Alcoholism Research, Division of Neuroscience and Behavioral Health, Division of Health Promotion and Disease Prevention, Institute of Medicine. Washington, D.C. : National Academy Press, 1997. xvii, 218 p.

97-069691   616.86   0309064015

Compulsive behavior. Substance abuse. Psychobiology.

RC564.R4376 2001

Relapse and recovery in addictions / edited by Frank M. Tims, Carl G. Leukefeld, Jerome J. Platt. New Haven, CT : Yale University Press, c2001. xii, 420 p. :

00-043598   616.86/0651   0300083831

Substance abuse -- Relapse -- Prevention. Substance abuse -- Patients -- Rehabilitation.

RC564.S8372 1996

Substance abuse sourcebook : basic health-related information about the abuse of legal and illegal substances such as alcohol, tobacco, prescription drugs, marijuana, cocaine, and heroin ; and inclu edited by Karen Bellenir. Detroit, MI. : Omnigraphics, c1996. x, 573 p. :

96-009511   616.86   0780800389

Substance abuse.

RC564.T55 1994
Thombs, Dennis L.

Introduction to addictive behaviors / Dennis L. Thombs. New York : Guilford Press, c1994. xiii, 236 p.

93-030812   616.86/071   0898623367

Substance abuse -- Etiology. Substance abuse -- Treatment.

RC564.T7347 1996

Treating substance abuse : theory and technique / edited by Frederick Rotgers, Daniel S. Keller, Jon Morgenstern. New York : Guilford Press, c1996. viii, 328 p.

95-025144   616.8606   1572300256

Substance abuse -- Treatment. Substance Abuse -- therapy. Substance Abuse -- psychology.

RC564.29.D87 1997
DuPont, Robert L.,

The selfish brain : learning from addiction / Robert L. DuPont. Washington, DC : American Psychiatric Press, c1997. xxxv, 553 p.

96-008593   362.29   0880486864

Substance abuse. Substance abuse -- Treatment. Recovering addicts.

RC564.5.W65.E77 1992
Ettorre, E. M.

Women and substance use / Elizabeth Ettorre. New Brunswick, N.J. : Rutgers University Press, c1992. x, 204 p. ;

92-007113   362.29/082   0813518636

Women -- Substance use. Feminist theory.

RC565.A394 1990

Alcohol and the family / edited by R. Lorraine Collins, Kenneth E. Leonard, John S. Searles. New York : Guilford Press, 1990. p. cm.

89-037204   362.29/23   0898621690

Alcoholism. Alcoholics -- Family relationships. Family psychotherapy.

RC565.M346 1983

Medical and social aspects of alcohol abuse / edited by Boris Tabakoff, Patricia B. Sutker, and Carrie L. Randall. New York : Plenum Press, c1983. xvi, 403 p. ;

83-004786   616.86/1   0306412217

Alcoholism. Alcohol -- Physiological aspects. Alcohol, Ethyl.

RC565.V332 1995
Vaillant, George E.,

The natural history of alcoholism revisited / George E. Vaillant. Cambridge, Mass. : Harvard University Press, 1995. xiii, 446 p. ;

          616.86/1   0674603788

Alcoholism. Alcoholism--Longitudinal studies. Alcoholism.

RC567.K65 2001
Kozlowski, Lynn T.

Cigarettes, nicotine, & health : a biobehavioral approach / Lynn T. Kozlowski, Jack E. Henningfield, Janet Brigham. Thousand Oaks, Calif. : Sage, c2001. xi, 192 p. :

00-012631   616.86/5071   080395946X

Tobacco -- Physiological aspects. Tobacco -- Psychological aspects. Nicotine -- Physiological aspects.

RC567.R56 2001
Smoking : risk, perception & policy / Paul Slovic, editor. Thousand Oaks, Calif. : Sage Publications, c2001. xiii, 378 p.
00-012865   362.29/6   0761923802
Smoking -- Health aspects. Nicotine -- Health aspects. Cigarette smokers -- Attitudes.

RC568.C6.C628 1987
Cocaine : clinical and biobehavioral aspects / edited by Seymour Fisher, Allen Raskin, E.H. Uhlenhuth. New York : Oxford University Press, 1987. ix, 256 p. :
86-000857   616.86/3   0195040686
Cocaine habit -- Congresses. Cocaine -- Physiological effect -- Congresses. Cocaine -- Psychological aspects -- Congresses.

RC568.C6.G653 1993
Gold, Mark S.
Cocaine / Mark S. Gold. New York : Plenum Medical Book Co., c1993. x, 238 p. :
92-045165   616.86/47   0306443864
Cocaine habit. Cocaine -- Physiological effect. Cocaine habit -- Treatment.

RC568.C6.P53 1997
Platt, Jerome J.
Cocaine addiction : theory, research, and treatment / Jerome J. Platt. Cambridge, Mass. : Harvard University Press, 1997. xiv, 458 p. ;
96-037435   616.86/47   0674136322
Cocaine habit. Cocaine. Narcotic Dependence.

RC568.C6.W46 1994
Weiss, Roger D.,
Cocaine / Roger D. Weiss, Steven M. Mirin, Roxanne L. Bartel. Washington, DC : American Psychiatric Press, c1994. xiv, 204 p. ;
93-015802   616.8647   0880485493
Cocaine habit. Cocaine -- Physiological effect. Cocaine.

RC568.H4.P55 1986
Platt, Jerome J.
Heroin addiction : theory, research, and treatment / Jerome J. Platt. Malabar, Fla. : R.E. Krieger Pub. Co., 1986-1995. 3 v. ;
83-019584   362.2/93   0898746949
Heroin habit. Heroin habit -- Treatment. Drugs of abuse -- Law and legislation -- United States.

RC569.F57 1997
Firestone, Robert.
Suicide and the inner voice : risk assessment, treatment, and case management / Robert W. Firestone. Thousand Oaks, Calif. : Sage Publications, c1997. xvi, 333 p. :
96-051212   616.85/8445   0761905545
Suicide. Suicidal behavior. Suicide -- Prevention.

RC569.M55 1998
Minois, Georges,
History of suicide : voluntary death in Western culture / Georges Minois ; translated by Lydia G. Cochrane. Baltimore : Johns Hopkins University Press, 1998. p. cm.
98-004069   179.7   0801859190
Suicide -- History. Right to die.

RC569.S3848 2001
Shneidman, Edwin S.
Comprehending suicide : landmarks in 20th-century suicidology / Edwin Shneidman. Washington, DC : American Psychological Association, c2001. xiv, 215 p. ;
00-065066   616.85/8445   1557987432
Suicide. Suicide -- Miscellanea.

RC569.5.A28.C66 1997
Construction and reconstruction of memory : dilemmas of childhood sexual abuse / edited by Charlotte Prozan. Northvale, N.J. : Jason Aronson, c1997. xx, 236 p. ;
95-051701   616.85/8369   1568217870
Adult child sexual abuse victims. Recovered memory. Repression (Psychology)

RC569.5.A28.G37 1999
Gartner, Richard B.
Betrayed as boys : psychodynamic treatment of sexually abused men / Richard B. Gartner. New York : Guilford Press, c1999. xii, 356 p. ;
98-055694   616.85/83690651
1572304677
Adult child sexual abuse victims. Male sexual abuse victims. Psychodynamic psychotherapy.

RC569.5.A28.P67 1996
Pope, Kenneth S.
Recovered memories of abuse : assessment, therapy, forensics / Kenneth S. Pope and Laura S. Brown. Washington, D.C. : American Psychological Ass., c1996. ix, 315 p. :
96-033009   616.85/8369   155798395X
Adult child sexual abuse victims. Recovered memory. False memory syndrome.

RC569.5.A28.S48 1995
Sexual abuse recalled : treating trauma in the era of the recovered memory debate / edited by Judith L. Alpert. Northvale, N.J. : Jason Aronson, c1995. xxiv, 410 p.
95-004702   616.85/8369   1568213638
Adult child sexual abuse victims. Recovered memory.

RC569.5.B67.E87 1986
Essential papers on borderline disorders : one hundred years at the border / Michael H. Stone, editor. New York : New York University Press, 1986. x, 580 p. ;
85-015384   616.89   0814778496
Borderline personality disorder.

RC569.5.C55.B56 1997
Bloom, Sandra L.,
   Creating sanctuary : toward the evolution of sane societies / Sandra L. Bloom. New York : Routledge, 1997. xi, 306 p. ;
96-037298   616.85/82239   0415915686
   Adult child abuse victims -- Rehabilitation. Adult child abuse victims -- Rehabilitation -- Case studies. Psychic trauma -- Social aspects.

RC569.5.C55.B75 1992
Briere, John.
   Child abuse trauma : theory and treatment of the lasting effects / John N. Briere. Newbury Park, Calif. : Sage Publications, c1992. xx, 203 p. ;
92-023606   616.85/822390651
0803937121
   Adult child abuse victims -- Rehabilitation. Adult child abuse victims -- Mental health. Psychotherapy.

RC569.5.C55.M33 1998
MacKinnon, Laurie K.
   Trust and betrayal in the treatment of child abuse / Laurie K. MacKinnon ; foreword by Virginia Goldner. New York : Guilford Press, c1998. xii, 260 p. ;
97-043972   616.85/82230651
1572302984
   Abusive parents -- Counseling of. Psychotherapist and patient. Family psychotherapy.

RC569.5.C55.R69 1998
Roy, R.
   Childhood abuse and chronic pain : a curious relationship? / Ranjan Roy. Toronto ; University of Toronto Press, c1998. xi, 160 p. ;
98-176843   616/.0472/019   0802007392
   Chronic pain -- Psychological aspects. Adult child sexual abuse victims -- Mental health. Pain -- psychology.

RC569.5.C55.S53 1999
Shengold, Leonard.
   Soul murder revisited : thoughts about therapy, hate, love, and memory / Leonard Shengold. New Haven, CT : Yale University Press, 1999. viii, 328 p.
98-027156   616.85/82239   0300075944
   Adult child abuse victims -- Mental health. Psychoanalysis. Child abuse in literature.

RC569.5.C55.W49 1996
Wiehe, Vernon R.
   Working with child abuse and neglect : a primer / Vernon R. Wiehe. Thousand Oaks, Calif. : Sage Publications, c1996. xiv, 245 p. ;
96-010040   616.85/8223   0761903488
   Child abuse. Child abuse -- Treatment. Child abuse -- Prevention.

RC569.5.C63.G74 1994
Greenberg, Gary,
   The self on the shelf : recovery books and the good life / Gary Greenberg. Albany : State University of New York Press, c1994. xiv, 287 p. ;
93-038024   158/.1/0973   0791420450
   Codependency literature. Interpersonal relations -- Moral and ethical aspects. Autonomy (Psychology) -- Moral and ethical aspects.

RC569.5.C63.I78 1999
Irvine, Leslie.
   Codependent forevermore : the invention of self in a twelve step group / Leslie Irvine. Chicago, Ill. : University of Chicago Press, c1999. vii, 210 p. ;
99-010350   362.2/04256   0226384713
   Codependency -- Social aspects -- United States. Self -- Social aspects. Identity (Psychology)

RC569.5.C63.R5 1995
Rice, John Steadman.
   A disease of one's own : psychotherapy, addiction, and the emergence of co-dependency / John Steadman Rice. New Brunswick, NJ : Transaction Publishers, c1996. viii, 253 p.
95-037866   616.86   1560002417
   Codependency -- Social aspects -- United States. Popular culture -- United States -- History -- 20th century. Self-actualization (Psychology) -- Social aspects -- United States. United States -- Civilization -- 1970-

RC569.5.C63.W469 1991
Whitfield, Charles L.
   Co-dependence : healing the human condition : the new paradigm for helping professionals and people in recovery / Charles L. Whitfield. Deerfield Beach, Fla. : Health Communications, Inc. c1991. viii, 327 p.
91-008606   158/.1   155874150X
   Codependency. Rehabilitation.

RC569.5.D47.W55 1998
Wilshire, Bruce W.
   Wild hunger : the primal roots of modern addiction / Bruce Wilshire. Lanham : Rowman & Littlefield Publishers, c1998. xv, 285 p. ;
98-003356   616.86   0847689670
   Dependency (Psychology). Compulsive behavior -- Psychological aspects. Senses and sensation.

RC569.5.E94.Y38 1991
Yates, Alayne.
   Compulsive exercise and the eating disorders : toward and integrated theory of activity / Alayne Yates. New York, N.Y. : Brunner/Mazel, c1991. ix, 259 p. :
90-015153   616.85/2   087630630X
   Exercise addiction. Eating disorders. Compulsive Behavior.

RC569.5.F3.A28 1988
   Abuse and victimization across the life span / edited by Martha B. Straus. Baltimore : Johns Hopkins University Press, c1988. x, 270 p. :
87-046306   616.85/82   0801836360
   Family violence. Child Abuse. Elder Abuse.

RC569.5.F3.D87 1998
Dutton, Donald G.,
   The abusive personality : violence and control in intimate relationships / Donald G. Dutton. New York : Guilford Press, c1998. ix, 214 p. :
98-023645   616.85/82   1572303700
   Abusive men -- Psychology. Object relations (Psychoanalysis) Attachment behavior.

RC569.5.F3.F35 1996
Family violence : a clinical and legal guide / edited by Sandra J. Kaplan ; with legal commentary by Howard A. Davidson. Washington, DC : American Psychiatric Press, c1996. xxi, 332 p. ;
95-000628   616.85/822   0890420106
Victims of family violence. Family violence -- Prevention. Family violence -- Law and legislation -- United States.

RC569.5.F3P787 2001
Psychological abuse in violent domestic relations / K. Daniel O'Leary and Roland D. Maiuro, editors. New York : Spring Pub. Co., c2001. xxi, 222 p. ;
          616.85/822   0826113214
Family violence--Psychological aspects. Psychological abuse.

RC569.5.H65.M35 1996
Malmquist, Carl P.
Homicide : a psychiatric perspective / Carl P. Malmquist. Washington, DC : American Psychiatric Press, c1996. xi, 395 p. :
95-011551   616.85/844   0880486902
Homicide -- Psychological aspects. Murderers -- Mental health. Mental Disorders -- psychology.

RC569.5.M8.H33 1995
Hacking, Ian.
Rewriting the soul : multiple personality and the sciences of memory / Ian Hacking. Princeton, N.J. : Princeton University Press, c1995. ix, 336 p. ;
94-041975   153.1/2   069103642X
Multiple personality -- Philosophy. Memory -- Social aspects. Multiple personality -- Social aspects.

RC569.5.M83.A38 1998
Allison, David B.
Disordered mother or disordered diagnosis? : Munchausen by proxy syndrome / David B. Allison, Mark S. Roberts. Hillsdale, NJ : Analytic Press, 1998. p. cm.
98-034172   616.85/8223   0881632902
Munchausen syndrome by proxy.

RC569.5.M83.M86 1995
Munchausen syndrome by proxy : issues in diagnosis and treatment / edited by Alex V. Levin, Mary S. Sheridan. New York : Lexington Books, c1995. xi, 479 p. :
95-003324   616.85/8223   0029186064
Munchausen syndrome by proxy. Munchausen Syndrome by Proxy -- diagnosis. Munchausen Syndrome by Proxy -- therapy.

RC569.5.S45.M54 1994
Miller, Dusty,
Women who hurt themselves : a book of hope and understanding / Dusty Miller. New York : BasicBooks, c1994. viii, 280 p.
93-047203   616.89/0082   0465092209
Self-destructive behavior. Women -- Mental health. Post-traumatic stress disorder.

RC569.5.V55.F56 1997
Flannery, Raymond B.
Violence in America : coping with drugs, distressed families, inadequate schooling, and acts of hate / Raymond B. Flannery, Jr. New York : Continuum, 1997. 167 p. ;
96-040431   155.9/2   0826410022
Violence. Violence -- United States. Violence -- United States -- Prevention.

RC569.5.V55.T62 1989
Toch, Hans.
The disturbed violent offender / Hans Toch and Kenneth Adams ; foreword by Lloyd E. Ohlin. New Haven : Yale University Press, c1989. xx, 183 p. ;
89-005771   364.3   0300045336
Violence. Prisoners -- Mental health.

RC569.5.V55.V54 1994
Violence and mental disorder : developments in risk assessment / edited by John Monahan and Henry J. Steadman. Chicago : University of Chicago Press, 1994. x, 324 p. :
93-001670   616.85/82   0226534057
Violence -- Forecasting. Insane, Criminal and dangerous. Violence -- Psychological aspects.

RC569.9-571 Neurosciences. Biological psychiatry. Neuropsychiatry — Psychiatry — Mental retardation. Developmental disabilities

RC569.9.L43 1984
Learning and cognition in the mentally retarded / edited by Penelope H. Brooks, Richard Sperber, Charley McCauley. Hillsdale, N.J. : L. Erlbaum Associates, 1984. xvii, 541 p.
84-010289   616.85/88   0898593743
Mental retardation -- Congresses.

RC569.95.L56 1989
Lindsey, Mary P.
Dictionary of mental handicap / Mary P. Lindsey. London ; Routledge, 1989. vi, 345 p. ;
89-190759   362.3/03   0415028108
Mental retardation -- Dictionaries.

RC570.C515 2002
Mental retardation : definition, classification, and systems of supports. 10th ed. Washington, DC : American Association on Mental Retardation, c2002. p. cm.
          616.85/88/0012   0940898810
Mental retardation--Classification.

RC570.Z54 1986
Zigler, Edward,
Understanding mental retardation / Edward Zigler and Robert M. Hodapp. Cambridge ; Cambridge University Press, 1986. xii, 292 p. :
85-031444   616.85/88   0521318785
Mental retardation. Mental Retardation.

RC570.2.R53 1996
Richardson, Stephen A.
  Twenty-two years : causes and consequences of mental retardation / Stephen A. Richardson and Helene Koller. Cambridge, Mass. : Harvard University Press, 1996. xvii, 328 p.
96-028834   616.85/88071   0674212975
  Mental retardation -- Etiology. Mental retardation -- Complications.

RC570.5.U6.S34 1987
Scheerenberger, R. C.
  A history of mental retardation : a quarter century of promise / R.C. Scheerenberger. Baltimore : P.H. Brookes Pub. Co., c1987. xv, 318 p. :
87-000675   362.3/8/0973   093371680X
  Mental retardation -- United States -- History -- 20th century. Mentally handicapped -- Services for -- United States -- History -- 20th century. Mentally handicapped -- Services for -- Government policy -- United States -- History -- 20th century.

RC571.G5
Gibson, David,
  Down's syndrome : the psychology of mongolism / David Gibson. Cambridge ; Cambridge University Press, 1978. xiii, 366 p.
77-087381   616.8/58842   0521219140
  Down syndrome.

RC584-596 Specialities of internal medicine — Immunologic diseases — Allergy. Hypersensitivity, Immediate and delayed

RC584.A3443 2002
  Allergies sourcebook :basic consumer health information about allergic disorders, triggers, reactions, and related symptoms, including anaphylaxis ... / edited by Annemarie S. Muth. 2nd ed. Detroit, MI : Omnigraphics, c2002. xv, 598 p. ;
          616.97   0780803760
  Allergy--Popular works.

RC584.A44 1998
  Allergy :principles & practice / edited by Elliott Middleton, Jr ... [et al.]. 5th ed. St. Louis : Mosby, c1998. 2 v. (xxix, 1249, [70] p.) :
          616.97   0815100728
  Allergy. Hypersensitivity.

RC585.N38 2001
Lipkowitz, Myron A.
  Encyclopedia of allergies / Myron A. Lipkowitz, Tova Navarra. 2nd ed. New York, N.Y. : Facts On File, c2001. xii, 340 p. ;
          616.97/003   081604404X
  Allergy--Encyclopedias.

RC585.R275 1997
Radetsky, Peter.
  Allergic to the twentieth century : the explosion in environmental allergies, from sick buildings to multiple chemical sensitivity / Peter Radetsky. Boston : Little, Brown, 1997. 264 p. ;
96-040192   616.97   0316732214
  Allergy. Environmentally induced diseases. Toxicology.

RC591.A84 2000
  Asthma sourcebook : basic comnsumer health information about asthma, including symptoms, traditional and nontraditional remedies ... / edited by Annemarie S. Muth. Detroit, Mich. : Omnigraphics, c2000. xiii, 627 p.
00-063716   616.2/38   0780803817
  Asthma -- Popular works.

RC591.B765 1994
Brookes, Tim.
  Catching my breath : an asthmatic explores his illness / Tim Brookes. New York : Times Books, c1994. xii, 291 p. ;
93-044737   616.2/38   0812921828
  Asthma.

RC591.L54 1999
Lieberman, Phil L.
  Understanding asthma / Phil Lieberman. Jackson : University Press of Mississippi, c1999. x, 124 p. :
99-013753   616.2/38   1578061415
  Asthma -- Popular works.

RC591.R56 1997
  The rising trends in asthma. Chichester, England ; Wiley, 1997. ix, 280 p. :
96-040339   616.2/38   0471970123
  Asthma -- Congresses. Asthma -- immunology -- congresses. Asthma -- epidemiology -- congresses.

RC596.A45 1984
  Adverse reactions to foods : American Academy of Allergy and Immunology Committee on Adverse Reactions to Foods, National Institute of Allergy and Infectious Disease. [Bethesda, Md.?] : U.S. Dept. of Health and Human Services, Public 1984. xv, 220, 101
84-603142   616.97/5
  Food allergy.

RC607 Specialities of internal medicine — Immunologic diseases — Immunodeficiency

RC607.A26.A34523 1996
  AIDS, a moral issue : the ethical, legal, and social aspects / edited by Brenda Almond. New York : St. Martin's Press, 1996. x, 162 p. ;
96-010822   362.1/969792   0312161522
  AIDS (Disease) -- Social aspects. AIDS (Disease) -- Moral and ethical aspects.

RC607.A26A3478 1999
The AIDS knowledge base :a textbook on HIV disease from the University of California, San Francisco and San Francisco General Hospital / editors, P.T. Cohen, Merle A. Sande, Paul A. Volberding ; associate editors, Dennis H. Osmond ... [et al.]. 3rd ed. Philadelphia, PA : Lippincott, Williams and Wilkins,, 1999. xxiii, 966 p., 29 col. plates :
616.97/92   0316149039
AIDS (Disease)

RC607.A26A3573 1999
AIDS sourcebook :basic consumer health information about acquired immune deficiency syndrome (AIDS) and human immunodeficiency virus (HIV) infection, featuring updated statistical data, reports on recent research and prevention initiatives, and other s edited by Karen Bellenir. 2nd ed. Detroit, Mich : Omnigraphics, 1999. xiii, 751 p. :
362.1/969792   078080225X
AIDS (Disease)

RC607.A26.A97 1996
Ayala, Victor.
Falling through the cracks : AIDS and the urban poor / Victor Ayala. Bayside, NY : Social Change Press, c1996. xviii, 125 p.
95-070518   362.1/969792   0964443708
AIDS (Disease) -- Social aspects. Poor -- Social conditions.

RC607.A26.C34 1993
Cameron, Miriam.
Living with AIDS : experiencing ethical problems / Miriam E. Cameron. Newbury Park : Sage Publications, c1993. xx, 251 p. :
93-025063   362.1/969792   080394778X
AIDS (Disease) -- Moral and ethical aspects.

RC607.A26.D56 1991
A Disease of society : cultural and institutional responses to AIDS / edited by Dorothy Nelkin, David P. Willis, Scott V. Parris. Cambridge [England] ; Cambridge University Press, 1991. vii, 287 p. ;
90-015071   362.1/969792   0521404118
AIDS (Disease) -- Social aspects.

RC607.A26.H38 1996
Haver, William Wendell,
The body of this death : historicity and sociality in the time of AIDS / William Haver. Stanford, Calif. : Stanford University Press, c1996. xviii, 221 p.
96-000856   306.4/61   0804727163
AIDS (Disease) -- Philosophy. AIDS (Disease) -- Social aspects.

RC607.A26.H5688 1998
HIV and community mental healthcare / edited by Michael D. Knox and Caroline H. Sparks. Baltimore : Johns Hopkins University Press, 1998. xv, 300 p. :
97-024462   362.1/969792/0019
0801858038
AIDS (Disease) -- Psychological aspects. Community mental health services. HIV Infections -- psychology.

RC607.A26.H5716 1999
HIV homecare handbook / Barbara Daigle ... [et al.]. Sudbury, Mass. : Jones and Bartlett, c1999. xvi, 382 p. :
98-043154   362.1/969792   0763707031
AIDS (Disease) -- Patients -- Home care -- Handbooks, manuals, etc. Home nursing -- Handbooks, manuals, etc.

RC607.A26.H5763 1997
HIV mental health for the 21st century / edited by Mark G. Winiarski. New York : New York University Press, c1997. xxxiv, 357 p.
96-035695   362.1/969792/0019
0814793126
AIDS (Disease) -- Patients -- Mental health.

RC607.A26.H8955 2000
Huber, Jeffrey T.
Encyclopedic dictionary of AIDS-related terminology / Jeffrey T. Huber, Mary L. Gillaspy. New York : Haworth Information Press, c2000. v, 246 p. ;
00-038919   616.97/92   0789012073
AIDS (Disease) -- Dictionaries.

RC607.A26.H896 1996
Huber, Jeffrey T.
HIV/AIDS and HIV/AIDS-related terminology : a means of organizing the body of knowledge / Jeffrey T. Huber, Mary L. Gillaspy. New York : Haworth Press, c1996. ix, 107 p. ;
96-001981   616.97/92/0014   1560249706
AIDS (Disease) -- Terminology. HIV infections -- Terminology. Subject headings -- HIV infections.

RC607.A26.J654 1995
Johnston, William I.
HIV-negative : how the uninfected are affected by AIDS / William I. Johnston ; foreword by Eric E. Rofes. New York : Plenum Press, c1995. xii, 332 p. ;
95-006962   155.9/16   0306449471
AIDS (Disease) -- Psychological aspects. Gay men. AIDS phobia.

RC607.A26K356 1998
Kalichman, Seth C.
Understanding AIDS : advances in research and treatment / Seth C. Kalichman. 2nd ed. Washington, DC : American Psychological Association, c1998. xviii, 509 p. :
616.97/92/0019   1557985308
AIDS (Disease) AIDS (Disease)--Psychological aspects. AIDS (Disease)--Social aspects.

RC607.A26.K5753 1998
Klein, Sandra Jacoby.
Heavenly hurts : surviving AIDS-related deaths and losses / Sandra Jacoby Klein. Amityville, N.Y. : Baywood Pub. Co., c1998. x, 153 p. ;
97-020522   362.1/969792/0019
0895031817
AIDS (Disease) -- Psychological aspects. AIDS (Disease) -- Patients -- Death. Bereavement.

RC607.A26.K5755 1997
Klitzman, Robert.
Being positive : the lives of men and women with HIV / Robert Klitzman. Chicago : Ivan R. Dee, 1997. xii, 244 p. ;
97-016116   362.1/969792   1566631645
HIV infections -- Psychological aspects. HIV-positive persons.

RC607.A26.K83 1987
Kubler-Ross, Elisabeth.
AIDS : the ultimate challenge / Elisabeth Kubler-Ross. New York : Macmillan, c1987. xii, 329 p. ;
87-024016   362.1/969792/00973
0025671707
AIDS (Disease) -- Palliative treatment. AIDS (Disease) -- Psychological aspects. Terminal care.

RC607.A26.L377 1997
Lather, Patricia Ann,
Troubling the angels : women living with HIV/AIDS / Patti Lather and Chris Smithies. Boulder, Colo. : Westview Press, 1997. p. cm.
97-003989   362.1/969792/0082
0813390176
AIDS (Disease) in women -- Sex factors.

RC607.A26.P686 1996
Powell, Josh.
AIDS and HIV-related diseases : an educational guide for professionals and the public / Josh Powell ; foreword by Amy Bourdeau. New York : Insight Books, c1996. xiii, 246 p.
96-029019   616.97/92   0306450852
AIDS (Disease) HIV infections. Health education.

RC607.A26.R65 1993
Root-Bernstein, Robert Scott.
Rethinking AIDS : the tragic cost of premature consensus / Robert S. Root-Bernstein. New York : Free Press ; c1993. xvii, 512 p.
92-026843   616.97/92071   0029269059
AIDS (Disease) -- Etiology. HIV infections. HIV (Viruses)

RC607.A26.S3738 1999
Schoub, B. D.
AIDS & HIV in perspective : a guide to understanding the virus and its consequences / Barry D. Schoub. Cambridge ; Cambridge University Press, 1999. xix, 274 p. :
98-011707   616.97/92   052162150X
AIDS (Disease) Acquired Immunodeficiency Syndrome. HIV Infections.

RC607.A26S75 1998
Stine, Gerald James.
Acquired immune deficiency syndrome : biological, medical, social, and legal issues / Gerald J. Stine. 3rd ed. Upper Saddle River, N.J. : Prentice Hall, c1998. xxx, 610 p. :
          362.1/969792   0137899912
AIDS (Disease) Acquired Immunodeficiency Syndrome. AIDS-Related Opportunistic Infections.

RC607.A26.T73 1997
Treating the psychological consequences of HIV / Michael F. O'Connor, editor ; Irvin D. Yalom, general editor. San Francisco : Jossey-Bass Publishers, c1997. xxxiv, 361 p.
96-031519   616.97/92/0019   0787903140
HIV infections -- Psychological aspects.

RC607.A26.W383 1998
Watstein, Sarah.
The AIDS dictionary / Sarah Barbara Watstein, with Karen Chandler. New York : Facts on File, c1998. ix, 340 p. ;
97-008114   616.97/92/003   0816031495
AIDS (Disease) -- Dictionaries.

RC621 Specialities of internal medicine — Immunologic diseases — Examination Diagnosis

RC621.G52 1990
Gibson, Rosalind S.
Principles of nutritional assessment / Rosalind S. Gibson. New York : Oxford University Press, 1990. xvi, 691 p. :
89-003411   613.2   0195058380
Nutrition -- Evaluation.

RC622 Specialities of internal medicine — Immunologic diseases — Nutritionally induced diseases

RC622.N8932 1996
Nutritional concerns of women / edited by Ira Wolinsky, Dorothy Klimis-Tavantzis. Boca Raton : CRC Press, c1996. 335 p. :
95-042174   616/.0082   0849385024
Nutritionally induced diseases -- Sex factors. Women -- Nutrition. Women -- Diseases.

RC627 Specialities of internal medicine — Nutritional diseases — Special diseases, states, and factors in disease, A-Z

RC627.B45.C37 2000
Carpenter, Kenneth J.
Beriberi, white rice, and vitamin B : a disease, a cause, and a cure / Kenneth J. Carpenter. Berkeley, CA : University of California Press, c2000. xiv, 282 p. :
99-053339   616.3/92/009   0520220536
Beri-beri -- History. Vitamin B1 -- History.

RC627.S36.C36 1986
Carpenter, Kenneth J.
The history of scurvy and vitamin C / Kenneth J. Carpenter. Cambridge ; Cambridge University Press, 1986. viii, 288 p.
85-025464   616.3/94/009   0521320291
Scurvy -- History. Vitamin C -- History. Ascorbic Acid -- history.

RC627.S36.C87 1994
Cuppage, Francis E.
 James Cook and the conquest of scurvy / Francis E. Cuppage. Westport, Conn. : Greenwood Press, 1994. ix, 163 p. :
94-003050   616.3/94/009   0313291810
Cook, James, -- 1728-1779 -- Journeys. Scurvy -- History -- 18th century.

RC628 Specialities of internal medicine — Metabolic diseases — Obesity

RC628.O297 2001
 Obesity sourcebook :basic consumer health information about diseases and other problems associated with obesity ... / edited by Wilma Caldwell and Chad T. Kimball. 1st ed. Detroit, MI : Omnigraphics, c2001. xii, 376 p. :
    616.3/98   0780803337
Obesity--Popular works.

RC628.P496 2000
 Physical activity and obesity / Claude Bouchard, editor. Champaign, IL : Human Kinetics, c2000. vii, 400 p. :
99-088071   616.3/98   0880119098
Obesity. Exercise -- Physiological aspects.

RC629 Specialities of internal medicine — Metabolic diseases — Gout

RC629.P67 1998
Porter, Roy,
 Gout : the patrician malady / Roy Porter and G.S. Rousseau . New Haven, Conn : Yale University Press, 1998. xiv, 393 p. :
98-016881   616.3/999/009   0300073860
Gout -- History.

RC630 Specialities of internal medicine — Metabolic diseases — Water, Electrolyte, and acid-base disorders

RC630.L68 1992
Lowenstein, Jerome.
 Acid and basics : a guide to understanding acid-base disorders / Jerome Lowenstein ; illustrations by Ronald Markman. New York : Oxford University Press, 1993. xii, 154 p. :
92-016192   616.3/9   0195075722
Acid base imbalances. Acid-Base Equilibrium. Acid-Base Imbalance.

RC630.R67 2001
Rose, Burton David,
 Clinical physiology of acid-base and electrolyte disorders / Burton David Rose, Theodore W. Post. 5th ed. New York : McGraw-Hill, Medical Pub. Division, c2001. x, 992 p. :
    616.3/992   0071346821
Acid-base imbalances. Water-electrolyte imbalances. Kidneys--Pathophysiology.

RC632 Specialities of internal medicine — Metabolic diseases — Other metabolic diseases, A-Z

RC632.H83.B97 1991
Byrne, Kevin P.,
 Understanding and managing cholesterol : a guide for wellness professionals / Kevin P. Byrne. Champaign, Ill. : Human Kinetics Books, c1991. ix, 334 p. :
90-005195   616.1/360654   0873223098
Hypercholesteremia -- Diet therapy. Hypercholesteremia -- Prevention. Atherosclerosis -- Etiology.

RC641.7 Specialities of internal medicine — Diseases of the blood and blood-forming organs — Anemia

RC641.7.H35D575 2001
 Disorders of hemoglobin : genetics, pathophysiology, and clinical management / edited by Martin H. Steinberg ... [et al.]. Cambridge ; Cambridge University Press, 2001. xiv, 1268 p. ;
    616.1/51   0521632668
Hemoglobinopathy. Hemoglobinopathies. Anemia, Sickle Cell.

RC641.7.S5.B56 1995
Bloom, Miriam.
 Understanding sickle cell disease / Miriam Bloom. Jackson : University Press of Mississippi, c1995. x, 126 p. :
94-044275   616.1/527   0878057447
Sickle cell anemia -- Popular works.

RC641.7.S5.S55 1992
 Sickle cell disease : pathophysiology, diagnosis, and management / edited by Vipul N. Mankad and R. Blaine Moore. Westport, Conn. : Praeger, 1992. x, 413 p. :
91-032168   616.1/527   027592503X
Sickle cell anemia. Anemia, Sickle Cell -- diagnosis. Anemia, Sickle Cell -- physiopathology.

RC642 Specialities of internal medicine — Diseases of the blood and blood-forming organs — Hemophilia

RC642.R47 1999
Resnik, Susan,
 Blood saga : hemophilia, AIDS, and the survival of a community / Susan Resnik. Berkeley : University of California Press, c1999. xvi, 292 p. :
98-014150   362.1/961572/00973
0520211952
Hemophilia -- United States -- History.

RC648-661 Specialities of internal medicine — Diseases of the endocrine glands. Clinical endocrinology

RC648.T48 2002
Williams textbook of endocrinology / P. Reed Larsen ... [et al.]. 10th ed. Philadelphia : W.B. Saunders, 2002. p. cm.
616.4   0721691846
Endocrinology. Endocrine glands--Diseases.

RC660.C4746 2001
Colberg, Sheri R.,
The diabetic athlete / Sheri R. Colberg. Champaign, IL : Human Kinetics, c2001. x, 261 p. :
00-031907   616.4/62/0088796
0736032711
Diabetic athletes. Diabetes -- Exercise therapy.

RC660.D542 2003
Ellenberg and Rifkin's diabetes mellitus :theory and practice. 6th ed. / edited by Daniel Porte, Jr., Robert S. Sherwin, Alain New York : McGraw-Hill, Health Professions Division, c2003. p. ;
616.4/62   0838521789
Diabetes. Diabetes Mellitus.

RC660.4.M37 2001
Mayo Clinic on managing diabetes / Maria Collazo-Clavell, editor in chief. 1st ed. Rochester, Minn. : Mayo Clinic, c2001. ix, 194 p. :
616.4/62   1893005062
Diabetes--Popular works. Diabetes Mellitus--Popular Works.

RC661.E94
The health professional's guide to diabetes and exercise / editors, Neil Ruderman, John T. Devlin. Alexandria, VA : American Diabetes Association, c1995. xiii, 335 p.
95-031497   616.4/620624   094544852X
Diabetes -- Exercise therapy -- Handbooks, manuals, etc. Diabetes Mellitus -- therapy -- handbooks. Exercise Therapy -- handbooks.

RC666.5 Specialities of internal medicine — Diseases of the circulatory (cardiovascular) system — History

RC666.5.B56 1999
Cardiology :the evolution of the science and the art / edited by Richard J. Bing. 2nd ed. New Brunswick, N.J. : Rutgers University Press, c1999. xiv, 360 p. :
616.1/2/009   0813526280
Cardiology--History. Cardiology--history. Physicians--biography.

RC667 Specialities of internal medicine — Diseases of the circulatory (cardiovascular) system — General works

RC667.H88 2001
Hurst's The heart / editors, Valentin Fuster ... [et al.]. 10th ed. New York : McGraw-Hill Health Professions Division, c2001. p. ;
616.1   0071356940
Cardiovascular system--Diseases. Heart--Diseases. Cardiovascular Diseases.

RC667.T44 2002
Textbook of cardiovascular medicine / editor, Eric J. Topol ; associate editors, Robert M. Califf ... [et al.]. 2nd ed. Philadelphia : Lippincott Williams & Wilkins, 2002. p. ;
616.16   0781732255
Cardiology. Cardiovascular system--Diseases. Cardiovascular Diseases.

RC672 Specialities of internal medicine — Diseases of the circulatory (cardiovascular) system — Popular works

RC672.H396 2000
Heart diseases and disorders sourcebook : basic consumer health information about heart attacks, angina, rhythm disorders, heart failure, valve disease, congenital heart disorders, and more ... / edited by Karen Bellenir. 2nd ed. Detroit, MI : Omnigraphics, c2000. xiii, 612 p. :
616.1/2   0780802381
Heart--Diseases--Popular works.

RC681-685 Specialities of internal medicine — Diseases of the circulatory (cardiovascular) system — Diseases of the heart

RC681.C56
Willius, Frederick A.
Classics of cardiology : a collection of classic works on the heart and circulation with comprehensive biographic accounts of the authors / by Fredrick A. Willius and Thomas E. Keys. New York : H. Schuman : 1961, c1941. 2 v. :
62005604
Cardiovascular system -- collected works.

RC681.H362 1997
Heart disease :a textbook of cardiovascular medicine / edited by Eugene Braunwald. 5th ed. Philadelphia : Saunders, c1997. xxviii, 1996, [56] p. :
616.1/2   0721656668
Heart--Diseases. Cardiovascular system--Diseases. Heart Diseases.

RC682.W65 1998
Women, stress, and heart disease / edited by Kristina Orth-Gomer, Margaret Chesney, Nanette K. Wenger. Mahwah, N.J. : Lawrence Erlbaum Associates, 1998. xiv, 298 p. :
97-044966   616.1/2/0082   0805821244
Heart diseases in women -- Risk factors. Women -- Health and hygiene. Stress (Psychology)

RC683.5.E94
Froelicher, Victor F.
　Exercise and the heart / Victor F. Froelicher, Jonathan N. Myers. Philadelphia : W.B. Saunders Co., c2000. viii, 456 p.
99-026385　　　　616.1/20754　　　0721684505
　Exercise tests. Heart function tests. Heart -- Diseases -- Diagnosis.

RC684.E4
Drake, James W.
　Automated external defibrillation / James W. Drake. Upper Saddle River, NJ : Brady/Prentice Hall Health, c2000. vi, 121 p. :
99-038345　　　　616.1/23025　　　0130843830
　Electric countershock. Defibrillators. Cardiac arrest.

RC684.P3
Greatbatch, Wilson.
　The making of the pacemaker : celebrating a lifesaving invention / Wilson Greatbatch ; foreword by Seymour Furman. Amherst, N.Y. : Prometheus Books, 2000. 260 p. :
00-023296　　　617.4/120645/09　　1573928062
　Cardiac pacemakers -- History.

RC685.C6.K53 2000
Klaidman, Stephen.
　Saving the heart : the battle to conquer coronary disease / Stephen Klaidman. Oxford ; Oxford University Press, 2000. xvi, 272 p. :
99-028930　　　　617.4/12059　　　0195112792
　Coronary heart disease -- Treatment -- History. Coronary heart disease -- Surgery -- History. Thoracic Surgery -- Biography.

RC685.H8.P34 1992
　Pathophysiology of hypertension in Blacks / edited by John C.S. Fray, Janice G. Douglas. New York : Published for the American Physiological Society 1993. xvi, 299 p. :
92-018761　　　　616.1/32/008996073
0195067207
　Hypertension -- Pathophysiology. Afro-Americans -- Diseases. Blacks -- Diseases.

RC731-774 Specialities of internal medicine — Diseases of the respiratory system

RC731.R468 1995
　Respiratory diseases and disorders sourcebook : basic information about respiratory diseases and disorders including asthma, cystic fibrosis, pneumonia, the common cold, influenza, and others, featu edited by Allan R. Cook and Peter D. Dresser. Detroit, MI : Omnigraphics, 1995. xiii, 771 p.
95-019214　　　　616.2　　　0780800370
　Respiratory organs -- Diseases.

RC733.D44 1998
Derickson, Alan.
　Black lung : anatomy of a public health disaster / Alan Derickson. Ithaca : Cornell University Press, 1998. xiv, 237 p. :
98-013612　　　　616.2/44　　　0801431867
　Lungs -- Dust diseases -- United States -- History. Coal miners -- United States -- Health and hygiene. Coal miners -- Legal status, laws, etc. -- United States.

RC735.I5.R4728 1999
Cairo, Jimmy M.
　Mosby's respiratory care equipment. St. Louis : Mosby, c1999. xxiv, 763 p.
98-055692　　　615.8/36/028　　　0815121482
　Respiratory therapy -- Equipment and supplies. Respiratory intensive care -- Equipment and supplies. Respiratory Therapy -- instrumentation.

RC756.T48 1998
　Textbook of pulmonary diseases / edited by Gerald L. Baum ... [et al.]. 6th ed. Philadelphia : Lippincott-Raven, 1998- 2 v. (xviii, 1503, 38 p.) :
　　　　　　616.2/4　　　0316084344
　Lungs--Diseases. Pleura--Diseases Lung Diseases.

RC774.R67 1991
Rosner, David,
　Deadly dust : silicosis and the politics of occupational disease in twentieth-century America / David Rosner and Gerald Markowitz. Princeton, N.J. : Princeton University Press, c1991. xiii, 229 p.
90-009218　　　　616.2/44　　　0691047588
　Silicosis -- United States. Occupational diseases -- Social aspects -- United States. Occupational diseases -- Political aspects -- United States.

RC801-862 Specialities of internal medicine — Diseases of the digestive system

RC801.G384 2002
　Sleisenger & Fordtran's gastrointestinal and liver disease : pathophy 7th ed. Lawrence S. Friedman, Marvin H. Sleisenger. Philadelphia : Saunders, c2002. 2 v. (xli, 2385, 98 p.) :
　　　　　　616.3/3　　　0721689736
　Gastrointestinal system--Diseases. Liver--Diseases. Gastrointestinal Diseases.

RC802.9.G368 1999
　Gastrointestinal pathology : an atlas and text / Cecilia M. Fenoglio-Preiser ... [et al.] ; drawings by Amy E. Noffsinger, drawings from the first edition by Michael Norviel 2nd ed. Philadelphia : Lippincott-Raven, c1999. xiii, 1296 p. :
　　　　　　616.3/307　　　0397516401
　Gastrointestinal system--Diseases. Gastrointestinal system--Histopathology--Atlases. Gastrointestinal Diseases--pathology.

RC815.S452 1999
Scully, Crispian.
   Oral disease / Crispian Scully, Roderick A. Cawson. 2nd ed. Edinburgh ; Churchill Livingstone, 1999. 170 p. :
               617.5/22   044306170X
   Oral medicine--Atlases. Mouth--Diseases--Atlases. Mouth Diseases--atlases.

RC815.W66 1997
Wood, Norman K.
   Differential diagnosis of oral and maxillofacial lesions / Norman K. Wood, Paul W. Goaz. 5th ed. St. Louis : Mosby, c1997. xii, 656 p. :
               616.3/1075   0815194323
   Mouth--Diseases--Diagnosis. Face--Diseases--Diagnosis. Maxilla--Diseases--Diagnosis.

RC848.H425.T87 1998
Turkington, Carol.
   Hepatitis C : the silent killer / Carol Turkington. Lincolnwood, Ill. : Contemporary Books, c1998. xviii, 188 p.
97-053202   616.3/623   0809229587
   Hepatitis C -- Popular works.

RC862.I53.Z66 2000
Zonderman, Jon.
   Understanding Crohn disease and ulcerative colitis / Jon Zonderman and Ronald Vender. Jackson, Miss. : University Press of Mississippi c2000. xiv, 116 p. :
99-052483   616.3/44   1578062020
   Inflammatory bowel diseases -- Popular works.

RC871 Specialties of internal medicine — Diseases of the genitourinary system. Urology — General works

RC871.C33 2002
   Campbell's urology / B. Retik editor-in-chief, Patrick C. Walsh ; editors, Alan ... [et al.] 8th ed. Philadelphia, PA : Saunders, c2002. 4 v (xl, 3954, 128 p.) :
               616.5   0721690580
   Urology.

RC883-889 Specialities of internal medicine — Diseases of the genitourinary system. Urology — Diseases and functional disorders of the genital organs (General and male). Andrology

RC883.D695 1998
Dreger, Alice Domurat.
   Hermaphrodites and the medical invention of sex / Alice Domurat Dreger. Cambridge, Mass. : Harvard University Press, 1998. xiii, 268 p.
97-040487   616.6/94   0674089278
   Hermaphroditism -- Treatment -- France -- History -- 19th century. Hermaphroditism -- Treatment -- Great Britain -- History -- 19th century. Hermaphroditism -- Treatment -- France -- History -- 20th century.

RC889.G665 2002
Gordon, John D.
   Handbook for clinical gynecologic endocrinology and infertility / John David Gordon, Leon Speroff. Philadelphia, PA : Lippincott Williams & Wilkins, c2002. p. ;
               618.1   078173164X
   Infertility--Handbooks, manuals, etc. Endocrine gynecology--Handbooks, manuals, etc. Genital Diseases, Female--Handbooks.

RC889.I556 1997
   Infertility :a comprehensive text / [edited by] Machelle M. Seibel.2nd ed. Stamford, CT : Appleton & Lange, c1997. xviii, 903 p. :
               616.6/92   0838542581
   Infertility. Infertility.

RC889.M368 1996
Marsh, Margaret S.,
   The empty cradle : infertility in America from Colonial times to the present / Margaret Marsh and Wanda Ronner. Baltimore : Johns Hopkins University Press, c1996. 326 p. :
95-035525   616.6/92/00973   0801852285
   Infertility -- United States -- History. Childlessness -- United States -- History. Motherhood -- United States -- History.

RC924.5 Specialities of internal medicine — Diseases of the genitourinary system. Urology — Diseases of the connective tissues

RC924.5.L85.W35 2000
Wallace, Daniel J.
   The lupus book : a guide for patients and their families / Daniel J. Wallace. New York : Oxford University Press, c2000. xii, 271 p. :
99-013841   616.7/7   0195132815
   Systemic lupus erythematosus -- Popular works.

RC925 Specialities of internal medicine — Diseases of the muscuskeletal system — Societies. Serials

RC925.D535 2001
   Disorders of voluntary muscle / edited by George Karpati, David Hilton-Jones, and Robert C. Griggs ; foreword by Lord Walton of Detchant. 7th ed. Cambridge ; Cambridge University Press, c2001. xiv, 775 p. :
               616.7/4   0521650623
   Muscles--Diseases. Muscular Diseases. Muscle, Skeletal--physiopathology.

RC925.5-933 Specialities of internal medicine — Diseases of the musculoskeletal system

RC925.5.E39 1994
Edwardson, Barbara M.,
   Musculoskeletal disorders : common problems / Barbara M. Edwardson. San Diego, Calif. : Singular Pub. Group, c1995. xv, 301 p. :
94-031570   616.7   156593170X
   Musculoskeletal system -- Diseases -- Physical therapy. Musculosketal Diseases -- therapy. Musculosketal Diseases -- diagnosis.

RC927.3.W53 1996
Williamson, Miryam Ehrlich.
Fibromyalgia : a comprehensive approach : what you can do about chronic pain and fatigue / Miryam Ehrlich Williamson ; foreword by David A. Nye. New York : Walker and Co., 1996. x, 216 p. :
96-003251   616.7/4   0802774849
Fibromyalgia -- Popular works.

RC930.S47 1998
Siegel, Irwin M., 1927-
All about bone : an owner's manual / Irwin M. Siegel. New York : Demos, 1998. p. cm.
98-009675   616.7/1   1888799161
Bones -- Diseases -- Popular works. Musculoskeletal system -- Diseases -- Popular works. Orthopedics -- Popular works.

RC933.A64 2001
Arthritis and allied conditions :a textbook of rheumatology. 14th ed. / [edited by] William J. Koopman ; with a foreword by Daneil Baltimore : Williams & Wilkins, c2001. 2 v. :
616.7/22   0781722403
Rheumatology. Arthritis. Arthritis.

RC952 Special situations and conditions — Geriatrics — General works

RC952.C53 1999
Reichel's care of the elderly :clinical aspects of aging / editors, Joseph J. Gallo ... [et al.]. 5th ed. Philadelphia : Williams & Wilkins, 1999. xxvii, 856 p. :
618.97   0683301691
Geriatrics. Aging. Geriatrics.

RC952.G393 2002
Geriatric medicine :an evidence-based approach / editors, Christine K. Cassel ... [et al.]. 4th ed. New York : Springer, c2002. p. ;
618.97   0387955143
Geriatrics. Evidence-based medicine. Geriatrics.

RC952.G54 1994
Gillick, Muriel R.,
Choosing medical care in old age : what kind, how much, wh4n to stop / Muriel R. Gillick. Cambridge, Mass. : Harvard University Press, 1994. ix, 213 p. ;
94-011333   362.1/9897   0674128125
Aged -- Medical care.

RC952.5 Special situations and conditions — Geriatrics — General special

RC952.5.E58 1996
Encyclopedia of gerontology : age, aging, and the aged / editor-in-chief, James E. Birren. San Diego : Academic Press, c1996. 2 v. :
95-047195   612.6/7/03   0122268601
Geriatrics -- Encyclopedias. Gerontology -- Encyclopedias. Geriatrics -- encyclopedias.

RC952.5.P48 1999
Physical and mental issues in aging sourcebook : basic consumer health information on physical and mental disorders associated with the aging process, including concerns about cardiovascular disease edited by Jenifer Swanson. Detroit, MI. : Omnigraphics, 1999. xiii, 660 p.
99-015540   618.97   0780802330
Geriatrics -- Popular works. Aged -- Diseases -- Popular works.

RC953 Special situations and conditions — Geriatrics — Handbooks, manuals, etc.

RC953.G34 2000
Handbook of geriatric assessment / Joseph J. Gallo ...[et al.].3rd ed. Gaithersburg, Md. : Aspen, c2000. x, 361 p. ;
618.97/075   083421248X
Aged--Diseases--Diagnosis--Handbooks, manuals, etc. Aged--Psychological testing--Handbooks, manuals, etc. Aged--Care--Handbooks, manuals, etc.

RC953.5 Special situations and conditions — Geriatrics — Therapeutics

RC953.5.F86 2001
Functional performance in older adults / [edited by] Bette R. Bonder, 2nd ed. Philadelphia : F.A. Davis, c2001. xxxi, 544 p. :
612.6/7   0803605439
Aged--Rehabilitation. Aging. Aging--physiology.

RC954 Special situations and conditions — Geriatrics — Nursing

RC954.E53 2001
The encyclopedia of elder care :the comprehensive resource on geriatric and social care / Mathy D. Mezey, editor-in-chief ; Barbara J. Berkman ... [et al.], associate editors ; Melissa M. Bottrell, managing editor. New York : Springer Pub., c2001. xl, 783 p. ;
362.1/9897   0826113680
Geriatric nursing--Encyclopedias. Aged--Care--Encyclopedias. Aged--Medical care--Encyclopedias.

RC954.G4735 2000
Gerontologic nursing / [edited by] Annette G. Lueckenotte.2nd ed. St. Louis : Mosby, c2000. xxix, 846 p. :
610.73/65   0323007570
Geriatric nursing. Geriatric Nursing. Aged--psychology.

RC954.H575 1999
Home care of the elderly / [edited by] Sheryl Mara Zang, Judith A. Allender. Philadelphia : Lippincott, c1999. xx, 524 p. :
610.73/65   0781715423
Geriatric nursing. Home nursing. Aged--Home care.

RC954.3 Special situations and conditions — Geriatrics — Hospital and nursing home care

RC954.3.L66 1995
Long-term care decisions : ethical and conceptual dimensions / edited by Laurence B. McCullough and Nancy L. Wilson. Baltimore : Johns Hopkins University Press, 1995. xiv, 246 p. :
94-037416   362.1/6/0846   0801849934
Aged -- Long-term care -- Moral and ethical aspects -- Congresses. Long-term care of the sick -- Moral and ethical aspects -- Congresses. Long-Term Care -- in old age -- congresses.

RC961 Special situations and conditions — Tropical medicine — General works

RC961.C87 1989
Curtin, Philip D.
Death by migration : Europe's encounter with the tropical world in the nineteenth century / Philip D. Curtin. Cambridge [England] ; Cambridge University Press, 1989. xix, 251 p. :
89-031414   614.4/0913   0521371627
Tropical medicine -- History. Soldiers -- India -- Mortality. Soldiers -- Algeria -- Mortality.

RC961.H84 2000
Hunter's tropical medicine and emerging infectious disease. 8th ed. / [edited by] G. Thomas Strickland ; associate editors, Alan Philadelphia : Saunders, c2000. xxviii, 1192 p. :
          616.9/883   0721662234
Tropical medicine. Tropical Medicine.

RC962 Special situations and conditions — Tropical medicine — By region or country, A-Z

RC962.G7.C66 1992
Cook, G. C.
From the Greenwich hulks to old St. Pancras : a history of tropical disease in London / G.C. Cook. London ; Athlone Press, 1992. xiii, 338 p.
92-010542   616.9/883/09421   0485114119
Tropical medicine -- England -- London -- History. Tropical Medicine -- history.

RC963 Special situations and conditions — Industrial medicine — General works

RC963.A3C66 1999
Confer, Robert G.
Occupational health and safety : terms, definitions, and abbreviations / Robert G. Confer, Thomas R. Confer. 2nd ed. Boca Raton, FL : Lewis Publishers, c1999. 275 p. ;
          616.9/803/03   1566703611
Industrial hygiene--Dictionaries. Industrial safety--Dictionaries.

RC963.O22 2000
Occupational health : recognizing and preventing work-related disease and injury / editors, Barry S. Levy, David H. Wegman. Philadelphia : Lippincott Williams & Wilkins, c2000. xxi, 842 p. :
99-035194   616.9/803   0781719542
Medicine, Industrial. Occupational Diseases -- prevention & control. Occupational Health.

RC963.6 Special situations and conditions — Industrial medicine — By age group, class, etc., A-Z

RC963.6.A78.R67 1994
Rossol, Monona.
The artist's complete health & safety guide / Monona Rossol. New York : Allworth Press, c1994. 343 p. :
94-070298   700/.28/9   1880559188
Artists -- Health and hygiene -- Handbooks, manuals, etc. Artists' materials -- Safety measures -- Handbooks, manuals, etc. Artists' materials -- Toxicology -- Handbooks, manuals, etc.

RC963.6.A78.S62 1993
Spandorfer, Merle,
Making art safely : alternative methods and materials in drawing, painting, printmaking, graphic design, and photography / Merle Spandorfer, Deborah Curtiss, Jack Snyder. New York : Van Nostrand Reinhold, c1993. xvi, 255 p. :
92-004841   363.11/976   0442234899
Artists -- Health and hygiene. Artists' materials -- Safety measures.

RC963.6.W65
Hepler, Allison L.
Women in labor : mothers, medicine, and occupational health in the United States, 1890-1980 / Allison L. Hepler. Columbus : Ohio State University Press, c2000. xii, 177 p. :
00-008776   616.98/03/082   0814208509
Women -- Employment -- Health aspects -- United States -- History. Industrial hygiene -- United States -- History.

RC963.6.W65.M47 1998
Messing, Karen.
One-eyed science : occupational health and women workers / Karen Messing ; foreword by Jeanne Mager Stellman. Philadelphia : Temple University Press, 1998. xx, 244 p. :
97-026885   616.9/803*/082   1566395976
Women -- Employment -- Health aspects. Occupational diseases -- Sex factors. Sex discrimination against women.

RC964-965 Special situations and conditions — Industrial medicine — Occupational diseases

RC964.H8 2000
Hunter's diseases of occupations. London : Arnold ; 2000. xii, 1001 p.
00-301068   0340677503
Occupational diseases.

RC964.T65 1993

Toxic circles : environmental hazards from the workplace into the community / Helen E. Sheehan, Richard P. Wedeen, editors. New Brunswick, N.J. : Rutgers University Press, c1993. xii, 277 p. :
92-048258　　　　363.11/2/0973　　　081351990X
Occupational diseases. Occupational diseases -- New Jersey. Environmental health.

RC965.C77.B68 1993
Botsch, Robert Emil,

Organizing the breathless : cotton dust, southern politics & the Brown Lung Association / Robert E. Botsch. Lexington, KY : University Press of Kentucky, c1993. x, 228 p. ;
92-042053　　　　363.11/967721/0975
0813118182
Byssinosis -- Social aspects -- Southern States. Cotton manufacture -- Health aspects -- Southern States. Cotton dust -- Health aspects -- Southern States.

RC965.M5.F73 1992
Frazier, Claude Albee,

Miners and medicine : West Virginia memories / by Claude A. Frazier with F.K. Brown ; foreword by Stuart McGehee. Norman : University of Oklahoma Press, c1992. xi, 131 p. :
92-054151　　　　616/.008/8622　　　0806124547
Coal miners -- Medical care -- West Virginia -- History. Coal Mining -- history -- West Virginia. Occupational Diseases -- history -- West Virginia.

RC965.T54R668 2000
Rossol, Monona.

The health & safety guide for film, TV, & theater / Monona Rossol. New York : Allworth Press, c2000. xxi, 233 p. :
　　　　　363.11/9792　　　1581150717
Theaters--Health aspects. Theaters--Safety measures. Television broadcasting--Health aspects.

RC965.U7.B35 1993
Ball, Howard,

Cancer factories : America's tragic quest for uranium self-sufficiency / Howard Ball. Westport, Conn. : Greenwood Press, 1993. xiv, 188 p. :
92-032225　　　　363.17/99/08622　　　0313275661
Uranium miners -- United States -- Health and hygiene. Uranium mines and mining -- United States -- History. Uranium industry -- United States -- Government policy -- History.

RC966 Special situations and conditions — Industrial medicine — Industrial nursing

RC966.R64 2001
Rogers, Bonnie.

Occupational health nursing :concepts and practice / Bonnie Rogers. 2nd Ed. Philadelphia : W.B. Saunders Co., c2001. xvi, 527 p. :
　　　　　610.73/46　　　0721685110
Industrial nursing.

RC967 Special situations and conditions — Industrial medicine — Industrial hygiene

RC967.P37 1991

Patty's industrial hygiene and toxicology / George D. Clayton, Florence E. Clayton, editors ; contributors, R.E. Allan ... [et al.]. 4th ed. New York : Wiley, c2001<1995> 9 vols. :
　　　　　613.6/2　　　0471319457
Industrial hygiene. Industrial toxicology.

RC967.S356 1997
Scott, Ronald McLean,

Basic concepts of industrial hygiene / Ronald Scott. Boca Raton, Fla : Lewis Publishers, c1997. 471 p. :
97-028597　　　　616.9/803　　　1566702925
Industrial hygiene.

RC967.S36 1995
Scott, Ronald M.

Introduction to industrial hygiene / Ronald M. Scott. Boca Raton : Lewis Publishers, c1995. xxiii, 468 p.
94-045567　　　　613.6/2　　　1566701406
Industrial hygiene.

RC967.S45 1997
Sellers, Christopher C.

Hazards of the job : from industrial disease to environmental health science / Christopher C. Sellers. Chapel Hill : University of North Carolina Press, c1997. xv, 331 p. :
96-025455　　　　363.11/09　　　0807823147
Industrial hygiene -- History. Environmental health -- History.

RC967.W668 2000

Workplace health and safety sourcebook : basic consumer health information about workplace health and safety, including the effect of workplace hazards on the lungs, skin, heart, ears, eyes, brain, edited by Chad T. Kimball. Detroit, MI : Omnigraphics, c2000. xv, 625 p. :
00-058477　　　　616.9/803　　　0780802314
Industrial hygiene -- Popular works. Industrial safety -- Popular works.

RC967.5 Special situations and conditions — Industrial medicine — Industrial psychiatry

RC967.5.H36 1998

Handbook of organizational health psychology : programs to make the workplace healthier / edited by Sam Klarreich. Madison, Conn. : Psychosocial Press, c1998. xvii, 296 p.
98-022824　　　　658.3/82　　　1887841172
Industrial psychiatry. Psychology, Industrial. Employees -- Mental health.

RC969 Special situations and conditions — Industrial medicine — Medical departments

RC969.H43.E26 1994
Economic impact of worksite health promotion / Joseph P. Opatz, editor. Champaign, IL : Human Kinetics Publishers, c1994. viii, 258 p.
93-019102   658.3/82   0873224361
Health promotion -- Economic aspects. Industrial hygiene.

RC971 Special situations and conditions — Military medicine — General works

RC971.C87 1998
Curtin, Philip D.
Disease and empire : the health of European troops in the conquest of Africa / Philip D. Curtin. Cambridge, U.K. ; Cambridge University Press, 1998. xiii, 256 p.
98-022027   616.9/8023/096   0521591694
Medicine, Military -- Africa.   Africa -- History, Military -- 19th century. Europe -- Colonies -- Africa.

RC971.G33 1992
Gabriel, Richard A.
A history of military medicine / Richard A. Gabriel and Karen S. Metz ; foreword by John Keegan. New York : Greenwood Press, 1992. 2 v. :
91-032404   616.9/8023   031327746X
Medicine, Military -- History.

RC986 Special situations and conditions — Naval medicine — General works

RC986.D78 2000
Druett, Joan.
Rough medicine : surgeons at sea in the age of sail / Joan Druett. New York : Routledge, 2000. x, 270 p. :
00-034474   616.9/8024/09034
0415924510
Medicine, Naval -- South Pacific Ocean -- History -- 19th century. Ship physicians -- South Pacific Ocean -- History -- 19th century. Whaling -- South Pacific Ocean -- History.

RC986.K36
Keevil, John J.
Medicine and the Navy, 1200-1900 / Introd. by Sir Henry Dale. Edinburgh : E. & S. Livingstone, 1957-63. 4 v. :
58000899   616.98024
Medicine, Naval -- history. Medicine, Naval -- History.

RC1005 Special situations and conditions — Submarine medicine — General works

RC1005.E35 2002
Diving and subaquatic medicine / Carl Edmonds ... [et al.].4th ed. London ; Arnold, c2002. viii, 719 p. :
          616.9/8022   0340806303
Submarine medicine.

RC1015 Special situations and conditions — Submarine medicine — Underwater physiology

RC1015.H45
Hempleman, H. V.
The physiology of diving in man and other animals / H. V. Hempleman, A. P. M. Lockwood. London : E. Arnold, 1978. 56, [2] p. :
79-307465   599/.01/9135   0713126914
Underwater physiology. Deep diving -- Physiological aspects. Marine mammals -- Physiology.

RC1062 Special situations and conditions — Aviation medicine — General works

RC1062.A95 1999
Aviation medicine / edited by John Ernsting, A.N. Nicholson, D.J. Rainford. 3rd ed. Oxford ; Butterworth-Heinemann, 1999. xv, 703 p. :
          616.9/80213   0750632526
Aviation medicine.

RC1062.F86 1996
Fundamentals of aerospace medicine / [edited by] Roy L. DeHart. 2nd ed. Baltimore, MD : Williams & Wilkins, c1996. xix, 1091 p. :
          616.9/8021   0683023969
Aviation medicine. Space medicine. Aerospace Medicine.

RC1075 Special situations and conditions — Aviation medicine — Aviation physiology

RC1075.P46
Physiology in the space environment. Washington, National Academy of Sciences, National Research 1967-68 [v. 1 2 v.
67-060044   612/.0145
Space flight -- Physiological effect.

RC1135 Special situations and conditions — Transportation medicine — Special topics, A-Z

RC1135.F86 1997
Fundamentals of space life sciences / edited by Susanne E. Churchill ; with a foreword by Heinz Oser. Malabar, Fla. : Krieger Pub. Co., 1997. 2 v. (xvi, 36
95-015029   616.9/80214   0894640518
Space medicine. Space biology.

RC1135.H37 1989
Harding, Richard
Survival in space : medical problems of manned spaceflight / Richard Harding. London ; Routledge, 1989. xix, 227 p.,
88-032091   616.9/80214   0415002532
Space medicine. Space Flight.

RC1135.S62 1993

Space biology and medicine / series edited by Arnauld E. Nicogossian ... [et al.] ; co-editors, L.F. Dietlein ... [et al.]. Washington, D.C. : American Institute of Aeronautics and Astronauti c1993-c1996 v. 1, 3, bks.

93-026189   616.9/80214   1563470616
Space medicine. Space biology.

RC1210 Special situations and conditions — Sports medicine — General works

RC1210.B395 1995
Berryman, Jack W.

Out of many, one : a history of the American College of Sports Medicine / Jack W. Berryman. Champaign, IL : Human Kinetics, c1995. x, 414 p. :

94-023876   617.1/027/06073   0873228154
Sports medicine -- Study and teaching -- United States -- History. Sports Medicine -- history. Societies, Scientific -- history.

RC1210.D73 1993
Dragoo, Jason L.

Handbook of sports medicine / by Jason L. Dragoo ; illustrations by Torey J. Arvik ; [foreword by Thomas Carter ; preface by Bruce McCall]. Temple, AZ : Renaissance Pub., c1993. 192 p. :

93-092722   617.1/027   0963714406
Sports medicine -- Handbooks, manuals, etc.

RC1210.E782 1997

Essentials of sports medicine / edited by Robert E. Sallis, Ferdy Massimino. St. Louis : Mosby-Year Book, c1997. xxi, 646 p. :

617.1/027   0815101570
Sports medicine. Sports Medicine. Athletic Injuries.

RC1210.O96 1998

Oxford textbook of sports medicine / edited by Mark Harries ... [et al.]. 2nd ed. Oxford ; Oxford University Press, 1998. xv, 957 p. :

617.1/027   0192627171
Sports medicine--Handbooks, manuals, etc. Athletic Injuries--handbooks. Sports Medicine--handbooks.

RC1210.P735 2001

Principles and practice of primary care sports medicine / editors, William E. Garrett, Jr., Donald T. Kirkendall, Deborah L. Squire ; medical illustrations by Marsha Dohrmann Kitkowski. Philadelphia : Lippincott Williams & Wilkins, c2001. xvii, 679 p. :

617.1/027   0781729564
Sports medicine. Primary care (Medicine) Athletic Injuries--therapy.

RC1210.S638 1992

Sport and exercise science : essays in the history of sports medicine / edited by Jack W. Berryman and Roberta J. Park. Urbana : University of Illinois Press, c1992. xvii, 372 p.

91-027220   617.1/027/09   0252018966
Sports medicine -- History.

RC1211 Special situations and conditions — Sports medicine — Handbooks, manuals, etc.

RC1211.H36 1999

Handbook of sports medicine :a symptom-oriented approach / [edited by] Wade A. Lillegard, Janus D. Butcher, Karen S. Rucker ; foreword by Karl B. Fields. 2nd ed. Boston : Butterworth-Heinemann, c1999. xvi, 431 p. :

617.1/027   0750690410
Sports medicine--Handbooks, manuals, etc. Sports Medicine--handbooks. Athletic Injuries--handbooks.

RC1218 Special situations and conditions — Sports medicine — By age group, class, etc., A-Z

RC1218.C45.B69 1999
Boyle, Daniel J.

Sports medicine for parents & coaches / Daniel J. Boyle. Washington, DC : Georgetown University Press, 1999. ix, 117 p. :

99-013392   617.1/027/083   0878407324
Pediatric sports medicine -- Handbooks, manuals, etc. Sports injuries in children -- Handbooks, manuals, etc.

RC1218.W65.D832

Women in sport / edited by Barbara L. Drinkwater ; in collaboration with the International Federation of Sports Medicine. Malden, MA : Blackwell Science, 2000. p. cm.

99-057719   617.1/027/082   0632050845
Woman athletes -- Health and hygiene.

RC1218.W65.O68 2000
Otis, Carol L.

The athletic woman's survival guide : how to win the battle against eating disorders, amenorrhea, and osteoporosis / Carol L. Otis, Roger Goldingay. Champaign, IL : Human Kinetics, c2000. xii, 264 p. :

99-055550   617.1/027/082   0736001212
Women athletes -- Health and hygiene. Women athletes -- Diseases. Eating disorders.

RC1220 Special situations and conditions — Sports medicine — Medical and physiological aspects of special activities. By activity, A-Z

RC1220.D35.H68 1988
Howse, Justin.

Dance technique and injury prevention / Justin Howse, Shirley Hancock ; foreword by Ninette de Valois. New York : Theatre Arts Books/Routledge, 1988. xii, 196 p. :

88-016094   617.1   0878309853
Dancing injuries -- Prevention.

RC1220.E53.E53 1991

Endurance in sport / edited by R.J. Shephard & P.-O. Astrand Oxford [England] ; Blackwell Scientific Publications ; 1992. xvi, 638 p. :

91-019548   613.7/1   0632030356
Endurance sports. Exercise -- Physiological aspects. Physical fitness.

RC1220.R8T49 2001
Textbook of running medicine / [edited by] Francis G. O'Connor, Robert P. Wilder ; surgical section editor, Robert Nirschl. New York : McGraw-Hill, Medical Pub. Division, c2001. xxiv, 696 p. :
617.1/027   007135977X
Running injuries--Treatment. Running--injuries. Athletic Injuries--therapy.

RC1220.S57.U88 1996
The U.S. soccer sports medicine book / editor-in-chief, William E. Garrett, Jr. ; associate editors, Donald T. Kirkendall, S. Robert Contiguglia. Baltimore : Williams & Wilkins, 1996. xv, 504 p. :
96-001088   617.1/027   0683182498
Soccer -- Physiological aspects. Soccer injuries. Soccer -- injuries -- congresses.

RC1225 Special situations and conditions — Sports medicine — Medical examination of athletes

RC1225.P47 1990
Physiological testing of the high-performance athlete / J. Duncan MacDougall, Howard A. Wenger, Howard J. Green, editors. Champaign, Ill. : Human Kinetics Books, c1991. x, 432 p. :
90-035488   613.7/11/0287   0873223004
Athletes -- Medical examinations. Physical fitness -- Testing.

RC1230 Special situations and conditions — Sports medicine — Doping in sports

RC1230.A522 2000
Anabolic steroids in sport and exercise / Charles E. Yesalis, editor. 2nd ed. Champaign, IL : Human Kinetics, c2000. xviii, 493 p. :
362.29/088/796   0880117869
Anabolic steroids--Health aspects. Doping in sports.

RC1230.D76 2001
Doping in elite sport : the politics of drugs in the Olympic movement / Wayne Wilson and Edward Derse, editors. Champaign, IL : Human Kinetics, c2001. xv, 295 p. :
00-033599   362.29/088/796   0736003290
Doping in sports. Olympics.

RC1230.M65 2001
Monaghan, Lee F.,
Bodybuilding, drugs, and risk / Lee F. Monaghan. New York : Routledge, 2001. p. cm.
362.29/088/796   041522683X
Doping in sports. Bodybuilders--Drug use. Anabolic steroids.

RC1230.T42 1991
Taylor, William N.
Macho medicine : a history of the anabolic steroid epidemic / by William N. Taylor. Jefferson, N.C. : McFarland, c1991. ix, 198 p. :
91-052506   362.29   0899506135
Doping in sports -- History. Anabolic steroids -- History.

RC1230.W295 2000
Waddington, Ivan.
Sport, health and drugs : a critical sociological perspective / Ivan Waddington. London ; E & FN Spon, 2000. x, 214 p. ;
99-053040   362.29/088/796   0419251901
Doping in sports -- Social aspects.

RC1230.W33 1989
Wadler, Gary I.,
Drugs and the athlete / Gary I. Wadler, Brian Hainline. Philadelphia : F.A. Davis Co., c1989. xxii, 353 p.
88-033612   362.2/9   0803690088
Doping in sports. Doping in Sports. Substance Abuse -- diagnosis.

RC1235-1245 Special situations and conditions — Sports medicine — Physiology of sports

RC1235.B37 1998
Bartlett, Roger.
Sports biomechanics : preventing injury and improving performance / Roger Bartlett. New York : E & FN Spon, 1998. p. cm.
98-021961   612/.044   0419184406
Sports -- Physiological aspects. Human mechanics. Sports injuries -- Prevention.

RC1235.B87 1990
Bursztyn, Peter.
Physiology for sportspeople : a serious user's guide to the body / Peter G. Bursztyn ; illustrated by Peter G. Jack. Manchester, U.K. ; Manchester University Press : c1990. xiii, 278 p.
90-006308   612/.044   0719030862
Sports -- Physiological aspects.

RC1235.D76 1996
Drowatzky, John N.
Ethical decision making in physical activity research / John N. Drowatzky. Champaign, IL : Human Kinetics, c1996. viii, 103 p.
95-042649   174/.28   0873224736
Sports medicine -- Research -- Moral and ethical aspects. Kinesiology -- Research -- Moral and ethical aspects. Exercise -- Research -- Moral and ethical aspects.

RC1235.E94 2000
Exercise and sport science / editors, William E. Garrett, Jr., Donald T. Kirkendall ; illustrator, Marsha Dohrmann. Philadelphia : Lippincott Williams & Wilkins, c2000. xix, 980 p. :
99-038884   612/.044   0683034219
Sports -- Physiological aspects. Exercise -- Physiological aspects. Human mechanics.

RC1235.O94 1998
Overtraining in sport / Richard B. Kreider, Andrew C. Fry, Mary L. O'Toole, editors. Champaign, IL : Human Kinetics, c1998. xi, 403 p. :
97-031205   617.1/027   0880115637
Sports -- Physiological aspects. Physical education and training. Stress (Physiology)

RC1236.N47.K53 1996
Klawans, Harold L.
   Why Michael couldn't hit : and other tales of the neurology of sports / Harold L. Klawans. [New York, NY] : W.H. Freeman, c1996. xii, 308 p. :
96-024097   362.1/968/0088796
0716730014
   Neurophysiology. Sports -- Physiological aspects. Nervous system -- Diseases -- Complications.

RC1245.S73 1997
Stainback, Robert D.,
   Alcohol and sport / Robert D. Stainback. Champaign, IL : Human Kinetics, c1997. xi, 219 p. :
96-048332   616.86/1/0088796
0873225317
   Athletes -- Alcohol use.

RD Surgery

RD19 History — General works

RD19.C38
Cartwright, Frederick Fox.
   The development of modern surgery [by] Frederick F. Cartwright. New York, T. Y. Crowell Co. [1968, c1967] x, 323 p.
68-011287   617/.09
   Surgery -- History.

RD19.H34
Haeger, Knut,
   The illustrated history of surgery / Knut Haeger. London ; Fitzroy Dearborn Pubishers, 2000. 295 p. :
01-268056   617/.09   1579583199
   Surgery -- History.

RD19.R88 1993
Rutkow, Ira M.
   Surgery : an illustrated history / Ira M. Rutkow. St. Louis : Published by Mosby-Year Book Inc. in collaboration with xiii, 550 p. :
          617/.09   0801660785
   Surgery--History. Surgery--history.

RD19.W36
Wangensteen, Owen Harding,
   The rise of surgery : from empiric craft to scientific discipline / by Owen H. Wangensteen and Sarah D. Wangensteen. Minneapolis : University of Minnesota Press, c1978. xviii, 785 p.
77-087933
   Surgery -- History. Surgery -- History.

RD19.Z5 1967
Zimmerman, Leo M.,
   Great ideas in the history of surgery / Leo M. Zimmerman , Ilza Veith. New York : Dover Publications, 1967. xii, 587 p. :
67014872   617/.09
   Surgery Surgery -- History. Surgery -- history

RD21 History — General special

RD21.B55 1970
Billings, John Shaw,
   The history and literature of surgery. [New York] Argosy-Antiquarian, 1970. 132 p.
78-115407   617/.09   0872660389
   Surgery -- History. Surgery -- Bibliography.

RD27 History — Modern

RD27.G553 1962
Glaser, Hugo,
   The road to modern surgery; the advances in medicine and surgery during the past hundred years. Translated by Maurice Michael. New York, Dutton, 1962 [c1960] 223p.
61012468   617.09
   Medicine -- History. History of Medicine Surgery -- History.

RD27.3 History — By region or country, A-Z

RD27.3.F8.P6813 1990
Pouchelle, Marie-Christine.
   The body and surgery in the Middle Ages / Marie-Christine Pouchelle ; translated by Rosemary Morris. New Brunswick, N.J. : Rutgers University Press, 1990. vi, 276 p., [
90-008126   617/.0944/09023   0813516056
   Mondeville, Henri de, -- 14th cent. Mondeville, Henri de, -- 14th cent. Medicine -- Philosophy. Surgery -- France -- History. Body, Human.

RD27.35 Biography — Individual

RD27.35.B365B36 2002
Bankston, John,
   Christiaan Barnard and the story of the first successful heart transplant / John Bankston. Bear, DE : Mitchell Lane Publishers, 2002. p. cm.
          158415120X
   Barnard, Christiaan, 1922- Barnard, Christiaan, 1922- Transplant surgeons--South Africa--Biography--Juvenile literature. Heart--Transplantation--Juvenile literature. Physicians.

RD27.35.B42.H67 1996
Horsman, Reginald.
   Frontier doctor : William Beaumont, America's first great medical scientist / Reginald Horsman. Columbia : University of Missouri Press, c1996. xiii, 320 p.
95-049849   610/.92   082621052X
   Beaumont, William, -- 1785-1853. Beaumont, William, -- 1785-1853. Physiologists -- United States -- Biography. Surgeons -- United States -- Biography. Physicians -- biography.

RD27.35.D74.L68 1996
Love, Spencie,
   One blood : the death and resurrection of Charles R. Drew / by Spencie Love, with a foreword by John Hope Franklin. Chapel Hill, NC : The University of North Carolina Press, 1996. xix, 373 p. :
95-035720   617/.092   0807822507
   Drew, Charles Richard, -- 1904-1950 -- Death and burial. Drew, Charles Richard, -- 1904-1950 -- Legends. Discrimination in medical care -- United States -- History -- 20th century. Race relations -- Folklore. United States -- Race relations.

RD27.35.H34.A33
Hall, Edwin Presley.
A doctor reminisces / Edwin Presley Hall. Huntsville, Ala. : Strode Publishers, c1978. 332 p. ;
77-094279   617/.092/4   0873971337
Hall, Edwin Presley.   Surgeons -- United States -- Biography.

RD27.35.M65.A33
Morgan, Elizabeth,
The making of a woman surgeon / Elizabeth Morgan. New York : Putnam, c1980. 368 p. ;
80-000269   617/.092/4   039912361X
Morgan, Elizabeth, -- 1947-   Women surgeons -- United States -- Biography. Plastic surgeons -- United States -- Biography. Residents (Medicine) -- United States -- Biography.

RD27.35.M68.A33
Moynihan, Donald T.
Skin deep : the making of a plastic surgeon / by Donald T. Moynihan and Shirley Hartman. Boston : Little, Brown, c1979. viii, 339 p.
79-010552   617/.95/00924   0316587001
Moynihan, Donald T.   Plastic surgeons -- California -- Biography. Residents (Medicine) -- California -- Biography.

RD27.35.M87.R46 1993
The Remarkable surgical practice of John Benjamin Murphy / edited by Robert L. Schmitz and Timothy T. Oh. Urbana : University of Illinois Press, c1993. x, 207 p. :
92-000524   617/.092   025201958X
Murphy, J. B. -- (John Benjamin), -- 1857-1916. Murphy, J. B. -- (John Benjamin), -- 1857-1916.   Surgery -- United States -- History. Surgeons -- United States -- Biography. Surgery -- bibliography.

RD27.35.N64.A3 1990
Nolen, William A.,
The making of a surgeon / William A. Nolen. Denver : Mid-List Press, c1990. xii, 269 p. ;
90-006699   617/.0092   0922811059
Nolen, William A., -- 1928-   Surgeons -- Minnesota -- Litchfield -- Biography.

RD27.35.P38.G65 1988
Goldowsky, Seebert J.
Yankee surgeon : the life and times of Usher Parsons, 1788-1868 / Seebert J. Goldowsky. Boston : Francis A. Countway Library of Medicine in coope 1988. xvi, 450 p. :
88-215105   617/.092   0881350885
Parsons, Usher, -- 1788-1868.   Surgeons -- Rhode Island -- Biography.

RD27.7 Surgical ethics

RD27.7.M33
MacKay, William,
Salesman surgeon : the incredible story of an amateur in the operating room / by William MacKay, as told to Maureen Mylander. New York : McGraw-Hill, c1978. xii, 187 p. ;
78-015631   617   0070443904
MacKay, William, -- 1943-   Surgeons -- Professional ethics. Sales personnel -- New York (State) -- Biography.

RD31.3 Popular works

RD31.3.B47 2001
Berman, Joel A.
Understanding surgery :a comprehensive guide for every family / by Joel A. Berman. Boston : Branden Books, c2001. 494 p. :
617   0828320616
Surgery--Popular works. Surgery--History--Popular works.

RD34 Clinical cases

RD34.P27 1960
Pare, Ambroise,
Case reports and autopsy records. Compiled and edited by Wallace B. Hamby. Translated from J.P. Malgaigne's Oeuvres completes d'Ambroisie Pare, Paris, 1840. Springfield, Ill., Thomas [1960] xx, 214 p.
60-012663   617.092
Surgery -- Case studies. Surgery -- Early works to 1800.

RD39 Addresses, essays, lectures

RD39.R58
Rives, James Davidson,
Essays of a Louisiana surgeon / by James D. Rives ; edited posthumously by Robert S. Sparkman. New Orleans : James D. Rives Surgical Society, 1977. xix, 136 p. :
77-151212   617
Rives, James Davidson, -- 1893-1975 -- Addresses, essays, lectures. Surgery -- Addresses, essays, lectures. Surgery -- Study and teaching -- Addresses, essays, lectures. Surgeons -- Louisiana -- Biography -- Addresses, essays, lectures.

RD39.W66
Woodruff, Michael F. A.,
On science and surgery / Michael Woodruff. Edinburgh : Edinburgh University Press, c1977. viii, 154 p.
77-675824   610   0852243030
Surgery -- Addresses, essays, lectures. Medicine -- Addresses, essays, lectures.

RD79 Anesthesiology — History — General works

RD79.C53 1985
Classical anesthesia files / [edited by] David M. Little, Jr. Park Ridge, Ill. : Wood Library-Museum of Anesthesiology, sponsored c1985. xvii, 335 p.
85-012088   617/.96   0961493208
Anesthesia -- History. Anesthesia -- history.

RD80.3 Anesthesiology — History — By region or country

RD80.3.P47 1985
Pernick, Martin S.
   A calculus of suffering : pain, professionalism, and anesthesia in nineteenth-century America / Martin S. Pernick. New York : Columbia University Press, 1985. xiii, 421 p.
84-012664   617/.96/0973   0231051867
   Anesthesia -- United States -- History -- 19th century. Medicine -- United States -- History -- 19th century. Surgery -- United States -- History -- 19th century.

RD81 Anesthesiology — General works

RD81.A54 1994
   Anesthesia / edited by Ronald D. Miller ; atlas of regional anesthesia procedures illustrated by Gwenn Afton-Bird. 4th ed. New York : Churchill Livingstone, 1994. 2 v. (xxi, 2696 p.) :
          617.9/6   044308906X
   Anesthesia. Anesthesia.

RD93 Emergency surgery. Wounds and injuries — General works

RD93.B32 1995
   Hamilton Bailey's emergency surgery. 12th ed. / edited by B.W. Ellis ; special editorial assistance given Oxford ; Butterworth-Heinemann, c1995. xiv, 866 p. :
          617/.026   0750627719
   Surgical emergencies. Emergencies. Surgery, Operative.

RD93.8 Emergency surgery. Wounds and injuries — By region or country — United States

RD93.8.R64 1998
Robertson, Leon S.
   Injury epidemiology : research and control strategies / Leon S. Robertson. New York : Oxford University Press, 1998. ix, 265 p. :
97-035804   614.5/99   019512202X
   Wounds and injuries -- United States -- Epidemiology. Wounds and injuries -- Epidemiology -- Research -- Methodology.

RD97 Emergency surgery. Wounds and injuries — Wounds by type or causative agent — Sports injuries

RD97.B655 1995
Booher, James M.
   Prevention and care of athletic injuries / James M. Booher. 3rd ed. Dubuque, Iowa : Eddie Bowers Pub., c1995. vi, 202 p. :
          617.1/027   0945483406
   Sports injuries--Prevention. Sports injuries. Athletes--Health and hygiene.

RD97.C665 2001
   Coping with sports injuries :psychological strategies for rehabilitation / [edited by] Jane Crossman. Oxford ; Oxford University Press, 2001. xviii, 202 p. :
          617.1/027   0192632159
   Sports injuries--Patients--Rehabilitation. Sports injuries--Patients--Rehabilitation--Psychological aspects. Sports injuries--Psychological aspects.

RD97.F86 1998
   Functional rehabilitation of sports and musculoskeletal injuries / [edited by] W. Ben Kibler, Stanley A. Herring, Joel M. Press ; with Patricia A. Lee. Gaithersburg, Md. : Aspen, 1998. xiv, 303 p. :
97-041935   617.1/027   0834206129
   Sports injuries -- Patients -- Rehabilitation. Sports physical therapy. Musculoskeletal system -- Wounds and injuries -- Patients -- Rehabilitation.

RD97.G373 1999
Garrick, James G.
   Sports injuries : diagnosis and management / James G. Garrick, David   R. Webb. 2nd ed. Philadelphia : W.B. Saunders, c1999. xiv, 429 p. :
          617.1/027   0721644341
   Sports injuries. Athletic Injuries--diagnosis. Athletic Injuries--therapy.

RD97.H45 1993
Heil, John,
   Psychology of sport injury / John Heil. Champaign, IL : Human Kinetics Publishers, c1993. xiv, 338 p. :
92-035854   617.1/027   0873224639
   Sports injuries -- Psychological aspects.

RD97.H68 2000
Houglum, Peggy A.,
   Therapeutic exercise for athletic injuries / Peggy A. Houglum. Champaign, IL : Human Kinetics, c2001. xix, 1011 p. :
          615.8/2/088796   0880118431
   Sports injuries--Exercise therapy.

RD97.M84 1996
Mueller, Frederick O.
   Catastrophic injuries in high school and college sports / Frederick O. Mueller, Robert C. Cantu, Steven P. Van Camp. Champaign, IL : Human Kinetics, c1996. vi, 114 p. :
95-031210   617.1/027   0873226747
   Sports injuries. College athletes -- Wounds and injuries. High school athletes -- Wounds and injuries.

RD97.S538 2000
Shultz, Sandra J.,
   Assessment of athletic injuries / Sandra J. Shultz, Peggy A. Houglum, David H. Perrin. Champaign, IL : Human Kinetics, 2000. xiii, 489 p.
00-025395   617.1/027/076   0736001581
   Sports -- Accidents and injuries -- Diagnosis -- Examinations, questions, etc. Sports medicine -- Examinations, questions, etc. Athletic Injuries -- diagnosis -- Examination Questions.

RD97.S736 1999
Sports injuries sourcebook ; basic consumer health information about common sports injuries ... edited by Heather E. Aldred. Detroit, MI : Omnigraphics, c1999. xiv, 606 p. :
99-029624   617.1/027   0780802187
Sports injuries. Sports medicine. Wounds and injuries.

RD118 Plastic surgery. Reparative surgery — General works

RD118.R365 2001
Reconstructive and cosmetic surgery sourcebook :basic consumer health information on cosmetic and reconstructive plastic surgery ... / edited by M. Lisa Weatherford. 1st ed. Detroit, MI : Omnigraphics, 2001. xii, 374 p. :
                617.9/5   0780802144
Surgery, Plastic. Consumer education.

RD118.S745 1999
Stedman's plastic surgery/ENT/dentistry words. Baltimore, Md. : Lippincott Williams & Wilkins, c1999. p. cm.
98-033791   617.9/5/014   0683404601
Surgery, Plastic -- Terminology. Otolaryngology -- Terminology. Dentistry -- Terminology.

RD118.5 Plastic surgery. Reparative surgery — Psychological aspects

RD118.5.G55 1998
Gilman, Sander L.
Creating beauty to cure the soul : race and psychology in the shaping of aesthetic surgery / Sander L. Gilman. Durham, N.C. : Duke University Press, 1998. p. cm.
98-023182   617.9/5/019   0822321114
Surgery, Plastic -- Psychological aspects. Beauty, Personal -- Psychological aspects. Surgery, Plastic -- Philosophy.

RD119 Plastic surgery. Reparative surgery — Cosmetic surgery — General works

RD119.H35 1997
Haiken, Elizabeth.
Venus envy : a history of cosmetic surgery / Elizabeth Haiken. Baltimore : Johns Hopkins University Press, 1997. ix, 370 p. :
97-019823   617.9/5   0801857635
Surgery, Plastic -- Social aspects -- United States. Surgery, Plastic -- United States -- History. Beauty, Personal -- Social aspects -- United States.

RD119.S85 2001
Sullivan, Deborah A.,
Cosmetic surgery : the cutting edge of commercial medicine in America / Deborah A. Sullivan. New Brunswick, NJ : Rutgers University Press , c2001. xiii, 233 p.
00-039028   617.9/5   0813528593
Surgery, Plastic. Surgery, Plastic -- Economic aspects. Surgery, Plastic -- Marketing.

RD120.7 Transplantation of organs, tissues, etc. — General works

RD120.7.F68 1992
Fox, Renee C.
Spare parts : organ replacement in American Society / Renee C. Fox and Judith P. Swazey ; with the assistance of Judith C. Watkins. New York : Oxford University Press, 1992. xviii, 254 p.
91-039727   362.1/9795/00973   0195076508
Transplantation of organs, tissues, etc. -- Moral and ethical aspects -- United States. Transplantation of organs, tissues, etc. -- Social aspects -- United States. Heart, Artificial -- History.

RD120.7.N49 1991
New harvest : transplanting body parts and reaping the benefits / edited by C. Don Keyes in collaboration with coeditor Walter E. Wiest. Clifton, N.J. : Humana Press, c1991. xiii, 299 p.
90-026049   174/.25   0896032000
Transplantation of organs, tissues, etc. -- Moral and ethical aspects. Homografts -- Moral and ethical aspects.

RD120.7.P365 2001
Parr, Elizabeth.
Coping with an organ transplant :a practical guide to understanding, preparing for, and living with an organ transplant / Elizabeth Parr and Janet Mize. New York, NY : Avery, c2001. xiv, 177 p. ;
                617.9/5   1583330925
Transplantation of organs, tissues, etc. Consumer education.

RD120.7.T657 2000
The transplant patient : biological, psychiatric, and ethical issues in organ transplantation / edited by Paula Trzepacz and Andrea F. DiMartini. Cambridge ; Cambridge Unitersity Press, 2000. xii, 311 p. :
                617.9/5   0521553547
Transplantation of organs, tissues, etc.--Physiological aspects. Transplantation of organs, tissues, etc.--Psychological aspects. Transplantation of organs, tissues, etc.--Moral and ethical aspects.

RD120.7.V43 2000
Veatch, Robert M.
Transplantation ethics / Robert M. Veatch. Washington, D.C. : Georgetown University Press, c2000. xvii, 427 p.
00-026843   174/.25   0878408118
Transplantation of organs, tissues, etc. -- Moral and ethical aspects.

RD129.5 Transplantation of organs, tissues, etc. — Donation of organs, tissues, etc.

RD129.5.O736 1996

Organ and tissue donation : ethical, legal, and policy issues / edited by Bethany Spielman. Carbondale : Southern Illinois University Press, c1996. xx, 192 p. ;
96-017115   174/.25   0809321076
Donation of organs, tissues, etc. -- Moral and ethical aspects -- Congresses. Donation of organs, tissues, etc. -- Law and legislation -- Congresses. Donation of organs, tissues, etc. -- Government policy -- United States -- Congresses.

RD130 Prothesis. Artificial organs

RD130.L64 1968
Longmore, Donald.

Spare-part surgery; the surgical practice of the future. Edited and illustrated by M. Ross-Macdonald. Garden City, N.Y., Doubleday, 1968. 192 p.
68-018093   617/.95
Heart, Artificial. Artificial kidney. Prosthesis.

RD137 Surgery in childhood — General works

RD137.P43 1993

Pediatric surgery / [edited by] Keith W. Ashcraft, Thomas M. Holder. 2nd ed. Philadelphia : Saunders, c1993. xviii, 1062 p. :
    617.9/8   072163737X
Children--Surgery. Surgery--in infancy & childhood.

RD137.S85 1990

Swenson's pediatric surgery. 5th ed. / edited by John G. Raffensperger. Norwalk, Conn. : Appleton & Lange, c1990. xvi, 994 p., [1] leaf of plates :
    617.9/8   0838587577
Children--Surgery. Surgery--in infancy & childhood.

RD137.3 Surgery in childhood — Atlases. Pictorial works

RD137.3.A84 1994
Ashcraft, Keith W.,

Atlas of pediatric surgery / Keith W. Ashcraft. Philadelphia : Saunders, c1994. x, 318 p. :
    617.9/8   0721637205
Children--Surgery--Atlases. Surgery, Operative--in infancy & childhood--atlases.

RD524 Surgery by region, system, or organ — Head and neck — Lips

RD524.B37 1991
Bardach, Janusz.

Surgical techniques in cleft lip and palate / Janusz Bardach, Kenneth E. Salyer ; with contributions by Ian T. Jackson, M. Samuel Noordhoff ; illustrations by Hani Elkadi. 2nd ed. St. Louis : Mosby-Year Book, [c1991]. xiii, 368 p. :
    617.5/22   0815105282
Cleft lip--Surgery. Cleft palate--Surgery. Cleft Lip--surgery.

RD525 Surgery by region, system, or organ — Head and neck — Palate

RD525.G78 2001
Gruman-Trinkner, Carrie T.

Your cleft-affected child :the complete book of information, resources, and hope / Carrie T. Gruman-Trinkner. 1st ed. Alameda, CA : Hunter House ; xii, 176 p. :
    618.92/0975225   0897931858
Cleft palate children. Cleft palate. Cleft lip.

RD529 Surgery by region, system, or organ — Head and neck — Skull

RD529.F85
Fulton, John Farquhar,

Frontal lobotomy and affective behavior, a neurophysiological analysis. New York, Norton [1951] 159 p.
51012058   617.51
Brain -- Localization of functions. Brain -- Surgery. Psychosurgery.

RD529.P4
Penfield, Wilder,

The cerebral cortex of man; a clinical study of localization of function, by Wilder Penfield and Theodore Rasmussen. New York, Macmillan, 1950. xv, 248 p.
50008617   617.48
Brain -- Surgery. Epilepsy. Brain -- Localization of functions.

RD535.8 Surgery by region, system, or organ — Chest. Thoracic surgery — Biography

RD535.8.G53.R66 1991
Romaine-Davis, Ada,

John Gibbon and his heart-lung machine / Ada Romaine-Davis. Philadelphia : University of Pennsylvania Press, c1991. xxii, 251 p.
91-040290   617.4/12/092   0812230736
Gibbon, John Heysham. Gibbon, John Heysham. Heart, Mechanical -- History. Thoracic surgeons -- United States -- Biography. Heart, Mechanical -- history.

RD539.8 Surgery by region, system, or organ — Breast

RD539.8.S24 2000
Safety of silicone breast implants / Stuart Bondurant, Virginia Ernster, and Roger Herdman, editors ; Committee on the Safety of Silicone Breast Implants, Division of Health Promotion and Disease Prevention, Institute of Medicine. Washington, D.C. : Institute of Medicine, c2000. xvi, 540 p. ;
99-040812   618.1/90592   0309065321
Breast implants -- Complications. Silicones -- Toxicology. Mammaplasty.

RD539.8.S74 1998
Stewart, Mary White,
Silicone spills : breast implants on trial / Mary White Stewart. Westport, Conn. : Praeger, 1998. xiv, 223 p. :
97-041006   618.1/90592   0275963594
Breast implants -- Complications. Body image in women. Breast implants -- Law and legislation -- United States.

RD539.8.S76 1994
Stott-Kendall, Pamela.
Torn illusions : one woman's tragic experience with the silicone conspiracy / Pamela Stott-Kendall. Far Hills, N.J. : New Horizon Press, c1994. xiii, 242 p.
93-061692   618.1/9059   0882820907
Breast implants -- Complications. Silicones -- Toxicology.

RD539.8.V38 1993
Vasey, Frank B.
The silicone breast implant controversy : what women need to know / by Frank B. Vasey and Josh Feldstein. Freedom, CA : Crossing Press, c1993. 153 p. ;
93-029670   618.1/9059   0895946092
Breast implants -- Complications. Silicones -- Toxicology. Consumer education.

RD559 Surgery by region, system, or organ — Extremities — Upper extremities

RD559.B67 2001
The hand :fundamentals of therapy / [edited by] Judith Boscheinen-Morrin, W. Bruce Conolly. 3rd ed. Oxford ; Butterworth-Heinemann, c2001. 243 p. :
              617.5/75   0750645776
Hand--Wounds and injuries--Patients--Rehabilitation. Hand--Surgery--Patients--Rehabilitation. Hand--Diseases--Patients--Rehabilitation.

RD559.C68 2001
Coppard, Brenda M.
Introduction to splinting :a critical-reasoning & problem-solving approach / Brenda M. Coppard, Helene Lohman ; editorial consultant, Karen Shultz-Johnson. 2nd ed. St. Louis : Mosby, c2001. xiv, 655 p. :
              617.5/75044   0323009344
Hand--Wounds and injuries--Treatment. Splints (Surgery) Splints.

RD593 Surgery by region, system, or organ — Nervous system. Neurosurgery — General works

RD593.W3
Walker, A. Earl
A history of neurological surgery. Contributors: William J. Atkinson [and others] Baltimore, Williams & Wilkins, 1951. xii, 583 p.
51003943   617.48
Nervous System -- surgery. Nervous system -- Surgery. Surgery -- History.

RD594.3 Surgery by region, system, or organ — Nervous system. Neurosurgery — Spinal cord

RD594.3.S497 1998
Seymour, Wendy.
Remaking the body : rehabilitation and change / Wendy Seymour. London ; Routledge, c1998. xvi, 202 p. ;
97-046633   155.9/16   0415186013
Paralysis -- Psychological aspects. Paralysis -- Social aspects. Paralytics -- Rehabilitation.

RD598 Surgery by region, system, or organ — Cardiovascular system — General works

RD598.H4 1968
Hawthorne, Peter,
The transplanted heart; the incredible story of the epic heart transplant operations by Professor Christiaan Barnard and his team. [1st U.S. ed.] Chicago, Rand McNally [1968] 192 p.
              617/.95/12
Barnard, Christiaan, 1922-   Heart--Transplantation.

RD598.L38
Leipold, L. Edmond,
Dr. Christiaan N. Barnard, the man with the golden hands, by L. E. Leipold. Minneapolis, Denison [1971] 179 p.
78-118161   617/.0924   0513011064
Barnard, Christiaan, -- 1922-   Transplant surgeons -- South Africa -- Biography. Heart -- Transplantation. Heart -- Transplantation.

RD598.M17
Malan, Marais.
Heart transplant; the story of Barnard and the "ultimate in cardiac surgery". Johannesburg, Voortrekkerpers, 1968. 196 p.
72-377176   617/.95/12
Barnard, Christiaan, -- 1922-   Heart -- Transplantation.

RD598.M523 2000
Miller, G. Wayne.
King of hearts : the true story of the maverick who pioneered open-heart surgery / G. Wayne Miller. New York : Times Books, c2000. xv, 302 p. :
99-038264   617.412/092   0812930037
Lillehei, C. Walton, -- 1918-   Surgeons -- United States -- Biography. Heart -- Surgery -- United States -- History.

RD598.N512 1976
Nolen, William A.,
    Surgeon under the knife / William A. Nolen. New York : Coward, McCann & Geoghegan, c1976. 223 p. :
75-045470   617/.092/4   0698107438
Nolen, William A., -- 1928- -- Health.   Heart -- Surgery -- Patients -- United States -- Biography. Surgeons -- Minnesota -- Litchfield -- Biography. Heart surgery -- Personal narratives.

RD598.S454 1992
Shumacker, Harris B,
    The evolution of cardiac surgery / Harris B Shumacker, Jr. Bloomington : Indiana University Press, c1992. xiii, 476 p.
91-035312   617.4/12/09   0253352215
Heart -- Surgery -- History. Heart Surgery -- history.

RD598.T475
Thompson, Thomas,
    Hearts; of surgeons and transplants, miracles and disasters along the cardiac frontier. New York, McCall Pub. Co. [1971] xii, 304 p.
70-154248   617/.412   0841501238
    Heart -- Transplantation.

RD651 Neoplasms. Tumors. Oncology — General works

RD651.M56 1995
    Minimal access surgical oncology / edited by Frederick L. Greene and R. David Rosin ; foreword by Alfred Cuschieri. Oxford ; Radcliffe Medical Press, c1995. p. cm.
95-005161   616.99/4059   1857750802
    Cancer -- Endoscopic surgery. Neoplasms -- surgery. Surgery, Laparoscopic -- methods.

RD651.S8833 2001
    Surgical oncology : an algorithmic approach / editors, Theodore J. Saclarides, Keith W. Millikan, Constantine V. Godellas. New York : Springer-Verlag, c2001. p. ;
          616.99/4059   0387952012
    Cancer--Surgery. Oncology. Algorithms.

RD701 Orthopedia. Orthopedic surgery — Societies. Serials

RD701.C58
Coffman, William Milo,
    American in the rough; the autobiography of W. M. (Bill) Coffman. New York, Simon and Schuster, 1955. 309 p.
55010058
Coffman, William Milo, -- 1883-

RD728 Orthopedia. Orthopedic surgery — Biography — Individual, A-Z

RD728.D38.A34
David, Solomon D.,
    Transfigured : the autobiography of Solomon D. David / as told to J. Robert Moffett ; [designed & edited by Larry Bouchard ; map by Julie Eileen Ryan]. New Braunfels, Tex. : Solomon D. & Victoria David Foundation ; c1979. ix, 82 p. :
79-128696   617/.3/00924
David, Solomon D., -- 1888-1977.   Orthopedists -- United States -- Biography.

RD736 Orthopedia. Orthopedic surgery — Special therapies, A-Z

RD736.P47.O78 1997
    Orthopedic and sports physical therapy. St. Louis : Mosby-Year Book, c1997. xiii, 633 p.
96-020127   615.8/2   0815190514
    Orthopedics. Physical therapy. Sports physical therapy.

RD755 Orthopedia. Orthopedic surgery — Orthopedic instruments, apparatus, and appliances — General works

RD755.U83
    The use of technology in the care of the elderly and the disabled : tools for living / edited by Jean Bray and Sheila Wright ; foreword by H. S. Wolff. Westport, Conn. : Greenwood Press, c1980. xii, 267 p. :
80-017847   617/.9   0313226164
    Orthopedic apparatus -- Congresses. Self-help devices for the disabled -- Congresses. Physically handicapped -- Rehabilitation -- Congresses.

RD768-771 Orthopedia. Orthopedic surgery — Deformities and disorders — Spine. Back

RD768.E39 1999
Edwards, B. C.
    Manual of combined movements : their use in the examination and treatment of musculoskeletal vertebral column disorders / Brian C. Edwards. 2nd ed. Oxford ; Butterworth-Heinemann, c1999. vi, 149 p. :
          617.4/7   0750642904
    Spine--Examination--Handbooks, manuals, etc. Spine--Movements--Handbooks, manuals, etc. Manipulation, Orthopedic--methods.

RD768.O646 1999
    Operative spine surgery / [edited by] William C. Welch, George B. Jacobs, Roger P. Jackson. Stamford, Conn. : Appleton & Lange, c1999. ix, 275 p. :
98-022965   617.5/6059   0838573932
    Spine -- Surgery. Spine -- surgery. Spinal Diseases -- surgery.

RD771.B217B669 2001
Borenstein, David G.
Back in control! :a conventional and complementary prescription for eliminating back pain / David Borenstein. New York : M. Evans, c2001. 208 p. :
     617.5/64   0871319454
    Backache. Backache--Alternative treatment.

RD771.B217N43 2000
Neck and back pain : the scientific evidence of causes, diagnosis, and treatment / editors, Alf L. Nachemson, Egon Jonsson. Philadelphia : Lippincott Williams & Wilkins, c2000. xv, 495 p. :
     617.5/64   078172760X
    Backache. Neck pain. Exercise therapy.

RD771.B217.P49 1994
Physical therapy of the low back / edited by Lance T. Twomey, James R. Taylor. New York : Churchill Livingstone, c2000. xii, 411 p. :
00-022470   617.5/64062   0443065527
    Backache -- Physical therapy. Backache. Back Pain -- rehabilitation.

RD797 Orthopedia. Orthopedic surgery — Physical rehabilitation — Societies. Serials

RD797.C55 1996
Clinical orthopaedic rehabilitation / editor, S. Brent Brotzman. St. Louis : Mosby, c1996. xii, 402 p. :
     617.3   0815110340
    People with disabilities--Rehabilitation. Orthopedics. Orthopedics--methods.

RD798 Orthopedia. Orthopedic surgery — Physical rehabilitation — General special

RD798.D4
DeLoach, Charlene.
Adjustment to severe physical disability : a metamorphosis / Charlene DeLoach, Bobby G. Greer. New York : McGraw-Hill, c1981. xv, 310 p. ;
80-017612   362.4/01/9   0070162816
    Physically handicapped -- Psychology. Adjustment (Psychology) Social adjustment.

RE Ophthalmology

RE26 History — General works

RE26.H53 1996
The history of ophthalmology / edited by Daniel M. Albert, Diane D. Edwards. Cambridge, Mass., USA : Blackwell Science, c1996. xvi, 394 p., [12] p. of plates :
617.7/009   0865423784
Ophthalmology--History. Ophthalmology--history.

RE36 Biography — Individual, A-Z

RE36.H56.A3 1993
Hine, Robert V.,
Second sight / Robert V. Hine. Berkeley : University of California Press, c1993. xv, 203 p. :
92-031096   362.4/1/092   0520081951
Hine, Robert V., -- 1921- -- Health.   Blind -- United States -- Biography.

RE48 Diseases of the eye (General) — General special

RE48.E445 2003
Emergency ophthalmology / [edited by] Kenneth C. Chern. New York : McGraw-Hill, Medical Pub. Division, c2003. p. ;
617.7/026   007137325X
Ophthalmologic emergencies. Eye Diseases--diagnosis. Eye Diseases--therapy.

RE48.F8
Fuchs, Adalbert,
Geography of eye diseases.   Wien, Verlag Notring der Wissenschaftlichen Verbande O 1962. 162 p.
63004709
Eye -- Diseases and defects. Medical geography.

RE48.M335 1998
Management of ocular injuries and emergencies / edited by Mathew W. MacCumber ; illustrations by Brent A. Bauer. Philadelphia : Lippincott-Raven, c1998. xxi, 486 p. :
617.7/025   0397514964
Ophthalmologic emergencies. Eye--Wounds and injuries. Eye Injuries--therapy.

RE48.W625 1995
Wilkins, Arnold J.
Visual stress / Arnold J. Wilkins. Oxford ; Oxford University Press, 1995. xxii, 194 p.
94-032441   617.7   019852174X
Eyestrain.

RE51 Diseases of the eye (General) — Outlines, syllabi, etc.

RE51.C48 2001
Chapman, Bill G.
Coping with vision loss :maximizing what you can see and do / Bill G. Chapman ; illustrated by George H. Pollock. Alameda, CA : Hunter House ; xviii, 282 p. :
617.7   0897933168
Vision disorders--Popular works. Low vision--Popular works. Large type books.

RE51.G75 2000
Grierson, Ian.
The eye book : eyes and eye problems explained / Ian Grierson. Liverpool : Liverpool University Press, 2000. 212 p., [8] p. of plates :
612.8/4   0853237557
Eye. Eye--Diseases--Popular works. Eye--Diseases--Treatment--Popular works.

RE51.L28 2001
Lavine, Jay B.
The eye care sourcebook / Jay B. Lavine. Chicago : Contemporary Books, c2001. xii, 340 p. :
617.7   0737303956
Eye--Care and hygiene--Popular works.

RE67 Clinical physiology of the eye

RE67.N88 1999
Nutritional and environmental influences on vision / edited by Allen Taylor. Boca Raton, FL : CRC Press, 1999. p. cm.
98-049170   617.7/071   0849385652
Eye -- Pathophysiology. Eye -- Diseases -- Nutritional aspects. Eye -- Diseases -- Environmental aspects.

RE68 Immunological aspects

RE68.A44 2000
Allergic diseases of the eye / [edited by] Mark B. Abelson ; illustrated by David Anders Tilden. Philadelphia : Saunders, c2000. xiii, 270 p. :
617.7/1   0721686796
Eye--Diseases--Immunological aspects. Allergy. Eye--Inflammation.

RE91 Vision disorders. Blindness — General works

RE91.B35 1990
Bailey, Ian L.
Visual impairment : an overview / Ian L. Bailey, Amanda Hall. New York, NY : American Foundation for the Blind, c1990. iii, 49 p. :
90-001099   617.7/12   0891281746
Low vision.

RE91.S27 2002

The encyclopedia of blindness and vision impairment / Jill Sardegna ... [et al.]. 2nd ed. New York : Facts on File, c2002. xiii, 333 p. :

362.4/1/03　　　　0816042802

Blindness--Dictionaries. Blind, Apparatus for the--Dictionaries. Vision disorders--Dictionaries.

RE91.S413
Senden, Marius von.

Space and sight; the perception of space and shape in the congenitally blind before and after operation. Translated by Peter Heath. Glencoe, Ill., Free Press c 1960 348 p.

61002883　　　　152.1

Blindness. Eye -- Surgery. Vision.

RE336 Diseases of the anterior segment — Diseases of the cornea — General works

RE336.R3 1993
Rabinowitz, Yaron S.

Color atlas of corneal topography : interpreting videokeratography / Yaron S Rabinowitz, Steven E. Wilson, Stephen D. Klyce. New York, N.Y. : Igaku-Shoin, c1993. ix, 115 p. :

93-000208　　　　617.7/19　　　　0896402355

Cornea -- Diseases -- Atlases. Computer-assisted videokeratography -- Atlases. Cornea -- anatomy & histology -- atlases.

RE551 Diseases of the posterior segment — Diseases of the retina — General works

RE551.R43 2001

Retina / editor-in-chief, Stephen J. Ryan. 3rd ed. St. Louis : Mosby, c2001. 3 v. (xxix, 2601, 53 p.) :

617.7/35　　　　0323008046

Retina--Diseases. Retina--Surgery. Retina--Physiology.

RE551.Y36 1995
Yannuzzi, Lawrence A.,

The retina atlas / Lawrence A. Yannuzzi, David R. Guyer, W. Richard Green. St. Louis : Mosby, c1995. xvii, 782 p.

94-031577　　　　617.7/3/0222　　　　0815134320

Retina -- Diseases -- Atlases. Retinal Diseases -- atlases.

RE661 Diseases of the posterior segment — Diseases of the retina — Other diseases of the retina, A-Z

RE661.D3G56 2001
Glaser, Bert,

The macular degeneration sourcebook :a guide for patients and families / Bert Glaser, Lester A. Picker. Omaha, Neb. : Addicus Books, 2001. p. cm.

617.7/35　　　　1886039534

Retinal degeneration--Popular works.

RE925 Refraction and errors of refraction and accommodation — General works

RE925.H8
Huxley, Aldous,

The art of seeing / by Aldous Huxley. New York : Harper, c1942. 273 p. ;

42024692　　　　617.7

Vision. Eye -- Accommodation and refraction. Eye -- Diseases and defects.

RF Otorhinolaryngology

RF25 History — General works

RF25.W45 1990
Weir, Neil.
Otolaryngology : an illustrated history / Neil Weir. London ; Butterworths, 1990. 290 p. :
617.5/1/009   0407009248
Otolaryngology--History. Otolaryngology--history

RF38 Biography — Individual, A-Z

RF38.R67.A3
Rosen, Samuel,
The autobiography of Dr. Samuel Rosen. New York, Knopf; [distributed by Random House] 1973. xiv, 268 p.
72-011041   617.8/00924   0394443438
Rosen, Samuel, -- 1897- Otolaryngologists -- New York (State) -- New York -- Biography.

RF46 General works — 1901-

RF46.L83 1999
Essentials of otolaryngology / editors, Frank E. Lucente, Gady Har-El ; associate editors, Ari J. Goldsmith ... [et al.]. 4th ed. Philadelphia : Lippincott Williams & Wilkins, c1999. xx, 488 p. :
617.5/1   078171463X
Otolaryngology. Otorhinolaryngologic Diseases.

RF52.5 Nursing

RF52.5.S54 1993
Sigler, Barbara A.
Ear, nose, and throat disorders / Barbara A. Sigler, Linda T. Schuring ; original illustratins by George J. Wassilchenko and Donald P. O'Connor ; original photography by Patrick Watson. St. Louis : Mosby, c1993. xiii, 290 p.
93-023154   617.5/1   0801680115
Otolaryngologic nursing. Otorhinolaryngologic Diseases -- nursing.

RF123 Otology. Diseases of the ear — Examination. Diagnosis — General works

RF123.R84 1986
Ruenes, Ramon.
Otologic radiology : with clinical correlations / Ramon Ruenes, Antonio De la Cruz ; House Ear Institute. New York : Macmillan ; c1986. xiii, 183 p.
85-024059   617.8/0757   0023261307
Ear -- Radiography. Ear -- Diseases -- Diagnosis. Diagnosis, Radioscopic.

RF225 Otology. Diseases of the ear — Diseases of the middle ear — Otitis media

RF225.B57 2000
Bluestone, Charles D.,
Otitis media in infants and children / Charles D. Bluestone, Jerome O. Klein. 3rd ed. Philadelphia : Saunders, c2001. 404 p. :
618.92/09784   0721687091
Otitis media in children. Child. Otitis Media--Infant.

RF235 Otology. Diseases of the ear — Diseases of the mastoid process

RF235.W5
Whiting, Frederick.
The modern mastoid operation, by Frederick Whiting, illustrated by twenty-five half-tone and twenty-three key plates made from original drawings. Philadelphia, P. Blakiston's Son & Co., 1905. xiii, p. 1 .
05003746
Mastoid -- surgery

RF290 Otology. Diseases of the ear — Audiology. Hearing disorders. Deafness — General works

RF290.E73 2001
Gelfand, Stanley A.,
Essentials of audiology / Stanley A. Gelfand.2nd ed. New York : Thieme, 2001. p. cm.
617.8   1588900177
Audiology.

RF290.M34 2002
Martin, Frederick N.
Introduction to audiology / Frederick N. Martin, John Greer Clark. 8th ed. Boston : Allyn and Bacon, 2002. p. cm.
617.8   0205366414
Audiometry. Audiology. Hearing disorders--Problems, exercises, etc.

RF290.M84 2000
Myers, David G.
A quiet world : living with hearing loss / David G. Myers. New Haven : Yale University Press, c2000. xi, 211 p. :
00-038153   617.8   0300084390
Deafness -- Popular works. Hearing disorders -- Popular works. Hearing aids.

RF290.N47 1992
Newby, Hayes A.
Audiology / Hayes A. Newby, Gerald R. Popelka. 6th ed. Englewood Cliffs, N.J. : Prentice Hall, c1992. viii, 552 p. :
617.8/9   0130519219
Audiology. Hearing disorders. Hearing.

RF290.T93 2000
Turkington, Carol.
The encyclopedia of deafness and hearing disorders / Carol Turkington and Allen E. Sussman. New York, NY : Facts On File, c2000. ix, 294 p. :
00-023288   617.8/003   081604046X
Deafness -- Encyclopedias. Ear -- Diseases -- Encyclopedias.

RF291 Otology. Diseases of the ear — Audiology. Hearing disorders. Deafness — General special

RF291.C63 1996
Communication therapy : an integrated approach to aural rehabilitation with deaf and hard of hearing adolescents and adults / Mary June Moseley, Scott J. Bally, editors. Washington, D.C. : Gallaudet University Press, 1996. xi, 394 p. :
96-016866   617.8/9   1563680548
Deaf -- Rehabilitation. Deaf children -- Rehabilitation. Hearing impaired -- Rehabilitation.

RF291.J63 1987
Jones, Lesley,
Words apart : losing your hearing as an adult / Lesley Jones, Jim Kyle, Peter Wood. London ; Tavistock Publications, 1987. vii, 267 p. :
87-017966   362.4/2   0422609706
Deafness -- Social aspects.

RF291.M9
Myklebust, Helmer R.
The psychology of deafness; sensory deprivation, learning, and adjustment. New York, Grune & Stratton [1960] xii, 393 p.
60014526   136.761
Deafness -- Psychological aspects.

RF291.35 Otology. Diseases of the ear — Audiology. Hearing disorders. Deafness — Popular works

RF291.35.S88 1999
Suss, Elaine.
When the hearing gets hard : winning the battle against hearing impairment / by Elaine Suss. Secaucus, NJ : Carol Pub. Group, c1999. p. cm.
       617.8/001/9   0806521406
Hearing impaired--Life skills guides. Hearing impaired-- Psychological aspects. Hearing impaired--Family relationships.

RF291.5 Otology. Diseases of the ear — Audiology. Hearing disorders. Deafness — By age group, class, etc., A-Z

RF291.5.C45.I54 1994
Infants and toddlers with hearing loss : family-centered assessment and intervention / edited by Jackson Roush and Noel D. Matkin. Baltimore : York Press, c1994. xiv, 360 p. :
94-022417   362.4/28/054   0912752289
Hearing disorders in children. Hearing disorders in infants. Hearing impaired children -- Family relationships.

RF291.5.C45N67 2001
Northern, Jerry L.
Hearing in children / Jerry L. Northern, Marion P. Downs. 5th ed. Philadelphia, PA : Lippincott Williams & Wilkins, 2001. p. cm.
       618.92/0978   0683307649
Hearing disorders in children.

RF292.8 Otology. Diseases of the ear — Audiology. Hearing disorders. Deafness — Congenital and hereditary deafness — Usher's syndrome

RF292.8.C37 2002
Carroll, Cathryn.
Orchid of the Bayou : a deaf woman faces blindness / Cathryn Carroll and Catherine Hoffpauir Fischer. Washington, DC : Gallaudet University Press, 2002. xiii, 253 p.
00-050410   362.4/1/092   1563681048
Fischer, Catherine Hoffpauir. Usher's syndrome -- Patients -- Biography. Usher's syndrome -- Popular works.

RF293.8 Audiology. Hearing disorders. Deafness — Tinnitus

RF293.8. H463 2002
Henry, Jane L.
Tinnitus :a self-management guide for the ringing in your ears / Jane L. Henry, Peter H. Wilson. Boston : Allyn and Bacon, c2002. xiv, 209 p. ;
       617.8   0205315372
Tinnitus. Tinnitus--Treatment. Tinnitus--Patients--Rehabilitation.

RF293.8.V47 2001
Vernon, Jack A.
Tinnitus :questions and answers / Jack A. Vernon, Barbara Tabachnick Sanders. Boston : Allyn and Bacon, c2001. xii, 276 p. :
       617.8   0205326854
Tinnitus--Examinations, questions, etc. Tinnitus--therapy-- Examination Questions. Tinnitus--diagnosis--Examination Questions.

RF294 Otology. Diseases of the ear — Audiology. Hearing disorders. Deafness — Clinical hearing tests. Audiometry

RF294.S55 1991
Silman, Shlomo.
Auditory diagnosis : principles and applications / Shlomo Silman, Carol A. Silverman. San Diego : Academic Press, c1991. xvi, 412 p. :
90-014465   617.8/075   0126434514
Audiometry. Hearing disorders -- Diagnosis. Hearing Disorders -- diagnosis.

RF297 Otology. Diseases of the ear — Audiology. Hearing disorders. Deafness — Other treatment

RF297.R44 2000
Rehabilitative audiology : children and adults / editors, Jerome G. Alpiner, Patricia A. McCarthy. Philadelphia, PA : Lippincott Williams & Wilkins, c2000. xii, 690 p. :
99-032657   617.8/9   0683306529
Hearing impaired -- Rehabilitation. Deaf -- Rehabilitation. Audiology.

RF510 Laryngology. Diseases of the throat — Diseases of the larynx, vocal cords, epiglottis, and trachea — General works

RF510.A53 1999
Andrews, Moya L.
Manual of voice treatment : pediatrics through geriatrics / Moya L. Andrews. 2nd ed. San Diego : Singular Pub. Group, c1999. xiv, 709 p. :
           616.85/5   1565939980
Voice disorders--Handbooks, manuals, etc. Voice disorders--Treatment--Handbooks, manuals, etc. Voice Disorders--therapy--handbooks.

RG Gynecology and Obstetrics

RG45 Dictionaries and encyclopedias

RG45.M45 2000
Melloni, June L.
Melloni's illustrated dictionary of obstetrics and gynecology / edited by I.G. Dox, J.L. Melloni, and H.H. Sheld. New York : Parthenon Pub. Group, c2000. 401 p. :
99-056573   618/.03   1850707103
Gynecology -- Dictionaries. Obstetrics -- Dictionaries. Gynecology -- Dictionary -- English.

RG51 History — General works

RG51.F55 1950
Graham, Harvey,
Eternal Eve, by Harvey Graham [pseud. London] Heinemann, 1950. xx, 699 p.
618.09
Gynecology--History. Obstetrics--History.

RG51.O36 1994
O'Dowd, Michael J.
The history of obstetrics and gynaecology / Michael J. O'Dowd and Elliot E. Philipp ; with a foreword by J.J. Sciarra. New York : Parthenon Pub. Group, c1994. x, 710 p. :
94-019129   618/.09   1850702241
Gynecology -- History. Obstetrics -- History. Obstetrics -- history.

RG76 Biography — Individual

RG76.L35G8813 2001
Gutmann, Caroline.
The legacy of Dr. Lamaze : the story of the man who changed childbirth / Caroline Gutmann ; translated by Bruce Henderson. 1st U.S. ed. New York : St. Martin's Press, 2001. xxi, 218 p., [8] p. of plates :
618.2/0092   031226190X
Lamaze, Fernand, 1890-1957. Obstetricians--France--Biography. Natural childbirth. Pregnancy.

RG85 General works — Through 1900 — Medieval

RG85.E53 1980
Medieval woman's guide to health : the first English gynecological handbook : Middle English text / with introd. and modern English translation by Beryl Rowland. Kent, Ohio : Kent State University Press, 1981. xvii, 192 p.
80-082201   618   0873382439
Gynecology -- Early works to 1800. Obstetrics -- Early works to 1800. Medicine, Medieval.

RG103.5 Psychological and psychosomatic aspects

RG103.5.B87 2001
Burt, Vivien K.,
Concise guide to women's mental health / Vivien K. Burt, Victoria C. Hendrick. 2nd ed. Washington, DC : American Psychiatric Pub., c2001. xv, 195 p. :
616.89/0082   1585620300
Gynecology--Psychological aspects. Obstetrics--Psychological aspects. Women--Mental health.

RG103.7 Decision making

RG103.7.F57 1986
Fisher, Sue,
In the patient's best interest : women and the politics of medical decisions / Sue Fisher. New Brunswick, N.J. : Rutgers University Press, c1986. ix, 214 p. :
85-030253   362.1/98   0813511623
Gynecology -- Decision making. Generative organs, Female -- Surgery -- Decision making. Gynecologist and patient.

RG107.5 Examination. Diagnosis — Special diagnostic methods, A-Z

RG107.5.U4R48 2001
Review of diagnostic ultrasound :abdomen and OB/GYN / Roger C. Sanders ... [et al.]. Philadelphia : Lippincott Williams & Wilkins, 2001. p. ;
618/.047543   0781717787
Ultrasonics in obstetrics--Examinations, questions, etc. Generative organs, Female--Ultrasonic imaging--Examinations, questions, Abdomen--Ultrasonic imaging--Examinations, questions, etc.

RG110 Handbooks, manuals, etc.

RG110.D36 1999
Danforth's obstetrics and gynecology / 8th ed. editors James R. Scott ... [et al.] ; illustrations by Jennifer Smith, medical illustrator. Philadelphia : Lippincott, Williams & Wilkins, c1999. xviii, 988 p. :
618   0781712068
Gynecology--Handbooks, manuals, etc. Obstetrics--Handbooks, manuals, etc. Obstetrics.

RG121 Popular works

RG121.H435 2001
Healthy women, healthy lives :a guide to preventing disease from the landmark Nurses' Health Study / senior editors, Susan E. Hankinson ... [et al.]. New York : Simon & Schuster Source, c2001. xxviii, 546 p. :
613/.04244   0743217748
Women--Diseases--Prevention. Women--Health and hygiene.

RG121.K218 1990
Kahn, Ada P.
The A-Z of women's sexuality / Ada P. Kahn, Linda Hughey Holt. New York : Facts on File, c1990. 362 p. :
89-028211   618/.03   0816019967
Gynecology -- Popular works. Obstetrics -- Popular works. Women -- Sexual behavior -- Dictionaries.

RG133.5 Reproductive technology

RG133.5.B434 2000
Becker, Gaylene.
The elusive embryo : how women and men approach new reproductive technologies / Gay Becker. Berkeley: University of California Press, 2000. x, 320 p. ;
00-055967   616.6/9206   0520224302
Human reproductive technology -- Case studies. Infertility -- Patients -- Interviews.

RG133.5.B625 2000
Bodies of technology : women's involvement with reproductive medicine / edited by Ann Rudinow Saetnan, Nelly Oudshoorn, and Marta Kirejczyk. Columbus, OH : Ohio State University Press, c2000. x, 461 p. ;
00-032368   618.1/7806   0814208460
Human reproductive technology -- Social aspects. Human reproductive technology -- Cross-cultural studies. Women -- Health and hygiene -- Social aspects.

RG133.5.D38 2001
Davis, Dena S.,
Genetic dilemmas : reproductive technology, parental choices, and children's futures / Dena S. Davis. New York : Routledge, c2001. ix, 153 p. ;
00-055336   176   0415924081
Human reproductive technology -- Moral and ethical aspects. Medical genetics -- Moral and ethical aspects.

RG133.5.F93 1998
The future of human reproduction : ethics, choice, and regulation / edited by John Harris and Soren Holm. Oxford ; Clarendon Press, 1998. p. cm.
98-016389   176   0198237618
Human reproductive technology -- Moral and ethical aspects. Human reproductive technology -- Government policy. Human reproductive technology -- Social aspects.

RG133.5.H38 1992
Harris, John,
Wonderwoman and Superman : the ethics of human biotechnology / John Harris. Oxford [England] ; Oxford University Press, 1992. viii, 271 p.
91-023939   176   0192177540
Human reproductive technology -- Moral and ethical aspects. Genetic engineering -- Moral and ethical aspects.

RG133.5.M846 1997
Mulkay, M. J.
The embryo research debate : science and the politics of reproduction / Michael Mulkay. New York : Cambridge University Press, 1997. xiii, 212 p.
96-029109   176/.0941   0521571804
Human reproductive technology -- Political aspects -- Great Britain. Human embryo -- Research -- Political aspects -- Great Britain.

RG133.5.P87 1996
Purdy, Laura M.
Reproducing persons : issues in feminist bioethics / Laura M. Purdy. Ithaca, NY : Cornell University Press, c1996. ix, 257 p. ;
95-052019   176   080143243X
Human reproductive technology -- Moral and ethical aspects. Abortion -- Moral and ethical aspects. Feminist ethics.

RG133.5.R38 1993
Raymond, Janice G.
Women as wombs : reproductive technologies and the battle over women's freedom / Janice G. Raymond. [San Francisco] : HarperSanFrancisco, c1993. xxxiii, 254 p
92-056139   176   0062508989
Human reproductive technology -- Moral and ethical aspects. Human reproductive technology -- Political aspects. Women -- United States -- Social conditions.

RG133.5.S77 1997
Strong, Carson.
Ethics in reproductive and perinatal medicine : a new framework / Carson Strong. New Haven : Yale University Press, 1997. viii, 247 p.
96-018957   174/.25   0300068328
Human reproductive technology -- Moral and ethical aspects. Perinatology -- Moral and ethical aspects. Ethics, Medical.

RG135 Reproductive technology — Fertilization in vitro

RG135.B66 1989
Bonnicksen, Andrea L.
In vitro fertilization : building policy from laboratories to legislatures / Andrea L. Bonnicksen. New York : Columbia University Press, c1989. x, 194 p. ;
88-034620   362.1/98178   0231069049
Fertilization in vitro, Human -- Social aspects -- United States. Fertilization in vitro, Human -- Government policy -- United States. Fertilization in vitro, Human -- Law and legislation -- United States.

RG136 Contraception. Birth control

RG136.G765 1985
Guillebaud, John.
Contraception : your questions answered / John Guillebaud. London : Pittman, 1985. 311 p. :
          613.9/4   0272798193
Contraception--Miscellanea.

RG137.45-137.5 Contraception. Birth control — Contraceptives — Contraceptive drugs

RG137.45.R53 1997
Riddle, John M.
Eve's herbs : a history of contraception and abortion in the West / John M. Riddle. Cambridge, Mass. : Harvard University Press, 1997. 341 p. :
96-040383   613.9/4   067427024X
Herbal contraceptives -- History. Herbal abortifacients -- History. Birth control -- Public opinion.

RG137.5.A76 1995
Asbell, Bernard.
The Pill : a biography of the drug that changed the world / Bernard Asbell. New York : Random House, c1995. xvii, 411 p.
94-023185   613.9/432   0679435557
Oral contraceptives -- Research -- History. Oral contraceptives -- Social aspects.

RG137.5.R53 1992
Riddle, John M.
Contraception and abortion from the ancient world to the Renaissance / John M. Riddle. Cambridge, Mass. : Harvard University Press, 1992. x, 245 p. :
91-033682   613.9/4/0901   0674168755
Contraception -- History. Oral contraceptives -- History. Mifepristone -- History.

RG161 Functional and systemic disorders. Endocrine gynecology — Menstrual disorders — General works

RG161.G35 1985
Gannon, Linda.
Menstrual disorders and menopause : biological, psychological, and cultural research / Linda R. Gannon. New York : Praeger, 1985. xii, 285 p. :
85-003629   618.1/72   0030038782
Menstruation disorders. Menopause. Menopause.

RG161.M47 1991
Menstrual health in women's lives / edited by Alice J. Dan and Linda L. Lewis. Urbana : University of Illinois Press, c1992. 301 p. :
90-011178   618.1/72   0252062094
Menstruation disorders -- Congresses. Menstrual cycle -- Congresses. Menstruation -- Miscellanea -- Congresses.

RG165 Functional and systemic disorders. Endocrine gynecology — Menstrual disorders — Premenstrual syndrome

RG165.F526 1996
Figert, Anne E.
Women and the ownership of PMS : the structuring of a psychiatric disorder / Anne E. Figert. New York : Aldine De Gruyter, c1996. xx, 191 p. :
96-003647   618.1/72   0202305503
Premenstrual syndrome -- Social aspects. Premenstrual syndrome -- Psychological aspects. Women -- Mental health.

RG186 Functional and systemic disorders. Endocrine gynecology — Menstrual disorders — Menopause

RG186.M42 1990
The meanings of menopause : historical, medical, and clinical perspectives / edited by Ruth Formanek. Hillsdale, NJ : Analytic Press : 1990. xxv, 322 p. :
89-017905   612.6/65   0881630802
Menopause. Menopause.

RG186.N67 2001
Northrup, Christiane.
The wisdom of menopause :creating physical and emotional health and healing during the change / Christiane Northrup. New York : Bantam Books, 2001. xvi, 589 p. :
          618.1/75   055380121X
Menopause. Menopause--Psychological aspects. Menopause--Religious aspects.

RG186.T73 1999
Treatment of the postmenopausal woman :basic and clinical aspects / editor, Rogerio A. Lobo.2nd ed. Philadelphia, PA : Lippincott Williams & Wilkins, c1999. xxi, 681 p. :
          618.1/75   0781715598
Menopause--Complications. Menopause--Hormone therapy. Climacteric--physiology.

RG483 Diseases of the female pelvis and pelvic supporting structures — Special, A-Z

RG483.E53E56 1995
The endometriosis sourcebook :the definitive guide to current treatment options, the latest research, common myths about the disease, and coping strategies-- both physical and emotional / [compiled by] Mary Lou Ballweg and the Endometriosis Association ; foreword by Dan Mart Chicago : Contemporary Books, c1995. xviii, 473 p. :
          618.1   0809232634
Endometriosis--Popular works.

RG483.E53E57 1997
Endometrium and endometriosis / edited by Michael P. Diamond, Kevin G. Osteen. Malden, Mass. : Blackwell Science, c1997. xiv, 384 p. :
          618.1   0865425027
Endometriosis. Endometrium--Pathophysiology. Endometriosis--therapy.

RG491 Diseases of the breast — General works

RG491.M58 2001
Mitchell, Deborah R.
Breast health the natural way / Deborah Mitchell and Deborah Gordon. New York : John Wiley, c2001. vi, 282 p. :
          618.1/9   0471379581
Breast--Care and hygiene. Alternative medicine. Women--Health and hygiene.

RG493.5 Diseases of the breast — Examination. Diagnosis — Special diagnostic methods, A-Z

RG493.5.R33A23 2001
Andolina, Valerie.
   Mammographic imaging :a practical guide / Valerie Fink Andolina, Shelly Lillé, Kathleen M. Willison. Baltimore, MD : Lippincott Williams & Wilkins, 2001. xvii, 498 p. :
          618.1/07572   0781716969
   Breast--Radiography. Breast--Imaging. Breast--Cancer--Diagnosis.

RG516 Obstetrics — History — 19th-20th centuries

RG516.L68 1992
Loudon, Irvine.
   Death in childbirth : an international study of maternal care and maternal mortality, 1800-1950 / Irvine Loudon. Oxford : Clarendon Press ; 1992. xxiii, 622 p.
92-020160   362.1/982   0198229976
   Prenatal care -- History -- 19th century. Prenatal care -- History -- 20th century. Mothers -- Mortality -- History -- 19th century.

RG518 Obstetrics — History — By region or country, A-Z

RG518.U5.L4 1986
Leavitt, Judith Walzer.
   Brought to bed : childbearing in America, 1750 to 1950 / Judith Walzer Leavitt. New York : Oxford University Press, 1986. ix, 284 p. :
85-030967   618.2/00973   0195038436
   Obstetrics -- United States -- History -- 18th century. Obstetrics -- United States -- History -- 19th century. Obstetrics -- United States -- History -- 20th century.

RG518.U5.W47 1989
Wertz, Richard W.
   Lying-in : a history of childbirth in America / Richard W. Wertz and Dorothy C. Wertz. New Haven : Yale University Press, 1989. xviii, 322 p.
89-050512   618.2/00973   0300040873
   Obstetrics -- United States -- History. Childbirth -- United States -- History. Obstetrics -- Social aspects -- United States -- History.

RG524 Obstetrics — General works — 1931-

RG524.W7 2001
   Williams obstetrics / F. Gary Cunningham ... [et al.]. 21st ed. New York : McGraw-Hill, c2001. x, 1668 p. :
          618.2   0071121951
   Obstetrics. Obstetrics.

RG525 Obstetrics — Popular works

RG525.P437 2001
Petrikovsky, Boris M.
   What your unborn baby wants you to know :a complete guide to a healthy pregnancy / Boris Petrikovsky, Jessica Jacob, and Lisa Aiken. New York, N.Y. : Perigee, 2001. xvii, 296 p. :
          618.2/4   039952682X
   Pregnancy--Popular works. Childbirth--Popular works. Prenatal care--Popular works.

RG525.P676 1997
   Pregnancy and birth sourcebook : basic information about planning for pregnancy, maternal health, fetal growth and development ... / edited by Heather E. Aldred. Detroit, MI : Omnigraphics, c1997. xiii, 737 p.
97-036154   618.2   0780802160
   Pregnancy. Childbirth. Pregnancy -- Complications.

RG525.V38 1996
Vaughan, Christopher C.,
   How life begins : the science of life in the womb / Christopher Vaughan ; illustrations, Marni Fylling. New York : Times Books, c1996. xiv, 290 p. :
94-048779   612.6/4   0812921038
   Fetus -- Growth. Human embryo. Human reproduction.

RG526 Obstetrics — General special

RG526.A76 1982
Arney, William Ray.
   Power and the profession of obstetrics / William Ray Arney. Chicago : University of Chicago Press, 1982. xi, 290 p. :
82-008410   362.1/982   0226027287
   Obstetrics -- Social aspects. Obstetrics -- Practice. Midwifery.

RG571 Obstetrics — Pregnancy — Obstetrical emergencies. Diseases and conditions in pregnancy — General works

RG571.M45 2000
   Cherry and Merkatz's complications of pregnancy. 5th ed. / editor, Wayne R. Cohen ; consulting editors, Sheldon H. Philadelphia : Lippincott Williams & Wilkins, c2000. xxii, 902 p. :
          618.3   0683016733
   Pregnancy--Complications. Pregnancy Complications.

RG613 Obstetrics — The embryo and fetus. Perinatology — Physiology of the fetus

RG613.J56 2001
Jirásek, Jan E.
  An atlas of the human embryo and fetus :a photographic review of human prenatal development / Jan E. Jirásek ; foreword by Louis G. Keith. New York : Parthenon Pub. Group, c2001. 144 p. :
           612.6/4/00222   185070659X
  Embryology, Human--Atlases. Fetus--Atlases. Fetus--Growth--Atlases.

RG627.5 Obstetrics — The embryo and fetus. Perinatology — Diseases and abnormalities

RG627.5.S57 1997
Jones, Kenneth Lyons.
  Smith's recognizable patterns of human malformation / Kenneth Lyons Jones. 5th ed. Philadelphia : Saunders, c1997. xviii, 857 p. :
           616/.043   0721661157
  Abnormalities, Human. Abnormalities.

RG629 Obstetrics — Diseases and abnormalities — Special diseases and abnormalities, A-Z

RG629.F45.I57 1996
  Fetal alcohol syndrome : diagnosis, epidemiology, prevention, and treatment / Kathleen Stratton, Cynthia Howe, and Frederick Battaglia, editors ; Committee to Study Fetal Alcohol Syndrome, Division of Biobehavioral Sciences and Mental Disorders, Institute of Medicine. Washington, D.C. : National Academy Press, 1996. xiii, 213 p.
  95-049289   618.3/268   0309052920
  Fetal alcohol syndrome. Fetal Alcohol Syndrome.

RG652 Obstetrics — Labor. Parturition — General special

RG652.A45 1986
  The American way of birth / edited by Pamela S. Eakins. Philadelphia : Temple University Press, 1986. xvii, 350 p.
  86-003803   304.6/3/0973   0877224323
  Childbirth -- Social aspects. Pregnancy -- Social aspects. Feminism.

RG652.B65 1995
Borst, Charlotte G.
  Catching babies : the professionalization of childbirth, 1870-1920 / Charlotte G. Borst. Cambridge, Mass. : Harvard University Press, 1995. xi, 254 p. :
  95-005261   618.2/009775   0674102622
  Childbirth -- Wisconsin -- History -- 19th century. Childbirth -- Wisconsin -- History -- 20th century. Midwifery -- Wisconsin -- History.

RG661-661.5 Obstetrics — Labor. Parturition — Natural childbirth

RG661.C656 2000
  Complementary therapies for pregnancy and childbirth / edited by Denise Tiran and Sue Mack. New York Bailliere Tindall, 2000. p. cm.
  99-053489   618.2   044306427X
  Pregnancy -- Alternative treatment. Childbirth -- Alternative treatment.

RG661.D5 1956
Dick-Read, Grantly,
  The natural childbirth primer. New York, Harper [1956, c1955] 52 p.
           618.4
  Childbirth--Psychology.

RG661.5.F56 1998
Flatto, Edwin.
  Home birth : step-by-step instruction for natural home birth and emergency childbirth / [Edwin W. Flatto]. 11th (rev.) ed. Miami, Fla. : Plymouth Press, c1998. 141 p. :
           618.4   0935540024
  Childbirth at home--Handbooks, manuals, etc.

RG761 Obstetrics — Obstetric operations. Operative obstetrics — Cesarean section

RG761.B48 1990
Blumenfeld-Kosinski, Renate,
  Not of woman born : representations of caesarean birth in medieval and Renaissance culture / Renate Blumenfeld-Kosinski. Ithaca : Cornell University Press, 1990. x, 204 p. :
  89-017421   618.8/6/0902   0801422922
  Cesarean section -- Europe -- History. Cesarean section in art. Medical illustration -- History.

RG811 Obstetrics — Puerperal state — Puerperal infection

RG811.C45 1995
  Childbed fever : a documentary history / edited by Irvine Loudon. New York : Garland Pub., 1995. lxv, 224 p. ;
  94-033390   618.7/4   081531079X
  Puerperal septicemia -- History -- Sources.

RG940 Obstetrics — Maternal care. Prenatal care services — General works

RG940.P74 1988
  Prenatal care : reaching mothers, reaching infants / Sarah S. Brown, editor ; Committee to Study Outreach for Prenatal Care, Division of Health Promotion and Disease Prevention, Institute of Medicine. Washington, D.C. : National Academy Press, 1988. ix, 254 p. :
  88-028991   362.1/982   0309038928
  Prenatal care. Women's health services. Prenatal Care.

RG940.W66 1992
   Women and children first ; international maternal and infant
welfare, 1870-1945 / edited by Valerie Fildes, Lara Marks, and
Hilary Marland. London ; Routledge, 1992. xxiii, 311 p.
92-007627   362.1/982/009   0415080908
   *Maternal health services -- History -- 20th century. Maternal
health services -- History -- 19th century. Infant health services --
History -- 20th century.*

RG950 Obstetrics — Maternal care. Prenatal care services — Midwifery. Midwives. Doulas

RG950.F7 1998
Fraser, Gertrude Jacinta.
   African American midwifery in the South : dialogues of
birth, race, and memory / Gertrude Jacinta Fraser. Cambridge,
Mass. : Harvard University Press, 1998. x, 287 p. ;
97-038661   618.2/0233
   *Afro-American midwives -- Virginia -- History -- 20th century.
Midwifery -- Virginia -- History -- 20th century. Childbirth -- Virginia
-- History -- 20th century.*

RG950.W48 2002
Wheeler, Linda A.
   Nurse-midwifery handbook : a practical guide to prenatal
and postpartum care / Linda Wheeler. 2nd ed. Philadelphia,
PA : Lippincott Williams & Wilkins, c2002. xx, 443 p. :
               618.2   0781729297
   *Midwifery--Handbooks, manuals, etc. Prenatal care--Handbooks,
manuals, etc. Postnatal care--Handbooks, manuals, etc.*

RG951 Obstetrics — Maternal care. Pernatal care services — Maternity nursing. Obstetrical nursing

RG951.M318 2000
   Maternity & women's health care / [edited by] Deitra
Leonard Lowdermilk, Shannon E. Perry, Irene M. Bobak. 7th
ed. St. Louis, Mo. : Mosby, c2000. xxvi, 1252 p. :
               610.73/678   0323009611
   *Maternity nursing. Gynecologic nursing. Obstetrical Nursing--
methods--Nurses' Instruction.*

RG951.O43 2000
Olds, Sally B.,
   Maternal-newborn nursing : a family and community-based
approach / Sally B. Olds, Marcia L. London, Patricia A.
Wieland Ladewig. Upper Saddle River, N.J. : Prentice Hall
Health, c2000. xxix, 1090 p.
99-028575   610.73/678   0805380701
   *Maternity nursing -- Handbooks, manuals, etc. Community health
nursing -- Handbooks, manuals, etc. CommunityHealth Nursing.*

RG960-962 Obstetrics — Maternal care. Prenatal care services — By region or country

RG960.S85 1988
Sullivan, Deborah A.,
   Labor pains : modern midwives and home birth / Deborah
A. Sullivan and Rose Weitz. New Haven : Yale University
Press, c1988. xii, 220 p. ;
87-023004   618.2/0233   0300040938
   *Midwives -- United States. Midwives -- United States -- History.
Midwives -- Social aspects.*

RG962.E98.S65 1996
Smith, Margaret Charles,
   Listen to me good : the life story of an Alabama midwife /
Margaret Charles Smith and Linda Janet Holmes. Columbus :
Ohio State University Press, c1996. xvii, 178 p.
96-015037   618.2/0233   0814207006
*Smith, Margaret Charles, -- 1906-   Afro-American midwives --
Alabama -- Eutaw -- Biography. Midwifery -- Alabama -- Eutaw --
History.*

RJ Pediatrics

RJ36 History — General works

RJ36.A2
Abt, Arthur F.
Abt-Garrison history of pediatrics. Philadelphia, Saunders, 1965. x, 316 p.
      618.92
Pediatrics--History.

RJ36.C65 1999
Colon, A. R.
Nurturing children : a history of pediatrics / A.R. Colon with P.A. Colon. Westport, Conn. : Greenwood Press, 1999. xvi, 329 p. :
99-025000   618.92/0009   0313310807
Pediatrics -- History. Pediatrics -- history.

RJ42 History — By region or country, A-Z

RJ42.G7.Y8
Yudkin, Simon.
The health and welfare of the immigrant child: a lecture. London, National Committee for Commonwealth Immigrants [1967]. 15 p.
68-092859   614.09/42
Children of immigrants -- Diseases -- Great Britain. Immigrants -- Health and hygiene -- Great Britain. Public health -- Great Britain.

RJ42.U5.H36 1988
Halpern, Sydney A.
American pediatrics : the social dynamics of professionalism, 1880-1980 / Sydney A. Halpern. Berkeley : University of California Press, c1988. xi, 228 p. ;
87-030222   362.1/9892/00973
0520051955
Pediatrics -- United States -- History. Pediatrics -- history -- United States. Professional Practice -- history -- United States.

RJ43 Biography

RJ43.Y36.A3 1995
Yamazaki, James N.
Children of the atomic bomb : an American physician's memoir of Nagasaki, Hiroshima, and the Marshall Islands / James N. Yamazaki with Louis B. Fleming. Durham : Duke University Press, 1995. xvi, 182 p. :
95-006683   618.92/9897/0092
0822316587
Yamazaki, James N. Pediatricians -- United States -- Biography. Atomic bomb victims -- Medical care -- Japan -- Hiroshima-shi. Atomic bomb victims -- Medical care -- Japan -- Nagasaki-shi.

RJ45 General works

RJ45.R87 2003
Rudolph's pediatrics / editors, Colin D. Rudolph ... [et al.]. 21st ed. New York : McGraw-Hill, Medical Pub. Division, c2003. xxxiv, 2688 p. :
      618.92   0071124578
Pediatrics. Pediatrics.

RJ47 General special

RJ47.D48 1999
Developmental-behavioral pediatrics / [edited by] Melvin D. Levine, William B. Carey, Allen C. Crocker. 3rd ed. Philadelphia : Saunders, c1999. xvi, 912 p. :
      618.92/8   0721671543
Pediatrics. Pediatrics--Psychological aspects. Child development.

RJ47.D55 2001
Ditchek, Stuart H.
Healthy child, whole child :integrating the best of conventional and alternative medicine to keep your kids healthy / Stuart H. Ditchek, Russell H. Greenfield with Lynn Murray Willeford ; foreword by Andrew Weil. 1st ed. New York, N.Y. : HarperResource, c2001. xxv, 434 p. :
      618.92   0062737457
Children--Health and hygiene. Children--Diseases--Alternative treatment. Alternative medicine.

RJ47.5 Psychological and psychosomatic aspects — General works

RJ47.5.C663 1991
This is our child : how parents experience the medical world / edited by Antonya Cooper and Valerie Harpin. Oxford [England] ; Oxford University Press, 1991. viii, 152 p.
90-014176   618.92/0001/9   0192618997
Sick children -- Psychology -- Case studies. Sick children -- Family relationships -- Case studies. Children -- Death -- Psychological aspects -- Case studies.

RJ47.5.H38 1995
Handbook of pediatric psychology / edited by Michael C. Roberts. 2nd ed. New York : Guilford Press, c1995. xviii, 814 p. :
      618.92/00019   0898621569
Pediatrics--Psychological aspects. Sick children--Psychology. Child Psychology.

RJ47.5.S77 1992
Stress and coping in child health / Annette M. La Greca ... [et al.], editors. New York : Guilford Press, c1992. xvi, 413 p. :
91-038224   618.92/0001/9   0898621127
Pediatrics -- Psychological aspects. Sick children -- Psychology. Teenagers -- Diseases -- Psychological aspects.

RJ47.53 Psychological and psychosomatic aspects — Child and adolescent health behavior

RJ47.53.W54 1988
Wilkinson, Simon R.
　The child's world of illness : the development of health and illness behaviour / Simon R. Wilkinson. Cambridge ; Cambridge University Press, 1988. x, 288 p. ;
87-026825　　　　155.4　　　052132873X
　Health behavior in children. Sick children -- Psychology. Attitude to Health -- in infancy & childhood.

RJ47.7 Social aspects

RJ47.7.P38 1996
Pawluch, Dorothy,
　The new pediatrics : a profession in transition / Dorothy Pawluch. Hawthorne, N.Y. : Aldine de Gruyter, c1996. xii, 175 p. :
96-001029　　　　618.92　　　0202305341
　Pediatrics -- Social aspects -- United States. Pediatrics -- Practice -- United States. Pediatrics -- United States -- Philosophy.

RJ48 Handbooks, manuals, etc.

RJ48.R67 1997
Rosenstein, Beryl J.
　Pediatric pearls : the handbook of practical pediatrics / Beryl J. Rosenstein, Patricia D. Fosarelli. 3rd ed. St. Louis : Mosby, c1997. xxvii, 492 p. :
　　　　　　618.92　　0815186827
　Pediatrics--Handbooks, manuals, etc. Pediatrics--handbooks.

RJ50 Examination. Diagnosis — General works

RJ50.G65 1983
Goodman, Richard M.
　The malformed infant and child : an illustrated guide / Richard M. Goodman, Robert J. Gorlin ; medical illustrator, Deborah Meyer. New York : Oxford University Press, 1983. ix, 460 p. :
82-014085　　　　618.92/0043　　　0195032543
　Children -- Diseases -- Diagnosis. Infants -- Diseases -- Diagnosis. Abnormalities, Human -- Diagnosis.

RJ51 Examination. Diagnosis — Special diagnostic methods, A-Z

RJ51.D48.B47 1994
Bergen, Doris.
　Assessment methods for infants and toddlers : transdisciplinary team approaches / Doris Bergen ; foreword by Stephen J. Bagnato. New York : Teachers College Press, c1994. xii, 339 p. :
94-012519　　　618.92/0075　　　0807733806
　Child development -- Testing. Infants -- Development -- Testing. Child development deviations -- Diagnosis.

RJ51.D48.W94 1997
Wyly, M. Virginia
　Infant assessment / M. Virginia Wyly. Boulder, CO : Westview Press, 1997. p. cm.
97-000510　　　　305.232　　　　0813330874
　Infants -- Psychological testing. Infants -- Development -- Testing. Child development deviations -- Diagnosis.

RJ53 Therapeutics — Special therapies, A-Z

RJ53.A27S36 1999
Scott, Julian.
　Acupuncture in the treatment of children / Julian Scott and Teresa Barlow. 3rd ed. Seattle, WA : Eastland Press, 1999. xii, 628 p. :
　　　　　　615.8/92/083　　　0939616300
　Acupuncture for children.

RJ53.O25
　Best practice occupational therapy : in community service with children and families / [edited by] Winnie Dunn. Thorofare, NJ : Slack Inc., c2000. 373 p. :
00-027243　　　　615.8/515/083　　　1556424566
　Occupational therapy for children -- Standards. Occupational therapy services -- Standards.

RJ53.O25O22 2001
　Occupational therapy for children / edited by Jane Case-Smith ; with illustrations by Jeanne Robertson, Jody Fulks, medical illustrator. 4th ed. St. Louis : Mosby, c2001. xiv, 918 p. :
　　　　　　615.8/515/0983　　　0323007643
　Occupational therapy for children. Occupational therapy for children--Practice. Occupational Therapy--in infancy & childhood.

RJ53.P5P52 2000
　Physical therapy for children / editor, Suzann K. Campbell ; associate editors, Darl W. Vander Linden, Robert J. Palisano. 2nd ed. Philadelphia, PA : Saunders, c2000. xvi, 1006 p. :
　　　　　　615.8/2/083　　　0721683169
　Physical therapy for children. Physical Therapy--methods--Child. Physical Therapy--methods--Infant.

RJ53.R43F56 1996
Therapeutic recreation for exceptional children :let me in, I want to   play / edited by Aubrey H. Fine ; Nya M. Fine, consultant ; with a foreword   by Chester L. Land. 2nd ed. Springfield, Ill., U.S.A. : C.C. Thomas, c1996. xix, 401 p. :
      616.8/5153/083   0398066620
Recreational therapy for children. Handicapped children-- Recreation. Play therapy.

RJ60 Infant and neonatal morbidity and mortality — By region or country, A-Z

RJ60.U5.B66 1989
Boone, Margaret S.
Capital crime : Black infant mortality in America / Margaret S. Boone ; foreword by John W. Scanlon. Newbury Park : Sage, c1989. 253 p. :
89-004046   362.1/982/00890730753
0803933738
Afro-American infants -- Mortality.

RJ60.U5.R33 1994
Racial differences in preterm delivery : developing a new research paradigm / edited by Diane Rowley, Heather Tosteson. New York : Oxford University Press, c1994. p. cm.
93-037572   614.5/992   0195090306
Afro-American infants -- Mortality -- Research. Birth weight, Low -- United States -- Research. Health and race -- United States -- Research.

RJ61 Infant and neonatal morbidity and mortality — Popular works

RJ61.S6345 1998
Small, Meredith F.
Our babies, ourselves : how biology and culture shape the way we parent / Meredith F. Small. New York : Anchor Books, 1998. xxii, 292 p.
97-044348   649/.122   0385482574
Infants -- Care -- Cross-cultural studies. Infants -- Development -- Cross-cultural studies. Parent and infant -- Cross-cultural studies.

RJ61.S75
Spock, Benjamin,
A baby's first year, by Benjamin Spock, John Reinhart [and] Wayne Miller, photographer. New York, Duell, Sloan and Pearce [1955] 178 p.
54005100   649.1
Infants -- Care and hygiene.

RJ61.S76 1992
Spock, Benjamin,
Dr. Spock's baby and child care / Benjamin Spock and Michael B. Rothanberg. 6th ed., fully rev. and updated for the 1990s. New York, NY : Pocket Books, 1992. xxv, 832 p. :
      649/.1   20   067
Infants--Care. Child care. Child rearing.

RJ91 Infant and neonatal morbidity and mortality — Supposed prenatal influence. Prenatal culture. Stirpiculture

RJ91.N235 1999
Nathanielsz, P. W.
Life in the womb : the origin of health and disease / Peter W. Nathanielsz. Ithaca, N.Y. : Promethean Press, 1999. p. cm.
98-051356   612.6/47   0916859568
Prenatal influences -- Popular works. Diseases -- Causes and theories of causation -- Popular works. Diseases -- Susceptibility -- Popular works.

RJ102 Child health. Child health services. Preventive health services for children — General works

RJ102.C487 1990
Children in a changing health system : assessments and proposals for reform / edited by Mark J. Schlesinger and Leon Eisenberg. Baltimore : Johns Hopkins University Press, c1990. xx, 372 p. ;
89-024406   362.1/9892/00973
0801839734
Child health services -- United States. Child health services -- Government policy -- United States. Child Health Services -- United States.

RJ102.G64 1987
Goggin, Malcolm L.,
Policy design and the politics of implementation : the case of child health care in the American states / Malcolm L. Goggin. Knoxville : University of Tennessee Press, c1987. xv, 296 p. :
86-011333   362.1/088054   0870495135
Child health services -- Government policy -- United States. Child health services -- United States -- Administration. Child Health Services -- organization & administration -- United States.

RJ102.K46 1993
King, Charles R.
Children's health in America : a history / Charles R. King. New York : Twayne Publishers ; c1993. xviii, 217 p.
93-006756   362.1/9892/000973
0805741011
Child health services -- United States -- History. Child health services -- Social aspects -- United States -- History. Pediatrics -- United States -- History.

RJ102.K5 1993
Klaus, Alisa,
Every child a lion : the origins of maternal and infant health policy in the United States and France, 1890-1920 / Alisa Klaus. Ithaca : Cornell University Press, c1993. viii, 298 p.
92-034682   362.1/9892/010973
080142447X
Infant health services -- Government policy -- United States -- History. Infant health services -- Government policy -- France -- History. Maternal health services -- Government policy -- United States -- History.

RJ102.M26 1997
Maternal and child health : programs, problems, and policy in public health / edited by Jonathan B. Kotch. Gaithersburg, Md. : Aspen Publishers, 1997. xiv, 481 p. :
96-048785   362.1/9892/000973
0834207710
Child health services -- United States. Maternal health services -- United States. Child Health Services -- United States.

RJ102.M27 1990
Maternal-child health policy : a nursing perspective / Janet Nielson Natapoff, Rita Reis Wieczorek, editors. New York : Springer Pub. Co., c1990. xiv, 343 p. :
90-009464   362.1/9892/00973
0826160506
Child health services -- United States. Medical policy -- United States. Maternal health services -- United States.

RJ102.M43 1990
Meckel, Richard A.,
"Save the babies" : American public health reform and the prevention of infant mortality, 1850-1929 / Richard A. Meckel. Baltimore : Johns Hopkins University Press, c1990. xi, 302 p., [
89-015389   362.1/9892/01097309034
0801838797
Infants -- Death -- United States -- Prevention -- History. Infant health services -- United States -- History. Maternal health services -- United States -- History.

RJ131 Physiology of children and infants — Growth and development — General works

RJ131.G46 1947
Gesell, Arnold,
Developmental diagnosis; normal and abnormal child development, clinical methods and pediatric applications, by Arnold Gesell, M.D. [and] Catherine S. Amatruda, M.D. New York [etc.] Hoeber [1947] xvi, 496 p.
47-002424   136.7
Child development -- Testing. Child development deviations.

RJ131.G47
Gesell, Arnold,
How a baby grows : a story in pictures / by Arnold Gesell ... Over 800 photographs arranged and interpreted with the assistance of Katherine Gesell Walden, A.B. New York ; Harper & Brothers, 1945. vii, 77, [3]
45000024   136.708
Child study. Child Development Infants -- Growth.

RJ131.L37 1983
Leach, Penelope.
Babyhood : stage by stage, from birth to age two : how your baby develops physically, emotionally, mentally / Penelope Leach. 2nd ed., rev. and expanded. New York : Knopf : 1983. xxi, 413 p. :
          612/.65   20   039
Infants--Development.

RJ131.R63 1987
The Role of culture in developmental disorder / edited by Charles M. Super. San Diego : Academic Press, c1987. xiii, 254 p.
87-001124   305.9/0816   0126768404
Developmental disabilities -- Social aspects. Cultural psychiatry. Developmental disabilities -- Cross-cultural studies.

RJ131.R66 1995
Rossetti, Louis Michael.
Infant-toddler assessment : an interdisciplinary approach / Louis M. Rossetti. Austin, Tex. : PRO-ED, [1995] xi, 294 p. ;
          618.92   0890793123
Child development--Research--Methodology. Child psychology--Research--Methodology. Child Development.

RJ131.T29 1990
Tanner, J. M.
Foetus into man : physical growth from conception to maturity / J.M. Tanner. Rev. and enl. ed. Cambridge, Mass. : Harvard University Press, 1990. vii, 280 p. :
          612.6   067430702X
Children--Growth. Growth.

RJ133 Physiology of children and infants — Growth and development — Motor development. Exercise

RJ133.R679 1996
Rowland, Thomas W.
Developmental exercise physiology / Thomas W. Rowland. Champaign, IL : Human Kinetics, c1996. x, 269 p. :
96-010886   612/.044/083   0873226402
Motor ability in children -- Physiological aspects. Exercise -- Physiological aspects.

RJ134 Physiology of children and infants — Growth and development — Infant growth and development

RJ134.B74 1994
Bremner, J. Gavin,
Infancy / J. Gavin Bremner. 2nd ed. Oxford, UK ; Blackwell, c1994. ix, 323 p. :
          305.23/2   063118466X
Infants--Development. Infant psychology.

RJ134.C85 1989
The Cultural context of infancy / edited by J. Kevin Nugent, Barry M. Lester, T. Berry Brazelton. Norwood, N.J. : Ablex Pub. Corp., c1989-1991 v. 1-2   :
88-026059   155.4/22   0893911909
Infants -- Development. Individual differences.

RJ134.R47 1986
Restak, Richard M.,
The infant mind / Richard M. Restak. Garden City, N.Y. : Doubleday, 1986. xi, 274 p. :
86-002033   155.4/22   0385195311
Infants -- Development. Brain. Infant psychology.

RJ135 Physiology of children and infants — Growth and development — Arrested development

RJ135.B38 2002
Children with disabilities / edited by Mark L. Batshaw. 5th ed. Balitmore : Paul H. Brookes, c2002. p. ;
618.92   1557665818
Child development deviations. Child development deviations--Etiology. Developmentally disabled children--Care.

RJ137 Physiology of children and infants — Growth and development — Growth and development of handicapped children

RJ137.H63 1998
Hodapp, Robert M.
Development and disabilities : intellectual, sensory, and motor impairments / Robert M. Hodapp. Cambridge ; Cambridge University Press, 1998. xiv, 270 p. ;
97-049940   155.45   0521482941
Handicapped children -- Development.

RJ138 Medical rehabilitation of handicapped children

RJ138.P45 1982
Physically handicapped children : a medical atlas for teachers / edited by Eugene E. Bleck, Donald A. Nagel. New York : Grune & Stratton, c1982. xxii, 530 p.
81-006804   618.92/7   0808913913
Physically handicapped children. Children -- Diseases. Physically handicapped children -- Education.

RJ141 Physiology of adolescents — Growth and development

RJ141.H43 1991
The Health of adolescents : understanding and facilitating biological, behavioral, and social development / William R. Hendee, editor. San Francisco : Jossey-Bass, 1991. xxxviii, 562
90-015627   613/.0433   1555423086
Teenagers -- Health and hygiene. Adolescence. Adolescent Behavior.

RJ206 Nutrition and feeding of children — General works

RJ206.W75
Growth and development of the child ... report of the Committee on Growth and Development, Kenneth D. Blackfan, M.D., chairman, White House Conference on Child Health and Protection. New York, The Century Co. [c1932-33] 4 v.
32026520   649.3
Children -- Nutrition. Growth. Children -- Care and hygiene.

RJ216 Nutrition and feeding of children — Nutrition of infants

RJ216.A58 1992
The Anthropology of breast-feeding : natural law or social construct / edited by Vanessa Maher. Oxford ; Berg ; 1992. xi, 185 p. ;
92-234084   392/.13   0854967214
Breast feeding -- Cross-cultural studies. Women -- Social conditions -- Cross-cultural studies.

RJ216.A65 1987
Apple, Rima D.
Mothers and medicine : a social history of infant feeding, 1890-1950 / Rima D. Apple. Madison, Wis. : University of Wisconsin Press, 1987. xv, 261 p. :
87-040137   362.1/9892   0299114805
Infants -- United States -- Nutrition -- History -- 19th century. Breast feeding -- United States -- History -- 19th century. Mothers -- United States -- History -- 19th century.

RJ216.B28 1995
Baumslag, Naomi.
Milk, money, and madness : the culture and politics of breastfeeding / Naomi Baumslag and Dia L. Michels ; foreword by Richard Jolly. Westport, Conn. : Bergin & Garvey, 1995. xxxi, 256 p.
95-014975   649/.33   0897894073
Breast feeding -- Health aspects. Breast feeding -- Social aspects. Breast milk.

RJ216.B7798 2002
Breastfeeding sourcebook / edited by Jenni Lynn Colson.1st ed. Detroit, MI : Omnigraphics, c2002. xiii, 388 p. :
649/.33   0780803329
Breast feeding. Consumer education.

RJ216.B85 1997
Briggs, Gerald G.
Drugs in lactation / Gerald G. Briggs, Roger K. Freeman, Sumner J. Yaffe. 2nd ed. Baltimore : Williams & Wilkins, c1997. xv, 59 p. ;
615/.704   0683303945
Breast feeding--Health aspects. Breast milk--Contamination. Infants (Newborn)--Effect of drugs on.

RJ216.F44 1987
Feeding the sick infant / editor, Leo Stern. Vevey, Switzerland : Nestle Nutrition ; c1987. xv, 301 p. :
87-012686   618.92/0654   0881673161
Infants -- Nutrition -- Congresses. Infants -- Disease -- Diet therapy -- Congresses. Infant, Newborn -- growth & development -- congresses.

RJ216.F5 1986
Fildes, Valerie A.
Breasts, bottles and babies : a history of infant feeding / by Valerie A. Fildes. Edinburgh : Edinburgh University Press, c1986. xxviii, 462 p
85045168   649.3/09   0852244622
Infants -- Nutrition -- History. Breast feeding -- History. Bottle feeding -- History.

RJ216.L354 2000
Lauwers, Judith,
  Counseling the nursing mother : a lactation consultant's reference / Judith Lauwers, Debbie Shinskie, with the assistance of Sandra Breck. Sudbury, Mass. : Jones and Bartlett, c2000. xvii, 540 p.
99-029436   649/.33   0763709751
  Breast feeding. Lactation.

RJ216.L36
Lawson, Donna.
  Superbaby cookbook, [by] Donna Lawson & Jean Conlon. New York, Macmillan [1974] x, 180 p.
73-013169   649/.3   0025695002
  Cookery (Baby foods) Cookery. Infant food -- Popular works.

RJ216.S9 1982
Sussman, George D.,
  Selling mothers' milk : the wet-nursing business in France, 1715-1914 / George D. Sussman. Urbana : University of Illinois Press, c1982. xi, 210 p., [
81-016277   338.4/76493   0252009193
  Wet-nurses -- France -- History -- 18th century. Wet-nurses -- France -- History -- 19th century. France -- Social conditions -- 18th century. France -- Social conditions -- 19th century.

RJ216.V36 1989
Van Esterik, Penny.
  Beyond the breast-bottle controversy / Penny Van Esterik. New Brunswick, N.J. : Rutgers University Press, c1989. xx, 242 p. ;
88-018494   363.8   0813513820
  Breast feeding -- Social aspects. Infant formulas -- Social aspects. Infants -- Developing countries -- Nutrition -- Social aspects.

RJ216.W37 2000
Ward, Jule DeJager.
  La Leche League : at the crossroads of medicine, feminism, and religion / Jule DeJager Ward. Chapel Hill : University of North Carolina Press, c2000. xi, 227 p. :
99-012921   649/.33   0807825093
  Breast feeding -- Social aspects. Breast feeding -- Religious aspects.

RJ235 Nutrition and feeding of children — Nutrition of adolescents

RJ235.D546 2001
  Diet information for teens : health tips about diet and nutrition, including facts about nutrients, dietary guidelines, breakfasts, school lunches, snacks, party food, weight control, eating disorders edited by Karen Bellenir. Detroit, MI : Omnigraphics, 2001. xii, 399 :
00-049213   613.2/0835   0780804414
  Teenagers -- Nutrition. Teenagers -- Health and hygiene. Diet.

RJ242 Hospital care of children

RJ242.B47 1989
Beuf, Ann H.,
  Biting off the bracelet : a study of children in hospitals / Ann Hill Beuf. 2nd ed. Philadelphia : University of Pennsylvania Press, c1989. xi, 206 p. ;
362.1/9892   0812212789
  Children--Hospital care. Children--Hospitals--Sociological aspects. Children--Sociological aspects.

RJ245 Nursing of children. Pediatric nursing — General works

RJ245.C477 1998
  Children and families in health and illness / Marion E. Broome ... [et al.], editors. Thousand Oaks, Calif. : Sage Publications, c1998. x, 363 p. :
97-045403   610.73/62   0803959028
  Pediatric nursing. Family nursing. Pediatric nursing -- Research.

RJ245.W47 1999
  Whaley & Wong's nursing care of infants and children / Donna L. Wong ... [et al.]. 6th ed. St. Louis : Mosby, c1999. xxxvii, 2119 p. :
610.73/62   0323001505
  Pediatric nursing. Pediatric Nursing.

RJ253.5 Newborn infants. Neonatology — Care and therapeutics — Intensive care. Neonatal emergencies

RJ253.5.A44 1995
Alecson, Deborah Golden,
  Lost lullaby / Deborah Golden Alecson. Berkeley : University of California Press, c1995. xii, 207 p. ;
94-011712   174/.24   0520088700
  Neonatal intensive care -- Moral and ethical aspects. Euthanasia -- Moral and ethical aspects.

RJ253.5.B34 1996
Baker, Jeffrey P.
  The machine in the nursery : incubator technology and the origins of newborn intensive care / Jeffrey P. Baker. Baltimore : Johns Hopkins University Press, c1996. x, 247 p. :
95-040320   618.92/01   0801851734
  Neonatal intensive care -- History. Incubators (Pediatrics) -- History.

RJ253.5.C65 1992
  Compelled compassion : government intervention in the treatment of critically ill newborns / edited by Arthur L. Caplan, Robert H. Blank, and Janna C. Merrick. Totowa, N.J. : Humana Press, c1992. xi, 336 p. ;
91-044190   618.92/01   0896032248
  Neonatal intensive care -- Law and legislation -- United States. Neonatal intensive care -- Moral and ethical aspects -- United States.

RJ253.5.E83

Ethics of newborn intensive care / edited by Albert R. Jonsen and Michael J. Garland. San Francisco : Health Policy Program, School of Medicine, University xv, 193 p. ;
     174/.2   0877722161
Neonatal intensive care--Moral and ethical aspects--Congresses. Ethics, Medical--Congresses. Infant, Newborn, Diseases--Therapy--Congresses.

RJ253.5.F76 1986
Frohock, Fred M.

Special care : medical decisions at the beginning of life / Fred M. Frohock. Chicago : University of Chicago Press, 1986. xiii, 263 p.
85-031806   362.1/9892/01   0226265811
Neonatal intensive care -- Decision making. Neonatal intensive care -- Moral and ethical aspects. Neonatal intensive care -- Economic aspects.

RJ253.5.G85 1986
Guillemin, Jeanne,

Mixed blessings : intensive care for newborns / Jeanne Harley Guillemin, Lynda Lytle Holmstrom. New York : Oxford University Press, 1986. x, 317 p. ;
85-028968   618.92/01   0195040325
Neonatal intensive care -- Decision making. Neonatal intensive care -- Moral and ethical aspects.

RJ253.5.G87 1986
Gustaitis, Rasa.

A time to be born, a time to die : conflicts and ethics in an intensive care nursery / Rasa Gustaitis and Ernle W.D. Young. Reading, Mass. : Addison Wesley, c1986. xvi, 267 p. ;
85-026804   362.1/9892/01   0201115557
Neonatal intensive care -- Economic aspects. Neonatal intensive care -- Moral and ethical aspects. Neonatal intensive care -- Decision making.

RJ253.5.L96 1985
Lyon, Jeff.

Playing God in the nursery / Jeff Lyon. New York : W.W. Norton, c1985. 366 p. ;
84-025457   174/.24   0393018989
Neonatal intensive care -- Moral and ethical aspects. Infanticide -- Moral and ethical aspects. Medical ethics.

RJ253.5.W44 1984
Weir, Robert F.,

Selective nontreatment of handicapped newborns : moral dilemmas in neonatal medicine / Robert F. Weir. New York : Oxford University Press, 1984. xii, 292 p. ;
83-019376   174/.24   0195033965
Neonatal intensive care -- Moral and ethical aspects. Infants (Newborn) -- Legal status, laws, etc. Infanticide.

RJ370 Diseases of children — Critical diseases. Emergencies. Intensive care

RJ370.O74 1983
O'Riordan, William D.

The parent's guide to emergency first aid / by William D. O'Riordan. Norwalk, Conn. : Appleton-Century-Crofts, c1983. xvii, 200 p.
83-002572   618.92/0025   0838577296
Pediatric emergencies. First aid in illness and injury.

RJ380 Diseases of children — Chronic diseases — General works

RJ380.C37 1989

Caring for children with chronic illness : issues and strategies / Ruth E.K. Stein, editor. New York : Springer Pub. Co., c1989. xxx, 301 p. :
88-020169   362.1/6/088054   0826159001
Chronically ill children -- Medical care -- United States. Chronically ill children -- Medical care -- Government policy -- United States. Child Health Services -- United States.

RJ380.E37 1990
Eiser, Christine.

Chronic childhood disease : an introduction to psychological theory and research / Christine Eiser. Cambridge [England] ; Cambridge University Press, 1990. x, 174 p. :
89-071299   618.92   0521385199
Chronic diseases in children -- Psychological aspects. Chronic diseases in children -- Patients -- Family relationships.

RJ380.G37 1989
Garrison, William T.

Chronic illness during childhood and adolescence : psychological aspects / William T. Garrison, Susan McQuiston. Newbury Park, Calif. : Sage Publications, c1989. 160 p. ;
89-005989   155.4   0803933320
Chronic diseases in children -- Psychological aspects. Chronic diseases in adolescence -- Psychological aspects. Chronic Disease -- in adolescence.

RJ380.M66 1997

Mosby's resource guide to children with disabilities and chronic illness / [edited by] Helen M. Wallace ... [et al.] ; with a foreword by C. St. Louis : Mosby, c1997. 504 p. :
     362.1/9892   0815190514
Chronically ill children--Services for. Exceptional children--Services for. Exceptional children--Rehabilitation.

RJ387 Diseases of children — Immunologic diseases — Other diseases, A-Z

RJ387.A25.A36 1992
Adolescents and AIDS : a generation in jeopardy / edited by Ralph J. DiClemente. Newbury Park, Calif. : Sage Publications, c1992. xiv, 314 p. :
92-019402   362.1/969792/00835
0803941811
AIDS (Disease) in adolescence -- United States. AIDS (Disease) in adolescence -- United States -- Prevention. AIDS (Disease) in adolescence -- Government policy -- United States.

RJ387.A25.C45 1989
Children, adolescents & AIDS / edited by Jeffrey M. Seibert & Roberta A. Olson. Lincoln : University of Nebraska Press, c1989. 243 p. ;
89-004866   362.1/989297/92   0803241860
AIDS (Disease) in children -- Social aspects. AIDS (Disease) in children -- Psychological aspects. AIDS (Disease) in adolescence -- Social aspects.

RJ387.A25.C48 1995
Children, families, and HIV/AIDS : psychosocial and therapeutic issues / editors, Nancy Boyd-Franklin, Gloria L. Steiner, Mary Boland ; foreword by James Oleske. New York : Guilford Press, 1995. xvii, 334 p.
93-034761   362.1/98929792   089862147X
AIDS (Disease) in children -- Social aspects. AIDS (Disease) in children -- Psychological aspects. AIDS (Disease) in children -- Patients -- Family relationships.

RJ387.A25.C68 1990
Courage to care : responding to the crisis of children with AIDS / edited by Gary R. Anderson. Washington, DC : Child Welfare League of America, c1990. xiv, 416 p. :
90-002085   362.1/98929792   0878684018
AIDS (Disease) in children -- Social aspects. AIDS (Disease) in children -- Patients -- Family relationships. AIDS (Disease) in children -- Patients -- Services for.

RJ387.A25.F36 1993
Families living with drugs and HIV : intervention and treatment strategies / edited by Richard P. Barth, Jeanne Pietrzak, Malia Ramler. New York : Guilford Press, c1993. xvi, 368 p. ;
92-001693   362.1/989297/9200973
0898628881
AIDS (Disease) in children -- Patients -- Services for -- United States. Children of narcotic addicts -- Services for -- United States. Drug abuse in pregnancy -- United States -- Prevention.

RJ387.A25.H39 2000
Hawkins, Anne Hunsaker,
A small, good thing : stories of children with HIV and those who care for them / Anne Hunsaker Hawkins. New York : W.W. Norton, c2000. xv, 286 p. ;
00-027018   362.1/98929792   0393049442
AIDS (Disease) in children -- Patients -- Biography. AIDS (Disease) in children -- Popular works.

RJ387.A25.H46 1992
Henggeler, Scott W.
Pediatric and adolescent AIDS : research findings from the social sciences / Scott W. Henggeler, Gary B. Melton, James R. Rodrigue. Newbury Park : Sage Publications, c1992. viii, 188 p.
92-013382   618.92/9792   0803939825
AIDS (Disease) in children. AIDS (Disease) in children -- Social aspects. AIDS (Disease) in adolescence.

RJ387.A25.H58 1991
HIV infection and developmental disabilities : a resource for service providers / edited by Allen C. Crocker, Herbert J. Cohen, and Theodore A. Kastner. Balitmore : P.H. Brookes Pub. Co., c1992. xxi, 292 p. :
91-023311   618.92/97/92   1557660832
AIDS (Disease) in children. Developmentally disabled children -- Diseases. Developmentally disabled -- Diseases.

RJ387.A25.K57 1989
Kirp, David L.
Learning by heart : AIDS and schoolchildren in America's communities / David L. Kirp, with Steven Epstein ... [et al.]. New Brunswick [N.J.] : Rutgers University Press, c1989. 304 p. ;
88-029789   362.1/9892/979200973
0813513960
AIDS (Disease) in children -- Social aspects -- United States -- Case studies. AIDS (Disease) in children -- Law and legislation -- United States -- Case studies. Students -- Health and hygiene -- United States -- Case studies.

RJ399 Diseases of children — Diseases and disorders of metabolism and nutrition — Other, A-Z

RJ399.A6.G68 1993
Gould, John A.,
The withering child / John A. Gould. Athens : University of Georgia Press, c1993. 232 p. ;
93-012351   618.92/85/2620092
0820315605
Gould, Gardner -- Health. Gould, John A., -- 1944- -- Family. Anorexia in children -- Patients -- Family relationships. Anorexia in children -- Patients -- Biography.

RJ399.C6C46 2002
Child and adolescent obesity : causes and consequences, prevention and management / edited by Walter Burniat ... [et al.]. New York : Cambridge University Press, 2002. p. cm.
               618.92/398   0521652375
Obesity in children. Obesity in adolescence. Children--Nutrition.

RJ399.C6N48 2001
Obesity in childhood and adolescence / editors, Chunming Chen, William H. Dietz. Philadelphia : Lippincott Williams & Wilkins, c2002. p. ;
               618.92/398   0781741327
Obesity in children--Congresses. Obesity in adolescence--Congresses. Children--Nutrition--Congresses.

RJ399.M26.M32 1993

Malnourished children in the United States : caught in the cycle of poverty / Robert J. Karp, editor. New York : Springer Pub. Co., c1993. xxviii, 266 p

93-018736   362.1/989239/00973

0826173306

Malnutrition in children -- United States. Poor children -- United States -- Nutrition. Child development deviations -- Nutritional aspects.

RJ399.N8

Clinical nutrition of the young child / editors, Oscar Brunser ... [et al.]. New York : Raven Press, c1991. viii, 315, 11

91-000114   618.92/39   0881677825

Nutrition disorders in children. Children -- Nutrition. Infants -- Nutrition.

RJ401 Diseases of children — Infectious and parasitic diseases — General works

RJ401.I563 1998

Krugman's infectious diseases of children. 10th ed. / [edited by] Samuel L. Katz, Anne A. Gershon, Peter J. St. Louis : Mosby, c1998. xiv, 785 p. :

618.92/9   0815152515

Communicable diseases in children. Communicable Diseases--in infancy & childhood.

RJ416 Diseases of children — Diseases of the hemic and lymphatic systems. Hematologic diseases. Pediatric hematology — By disease, A-Z

RJ416.S53.S53 1986

Sickle cell disease : psychological and psychosocial issues / edited by Anita Landau Hurtig and Carol Therese Viera. Urbana : University of Illinois Press, c1986. viii, 155 p.

85-005400   616.1/527/0019   0252011864

Sickle cell anemia in children -- Psychological aspects. Sickle cell anemia in children -- Social aspects. Anemia, Sickle Cell -- psychology.

RJ418 Diseases of children — Diseases of the endocrine system. Pediatric endocrinology. Pediatric neuroendocrinology — General works

RJ418.P42 2002

Pediatric endocrinology / [edited by] Mark A. Sperling. 2nd ed. Philadelphia : Saunders, 2002. xvii, 796 p. :

618.92/4   0721695396

Pediatric endocrinology. Endocrine Diseases--Child. Endocrine Diseases--Infant.

RJ423 Diseases of children — Diseases of the cardiovascular system — Examination. Diagnosis

RJ423.L56

Lind, John,

Heart volume in normal infants, a roentgenological study. [Translated by Ulla Schott] Stockholm, Bonniers boktr., 1950. 126, [1] p.

51-002584

Heart -- Measurement. Heart -- Radiography. Infants.

RJ426 Diseases of children — Diseases of the cardiovascular system — By disease, A-Z

RJ426.A7P394 2001

Practical management of pediatric cardiac arrhythmias / edited by Vicki L. Zeigler and Paul C. Gillette. Armonk, NY : Futura, c2001. ix, 422 p. :

618.92/128   0879934662

Arrhythmia in children. Arrhythmia--diagnosis--Child. Arrhythmia--therapy--Child.

RJ426.C64N45 2001

Neill, Catherine A.

The heart of a child :what families need to know about heart disorders in children / Catherine A. Neill, Edward B. Clark, Carleen Clark. 2nd ed. Baltimore : Johns Hopkins University Press, 2001. p. cm.

618.92/12   0801866367

Congenital heart disease in children. Heart--Diseases. Children--Diseases.

RJ426.C64.P43 1992

Pediatric cardiovascular imaging / [edited by] Ina Lynn Dyer Tonkin. Philadelphia, PA : Saunders, c1992. xix, 288 p.,

91-006876   618.92/120754   0721636659

Congenital heart disease in children -- Imaging. Diagnostic Imaging -- in infancy & childhood. Heart Defects, Congenital -- diagnosis.

RJ496 Diseases of children — Diseases of the nervous system. Pediatric neurology — By disease, A-Z

RJ496.A6.E57 1984

Eisenson, Jon,

Aphasia and related disorders in children / Jon Eisenson. New York : Harper & Row, c1984. x, 294 p. ;

83-012740   618.92/8552   0060418893

Aphasic children. Language disorders in children. Aphasia -- In infancy and childhood.

RJ496.A86.B73 1991

Braswell, Lauren.

Cognitive-behavioral therapy with ADHD children : child, family, and school interventions / Lauren Braswell, Michael L. Bloomquis ; foreword by Russell A. Barkley. New York : Guilford Press, c1991. xvii, 391 p.

91-016596   618.92/8589   0898627648

Attention-deficit hyperactivity disorder -- Treatment. Cognitive therapy for children. Attention Deficit Disorder with Hyperactivity -- therapy.

RJ496.B7C49 2001
Children with traumatic brain injury :a parent's guide / edited by Lisa Schoenbrodt. Bethesda, MD : Woodbine House, 2001. xi, 482 p. :
         618.92/8043   0933149999
Brain-damaged children--Rehabilitation. Brain--Wounds and injuries--Patients--Rehabilitation. Brain damage--Complications.

RJ496.B7.T73 1995
Traumatic head injury in children / edited by Sarah H. Broman, Mary Ellen Michel. New York : Oxford University Press, 1995. xv, 299 p. :
94-045129   617.4/81044/083   019509428X
Brain-damaged children. Brain -- Wounds and injuries -- Complications. Brain Injuries -- in infancy & childhood.

RJ496.C4C34 1998
Caring for children with cerebral palsy :a team approach / edited by John P. Dormans and Louis Pellegrino. Baltimore : P.H. Brookes Pub. Co., c1998. xiv, 533 p. :
         618.92/836   155766322X
Cerebral palsied children--Rehabilitation. Cerebral palsied children--Life skills guides. Cerebral Palsy--in infancy & childhood.

RJ496.C4S348 1993
Schleichkorn, Jay.
Coping with cerebral palsy : answers to questions parents often ask / by Jay Schleichkorn. 2nd ed. Austin, Tex. : PRO-ED, c1993. xviii, 252 p. :
         618.92/836   0890795762
Cerebral palsied children. Cerebral palsy.

RJ496.H3C48 2001
The child with headache : diagnosis and treatment / editors, Patricia A. McGrath, Loretta M. Hillier. Seattle : IASP Press, c2001. xi, 292 p. :
         618.92/8491   0931092302
Headache in children. Headache Disorders--diagnosis--Child. Headache Disorders--therapy--Child.

RJ496.H3.I57 1988
Headache in children and adolescents : proceedings of the First International Symposium on Headache in Children and Adolescents, Pavia, Italy, 19-20 May 1988 / editors, G. Lanzi, U. Balottin, A. Cernibori. Amsterdam ; Excerpta Medica ; 1989. xi, 371 p. :
89-001220   618.92/849   0444810749
Headache in children -- Congresses. Headache in adolescence -- Congresses. Headache -- in adolescence -- congresses.

RJ496.L35.L46 1998
Leonard, Laurence B.
Children with specific language impairment / Laurence B. Leonard. Cambridge, Mass. : The MIT Press, c1998. viii, 339 p.
96-037594   618.92/855   0262122065
Language disorders in children.

RJ496.L35P38 2001
Paul, Rhea.
Language disorders from infancy through adolescence : assessment & intervention / Rhea Paul ; photographs by Shelah Johnson and Patrick Watson ; drawings by Ruth Chapin Finn. 2nd ed. St. Louis : Mosby, c2001. xvi, 650 p. :
         618.92/855   0323006604
Language disorders in adolescence. Language disorders in children.

RJ496.L4.L433 1986
Learning disabilities and prenatal risk / edited by Michael Lewis. Urbana : University of Illinois Press, c1986. xi, 364 p. :
85-020896   618.92/89   0252011880
Learning disabilities -- Etiology -- Congresses. Pregnancy -- Complications -- Congresses. Prenatal care -- Congresses.

RJ499 Diseases of children — Mental disorders of children and adolescents. Child psychiatry. Child mental health services — General works

RJ499.A1.C3
Caplan, Gerald,
Prevention of mental disorders in children; initial exploration. New York, Basic Books [1961] 425 p.
61-006400   131.3
Child psychiatry.

RJ499.A1.T7 1972
Trapp, E. Philip,
Readings on the exceptional child; research and theory, edited by E. Philip Trapp [and] Philip Himelstein. New York, Appleton-Century-Crofts [1972] xiii, 714 p.
74-186622   155.4/5   0390884847
Exceptional children.

RJ499.B3
Baruch, Dorothy (Walter)
One little boy. Medical collaboration by Hyman Miller. New York, Julian Press [1952] 242 p.
52-007068   618.92
Child psychiatry -- Case studies.

RJ499.B48
Bettelheim, Bruno.
Truants from life; the rehabilitation of emotionally disturbed children. Glencoe, Ill., Free Press [1955] 511 p.
55-007331   136.708
Mentally ill children.

RJ499.B73
Burlingham, Dorothy T.
Psychoanalytic studies of the sighted and the blind. New York, International Universities Press [1972] vi, 396 p.
76-184213   618.9/28/91708   082364510X
Child psychiatry. Blind -- Psychology. Child analysis.

RJ499.C26
Caplan, Gerald,
Emotional problems of early childhood. New York, Basic Books [1955] xiv, 544 p.
55-012177   618.92
Child psychiatry. Emotional problems of children.

RJ499.C299 1990
Catalano, Stephen.
Children's dreams in clinical practice / Stephen Catalano. New York : Plenum, c1990. p. cm.
89-028470   154.6/34/083   0306433087
Child psychopathology. Child psychology. Children s dreams.

RJ499.F36 1996
Families and the mental health system for children and adolescents : policy, services, and research / Craig Anne Heflinger and Carol T. Nixon, editors. Thousand Oaks : Sage Publications, c1996. ix, 261 p. :
95-050162   362.2/0835   0761902678
Child mental health services. Teenagers -- Mental health services. Family -- Mental health services.

RJ499.H87 1991
Husain, Syed Arshad.
Fundamentals of child and adolescent psychopathology / Syed Arshad Husain, Dennis P. Cantwell. Washington, DC : American Psychiatric Press, c1991. xiv, 333 p. ;
90-000565   618.92/89   0880482273
Child psychopathology. Adolescent psychopathology. Child Behavior Disorders.

RJ499.I68 1987
The Invulnerable child / edited by E. James Anthony and Bertram J. Cohler. New York : Guilford Press, c1987. xiv, 432 p. ;
86-027120   618.92/89   0898622271
Child mental health -- Forecasting. Resilience (Personality trait) in children. Adjustment (Psychology) in children.

RJ499.K64 1990
Koocher, Gerald P.
Children, ethics, & the law : professional issues and cases / Gerald P. Koocher & Patricia C. Keith-Spiegel. Lincoln : University of Nebraska Press, c1990. xii, 230 p. ;
89-078514   174/.2   0803247311
Child mental health services -- Moral and ethical aspects. Child psychotherapy -- Moral and ethical aspects. Children -- Counseling of -- Moral and ethical aspects.

RJ499.M234
Mahler, Margaret S.
The selected papers of Margaret S. Mahler, M.D. New York : J. Aronson, c1979. 2 v. ;
79-051915   618.92/89   0876683715
Child psychiatry. Child psychology. Separation-individuation.

RJ499.M3
Masland, Richard L.
Mental subnormality: biological, psychological, and cultural factors [by] Richard L. Masland, Seymour B. Sarason [and] Thomas Gladwin. New York, Basic Books [1959, c1958] 442 p.
58-013161   136.766
Mentally handicapped children.

RJ499.M46
Michal-Smith, Harold.
The special child: diagnosis, treatment, habilitation; [selected papers on certain aspects of diagnosis, treatment, habilitation, by Harold Michal-Smith and Shulamith Kastein. Seattle, New School for the Special Child, Bureau of Publ 1962] 334 p.
62051818   618.9289
Mentally handicapped children.

RJ499.R5
Riese, Hertha (Pataky)
Heal the hurt child; an approach through educational therapy with special reference to the extremely deprived Negro child. Foreword by Nathan W. Ackerman. [Chicago] University of Chicago Press [1962] 615 p.
62019623   618.9289
Socially handicapped children -- Education. Cultural Deprivation Negroes -- United States.

RJ499.R66 1980
Ross, Alan O.
Psychological disorders of children : a behavioral approach to theory, research, and therapy / Alan O. Ross. 2d ed. New York : McGraw-Hill, c1980. xvii, 362 p. ;
          618.9/28/9   0070538832
Child psychiatry.

RJ499.R67
Rothstein, Jerome H.,
Mental retardation; readings and resources. New York, Holt, Rinehart and Winston [1961] 628 p.
61-012770   136.766
Mentally handicapped children -- Addresses, essays, lectures. Mentally handicapped children -- Education -- Addresses, essays, lectures. Mentally handicapped -- United States -- Addresses, essays, lectures.

RJ499.S8
Strauss, Alfred A.,
Psychopathology and education of the brain-injured child, by Alfred A. Strauss and Laura E. Lehtinen. New York, Grune & Stratton, 1947-55. 2 v.
48000889   616.83
Disabled -- education. Child Psychiatry Brain Damage, Chronic

RJ499.T47 1997
Textbook of child & adolescent psychiatry / edited by Jerry M. Wiener. 2nd ed. Washington, DC : American Psychiatric Press, c1997. xviii, 940 p. :
          618.92/89   1882103033
Child psychiatry. Adolescent psychiatry. Mental Disorders--in infancy & childhood.

RJ499.T53
Thomas, Alexander,
Temperament and behavior disorders in children [by] Alexander Thomas, Stella Chess [and] Herbert G. Birch. New York, New York University Press, 1968. vii, 309 p.
68-013025   618.92/89
Child psychiatry. Temperament in children.

RJ499.W42
Western Reserve University.
Communication problems and their effect on the learning potential of the mentally retarded child [by] Nancy E. Wood. Cleveland, Western Reserve University and the Cleveland Hea 1960. 1 v. (various
61060600   136.766
Mentally handicapped children. Mentally handicapped children -- Education.

RJ499.W45 2000
Wicks-Nelson, Rita,
Behavior disorders of childhood / Rita Wicks-Nelson, Allen C. Israel. 4th ed. Upper Saddle River, NJ : Prentice Hall, c2000. xvi, 544 p. :
618.92/89   0130835366
Child psychopathology.

RJ499.W493 1996
Winnicott, D. W.
Thinking about children / D.W. Winnicott ; edited by Jennifer Johns, Ray Shepherd, and Helen Taylor Robinson ; bibliography compiled by Harry Karnac. Reading, Mass. : Addison-Wesley Pub., c1996. xxxii, 343 p.
96-011007   618.92/89   0201407000
Child mental health. Child psychology. Child analysis.

RJ499.W52
Witmer, Helen Leland,
Psychiatric interviews with children ... New York, Commonwealth Fund, 1946. vii, 443 p.
47000294   618.92
Child psychiatry.

RJ499.3 Diseases of children — Mental disorders of children and adolescents. Child psychiatry. Child mental health services — Handbooks, manuals, etc.

RJ499.3.H356 1997
Handbook of child and adolescent psychiatry / Joseph D. Noshpitz, editor-in-chief ; Stanley Greenspan, Serena Wieder, Joy Osofsky, editors. New York : Wiley, c1997-c1998. 7 v. :
618.92/89   0471193283
Child psychiatry--Handbooks, manuals, etc. Adolescent psychiatry--Handbooks, manuals, etc.

RJ499.3.H368 2002
Handbook of serious emotional disturbance in children and adolescents / edited by Diane T. Marsh and Mary A. Fristad. New York : J. Wiley, c2002. xiii, 509 p. :
305.9/0824   0471398144
Mentally ill children--Handbooks, manuals, etc. Children with mental disabilities--Handbooks, manuals, etc. Emotional problems of children--Handbooks, manuals, etc.

RJ501-502 Diseases of children — Mental disorders of children and adolescents. Child psychiatry. Child mental health services — By region or country

RJ501.A2.H67 1989
Horn, Margo.
Before it's too late : the child guidance movement in the United States, 1922-1945 / Margo Horn. Philadelphia : Temple University Press, 1989. xii, 224 p. ;
88-033709   362.2/088054   0877225893
Child guidance clinics -- United States -- History. Child mental health services -- United States -- History.

RJ501.A2.J64 1999
Jones, Kathleen W.
Taming the troublesome child : American families, child guidance, and the limits of psychiatric authority / Kathleen W. Jones. Cambridge, Mass : Harvard University Press, 1999. x, 310 p. :
99-011588   362.2/083/0973   0674868110
Child mental health services -- United States -- History -- 20th century. Child guidance clinics -- United States -- History -- 20th century. Problem children -- United States -- History -- 20th century.

RJ501.A2.R53 1989
Richardson, Theresa R.,
The century of the child : the mental hygiene movement and social policy in the United States and Canada / Theresa R. Richardson. Albany, N.Y. : State University of New York Press, c1989. xii, 273 p. ;
88-024894   362.2/088054   0791400204
Child mental health services -- United States -- History -- 20th century. Child mental health services -- Canada -- History -- 20th century. Child mental health services -- Government policy -- United States -- History -- 20th century.

RJ501.A2.S83 1989
Substance abuse & kids : a directory of education, information, prevention, and early intervention programs. Phoenix, Ariz. : Oryx Press, 1989. x, 466 p. :
89-008848   362.29/083   0897745833
Child mental health services -- United States -- Directories. Substance abuse -- Treatment -- United States -- Directories.

RJ502.S6.H53 1996
Hickson, Joyce.
Multicultural counseling in a divided and traumatized society : the meaning of childhood and adolescence in South Africa / Joyce Hickson and Susan Kriegler ; foreword by Paul Pedersen. Westport, Conn. : Greenwood Press, 1996. xiv, 186 p. ;
95-041697   362.2/0968   0313285543
Child mental health services -- South Africa. Cross-cultural counseling -- South Africa. Counselor and client -- South Africa.

RJ502.5 Diseases of children — Mental disorders of children and adolescents. Child psychiatry. Child mental health services — Infant psychiatry. Infant analysis

RJ502.5.I465 2002
Infant and toddler mental health : models of clinical intervention with infants and their families / edited by J. Martín Maldonado-Durán. 1st ed. Washington, DC : American Psychiatric Pub., c2002. xxvii, 392 p. :
            618.92/89   1585620866
  Infants--Mental health. Toddlers--Mental health. Family psychotherapy.

RJ502.5.K57 1987
Klein, Josephine.
  Our need for others and its roots in infancy / Josephine Klein. London ; Tavistock Publications, 1987. xviii, 444 p.
87-001935   155.4/8   0422614106
  Object relations (Psychoanalysis) Self in infants. Need (Psychology)

RJ502.5.S65 1983
Spitz, Rene A.
  Rene A. Spitz, dialogues from infancy : selected papers / edited by Robert N. Emde. New York : International Universities Press, c1983. x, 484 p. :
83-026461   618.92/89   0823657876
  Infant psychiatry.

RJ503 Diseases of children — Mental disorders of children and adolescents. Child psychiatry. Child mental health services — Adolescent psychiatry. Adolescent psychotherapy. Adolescent analysis

RJ503.C635 1996
Cohen, Patricia.
  Life values and adolescent mental health / Patricia Cohen, Jacob Cohen. Mahwah, N.J. : L. Erlbaum Associates, 1996. xiii, 181 p.
95-041474   616.89/022   0805817743
  Teenagers -- Mental health. Values in adolescence.

RJ503.E84 1990
  Ethnic issues in adolescent mental health / edited by, Arlene Rubin Stiffman, Larry E. Davis. Newbury Park, Calif. : Sage Publications, c1990. 360 p. ;
90-008735   362.2/0835   0803939841
  Minority teenagers -- Mental health -- United States. Minority teenagers -- United States -- Sexual behavior.

RJ503.F57 1988
Fishman, H. Charles
  Treating troubled adolescents : a family therapy approach / H. Charles Fishman. New York : Basic Books, c1988. xii, 318 p. ;
87-047838   616.89/156   0465087426
  Adolescent psychotherapy. Family psychotherapy.

RJ503.G74 1991
Greenspan, Stanley I.
  The clinical interview of the child / Stanley I. Greenspan, with the collaboration of Nancy Thorndike Greenspan. 2nd ed. Washington, DC : American Psychiatric Press, c1991. 245 p. ;
            618.92/89075   0880484209
  Mental illness--Diagnosis. Interviewing in child psychiatry. Child psychology.

RJ503.M44
Meeks, John E.
  The fragile alliance : an orientation to psychotherapy of the adolescent / John E. Meeks, William Bernet. Malabar, Fla. : Krieger Pub. Co., 2001. xiii, 486 p.
00-061708   616.89/14/0835   1575241250
  Adolescent psychotherapy. Psychotherapy -- Adolescence.

RJ503.M495 1998
Micucci, Joseph A.
  The adolescent in family therapy : breaking the cycle of conflict and control / Joseph A. Micucci. New York : Guildford Press, c1998. xi, 336 p. :
98-037859   616.89/156/0835   1572303891
  Adolescent psychotherapy. Family psychotherapy. Family -- Psychological aspects.

RJ503.M55 1983
Miller, Derek.
  The age between : adolescence and therapy / Derek Miller. New York : J. Aronson, c1983. xiv, 441 p. ;
83-003893   616.89   0876686390
  Adolescent psychiatry. Adolescent psychology. Adolescent psychiatry.

RJ503.R63 1989
Robin, Arthur L.
  Negotiating parent-adolescent conflict : a behavioral-family systems approach / Arthur L. Robin, Sharon L. Foster ; foreword by K. Daniel O'Leary. New York : Guilford Press, c1989. xii, 338 p. ;
87-031502   616.89/022   0898620724
  Behavior therapy for teenagers. Family psychotherapy. Adolescent Psychology.

RJ503.W67 1991
Worden, Mark,
  Adolescents and their families : an introduction to assessment and intervention / Mark Worden. New York : Haworth Press, c1991. xii, 209 p. ;
91-007909   616.89/022   1560241012
  Adolescent psychotherapy. Teenagers -- Family relationships.

RJ503.3 Diseases of children — Mental disorders of children and adolescents. Child psychiatry. Child mental health services — Clinical psychology

RJ503.3.C37 1999
Carr, Alan,
  The handbook of child and adolescent clinical psychology : a contextual approach / Alan Carr. New York : Routledge, 1999. xxi, 1000 p.
98-025289   618.92/89   0415194911
  Child psychology -- Handbooks, manuals, etc. Adolescent psychology -- Handbooks, manuals, etc.

RJ503.5 Diseases of children — Mental disorders of children and adolescents. Child psychiatry. Child mental health services — Examination. Assessment. Diagnosis

RJ503.5.G33 1986
Gabel, Stewart,
  Understanding psychological testing in children : a guide for health professionals / Stewart Gabel, Gerald D. Oster, Steven M. Butnik. New York : Plenum Medical Book Co., c1986. x, 184 p. :
86-015104   155.4   0306422441
  Psychological tests for children. Psychological Tests -- in infancy & childhood.

RJ504-506 Diseases of children — Mental disorders of children and adolescents. Child psychiatry. Child mental health services — Child psychotherapy

RJ504.A43 1988
Allan, John A. B.
  Inscapes of the child's world : Jungian counseling in schools and clinics / John Allan. Dallas, Tex. : Spring Publications, c1988. xxvi, 235 p.
88-027831   618.92/891/14   0882143387
Jung, C. G. -- (Carl Gustav), -- 1875-1961. Child psychotherapy. Children -- Counseling of.

RJ504.B758 1997
Bromfield, Richard.
  Playing for real : exploring the world of child therapy and the inner worlds of children / Richard Bromfield. Northvale, N.J. : Jason Aronson, 1997. x, 241 p. ;
          618.92/8914   0765701294
  Child psychotherapy. Child psychotherapy--Case studies.

RJ504.C463 2000
Chethik, Morton.
  Techniques of child therapy : psychodynamic strategies / Morton Chethik. 2nd ed. New York : Guilford Press, c2000. x, 307 p. :
          618.92/8914   1572305282
  Child psychotherapy.

RJ504.D65 1990
Donovan, Denis M.
  Healing the hurt child : a developmental-contextual approach / Denis M. Donovan, Deborah McIntyre. New York : Norton, 1990. p. cm.
89-049420   618.92/8914   0393700933
  Child psychotherapy. Abused children -- Mental health. Contextual therapy.

RJ504.I57 1999
  Innovative psychotherapy techniques in child and adolescent therapy / edited by Charles E. Schaefer. 2nd ed. New York : Wiley, c1999. xii, 514 p. :
          618.92/8914   047124404X
  Child psychotherapy. Adolescent psychotherapy. Psychotherapy-- in infancy & childhood.

RJ504.S59 1989
Spiegel, Stanley.
  An interpersonal approach to child therapy : the treatment of children and adolescents from an interpersonal point of view / Stanley Spiegel. New York : Columbia University Press, c1989. xxii, 228 p.
89-030772   618.92/8914   0231062923
  Child psychotherapy.

RJ504.S77 1988
Strayhorn, Joseph M.
  The competent child : an approach to psychotherapy and preventive mental health / Joseph M. Strayhorn. New York : Guilford Press, c1988. ix, 310 p. ;
87-021086   618.92/8914   0898627109
  Child psychotherapy. Mental illness -- Prevention. Parent and child.

RJ504.2.H4513 1990
Heller, Peter,
  A child analysis with Anna Freud / Peter Heller ; translated by Salome Burckhardt and Mary Weigand and revised by the author. Madison, Conn. : International Universities Press, c1990. li, 383 p., [
89-002146   618.92/8914
Freud, Anna, -- 1895- Heller, Peter, -- 1920-- -- Mental health. Child analysis -- Case studies. Psychotherapy patients -- Austria -- Biography.

RJ504.2.K4413 1984
Klein, Melanie.
  The psycho-analysis of children / by Melanie Klein ; authorized translation by Alix Strachey ; revised in collaboration with Alix Strachey by H.A. Thorner. New York : Free Press, 1984, c1975. xvi, 326 p. ;
84-013774   618.92/8917   0029184304
  Child analysis. Personality in children. Psychoanalysis.

RJ504.2.P4613 1991
Petot, Jean-Michel.
Melanie Klein : Volume II, the ego and the good object, 1932-1960 / Jean-Michel Petot ; translated from the French by Christine Trollope. Madison, Conn. : International Universities Press, c1991. xi, 281 p. ;
90004775   618.92/8917   0823633292
Klein, Melanie.   Object relations (Psychoanalysis) Child analysis. Ego (Psychology)

RJ505.A7.W67 1990
Working with children in art therapy / edited by Caroline Case and Tessa Dalley. London ; Routledge, 1990. xiii, 224 p.,
88-032538   615.8/5156/088054
0415017378
Art therapy for children.

RJ505.B4.G723 1984
Graziano, Anthony M.,
Children and behavior therapy / Anthony M. Graziano, Kevin C. Mooney. New York : Aldine, c1984. xii, 486 p. ;
83-025724   618.92/89142   0202260879
Behavior therapy for children. Child psychotherapy. Behavior therapy -- In infancy and childhood.

RJ505.C63R658 2002
Ronen, Tammie.
Cognitive-constructivist psychotherapy with children and adolescents / by Tammie Ronen. New York : Kluwer Academic/Plenum Publishers, c2002. p. ;
          618.92/89142   0306473674
Cognitive therapy for children--Case studies. Cognitive therapy for teenagers--Case studies. Constructionism (Psychology)

RJ505.C63.Z37 1992
Zarb, Janet M.
Cognitive-behavioral assessment and therapy with adolescents / Janet M. Zarb. New York : Brunner/Mazel, c1992. x, 239 p. ;
92-016165   616.89/142/0835
Cognitive therapy for teenagers. Behavioral assessment of teenagers. Adolescent Psychology.

RJ505.G7G768 1996
Group therapy with children and adolescents / edited by Paul Kymissis and David A. Halperin. 1st ed. Washington, DC : American Psychiatric Press, c1996. xix, 405 p. ;
          616.89/152/083   0880486546
Group psychotherapy for teenagers. Group psychotherapy for children. Psychotherapy, Group--in infancy & childhood.

RJ505.P33S45 1998
Selman, Robert L.
Making a friend in youth : developmental theory and pair therapy / Robert L. Selman and Lynn Hickey Schultz. 1st pbk. ed. New York : Aldine de Gruyter, 1998. p. cm.
          618.92/8914   0202306054
Pair therapy. Friendship in children. Friendship in adolescence.

RJ505.P37.T74 1998
Treating children with sexually abusive behavior problems : guidelines for child and parent intervention / Jan Ellen Burton ... [et al.] ; David H. Justice, contributor. New York : Haworth Maltreatment and Trauma Press, c1998. xiii, 279 p.
98-006095   618.92/858306   0789004720
Sexual disorders in children -- Treatment. Behavior disorders in children -- Treatment. Children -- Sexual behavior.

RJ505.P6O26 2000
O'Connor, Kevin J.
The play therapy primer / Kevin J. O'Connor. 2nd ed. New York : John Wiley & Sons, c2000. xii, 478 p. ;
          615.8/5153/083   0471248738
Play therapy.

RJ505.P6S27 2002
Play therapy techniques / edited by Charles E. Schaefer and Donna M. Cangelosi. 2nd ed. Northvale, N.J. : Jason Aronson, 2002. p. cm.
          618.92/891653   0765703602
Play therapy--Methodology.

RJ506.A58.H87 1992
Husain, Syed Arshad.
Anxiety disorders in children and adolescents / Syed Arshad Husain, Javad H. Kashani. Washington, DC : American Psychiatric Press, c1992 [i.e. 1 xii, 184 p. ;
91-022233   618.92/85223   0880484675
Anxiety in children. Anxiety in adolescence. Anxiety Disorders -- in adolescence.

RJ506.A58I57 1994
International handbook of phobic and anxiety disorders in children and adolescents / edited by Thomas H. Ollendick, Neville J. King, and William Yule. New York : Plenum Press, c1994. xiii, 496 p. :
          618.92/8522   0306447592
Anxiety in children. Phobias in children. Anxiety in adolescence.

RJ506.A9A8928 1998
Autism and pervasive developmental disorders / edited by Fred R. Volkmar. Cambridge ; Cambridge University Press, 1998. xvi, 278 p. :
          618.92/8982   0521553865
Autism in children. Developmental disabilities. Autism, Infantile.

RJ506.A9.B4
Bettelheim, Bruno.
The empty fortress; infantile autism and the birth of the self. New York, Free Press [1967] xiv, 484 p.
67-010886   618.9289
Autism in children.

RJ506.A9.M39 1993
Maurice, Catherine.
Let me hear your voice : a family's triumph over autism / Catherine Maurice. New York : Knopf, 1993. xx, 371 p. ;
92-002471   618.92/8982/0092
0679408630
Autistic children -- United States -- Biography. Autistic children -- United States -- Family relationships. Autistic children -- Rehabilitation -- United States.

RJ506.A9.M48 1997
Mesibov, Gary B.
Autism : understanding the disorder / Gary B. Mesibov and Lynn W. Adams and Laura G. Klinger. New York : Plenum Press, c1997. xii, 124 p. ;
97-035645   618.92/8982   0306455463
Autism in children -- Psychological aspects. Autism.

RJ506.A9.U5 1993
Understanding other minds : perspectives from autism / edited by Simon Baron-Cohen, Helen Tager-Flusberg, and Donald J. Cohen. Oxford ; Oxford University Press, 1993. xiii, 515 p.
92-048765   618.92/8982   0192620541
Autism in children. Philosophy of mind in children. Autism, Infantile.

RJ506.B44C36 2002
Campbell, Susan B.
Behavior problems in preschool children : clinical and developmental issues / Susan B. Campbell. 2nd ed. New York : Guilford Press, 2002. p. cm.
        618.92/89   1572307846
Behavior disorders in children. Child development. Preschool children--Mental health.

RJ506.B44.H25 1999
Handbook of disruptive behavior disorders / edited by Herbert C. Quay and Anne E. Hogan. New York : Kluwer Academic/Plenum Publishers, c1999. xiii, 695 p.
98-056517   618.92/89   0306459744
Behavior disorders in children. Attention-deficit disorder in adolescence. Conduct disorders in adolescence.

RJ506.B44.S77 1990
Straight and devious pathways from childhood to adulthood / edited by Lee N. Robins and Michael Rutter. Cambridge ; Cambridge University Press, 1990. xix, 389 p. :
89-000913   618.92/89   0521364086
Behavior disorders in children -- Longitudinal studies. Developmental psychology. Child Behavior Disorders.

RJ506.C48.B44 1993
Behind the playground walls : sexual abuse in preschools / Jill Waterman ... [et al.]. New York : Guilford Press, c1993. xii, 308 p. :
91-035420   616.85/83   0898625238
Sexually abused children. Sexually abused children -- Family relationships. Preschool children.

RJ506.C48.F74 1996
Freyd, Jennifer J.
Betrayal trauma : the logic of forgetting childhood abuse / Jennifer J. Freyd. Cambridge, Mass. : Harvard University Press, 1996. 232 p. :
96-009059   616.85/82239   067406805X
Child sexual abuse. Betrayal -- Psychological aspects. Psychic trauma.

RJ506.C65.F75 1998
Frick, Paul J.
Conduct disorders and severe antisocial behavior / Paul J. Frick. New York : Plenum Press, c1998. viii, 152 p.
98-015094   618.92/89   0306458403
Conduct disorders in children.

RJ506.D4.C59 1992
Clinical guide to depression in children and adolescents / edited by Mohammad Shafii, Sharon Lee Shafii. Washington, DC : American Psychiatric Press, c1992. xv, 304 p. :
91-022112   618.92/8527   0880483563
Depression in children. Depression in adolescence. Manic-depressive illness in children.

RJ506.D4.C97 1996
Cytryn, Leon.
Growing up sad : childhood depression and its treatment / Leon Cytryn, Donald H. McKnew, Jr. New York : Norton, c1996. 216 p. ;
95-041233   618.92/8527   0393038270
Depression in children.

RJ506.D4M47 2001
Merrell, Kenneth W.
Helping students overcome depression and anxiety : a practical guide / Kenneth W. Merrell. New York : Guilford Press, c2001. xxiv, 231 p. :
        618.92/8527   1572306173
Depression in children--Treatment. Depression in adolescence--Treatment. Anxiety in children--Treatment.

RJ506.D47.B47 1993
Berkson, Gershon.
Children with handicaps : a review of behavioral research / Gershon Berkson. Hillsdale, N.J. : Lawrence Erlbaum Associates, 1993. xi, 479 p. ;
92-049570   155.45/1   0898599873
Developmentally disabled children -- Psychology -- Abstracts. Developmentally disabled children -- Abstracts. Child Development Disorders.

RJ506.D78.A365 2001
Adolescents, alcohol, and substance abuse : reaching teens through brief interventions / edited by Peter M. Monti, Suzanne M. Colby, Tracy A. O'Leary ; foreword by William R. Miller. New York : Guilford Press, c2001. xvi, 350 p. :
        616.86/00835   1572306580
Teenagers--Substance use. Teenagers--Alcohol use. Substance abuse--Prevention.

RJ506.E18.B47 1997
Berg, Francie M.
    Afraid to eat : children and teens in weight crisis / Frances M. Berg ; edited by Kendra Rosencrans. Hettinger, ND : Healthy Weight Journal, c1997. 310 p. :
96-231691   618.92/8526   0918532515
    Eating disorders in children. Eating disorders in adolescence. Obesity in children.

RJ506.E18B47 2001
Berg, Francie M.
    Children and teens afraid to eat :helping youth in today's weight-obsessed world / Frances M. Berg ; edited by Kendra Rosencrans.3rd ed. Hettinger, ND : Healthy Weight Network, c2001. 339 p. :
        618.92/8526   0918532566
    Eating disorders in children. Eating disorders in adolescence. Obesity in children.

RJ506.E18.M35 1991
Maine, Margo.
    Father hunger : fathers, daughters & food / Margo Maine. Carlsbad, CA : Gurze Books, c1991. xv, 254 p. ;
91-030915   616.85/26/008352 0936077093
    Eating disorders in adolescents. Teenage girls -- Mental health. Fathers and daughters.

RJ506.H65.H43 2001
Heckel, Robert V.
    Children who murder : a psychological perspective / Robert V. Heckel and David M. Shumaker ; foreword by Eugene Arthur Moore. Westport, Conn. : Praeger, 2001. xxii, 177 p.
00-042776   618.92/85844   0275966186
    Juvenile homicide -- Psychological aspects. Forensic psychiatry. Child psychotherapy.

RJ506.H9.A593 2001
Anastopoulos, Arthur D.,
    Assessing attention-deficit/hyperactivity disorder / Arthur D. Anastopoulos and Terri L. Shelton. New York : Kluwer Academic/Plenum Publishers, c2001. xvi, 349 p. :
00-049780   618.92/8589   0306463881
    Attention-deficit hyperactivity disorder -- Diagnosis. Attention-deficit hyperactivity disorder -- Treatment -- Evaluation.

RJ506.H9B47 2002
Berne, Samuel A.
    Without ritalin :a natural approach to ADD / Samuel A. Berne. Chicago : Keats Pub., c2002. xiv, 146 p. ;
        616.85/89   0658012150
    Attention-deficit hyperactivity disorder--Alternative treatment. Attention-deficit disorder in children--Alternative treatment. Holistic medicine.

RJ506.H9.D476 1999
DeGrandpre, Richard J.
    Ritalin nation : rapid-fire culture and the transformation of human consciousness / Richard DeGrandpre. New York : W.W. Norton, c1999. 284 p. ;
98-020687   618.92/8589   0393046850
    Attention-deficit hyperactivity disorder -- Social aspects -- United States. Methylphenidate hydrochloride. United States -- Civilization -- 1945-

RJ506.H9.G652 1998
Goldstein, Sam,
    Managing attention deficit hyperactivity disorder in children : a guide for practitioners / Sam Goldstein, Michael Goldstein ; contributions by Clare B. Jones, Lauren Braswell, Susan Sheridan. New York : Wiley, c1998. xx, 876 p. :
97-036626   618.92/8589   0471121584
    Attention-deficit hyperactivity disorder. Attention Deficit Disorder with Hyperactivity -- therapy.

RJ506.H9H86 1995
Hunter, Diana.
    The ritalin-free child :managing hyperactivity & attention deficits without drugs / by Diana Hunter. Ft. Lauderdale, Fla. : Consumer Press, c1995. 155, [2] p. ;
        618.92/858906   0962833681
    Attention-deficit hyperactivity disorder--Alternative treatment.

RJ506.H9.M42326 1999
Mate, Gabor.
    Scattered : how attention deficit disorder originates and what you can do about it / Gabor Mate. New York, N.Y., U.S.A. : Dutton, 1999. p. cm.
99-012999   616.85/89   0525944125
    Attention-deficit hyperactivity disorder -- Psychological aspects. Attention-deficit hyperactivity disorder -- Environmental aspects.

RJ506.H9.S68 1999
Stein, David B.
    Ritalin is not the answer : a drug-free, practical program for children diagnosed with ADD or ADHD / David B. Stein ; forward by Peter R. Breggin. San Francisco : Jossey-Bass, c1999. xviii, 203 p.
98-025535   618.92/858906   0787945145
    Attention-deficit hyperactivity disorder -- Alternative treatment.

RJ506.H9T383 2001
Taylor, John F.,
    Helping your ADD child:hundreds of practical solutions for parents and teachers of ADD children and teens (with or without hyperactivity) / John F. Taylor. Roseville, Calif. : Prima Health, 2001. p. cm.
        618.92/8589   0761527567
    Attention-deficit-disordered children. Attention-deficit disorder in adolescence. Problem children--Behavior modification.

RJ506.H9.T44 1998
Teeter, Phyllis Anne.
Interventions for ADHD : treatment in developmental context / Phyllis Anne Teeter ; foreword by Sam Goldstein. New York : Guilford Press, c1998. xxi, 378 p. ;
98-039158   618.92/8589   1572303840
Attention-deficit hyperactivity disorder. Attention-deficit disorder in adults.

RJ506.J88W56 1984
Winnicott, D. W.
Deprivation and delinquency / D.W. Winnicott ; edited by Clare Winnicott, Ray Shepherd, and Madeleine Davis. London ; Tavistock Publications ; vi, 294 p. ;
            616.85/82071/088055   0422791806
Juvenile delinquency. Antisocial personality disorders. Deprivation (Psychology)

RJ506.L4.A33
Advances in learning and behavioral disabilities. Greenwich, Conn. : JAI Press, c1982- v. ;
82-645749   618.92/89
Learning disabilities -- Periodicals. Problem children -- Periodicals. Behavior -- yearbooks.

RJ506.M4H36 1998
Handbook of mental retardation and development / edited by Jacob A. Burack, Robert M. Hodapp, Edward Zigler. Cambridge ; Cambridge University Press, 1998. xviii, 764 p. ;
            618.92/8588   0521446686
Mental retardation. Handicapped children--Development. Mentally handicapped children.

RJ506.M4.M84 1983
Mulliken, Ruth K.
Assessment of multihandicapped and developmentally disabled children / Ruth K. Mulliken, John J. Buckley. Rockville, Md. : Aspen Systems Corp., 1983. x, 343 p. ;
83-003739   618.92/8588075   089443876X
Mentally handicapped children -- Psychological testing. Developmentally disabled children -- Testing.

RJ506.M4.R62 1976
Robinson, Nancy M.
The mentally retarded child : a psychological approach / Nancy M. Robinson, Halbert B. Robinson ; with contributions by Gilbert S. Omenn, Joseph C. Campione. New York : McGraw-Hill, c1976. xvi, 592 p. :
75-030903   618.9/28/588   0070532028
Mentally handicapped children. Mental retardation. Mental retardation.

RJ506.P38.K56 1988
King, Neville J.
Children's phobias : a behavioural perspective / Neville J. King, David I. Hamilton and Thomas H. Ollendick. Chichester ; Wiley, c1988. x, 260 p. :
87-018894   618.92/85225   0471102768
Phobias in children. Behavior therapy. Behavior Therapy -- in infancy & childhood.

RJ506.P63.A57 1998
Antisocial behavior and mental health problems : explanatory factors in childhood and adolescence / Rolf Loeber ... [et al.]. Mahwah, N.J. : L. Erlbaum Associates, 1998. viii, 330 p.
97-038123   618.92/89   0805829563
Problem youth -- Pennsylvania -- Pittsburgh -- Longitudinal studies. Problem children -- Pennsylvania -- Pittsburgh -- Longitudinal studies.

RJ506.P63.S45 1998
Sells, Scott P.
Treating the tough adolescent : a family-based, step-by-step guide / Scott P. Sells ; forewords by Jay Haley and Neil Schiff. New York : Guilford Press, c1998. xvi, 320 p. :
98-039683   616.89/00835   1572304227
Problem youth -- Counseling of. Family psychotherapy. Problem youth -- Family relationships.

RJ506.P66.C47 1998
Children of trauma : stressful life events and their effects on children and adolescents / edited by Thomas W. Miller. Madison, Conn. : International Universities Press, c1998. xx, 267 p. :
97-015597   618.92/8521   0823608107
Psychic trauma in children. Psychic trauma in adolescence. Stress in children.

RJ506.P66M366 1997
Monahon, Cynthia.
Children and trauma : a guide for parents and professionals / Cynthia Monahon. San Francisco : Jossey-Bass Publishers, 1997. p. cm.
            618.92/85210651   0787910716
Psychic trauma in children.

RJ506.P69.M37 1984
Massie, Henry N.
Childhood psychosis in the first four years of life / Henry N. Massie, Judith Rosenthal. New York : McGraw-Hill, c1984. x, 315 p. :
83-026799   618.92/89   0070407657
Psychoses in children. Infant psychiatry. Child development disorders.

RJ506.S3.C36 1988
Cantor, Sheila.
Childhood schizophrenia / Sheila Cantor. New York : Guilford Press, c1988. viii, 193 p.
88-005180   618.92/8982   0898627133
Schizophrenia in children. Schizophrenia, Childhood.

RJ506.S33.B58 1987
Blagg, Nigel.
School phobia and its treatment / Nigel Blagg. London ; Croom Helm, c1987. ix, 228 p. ;
87-013444   618.92/85/225   0709939388
School phobia -- Treatment.

RJ506.S33.K42 2001
Kearney, Christopher A.
  School refusal behavior in youth : a fundamental approach to assessment and treatment / Christopher A. Kearney. Washington, D.C. : American Psychological Association, 2001. xiii, 265 p.
00-044174   618.92/89   1557986991
  School phobia.

RJ506.S33.W48 1990
  Why children reject school : views from seven countries / Colette Chiland, J. Gerald Young. New Haven : Yale University Press, c1990. p. cm.
89-049522   618.92/85225   0300044380
  School phobia -- Cross-cultural studies.

RJ506.S9.O73 1988
Orbach, Israel.
  Children who don't want to live : understanding and treating the suicidal child / Israel Orbach. San Francisco, Calif. : Jossey-Bass, c1988. 267 p.
87046338   618.92/858445   1555420761
  Children -- Suicidal behavior. Suicide -- in infancy & childhood Suicide -- in adolescence

RJ506.S9.S53 1994
Slaby, Andrew Edmund.
  No one saw my pain : why teens kill themselves / Andrew E. Slaby, Lili Frank Garfinkel. New York : Norton, c1994. xi, 208 p. ;
93-028398   616.85/8445/00835
0393035832
  Teenagers -- Suicidal behavior -- Case studies. Depression in adolescence -- Case studies.

RJ507 Diseases of children — Mental disorders of children and adolescents. Child psychiatry. Child mental health services — Specific causative factors, situations, abilities, etc., A-Z

RJ507.A29.H45 1998
Heineman, Toni Vaughn.
  The abused child : psychodynamic understanding and treatment / Toni Vaughn Heineman ; foreword by Alicia F. Lieberman. New York : Guilford Press, c1998. xi, 243 p. ;
98-015497   618.92/858223   1572303751
  Abused children -- Mental health. Psychodynamic psychotherapy for children.

RJ507.A29.P55 1991
Pillari, Vimala.
  Scapegoating in families : intergenerational patterns of physical and emotional abuse / Vimala Pillari. New York : Brunner/Mazel, c1991. xviii, 215 p.
91-003452   618.92/85822   0876306393
  Abused children -- Mental health. Psychologically abused children -- Mental health. Scapegoat -- Psychological aspects.

RJ507.A29.R95 1993
Rymer, Russ.
  Genie : an abused child's flight from silence / Russ Rymer New York, NY : HarperCollins Publishers, c1993. xii, 221 p. ;
92-053327   362.7/6/092   0060169109
  Genie, -- 1957-   Abused children -- California -- Biography.

RJ507.A36.M37 1988
McRoy, Ruth G.
  Emotional disturbance in adopted adolescents : origins and development / Ruth G. McRoy, Harold D. Grotevant, Louis A. Zurcher, Jr. New York : Praeger, 1988. xiv, 212 p. ;
88-001053   616.89/022   0275929132
  Adopted children -- Mental health. Adopted children -- Family relationships. Adolescent psychopathology.

RJ507.A36.P37 1998
Pardeck, John T.
  Children in foster care and adoption : a guide to bibliotherapy / John T. Pardeck and Jean A. Pardeck. Westport, Conn. : Greenwood Press, 1998. x, 103 p. ;
98-015323   615.8/516/083   031330775X
  Adopted children -- Mental health. Foster children -- Mental health. Bibliotherapy for children.

RJ507.A42.J47 1989
Jesse, Rosalie Cruise.
  Children in recovery / Rosalie Cruise Jesse. New York : Norton, c1989. xi, 276 p. :
88-037155   618.92/89156   0393700747
  Children of alcoholics -- Mental health. Family psychotherapy. Parent and child.

RJ507.A77.B69 1988
Bowlby, John.
  A secure base : parent-child attachment and healthy human development / John Bowlby. New York : Basic Books, c1988. xii, 205 p. :
88-047669   155.4/18   0465075983
  Attachment behavior in children. Parent and child. Child psychopathology.

RJ507.D59E44 1999
Emery, Robert E.
  Marriage, divorce, and children's adjustment / Robert E. Emery. 2nd ed. Thousand Oaks, Calif. : Sage Publications, c1999. 164 p. :
           155.4   076190252X
  Children of divorced parents--Mental health. Adjustment (Psychology) in children. Family--Psychological aspects.

RJ507.D59H63 1991
Hodges, William F.
  Interventions for children of divorce : custody, access, and psychotherapy / William F. Hodges. 2nd ed. New York : Wiley, c1991. xi, 387 p. ;
           306.8/9   0471522554
  Children of divorced parents--Mental health. Custody of children. Custody of children--Psychological aspects.

RJ507.F35.K37 1998
Kashani, Javad H.,
The impact of family violence on children and adolescents / Javad H. Kashani, Wesley D. Allan. Thousand Oaks, CA : Sage Publications, c1998. xii, 111 p. ;
97-033814   616.85/822   0761908978
Family violence -- Psychological aspects. Abused children -- Mental health. Abused teenagers -- Mental health.

RJ507.M54.G53 1989
Gibbs, Jewelle Taylor.
Children of color : psychological interventions with minority youth / Jewelle Taylor Gibbs, Larke Nahme Huang, and associates ; forewords by George Miller and Stanley Sue. San Francisco : Jossey-Bass Publishers, 1989. xxviii, 423 p
88-046098   618.92/89   1555421563
Children of minorities -- Mental health -- United States. Ethnic Groups -- psychology -- United States. Mental Health Services -- in adolescence -- United States.

RJ507.P35.A87 1995
Assessment of parenting : psychiatric and psychological contributions / edited by Peter Reder and Clare Lucey. London ; Routledge, 1995. xvi, 291 p. ;
95-007618   618.92/89   0415114535.
Parental influences. Child abuse -- Investigation. Family assessment.

RJ507.R44.R44 1991
Refugee children : theory, research, and services / edited by Frederick L. Ahearn, Jr. and Jean L. Athey. Baltimore : Johns Hopkins University Press, c1991. xii, 230 p. ;
90-025554   618.92/89/008694   0801841607
Refugee children -- Mental health -- United States. Refugee children -- Mental health services -- United States.

RJ507.S49.E94 1989
Everstine, Diana Sullivan,
Sexual trauma in children and adolescents : dynamics and treatment / by Diana Sullivan Everstine & Louis Everstine. New York : Brunner/Mazel, c1989. xii, 206 p. ;
88-026309   618.92/89   087630529X
Sexually abused children -- Mental health. Sexually abused teenagers -- Mental health. Family psychotherapy.

RJ507.S49.F35 1988
Faller, Kathleen Coulborn.
Child sexual abuse : an interdisciplinary manual for diagnosis, case management, and treatment / Kathleen Coulborn Faller. New York : Columbia University Press, 1988. 428 p. :
87-015064   616.85/83   0231064705
Sexually abused children -- Mental health. Sexually abused children -- Mental health services. Child psychotherapy.

RJ507.S49.S49 1990
The Sexually abused male / edited by Mic Hunter. Lexington, Mass. : Lexington Books, c1990. 2 v. :
90-006352   616.85/83   066921518X
Male sexual abuse victims -- Mental health. Sexually abused children -- Mental health. Adult child sexual abuse victims -- Mental health.

RJ507.S49.W544 1998
Wieland, Sandra.
Techniques and issues in abuse-focused therapy with children & adolescents : addressing the internal trauma / Sandra Wieland. Thousand Oaks : Sage Publications, c1998. xiv, 238 p. :
98-025306   618.92/8583606   0761904816
Sexually abused children -- Mental health. Sexually abused teenagers -- Mental health. Psychic trauma -- Treatment.

RJ507.S53.C34 1998
Caffaro, John V.
Sibling abuse trauma : assessment and intervention strategies for children, families, and adults / John V. Caffaro, Allison Conn-Caffaro. New York : Haworth Maltreatment and Trauma Press, c1998. xiv, 303 p. :
98-008166   616.85/822   0789004917
Sibling abuse.

RJ507.S77.H36 1997
Handbook of children's coping : linking theory and intervention / edited by Sharlene A. Wolchik and Irwin N. Sandler. New York : Plenum Press, c1997. xv, 549 p. :
97-016901   155.4/18   0306455366
Stress in children. Adjustment disorders in children. Adjustment (Psychology) in children.

RJ520 Diseases of children — Other diseases, A-Z

RJ520.P74.C46 1997
The challenge of fetal alcohol syndrome : overcoming secondary disabilities / edited by Ann Streissguth and Jonathan Kanter ; foreword by Mike Lowry ; introduction by Michael Dorris. Seattle : University of Washington Press, c1997. xxvii, 250 p.
97-018618   618.3/268   0295976500
Children of prenatal alcohol abuse -- Development. Children of prenatal alcohol abuse -- Services for. Fetal alcohol syndrome -- Complications.

RJ570 Materia medica and pharmacology — Trade publications

RJ570.M36 1996
Manual of diagnosis and professional practice in mental retardation / edited by John W. Jacobson and James A. Mulick ; [prepared by APA Division 33, Mental Retardation and Developmental Disabilities, for the American Psychological Association]. Washington, DC.: American Psychological Association, c1996. xv, 540 p. :
95-053053   618.92/8588   1557983216
Mental retardation -- Handbooks, manuals, etc.

RK Dentistry

RK27 Dictionaries and encyclopedias

RK27.M67 1998
Mosby's dental dictionary / [edited by] Thomas J. Zwemer.1st ed. St. Louis : Mosby, 1998. xiv, 658 p. :
617.6/003   0815198884
Dentistry--Dictionaries. Dictionaries, Dental.

RK29 History — General works

RK29.R54 1985
Ring, Malvin E.
Dentistry : an illustrated history / Malvin E. Ring. New York : Abrams ; 1985. 12, 319 p. :
85-003883   617.6/009   0810911000
Dentistry -- History. Dentistry -- History -- Pictorial works. History of Dentistry.

RK43 Biography — Individual, A-Z

RK43.W4.I2 1994
I awaken to glory : essays celebrating the sesquicentennial of the discovery of anesthesia by Horace Wells, December 11, 1844-December 11, 1994 / edited by Richard J. Wolfe and Leonard F. Menczer. Boston, Mass. : Published by the Boston Medical Library in the F 1994. xvii, 442 p.
95-113558   617.9/6/09   088135161X
Wells, Horace, -- 1815-1848. Anesthetics -- History. Dentistry -- history. Anesthesia -- history.

RK51.5 General special

RK51.5.N66 1999
Noonan, Melvin A.
They never came back : how to lose patients / Melvin A. Noonan. Birmingham, Mich. : Timbritom Press, c1999. 93 p. :
98-096363   617.6   0966593405
Dentistry -- Anecdotes. Dentistry -- Humor.

RK52 Public health aspects — General works

RK52.B87 1999
Burt, Brian A.
Dentistry, dental practice, and the community / Brian A. Burt, Stephen A. Eklund ; with a chapter contributed by Amid I. Ismail. 5th ed. Philadelphia : Saunders, c1999. x, 384 p. :
617.6   0721673090
Dental public health. Dentistry--Practice. Public Health Dentistry.

RK54 Aesthetic aspects

RK54.G64 1998
Goldstein, Ronald E.
Esthetics in dentistry / Ronald E. Goldstein.2nd ed. Hamilton, Ont. : B.C. Decker, <1998-   > v. <1-2 >, [13] leaves of plates :
617.6   155009047X
Dentistry--Aesthetic aspects. Esthetics, Dental.

RK55 By age group, class, etc., A-Z

RK55.C5P448 1999
Pediatric dentistry : infancy through adolescence / senior editor, J.R. Pinkham ; associate editors, Paul S. Casamassimo ... [et al.]. 3rd ed. Philadelphia : W.B. Saunders, c1999. xix, 675 p. :
617.6/45   0721682383
Pedodontics.

RK55.S53L57 2002
Dental management of the medically compromised patient / James W. Little ... [et al.]. 6th ed. St. Louis : Mosby, c2002. xi, DM-87, 617 p. :
617.6   0323011713
Sick--Dental care. Chronically ill--Dental care. Oral manifestations of general diseases.

RK58 Practice of dentistry. Dental economics — General works

RK58.P65 2002
Pollack, Burton R.,
Law and risk management in dental practice / Burton R. Pollack. Chicago : Quintessence Pub. Co., c2002. xii, 284 p. ;
617.6/0068   0867154160
Dentistry--Practice. Risk management. Dentists--Malpractice.

RK60 Dentistry as a profession. Dental hygiene as a profession — General works

RK60.K44 2001
Kendall, Bonnie L.
Opportunities in dental care careers / Bonnie L. Kendall ; foreword by Elizabeth C. Sidney. Rev. ed. / by Blythe Camenson. Chicago, IL: VGM Career Horizons, c2001. x, 149 p. ;
617.6/023   0658004786
Dentistry--Vocational guidance.

RK60.5 Dentistry as a profession. Dental hygiene as a profession — Dental hygienists

RK60.5.M63 1995
Mosby's comprehensive dental assisting : a clinical approach / [edited by] Betty Ladley Finkbeiner, Claudia Sullens Johnson. St. Louis : Mosby, c1995. x, 1186 p. :
94-031991   617.6   0815132395
Dental assistants. Dental Assistants.

RK60.5.T67 2003
Bird, Doni.
Torres and Ehrlich modern dental assisting Philadelphia : W.B. Saunders, c2003 xxii, 714 p.
98-040582   617.6/0233   0721693741
Dental assistants. Dental Assistants. Dental Care.

RK60.5.W5 1999
Wilkins, Esther M.
Clinical practice of the dental hygienist [by] Esther M. Wilkins. Philadelphia, Lippincott Williams & Wilkins, 1999 xiv, 529 p.
79-123418   617.6/01   0683303627
Dental hygiene.

RK60.7 Preventive dentistry — General works

RK60.7.H37 1999
Primary preventive dentistry / [edited by] Norman O. Harris, Franklin Garcia-Godoy. 5th ed. Stamford, Conn. : Appleton & Lange, c1999. xiii 658 p. :
              617.6/01   0838581293
Preventive dentistry. Preventive dentistry--Examinations, questions, etc. Dental caries--Examinations, questions, etc.

RK60.7.M67 1998
Mosby's comprehensive review of dental hygiene / edited by Michele Leonardi Darby. 4th ed. St. Louis : Mosby, c1998. ix, 902, 31 p. :
              617.6/01/076   0815122675
Dental hygiene--Outline, syllabi, etc. Dental hygiene--Case studies. Dental hygiene--Examinations, questions, etc.

RK61 Popular works. Care and hygiene for nonprofessionals

RK61.C57 2002
Christensen, Gordon J.
A consumer's guide to dentistry / Gordon J. Christensen.2nd ed. St. Louis, Mo. : Mosby, c2002. x, 214 p. :
              617.6   0323014836
Dentistry--Popular works. Dental Care. Dental Auxiliaries.

RK61.D52 2000
Diamond, Richard,
Dental first aid for families / Richard Diamond. Ravensdale, WA : Idyll Arbor, c2000. viii, 134 p. :
              617.6/01   188288339X
Teeth--Care and hygiene. Dental emergencies--Popular works.

RK61.M75 2001
Mittelman, Jerome S.
Healthy teeth for kids :a preventive program: from pre-birth through the teens / Jerome S. Mittelman, Beverly D. Mittelman, Jean Barilla. New York, NY : Twin Streams, c2001. xv, 288 p. ;
              617.6/01/083   1575666111
Teeth--Care and hygiene. Dental caries--Prevention--Popular works.

RK280 Study and teaching — Oral and dental anatomy and physiology

RK280.A74 1993
Ash, Major M.,
Wheeler's Dental anatomy, physiology, and occlusion / Major M. Ash, Jr. 7th ed. Philadelphia : W.B. Saunders, c1993. xi, 478 p. :
              611/.314   0721643744
Teeth. Occlusion (Dentistry) Dental Occlusion.

RK318 Oral and dental medicine. Pathology. Diseases — Therapeutics — General works

RK318.D43 1998
Decision making in dental treatment planning / [edited by] Walter B. Hall ... [et al.]. 2nd ed. St. Louis, Mo. : Mosby, c1998. xvii, 268 p. :
              617.6   0815141947
Dental therapeutics--Planning. Dental therapeutics--Decision making. Dental Care.

RK318.T74 2001
Treatment planning in dentistry / [edited by] Stephen J. Stefanac, Samuel Paul Nesbit. St. Louis, Mo. : Mosby, c2001. xxvi, 317 p. :
              617.7   0323003958
Dental therapeutics--Planning.

RK351 Oral and dental medicine — Diseases of the dental pulp, root, and periapical — General works

RK351.P37 2002
Pathways of the pulp / edited by Stephen Cohen, Richard C. Burns.8th ed. St. Louis : Mosby, c2002. xviii, 1031 p. :
              617.6/342   0323011624
Endodontics. Dental pulp--Diseases. Dental Pulp.

RK361 Oral and dental medicine. Pathology. Diseases — Diseases of the supporting structures of teeth. Periodontics — Societies. Serials

RK361.D43 1998
Decision making in periodontology / [edited by] Walter B. Hall.3rd ed. St. Louis : Mosby, c1998. xvi, 293 p. :
    617.6/32   0815141939
Periodontics--Decision making. Periodontal Diseases--diagnosis. Periodontal Diseases--therapy.

RK361.G58 2002
Carranza's clinical periodontology / [edited by] Michael G. Newman,9th ed. Philadelphia : W.B. Saunders Co., c2002. xv, 1033 p. :
    617.6/32   0721683312
Periodontics. Periodontal Diseases. Oral Surgical Procedures.

RK361.P4614 1998
Periodontal therapy :clinical approaches and evidence of success / edited by Myron Nevins, James T. Mellonig. Chicago : Quintessence Pub. Co., c1998- v. <1 > :
    617.6/3206   0867153091
Periodontal disease--Treatment. Periodontal disease--Atlases. Periodontal Diseases--therapy.

RK361.S2813 2000
Sato, Naoshi.
Periodontal surgery :a clinical atlas / Naoshi Sato. Chicago : Quintessence Pub. Co., c2000. 447 p. :
    617.6/32059   0867153776
Periodontium--Surgery--Atlases. Periodontics--Atlases. Periodontics--methods--Atlases.

RK501 Operative dentistry. Restorative dentistry — General works

RK501.S436 1996
Schwartz, Richard S.
Fundamentals of operative dentistry : a contemporary approach / Richard S. Schwartz, James B. Summitt, J. William Robbins ; illustrations by Jose dos Santos, Jr. Chicago : Quintessence Pub., c1996. xii, 424 p. :
    617.6/05   0867153113
Dentistry, Operative. Dentistry, Operative.

RK510 Operative dentistry. Restorative dentistry — Anesthesia in dentistry — General works

RK510.M33 1997
Malamed, Stanley F.,
Handbook of local anesthesia / Stanley F. Malamed ; original drawings by Susan B. Clifford. 4th ed. St. Louis : Mosby, c1997. xv, 327 p. :
    617.9/676   0815164238
Anesthesia in dentistry. Local anesthesia. Anesthesia, Dental.

RK521 Orthodontics — History

RK521.G673 2000
Orthodontics :current principles and techniques / edited by Thomas M. Graber, Robert L. Vanarsdall. 3rd ed. St. Louis : Mosby, c2000. xiv, 1040 p. :
    617.6/43   0815193637
Orthodontics. Orthodontics.

RK529 Oral surgery — General works

RK529.M37 1997
Manual of oral and maxillofacial surgery / [edited by] R. Bruce Donoff. 3rd ed. St. Louis : Mosby, c1997. xii, 427 p. :
    617.5/2059   0815127553
Mouth--Surgery--Handbooks, manuals, etc. Maxilla--Surgery--Handbooks, manuals, etc. Face--Surgery--Handbooks, manuals, etc.

RK652.5 Prosthetic dentistry. Prosthodontics — Dental materials — General works

RK652.5.F47 2001
Ferracane, Jack L.
Materials in dentistry :principles and applications / Jack L. Ferracane. 2nd ed. Philadelphia : Lippincott Williams & Wilkins, c2001. xiv, 354 p. :
    617.6/95   0781727332
Dental materials.

RK652.5.P47 2002
Restorative dental materials / edited by Robert G. Craig, John M. Powers. 11th ed. St. Louis : Mosby, c2002. xvi, 704 p. :
    617.6/95   0323014429
Dental materials. Dental Materials.

RK652.5.P495 1996
Phillips' science of dental materials / [edited by] Kenneth J. Anusavice. 10th ed. Philadelphia : W.B. Saunders, c1996. xiv, 709 p., [8] p. of plates :
    617.6/95   0721657419
Dental materials. Dental Materials.

RK666 Prosthetic dentistry. Prosthodontics — Dentures. Complete dentures — Partial dentures

RK666.R65 2001
Rosenstiel, Stephen F.
Contemporary fixed prosthodontics / Stephen F. Rosenstiel, Martin F. Land, Junhei Fujimoto ; artwork by Donald O'Connor, Sue E. Cottrill, Kerrie Marzo ; photographic services by James Cockerill. 3rd ed. St. Louis : Mosby, c2001. xi, 868 p. :
    617.6/92   081515559X
Bridges (Dentistry) Crowns (Dentistry)

RK667 Prosthetic dentistry. Prosthodontics — Special topics, A-Z

RK667.I45C66 1999
Misch, Carl E.
   Contemporary implant dentistry / Carl E. Misch. 2nd ed. St. Louis : Mosby, c1999. xviii, 684 p. :
             617.6/92   0815170599
   Dental implants. Dental Implantation. Dental Implants.

RK667.I45C7 1999
Cranin, A. Norman.
   Atlas of oral implantology / A. Norman Cranin, Michael Klein, Alan Simons. 2nd ed. St. Louis : Mosby, / c1999. xvi, 489 p. :
             617.6/92   155664552X
   Dental implants. Dental implants--Atlases. Dental Implantation--methods--atlases.

RK667.I45I466 1998
   Implant therapy :clinical approaches and evidence of success / edited by Myron Nevins, James T. Mellonig ; associate editor, Joseph P. Fiorellini. Chicago : Quintessence, c1998. ix, 257 p. :
             617.6/9   0867153415
   Dental implants. Dental Implants. Dental Implantation--methods.

RK701 Materia medica and pharmacology — General works

RK701.A33 2000
   ADA guide to dental therapeutics. 2nd ed. Chicago, Ill. : ADA Pub., c2000. xii, 658 p. ;
             615/.1/0246176   1891748017
   Dental pharmacology. Dental therapeutics. Dentistry.

RK701.M58
   Mosby's dental drug reference. St. Louis, Mo. : Mosby, c1994- v. ;
             615/.1/0246176
   Dental pharmacology--Handbooks, manuals, etc. Pharmaceutical Preparations--Handbooks. Dentistry--Handbooks.

RK715 Materia medica and pharmacology — Individual drugs and other agents, A-Z

RK715.A58G85 2001
   Antibiotic and antimicrobial use in dental practice / edited by Michael G. Newman, Arie J. van Winkelhoff. 2nd ed. Chicago : Quintessence Pub. Co., c2001. xv, 288 p. :
             617.6/061   0867153970
   Antibiotics. Materia medica, Dental. Antibiotics--adverse effects.

RL Dermatology

RL46 History

RL46.P8
Pusey, William Allen,
The history of dermatology, by Wm. Allen Pusey. Springfield, Ill., C.C. Thomas, 1933. xiii p., 3 l., 3-223 p., 1 l.
616.509
Dermatology--History.

RL46.W49 1998
Weyers, Wolfgang.
Death of medicine in Nazi Germany : dermatology and dermatopathology under the swastika / Wolfgang Weyers ; foreword by A. Bernard Ackerman. Philadelphia : Lippincott-Raven, c1998. xxii, 442 p.
97-052091   616.5/00943/0904
0781717140
Dermatology -- Germany -- History -- 20th century. Medicine -- Germany -- History -- 20th century. World War, 1939-1945 -- Atrocities.

RL71 General works — 1901-

RL71.D46 1999
Fitzpatrick's dermatology in general medicine. 5th ed. / editors, Irwin M. Freedberg ... [et al.]. New York : McGraw-Hill, Health Professions Division, c1999. 2 v. (xxxi, 3002 p.) :
616.5   0070219435
Dermatology. Skin--Diseases. Cutaneous manifestations of general diseases.

RL71.O33 2000
Odom, Richard B.,
Andrews' diseases of the skin :clinical dermatology Richard B. Odom, William D. James, Timothy G. Berger. 9th ed. Philadelphia : W. B. Saunders Co., c 2000. x, 1135 p. :
616.5   0721658326
Skin--Diseases. Dermatology.

RL72 General special

RL72.D54 1988
Difficult diagnoses in dermatology / edited by Mark Lebwohl. New York : Churchill Livingstone, 1988. xvi, 450 p. :
616.5/075   0443084602
Skin--Diseases--Diagnosis. Skin Diseases--diagnosis.

RL74 Handbooks, manuals, etc.

RL74.S25 2000
Hall, John C.,
Sauer's manual of skin diseases / John C. Hall ; with 13 contributing authors. 8th ed. Philadelphia : Lippincott Williams & Wilkins, c2000. xvii, 442 p. :
616.5   0781716292
Skin--Diseases--Handbooks, manuals, etc. Skin Diseases.

RL81 Atlases. Pictorial works

RL81.C665 2000
Color atlas of dermatology / Jeffrey P. Callen ... [et al.]. 2nd ed. Philadelphia : W.B. Saunders, c2000. 395 p. :
616.5/0022/2   0721682561
Dermatology--Atlases. Skin--Diseases--Atlases. Skin Diseases--Atlases.

RL85 Popular works

RL85.J33 2001
Jacknin, Jeanette.
Smart medicine for your skin :a comprehensive guide to understanding conventional and alternative therapies to heal common skin problems / Jeanette Jacknin. New York : Avery, c2001. xvi, 414 p. :
616.5   1583330984
Skin--Diseases--Popular works. Skin--Care and hygiene--Popular works.

RL95 Pathological anatomy

RL95.L48 1997
Lever's histopathology of the skin. 8th ed. / editor-in-chief, David Elder ; associate editors, Rosalie Philadelphia : Lippincott-Raven, c1997. xvii, 1073 p. :
616.5/07   0397515006
Skin--Histopathology. Skin Diseases--pathology.

RL100 Skin manifestations of systematic disease

RL100.B7 1998
Braverman, Irwin M.,
Skin signs of systemic disease / Irwin M. Braverman. 3rd ed. Philadelphia : Saunders, c1998. xvi, 682 p., [53] p. of plates :
616.5   0721637450
Cutaneous manifestations of general diseases. Skin Manifestations.

RL100.L43 1995
Lebwohl, Mark.
Atlas of the skin and systemic disease / Mark G. Lebwohl.
New York : Churchill Livingstone, 1995. xiii, 238 p. :
    616.5   0443087393
Cutaneous manifestations of general diseases--Atlases. Skin Diseases--complications--atlases. Skin Diseases--pathology--atlases.

RL120 Therapeutics — Other therapies, A-Z

RL120.L37A45 1997
Alster, Tina S.
Manual of cutaneous laser techniques / Tina S. Alster. Philadelphia : Lippincott-Raven, c1997. xi, 190 p. :
    617.4/77059   0397584296
Skin--Laser surgery--Handbooks, manuals, etc. Laser Surgery--methods. Skin Diseases--surgery.

RL120.L37L357 1997
Lasers in cutaneous and aesthetic surgery / editors, Kenneth A. Arndt, Jeffrey S. Dover, Suzanne M. Olbricht. Philadelphia : Lippincott-Raven Publishers, c1997. xvi, 480 p. :
    617.4/77059   0316051772
Skin--Laser surgery. Surgery, Plastic. Lasers in surgery.

RL241 Hyperemias, inflammations, and infections of the skin — Dermatitus — Occupational dermatitus due to drugs, radiation, etc.

RL241.O27 1999
Occupational skin disease / [edited by] Robert M. Adams. 3rd ed. Philadelphia : Saunders, c1999. xiii, 792 p., [2] p. of colored plates :
    616.5   0721670377
Occupational dermatitis. Skin--Diseases. Occupational diseases.

RL721 Diseases due to psychosomatic and nerve disorders — Dermatalgia. Pruritis and related conditions

RL721.F56 2000
Fleischer, Alan B.
The clinical management of itching / Alan B. Fleischer, Jr. New York : Parthenon Pub. Group, c2000. xxiii, 186 p. :
    616.5   1850707790
Itching. Pruritus.

RM Therapeutics. Pharmacology

RM16 Yearbooks

RM16.A63
Annual review of pharmacology. Palo Alto, Calif., Annual Reviews, inc. 15 v.
61-005649   615.1058
Pharmacology -- Yearbooks. Pharmacology -- yearbooks.

RM45 History — Modern

RM45.W43 1990
Weatherall, M.
In search of a cure : a history of pharmaceutical discovery / M. Weatherall. Oxford ; Oxford University Press, 1990. xiv, 298 p.,
90-007426   615/.1/09   0192617478
Pharmacology -- History. Therapeutics -- History. Pharmaceutical industry -- History.

RM62 Biography — Individual, A-Z

RM62.A24.P37 1992
Parascandola, John,
The development of American pharmacology : John J. Abel and the shaping of a discipline / John Parascandola. Baltimore : Johns Hopkins University Press, c1992. xvii, 212 p.
92-011545   615/.1/092   0801844169
Abel, John Jacob, -- 1857-1938. Abel, John Jacob, -- 1857-1938. Pharmacology -- United States -- History. Pharmacologists -- United States -- Biography. Pharmacology -- biography.

RM146 Misuse of therapeutic drugs. Medication errors — General works

RM146.M415 1999
Medication errors / edited by Michael R. Cohen. Washington, D.C. : American Pharmaceutical Association, c1999. 1 v. (various
99-031972   615.5/8   0917330897
Medication errors. Medication Errors.

RM170 Administration of drugs and other therapeutic agents — Infusion. Transfusion — General works

RM170.G33 2000
Gahart, Betty L.
Intravenous medications : a handbook for nurses and allied health professionals / Betty L. Gahart, Adrienne R. Nazareno. 16th ed. St Louis : Mosby, c2000. xviii, 987 p. ;
615.5/8   0815127294
Intravenous therapy--Handbooks, manuals, etc. Nursing--Handbooks, manuals, etc. Allied health personnel--Handbooks, manuals, etc.

RM172 Administration of drugs and other therapeutic agents — Infusion. Transfusion — Blood transfusion

RM172.S728 1998
Starr, Douglas P.
Blood : an epic history of medicine and commerce / Douglas Starr. New York : Alfred A. Knopf, 1998. xv, 441 p. :
97-046815   362.1/784/09   067941875X
Blood banks -- History.

RM184 Other therapeutic procedures — Cupping. Acupuncture. Artificial hyperemia. Mustard plasters

RM184.C37 1994
Cargill, Marie.
Acupuncture : a viable medical alternative / Marie Cargill. Westport, Conn. : Praeger ; 1994. xii, 176 p. :
94-012069   615.8/92   0275948811
Acupuncture -- Popular works.

RM184.C635 2000
Clinical acupuncture : scientific basis / G. Stux, R. Hammerschlag (eds.). Berlin ; Springer, 2000. p. ;
615.8/92   3540640541
Acupuncture. Acupuncture. Research.

RM184.K526 2000
Kidson, Ruth.
Acupuncture for everyone :what it is, why it works, and how it can help you / Ruth Kidson.1st U.S. ed. Rochester, VT : Healing Arts Press, 2000. 168 p. :
615.8/92   0892818999
Acupuncture.

RM184.U433 2002
Ulett, George A.
The biology of acupuncture / by George A. Ulett and SongPing Han. St. Louis, Mo : Warren H. Green, c2002. 160 p. :
615.8/92   0875275346
Acupuncture. Electroacupuncture.

RM216 Diet therapy. Clinical nutrition — General works — 1901-

RM216.G946 2000
Grodner, Michele.
Foundations and clinical applications of nutrition : a nursing approach / Michele Grodner, Sara Long Anderson, and Sandra DeYoung. St. Louis, Mo. ; Mosby, c2000. xix, 868 p. :
00-269915   615.8/54   0323003907
Diet therapy. Nutrition. Nursing.

RM216.M285 2000
Krause's food, nutrition, & diet therapy / edited by L. Kathleen Mahan, Sylvia Escott-Stump. 10th ed. Philadelphia : W.B. Saunders, c2000. xxxiv, 1194 p. :
615.8/54   0721679048
Diet therapy. Nutrition. Food.

RM216.N875 2001
Nutrition in the prevention and treatment of disease / edited by Ann M. Coulston, Cheryl L. Rock, and Elaine R. Monsen. San Diego, Calif. : Academic Press, c2001. xix, 801 p. :
615.8/54   0121931552
Dietetics. Nutrition. Diet in disease.

RM216.P67 1999
Peckenpaugh, Nancy J.
Nutrition essentials and diet therapy / Nancy J. Peckenpaugh, Charlotte M. Poleman. 8th ed. Philadelphia : W.B. Saunders, c1999. xviii, 635 p. :
613.2   072167707X
Diet therapy. Nutrition. Nutrition--nurses' instruction.

RM216.W682 2001
Williams, Sue Rodwell.
Basic nutrition and diet therapy / Sue Rodwell Williams.11th ed. St. Louis : Mosby, c2001. xx, 465, 176 p. :
613.2   0323005691
Diet therapy. Nutrition.

RM217 Diet therapy. Clinical nutrition — General special

RM217.L88 2001
Lutz, Carroll A.
Nutrition and diet therapy / Carroll A. Lutz, Karen Rutherford Przytulski. 3rd ed. Philadelphia, PA : F.A. Davis Co., c2001. xiii, 668 p. :
613.2   0803608047
Dietetics. Diet therapy. Nutrition.

RM222.2 Diet therapy. Clinical nutrition — Diets to control weight — Reducing weight

RM222.2.B443 1982
Bennett, William,
The dieter's dilemma : eating less and weighing more / William Bennett & Joel Gurin. New York : Basic Books, c1982. xiv, 315 p. ;
81-068403   613.2/5/019   0465016529
Reducing diets. Obesity. Body image.

RM222.2.B4522 1993
Berg, Francie M.
The health risks of weight loss / Frances M. Berg. Hettinger, N.D. : Obesity & Health, c1993. p. 62-190 :
94-175727   613.2/5   0918532426
Weight loss. Reducing diets. Weight Loss

RM222.2.D486 1999
Diet and weight control. Pleasantville, N.Y. : Reader's Digest Assoc., 1999. p. cm.
613.2/5   0762101458
Weight loss.

RM222.2.S755 1997
Stearns, Peter N.
Fat history : bodies and beauty in the modern West / Peter N. Stearns. New York : New York University Press, c1997. xvi, 294 p. :
96-045878   613.2/509   0814780695
Weight loss -- United States -- History. Weight loss -- France -- History. Body image -- United States -- History.

RM236 Diet therapy. Clinical nutrition — Vegetable diet

RM236.V43 2001
Vegetarian nutrition / edited by Joan Sabate ; in collaboration with Rosemary Ratzin-Turner. Boca Raton : CRC Press, c2001. 551 p. :
00-068871   613.2/62   0849385083
Vegetarianism.

RM237.8 Diet therapy. Clinical nutrition — Salt-free diet

RM237.8.S73 2001
American Heart Association low-salt cookbook :a complete guide to reducing sodium and fat in your diet / American Heart Association.2nd ed. New York : Clarkson Potter, c2001. xiv, 353 p. ;
641.5/632   0812991079
Salt-free diet--Recipes.

RM263 Chemotherapy — General special

RM263.P56 2002
Pharmacotherapy :a pathophysiologic approach / editors, Joseph T. DiPiro ... [et al.]. 5th ed. Stamford, Conn. : Appleton & Lang, c2002. xxv, 2440 p. :
      615.5/8   0071363610
Chemotherapy. Physiology, Pathological.

RM267 Antibiotic therapy. Antibiotics — General works

RM267.L36
Lappe, Marc.
Germs that won't die : medical consequences of the misuse of antibiotics / Marc Lappe. Garden City : Anchor Press/Doubleday, 1982. xvi, 246 p. :
81-043146   615/.329   0385150938
Antibiotics. Drug resistance in microorganisms. Medication abuse -- Complications.

RM300 Drugs and their actions — General works

RM300.F72 1997
Freeman, Julia B.
Pharmacologic basis of nursing practice / Julia B. Freeman Clark, Sherry F. Queener, Virginia Burke Karb.5th ed. St. Louis : Mosby, c1997. xv, 889 p. :
      615/.1/024613   0815115148
Pharmacology. Nursing. Drug Therapy--nurses' instruction.

RM300G644 2001
Goodman & Gilman's the pharmacological basis of therapeutics. 10th ed. / editors, Joel G. Hardman, Lee E. Limbird ; consulting New York : McGraw-Hill, c2001. xxvii, 2148 p. :
      615/.7   0071124322
Pharmacology. Chemotherapy. Pharmacology.

RM300. G717 2000
Grajeda-Higley, Leilani.
Understanding pharmacology : a physiologic approach / Leilani Grajeda-Higley. Stamford, CT : Appleton & Lang, c2000. xvii, 349 p.
99-073102   615/.1   0838581366
Pharmacology. Drugs. Nursing.

RM300.H65 2003
Hollinger, Mannfred A.
Introduction to pharmacology / Mannfred A. Hollinger. 2nd ed. London ; Taylor & Francis, 2003. p. ;
      615/.1   0415280346
Pharmacology. Pharmacology. Pharmaceutical Preparations.

RM300.J85 1988
Julien, Robert M.
Drugs and the body / Robert M. Julien. New York : W.H. Freeman, c1988. xvi, 297 p. :
86-031873   615/.7   0716718421
Pharmacology. Drug Therapy. Drugs -- metabolism.

RM300.R53 2002
Rice, Jane.
Medications and mathematics for the nurse. 9th ed. / Jane Rice. Albany, N.Y. : Delmar Publishers, c2002. xviii, 717 p. :
      615.5/8   0766830802
Pharmacology. Drugs--Administration. Pharmaceutical arithmetic.

RM300.S638 1999
Snyder, Katherine.
Pharmacology for the surgical technologist / Katherine Snyder, Chris Keegan. Philadelphia : W.B. Saunders Co., c1999. xii, 268 p. :
98-033323   615/.1   0721663214
Pharmacology. Operating room technicians. Pharmaceutical Preparations -- administration & dosage -- nurses' instruction.

RM300.15 Drugs and their actions — Popular works

RM300.15.B87 1986
Burger, Alfred,
Drugs and people : medications, their history and origins, and the way they act / Alfred Burger. Charlottesville [Va.] : University Press of Virginia, 1986. viii, 176 p.
85-026440   615/.1   0813910854
Drugs. Drugs -- History. Pharmacy -- Popular works.

RM301 Drugs and their actions — General special

RM301.H33 2001
McKenry, Leda M.
Mosby's pharmacology in nursing / Leda M. McKenry, Evelyn Salerno. 21st ed. St. Louis, Mo. : Mosby, 2001. xix, 1324 p. :
      615/.1   0323010059
Pharmacology. Nursing. Pharmacology--Nurses' Instruction.

RM301.K44 2003
Kee, Joyce LeFever.
Pharmacology :a nursing process approach / Joyce LeFever Kee, Evelyn R. Hayes. 4th ed. Philadelphia : Saunders, c2003. p. ;
      615.5/8   0721693458
Pharmacology. Nursing. Pharmacology--Nurses' Instruction.

RM301.12 Drugs and their actions — Handbooks, manuals, etc.

RM301.12.A2 1999
A to Z drug facts / [editor, David S. Tatro ; assistant editors, Larry R. Borgsdorf ... et al.]. St. Louis, Mo. : Facts and Comparisons, c1999. xvi, 1242, 47 p. :
       615/.1   1574390627
Drugs--Handbooks, manuals, etc. Pharmacology--Handbooks, manuals, etc.

RM301.12.D44 2000
Deglin, Judith Hopfer,
Davis's drug guide for nurses / Judith Hopfer Deglin, April Hazard Vallerand. 7th ed. Philadelphia : Davis, c2001. 59, 1245 p., [16] p. of col. plates :
      615/.1/024613   0803604955
Drugs--Handbooks, manuals, etc. Nursing--Handbooks, manuals, etc. Clinical pharmacology--Handbooks, manuals, etc.

RM301.15 Drugs and their actions — Popular works

RM301.15.A43 1998
Aldridge, Susan.
Magic molecules : how drugs work / Susan Aldridge. Cambridge, UK ; Cambridge University Press, 1998. xiii, 269 p.
98-021346   615/.7   0521584140
Drugs -- Mechanism of action -- Popular works.

RM301.15.B873 1995
Burger, Alfred,
Understanding medications : what the label doesn't tell you / Alfred Burger. Washington, DC : American Chemical Society, 1995. xiv, 206 p. :
95-017498   615/.1   0841232105
Drugs -- Popular works.

RM301.15.P39 2000
The PDR family guide to prescription drugs. 8th ed., [completely rev. and updated]. New York : Three Rivers Press, c2000. xv, 927 p., 16 p. of col. plates :
      615/.1   0609807668
Drugs--Popular works. Pharmaceutical Preparations--Handbooks. Pharmaceutical Preparations--Popular Works.

RM301.25 Drugs and their actions — Research. Experimental pharmacology. Drug development

RM301.25.M36 1999
Mann, J.
The elusive magic bullet : the search for the perfect drug / John Mann. Oxford ; Oxford University Press, 1999. x, 209 p. :
      615/.1/09   0198500939
Drugs--Research--History. Pharmacology--History.

RM301.28 Drugs and their actions — Clinical pharmacology

RM301.28.E33 2002
Edmunds, Marilyn W.
Introduction to clinical pharmacology / Marilyn W. Edmunds. St. Louis : Mosby, c2002. xiii, 487 p.
99-042911   615.5/8   0323019102
Clinical pharmacology. Nursing. Pharmacology, Clinical -- Nurses' Instruction.

RM302 Drugs and their actions — Drug interactions

RM302.H47 2000
Herr, Sharon M.
Herb-drug interaction handbook / Sharon M. Herr. Nassau, NY : Church Street Books, c2000. vii, 287 p. ;
00-710562   615/.7045   096787730X
Drug-herb interactions -- Handbooks, manuals, etc.

RM302.N38 2001
Meletis, Chris D.
Instant guide to drug-herb interactions / by Chris D. Meletis and the editors of Natural health magazine with Sheila Buff. 1st American ed. New York, N.Y. : Dorling Kindersley Pub., 2001. 160 p. :
      615/.7045   0789471507
Drug-herb interactions.

RM302.5 Drugs and their actions — Drug side effects (General)

RM302.5.D784
Drug eruption reference manual : DERM. New York : Parthenon Pub. Group, v. :
      616
Dermatotoxicology--Handbooks, manuals, etc. Drug-exanthems--Handbooks, manuals, etc. Drugs--Side effects--Handbooks, manuals, etc.

RM315 Drugs and their actions — Drugs acting on the nervous system — General works

RM315.K44 2000
Keen, Ernest,
Chemicals for the mind : psychopharmacology and human consciousness / Ernest Keen. Westport, Conn. : Praeger, 2000. xviii, 142 p.
99-016058   615/.78   0275967751
Psychopharmacology. Consciousness. Altered states of consciousness.

RM315.P365 2001
Pardridge, William M.
  Brain drug targeting :the future of brain drug development / William M. Pardridge. Cambridge ; Cambridge University Press, 2001. xvii, 353 p., [4] plates :
         615/.78   0521800773
  Neuropharmacology. Drug targeting. Brain--Effect of drugs on.

RM316 Drugs and their actions — Drugs acting on the nervous system — Drugs of abuse. Designer drugs

RM316.D76 1998
  Drug abuse handbook / editor-in-chief, Steven B. Karch. Boca Raton, Fla. : CRC Press, c1998. 1138 p. :
97-045100   616.86   0849326370
  Drugs of abuse -- Handbooks, manuals, etc. Drug abuse -- Handbooks, manuals, etc. Forensic toxicology -- Handbooks, manuals, etc.

RM316.K84 1998
Kuhn, Cynthia.
  Buzzed : the straight facts about the most used and abused drugs from alcohol to ecstasy / Cynthia Kuhn, Scott Swartzwelder, Wilkie Wilson ; with Leigh Heather Wilson and Jeremy Foster. New York : W.W. Norton, c1998. 317 p. :
97-017914   615/.78   0393317323
  Drugs of abuse -- Popular works.

RM332 Drugs and their actions — Drugs acting on the nervous system — Stimulants. Antidepressants

RM332.H42 1997
Healy, David,
  The antidepressant era / David Healy. Cambridge, Mass. : Harvard University Press, 1997. x, 317 p. :
97-023118   616.85/27061   0674039572
  Antidepressants -- History.

RM332.I43 1997
Inaba, Darryl.
  Uppers, downers, all arounders : physical and mental effects of psychoactive drugs / Darryl S. Inaba, William E. Cohen, Michael E. Holstein. 3rd ed. Ashland, Or. : CNS Publications, c1997. viii, 488 p. :
         616.86   092654425X
  Psychotropic drugs--Side effects. Drug abuse--Complications.

RM333 Drugs and their actions — Drugs acting on the nervous system — Tranquilizing drugs

RM333.U53 1991
  Understanding tranquilliser use : the role of the social sciences / edited by Jonathan Gabe. London ; Tavistock/Routledge, 1991. 215 p. ;
90-008436   306.4/61   0415030803
  Tranquilizing drugs -- Social aspects.

RM334 Drugs and their actions — Drugs acting on the nervous system — Nootropic agents

RM334.G76 2001
Group, David.
  Encyclopedia of mind enhancing foods, drugs, and nutritional substances / David W. Group. Jefferson, NC : McFarland, c2001. v, 215 p. ;
00-058678   615/.78   0786408537
  Nootropic agents. Dietary supplements.

RM409 Drugs and their actions — Antibacterial agents

RM409.R87 1990
Russell, A. D.
  Understanding antibacterial action and resistance / A.D. Russell, I. Chopra. New York : E. Horwood, 1990. 246 p. :
89-071647   616/.014   0745804063
  Antibacterial agents -- Physiological effect. Drug resistance in microorganisms. Antibiotics -- pharmacology.

RM411 Drugs and their actions — Antiviral agents

RM411.A576 1997
  Antiviral therapy / E. Blair ... [et al.]. New York : Springer, c1997. p. cm.
97-041321   616.9/25061   0387915109
  Antiviral agents. Virus diseases -- Chemotherapy. Virus Diseases -- drug therapy.

RM666 Drugs and their actions — Individual drugs and other agents, A-Z

RM666.A79.P3
Pauling, Linus,
  Vitamin C and the common cold [by] Linus Pauling. San Francisco, W. H. Freeman [1970] 122 p.
76-140232   616.2/05/061   0716701596
  Vitamin C -- Therapeutic use. Cold (Disease)

RM666.C266R3813 2001
Rätsch, Christian,
  Marijuana medicine :a world tour of the healing and visionary powers of cannabis / Christian Rätsch ; translated by John Baker. Rochester, VT : Healing Arts Press, 2001. xix, 204 p. :
         615/.7827   0892819332
  Marijuana--Therapeutic use. Traditional medicine. Medical anthropology.

RM666.H33C522 2001
Chevallier, Andrew.
  Herbal remedies handbook : essential tips / Andrew Chevallier. 1st American ed. New York : Dorling Kindersley Pub., 2001. 128 p. :
         615/.321   0789471779
  Herbs--Therapeutic use--Popular works.

RM666.H33C585 2001
Cichoke, Anthony J.
  Secrets of Native American herbal remedies :a comprehensive guide to the Native American tradition of using herbs and the mind/body/spirit connection for improving health and well-being / Anthony Cichoke. New York : Avery, 2001. xiv, 274 p. ;
          615/.321/08997   158333100X
  Herbs--Therapeutic use. Indians of North America--Medicine. Spiritual healing.

RM666.H33C67 1998
  The complete German Commission E monographs, herbal medicines / developed by a special expert committee of the German Federal Institute for Drugs and Medical Devices ; senior editor, Mark Blumenthal ; associate editors, Werner R. Busse ... [et al.]. Austin, Texas : American Botanical Council ; xxii, 685 p. ;
          615/.321   096555550X
  Herbs--Therapeutic use. Materia medica, Vegetable--Germany.

RM666.H33.D378 2000
Davidson, Jonathan R. T.,
  Herbs for the mind : what science tells us about nature's remedies for depression, stress, memory loss, and insomnia / Jonathan R. T. Davidson, Kathryn M. Connor. New York : Guilford Press, c2000. x, 278 p. :
00-026341   615/.78   157230572X
  Herbs -- Therapeutic use. Mental illness -- Nutritional aspects. Neuropharmacology.

RM666.H33.H466 2000
  Herbal medicine : a concise overview for professionals / edited by Edzard Ernst. Boston : Butterworth-Heinemann, 2000. 120 p. :
99-056378   615/.321   0750645407
  Herbs -- Therapeutic use. Materia medica, Vegetable.

RM666.H33K84 2000
Kuhn, Merrily A.,
  Herbal therapy & supplements :a scientific & traditional approach / Merrily A. Kuhn, David Winston ; text consultant, Ara DerMarderosian. Philadelphia : Lippincott, c2000. xviii, 430 p. ;
          615/.321   0781726433
  Herbs--Therapeutic use--Handbooks, manuals, etc. Dietary supplements--Handbooks, manuals, etc. Medicine, Herbal-- Handbooks.

RM666.H33K8713 2000
  Sauer's herbal cures : America's first book of botanic healing / translated and edited by William Woys Weaver. New York : Routledge, 2000. p. cm.
          615/.321/0973   0415923603
Sower, Christopher, 1721-1784. Kurtzgefasstes Kräuterbuch. Herbs--Therapeutic use--United States--Early works to 1800.

RM666.H33.R6 1999
Robbers, James E.
  Tyler's Herbs of choice : the therapeutic use of phytomedicinals / James E. Robbers, Varro E. Tyler. New York : Haworth Herbal Press, c1999. x, 287 p. :
98-028809   615/.321   0789001594
  Herbs -- Therapeutic use.

RM666.H33S575 2001
Skidmore-Roth, Linda.
  Mosby's handbook of herbs & natural supplements / Linda Skidmore-Roth. St. Louis, Mo. : Mosby, 2001. xxvi, 933 p. :
          615/.321   0323012086
  Herbs--Therapeutic use--Handbooks, manuals, etc. Dietary supplements--Handbooks, manuals, etc. Medicine, Herbal-- Handbooks.

RM666.H33.T94 1999
Foster, Steven,
  Tyler's honest herbal : a sensible guide to the use of herbs and related remedies / Steven Foster, Varro E. Tyler. New York : Haworth Herbal Press, c1999. xxi, 442 p. ;
98-043234   615/.321   0789007053
  Herbs -- Therapeutic use. Materia medica, Vegetable.

RM666.P48.H9
Huxley, Aldous,
  The doors of perception. New York] Harper [1954] 79 p.
54-005833   615.323471
  Peyote. Mescaline.

RM671 Nonprescription drugs. Patent medicines

RM671.A1.P48
  Physicians' desk reference for nonprescription drugs. [Oradell, N.J., Medical Economics Co.] v.
80-644575   615/.1/05
  Drugs, Nonprescription -- Periodicals. Drugs, Non-Prescription -- catalogs.

RM700 Physical medicine. Physical therapy — General works

RM700.M36 1989
  Manual of natural therapy : a succinct catalog of complementary treatments / Moshe Olshevsky ... [et al.]. New York : Facts On File, c1989. xii, 372 p. :
88-024410   615.5   0816012431
  Therapeutics, Physiological. Alternative medicine.

RM700.P34 2001
  Introduction to physical therapy / [edited by] Michael A. Pagliarulo.2nd ed. St. Louis : Mosby, 2001. xii, 340 p. :
          615.8/2   0323010571
  Physical therapy. Physical Therapy.

RM700.P464 1999
Physical agents in rehabilitation : from research to practice / [edited by] Michelle H. Cameron. Philadelphia : W.B. Saunders, c1999. xvi, 490 p. :
98-021395   615.8/2   0721662447
Physical therapy. Medicine, Physical. Physical Therapy -- methods.

RM706 Physical medicine. Physical therapy — Study and teaching — General works

RM706.H36 2002
Handbook of teaching for physical therapists / edited by Katherine F. Shepard, Gail M. Jensen ; with 14 contributing authors. 2nd ed. Boston : Butterworth-Heinemann, c2002. xxv, 518 p. :
          615.8/2/071   0750673095
Physical therapy--Study and teaching--Handbooks, manuals, etc. Patient education--Handbooks, manuals, etc. Physical Therapy--education.

RM721-723 Physical medicine. Physical therapy — Mechanotherapy. Massage, exercise, etc. — Massage

RM721.F54 2000
Field, Tiffany.
Touch therapy / Tiffany Field. Edinburgh ; Churchill Livingstone, 2000. p. cm.
99-035908   615.8/22   0443057915
Massage therapy. Therapeutic Touch. Massage.

RM723.A27C76 2000
20 common problems in dermatology / [editors] , Alan B. Fleischer, Jr. ... [et al.]. New York : McGraw-Hill, Health Professions Division, c2000. viii, 303 p. :
          616.5   0070220670
Skin--Diseases--Handbooks, manuals, etc. Dermatology--Handbooks, manuals, etc. Skin Diseases--diagnosis.

RM725 Physical medicine. Physical therapy — Mechanotherapy. Massage, exercise, etc. — Exercise

RM725.C585 1997
Clinical exercise testing and prescription : theory and application / edited by Scott O. Roberts, Robert A. Robergs, Peter Hanson. Boca Raton : CRC Press, c1997. 316 p. :
96-024940   615.8/2   0849345936
Exercise therapy. Exercise tests. Exercise Therapy -- methods.

RM725.G75 1998
Griffin, John C.
Client-centered exercise prescription / John C. Griffin. Champaign, IL : Human Kinetics, c1998. xiii, 264 p.
97-045094   615.8/2   0880117079
Exercise therapy. Exercise. Physical fitness.

RM725.H33 1998
Hall, Carrie M.
Therapeutic exercise : moving toward function / Carrie M. Hall, Lori Thein Brody. Philadelphia : Lippincott Williams & Wilkins, c1999. xxiii, 707 p. :
          615.8/2   0397552602
Exercise therapy.

RM725.R42 2001
ACSM's resource manual for Guidelines for exercise testing and prescription / American College of Sports Medicine ; senior editor, Jeffrey L. Roitman ; section editors, Matt Herridge ... [et al.]. 4th ed. Philadelphia : Lippincott Williams & Wilkins, c2001. xxxvi, 732 p. :
          615.8/2   0781725259
Exercise therapy--Handbooks, manuals, etc. Exercise tests--Handbooks, manuals, etc. Exercise Test.

RM725.T47 1990
Therapeutic exercise / edited by John V. Basmajian, Steven L. Wolf. 5th ed. Baltimore : Williams & Wilkins, c1990. xiii, 460 p. :
          615.8/24   0683004336
Exercise therapy. Exercise Therapy.

RM735-735.36 Physical medicine. Physical therapy — Occupational therapy. Rehabilitation

RM735.H68 2001
Howe, Margot C.
A functional approach to group work in occupational therapy / Margot C. Howe, Sharan L. Schwartzberg. 3rd ed. Philadelphia : Lippincott Williams & Wilkins, c2001. xvii, 267 p. :
          615.8/515   0781721091
Occupational therapy. Group psychotherapy.

RM735.J345 2001
Quick reference dictionary for occupational therapy / edited by Karen Jacobs and Laela Jacobs. 3rd ed. Thorofare, NJ : Slack, c2001. vi, 547 p. :
          615.8/515/03   1556424957
Occupational therapy--Dictionaries. Occupational Therapy--Terminology--English.

RM735.T44 2000
The texture of life : purposeful activities in occupational therapy / Jim Hinojosa, Marie-Louise Blount, editors. Bethesda, MD : American Occupational Therapy Association, c2000. x, 445 p. :
01-269561   615.8/515   1569001456
Occupational therapy -- Evaluation. Occupational Therapy.

RM735.36.O29 1984
Occupational therapy strategies and adaptations for independent daily living / Florence S. Cromwell, editor. New York : Haworth Press, c1984. 186 p. :
84-019157   615.8/515   0866563504
Occupational therapy. Life skills.

**RM811 Physical medicine. Physical therapy —
Hydrotherapy and balneotherapy — General works**

RM811.A65 1997
Aquatic rehabilitation / [edited by] Richard G. Ruoti, David
M. Morris, Andrew J. Cole. Philadelphia : Lippincott, c1997.
xiv, 417 p. :
96-002682   615.8/53   0397551525
*Hydrotherapy. Hydrotherapy -- methods. Exercise Therapy --
methods.*

RM931 Rehabilitation therapy

RM931.A65.C88 1984
Cusack, Odean.
Pets and the elderly : the therapeutic bond / Odean Cusack,
Elaine Smith. New York : Haworth Press, c1984. 257 p., [1] 1
83-026409   615.8/515   0866562591
Pets -- Therapeutic use. Aged -- Rehabilitation.

RM931.D35.H34 2000
Halprin, Anna.
Dance as a healing art : returning to health through
movement and imagery / Anna Halprin. Medocino, CA :
LifeRhythm, 2000. p. cm.
99-042779   616.8/5155   0940795191
Dance therapy.

RM950 Rehabilitation therapy —
Rehabilitation technology

RM950.C554 2002
Clinician's guide to assistive technology / edited by Don A.
Olson, Frank DeRuyter. St. Louis : Mosby, c2002. xvii, 484 p.
:
              617/.03   0815146019
*Self-help devices for people with disabilities. Self-Help Devices.
Disabled Persons--rehabilitation.*

RS Pharmacy and Materia Medica

RS51 Dictionaries and encyclopedias

RS51.D4795 1997
Dictionary of pharmacological agents. 1st ed. London ; Chapman & Hall, 1997. 3 v. :
615/.1/03   0412466309
Drugs--Dictionaries.

RS51.D776 2000
Drugs : synonyms and properties / edited by G.W.A. Milne. Aldershot, Hampshire, England ; Ashgate, c 2000. xx, 1267 p. ;
99-049084   615/.1/03   0566082284
Drugs -- Dictionaries. Drugs -- Indexes. Synonyms.

RS51.G85 2001
Grogan, F. James
Pharmacy simplified :a glossary of terms / F. James Grogan. Auatralia ; Delmar Thomson Learning, c2001. viii, 455 p. ;
615/.1/03   0766828581
Pharmacy--Dictionaries. Pharmacy--Abbreviations.

RS51.M67 1999
Morton, Ian,
Concise dictionary of pharmacological agents : properties and synonyms / by Ian K.M. Morton and Judith M. Hall. Boston : Kluwer Academic, 1999. viii, 342 p.
99-042527   615/.1/03   0751404993
Drugs -- Dictionaries. Pharmacology -- Dictionaries.

RS51.U65
The Complete drug reference. Yonkers, N.Y. : Consumer Reports Books, c1991-c2001. v. :
615/.1
Drugs--Dictionaries. Drugs--Side effects--Dictionaries. Drugs-- Safety measures--Dictionaries.

RS55.2 Generic drugs. Generic drug substitution

RS55.2.P37
PDR generics. Montvale, NJ : Medical Economics, c1995-c1998. 4 v. :
95-657702   615/.1
Generic drugs -- Periodicals. Catalogs, Drug. Drugs, Generic -- catalogs.

RS57 Pharmaceutical arithmetic. Statistical methods. Handbooks, manuals, calculations, etc.

RS57.J64 1986
Johnson, Grace G.
Mathematics for nurses / Grace G. Johnson. Norwalk, Conn. : Appleton-Century-Crofts, c1986. x, 214 p. ;
85-015746   615.5/8   0838561756
Pharmaceutical arithmetic -- Programmed instruction. Nursing -- Mathematics -- Programmed instruction. Drugs -- administration & dosage -- nurses' instruction.

RS61 History — General works

RS61.C69 1988
Cowen, David L.
Pharmacy : an illustrated history / by David L. Cowen and William H. Helfand. New York : Abrams, 1990. 272 p. :
88-006273   362.1/782/09   0810914980
Pharmacy -- History. Pharmacy -- history.

RS61.K73 1976
Kremers, Edward,
Kremers and Urdang's History of pharmacy. 4th ed. / rev. by Glenn Sonnedecker. Philadelphia : Lippincott, c1976. xv, 571 p. :
615/.4/09   0397520743
Pharmacy--History. Pharmacy--History.

RS67 History — By region or country

RS67.S65.C66 1994
Conroy, Mary Schaeffer,
In health and in sickness : pharmacy, pharmacists, and the pharmaceutical industry in late imperial, early Soviet Russia / Mary Schaeffer Conroy. Boulder : East European Monographs ; 1994. viii, 703 p.
94-070069   615/.1/0947   0880332832
Pharmacy -- Soviet Union -- History. Pharmacists -- Soviet Union -- History. Pharmaceutical industry -- Soviet Union -- History.

RS68 History — Pharmaceutical companies

RS68.A4.C5
Chapman-Huston, Desmond,
Through a city archway ; the story of Allen and Hanburys, 1715-1954, by Desmond Chapman-Huston and Ernest C. Cripps. London, J. Murray [1954] xv, 326 p.
55019071   615.4065

RS100.5 Pharmaceutical ethics

RS100.5.B839 1999
Buerki, Robert A.
　　Ethical practices in pharmacy :a guidebook for pharmacy technicians / Robert A. Buerki, Louis D. Vottero. Madison, Wis. : American Institute of the History of Pharmacy, 1999 viii, 55 p. :
　　　　174/.2　　093129228X
　　Pharmaceutical ethics. Pharmacy technicians. Pharmaceutical services--Moral and ethical aspects.

RS100.5.B84 1994
Buerki, Robert A.
　　Ethical responsibility in pharmacy practice / Robert A. Buerki, Louis D. Vottero. Madison, Wis. : American Institute of the History of Pharmacy, 1994. xiii, 194 p. :
　　　　174/.2　　0931292255
　　Pharmaceutical ethics. Ethics, Pharmacy

RS100.5.E845 1996
　　Ethical issues in pharmacy / Bruce D. Weinstein, editor. Vancouver, Wash. : Applied Therapeutics, Inc., c1996. xiii, 327 p. ;
　　　　174/.2　　0915486253
　　Pharmaceutical ethics. Ethics, Pharmacy.

RS100.5.I56 1991
　　Improving drug safety--a joint responsibility / R. Dinkel, B. Horisberger, K. Tolo (eds.). Berlin ; Springer-Verlag, c1991. xxi, 338 p. :
　　　　362.1/782　　　　3540535055
　　Pharmaceutical ethics--Congresses. Drugs--Safety measures--Congresses. Drug Evaluation--congresses.

RS100.5.P475 2002
　　Pharmaceutical ethics / edited by Sam Salek, Andrew Edgar. New York : J. Wiley, 2002. p. cm.
　　　　174/.2　　0471490571
　　Pharmaceutical ethics.

RS100.5.P48 1993
　　Pharmaceutical medicine / 2nd ed. edited by D.M. Burley and T.B. Binns ; with a foreword by Sir Abraham Goldberg. London ; E. Arnold, 1993 xiii, 299 p. :
　　　　615/.1　　0340525177
　　Pharmaceutical ethics. Drugs--Testing. Clinical trials.

RS154 Materia medica — Organic materia medica (General)

RS154.N428 2001
Negwer, Martin.
　　Organic-chemical drugs and their synonyms :an international survey / Martin Negwer, Hans-Georg Scharnow.8th extensively enl. ed. Weinheim ; Wiley-VCH, 2001. 6 v. (xvii, 4680 p.) :
　　　　615/.1　　3527302476
　　Drugs--Dictionaries. Chemistry, Pharmaceutical. Drugs--terminology.

RS160.7 Materia medica — Pharmacognosy. Pharmaceutical substances (Plant, animal, and inorganic) — Marine substances

RS160.7.D79 2000
　　Drugs from the sea / editor, Nobuhiro Fusetani. Basel ; Karger, 2000. vi, 158 p. :
　　　　615/.3　　3805570988
　　Marine pharmacology. Biological Products--pharmacology. Biological Factors--pharmacology.

RS164-165 Materia medica — Pharmacognosy. Pharmaceutical substances (Plant, animal, and inorganic) — Organic substances

RS164.B324.C74 1990
Crellin, J. K.
　　Herbal medicine past and present / John K. Crellin, and Jane Philpott. Durham : Duke University Press, 1990. 2 v. :
　　88-030906　　615/.321/0974　　0822308770
　　Bass, A. L. Tommie -- Interviews. Bass, A. L. Tommie. Medicinal plants -- Appalachian Region. Herbs -- Therapeutic use -- Appalachian Region. Materia medica, Vegetable -- Appalachian Region.

RS164.B412 1992
Bellamy, David J.
　　World medicine : plants, patients, and people / David Bellamy and Andrea Pfister. Oxford ; Blackwell, 1992. xx, 456 p. :
　　91-039201　　　　610　　　　0631169334
　　Materia medica, Vegetable -- History. Medicine -- History. Alternative medicine -- History.

RS164.C4437 1996
Chevallier, Andrew.
　　The encyclopedia of medicinal plants / Andrew Chevallier. New York : DK Pub. ; c1996. 336 p. :
　　96-015192　　　　615/.32/03　　　　0789410672
　　Materia medica, Vegetable -- Encyclopedias. Medicinal plants -- Encyclopedias.

RS164.C83 1997
Crellin, J. K.
　　A reference guide to medicinal plants : herbal medicine past and present / John K. Crellin and Jane Philpott. Durham, NC : Duke University Press, [1997] 551 p. :
　　　　615/.321/0974　　　　0822320681
　　Materia medica, Vegetable--Appalachian Region.

RS164.H88 1993
　　Human medicinal agents from plants / [editors], A. Douglas Kinghorn, Manuel F. Balandrin. Washington, DC : American Chemical Society, 1993. xii, 356 p. :
　　93-022180　　　　615/.32　　　　0841227055
　　Materia medica, Vegetable -- Congresses. Medicinal plants -- Congresses. Pharmacognosy -- Congresses.

RS164.I84 1993
Iwu, Maurice M.
Handbook of African medicinal plants / Maurice M. Iwu. Boca Raton : CRC Press, c1993. 435 p. :
92-049260   615/.321/096   084934266X
Materia medica, Vegetable -- Africa -- Handbooks, manuals, etc. Medicinal plants -- Africa -- Handbooks, manuals, etc. Medicine, Traditional -- Africa -- handbooks.

RS164.J69 1994
Joyce, Christopher,
Earthly goods : medicine-hunting in the rainforest / by Christopher Joyce. Boston : Little, Brown, c1994. xvi, 304 p. ;
93-049736   615/.32/0913   0316474088
Materia medica, Vegetable. Medicinal plants. Rain forest plants.

RS164.L475
Lewis, Walter Hepworth.
Medical botany : plants affecting man's health / Walter H. Lewis, Memory P. F. Elvin-Lewis. New York : Wiley, c1977. xv, 515 p. :
76-044376   615/.32   0471533203
Materia medica, Vegetable. Medicinal plants. Plants, Medicinal.

RS164.M377 1996
Medicinal resources of the tropical forest : biodiversity and its importance to human health / edited by Michael J. Balick, Elaine Elisabetsky, Sarah A. Laird. New York : Columbia University Press, c1996. xiv, 440 p. :
95-013809   615/.32/0913   0231101708
Materia medica, Vegetable. Rain forest plants. Ethnobotany.

RS164.R676 1999
Ross, Ivan A.
Medicinal plants of the world : chemical constituents, traditional, and modern medicinal uses / by Ivan A. Ross. Totowa, N.J. : Humana Press, c1999. xi, 415 p. :
98-034758   615/.32   0896035425
Medicinal plants -- Encyclopedias.

RS164.S1
Sayre, James Kedzie,
Ancient herb and modern herbs : a comprehensive reference guide to medicinal herbs, human ailments, and possible herbal remedies / by James Kedzie Sayre. San Carlos, Calif. : Bottlebrush Press, c2001. vi, 449 p. ;
01-116501   0964503913
Medicinal plants -- Encyclopedias. Herbs -- Therapeutic use -- Encyclopedias. Materia medica, Vegetable -- Encyclopedias.

RS164.T556 1998
Tilford, Gregory L.
From earth to herbalist : an earth-conscious guide to medicinal plants / Gregory L. Tilford ; with a foreword by Rosemary Gladstar ; illustrations by Nadja Cech Lindley. Missoula, Mont. : Mountain Press Pub. Co., c1998. xiii, 249 p.
98-030002   615/.32   0878423729
Medicinal plants.

RS165.O6.K37 1995
Kapoor, L. D.
Opium poppy : botany, chemistry, and pharmacology / L.D. Kapoor. New York : Food Products Press, c1995. xviii, 326 p.
94-020779   615/.323122   1560249234
Opium. Opium poppy.

RS172 Materia medica — Geographical distribution. Natural sources — By region or country

RS172.N67.S75 1998
Still, Cecil C.,
Botany and healing : medicinal plants of New Jersey and the region / Cecil C. Still. New Brunswick, N.J. : Rutgers University Press, c1998. xi, 261 p. :
97-045725   615/.32/0974   0813525071
Medicinal plants -- Northeastern States. Materia medica, Vegetable -- Northeastern States.

RS172.W4.K38 1996
Kay, Margarita Artschwager.
Healing with plants in the American and Mexican West / Margarita Artschwager Kay ; with a foreword by Andrew Weil. Tucson : University of Arizona Press, c1996. xvii, 315 p.
96-010101   615/.32/0978   0816516456
Materia medica, Vegetable -- West (U.S.) Materia medica, Vegetable -- Mexico.

RS356 Materia medica — Pharmaceutical supplies — Commercial publications

RS356.M524 1968
The Merck index; an encyclopedia of chemicals and drugs. Rahway, N.J., Merck, 1968. xii, 1713 p.
68-012252   615/.1/03
Materia medica. Drugs.

RS380 Materia medica — Pharmaceutical biotechnology

RS380.B5526 2000
Biopharmaceutical process validation / edited by Gail Sofer, Dane W. Zabriskie. New York : Marcel Dekker, c2000. xiv, 382 p. :
615/.19   0824702492
Pharmaceutical biotechnology--Quality control.

RS380.B553 1999
Biopharmaceuticals, an industrial perspective / edited by Gary Walsh and Brendan Murphy. Dordrecht ; Kluwer Academic, c1999. x, 514 p. :
615/.19   0792357469
Pharmaceutical biotechnology. Biological products--Therapeutic use.

RS380.B56 1990
Biotechnological innovations in health care. Oxford ; Butterworth-Heinemann, 1991. x, 299 p. :
615/.36   0750614978
Pharmaceutical biotechnology. Biological Products. Biotechnology.

RS380.D78 1991
Drug biotechnology regulation :scientific basis and practices / edited by Yuan-yuan H. Chiu, John L. Gueriguian. New York : M. Dekker, c1991. xxiii, 563 p. :
615/.19   0824784200
Pharmaceutical biotechnology. Pharmaceutical biotechnology--Law and legislation.

RS380.G75 2000
Understanding biopharmaceuticals :manufacturing and regulatory issues / edited by June N. Grindley and Jill E. Ogden. Denver, Colo. : Interpharm Press, c2000. xv, 325 p. :
615/.19   1574910833
Pharmaceutical biotechnology. Pharmaceutical biotechnology industry. Pharmaceutical biotechnology industry--Law and legislation.

RS380.H363 2002
Handbook of pharmaceutical biotechnology / Jay P. Rho, Stan G. Louie, editors. New York : Pharmaceutical Products Press, 2002. p. cm.
615/.19   0789016354
Pharmaceutical biotechnology--Handbooks, manuals, etc.

RS380.H88 1994
Huxsoll, Jean F.
Quality assurance for biopharmaceuticals / Jean F. Huxsoll. New York : Wiley, c1994. 206 p. :
615/.19   0471036560
Pharmaceutical biotechnology--Quality control.

RS380.M65 1999
Biopharmaceutical drug design and development / edited by Susanna Wu-Pong and Yongyut Rojanasakul ; foreword by Joseph R. Robinson. Totowa, N.J. : Humana Press, c1999. xii, 435 p. :
615/.19   089603691X
Pharmaceutical biotechnology. Gene therapy. Biotechnology.

RS380.P48 1997
Pharmaceutical biotechnology :a programmed text / edited by S. William Zito. 2nd ed. Lancaster, Pa. : Technomic Pub. Co., c1997. xii, 282 p. :
615/.19   1566765196
Pharmaceutical biotechnology.

RS380.W47 1994
Werth, Barry.
The billion-dollar molecule : one company's quest for the perfect drug / Barry Werth. New York : Simon & Schuster, c1994. 445 p. ;
93-032566   615/.19   0671723278
Pharmaceutical biotechnology. Pharmaceutical industry -- United States.

RS402 Materia medica — Pharmaceutical chemistry — Collected works (nonserial)

RS402.C65 1990
Comprehensive medicinal chemistry : the rational design, mechanistic study & therapeutic application of chemical compounds / chairman of the editorial board, Corwin Hansch ; joint executive editors, Peter G. Sammes, John B. Taylor. Oxford ; Pergamon Press, 1990. 6 v. :
89-016329   615/.19   0080325300
Pharmaceutical chemistry. Chemistry, Pharmaceutical.

RS403 Materia medica — Pharmaceutical chemistry — General works

RS403.B43 1988
Beckett, A. H.
Practical pharmaceutical chemistry / A.H. Beckett and J.B. Stenlake .4th ed. London : Athlone Press, 1988- v. <1 > :
615/.1901   20   048
Pharmaceutical chemistry. Chemistry, Pharmaceutical.

RS403.G76 1997
Gringauz, Alex,
Introduction to medicinal chemistry : how drugs act and why / Alex Gringauz. New York : Wiley-VCH, c1997. xiii, 721 p.
95-049331   615/.7   0895733250
Pharmaceutical chemistry. Chemistry, Pharmaceutical. Pharmacology.

RS403.P38 2001
Patrick, Graham L.
An introduction to medicinal chemistry / Graham L. Patrick. 2nd ed. Oxford ; Oxford University Press, 2001. xxiii, 620 p. :
615/.19   0198505337
Pharmaceutical chemistry.

RS403.R46 1998
Repic, Oljan,
Principles of process research and chemical development in the pharmaceutical industry / Oljan Repic. New York : Wiley, c1998. xvi, 213 p. :
97013904   0471165166
Chemical engineering. Pharmaceutical chemistry. Chemical process control.

RS419 Materia medica — Pharmaceutical chemistry — Combinatorial chemistry

RS419.T47 1998
Terrett, Nicholas K.
Combinatorial chemistry / Nicholas K. Terrett. Oxford ; Oxford University Press, 1998. xiv, 186 p. :
97-032698   615/.19   0198502206
Combinatorial chemistry.

RS420 Materia medica — Pharmaceutical chemistry — Drug design

RS420.M38 1990
Maxwell, Robert A.,
   Drug discovery : a casebook and analysis / by Robert A. Maxwell and Shohreh B. Eckhardt. Clifton, N.J. : Humana Press, c1990. xxv, 438 p. :
90-004915   615/.19   0896031802
   Drugs -- Design. Pharmacy -- Technological innovations. Drug Design.

RS431 Materia medica — Pharmaceutical chemistry — Individual substances, A-Z

RS431.A6.D53 1988
   Dictionary of antibiotics and related substances / edited by B.W. Bycroft ; contributors, A.A. Higton, A.D. Roberts. London ; Chapman and Hall, 1988. xviii, 944 p.
87-024902   615/.329/0321   0412254506
   Antibiotics -- Dictionaries. Anti-infective agents -- Dictionaries. Antibiotics -- dictionaries.

RT Nursing

RT3 Congresses

RT3.N78 1988

Nursing 2020 : a study of the future of hospital based nursing / Myrna Warnick, project director, Toni Sullivan, co-project director ; Deborah Smith, editor. New York : National League for Nursing, c1988. x, 166 p. ;
88-201398   362.1/73/0112   0887373976
Nursing -- Forecasting -- Congresses. Nursing services -- Forecasting -- Congresses.

RT4 By region or country — North America — United States

RT4.E53 2001

Enduring issues in American nursing / Ellen D. Baer ... [et al.], editors. New York : Springer Pub. Co., c2001. x, 377 p. :
00-063528   610.73/0973   0826113737
Nursing -- United States -- History. Nurses -- United States -- History.

RT4.L49 1996
Lewenson, Sandra.

Taking charge : nursing, suffrage, and feminism in America, 1873-1920 / Sandra Beth Lewenson. New York : National League for Nursing Press, c1996. xxiv, 273 p. :
     610.73/0973   0887376843
Nurses--United States--Political activity--History--19th century. Nurses--United States--Political activity--History--20th century.

RT4.S375 1999
Schorr, Thelma M.

100 years of American nursing : celebrating a century of caring / Thelma M. Schorr with Maureen Shawn Kennedy. Philadelphia, PA : Lippincott Williams & Wilkins, c1999. xvi, 222 p. :
99-010472   610.73/0973   0781718651
Nursing -- United States -- History. History of Nursing -- United States.

RT21 Dictionaries and encyclopedias

RT21.G353 2002

The Gale encyclopedia of nursing and allied health / Kristine Krapp, editor. Detroit : Gale Group, c2002. p. ;
     610.73/03   0787649392
Nursing--Encyclopedias. Medicine--Encyclopedias. Nursing Care--Encyclopedias--English.

RT23 Communication in nursing — General works

RT23.L83 1999
Luckmann, Joan.

Transcultural communication in nursing / Joan Luckmann. Albany, N.Y. : Delmar Publishers, c1999. xviii, 346 p. :
     610.73   0766802566
Communication in nursing--Cross-cultural studies. Transcultural nursing. Nursing--Social aspects.

RT31 History — General works

RT31.D64 1983
Dolan, Josephine A.

Nursing in society : a historical perspective / Josephine A. Dolan, M. Louise Fitzpatrick, Eleanor Krohn Herrmann. Philadelphia : Saunders, 1983. viii, 417 p.
82-048503   362.1/73   0721631355
Nursing -- History. Nursing -- Social aspects -- History. History of nursing.

RT31.D66 1996
Donahue, M. Patricia.

Nursing, the finest art :an illustrated history / M. Patricia Donahue. 2nd ed. St. Louis : Mosby, c1996. xix, 535 p. :
     610.73/09   0815127278
Nursing--History. Nursing--United States--History. Nursing in art.

RT31.J4 1969
Jensen, Deborah (MacLurg)

Jensen's History and trends of professional nursing [by] Gerald Joseph Griffin [and] Joanne King Griffin. Saint Louis, C. V. Mosby Co., 1969. xiii, 339 p.
69-018835   610.73/09   0801619769
Nursing -- History.

RT31.S66 1999
Snodgrass, Mary Ellen.

Historical encyclopedia of nursing / Mary Ellen Snodgrass. Santa Barbara, Calif. : ABC-CLIO, c1999. xvii, 354 p.
99-042670   610.73/09   1576070867
Nursing -- History -- Encyclopedias. Nursing -- History -- Encyclopedias.

RT34 Biography — Collective

RT34.A44 1988

American nursing : a biographical dictionary / [edited by] Vern L. Bullough, Olga Maranjian Church, Alice P. Stein. New York : Garland, 1988-1992. 2 v. :
87-029076   610.73/092/2   082408540X
Nurses -- United States -- Biography -- Dictionaries. History of Nursing -- United States. Nurses -- United States -- biography.

RT37 Biography — Individual, A-Z

RT37.N5.D67 2000
Dossey, Barbara Montgomery.
   Florence Nightingale : mystic, visionary, healer / Barbara Montgomery Dossey. Springhouse, PA : Springhouse Corp., c2000. vii, 440 p. :
99-023725   610.73/092   0874349842
Nightingale, Florence, -- 1820-1910.   Nurses -- England -- Biography.

RT37.N5.F55 1990
   Florence Nightingale and her era : a collection of new scholarship / edited by Vern Bullough, Bonnie Bullough, Marietta P. Stanton. New York : Garland, 1990. xvi, 365 p. ;
89-025949   610.73/092   0824069986
Nightingale, Florence, -- 1820-1910 -- Congresses.   Nurses -- England -- Biography -- Congresses. Nursing -- United States -- History -- Congresses.

RT37.N87.M37
Marshall, Helen E.
   Mary Adelaide Nutting, pioneer of modern nursing [by] Helen E. Marshall. Baltimore, Johns Hopkins University Press [1972] ix, 396 p.
72-174557   610.73/092/4   0801813654
Nutting, M. Adelaide -- (Mary Adelaide), -- 1858-1948.

RT40 General works — Through 1900

RT40.N5 1992
Nightingale, Florence,
   Notes on nursing : what it is, and what it is not / by Florence Nightingale ; with an introduction by Barbara Stevens Barnum and commentaries by contemporary nursing leaders. Commemorative ed. Philadelphia : Lippincott, c1992. 79 :
          610.73   0397550073
Nightingale, Florence, 1820-1910. Notes on Nursing. Nightingale, Florence, 1820-1910. Nursing. Nursing Care.

RT41 General works — 1901-

RT41.C7787 2001
Cooper, Carolyn,
   The art of nursing :a practical introduction / Carolyn Cooper. Philadelphia : W.B. Saunders, c2001. xi, 268 p. ;
          610.73   0721682162
Nursing. Nurse and patient. Nursing Care--methods.

RT41.C86 2000
   Fundamentals of nursing : concepts, process, and practice / Barbara Kozier ... [et al.]. Upper Saddle River, N.J. : Prentice Hall Health, c2000. xxiv, 1479 p.
99-033333   610.73   0805331840
Nursing. Nursing Process. Nursing Care.

RT41.F882 2001
Taylor, Carol,
   Fundamentals of nursing :the art & science of nursing care / Carol Taylor, Carol Lillis, Priscilla LeMone. 4th ed. Philadelphia : Lippincott, c2001. xxxv, 1387 p. :
          610.73   078172273X
Nursing. Nursing. Health Promotion.

RT41.H65 1996
   Medical-surgical nursing : total patient care / [edited by] Gail A. Harkness, Judith R. Dincher. 9th ed. St. Louis : Mosby, c1996. xviii, 1197 p. :
          610.73   0815140843
Nursing. Nursing Care.

RT41.I53 2002
   Complementary / alternative therapies in nursing / Mariah Snyder, Ruth Lindquist, editors. 4th ed. New York : Springer Pub. Co., c2002. xv, 335 p. :
          610.73   0826114466
Holistic nursing. Nurse and patient. Alternative medicine.

RT41.L53 1998
Leddy, Susan.
   Conceptual bases of professional nursing / Susan Kun Leddy, [J. Mae Pepper]. 4th ed. Philadelphia : Lippincott, c1998. xvi, 477 p. :
          610.73   0397552777
Nursing. Nursing. Nursing Theory.

RT41.L67 2001
Timby, Barbara Kuhn.
   Fundamental skills and concepts in patient care / Barbara Kuhn Timby. Philadelphia : Lippincott Williams & Wilkins, c2001. xxi, 866 p. :
00-025008   610.73   0781718783
Nursing. Nursing Care.

RT41.M49 1995
   Medical-surgical nursing : concepts and clinical practice / edited by Wilma J. Phipps ... [et al.]. 5th ed. St. Louis : Mosby, c1995. 1 v. (various pagings) :
          610.73   0801678889
Nursing. Surgical nursing. Nursing Care.

RT41.P844 2001
Potter, Patricia Ann.
   Fundamentals of nursing / Patricia A. Potter, Anne Griffin Perry. 5th ed. St. Louis : Mosby, c2001. xxxvii, 1785 p. :
          610.73   032301141
Nursing. Nursing Care. Nurse-Patient Relations.

RT41.S38 2003
Timby, Barbara Kuhn.
   Introductory medical-surgical nursing / Barbara K. Timby, Nancy E. Smith. 8th ed. Philadelphia : Lippincott William & Wilkins, c2003. p. ;
          610.73   078173553X
Nursing. Surgical nursing. Nursing Care.

RT41.T46 1996
Brunner and Suddarth's textbook of medical-surgical nursing. 8th ed./ [edited by] Suzanne C. Smeltzer, Brenda G. Bare. Philadelphia : J.B. Lippincott, c1996. xxxi, 2066, 78 p. :
610.73   0397550731
Nursing. Surgical nursing. Nursing Care.

RT42 General special

RT42.B576 2000
Blows, William T.,
The biological basis for nursing :clinical observations / William T. Blows. London ; Routledge, 2000. p. ;
610.73   0415212553
Nursing. Clinical medicine. Biology.

RT42.F64 2000
Fontaine, Karen Lee,
Healing practices : alternative therapies for nursing / Karen Lee Fontaine. Upper Saddle River, NJ : Prentice Hall, c2000. xi, 452 p. :
99-032976   615.5   0838503853
Nursing. Alternative medicine. Nursing Care.

RT42.H65 2000
Dossey, Barbara Montgomery.
Holistic nursing : a handbook for practice / Barbara Montgomery Dossey, Lynn Keegan, Cathie E. Guzzetta. Gaithersburg, Md. : Aspen Publishers, c2000. xxxiii, 812 p
99-027912   610.73   0834216299
Holistic nursing -- Handbooks, manuals, etc. Holistic Nursing.

RT42.M243 1996
The managed care challenge for nurse executives / American Organization of Nurse Executives. Chicago : American Hospital Pub., c1996. xiii, 110 p.
96-024117   362.1/73/068   1556481640
Nursing -- Effect of managed care on. Nurse Administrators. Nursing Services -- organization & administration.

RT42.M246 1999
Martinez de Castillo, Sandra Luz.
Strategies, techniques, and approaches to thinking : case studies in clinical nursing / Sandra Luz Martinez de Castillo. Philadelphia : Saunders, c1999. p. cm.
98-055263   610.73   0721676480
Nursing -- Case studies -- Handbooks, manuals, etc. Nursing -- Decision making -- Handbooks, manuals, etc. Nursing Care -- case studies.

RT42.N864 2001
Nursing leaders speak out : issues and opinions / Harriet R. Feldman, editor. New York : Springer Pub. Co., 2001. p. ;
00-069816   362.1/73/068   0826114164
Nursing services -- Administration. Nurses -- Interviews. Leadership.

RT42.P754 1998
Adult health nursing / edited by Patricia Gauntlett Beare, Judith L. Myers. 3rd ed. St. Louis : Mosby, c1998. p. cm.
610.73   0815110065
Nursing. Surgical nursing. Nursing Care.

RT42.R64
Rogers, Martha E.
An introduction to the theoretical basis of nursing [by] Martha E. Rogers. Philadelphia, F. A. Davis Co. [1970] xii, 144 p.
71-103539   610.73/01
Nursing -- Philosophy.

RT42.S47 2001
Sharpe, Charles C.,
Telenursing : nursing practice in cyberspace / Charles C. Sharpe. Westport, Conn. : Auburn House, 2001. x, 267 p. ;
00-038047   610.73   0865693048
Nursing -- Technological innovations. Medical telematics. Telecommunication in medicine.

RT42.T48 2002
Thomas, Sandra P.
Listening to patients : a phenomenological approach to nursing research and practice / Sandra P. Thomas, Howard R. Pollio. New York : Springer Pub. Co., c2002. xiii, 294 p.
00-1034183   610.73/06/99   0826114660
Nurse and patient. Existentialism. Interpersonal communication.

RT48 Nursing assessment

RT48.H38 2001
Barkauskas, Violet.
Health and physical assessment / Violet H. Barkauskas, Linda Ciofu Baumann, Cynthia S. Darling-Fisher. 3rd ed. St. Louis, MO : Mosby, 2001. xiv, 760 p. :
616.07/5   0323012140
Nursing assessment. Medical history taking. Physical diagnosis.

RT48.H425 2002
Estes, Mary Ellen Zator.
Health assessment & physical examination / Mary Ellen Zator Estes.   2nd ed. Albany, N.Y. : Delmar/Thomson Learning, c2002. xxvii, 932 p. :
616.07/5   0766824101
Nursing assessment. Physical diagnosis.

RT48.I57 1997
Instruments for clinical health-care research / editors, Marilyn Frank-Stromborg, Sharon J. Olsen ; with foreword by Nola J. Pender. Boston : Jones and Bartlett Publishers, c1997. xx, 620 p. :
97-003049   610.73/072   0763703168
Nursing assessment. Nursing. Research -- methods.

RT48.M8 2001
Murray, Ruth Beckmann.
Health promotion strategies through the life span / Ruth Beckmann Murray, Judith Proctor Zentner. 7th ed. Upper Saddle River, N.J. : Prentice Hall, c2001. xiv, 881 p. :
   613   0838536883
Nursing assessment. Health promotion. Life cycle, Human.

RT48.6 Nursing assessment — Nursing diagnosis

RT48.6.S66 1998
Sparks, Sheila M.
Nursing diagnosis reference manual / Sheila M. Sparks, Cynthia M. Taylor. 4th ed. Springhouse, Pa. : Springhouse Corp., c1998. viii, 696 p. :
   610.73   0874348978
Nursing diagnosis--Handbooks, manuals, etc. Nursing Diagnosis--handbooks. Patient Care Planning--handbooks.

RT49 Nursing care plans. Planning

RT49.C38 1999
Carpenito, Lynda Juall.
Nursing care plans & documentation :nursing diagnoses and collaborative problems / Lynda Juall Carpenito. 3rd ed. Philadelphia : Lippincott, c1999. xx, 825 p. :
   610.73   0781717426
Nursing care plans. Nursing assessment. Nursing diagnosis.

RT49.D64 2002
Doenges, Marilynn E.,
Nursing care plans :guidelines for individualizing patient care / Marilynn E. Doenges, Mary Frances Moorhouse, Alice C. Geissler-Murr.Ed. 6. Philadelphia : F.A. Davis, 2002. p. ;
   610.73   0803604920
Nursing care plans--Handbooks, manuals, etc. Patient Care Planning--Handbooks. Nursing Process--Handbooks.

RT50 Nursing records

RT50.M37 2000
Marrelli, T. M.
Nursing documentation handbook / T.M. Marrelli, with the assistance of Deborah S. Harper. St. Louis, Mo. : Mosby, 2000. p. ;
00-025398   610.73   0323010970
Nursing records -- Handbooks, manuals, etc. Nursing Records -- Handbooks. Documentation -- Handbooks.

RT50.M38 1999
Mastering documentation. 2nd ed. Springhouse, Pa. : Springhouse Corp., c1999. x, 435 p. :
   610.73   0874349524
Nursing records.

RT50.W457 2002
White, Lois.
Documentation & the nursing process / Lois White. Clifton Park, NY : Delmar Learning, 2002. p. cm.
   651.5/04261   0766850099
Nursing records--Handbooks, manuals, etc.

RT50.5 Computer applications

RT50.5.E36 2002
Edwards, Margaret J. A.
The Internet for nurses and allied health professionals / Margaret J.A. Edwards. 3rd ed. New York : Springer, c2002. ix, 138 p. :
   004.67/8   0387952365
Nursing--Computer network resources. Internet. Medical care--Computer network resources.

RT50.5.H43 2001
Hebda, Toni.
Handbook of informatics for nurses and health care professionals / Toni Hebda, Patricia Czar, Cynthia Mascara.2nd ed. Upper Saddle River, NJ : Prentice Hall, c2001. xxiv, 387 p. :
   610.73/0285   0130311022
Nursing informatics--Handbooks, manuals, etc. Medical informatics--Handbooks, manuals, etc. Medical Informatics.

RT50.5.N87 2000
Nursing informatics :where caring and technology meet / Marion J. Ball ... [et al.] editors ; forewords by Sue Karen Donaldson and Ulla Gerdin. 3rd ed. New York : Springer, c2000. xx, 445 p. :
   610.73/0285   0387989234
Nursing informatics. Information storage and retrieval systems--Nursing. Computers.

RT51 Handbooks, manuals, etc.

RT51.B78 2001
The Lippincott manual of nursing practice. 7th ed. / [edited by Sandra M. Nettina]. Philadelphia : Lippincott Williams & Wilkins, c2001. xx, 1746 p. :
   610.73   0781722969
Nursing--Handbooks, manuals, etc. Nursing Care--Handbooks.

RT51.P365 1994
Perry, Anne Griffin.
Clinical nursing skills & techniques / Anne Griffin Perry, Patricia A. Potter. 3rd ed. St. Louis : Mosby, c1994. xvii, 1198 p. :
   610.73   0801670071
Nursing--Handbooks, manuals, etc. Nursing Care--handbooks.

RT55 Problems, exercises, examinations

RT55.S28 2002

Saunders comprehensive review for NCLEX-RN / [edited by] Linda Anne Silvestri. 2nd ed. Philadelphia : W.B. Saunders, c2002. xxiv, 1195 p. :
   610.73/076   0721692354
Nursing--Examinations, questions, etc. Nursing Care--examination questions. Nursing Process--examination questions.

RT62 Practical nursing

RT62.B698 2003
Brown, Nancy J.

LPN/LVN student nurse handbook / Nancy J. Brown, B. Gayle Twiname, Sandra M. Boyd. Upper Saddle River, NJ : Prentice Hall, 2003. p. cm.
   610.73/06/93   0130941824
Practical nursing--Handbooks, manuals, etc. Practical nursing--Study and teaching--Handbooks, manuals, etc. Nursing, Practical--Handbooks.

RT62.W455 2002
White, Lois.

Career success in nursing / Lois White. Albany, NY : Delmar/Thomson Learning, c2002. v, 77 p. :
   610.73/06/93   0766835456
Practical nursing--Vocational guidance.

RT63 Addresses, essays, lectures

RT63.C87 2001

Current issues in nursing / [edited by] Joanne McCloskey Dochterman, Helen Kennedy Grace. 6th ed. St. Louis : Mosby, c2001. xxiii, 693 p. :
   610.73   0323012760
Nursing. Nursing--Social aspects--United States. Nursing--Practice--United States.

RT65 Medicine and surgery for nurses

RT65.P69 2001

Professional guide to diseases. 7th ed. Springhouse, Pa. : Springhouse Division, Lippincott Williams & 2001 xiv, 1376 p. :
   616   1582550735
Medicine--Handbooks, manuals, etc. Diseases--Handbooks, manuals, etc. Nursing--Handbooks, manuals, etc.

RT67 Hygiene for nurses

RT67.P56 2002
Pender, Nola J.,

Health promotion in nursing practice / Nola J. Pender, Carolyn L. Murdaugh, Mary Ann Parsons. 4th ed. Upper Saddle River, NJ : Prentice Hall, c2002. xi, 340 p. :
   613   0130319503
Health promotion. Preventive health services. Nursing.

RT68.S23 1996
Sackheim, George I.

Programmed mathematics for nurses / George I. Sackheim, Lewis Robins. 8th ed. New York : McGraw-Hill, Health Professions Division, c1996. ix, 313 p. :
   615/.14   0071053980
Nursing--Mathematics--Programmed instruction. Pharmacy--programmed instruction. Pharmacy--nurses' instruction.

RT69 Textbooks combining several basic subjects

RT69.W48 2001
Waugh, Anne.

Ross and Wilson anatomy and physiology in health and illness. 9th ed. / Anne Waugh, Allison Grant ; illustrations by Graeme Edinburgh ; Churchill Livingstone, 2001. p. ;
   612   0443064687
Human anatomy. Human physiology. Pathology.

RT71 Study and teaching — General works

RT71.R6
Rogers, Martha E.

Reveille in nursing [by] Martha E. Rogers. Philadelphia, Davis [1966, c1964] 97 p.
64023981   610.7307
Nursing -- Study and teaching. Education, Nursing

RT73 Study and teaching — General special

RT73.B27 1999
Barnum, Barbara Stevens.

Teaching nursing in the era of managed care / Barbara Stevens Barnum. New York : Springer Pub. Co., c1999. ix, 137 p. ;
   610.73/071/1   0826112544
Nursing--Study and teaching. Nursing--Effect of managed care on. Medical education.

RT73.D79 2001
Dunham, Kelli S.

How to survive and maybe even love nursing school! :a guide for students by students / by Kelli S. Dunham. Philadelphia, PA : F.A. Davis Co., c2001. xxv, 275 p. :
   610.73/071/1   0803607997
Nursing--Study and teaching. Nursing students--Psychology. Nursing students--Anecdotes.

RT73.T94 1999
Twiname, B. Gayle.
   Student nurse handbook : difficult concepts made easy / B. Gayle Twiname, Sandra M. Boyd. Stamford, Conn. : Appleton & Lange, c1999. xvi, 398 p. :
               610.73   0838586813
   Nursing students--Handbooks, manuals, etc. Nursing--Study and teaching--Handbooks, manuals, etc. Nursing.

RT74.7 Study and teaching — Preceptorships in nursing education

RT74.7.R65 1997
   The role of the preceptor : a guide for nurse educators and clinicians / Jean Pieri Flynn, editor. New York : Springer Pub. Co., c1997. xiv, 143 p. :
96-041728   610.73/071/55   0826194605
   Nursing -- Study and teaching (Preceptorship) Preceptorship -- organization & administration. Education, Nursing -- organization & administration.

RT76 Study and teaching — Continuing nursing education

RT76.S366 2000
   Scope and standards of practice for nursing professional development. Washington, D.C. : American Nurses Association, c2000. vii, 35 p. ;
           610.73/071/55
   Nursing--Study and teaching (Continuing education)--Standards-- United Nurses--In-service training--Standards--United States. Education, Nursing, Continuing--standards--United States.

RT76.U46 1999
Ulrich, Deborah L.
   Interactive group learning : strategies for nurse educators / Deborah L. Ulrich, Kellie J. Glendon. New York : Springer, c1999. xiii, 115 p.
98-031025   610.73/071/1   0826112382
   Nursing -- Study and teaching (Continuing education) Social groups. Education, Nursing -- methods.

RT79 Study and teaching — By region or country — United States

RT79.P48
   Peterson's guide to nursing programs. Princeton, N.J. : Peterson's Guides, c1994- v. :
94-660055   610.73/071/173
   Nursing schools -- United States -- Directories. Nursing schools -- Canada -- Directories. Education, Nursing, Baccalaureate -- Canada -- directories.

RT81.5 Research. Experimentation

RT81.5.B74 1994
Brink, Pamela J.
   Basic steps in planning nursing research : from question to proposal / Pamela J. Brink, Marilynn J. Wood. 4th ed. Boston : Jones and Bartlett Publishers, c1994. xiv, 386 p. :
          610.73/072   0867206772
   Nursing--Research--Planning. Nursing Research--methods. Research Design--nurses' instruction.

RT81.5.B86 2001
Burns, Nancy,
   The practice of nursing research :conduct, critique & utilization / Nancy Burns, Susan K. Grove. 4th ed. Philadelphia : Saunders, c2001. xx, 840 p. :
          610.73/072   0721691773
   Nursing--Research--Methodology. Nursing Research.

RT81.5.B863 1999
Burns, Nancy,
   Understanding nursing research / Nancy Burns, Susan K. Grove. 2nd ed. Philadelphia : W.B. Saunders, c1999. xiii, 509 p. :
          610.73/072   0721681069
   Nursing--Research--Philosophy. Nursing Research--methods.

RT81.5.E53 1998
   Encyclopedia of nursing research / Joyce J. Fitzpatrick, editor. New York : Springer Pub. Co., c1998. p. cm.
98-015853   610.73/072   082611170X
   Nursing -- Research -- Encyclopedias. Nursing Research -- encyclopedias.

RT81.5.M86 2001
Munro, Barbara Hazard.
   Statistical methods for health care research / Barbara Hazard Munro. 4th ed. Philadelphia : Lippincott Williams & Wilkins, c2001. xiii, 459 p. :
          610/.7/27   078172175X
   Nursing--Research--Statistical methods. Medical care--Research-- Statistical methods. Health Services Research--methods.

RT81.5.N8665 2001
   Nursing research :methods, critical appraisal, and utilization / [edited by] Geri LoBiondo-Wood, Judith Haber. 5th ed. St. Louis, Mo. : Mosby, 2001. p. ;
          610.73/07/2   0323012876
   Nursing--Research. Nursing Research.

RT81.5.P64 1999
Polit, Denise F.
   Nursing research :principles and methods / Denise F. Polit, Bernadette P. Hungler. 6th ed. Philadelphia : Lippincott, c1999. xviii, 757 p. :
          610.73/072   0781715628
   Nursing--Research--Methodology. Nursing Research--methods.

RT81.5.R66 2000
Roper, Janice M.
   Ethnography in nursing research / by Janice M. Roper, Jill Shapira. Thousand Oaks, Calif. : Sage Publications, 2000. p. cm.
99-050407   610.73/072   0761908730
   Nursing -- Research -- Methodology. Ethnology. Qualitative research.

RT82 Nursing as a profession

RT82.E45 2001
Ellis, Janice Rider.
   Nursing in today's world : challenges, issues, and trends / Janice Rider Ellis, Celia Love Hartley ; illustrations by Kari Berger. 7th ed. Philadelphia : Lippincott, c2001. xiv, 572 p. :
         610.73   0781724554
   Nursing. Nursing--Practice--United States. Nursing--trends--United States.

RT82.H37 1996
Harrington, Nicki.
   LPN to RN transitions / Nicki Harrington, Nancy E. Smith, Wanda E. Spratt. Philadelphia : Lippincott, c1996. xvii, 398 p. :
         610.73/06/9   0397550650
   Nursing--Vocational guidance. Practical nurses. Nursing--examination questions.

RT82.K4 1999
Kelly, Lucie Young.
   Dimensions of professional nursing / Lucie Young Kelly, Lucille A. Joel. 8th ed. New York : McGraw-Hill, Health Professions Division, c1999. p. cm.
         610.73   007034440X
   Nursing. Nursing--United States. Nursing.

RT82.K43 2002
Joel, Lucille A.
   The nursing experience :trends, challenges, and transitions / Lucille A. Joel, Lucie Young Kelly. 4th ed. New York : McGraw-Hill, c2002. xvii, 767 p. :
         610.73   0071363157
   Nursing--Vocational guidance. Nursing. Nursing.

RT82.N874 1997
   Nursing today : transition and trends / [edited by] JoAnn Zerwekh, Jo Carol Claborn. 2nd ed. Philadelphia : Saunders, c1997. xv, 535 p. :
         610.73/06/9   0721668992
   Nursing--Vocational guidance. Nursing--Social aspects. Nursing.

RT82.P755 2001
   Professional nursing : concepts & challenges / Kay Kittrell Chitty. Philadelphia : W.B. Saunders, c2001. xviii, 622 p.
00-024856   610.73/06/9   0721687113
   Nursing -- Vocational guidance. Nursing -- Social aspects. Nursing.

RT82.8 Nurse practitioners

RT82.8.C64 1999
Colyar, Margaret R.,
   Ambulatory care procedures for the nurse practitioner / Margaret R. Colyar, Cynthia R. Ehrhardt. Philadelphia : F.A. Davis, c1999. xvi, 472 p. :
         610.73   0803603649
   Nurse practitioners. Ambulatory medical care. Nursing.

RT82.8.C67 2001
   Core concepts in advanced practice nursing / [edited by] Denise Robinson, Cheryl Pope Kish. St. Louis, Mo. : Mosby, c2001. xxiii, 710 p. :
         610.73   0323008976
   Nurse practitioners. Nursing ethics. Nursing.

RT83.5 Minorities in nursing — Black nurses

RT83.5.C37 1995
Carnegie, Mary Elizabeth.
   The path we tread :Blacks in nursing worldwide, 1854-1994 / Mary Elizabeth Carnegie ; foreword by Josephine A. Dolan. 3rd ed. New York : National League of Nursing Press, c1995. xxi, 329 p. :
         610.73/089/96073   0887376401
   African American nurses--History. Nursing--United States--History. Nurses, Black--Caribbean, English-speaking--History.

RT83.5.H56 1989
Hine, Darlene Clark.
   Black women in white : racial conflict and cooperation in the nursing profession, 1890-1950 / Darlene Clark Hine. Bloomington : Indiana University Press, c1989. xxiii, 264 p.
88-046023   362.1/73/08996073   0253327733
   Afro-American nurses -- History. Nursing -- United States -- History. United States -- Race relations -- History.

RT84.5 Philosophy of nursing. Nursing models

RT84.5.B37 1998
Barnum, Barbara Stevens.
   Nursing theory :analysis, application, evaluation / Barbara Stevens Barnum. 5th ed. Philadelphia : Lippincott, c1998. xvii, 301 p. :
         610.73/01   0781711045
   Nursing--Philosophy. Nursing Theory.

RT84.5.C664 1996
   Conceptual models of nursing : analysis and application / [edited by] Joyce J. Fitzpatrick, Ann L. Whall. Stamford, Conn. : Appleton & Lange, c1996. p. cm.
96-004864   610.73/01   0838510647
   Nursing -- Philosophy. Nursing models. Models, Nursing.

RT84.5.J637 2001
Johnson, Betty M.
  An introduction to theory and reasoning in nursing / Betty M. Johnson, Pamela B. Webber. Philadelphia, PA : Lippincott, c2001. xxiii, 248 p. :
              610.73/01   0781721539
  Nursing--Philosophy. Reasoning.

RT84.5.N8795 1999
  Nursing theories : conceptual and philosophical foundations / Hesook Suzie Kim and Ingrid Kollak, editors. New York : Springer Pub. Co., c1999. xiii, 223 p.
99-027969   610.73/01   0826112870
  Nursing -- Philosophy. Nursing Theory. Models, Nursing.

RT84.5.N89 2002
  Nursing theories :the base for professional nursing practice / [edited by] Julia B. George. 5th ed. Upper Saddle River, N.J. : Prentice Hall, c2002. xi, 611 p. :
              610.73/01   0838571107
  Nursing--Philosophy. Nursing Theory.

RT84.5.N9 2002
  Nursing theorists and their work / [edited by] Ann Marriner Tomey, Martha Raile Alligood. 5th ed. St. Louis, Mo. : Mosby, c2002. xvi, 672 p. :
              610.73/01   0323011934
  Nursing--Philosophy. Nursing models.

RT84.5.O73 2001
Orem, Dorothea E.
  Nursing :concepts of practice / Dorothea E. Orem, with a contributed chapter by Susan G. Taylor and Kathie McLaughlin Renpenning. 6th ed. St. Louis : Mosby, c2001. xviii, 542 p. :
              610.73   032300864X
  Nursing--Philosophy.

RT84.5.P53 1999
  Philosophical and theoretical perspectives for advanced nursing practice / edited by Janet W. Kenney. 2nd ed. Sudbury, Mass. : Jones and Bartlett, c1999. xiii, 353 p. :
              610.73/01   0763709174
  Nursing--Philosophy. Nursing models. Nursing Theory.

RT85 Nursing ethics

RT85.B766 2002
Burkhardt, Margaret A.
  Ethics & issues in contemporary nursing / Margaret A. Burkhardt, Alvita K. Nathaniel. 2nd ed. Australia ; Delmar/Thomson Learning, 2002. xvi, 439 p. ;
              174/.2   0766836290
  Nursing ethics.

RT85.R79 1999
Rumbold, Graham.
  Ethics in nursing practice / Graham Rumbold. Edinburgh ; Bailliere Tindall, c1999. xi, 275 p. :
98-031648   174/.2   0702023124
  Nursing ethics. Nursing -- Moral and ethical aspects. Medical ethics.

RT85.V4 2000
Fry, Sara T.
  Case studies in nursing ethics / Sara T. Fry, Robert M. Veatch. Sudbury, Mass. : Jones & Bartlett, 2000. p. cm.
00-022091   174/.2   0763713333
  Nursing ethics -- Case studies.

RT85.2 Religious aspects

RT85.2.B37 1996
Barnum, Barbara Stevens.
  Spirituality in nursing : from traditional to new age / Barbara Stevens Barnum. New York : Springer Pub. Co., c1996. viii, 168 p.
95-025630   610/.73/01   0826191800
  Nursing -- Religious aspects. Nursing -- Philosophy. Nursing -- Psychological aspects.

RT85.2.M33 2001
Macrae, Janet,
  Nursing as a spiritual practice : a contemporary applicaton of Florence Nightingale's views / Janet A. Macrae. New York : Springer Pub., c2001. xi, 130 p. ;
00-064096   610.73   0826113877
  Nightingale, Florence, -- 1820-1910.   Nursing -- Religious aspects. Spiritual life.

RT85.2.O37 2002
O'Brien, Mary Elizabeth.
  Spirituality in nursing :standing on holy ground / Mary Elizabeth O'Brien. 2nd ed. Sudbury, Mass. : Jones and Bartlett, 2002. p. ;
              610.73/01   0763700525
  Nursing--Religious aspects--Christianity. Nursing--Moral and ethical aspects. Nursing--Philosophy.

RT85.5 Standards for nursing care. Nursing audit. Evaluation and quality control of nursing care

RT85.5.S53 1998
Sidani, Souraya.
  Evaluating nursing interventions : a theory-driven approach / by Souraya Sidani and Carrie Jo Braden. Thousand Oaks, Calif. : Sage Publications, c1998. x, 190 p. :
97-021227   610.73   0761903151
  Nursing audit. Outcome assessment (Medical care)

RT86 Psychology of nursing

RT86.N886 1999
Nursing and the experience of illness : phenomenology in practice / edited by Irena Madjar & JoAnn Walton ; with a foreword by Max van Manen. London ; Routledge, 1999. xvi, 198 p. ;
98-033321   610.73/019   0415207827
Nursing -- Psychological aspects. Phenomenology. Nursing -- Research.

RT86.3 Study and teaching — Nurse and patient

RT86.3.A76 1999
Arnold, Elizabeth.
Interpersonal relationships :professional communication skills for nurses / Elizabeth Nolan Arnold, Kathleen Underman Boggs. 3rd ed. Philadelphia : Saunders, c1999. xvi, 573 p. :
          610.73/06/99   0721681034
Nurse and patient. Interpersonal communication.

RT86.3.S54 1988
Shelly, Judith Allen.
Spiritual care :the nurse's role / Judith Allen Shelly & Sharon Fish. 3rd ed. Downers Grove, Ill. : InterVarsity Press, c1988. 251 p. :
          253   0830812547
Nurse and patient. Pastoral medicine. Nurses--Religious life.

RT86.5 Study and teaching — Social aspects

RT86.5.N875 2001
Nursing issues in the 21st century :perspectives from the literature / edited by Eleanor C. Hein. Philadelphia : Lippincott, c2001. xvi, 541 p. ;
          610.73/0973   0781730171
Nursing--Social aspects--United States. Nursing--Practice--United States. Nursing--United States--Forecasting.

RT86.54 Social aspects — Transcultural nursing

RT86.54.G35 1997
Galanti, Geri-Ann.
Caring for patients from different cultures : case studies from American hospitals / Geri-Ann Galanti. 2nd ed. Philadelphia : University of Pennsylvania Press, c1997. xii, 172 p. ;
          610.73   0812216083
Transcultural nursing--Case studies. Transcultural medical care--Case studies. Hospital care--Psychological aspects--Case studies.

RT86.7 Study and teaching — Practice of nursing. Nursing economics — General works

RT86.7.C47 2001
Chang, Cyril F.
Economics and nursing :critical professional issues / Cyril F. Chang, Sylvia A. Price, Susan K. Pfoutz. Philadelphia : F.A. Davis Co., c2001. xxiii, 507 p. :
          338.4/3362173   0803604653
Nursing--Economic aspects. Nursing--Supply and demand. Nursing--Effect of managed care on.

RT87 Special topics in basic nursing care, A-Z

RT87.P35M325 1999
McCaffery, Margo.
Pain : clinical manual / Margo McCaffery, Chris Pasero. 2nd ed. St. Louis : Mosby, c1999. xvii, 795 p. :
          616/.0472   081515609x
Pain--Nursing--Handbooks, manuals, etc. Pain--Handbooks, manuals, etc. Pain--nursing.

RT87.T45
Palliative care nursing : quality care to the end of life / Marianne LaPorte Matzo and Deborah Witt Shermann, editors. New York : Springer Pub., 2001. p. cm.
00-064094   362.1/75   0826113842
Terminal care. Palliative treatment.

RT87.T45K45 1999
Kemp, Charles,
Terminal illness :a guide to nursing care / Charles Kemp. 2nd ed. Philadelphia : Lippincott, c1999. xiv, 353 p. ;
          610.73/61   0781717728
Terminal care. Nursing. Terminal Care--methods.

RT87.T72M56 1999
Minor, Mary Alice D.,
Patient care skills / Mary A. Duesterhaus Minor, Scott Duesterhaus Minor ; photography by Robert Morrison. 4th ed. Stamford, Conn. : Appleton & Lange, c1999. xii, 501 p. :
          610.73   0838581579
Transport of sick and wounded--Handbooks, manuals, etc. Patients--Positioning--Handbooks, manuals, etc. Nursing--Handbooks, manuals, etc.

RT89 Specialities in nursing — Administration — General works

RT89.F34 2000
Fagin, Claire M.
Essays on nursing leadership / Claire Fagin. New York : Springer, c2000. xviii, 212 p.
00-030055   362.1/73/068   0826113575
Fagin, Claire M.   Nursing services -- Administration. Leadership. Nursing -- Essays.

RT89.N635 2000
Nurses taking the lead : personal qualities of effective leadership / [edited by] Fay L. Bower. Philadelphia : W.B. Saunders Co., c2000. xix, 337 p. :
99-031083   362.1/73/068   0721681697
Nursing services -- Administration. Leadership. Nursing.

RT89.N793 1999
Nursing issues in leading and managing change / [edited by] Jeanette Lancaster. St. Louis : Mosby, c1999. xxvi, 656 p. :
          362.1/73/068   0323002501
Nursing services--Administration. Organizational change. Medical care--United States.

RT89.S775 2001
Strategies for nursing leadership / Harriet R. Feldman, editor. New York : Springer Pub. Co., 2001. p. ;
00-069815   362.1/73/068   0826114148
Nursing services -- Administration. Leadership. Leadership -- Collected Works.

RT89.3.M37 2000
Marriner-Tomey, Ann,
Guide to nursing management and leadership / Ann Marriner-Tomey. 6th ed. St. Louis, Mo. : Mosby, c2000. xvii, 525 p. :
          362.1/73/068   0323010660
Nursing services--Administration. Leadership. Nursing, Supervisory.

RT90 Specialities in nursing — Teaching — General works

RT90.C36 2000
Canobbio, Mary M.
Mosby's handbook of patient teaching / Mary M. Canobbio. 2nd ed. St. Louis : Mosby, c2000. xxiv, 822 p. ;
          615.5/071   0323011039
Patient education--Handbooks, manuals, etc. Nurse and patient--Handbooks, manuals, etc. Patient Education--methods--handbooks.

RT90.R35 2000
Rankin, Sally H.
Patient education :principles & practices / Sally H. Rankin, Karen Duffy Stallings. 4th ed. Philadelphia, PA : Lippincott, c2000. xv, 432 p. :
          615.5/071   0781720222
Patient education. Nurse and patient.

RT90.R43 2001
Redman, Barbara Klug.
The practice of patient education / Barbara Klug Redman. 9th ed. St. Louis, Mo. : Mosby, 2001. xi, 314 p. :
          615.5/071   0323012795
Patient education. Nurse and patient.

RT90.7 Specialities in nursing — Primary nursing

RT90.7.P75 2000
Primary care across the lifespan / [edited by] Denise Robinson, Pamela Kidd, Karen Mangus Rogers. 1st ed. St. Louis : Mosby, c2000. xviii, 1470 p. :
          610.73   0323001483
Primary nursing. Primary care (Medicine) Nurse practitioners.

RT98 Specialities in nursing — Public health nursing

RT98.C625 2000
Community & public health nursing / [edited by] Marcia Stanhope, Jeanette Lancaster. St. Louis : Mosby, c2000. p. ;
99-047288   610.73/43   032300749X
Community health nursing. Community Health Nursing. Public Health Nursing.

RT98.M28 2001
Masson, VeNeta.
Ninth street notebook :voice of a nurse in the city / Veneta Masson. 1st ed. Washington, DC : Sage Femme Press, c2001. 206 p. :
          610.73/43   0967368812
Community health nursing. Community Health Nursing--Personal Narratives.

RT98.N88 2003
Clark, Mary Jo Dummer.
Community health nursing :caring for populations / Mary Jo Clark.4th ed. Upper Saddle River, N.J. : Prentice Hall, 2003. xxvi, 822 p. :
          610.73/43   0130941492
Community health nursing. Community Health Nursing. Nursing Process.

RT98.S78197 2002
Stanhope, Marcia.
Foundations of community health nursing : community-oriented practice / Marcia Stanhope, Jeanette Lancaster. St. Louis, Mo. : Mosby, c2002. xv, 671 p. :
          610.73/43   0323008615
Community health nursing. Community Health Nursing. Community Health Services.

RT98.S782 2000
Stanhope, Marcia.
Handbook of community-based and home health nursing practice : tools for assessment, intervention, and education / Marcia Stanhope, Ruth N. Knollmueller. St. Louis : Mosby, c2000. xviii, 668 p.
00-267319   610.73/43   0323008755
Community health nursing -- Handbooks, manuals, etc. Public health nursing -- Handbooks, manuals, etc. Home nursing -- Handbooks, manuals, etc.

RT120 Specialities in nursing — Other special types of nursing, A-Z

RT120.C45M55 2000
Miller, Judith Fitzgerald.
Coping with chronic illness :overcoming powerlessness / Judith Fitzgerald Miller. Ed. 3. Philadelphia : F.A. Davis, c2000. xiv, 573 p. :
        610.73/61   0803602987
Chronic diseases--Nursing. Chronic diseases--Psychological aspects. Control (Psychology)--Health aspects.

RT120.E4M69 2000
Mosby's emergency nursing reference / [edited by] Pamela S. Kidd, Patty Ann Sturt, Julia Fultz. 2nd ed. St. Louis : Mosby, c2000. xv, 959 p. :
        610.73/61   032301108X
Emergency nursing--Handbooks, manuals, etc.

RT120.F34F355 1998
Family nursing practice / [edited by] Beth Vaughan-Cole ... [et al.]. Philadelphia : Saunders, c1998. xvi, 368 p. :
        610.73   072166492X
Family nursing. Nursing. Family Health.

RT120.H65B84 2001
Buhler-Wilkerson, Karen.
No place like home :a history of nursing and home care in the United States / Karen Buhler-Wilkerson. Baltimore : John Hopkins University Press, 2001. p. cm.
        362.1/4/0973   0801865980
Home nursing--History.

RT120.H65 M36 1995
Rice, Robyn.
Manual of home health nursing procedures / Robyn Rice. St.Louis, Mo. : Mosby, c2000. xxiii, 445 p.
99-026972   610.73   0323009123
Home nursing -- Handbooks, manuals, etc. Nursing Care -- methods -- United States -- Legislation. Home Care Services -- standards -- United States -- Legislation.

RT120.H65R535 2001
Rice, Robyn.
Home care nursing practice : concepts and application / Robyn Rice. 3rd ed. St. Louis, Mo. : Mosby, c2001. xviii, 538 p. :
        362.1/4   0323011071
Home nursing.

RT120.I5C752 2002
Thelan's critical care nursing :diagnosis and management / Linda D. Urden, Kathleen M. Stacy, Mary E. Lough [editors]. 4th ed. St. Louis : Mosby, c2002. 1183 p. :
        610.73/61   0323014615
Intensive care nursing. Emergency nursing. Critical Care--nurses' instruction.

RT120.I5E83 2000
Priorities in critical care nursing / [edited by] Linda D. Urden, Kathleen M. Stacy. 3rd ed. St. Louis : Mosby, c2000. xi, 543 p. :
        610.73/61   0323010008
Intensive care nursing. Critical Care--nurses' instruction. Nursing Care.

RT120.R87
Bushy, Angeline.
Orientation to nursing in the rural community / by Angeline Bushy, with Kathryn Baird-Crooks ... [et al.]. Thousand Oaks, Calif. : Sage Publications, c2000. xii, 284 p. :
00-008364   610.73/43   0761911561
Rural nursing.

RV Botanic, Thomsonian, and Eclectic Medicine

RV5 General works — 1851-

RV5.B47 2000
Berman, Alex,
America's botanico-medical movements :vox populi / Alex Berman, Michael A. Flannery. New York : Pharmaceutical Products Press, c2001. xxiii, 289 p., 29 p. of plates :
615/.32/0973   0789012359
Berman, Alex, 1914-   Medicine, Botanic--United States--History. Materia medica--United States--History. Medicine, Herbal--history--United States.

RV8 Biography — Individual, A-Z

RV8.T47
Haller, John S.
The people's doctors : Samuel Thomson and the American botanical movement, 1790-1860 / John S. Haller, Jr. Carbondale : Southern Illinois University Press, c2000. xiv, 377 p. ;
99-087340   615.5/3   0809323397
Thomson, Samuel, -- 1769-1843.   Physicians -- United States -- Biography. Medicine, Botanic -- United States. Alternative medicine -- United States.

RV9 Addresses, essays, lectures

RV9.B87
Brown, John A.,
Quackery exposed!!! or, A few remarks on the Thomsonian system of medicine; introductory remarks. By John A. Brown ... Boston, 1833. 22 p.
Medicine, Botanic.

RV41 Eclectic medicine — General works

RV41.F8
Fyfe, John William,
Specific diagnosis and specific medication, by John William Fyfe ... Together with abstracts from the writings of John M. Scudder, M.D., and other leading authors. Cincinnati, O., The Scudder brothers company, 1909. 784 p.
20 5.
Medicine, Eclectic.

RV61 Eclectic medicine — History

RV61.H35 1994
Haller, John S.
Medical protestants : the eclectics in American medicine, 1825-1939 / John S. Haller, Jr. Carbondale : Southern Illinois University Press, c1994. xix, 340 p. :
93-007389   615.5/3   0809318946
Medicine, Eclectic -- United States -- History. History of Medicine, 19th Cent. -- United States. History of Medicine, 20th Cent. -- United States.

RV76 Eclectic medicine — Biography — Individual, A-Z

RV76.L56.F53 1998
Flannery, Michael A.,
John Uri Lloyd : the great American eclectic / Michael A. Flannery. Carbondale : Southern Illinois University Press, c1998. xviii, 234 p.
97-029242   615/.1/092   080932167X
Lloyd, John Uri, -- 1849-1936.   Medicine, Eclectic -- Ohio -- Cincinnati -- Biography. Pharmacists -- Ohio -- Cincinnati -- Biography.

RV81 Eclectic medicine — Addresses, essays and lectures

RV81.M64
Millen, Charles W.
Address by the Rev. Charles W. Millen, D. D. delivered at the 25th commencement of the Eclectic medical college of the city of New York, New York, The Day star, 1886. p. cm.
Medicine, Eclectic--Addresses, essays, lectures. [from old catalog]

RV401 Eclectic medicine — Materia medica and therapeutics — General works

RV401.F4
Felter, Harvey Wickes,
The eclectic materia medica, pharmacology and therapeutics, by Harvey Wickes Felter. Cincinnati, O., J. K. Scudder, 1922. 743 p.
Materia medica. Pharmacology. Therapeutics.

RX Homeopathy

RX41 Dictionaries and encyclopedias

RX41.C48 2000
Churchill Livingstone's international dictionary of homeopathy / prepared in collaboration with the faculty of Homoeopathy and the Homoepathic Trust ; [editor], Jeremy Swayne. Edinburgh ; Churchill Livingstone, 2000. xix, 251 p. :
          615.5/32/03   0443060096
Homeopathy--Dictionaries.

RX71 General works

RX71.D69 1997
Downey, Paul.
Homoeopathy for the primary health care team : a guide for GPs, midwives, district nurses, and other health professionals / Paul Downey. Oxford ; Butterworth-Heinemann, 1997. vii, 184 p. ;
          615.5/32   0750629991
Homeopathy. Homeopathy--methods. Primary Health Care--methods.

RX71.H65 1998
Homoeopathy : a critical appraisal / editors, Edzard Ernst, Eckhart G. Hahn ; assistant editors, Benno Brinkhaus, Christian Hentschel, Gernot Schindler. Oxford ; Butterworth-Heinemann, c1998. x, 240 p. :
          615.5/32   0750635649
Homeopathy. Medicine--Practice.

RX71.U46 1991
Ullman, Dana.
Discovering homeopathy : medicine for the 21st century / Dana Ullman. Rev. ed. Berkeley, Calif. : North Atlantic Books, c1991. xxxiv, 277 p. ;
          615.5/32   1556431082
Homeopathy. Homeopathy.

RX72 General special

RX72.S556 2000
Skinner, Sidney.
An introduction to homeopathic medicine in primary care / Sidney E. Skinner. Gaithersburg, MD : Aspen Publishers, 2001. xxii, 473 p. ;
          615.5/32   0834216760
Homeopathy. Primary care (Medicine)

RX72.S93 1998
Swayne, Jeremy.
Homeopathic method : implications for clinical practice and medical science / Jeremy Swayne ; foreword by Conrad Harris. New York : Churchill Livingstone, 1998. xiv, 228 p. :
          615.5/32   0443059268
Homeopathy.

RX73 Handbooks, manuals, etc.

RX73.L59 2001
Lockie, Andrew.
Homeopathy handbook / Andrew Lockie. 1st American ed. New York : Dorling Kindersley Pub., 2001. 128 p. :
          615.5/32   0789471787
Homeopathy--Handbooks, manuals, etc.

RX76 Popular works

RX76.U467 1999
Ullman, Dana.
Homeopathy A-Z / Dana Ullman. Carlsbad, CA : Hay House, c1999. 155 p. :
          615.5/32   156170573X
Homeopathy--Popular works.

RX601 Materia medica and therapeutics — General works

RX601.R59 1994
Roy, Margaret.
A first materia medica for homoeopathy : a self-directed learning text / Margaret Roy ; foreword by Vassilis Ghegas. Edinburgh ; Churchill Livingstone, 1994. 261 p. :
94-004032   615.5/32   0443048207
Homeopathy -- Materia medica and therapeutics. Homeopathy -- programmed instruction. Materia Medica -- programmed instruction.

RX615 Materia medica and therapeutics — Remedies, A-Z

RX615.F55S3413 2001
Scheffer, Mechthild.
The encyclopedia of Bach flower therapy / Mechthild Scheffer. Rochester, Vt. : Healing Arts Press, 2001. p. cm.
          615/.321   0892819413
Flowers--Therapeutic use.

RZ Other Systems of Medicine

RZ401 Mental healing

RZ401.G35 2001
Gerber, Richard,
  Vibrational medicine :the #1 handbook of subtle-energy therapies / Richard Gerber. 3rd ed. Rochester, VT : Bear & Co., c2001. 605 p. :
        615.5   1879181584
  Mental healing--Handbooks, manuals, etc. Vital force--Therapeutic use--Handbooks, manuals, etc. Alternative medicine--Handbooks, manuals, etc.

RZ401.W56 2000
Winkelman, Michael.
  Shamanism : the neural ecology of consciousness and healing / Michael Winkelman. Westport, CT : Bergin & Garvey, 2000. xvi, 309 p. ;
99-040489   291.1/44/019   0897897048
  Mental healing. Shamanism. Shamanism -- Physiological aspects.

RZ440 Miscellaneous systems and treatments — Naturopathy — General works

RZ440.M476 2001
Meyer, Eric.
  Mother nature, M.D. / Eric Meyer ; foreword by James A. Duke. Paramus, NJ : Prentice Hall, c2001. x, 298 p. ;
        615.5/35/03   0735202311
  Naturopathy--Encyclopedias. Herbs--Therapeutic use--Encyclopedias. Dietary supplements--Encyclopedias.

RZ440.S746 2001
Stengler, Mark.
  The natural physician's healing therapies / Mark Stengler ; foreword by James F. Balch. Paramus, NJ : Prentice Hall, 2001. xiv, 562 p. :
        615.5/35   0735202508
  Naturopathy--Popular works.

INDEXES

Ecology of the body : styles of behavior in human life ; BF698.3.L94 1987

Economic impact of worksite health promotion ; RC969.H43.E26 1994

Economics and nursing :critical professional issues ; RT86.7.C47 2001

Ecopsychology : restoring the earth, healing the mind ; BF353.5.N37.E26 1995

Ecstatic imagination : psychedelic experiences and the psychoanalysis of self-actualization, The ; RC553.H3.M47 1998

Education and class : the irrelevance of IQ genetic studies ; BF431.S285 1986

Effectiveness of drug abuse treatment : Dutch and American perspectives, The ; RC564.E3658 1990

Effects of atomic radiation : a half-century of studies from Hiroshima and Nagasaki ; RA648.3.S38 1995

Ego and the dynamic ground : a transpersonal theory of human development, The ; BF204.7.W37 1995

Ego and the id, The ; BF173.F645 1961

Ego and the mechanisms of defence, The ; BF173.F6173 1946, BF721.F692 vol. 2

E-Health, telehealth, and telemedicine :a guide to start-up and success ; R119.95.M344 2001

Electric and magnetic fields : invisible risks? ; RA569.3.S24 1996

Ellenberg and Rifkin's diabetes mellitus :theory and Practice ; RC660.D542 2003

Elusive embryo : how women and men approach new reproductive technologies, The ; RG133.5.B434

Elusive magic bullet : the search for the perfect drug, The ; RM301.25.M36 1999

Elusive quarry : a scientific appraisal of psychical research, The ; BF1042.H96 1989

Elusive science : origins of experimental psychical research, The ; BF1028.M38

Embarrassment : poise and peril in everyday life ; BF575.E53.M55 1996

Embryo research debate : science and the politics of reproduction, The ; RG133.5.M846 1997

EMDR : the breakthrough therapy for overcoming anxiety, stress, and trauma ; RC489.E98.S53 1997

Emergency ophthalmology ; RE48.E445 2003

Emerging issues in biomedical policy ; R855.5.U6.E44 1992

Emerging minds : the process of change in children's thinking ; BF723.C5.S53 1996

Emerging self : a developmental, self, and object relations approach to the treatment of the closet narcissistic disorder of the self , The; RC553.N36.M369 1993

Emotion : the science of sentiment ; BF531.E79 2001

Emotion and spirit : questioning the claims of psychoanalysis and religion ; BF175.4.R44.S94

Emotion, psychotherapy, and change ; RC489.E45.E46 1991

Emotional difficulties in reading; a psychological approach to study problems ; BF456.R2.E65

Emotional disturbance in adopted adolescents : origins and development ; RJ507.A36.M37 1988

Emotional nature of qualitative research, The; BF76.5.E47 2001

Emotional problems in later life : intervention strategies for professional caregivers ; RC451.4.A5B56 1998

Emotional problems of early childhood ; RJ499.C26

Emotions : outline of a theory, The ; BF531.S314

Emotions in the practice of psychotherapy : clinical implications of affect theories ; RC489.E45.P58

Emotions, cognition, and behavior ; BF713.E47 1984

Emotions, the social bond, and human reality : part;whole analysis ; BF531.S35 1997

Empathy reconsidered : new directions in psychotherapy ; RC489.E46.E48 1997

Empty cradle : infertility in America from Colonial times to the present, The ; RC889.M368 1996

Empty fortress; infantile autism and the birth of the self, The ; RJ506.A9.B4

Encountering the world : toward an ecological psychology ; BF353.R44 1996

Encyclopedia of adult development ; BF724.5.E53 1993

Encyclopedia of alien encounters, The ; BF2050.B35 2000

Encyclopedia of allergies ; RC585.N38 2001

Encyclopedia of Bach flower therapy, The ; RX615.F55S3413 2001

Encyclopedia of biostatistics ; RA409.E53 1998

Encyclopedia of blindness and vision impairment, The ; RE91.S27 2002

Encyclopedia of cancer ; RC262.E558 2002

Encyclopedia of complementary health practice ; R733.E525 1999

Encyclopedia of creativity ; BF408.E53 1999

Encyclopedia of deafness and hearing disorders, The ; RF290.T93 2000

Encyclopedia of depression, The ; RC537.R63 2001

Encyclopedia of dreams : symbols and interpretations, The ; BF1091.G84 1993

Encyclopedia of elder care : the comprehensive resource on geriatric and social care, The ; RC954.E53 2001

Encyclopedia of evolving techniques in psychodynamic therapy, The ; RC501.4.S65 1992

Encyclopedia of genetic disorders and birth defects, The ; RB155.5.W96 2000

Encyclopedia of gerontology : age, aging, and the aged ; RC952.5.E58 1996

Encyclopedia of human behavior ; BF31.E5 1994

Encyclopedia of human emotions ; BF531.E55 1999

Encyclopedia of human intelligence ; BF431.E59 1994

Encyclopedia of medicinal plants, The ; RS164.C4437 1996

Holistic conceptualization of stress and disease, A ; RC49.N493 1991

Holistic nursing : a handbook for practice ; RT42.H65 2000

Home birth : step-by-step instruction for natural home birth and emergency childbirth ; RG661.5.F56 1998

Home care nursing practice : concepts and application ; RT120.H65R535 2001

Home care of the elderly ; RC954.H575 1999

Homeopathic method : implications for clinical practice and medical science ; RX72.S93 1998

Homeopathy handbook ; RX73.L59 2001

Homicide : a psychiatric perspective ; RC569.5.H65.M35 1996

Homoeopathy : a critical appraisal ; RX71.H65 1998

Homeopathy A-Z ; RX76.U467 1999

Homoeopathy for the primary health care team : a guide for GPs, midwives, district nurses, and other health professionals ; RX71.D69 1997

Homosexualities and the therapeutic process, The ; RC558.H63 1991

Homosexuality & psychoanalysis ; RC506.H66 2001

Homosexuality : a practical guide to counseling lesbians, gay men, and their families ; RC558.M43 1990

Honoring patient preferences :a guide to complying with multicultural patient requirements ; RA418.5.T73H65 1999

Horse and buggy doctor, The; R154.H39.A3 1970

House of cards : psychology and psychotherapy built on myth ; RC480.5.D38 1994

House of make-believe : children's play and the developing imagination, The ; BF717.S514 1990

Household chemicals and emergency first aid ; RC86.8.F64 1993

How a baby grows : a story in pictures ; RJ131.G47

How children think and learn ; BF723.C5.W66 1988

How emotions work ; BF531.K38 1999

How Freud worked : first-hand accounts of patients ; BF109.F74.R632 1995

How implicit is implicit learning? – edited by Dianne C. Berry ; BF319.5.I45.H68 1997

How life begins : the science of life in the womb ; RG525.V38 1996

How to find health information on the Internet ; RA773.6.M39 1998

How to report statistics in medicine : annotated guidelines for authors, editors, and reviewers ; RA409.L357 1997

How to resolve the health care crisis : affordable protection for all Americans ; RA395.A3.H685

How to survive and maybe even love nursing school! : a guide for students by students ; RT73.D79 2001

How to use Index medicus, Psychological abstracts, Excerpta medica ; R119.S773 1994

How we grieve : relearning the world ; BF575.G7.A79 1996

Human behavior and environment : advances in theory and research ; BF353.H85

Human change processes : the scientific foundations of psychotherapy ; BF637.C4.M29 1991

Human development across the lifespan ; BF713.D33 1999

Human differences ; BF697.A55 1999

Human lead exposure ; RC347.5.H86 1991

Human lives : critical essays on consequentialist bioethics ; R724.H784 1997

Human medicinal agents from plants ; RS164.H88 1993

Human memory and amnesia ; BF371.H757 1982

Human mind, The ; BF173.M36 1945

Human model : primate perspectives, The ; BF671.H37

Human nature and conduct; an introduction to social psychology ; BF57.D4 1930

Human nature and suffering ; RC454.4.G54 1992

Human paleopathology : current syntheses and future options ; R134.8.H86 1991

Human sexual inadequacy RC556.M37

Human values in critical care medicine ; RC86.95.H86 1986

Human zoo, The ; BF701.M6 1969

Humane medicine ; R727.3.L565 1995

Humanism and the physician ; R723.P38

Hundred years of psychology,1833-1933, additional part: 1933-1963, by Donald J. West, A ; BF95.F5

Hunter's diseases of occupations ; RC964.H8 2000

Hunter's tropical medicine and emerging infectious Disease ; RC961.H84 2000

Hurried child : growing up too fast too soon, The ; BF723.S75.E44 1981

Hurst's The heart ; RC667.H88 2001

Hypnosis in therapy ; RC495.G464 1991

Hypnotic leadership : leaders, followers, and the loss of self ; BF637.L4

Hypnotism :a history ; RC497.F67 2000

Hypnotism; an objective study in suggestibility ; BF1141.W38

Hypothesis and evidence in psychoanalysis ; BF175.E29 1984

Hystories : hysterical epidemics and modern culture ; RC532.S46 1997

I awaken to glory : essays celebrating the sesquicentennial of the discovery of anesthesia by Horace Wells, December 11, 1844-December 11, 1994 ; RK43.W4.I2 1994

I knew a woman :the experience of the female body ; RA564.85.D38 2001

Ideas and realities of emotion ; BF311.P31367 1995

Identity in adolescence : the balance between self and other ; BF724.3.I3.K76 1989

Identity, youth, and crisis ; BF697.E7

Ideologies of breast cancer : feminist perspectives ; RC280.B8.I34 1999

Medical tests sourcebook : basic consumer health information about medical tests, including periodic health exams, general screening tests, tests you can do at home, findings of the U.S. Preventive ; RC71.3.M45 1999

Medical word finder : a reverse medical dictionary, The ; R121.H232 1987

Medical world of the eighteenth century, The ; R148.K5

Medical writing; the technic and the art ; R119.F55 1972

Medical-surgical nursing : concepts and clinical practice ; RT41.M49 1995

Medical-surgical nursing : total patient care ; RT41.H65 1996

Medicating schizophrenia : a history ; RC514.G44 1999

Medication errors ; RM146.M415 1999

Medications and mathematics for the nurse ; RM300.R53 2002

Medicinal plants of the world : chemical constituents, traditional, and modern medicinal uses ; RS164.R676 1999

Medicinal resources of the tropical forest : biodiversity and its importance to human health ; RS164.M377 1996

Medicine : an illustrated history ; R131.L95

Medicine and its technology : an introduction to the history of medical instrumentation ; R856.A5.D38

Medicine and society in America, 1660-1860 ; R148.S45

Medicine and the German Jews : a history ; R694.E376 2001

Medicine and the Navy, 1200-1900 ; RC986.K36

Medicine before the plague : practitioners and their patients in the crown of Aragon, 1285-1345 ; R557.A7.M38 1993

Medicine in America : a short history ; R151.C375 1991

Medicine in Chicago, 1850-1950 : a chapter in the social and scientific development of a city ; R210.C4.B6 1991

Medicine in quotations : views of health and disease through the ages ; R705.M465 2000

Medicine in the English Middle Ages ; R487.G47 1998

Medicine, philosophy and religion in ancient China : researches and reflections ; R601.S58 1995

Medicine's 10 greatest discoveries ; R145.F75 1998

Medicine's dilemmas : infinite needs versus finite resources ; RA410.53.K55 1994

Medieval & early Renaissance medicine : an introduction to knowledge and practice ; R141.S546 1990

Medieval medicus : a social history of Anglo-Norman medicine ; R141.K4

Medieval woman's guide to health : the first English gynecological handbook : Middle English text ; RG85.E53 1980

Melancholy scene of devastation : the public response to the 1793 Philadelphia yellow fever epidemic, A ; RC211.P5.M44 1997

Melanie Klein : Volume II, the ego and the good object, 1932-1960 ; RJ504.2.P4613 1991

Melloni's illustrated dictionary of obstetrics and gynecology ; RG45.M45 2000

Memoir of James Jackson, Jr., M.D., with extracts from his letters to his father, and medical cases, collected by him, A ; R154.J315.J2 1972

Memory ; BF371.W385 1987

Memory : phenomena, experiment, and theory ; BF371.P277 1993

Men and their motives; psycho-analytical studies ; BF173.F58 1947

Men and women of parapsychology : personal reflections ; BF1031.M537 1987

Mending bodies, saving souls : a history of hospitals ; RA964.R57 1999

Mending minds : a guide to the new psychiatry of depression, anxiety, and other serious mental disorders ; RC460.H47 1991

Menninger : the family and the clinic ; RC445.K3.T626 1990

Mens silences : predicaments in masculinity ; BF175.5.M37.R87 1992

Menstrual disorders and menopause : biological, psychological, and cultural research ; RG161.G35 1985

Menstrual health in women's lives ; RG161.M47 1991

Mental disorders in older adults : fundamentals of assessment and treatment ; RC451.4.A5.Z374 1998

Mental growth of the pre-school child; a psychological outline of normal development from birth to the sixth year, including a system of developmental diagnosis, The ; BF721.G5

Mental health & mental illness ; RC454.4.B372 2002

Mental health diagnostic desk reference : visual guides and more for learning to use the Diagnostic and statistical manual (DSM-IV-TR), The ; RC455.2.C4.M86 2001

Mental health disorders sourcebook : basic consumer health information about anxiety disorders, depression, and other mood disorders ... ; RC454.4.M458 1999

Mental health in a multi-ethnic society : a multi-disciplinary handbook ; RC451.5.A2.M465 1995

Mental health nursing : an introductory text ; RC440.B353 2000

Mental health nursing in the community ; RC440.M3544 1997

Mental health of Asian Americans, The ; RC451.5.A75.S93 1982

Mental health outcome evaluation ; RA790.5.S64 1998